Teacher Guidebook
Level E

A Reason For Spelling® Teacher's Guidebook - Level E
2nd Edition

EAN#: 978-1-58938-268-8
ISBN#: 1-58938-268-4
TL#: SPTGE2020JPS
Published by Concerned Communications, LLC
P.O. Box 1000, Siloam Springs, AR 72761

Authors: Rebecca Burton, Eva Hill, Leah Knowlton, Kay Sutherland
Illustrations: James McCullough & Mark Decker

For more information about *A Reason For Spelling*,® *A Reason For Handwriting*,®
A Reason For Science® and *A Reason For Guided Reading*®
go to: *www.AReasonFor.com*

Contents:

Acknowledgments:

Field Test Participants:

Virginia Allen, East Rockaway, New York • Mrs. Christine Baker, Belleville, Pennsylvania • Judy M. Banks, Carmichael, California • Darya Birch, San Clemente, California • Mari Anne Burns, Baton Rouge, Louisiana • Karen Dafflitto, St. Louis, Missouri • Kristen J. Dorsett, Prescott, Arizona • Ms. Laura Guerrera, East Rockaway, New York • Mrs. Anne Gutierrez, San Antonio, Texas • Jeanette O. Kappel, Winstead, Minnesota • Sharon K. Kobilka, San Antonio, Texas • Connie Kozitza, Winsted, Minnesota • Vivian I. Sawyer, Carmichael, California • Harold W. Souther, San Antonio, Texas • Cleo F. Staples, Auburn, California • Suezy Tucker, Auburn, California • Martha Woodbury, Los Angeles, California

Special thanks to:

Dr. Larry Burton, Dr. Carol Campbell, Dr. Lee Netherton, Melvin Northrup, Phyllis Paytee, Dr. Linda Romig

Placement Tests

In order to evaluate readiness and accurately meet individual student need, a simple placement test is recommended at the beginning of each school year.

Step 1: *Administer the test*

 Say

Number your paper from one to twenty. I will say the word once, use the word in a sentence, then say the word again. Write a word beside each number on your paper.

(Allow ample time and carefully monitor progress.)

Step 2: *Evaluate the corrected tests using the following criteria:*

If the student correctly spells 17 to 20 words:
• Assign the student to Level E program
• Encourage the student to work independently
• Select and assign several Other Word Forms to spell and test

If the student correctly spells 8 to 16 words:
• Assign the student to Level E program
• Allow opportunities to work independently
• Offer Other Word Forms activities

If the student correctly spells 0 to 7 words:
• Assign student to Level E, but use regular lessons without Other Word Forms
• Be sure student completes all regular activities
• May wish to administer Level D test

Placement Test Level E

1. athlete — He is my favorite **athlete.**
2. respect — I always show **respect** for God.
3. launch — Come help me **launch** my rocket.
4. museum — I like to visit this **museum.**
5. piece — I need a **piece** of paper.
6. gallon — He spilled a **gallon** of milk.
7. deposit — I will **deposit** money in the bank.
8. carton — This **carton** is sturdy.
9. narrow — The cave had a **narrow** passage.
10. dining — We will eat in the **dining** room.
11. dolphin — I like the **dolphin** at the zoo.
12. plunge — Watch her **plunge** into the pool!
13. chorus — I just know the **chorus** of the song.
14. design — My painting has a nice **design.**
15. dribble — He learned to **dribble** the ball.
16. version — Which game **version** do you like?
17. citrus — **Citrus** fruits are good for you.
18. formula — We mixed **formula** for the calves.
19. account — I have an **account** at the bank.
20. rhyme — What will **rhyme** with "skating?"

Placement Test Level D

1. practice — I have to **practice** the piano.
2. meant — I **meant** to finish my project.
3. station — I painted at the art **station.**
4. hollow — The log is **hollow.**
5. rescue — We will **rescue** the kitten.
6. dream — She had a funny **dream.**
7. pretend — I **pretend** to be a gorilla.
8. wreath — He put a **wreath** on the door.
9. cough — His **cough** is getting better.
10. decide — I can't **decide** what to buy.
11. bounce — I shouldn't **bounce** on the bed.
12. fault — It is my **fault** the books fell.
13. garbage — The **garbage** truck came today.
14. curious — She is **curious** about the package.
15. choice — We made a **choice** to obey.
16. rather — I'd **rather** play tag than swing.
17. castle — I made a large cardboard **castle.**
18. fountain — The **fountain** is lit up at night.
19. cereal — That is my favorite **cereal.**
20. herself — She made cookies by **herself.**

Day One

Literature Connection - Each week begins with a Scripture verse, followed by a theme story that develops the principles found in that verse. Topic and description are provided to inform the teacher of story content. Some teachers may choose to use this theme story for the Monday morning devotional.

Discussion Time *(optional)* - Discussion questions follow each story, giving the teacher the opportunity to evaluate student understanding, and to encourage students to apply the values found in the Scripture to their own lives.

Day One (cont.)

Preview - The test—study—test sequence begins with this pre-test which primarily uses sentences related to the story. Research has shown that immediate correction by the student—under teacher supervision—is one of the best ways to learn to spell.

Customize Your List *(notepaper graphic)* - An opportunity is provided to test additional words of the teacher's choice.

Say *(bubble graphic)* - Instructions to the students that are to be read aloud by the teacher are marked with the Say symbol for easy identification.

Progress Chart *(chart graphic)* - Students may record their Preview scores for later comparison against their Posttest scores. (Reproducible master provided in Appendix B.)

Day One (cont.)

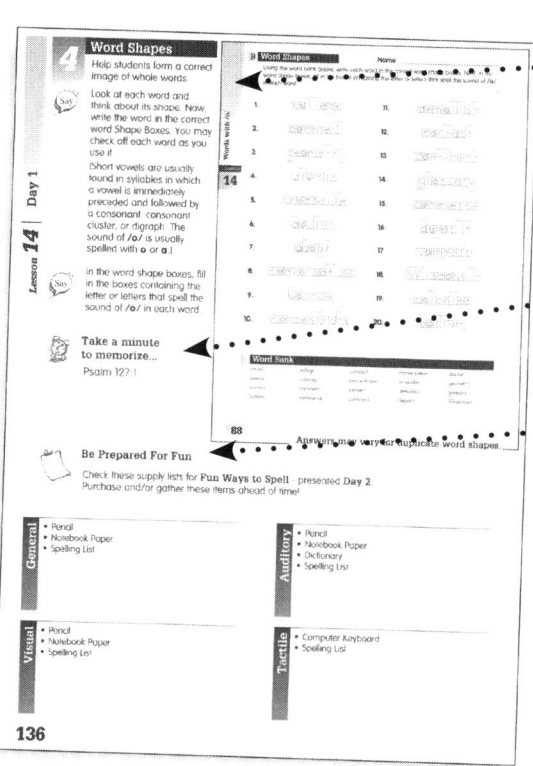

Word Shapes - The use of "Shape Boxes" is a research-based method that helps students form a correct visual image of each spelling word. An additional exercise is provided to enhance student identification of spelling patterns and thus strengthen phonemic awareness.

Take a Minute (clock graphic) - Reminders are provided for committing to memory the Scripture verses upon which the stories are based.

Be Prepared for Fun (list graphic) - For teacher convenience, a weekly supply list is provided for "Fun Ways to Spell" on Day 1. Supplies for the "General" activity are readily available in most classrooms. Other categories may require minimal extra planning.

Day Two

Hide & Seek - This research-proven method of spelling instruction is highly effective for dealing with multiple intelligences and varying learning styles.

Other Word Forms (optional) - A variety of activities allow students to become familiar with other forms of the week's spelling words.

Fun Ways to Spell - Four options are offered each week. In addition to a "General" activity, "Auditory," "Tactile," and "Visual" options are provided for students with different learning styles. Suggestions are also given for adapting these activities to various classroom settings.

Day Three

Language Arts Activity - Research studies show that meaningful, practical use of spelling words helps students become more familiar with the words they are studying. The weekly "Working with Words" activity is designed to offer practice in this area.

Take a Minute - Reminders to commit Scripture verses to memory are provided periodically.

Day Four

Dictation - Students write dictated words to complete sentences. This strengthens their word usage and context skills. Previously taught spelling words are also included in this activity, providing maintenance of spelling skills.

Proofreading - Proofreading allows students to become familiar with the format of standardized tests as they mark misspelled words. Proofreading is also a critical skill that can be incorporated in students' own writing.

Day Four (cont.)

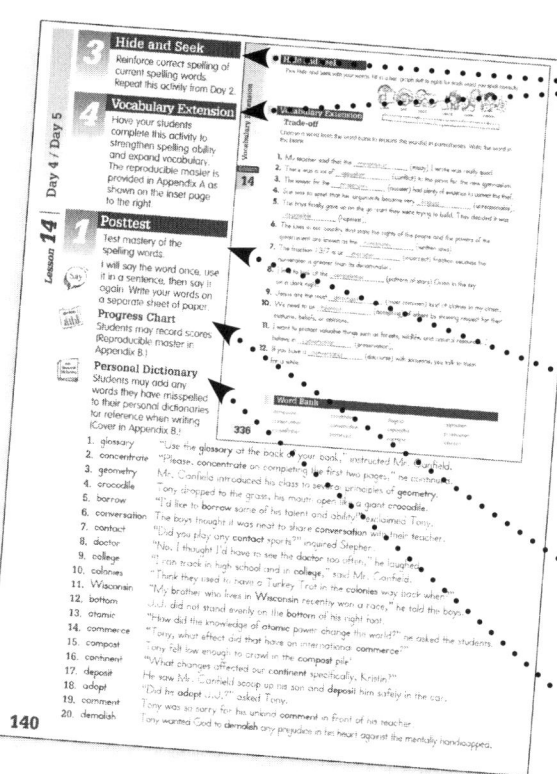

> ***Hide & Seek/Vocabulary Extension*** (optional) - Through practice of additional words similar to the weekly spelling lists, students are provided with vocabulary extension opportunities. (Note: These pages are not in the Student Worktext. Reproducible masters are provided for each week in Appendix A.)

Day Five

> ***Posttest*** - The test—study—test sequence of learning is completed with the posttest. Again, most sentences relate to the theme story. Visit the *A Reason For* website to download free, printable Posttest pages.

> ***Progress Chart*** (chart graphic) - Students may now record their posttest scores to evaluate their weekly progress.

> ***Personal Dictionary*** (dictionary graphic) - Students may add any words they have misspelled to their personal dictionaries. Each student may refer to his/her custom dictionary while journaling or during other writing activities. (Reproducible cover in Appendix B.)

Day Five (cont.)

> ***Learning Game*** (optional) - The weekly "board game" may be used to reinforce spelling skills and produce motivation and interest in good spelling. Most games can be played multiple times.

> ***Journal Entry*** - The underlying goal of spelling instruction is to create better writers. This weekly journaling activity allows students to apply their spelling skills in a meaningful way, while encouraging them to make the featured value their own. Guided discussion questions are provided to assist in reviewing the value taught by the story.

> ***Word Wow!*** - Interesting insights into words and their meanings are provided to capture student interest.

Research Basis

A Reason For Spelling® emphasizes a balance between spelling skills, application, and student enjoyment. In short, it is designed to be both meaningful and fun! Each level promotes successful classroom practices while incorporating the following research findings:

Research Findings:

Application:

Daily Practice. A daily period of teacher-directed spelling activities based on meaningful content greatly enhances student proficiency in spelling.

Daily lessons in *A Reason For Spelling*® provide systematic development of spelling skills with a focus on Scripture verses and values.

Spelling Lists. The most productive spelling lists feature developmentally-appropriate words of highest frequency in writing.

Through daily lessons, challenge words, and other word forms, *A Reason For Spelling*® focuses on the high frequency words children and adults use in daily writing.

Test—Study—Test. Effective educational programs are built on the learning model of "Test—Study—Test."

A Reason For Spelling® follows a weekly pretest/posttest format, and also includes a cumulative review for each unit.

Accurate Feedback. Pretest and proofreading results are crucial in helping students identify words that require their special attention.

Regular pretests and proofreading activities in *A Reason For Spelling*® help students identify words requiring their special attention.

Visual Imaging. Learning to spell a word involves forming a correct visual image of the whole word, rather than visualizing syllables or parts.

Every lesson in *A Reason For Spelling*® features word shape grids to help students form a correct visual image of each spelling word.

Study Procedures. The most effective word-study procedures involve visual, auditory, and tactile modalities.

A Reason For Spelling® uses the "look, say, hide, write, seek, check" method as a primary teaching tool.

Learning Games. Well-designed games motivate student interest and lead to spelling independence.

A Reason For Spelling® includes a wide variety of spelling games at each instructional level.

Self-Correction. Student focus, accomplished through such activities as self-correction of pretests, is an essential strategy for spelling mastery at every grade and ability level.

Teacher directed self-correction of pretests and reviews is encouraged throughout *A Reason For Spelling*®.

Regular Application. Frequent opportunities to use spelling words in everyday writing contribute significantly to the maintenance of spelling ability.

A Reason For Spelling® provides opportunities for journaling in each lesson to promote the use of assigned spelling words in personal writing.

Cohen, Leo A. 1969. *Evaluating Structural Analysis Methods Used in Spelling Books*. Doctoral Thesis, Boston University.

Davis, Zephaniah T. 1987. Upper Grades Spelling Instruction: What Difference Does It Make? *English Journal*, March: 100-101.

Dolch, E.W. 1936. A Basic Sight Vocabulary. *The Elementary School Journal*, Vol. 36: 456-460.

Downing, John, Robert M. Coughlin and Gene Rich. 1986. Children's Invented Spellings in the Classroom. *The Elementary School Journal*, Vol. 86, No. 3, January: 295-303.

Fiderer, Adele. 1995. *Practical Assessments for Literature-Based Reading Classrooms*. New York: Scholastic Professional Books.

Fitzsimmons, Robert J., and Bradley M. Loomer. 1980. *Spelling: The Research Basis*. Iowa City: The University of Iowa.

Gardner, Howard. 1993. *Multiple Intelligences: The Theory in Practice*. New York: Basic-Books.

Gentry, J. Richard. 1997. *My Kid Can't Spell*. Portsmouth, NH: Heinemann Educational Books.

Gentry, J. Richard and Jean Wallace Gillet. 1993. *Teaching Kids to Spell*. Portsmouth, NH:Heinemann Educational Books.

Gentry, J. Richard. 1985. You Can Analyze Developmental Spelling-And Here's How To Do It! *Early Years K-8*, May:1-4.

Goswami, Usha. 1991. Learning about Spelling Sequences: The Role of Onsets and Rimes in Analogies in Reading. *Child Development*, 62, 1110-1123.

Graves, Donald H. 1977. Research Update: Spelling Texts and Structural Analysis Methods. *Language Arts 54* January: 86-90.

Harp, Bill. 1988. When the Principal Asks, "Why Are Your Kids Giving Each Other Spelling Tests?" *Reading Teacher*, Vol. 41, No. 7, March: 702-704.

Hoffman, Stevie and Nancy Knipping. 1988. Spelling Revisited: The Child's Way. *Childhood Education*, June: 284-287.

Horn, Ernest. 1926. *A Basic Writing Vocabulary: 10,000 Frequently Used Words in Writing*. Monograph First Series, No. 4. Iowa City: The University of Iowa.

Horn, Thomas. 1946. *The Effect of the Corrected Test on Learning to Spell*. Master's Thesis, The University of Iowa.

Horsky, Gregory Alexander. 1974. *A Study of the Perception of Letters and Basic Sight Vocabulary Words of Fourth and Fifth Grade Children*. Doctoral Thesis, The University of Iowa.

Lacey, Cheryl. 1994. *Moving On In Spelling*. Jefferson City, Missouri: Scholastic.

Lutz, Elaine. 1986. ERIC/RCS Report: Invented Spelling and Spelling Development. *Language Arts*, Vol. 63, No. 7, November: 742-744.

Macmillan Dictionary for Children. 1997. New York: Simon and Schuster Books for Young Readers.

Marino, Jacqueline L. 1978. *Children's Use of Phonetic, Graphemic, and Morphophonemic Cues in a Spelling Task*. Doctoral Thesis, State University of New York at Albany.

Morris, Darrell, Laurie Nelson and Jan Perney. 1986. Exploring the Concept of 'Spelling Instructional Level' Through the Analysis of Error-Types. *The Elementary School Journal*, Vol. 87, No. 2, 195-197.

Nicholson, Tom and Sumner Schachter. 1979. Spelling Skill and Teaching Practice-Putting Them Back Together Again. *Language Arts*, Vol. 56, No. 7, October: 804-809.

Rothman, Barbara. 1997. *Practical Phonics Strategies to Build Beginning Reading and Writing Skills*. Medina, Washington: Institute for Educational Development.

Scott, Jill E. 1994. Spelling for Readers and Writers. *The Reading Teacher*, Vol. 48, No. 2, October: 188-190.

Simmons, Janice L. 1978. *The Relationship Between an Instructional Level in Spelling and the Instructional Level in Reading Among Elementary School Children*. Doctoral Thesis, University of Northern Colorado.

Templeton, Shane. 1986. Synthesis of Research on the Learning and Teaching of Spelling. *Educational Leadership*, March: 73-78.

Tireman, L.S. 1927. *The Value of Marking Hard Spots in Spelling*. Doctoral Thesis, University of Iowa.

Toch, Thomas. 1992. Nu Waz for Kidz tu Lern Rdn, Rtn. *U.S. News & World Report*, September 14: 75-76.

Wagstaff, Janiel M. *Phonics That Work! New Strategies for the Reading/Writing Classroom*. Jefferson City, Missouri: Scholastic.

Watson, Alan J. 1988. Developmental Spelling: A Word Categorizing Instructional Experiment. *Journal of Educational Research*, Vol. 82, No. 2, November/December: 82-88.

Wilde, Sandra. 1990. A Proposal for a New Spelling Curriculum. *The Elementary School Journal*, Vol. 90, No. 3, January: 275-289.

Introduction

Level *E*

English as a Second Language (ESL)

Effective teachers are always sensitive to the special spelling challenges faced by ESL students. While it is not practical to provide specific guidelines for every situation where the teacher may encounter students with limited English proficiency, the following general guidelines for two of the most prominent cultural groups (Asian & Hispanic) may prove helpful.

alphabet — Many Asian languages have a significantly different kind of alphabet and students may need considerable practice recognizing English letters and sounds.

vowels — Some Asian languages do not have certain English vowel sounds. Speakers often substitute other sounds. Spanish vowels have a single sound: *a* as in *ball*, *e* as in *eight*, *i* as in *ski*, *o* as in *over*, *u* as in *rule*. The Spanish *a* is spelled *e*, *e* is spelled *i* or *y*, and *i* is often spelled *ai* or *ay*.

ô — The variety of *ô* spellings may cause some problems for Spanish-speaking students.

ü, ů — The *u* sound does not occur in Spanish, and may cause problems.

ou — This sound is spelled *au* in Spanish.

r — This sound does not exist in Spanish. Many Asian languages do not have words ending with *r*.

b, d, h, j — Spanish and Asian speakers often confuse the sounds of *b / d* and *h / j*.

ge, gi, j — In Spanish, *ge*, *gi*, and *j* most closely resemble the English *h*.

l, f — Many Asian languages do not have these sounds.

k, q — The letter *k* does not exist in Spanish, but the sound *k* is spelled with either *c* or *qu*. The letter *q* always occurs with *ue* or *ui*.

p, g — In most Asian languages, the consonants *p* and *g* do not exist.

v — In Spanish, the letter *v* is pronounced *b*.

w — There are no Spanish-originated words with the letter *w*.

y — In Spanish, *y* is spelled *ll*.

x, z — In Spanish, *x* is never used in the final position. There is no letter or sound for *z*.

ch, sh — The Spanish language does not have the sound *sh*. Spellers often substitute *ch*. Many Asian languages do not contain *sh* or *ch*.

wh, th — The initial *wh* and *th* sounds do not exist in most Spanish and some Asian languages. The Spanish *d*, however, is sometimes pronounced almost like the *th*.

kn — This sound may be difficult for native speakers of Spanish or Asian languages.

s clusters — Spanish clusters that begin with *s* are always preceded by the vowels *a* or *e*. The most common clusters that will cause problems are *sc*, *sk*, *sl*, *sm*, *sn*, *sp*, *sq*, *st*, and *sw*. Many of these do not occur in Asian languages.

pl, fl, tr, fr, dr — These sounds are used in Spanish, but may not be present in some Asian languages.

ng, nk, nt, nd — Many Asian languages don't have *ng*, *nk*, *nt*, or *nd*. Spanish doesn't include the *ng* ending.

silent letters — The only silent letter in Spanish is *h*. Silent consonants such as those in *mb*, *lk*, and *gh* do not occur in Spanish or Asian languages.

double consonants — The only double consonants in Spanish are *cc*, *ll*, and *rr*.

ed — In Spanish, the suffix *ed* is pronounced aid. This can be very confusing, especially when the *ed* has the soft *t* sound as in *dropped*.

plurals — Spanish rules for adding plurals are: For words ending in a vowel, add *s*. For words ending in a consonant, add *es*. This may cause confusion both in pronunciation and spelling of English words.

contractions — Only two contractions are used in Spanish: *a el* becomes *al*, and *de el* becomes *del*. Apostrophes do not exist.

syllables — Many Asian languages consist entirely of one and two syllable words. Thus, many longer English words are often confusing.

Spelling Generalizations

In the English language, spelling cannot be taught primarily by rules or generalizations. It's a complex language that has evolved from many other languages and therefore contains many irregularities. There are exceptions to almost all spelling rules.

Research, however, indicates that some generalizations are of value in teaching children to spell. These generalizations have few exceptions and apply to a large number of words. Familiarity with these spelling rules can be helpful to many learners. In addition, generalizations that deal with adding suffixes to words can be quite valuable in expanding a student's ability to spell other word forms.

The following generalizations may prove to be helpful:

• The letter *q* is always followed by *u*.

• Every syllable contains a vowel. *Y* can also serve as a vowel.

• Words that end in silent *e*:
   … drop the *e* when adding a suffix beginning with a vowel. (live, living)
   … keep the *e* when adding a suffix beginning with a consonant. (time, timely)

• Words that end in *y*:
   … are not changed when adding suffixes if the *y* is preceded by a vowel. (say, saying)
   … change the *y* to *i* when adding suffixes if the *y* is preceded by a consonant, unless the suffix begins with *i*. (try, tried, trying)

• When *ei* or *ie* are used in a word, the *i* usually comes before the *e* except when they make the /$\bar{a}$/ sound, or follow after a *c*. (believe, eight, ceiling)

• Words ending in one consonant preceded by a single vowel usually double the final consonant when adding a suffix beginning with a vowel. (begin, beginning)

• Words ending with the sounds made by *x*, *s*, *sh*, and *ch* add the suffix *es* to form plurals. (mix, mixes)

• Proper nouns and most proper adjectives begin with capital letters.

Multiple Intelligences

In recognition of the multiple intelligences theory, *A Reason For Spelling*® provides activities to meet the varied needs of your students. (See "Fun Ways to Spell," and "Hide & Seek.")

Scripture Translation

Each weekly lesson in *A Reason For Spelling*® begins with a Scripture verse. This is followed by a contemporary theme story designed to bring out key values found in the verse.

Teachers are strongly encouraged to introduce each lesson by reading the "Theme Text" aloud (or have a student read the verse aloud to the class). This helps set the stage for the principles and values students will be focusing on that week.

Scripture verses used in *A Reason For Spelling*® are similar in most translations, allowing teachers to use the Scripture translation their school prefers, without affecting academic content.

Personal Spelling Dictionary

A great way to encourage students' spelling awareness is to help them develop and maintain their own Personal Spelling Dictionary at their desk to refer to when writing. This can be either a spiral-bound or loose-leaf notebook with a few pages designated for each letter of the alphabet. Throughout the school year, encourage students to constantly add words to their Personal Spelling Dictionary, not only from spelling class, but from other classes as well. These should include words a student finds difficult to spell, as well as words of particular interest. (Reproducible cover in Appendix B.)

Word Walls

Another excellent method of promoting spelling awareness in your classroom is to create a word wall. This wall (often a large bulletin board) contains commonly used words and words of special interest to your class. The classroom word wall becomes a permanent reference list that students may refer to as they read and write.

Words may be arranged in a variety of ways. Some examples include traditional alphabetical order; groups (such as math words, weather words, color words); or by the targeted vowel, for example:

A	E	I	O	U
April	cheese	listen	worry	judge
capture	leather	price	bought	curious
carpet	perfect	tonight	knock	pollute

Some words could even have picture or context clues added. Sample words from word families being studied, or interesting words students want to know how to spell are added throughout the year. Students should be reminded not to simply copy the words from the wall, but to look at the word needed, then write it from memory—or write the word they are having difficulty with, then check it against the word wall.

Games can be played using the word wall as well.
• Rhyming Words: Ask students to find a word that "rhymes with phone."

• Sentence Sense: Write the letter **w** on the board, then say "Look for a word that begins with a **w** and fits this sentence: I _ _ _ _ _ _ _ Jesus."

• Dictate & Write: Dictate a sentence for students to write using words found only on the wall.

• Read My Mind:

I am thinking of one of the words on the wall. It has _____ letters. It begins with _____ . The vowel is _____. It fits in this sentence: _____.

Flip Folders

The Flip Folder is a great way for students to use the research-based, time-tested "Look—Say—Hide—Write—Seek—Check" method to learn spelling words. They may do this activity on their own or with a partner.

On the front of a standard file folder, make two cuts to create three flaps (see diagram below). On a separate piece of paper, have students make three columns, then write the words they need to study in the first column. Now have students slide the paper into the folder so that the words are under the first flap.

- Open Flap 1 and **Look** at the first word.
- **Say** the word out loud
- Now **Hide** the word by closing the flap.
- Open Flap 2 and **Write** the word in the middle column.
- Open Flaps 1 & 2 and **Seek** the word to **Check** your spelling. If the word is misspelled. . .
- Open Flap 3 and **Write** the word correctly in the third column.

The goal of *A Reason For Spelling*® is to create proficient and self-reliant spellers and writers. By combining inventive spelling (through journaling) with formal spelling instruction, an excellent environment is created for students to develop into expert spellers. (Reproducible Journal cover in Appendix B.)

Inventive Spelling/Journaling

As children learn to spell, they go through several stages. The move from one stage to another is gradual even though students may spell from more than one stage at one time. Just as a toddler who is talking in complete sentences doesn't suddenly regress to babbling, so students tend to remain relatively stable within and between stages. Recognized stages of spelling development include:

Precognitive Stage: Children use symbols from the alphabet for writing words, but letters are random and do not correspond to sound. (eagle = dfbrt; eighty = acbp)

Semiphonetic Stage: Children understand and consistently represent sounds with letters. Spellings are often abbreviated representing only the initial and/or final sounds. (eagle = e; eighty = a)

Phonetic Stage: Students in this stage spell words like they sound. The speller perceives and represents every sound in a word, though spellings may be unconventional. (eagle = egl; eighty = aty)

Transitional Stage: Students think about how words appear visually. Spelling patterns are apparent. Spellings exhibit customs of English spelling such as vowels in every syllable, correct e-marker and vowel digraph patterns, inflectional endings, and frequent English letter sequences. (eagle = egul; eighty = eightee)

Conventional Stage: This stage develops over years of word study and writing. Correct spelling has different instructional levels. Correct spelling for a group of words that can be spelled by the average third grader would be "third grade level correct" spelling. (eagle = eagle; eighty = eighty)

An effective way to help students transition through the stages is to edit their first drafts, then talk with them about corrections. Discuss why changes are necessary. Encourage students to rewrite journal entries so others can read them easily. Display student work whenever possible. Teach students that invented spelling makes it easier for the writer, but that revision to standard spelling is a courtesy to the reader.

Word Lists

Word lists in *A Reason For Spelling*® are based on frequency of use in student and adult writing; frequency of use in reading materials; spelling difficulty; and grade level familiarity.

Studies used in the development of these lists include: *Dolch Basic Sight Vocabulary* (a list of 220 high frequency words); *The American Heritage Word Frequency Book* (a study of word frequency in print materials for grades three through nine); *Starter Words* (the 190 most frequently used words in children's writing, school materials, and adult print materials); and *A Basic Vocabulary of Elementary School Children*.

These standard references were extensively cross-checked with other respected studies (Gates; Horn; Greene & Loomer; Harris & Jacobson). It is significant to note that very few differences were found among these sources.

For teacher convenience, lesson numbers follow each word.

Level-D

accept-2
across-14
against-3
agree-4
ahead-3
alike-5
all right-16
almost-16
aloud-15
alphabet-13
already-16
although-11
among-10
annoy-21
anyway-29
anywhere-26
apartment-10
appear-27
applause-16
appointment-21
April Fools' Day-31
Arbor Day-31
arrest-2
arrow-2
attic-2
author-16
avenue-7
avoid-21
awful-16
backyard-29
bandage-2
barber-17
bare-26
barnyard-17
bathroom-29

bathtub-29
battle-23
beard-27
beast-14
beautiful-7
became-4
bedroom-29
bedspread-29
behave-4
believe-4
belt-10
bent-10
birth-19
blade-8
blank-10
blanket-8
blood-1
bloom-7
bluff-13
bomb-11
bounce-15
branch-1
brand-1
breakfast-3
bridge-8
broom-7
built-3
bulldozer-20
bulletin-20
burst-19
butcher-20
button-25
cabbage-2
cane-4
cape-4
capture-22
cardboard-17

carnival-17
carpet-17
cart-17
castle-23
cave-4
cellar-14
cereal-27
champion-25
chance-14
cheer-27
chef-13
chicken-25
chief-4
choice-21
chose-5
Christmas-31
citizen-14
clear-8
climb-11
clue-7
coach-5
collect-2
Columbus Day-31
comb-11
comfort-3
common-25
compare-26
cord-16
cotton-25
cough-13
couldn't-28
county-15
couple-3
cousin-3
crack-8
craft-13
cream-8

crooked-20
crow-5
crust-10
cure-20
curious-20
curl-19
curtain-25
curve-19
dairy-26
damage-2
danger-22
dare-26
dead-3
decide-14
deer-27
delight-11
depend-2
dessert-19
destroy-21
dew-7
didn't-28
disappear-27
disappoint-21
dive-5
dock-1
dollhouse-15
donor-22
dragon-25
dream-8
drift-13
drum-8
due-7
dumb-11
during-20
dust-1
Easter-31
either-22

elephant-13
else-14
employ-21
enjoyment-21
enough-13
enter-22
everybody-29
evil-23
except-2
exciting-14
fail-4
fair-26
false-16
famous-14
fare-26
farmer-17
farther-17
fault-16
favor-22
fear-27
feather-22
fence-14
festival-23
fierce-27
final-23
finger-22
fireplace-29
firm-19
fist-1
flock-1
flour-8
flow-8
flute-7
fog-16
folks-11
footprint-20
forest-16
forward-10
fountain-25
freight-4
frost-10
frown-15
fry-8
fully-20
furious-20
furniture-19
further-19
garbage-17
garden-17
gear-27
general-23
gentle-23
germ-19
glance-14
glare-26
glue-7
goodness-20
government-10

gown-15
graph-13
grave-8
groan-8
Groundhog Day-31
growl-15
guard-10
hadn't-28
hair-26
Halloween-31
handful-20
Hanukkah-31
hardly-17
hare-26
harm-17
harsh-17
haul-16
hawk-16
he'd-28
he'll-28
here's-28
herself-29
hollow-5
homemade-29
homework-29
honor-22
hospital-23
however-15
human-7
humor-22
hung-1
I'd-28
Independence Day-31
instead-3
iron-5
it'll-28
jelly-4
joint-21
jungle-23
kitchen-25
knife-11
knob-11
label-23
Labor Day-31
laid-4
laugh-13
lazy-4
lead-3
lean-4
least-4
leather-3
legend-10
lemon-25
level-23
limb-11
lion-25
listen-25

E Level

Texas-2
tomb-11
trophy-19
truly-11
tulip-11
tundra-5
umbrella-2
umpire-5
useless-11
Utah-11
valley-13
valve-13
veil-7
vein-7
Vermont-4
version-26
vetoes-8
view-11
Virginia-3
virus-27
voltage-10
walrus-27
Washington-4
weapon-2
weather-2
West Virginia-26
wharves-31
whereabouts-29
wield-8
wife-9
willpower-29
Wisconsin-14
wisdom-5
witness-27
wreck-31
Wyoming-10

Level-F

abandon-1
abdomen-1
ability-3
abolish-4
absence-31
abundant-27
accelerator-21
accessory-21
accurate-21
achievement-31
acquaintance-15
acquire-15
acquittal-15
acreage-14
action-25
actual-1
adjective-19
admonish-4
adobe-10

advantage-14
advertise-16
advice-9
advise-16
advocate-28
aggressive-19
agreeable-5
alfalfa-1
alligator-1
altogether-21
amazement-27
amendment-27
analysis-1
ancestor-1
apology-14
appearance-31
approximately-26
apricot-4
archaeology-14
architecture-15
arrogance-31
ashamed-13
assembly-26
assistance-31
associate-28
assurance-31
astronomy-4
atmosphere-11
attempt-2
attention-25
attorney-21
attractive-19
automotive-19
bacteria-11
balance-1
barometer-20
bazaar-29
behavior-21
beliefs-8
bellow-2
benefit-2
betrayed-13
bewildered-13
beyond-4
bilingual-5
billion-25
binoculars-20
biography-4
biology-14
bizarre-29
boarder-29
boast-10
border-29
botanist-4
brackets-1
brakes-29
breaks-29
breathe-8

cafeteria-11
calcium-1
calculate-1
calendar-20
calorie-1
capital-29
capitol-29
capsule-1
captain-1
career-11
cashier-11
caution-25
cavalry-1
ceiling-8
centimeter-20
certificate-21
challenge-1
chameleon-15
chandelier-11
channel-1
character-15
chemical-15
cherish-2
chimney-3
chronic-15
cinema-3
civilize-16
classified-13
clenched-13
clockwise-16
coarse-29
coastal-10
coax-10
cocoa-10
coincidence-31
collision-25
colon-10
comfortable-5
commandment-27
community-26
compact-28
comparative-19
complain-7
complete-8
compress-28
compromise-16
computer-20
conceal-8
conceit-8
concerned-13
concert-28
condense-2
conflict-28
congratulations-17
connect-2
conscience-31
consequence-15
consumer-20

contaminated-1
content-28
contest-28
convertible-5
cooperate-21
correct-21
council-29
counsel-29
courage-14
creased-13
creation-25
crescent-31
criminology-14
criteria-11
critical-5
crucial-5
cruelty-26
cunning-13
current-27
cursive-19
cushion-25
customer-20
customize-16
cyclone-9
cylinder-3
decision-25
declarative-19
defeat-8
definitely-26
definition-25
degree-8
dehydrated-13
delete-8
deliberate-28
delicate-2
delightful-9
density-2
dentist-2
deodorant-27
dependence-31
depth-2
describe-9
desolate-28
detective-19
determination-17
develop-2
devotion-25
diagonal-5
diagram-9
diameter-1
diamond-9
diesel-8
digestive-19
dimensions-17
direction-25
disagree-22
disappearance-22
disappointment-22

disbelief-22
discard-22
discharge-22
disclose-22
discomfort-22
disconnect-22
discontinue-22
discount-22
discourage-22
discover-22
disengage-22
disgrace-22
disguised-13
disgust-22
dishonest-22
dislike-22
dismay-22
dismiss-22
disorder-22
displease-22
dispute-22
dissatisfy-22
distance-31
distrust-22
division-25
document-27
dreary-11
drenched-13
dripped-13
duplicate-7
durable-5
dyeing-29
dying-29
dynamite-9
eclipse-3
ecology-14
economy-4
edible-5
editorial-5
eerie-11
elective-19
electrical-5
electron-4
elementary-2
elevator-21
eligible-5
emotion-25
empathize-16
enable-7
encourage-14
endanger-20
endeavor-21
engrave-7
enterprise-16
entertain-7
entirely-9
entrance-28
environment-27

equality-15
equipment-15
equivalent-15
erode-10
erosion-25
especially-26
estimate-28
ethnic-2
evacuate-7
eventually-26
evidence-31
excellent-27
excessive-19
exchange-7
excitement-27
excursion-17
excuse-28
executive-19
exercise-16
expense-2
experience-11
explain-7
exploration-17
extent-27
extinct-3
familiar-20
fascinating-13
fashion-25
favorable-5
federal-5
fertilize-16
fiction-25
finalize-16
foliage-14
fraction-25
fragment-27
franchise-16
frontier-11
function-25
galaxy-1
gallery-1
gemology-14
gently-26
geology-14
geranium-7
glacier-20
gnarled-13
gorilla-3
graceful-7
graduation-17
grammar-20
gravity-26
greedy-8
growth-10
headache-15
headquarters-15
hemisphere-11
heredity-26

Curriculum Objectives

Literature Connection
To increase comprehension and vocabulary development through a value-based story.

Discussion Time
To check understanding of the story and encourage personal value development.

Preview
To test for knowledge of correct spellings of current spelling words.

Word Shapes
To help students form a correct visual image of whole words and to help students recognize common spelling patterns.

Hide & Seek
To reinforce correct spelling of current spelling words.

Other Word Forms
To strengthen spelling ability and expand vocabulary.

Fun Ways to Spell
To reinforce correct spelling of current words with activities that appeal to varying learning styles.

Dictation
To reinforce using current and previous spelling words in context.

Proofreading
To reinforce recognition of misspelled words, and to familiarize students with standardized test format.

Language Arts Activity
To familiarize students with word meaning and usage.

Posttest
To test mastery of the current spelling words.

Learning Game
To reinforce correct spelling of test words.

Vocabulary Extension
To provide advanced spellers with the opportunity to enrich their vocabulary.

Journaling
To provide a meaningful reason for correct spelling through personal writing.

Unit Tests
To test mastery of the correct spelling of the words from each unit.

Action Game
To provide a fun way to review spelling words from the previous unit.

Certificate
To provide opportunity for parents or guardians to encourage and assess their child's progress.

Parent Letter
To provide the parent or guardian with the spelling word lists for the next unit.

Phonics Units (Levels A and B only)
To provide a supplement for promoting phonemic awareness, and a review of basic phonic skills.

Common Spelling Patterns

The following list of sounds and spelling patterns will help you easily identify words with similar patterns.

Sounds	Sample Words	Sounds	Sample Words
a	ask, hat	ō	old, boat, hoe, globe, blow
ā	apron, late, mail, play	ô	talk, cause, draw, soft, thought
ä	father, part, heart	ôr	story, more, ward, four
âr	aware, fair, bear, there	oi	point, boy
b	berry, able, scrub	ou	about, plow
ch	cheese, bunch, latch, nature	p	plan, reply, snap, supply
d	dog, ladder	r	ran, merry, more, write
e	bed, heavy, said	s	say, guess, scent, price, city
ē	she, heat, free, niece, key	sh	ship, cash, mission, machine, special, vacation
f	fish, loaf, off, enough, prophet		
g	give, forgot, shrug	t	ten, put, butter, creased
h	has, anyhow, whole	th	thin, ethnic, with
wh	whine, which	<u>th</u>	them, worthy, smooth
i	dig, gym	u	cup, done, what, young
ī	find, pie, mice, try	ū	human, you, new, tune
îr	clear, deer, pierce, cereal, here	ü	clue, do, soon, fruit
j	just, enjoy, germ, huge, budge	u̇	took, should, push
k	keep, hook, stick, school, can	ûr	earn, stern, first, work, Thursday
l	left, July, haul, fully, tell	v	visit, avoid, arrive
m	meal, calm, climb, common, hymn	w	wash, driveway
		y	young, familiar
n	nice, fun, tunnel, know	z	lazy, jazz, prize, raise, reins, example
ng	along, bringing, think	zh	measure, erosion
o	not, pond, watch	ə	above, water, animal, gallon, thankful

Daily Lesson Plans

Letter

Provide the parent or guardian with the spelling word lists for the first unit.

Give your parents or guardian this letter that lists your spelling words for the next unit. Put it where you will remember to practice the words together.

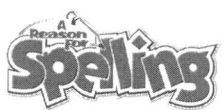

Dear Parent,

We are about to begin our first spelling unit containing five weekly lessons. A set of twenty words will be studied each week. All the words will be reviewed in the sixth week. Values based on the Scriptures listed below will be taught in each lesson.

Lesson 1	Lesson 2	Lesson 3	Lesson 4	Lesson 5
accent	attend	admit	alcohol	adult
acid	credit	assist	astronaut	album
adapt	delta	cliffs	audience	circuit
aspect	denim	discuss	Australia	construct
athlete	healthy	disk	automatic	crumb
atlas	heifer	England	automobile	District of Columbia
banana	lever	glisten	awkward	freedom
banner	Maryland	glitter	clause	gruffly
batch	method	history	coffee	hungry
California	New Mexico	hymn	crawl	minutes
camera	respect	income	exhaust	museum
Canada	selfish	index	launch	numb
cavern	shelter	infant	laundry	opossum
cavity	strength	insist	lawyers	pulse
gram	tennis	kidnap	online	shrug
latch	tense	limit	precaution	suffix
mass	Texas	lizard	somersault	summary
Montana	umbrella	Michigan	strawberry	tundra
panic	weapon	Mississippi	Vermont	umpire
planet	weather	Virginia	Washington	wisdom
Psalm 71:8	Psalm 25:6,7	Psalm 51:10,12	Psalm 92:2,4	Psalm 16:8,9

Have each student remove this letter from his or her Worktext prior to beginning Lesson 1.

Home Alone? - NOT!

Katelynn learns God is with her when she feels her need for Him, and also when she doesn't.

"*I* don't know what the big deal is. I've been home alone before." Katelynn Hatasaki fastened her house key to the shiny chain heaped on the kitchen counter.

"You have your key, Katie?" Mr. Hatasaki checked his watch as he opened the front door for his two daughters.

Katelynn lifted the key she had just hung around her neck. "Right here. Don't worry, Dad." She patted his arm as she followed her older sister, Jennifer, out the front door of the apartment.

"Now remember to turn the thermostat to 74° as soon as you come in—just like I showed you. It will take a while for the apartment to cool down, but don't keep adjusting the temperature." Mr. Hatasaki surveyed the room before he shut the door behind them.

"You can call Dad at the gas station or I'll just be in the next building at Krugers' apartment." Jennifer grabbed Katelynn's shoulder, "Do you have Krugers' number? You can always dial 911 if you have a bad asthma attack or something. They'll find you even if you can't talk."

"Don't be so dramatic, you guys. All the phone numbers are programmed. I'll be fine. It's just until Mom's off work." Katelynn held her head high and sauntered down the stairs towards the family car.

Katelynn hummed to herself that afternoon as she climbed the stairs to her family's third-floor apartment. She pulled the shiny new chain from around her neck. The 10-year-old girl gripped the key tightly in her hand and twirled the chain as she marched past her neighbors' apartments. "I wonder how long Jennifer will be at the Krugers'

babysitting?" She stopped in front of the red door marked 308-B.

A car door slammed in the parking lot. Katelynn looked over the railing and saw a tall, dark-haired man locking the door of a big black pickup. The back of the loaded truck was covered with a green tarp. The man glanced up at her as he started toward the stairs. Their eyes met for an instant before Katelynn turned back toward her apartment.

"I don't recognize him," she mumbled. "I wonder if he's coming up here?" Katelynn hurriedly slipped the key into the lock and pushed the door open. "I don't want him to know I'm by myself." She quickly stepped into the dark interior and slammed the door. She hastily locked the doorknob, turned the deadbolt, and slid the chain into place. "He can't be a salesman," she said to herself. "I wonder what he's doing here?"

Katelynn leaned against the warm door and surveyed the room. She could feel her heart thumping loudly. She wiped away the sweat dripping into her eyes and reached over to open the blinds when she remembered her mom's warning, "Katelynn, leave the front blinds closed. Someone walking by may notice you're alone. Don't answer the phone or the door. I'll be home by 4:00."

Katelynn slung her backpack on the kitchen counter. She poured herself a glass of juice before she turned on the air conditioner. The baby next door cried. The refrigerator hummed. She froze when she heard footsteps outside the apartment—and relaxed when they continued on. "It's too quiet! I hear every little sound." Her own voice sounded loud in the empty apartment.

The phone jangled. She

automatically reached for it, then jerked her hand back as if she'd been burned. *I'm not supposed to answer that thing; but maybe it's Beth. I could talk to her for a while,* she reasoned. The caller didn't leave a message. Katelynn sighed and picked up the phone. *Maybe I'll call Beth. Mom just said not to answer the phone.*

Whew! It's hot in here. She fanned herself with a magazine. *I'm going to change into something cooler.* As she passed the bathroom she noticed her favorite shirt on the floor. "I think I'll do a load of wash." She talked to herself as she collected more dirty clothes. "This should be enough to do a small load." She dumped the clothes into the washer. *It's so hot in here. I wonder if I did that thermostat right?* She closed the lid of the machine and smiled. *That's good. Now, where did I put the phone?*

Katelynn wiped the moisture off her forehead with a towel and picked up the cordless phone. She checked the thermostat again. It was set right on 74°. She nudged the dial a little lower. Warm sunlight streamed in through the sliding-glass door beside her. She reached over to pull the heavy drapes closed when movement below caught her eye.

A young girl in front of the next apartment building was wildly waving her arms. When she paused, a woman started gesturing with her hands. A little blond-haired boy came running around the end of a U-Haul truck and tapped the girl on the shoulder. He pointed to a door on the second floor. Katelynn unlocked the sliding-glass door and stepped out onto the balcony to get a better view. She soon realized that none of the three was saying a word. The young girl seemed to be the most expressive. It looked as if she were angry about something. *They must be moving in today. I bet the girl is about my age.*

Mr. Rippy roared by between the apartments on his big riding mower. The new girl didn't turn around—or even seem to notice the deafening noise right behind her.

3

Suddenly it hit Katelynn—the girl was deaf! She was using sign language to talk to her family. Katelynn jumped when the phone in her hand rang. She remembered not to answer it, though. *That girl can't hear anything! It's always quiet for her.* Katelynn reached behind her and shut the screen door. It was actually cooler outside than it was in the apartment. She continued to watch the family. A teenage boy joined them. When he unlocked the door of apartment 205-B, she decided he must be the older brother.

I wonder if they're all deaf? Maybe the girl will go to Knowlton Elementary. Katelynn was so busy watching the family that she ignored the spasms of her bronchial tubes until it was hard to force air into her lungs. Whee-heee. Whee-heee. She wheezed in the hot, grassy-smelling air. It was so interesting watching the family talk to each other with their hands she hadn't stopped to use the inhaler at the first sign of her asthma attack.

She reluctantly walked back into the kitchen without shutting the door and picked up her backpack. She rummaged through it until she found the small aerosol dispenser. *What's triggering this episode, I wonder?* She walked back onto the balcony. As the asthma flared, it was getting harder and harder for her to breathe. She inhaled two puffs of the medication and held her breath. It helped, but the wheezing didn't stop. "I wonder…whee-heee… when Mom…whee-heee…will get here?"

She shuffled back into the apartment and flopped onto the couch. The apartment was unbearably hot. She started to get up to check the thermostat again, when she heard footsteps. They slowed as they approached and stopped right outside the door. Her eyes widened as she watched the doorknob turn. She heard the sound of a key in the deadbolt! She huddled on the couch and stuffed a fist

into her mouth as the door opened— until it was stopped by the chain.

"Katelynn, open the door. I'm home." Mrs. Hatasaki peeked in through the crack in the door.

Katelynn let out the breath she had been holding. "Whee-hee. I'm…whee-hee…coming.…"

"Katie, have you taken your medication?" The girl nodded. "Why is the sliding-glass door open? You know that cut grass always triggers an episode. How come the air-conditioner isn't turned on? It's like an oven in here." Mrs. Hatasaki bustled around the apartment. She turned the switch on the thermostat to "cool"—and the air-conditioner cycled on immediately. She shut the sliding-glass door and the dryer door. "When did you take your last dose of medication?"

Katelynn looked at her watch. "About…whee-hee…10 minutes ago."

"Take another dose at 4:00." Mrs. Hatasaki sat down beside her daughter and wiped her face with a cool cloth.

"I'm glad you're…whee-hee… home, Mom." Katelynn smiled weakly. "I did remember not to answer the phone…whee-hee…or open the blinds. I started the wash."

Mother and daughter sat quietly on the couch as the apartment cooled down. Mrs. Hatasaki rubbed Katelynn's back and wiped her face with a damp washcloth. Her breathing became less labored after she took the next dose of medication, so Mom got up and went into the kitchen to start supper.

"Katelynn, why don't you put that load of clothes into the dryer?" Mrs. Hatasaki closed the oven door and set the timer.

Katelynn stood up, stretched, and walked over to the sliding glass door. Mr. Rippy was almost finished mowing the lawn. She silently watched the new family carrying things up to their apartment. The dark-haired man from the black pickup was helping the teenage boy carry a dresser up the stairs. When he got to the door, he set his end of the dresser down and turned to sign something to the girl following them. They laughed and went together into the apartment. *He must be their Dad*, Katelynn mused. *I was*

so worried about him I forgot to turn the thermostat to 'cool,' I stood on the balcony while the grass was being mowed, and I nearly forgot to start the washer.

She smiled and took a deep breath. As she relaxed, she knew who had been with her all day long—when she was confident and sure of herself AND when she was afraid and all alone. "Thanks, God," she breathed.

Discussion Time

Check understanding of the story and development of personal values.

- Tell about a time you stayed alone.
- How did you feel?
- How did Katelynn feel about staying home at the beginning of the story?
- How did she feel when she noticed the stranger from the black pickup coming up the stairs?
- What did Katelynn do when she heard footsteps stop outside the apartment and then saw the doorknob turn?
- Later as Katelynn stood at the sliding glass doors and watched the new family move in, why did she feel thankful?

1. latch
2. aspect
3. accent
4. acid
5. adapt
6. camera
7. gram
8. mass
9. batch
10. banana
11. banner
12. atlas
13. Canada
14. athlete
15. Montana
16. planet
17. California
18. panic
19. cavern
20. cavity

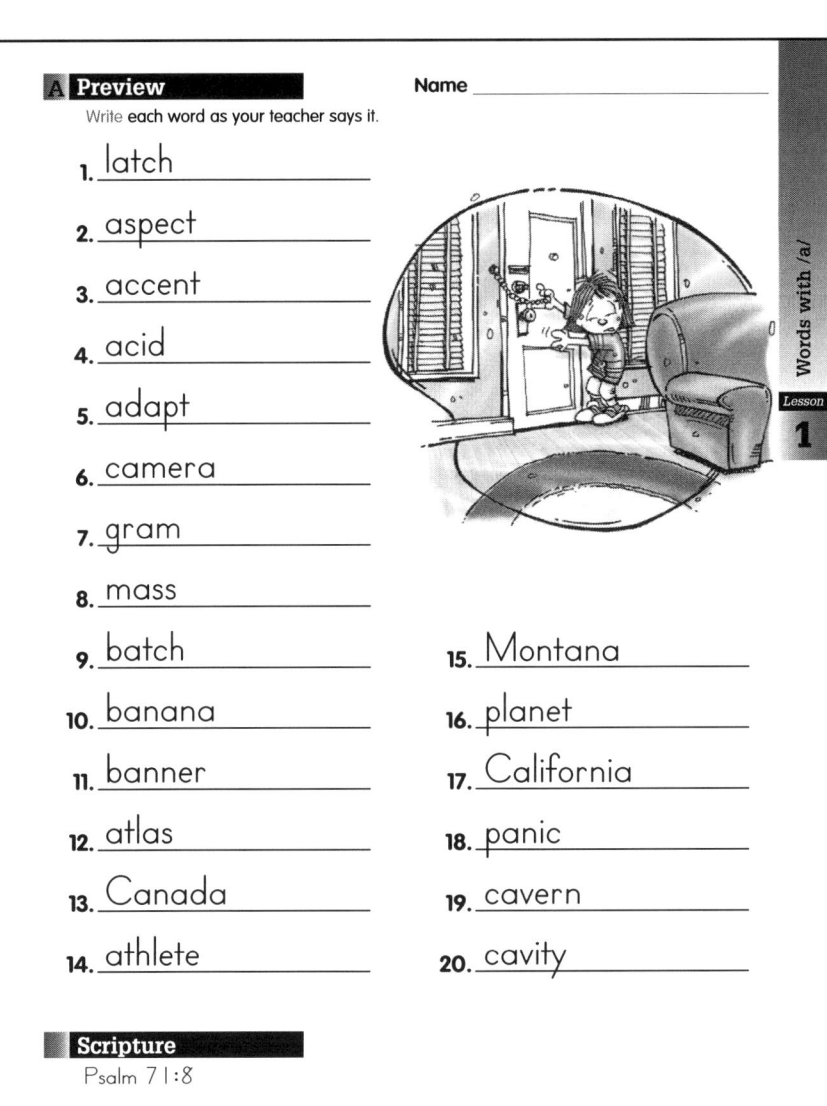

Words with /a/

Lesson **1**

Scripture
Psalm 71:8

5

 Customize Your List
On a separate sheet of paper, additional words of your choice may be tested.

 (Say) I will say each word once, use the word in a sentence, then say the word again. Write the words on the lines in your Worktext.

 (Say) **Correct Immediately!**
Let's correct our Preview. I will spell each word out loud. If you spelled a word incorrectly, rewrite it correctly.

 Progress Chart
Students may record scores. (Reproducible master provided in Appendix B.)

Lesson **1** | Day 1

1.	latch	Katelynn reached for the chain to **latch** the door.
2.	aspect	Mr. and Mrs. Hatasaki tried to teach Katelynn every **aspect** of safety.
3.	accent	Being alone seemed to **accent** every little sound.
4.	acid	The natural **acid** in the orange juice burned Katelynn's dry throat.
5.	adapt	It would be difficult to **adapt** to not being able to hear.
6.	camera	She looked through the lens of her dad's **camera**.
7.	gram	Katelynn tried to remember Mr. Canfield's definition of **gram**.
8.	mass	She knew that **mass** meant a body of matter.
9.	batch	She saw a **batch** of cookies in the jar on the counter.
10.	banana	Katelynn peeled a **banana**, but felt too hot to eat.
11.	banner	Katelynn straightened the school **banner** she had hanging on her wall.
12.	atlas	Next, she aimlessly leafed through the giant **atlas** on the coffee table.
13.	Canada	She tried to memorize the provinces of **Canada**.
14.	athlete	A famous **athlete** was pictured beside the facts about the country.
15.	Montana	She also read about the thoroughbreds in **Montana**.
16.	planet	Katelynn felt as if she were alone on the **planet**.
17.	California	The pictures of the beaches of **California** made her feel more hot.
18.	panic	Katelynn knew **panic** would worsen her asthma attack.
19.	cavern	Noises in the hallway outside the apartment echoed like in a **cavern**.
20.	cavity	Her chest **cavity** ached as her bronchial tubes tightened.

4 Word Shapes

Help students form a correct image of whole words.

Say

Look at each word and think about its shape. Now, write the word in the correct Word Shape Boxes. You may check off each word as you use it.

(Short vowels are usually found in syllables in which a vowel is immediately preceded and followed by a consonant, consonant cluster, or digraph.)

Say

In the Word Shape Boxes, fill in the boxes containing the letter or letters that spell the sound of /a/ in each word.

Take a minute to memorize...

Psalm 71:8

B Word Shapes   Name _____

Using the word bank below, write each word in the correct Word Shape Boxes. Next, in the Word Shape Boxes, fill in the boxes containing the letter or letters that spell the sound of /a/ in each word.

Words with /a/

Lesson 1

1. Montana
2. California
3. cavern
4. panic
5. athlete
6. banner
7. aspect
8. adapt
9. atlas
10. accent

11. planet
12. Canada
13. cavity
14. camera
15. mass
16. acid
17. gram
18. batch
19. latch
20. banana

Word Bank

accent	athlete	batch	cavern	mass
acid	atlas	California	cavity	Montana
adapt	banana	camera	gram	panic
aspect	banner	Canada	latch	planet

6

Answers may vary for duplicate word shapes.

Be Prepared For Fun

Check these supply lists for **Fun Ways to Spell** - presented **Day 2**. Purchase and/or gather these items ahead of time!

General
- Pencil
- Graph Paper (1 sheet per child)
- Spelling List

Auditory
- Voice Recorder
- Spelling List

Visual
- American Sign Language reproducible master (provided in Appendix B)
- Spelling List

Tactile
- Soccer Ball, Basketball, Tennis Ball, or 4-Square Ball
- Spelling List

C Hide and Seek

Name _____

Play **Hide and Seek** with your words. Fill in a box on the bar graph (left to right) for each word you spell correctly.

LOOK   SAY   SPELL ALOUD   WRITE   SEEK   CHECK

D Other Word Forms

Using the words below, follow the instructions given by your teacher.

accented	athletic	Canadian	masses
accentuate	atlases	cavernous	Montanan
acidic	bananas	caverns	panicked
acids	banners	cavities	panicking
adaptable	batches	grams	planetarium
adapting	Californian	latched	planets
aspects	cameraman	latching	vaster
athletes	cameras	massed	vastest

E Fun Ways to Spell

Initial the box of each activity you finish.

1. ☐
Create a crossword puzzle with clues.

2. w·o·r·d ☐
Spell your words with sign language.

3. W·O·R·D ☐
Spell your words on a voice recorder.

4. B·A·T·C·H ☐
Bounce a ball as you spell your words.

Words with /a/

Lesson 1

7

---

1 Hide and Seek

Reinforce spelling by using multiple styles of learning.

On a white board, Teacher writes each word — one at a time. **Have students:**

- **Look** at the word.
- **Say** the word out loud.
- **Spell** the word out loud.
- **Hide** (teacher erases word.)
- **Write** the word on paper.
- **Seek** (teacher rewrites word.)
- **Check** spelling. If incorrect, rewrite word correctly.

2 Other Word Forms

This activity is optional. Have students write original sentences using these Other Word Forms:

acidic
Montanan
massed
cavernous

3 Fun Ways to Spell

Four activities are provided. Use one, two, three, or all of the activities. Have students initial the box for each activity they complete.

Options:

- assign activities to students according to their learning styles
- set up the activities in learning centers for the students to do throughout the day
- divide students into four groups and assign one activity per group
- do one activity per day

General
To create a crossword puzzle...
- Use a pencil to arrange your words on graph paper.
- Overlap words where letters are shared.
- Don't create any new words.
- Outline each word with a marker and number it.
- Write a clue for each word.
- Erase your words.
- Trade with a classmate and work each other's puzzles.

Auditory
To spell your words using a voice recorder...
- Record yourself as you say and spell each word on your spelling list.
- Listen to your recording and check your spelling.

Visual
To spell your words with sign language...
- Have a classmate read a spelling word to you from the list.
- Spell the word using the American Sign Language alphabet.
- Do this with each word on your list.

Tactile
To bounce a ball as you spell your words...
- Look at the first word on your list.
- Bounce the ball as you say each letter of the word aloud.
- Do this with each word on your list.

Working with Words

Familiarize students with word meaning and usage.

Scrambled Words

Say

Write the letters **alst** on the board. Have a student unscramble the letters to make the word **last**.

Unscramble each spelling word. Write the word correctly on the line. Remember to use capital letters where they are needed.

Word Clues

Say

Use your word bank to help you match the spelling words to the clues. Some of the clues are synonyms, words that have the same meaning as the spelling word. You may use a dictionary or thesaurus to help you.

Take a minute to memorize...

Psalm 71:8

F Working with Words   Name _____

Scrambled Words

Unscramble each word. Write the unscrambled word on the line. Use capital letters where they are needed.

1. aeehltt — athlete
2. aamnnot — Montana
3. aaabnn — banana
4. acdi — acid
5. acitvy — cavity
6. abcht — batch
7. aacfiilnor — California
8. agmr — gram
9. catcne — accent
10. aalst — atlas
11. amss — mass
12. abennr — banner
13. aadpt — adapt
14. aaacdn — Canada
15. acinp — panic
16. acepst — aspect
17. aelnpt — planet
18. achlt — latch
19. acenrv — cavern
20. aacemr — camera

Word Clues

Match the spelling words to the clues. You may use a dictionary or thesaurus to help you.

1. emphasize, stress — accent
2. void, depression — cavity
3. alarm, scare — panic
4. runner, swimmer — athlete
5. cave, hollow — cavern
6. appearance, condition — aspect
7. quantity, bulk — mass
8. corrosive, erosive — acid
9. adjust, accommodate — adapt
10. Earth, Mars — planet
11. pennant, flag — banner
12. tropical fruit — banana
13. unit of mass — gram
14. photographic tool — camera
15. charts, maps — atlas
16. group, bunch — batch
17. coastal state — California
18. fasten, secure — latch

Word Bank

accent	athlete	batch	cavern	mass
acid	atlas	California	cavity	Montana
adapt	banana	camera	gram	panic
aspect	banner	Canada	latch	planet

8

8

G Dictation

Name _____

Write **each sentence as your teacher dictates**. Use **correct punctuation**.

1. Katelynn <u>began to panic when the tall man</u> <u>looked at her.</u>

2. <u>Mom made a batch of cookies after supper.</u>

3. Katelynn <u>got the atlas to find a map</u> <u>of Canada.</u>

H Proofreading

If a word is misspelled, fill in the oval by that word. If all the words are spelled correctly, fill in the oval by **no mistake**.

1. ○ adapt
   ● acsent
   ○ gram
   ○ no mistake

2. ● camra
   ○ latch
   ○ banner
   ○ no mistake

3. ● asid
   ○ California
   ○ batch
   ○ no mistake

4. ○ athlete
   ○ mass
   ● canada
   ○ no mistake

5. ● panick
   ○ Canada
   ○ rake
   ○ no mistake

6. ○ cavity
   ○ planet
   ○ love
   ● no mistake

7. ○ banana
   ● aspekt
   ○ cavern
   ○ no mistake

8. ● planit
   ○ aspect
   ○ panic
   ○ no mistake

9. ● lacth
   ○ atlas
   ○ camera
   ○ no mistake

10. ○ acid
    ○ Montana
    ● atlus
    ○ no mistake

11. ○ broom
    ● cavirn
    ○ accent
    ○ no mistake

12. ○ flute
    ● Montanna
    ○ look
    ○ no mistake

9

---

1 Dictation

Reinforce correct spelling by using current and previous words in context.

(Say) Listen as I read each sentence and then write it in your Worktext. Remember to use correct capitalization and punctuation. (Slowly read each sentence twice. Sentences are found in the Student Worktext to the left.)

2 Proofreading

Familiarize students with standardized test format and reinforce recognition of misspelled words.

(Say) Look at each set of words. If a word is misspelled, fill in the oval by that word. If all the words are spelled correctly, fill in the oval by **no mistake**.

9

3 Hide and Seek

Reinforce correct spelling of current spelling words. Repeat this activity from Day 2.

4 Vocabulary Extension

Have your students complete this activity to strengthen spelling ability and expand vocabulary. The reproducible master is provided in Appendix A as shown on the inset page to the right.

1 Posttest

Visit the **A Reason For** website to download free, printable Posttest pages.

Say

I will say the word once, use it in a sentence, then say it again. Write your words on a separate sheet of paper.

Progress Chart

Students may record scores. (Appendix B)

Personal Dictionary

Students may add any words they have misspelled to their personal dictionaries. (Appendix B)

Hide and Seek

Play Hide and Seek with your words. Fill in a bar graph (left to right) for each word you spell correctly.

LOOK   SAY   HIDE   WRITE   SEEK   CHECK.

Vocabulary Extension

Crossword Puzzle

Use the clues below to complete the puzzle.

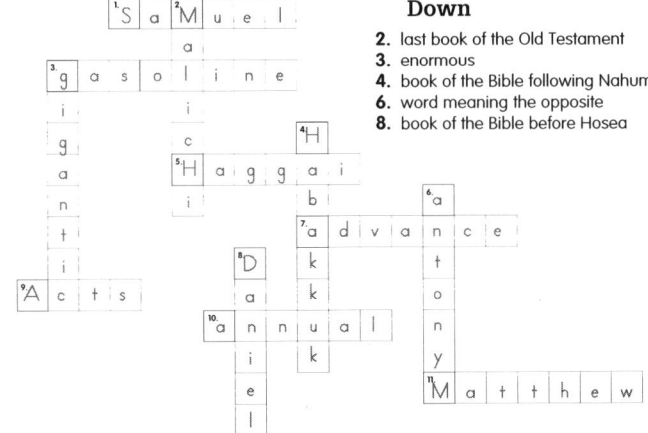

Down

2. last book of the Old Testament
3. enormous
4. book of the Bible following Nahum
6. word meaning the opposite
8. book of the Bible before Hosea

Across

1. book of the Bible that follows Ruth
3. motor fuel
5. book of the Bible between Zephaniah and Zechariah
7. move forward
9. fifth book of the New Testament
10. occurring every year
11. one of the four gospels

Word Bank

Acts	antonym	gigantic	Malachi
advance	Daniel	Habakkuk	Matthew
annual	gasoline	Haggai	Samuel

325

---

1. **accent** — Katelynn tripped over the **accent** rug just inside the door.
2. **batch** — Katelynn thought about making a **batch** of muffins to go with dinner.
3. **gram** — Katelynn noticed the juice did not have a single **gram** of fat.
4. **cavity** — The cold juice made the **cavity** in her upper molar throb.
5. **acid** — The **acid** in the juice burned her throat as she drank.
6. **mass** — Mr. Canfield defined **mass** for his class that day.
7. **camera** — Katelynn put her dad's **camera** back in its case.
8. **adapt** — She wondered how a person could **adapt** to not hearing.
9. **aspect** — She began to consider every possible **aspect** of being home alone.
10. **banner** — Her school **banner** is bright green with gold letters.
11. **atlas** — The giant picture **atlas** on the coffee table was very heavy.
12. **Montana** — There were photos of beautiful horses on the pages about **Montana**.
13. **Canada** — She imagined standing by the great Niagara Falls in **Canada**.
14. **athlete** — Katelynn does not plan to become a professional **athlete**.
15. **banana** — She put the uneaten **banana** on the top shelf of the refrigerator.
16. **panic** — Each noise increased Katelynn's feelings of **panic**.
17. **planet** — Katelynn felt like she was alone on the **planet**.
18. **cavern** — The empty apartment seemed to echo like a **cavern**.
19. **latch** — When her mom got home, Katelynn had to remove the chain from the **latch**.
20. **California** — The book lay open to pictures and information about **California**.

I Game

Name _____

Go upstairs with Katelynn to her family's apartment. Move one step for each word you or your team spells correctly.

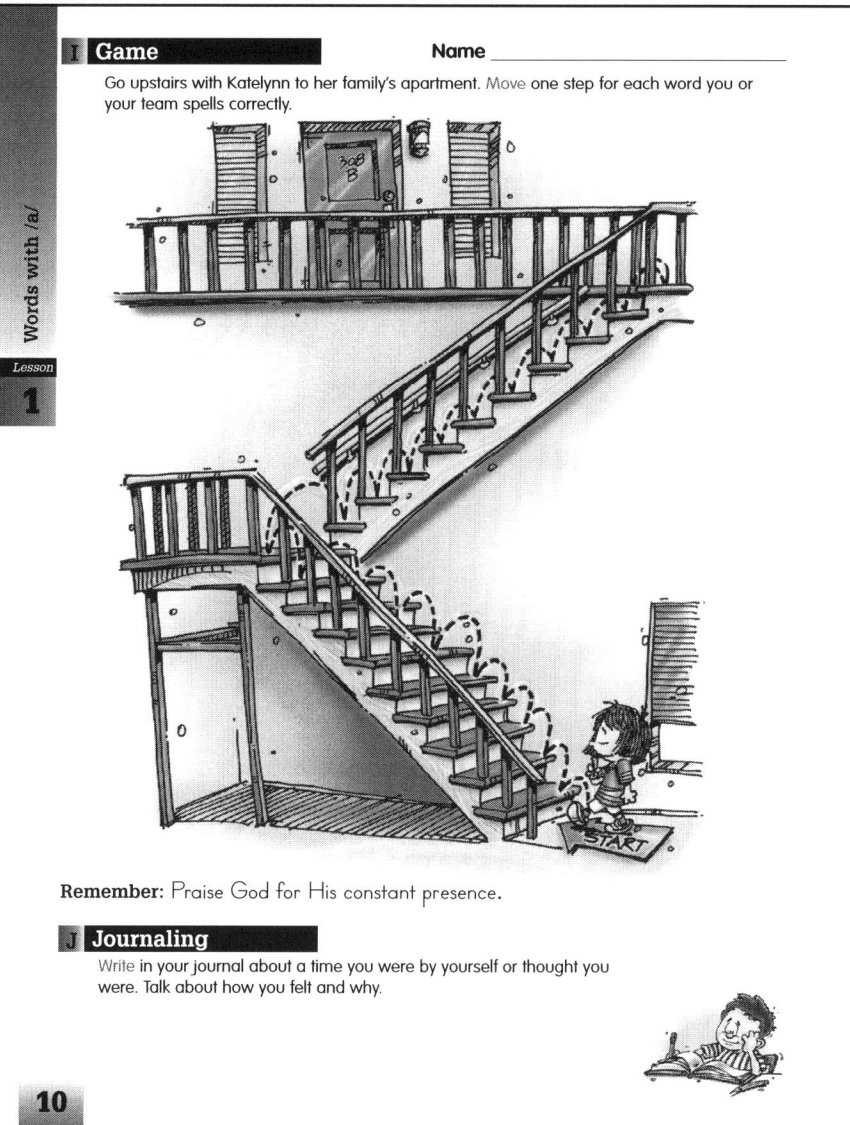

Remember: Praise God for His constant presence.

J Journaling

Write in your journal about a time you were by yourself or thought you were. Talk about how you felt and why.

10

How to Play:

- Divide the class into two teams.
- Have each student place his/her game piece on Start.
- Have a student from team A go to the board.
- Say the spelling word.
- Have the student write the word on the board.
- If correct, instruct each member of team A to move his/her game piece forward one space.
- Alternate between teams A and B.
- The team to reach the apartment first is the winner.
- **Small Group Option**: Students may play this game without teacher direction in small groups of two or more.

2 Game

Reinforce spelling skills and provide motivation and interest.

Materials

- game page (from student text)
- game pieces (1 per child)
- game word list

Game Word List

1. accent
2. acid
3. adapt
4. camera
5. gram
6. banana
7. banner
8. Canada
9. Montana
10. panic
11. planet
12. aspect
13. mass
14. California
15. batch
16. latch
17. athlete
18. atlas
19. cavern
20. cavity

3 Journaling

Provide a meaningful reason for correct spelling through personal writing.

Review the story using discussion leads provided on the following page. Encourage students to apply the Scriptural value in their journaling.

Journaling (continued)

Say

- As she left for school, how did Katelynn feel about being left alone later in the afternoon? (She was confident and sure of herself.)

- What did Katelynn see on her way up to the apartment that worried her? (A stranger in a black pickup truck.)

- After Katelynn locked the apartment door, why was she so aware of all the little noises? (She was scared.)

- Why was Katelynn fascinated by the new neighbors moving in? (There was a girl her age waving her arms around.)

- When Mr. Rippy roared by on the lawn mower what did Katelynn discover about the new girl? (She was deaf.)

- Later as she watched the family finish moving in what did she realize? (God was with her all the time.)

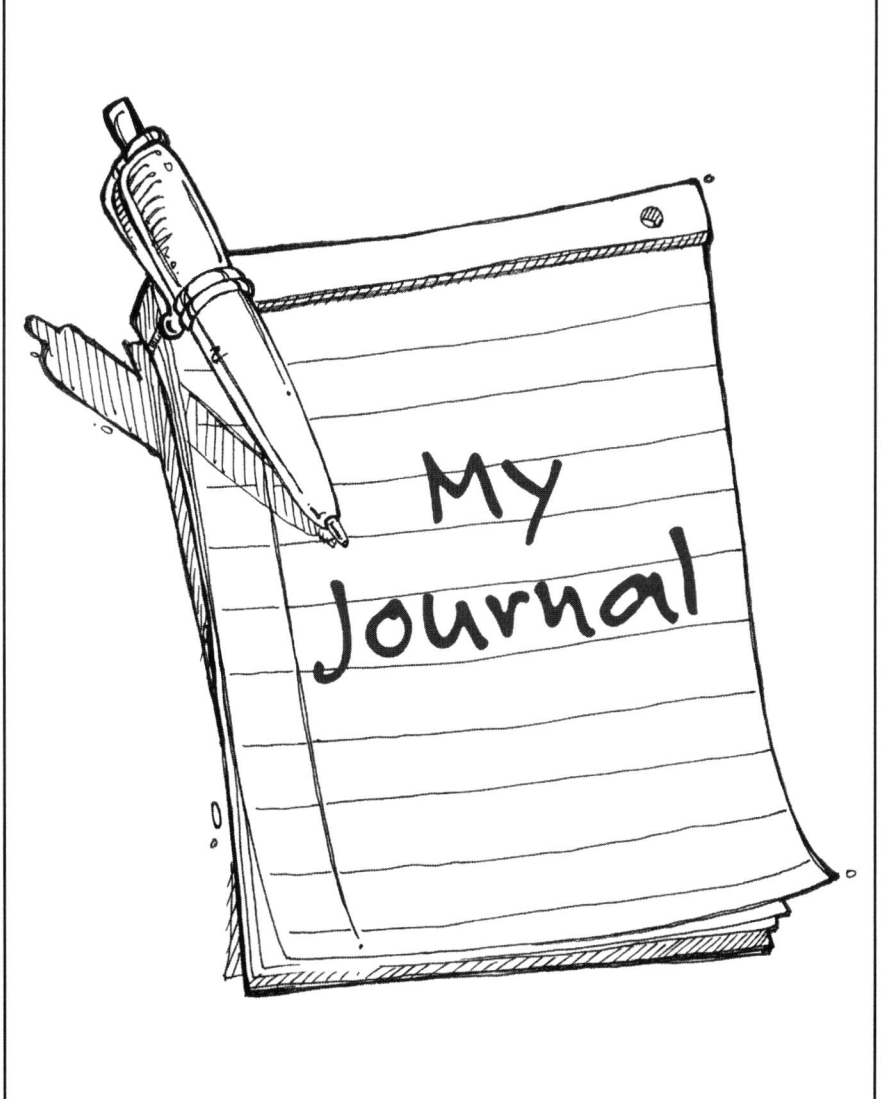

Some Common Abbreviations:

a.m. = Ante Meridiem or Before Noon

AWOL = Absent Without Official Leave

rpm = Revolutions Per Minute

RSVP = Repondez S'il Vous Plait or Respond, please

"R.S.V.P. by _____"

*When Beth doesn't get an invitation to Laney's slumber party,
she learns things are not always as they appear.*

Dear Megan,

Mom finally let me get my own email account! My address is: smalltowngirl@kmail.com. This will be fun writing back and forth! Mom says I'm old enough to email my father in New York on my own. I know he's busy, but maybe this way he will write more often.

I finally get to have a slumber party! Mom said I could invite whoever I want, so I'm asking all the girls in my class. I wish you lived here. It's going to be this weekend. Rachel and Katelynn are helping me plan it. I've decided on a 50's theme. I want everyone to dress up in clothes like they wore back in the olden days. You know—those poodle skirts, blouses, white bobby socks, and saddle shoes—stuff like that. I've gotten cat-eye glasses and white scarves for everyone's hair. It should be funny. Mom's going to take lots of pictures. I'll send you some later. Do you or Brittany have any ideas for a 50's party? Our school has already started. Has yours? Mr. Canfield is our teacher. The boys like him because he is so good at sports!

Laney

Dear Diary,

Laney, Rachel, and Katelynn have been talking about Laney's sleep-over all week. Laney asked Rachel and Katelynn to help her plan it. Laney missed my last sleep-over. She came to one a long time ago, though. It was the first week she moved here from New York City. I bet she'll do something really different. Maybe it's because she's from such a big city. She always comes up with ideas that nobody else ever thinks of. She draws really well too.

Beth

Dear Megan,

Got your e-mail last night. Thanks for the ideas. Tell Brittany hi for me. I wish you guys were here. No, I haven't been to the Skatepark here. Some towns don't have tracks for BMX bikes or skateboards. Mom and I went shopping again last night. We bought little Slinkys, yo-yos, and bouncy glitter balls for game prizes. The shopping here isn't like New York City. But we finally found the tissue paper stuff for everyone to make wrist corsages like you told me about. We even got some of those long, skinny, pink balloons. One of my books shows how to twist the balloons into the shape of a poodle. You know, poodles—to remind you of poodle skirts. This is going to be so much fun! Rachel and I made some neat invitations. I'm going to pass them out at school tomorrow.

Laney

Dear Diary,

Everyone is talking about Laney's sleep-over. Katelynn said it's going to be a 50s theme. I don't have any saddle shoes like they were talking about, but I have a white blouse and Mom is going to cut off a pair of my old pants to make pedal pushers. I told her about the poodle skirts, and she showed me a picture of Grandma in pedal pushers. Grandma didn't have any wrinkles and Grandpa was with her. Grandpa had his arm around Grandma and she was wearing a pair of pants that came just past her knees. They had little slits in the legs so she could move better. They were standing in front of two funny-looking bikes. I can borrow some of Mom's white socks. Mine never stay white very long.

Beth

Dear Megan,

I've finished the invitations. We've asked everybody to R.S.V.P. by tomorrow. Mom is taking me to school early this morning. I'm going to put one on every girl's desk. They'll see them when they first come in.

To answer your question. I skate and ride with two boys—Stephen and Tony. (Don't get any ideas, now.) We don't have a Skatepark, but a man named Mr. Sample lets us ride in an empty lot he owns. We've kind of made our own track with jumps and everything for the bikes. We skate on the sidewalks and a parking lot in Mason Springs Park.

I like your idea about a vinyl record-shaped cake. Gotta go if I'm going to get to school early this morning.

Laney

Dear Diary,

Everyone got an invitation to Laney's slumber party—except for me. "R.S.V.P by Thursday," they say. That's French for "tell me if you're coming." Can you believe she expects everyone to write and tell her if they want to come? What's wrong with the phone? She even invited Sarah. I don't know what her problem is. Maybe I'm just not good enough for her New York tastes. She skipped my sleep-over. She told me she forgot all about it. I bet she just didn't want to come. She went skating with Tony or something. I can't remember now. It was last year during Spring Break. She was supposed to go back to New York and see her father. I wish Laney would just go back to New York—and stay.

Beth

Dear Megan,

Mom can't believe how much I email you. How is Brit doing? Has she gotten any new pets lately? The strangest thing happened today. I passed out the invitations this morning, you know. And everyone is excited about it except for this girl in my class

13

named Beth. She doesn't say a word. She acts mad or something. I missed her party last spring but it was an accident. She was real nice about it. She ate with the boys at lunch today. She's good at sports and has been friends with Tony and Stephen since before first grade. She's acting so weird. We're not best friends but she didn't even talk with the girls at recess. She played catch with Tony. Who knows?

Laney

Dear Diary,

I wasn't planning on writing in here so often, but I am so mad! I wish I could make Laney feel as left out as I do. I can't believe she didn't invite me to the slumber party!! I've never liked her very much. She always spends so much money on clothes. I don't like her hair either. It looks like a boy's hair cut. Katelynn asked me what I'm going to wear to the slumber party. I told her I wasn't in the mood to make a fool out of myself and dress up like my grandma. I don't like the goofy glasses they wore back then or the music or the white socks. I told her Luke and I were going to camp by our creek this weekend. I'd better go tell Luke.

Beth

Dear Megan,

Yes, I'm sure Beth got her invitation. Katelynn told me Beth doesn't like my 50's theme. She's going to camp out by their creek this weekend with her brother Luke. She told Katelynn she wouldn't be caught dead in cat-eye glasses and she doesn't like 50's music either. I wish she'd tell me instead of everyone else. Sarah told me she didn't think she would be able to come. Her mom is sick or something. Beth hasn't said a word—except to Katelynn. I guess I should go talk to her. Everyone else is coming.

Laney

Dear Diary,

I don't even want to go to school tomorrow. All everyone can talk about is Laney's party. I'm sick of Laney this and Laney that. I'm sick of hearing about the 50's. I'm sick of being sick of it!

Beth

Dear Megan,

It all makes sense now. Tony found Beth's invitation by the computer at the back of our classroom. I must have dropped it there. It wasn't opened. She thought I didn't want her to come to the party. I'll have to agree it sure looked that way. I wish she had just come and told me. She didn't even tell her best friend, Katelynn. I guess she was embarrassed that she was the only girl in the class who wasn't invited. What a mess! I told her I was sorry. I think she believes me.

Laney

Dear Diary,

Whew….What a mess. I just responded to Laney's invitation. Tony found my invitation today. Laney had dropped it. She told me she was sorry. I told her I was sorry. I don't know why I have such a hard time seeing the good in her. I didn't say very kind things about her. I think I'll tear out those pages in my diary. On second thought, I don't think I will. I need to leave them there to remind me to look for the good in people—like the Lord looks at me.

Beth

Discussion Time

Check understanding of the story and development of personal values.

- Why was Laney e-mailing Megan in New York?
- Have any of you ever kept a diary or journal?
- Raise your hand if you have your own e-mail account.
- What did you like or dislike about putting your thoughts and ideas in print?
- What is Laney planning for all the girls in her class?
- How did Beth react when she didn't get an invitation?
- How did Laney respond when Beth didn't want to come to her party?
- What could they have done to solve the problem more quickly?
- How does the Lord look at us?

14

Dear Diary,

A Preview

Write **each word as your teacher says it.**

Name _____

1. weather
2. attend
3. tennis
4. heifer
5. delta
6. method
7. New Mexico
8. Texas
9. selfish
10. lever
11. credit
12. Maryland
13. weapon
14. shelter
15. umbrella
16. denim
17. tense
18. strength
19. respect
20. healthy

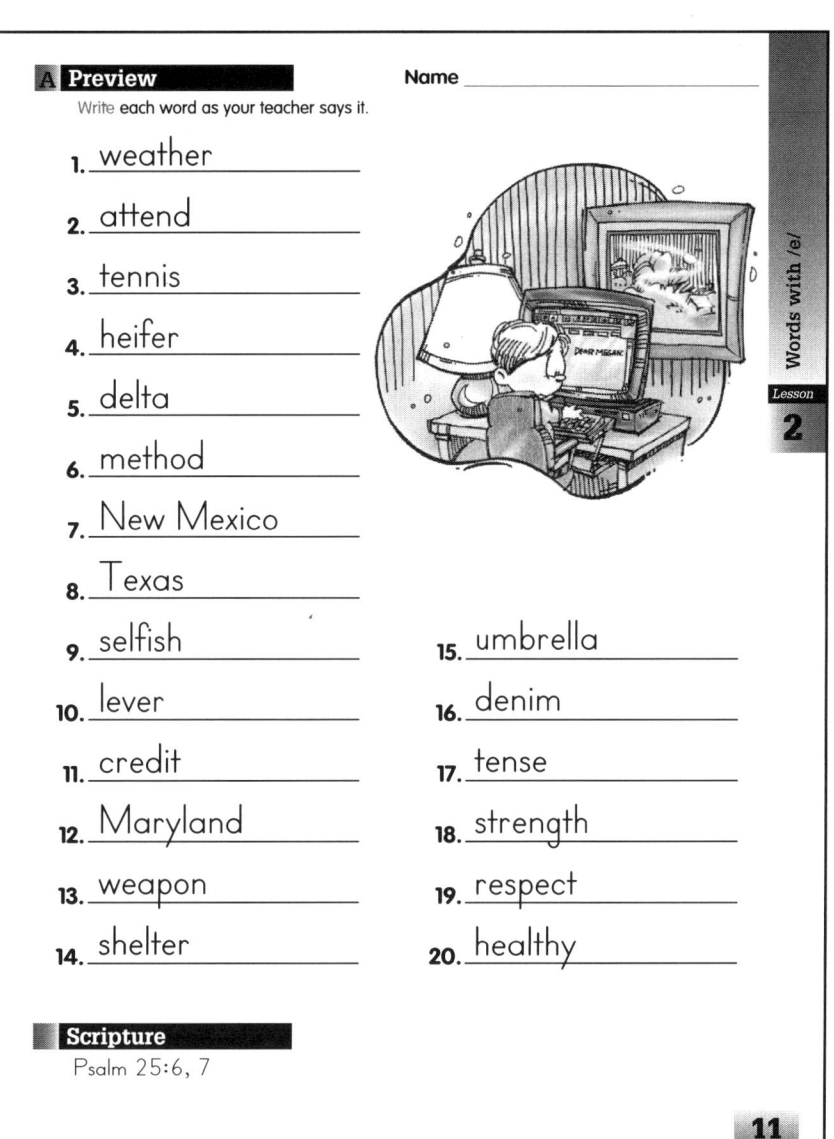

Words with /e/

Lesson **2**

Scripture
Psalm 25:6, 7

11

 ## Preview
3 Test for knowledge of the correct spellings of these words.

 Customize Your List
On a separate sheet of paper, additional words of your choice may be tested.

I will say each word once, use the word in a sentence, then say the word again. Write the words on the lines in your Worktext.

 Correct Immediately!
Let's correct our Preview. I will spell each word out loud. If you spelled a word incorrectly, rewrite it correctly.

 Progress Chart
Students may record scores. (Reproducible master provided in Appendix B.)

1.	weather	Laney hoped the **weather** would be nice the day of her party.
2.	attend	She bought prizes and favors for everyone she'd asked to **attend**.
3.	tennis	Each glitter ball bounced high like a **tennis** ball.
4.	heifer	Beth was thinking of raising a **heifer** for her 4-H project.
5.	delta	Mr. Canfield taught his class that "**delta**" can describe anything triangular.
6.	method	Mr. Canfield's **method** of teaching is interesting and unique.
7.	New Mexico	He pointed out some interesting facts about **New Mexico**.
8.	Texas	**Texas** borders New Mexico.
9.	selfish	"I think Laney is so **selfish**," wrote Beth.
10.	lever	Beth twisted the **lever** on the water fountain angrily.
11.	credit	Beth did not give Laney any **credit** for being thoughtful.
12.	Maryland	"I wish she'd move back to **Maryland**, or New York, or wherever!" Beth fumed.
13.	weapon	She used her anger as a **weapon** to defend her hurt feelings.
14.	shelter	Beth tried to **shelter** her feelings by acting uninterested in the party.
15.	umbrella	She grabbed her **umbrella** before walking grumpily to her family's truck.
16.	denim	Her **denim** jumper felt hot in the afternoon sun.
17.	tense	Beth felt **tense** and hurt as she wrote in her diary.
18.	strength	She asked God to give her the **strength** to treat Laney with kindness.
19.	respect	God wants us to **respect** each other's feelings.
20.	healthy	Beth prayed for a **healthy** attitude toward Laney.

15

4 Word Shapes

Help students form a correct image of whole words.

 Look at each word and think about its shape. Now, write the word in the correct Word Shape Boxes. You may check off each word as you use it.

(Short vowels are usually found in syllables in which a vowel is immediately preceded and followed by a consonant, consonant cluster, or digraph.)

 In the Word Shape Boxes, fill in the boxes containing the letter or letters that spell the sound of **/e/** in each word.

 Take a minute to memorize...

Psalm 25:6,7

 Lesson 2 | **Day 1**

B Word Shapes   Name _____

Using the word bank below, write each word in the correct Word Shape Boxes. Next, in the Word Shape Boxes, fill in the boxes containing the letter or letters that spell the sound of /e/ in each word.

Words with /e/ **Lesson 2**

1. respect
2. denim
3. umbrella
4. Texas
5. delta
6. method
7. strength
8. credit
9. Maryland
10. selfish

11. shelter
12. healthy
13. New Mexico
14. heifer
15. lever
16. weather
17. weapon
18. tennis
19. tense
20. attend

Word Bank

attend	healthy	method	shelter	Texas
credit	heifer	New Mexico	strength	umbrella
delta	lever	respect	tennis	weapon
denim	Maryland	selfish	tense	weather

12

Answers may vary for duplicate word shapes.

 Be Prepared For Fun

Check these supply lists for **Fun Ways to Spell** - presented **Day 2**.
Purchase and/or gather these items ahead of time!

General
- Pencil
- Notebook Paper
- Spelling List

Auditory
- Pencil
- Notebook Paper
- Dictionary
- Spelling List

Visual
- Pencil
- Notebook Paper
- Spelling List

Tactile
- Clay
- Spelling List

16

C Hide and Seek Name _____

Play **Hide and Seek** with your words. Fill in a box on the bar graph (left to right) for each word you spell correctly.

LOOK   SAY   SPELL ALOUD   WRITE   SEEK   CHECK

D Other Word Forms

Using the words below, follow the instructions given by your teacher.

attendance	leverage	selfishness	Texan
attending	levering	sheltered	umbrellas
credited	Marylander	sheltering	weaponry
credits	methodical	strengthen	weapons
deltaic	methodology	strengthening	weathered
denims	New Mexican	tennis elbow	weathering
healthier	respectable	tennis shoe	
healthiest	respected	tensed	
heifers	selfishly	tensely	

E Fun Ways to Spell

Initial the box of each activity you finish.

1. [ ]
Encode your spelling words.

2. [ ]
Find hidden words in your spelling words.

3. [ ]
Define your spelling words.

4. [ ]
Spell your words with clay.

13

Words with /e/

Lesson **2**

Hide and Seek

1

Reinforce spelling by using multiple styles of learning.

On a white board, Teacher writes each word — one at a time. **Have students:**

- **Look** at the word.
- **Say** the word out loud.
- **Spell** the word out loud.
- **Hide** (teacher erases word.)
- **Write** the word on paper.
- **Seek** (teacher rewrites word.)
- **Check** spelling. If incorrect, rewrite word correctly.

Day 2

Other Word Forms

2

This activity is optional. Have students find and circle the Other Word Forms that are antonyms of the following:

relaxed
unprotected
weaken
sickliest

Lesson **2**

Fun Ways to Spell

3

Four activities are provided. Use one, two, three, or all of the activities. Have students initial the box for each activity they complete.

Options:

- assign activities to students according to their learning styles
- set up the activities in learning centers for the students to do throughout the day
- divide students into four groups and assign one activity per group
- do one activity per day

General

To encode your spelling words...
- Write the alphabet on your paper.
- Write your own code for each letter underneath it.
- Write your spelling words in your code.
- Trade papers with a classmate and decode the words.
- Check to make sure your classmate spelled the words correctly.

Auditory

To define your spelling words...
- Ask a classmate to look up a word from your spelling list in the dictionary and read the definition to you, but not the spelling word.
- Decide which word on your list matches this definition and write the word.
- Ask your classmate to check your spelling.
- Switch with a classmate and continue taking turns.

Visual

To find hidden words in your spelling words...
- Choose a word from your spelling list.
- Write it on your paper.
- Find and write as many smaller words as you can that are contained within your spelling word.
- Do this with each word.

Tactile

To spell your words with clay...
- Roll pieces of clay into ropes.
- Use the ropes to make the letters of each word.
- Put them in the right order to spell each word.
- Check your spelling.

Working with Words

Familiarize students with word meaning and usage.

Hidden Words

Explain that the spelling words for this week are hidden in the puzzle. After finding each word, the student should write the word under the correct heading.

Say

Use the word bank to help you find each of the words in the puzzle. Words may go across, down, or diagonally. Circle, then write the words.

Take a minute to memorize...

Psalm 25:6,7

F Working with Words

Name _____

Hidden Words

Use the word bank to help you find each of the words in the puzzle. Words may go across, down, or diagonally. Circle and write the words.

Words with /e/
Lesson 2

Across
1. denim
2. healthy
3. method
4. New Mexico
5. respect
6. shelter
7. strength
8. Maryland
9. delta

Down
10. attend
11. credit
12. heifer
13. lever
14. tennis
15. Texas
16. umbrella
17. weapon

Diagonal
18. selfish
19. tense
20. weather

Word Bank

attend	healthy	method	shelter	Texas
credit	heifer	New Mexico	strength	umbrella
delta	lever	respect	tennis	weapon
denim	Maryland	selfish	tense	weather

14

18

G Dictation

Name _____

Write **each sentence as your teacher dictates**. Use **correct punctuation**.

1. Beth <u>said, "I think she is just plain selfish not</u> <u>to ask me to her house!"</u>

2. <u>I would rather wear tennis shoes than dress</u> <u>like my grandmother.</u>

3. <u>The weather man is calling for rain, so I'm</u> <u>going to take my umbrella.</u>

Words with /e/

Lesson **2**

H Proofreading

If a word is misspelled, fill in the oval by that word. If all the words are spelled correctly, fill in the oval by **no mistake**.

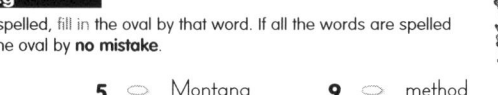

1. ○ acid
    ○ credit
    ● wepon
    ○ no mistake

2. ● heffer
    ○ latch
    ○ athlete
    ○ no mistake

3. ● helthy
    ○ batch
    ○ delta
    ○ no mistake

4. ○ mass
    ○ atlas
    ○ selfish
    ● no mistake

5. ○ Montana
    ● umbrela
    ○ shelter
    ○ no mistake

6. ● teniss
    ○ planet
    ○ cavern
    ○ no mistake

7. ● tinse
    ○ Canada
    ○ California
    ○ no mistake

8. ○ banner
    ● Mariland
    ○ respect
    ○ no mistake

9. ○ method
    ● wethar
    ○ camera
    ○ no mistake

10. ○ accent
    ○ lever
    ● new mexico
    ○ no mistake

11. ○ panic
    ○ adapt
    ○ Texas
    ● no mistake

12. ○ attend
    ○ denim
    ● strenth
    ○ no mistake

15

Dictation

1 Reinforce correct spelling by using current and previous words in context.

(Say) Listen as I read each sentence and then write it in your Worktext. Remember to use correct capitalization and punctuation. (Slowly read each sentence twice. Sentences are found in the Student Worktext to the left.)

Proofreading

2 Familiarize students with standardized test format and reinforce recognition of misspelled words.

(Say) Look at each set of words. If a word is misspelled, fill in the oval by that word. If all the words are spelled correctly, fill in the oval by **no mistake**.

Lesson **2**

3 Hide and Seek

Reinforce correct spelling of current spelling words. Repeat this activity from Day 2.

4 Vocabulary Extension

Have your students complete this activity to strengthen spelling ability and expand vocabulary. The reproducible master is provided in Appendix A as shown on the inset page to the right.

1 Posttest

Visit the **A Reason For** website to download free, printable Posttest pages.

(Say) I will say the word once, use it in a sentence, then say it again. Write your words on a separate sheet of paper.

Progress Chart
Students may record scores. (Appendix B)

Personal Dictionary
Students may add any words they have misspelled to their personal dictionaries. (Appendix B)

Lesson 2 | Vocabulary Extension

Hide and Seek
Play Hide and Seek with your words. Fill in a bar graph (left to right) for each word you spell correctly.

LOOK   SAY   HIDE   WRITE   SEEK   CHECK

Vocabulary Extension
Trade-off
Choose a word from the word bank to replace the word(s) in parentheses. Write the word in the blank.

1. ___Genesis___ (book of the Bible meaning beginning) tells sacred history from the first day of creation to the death of Joseph.
2. I don't ___recommend___ (suggest) that you wait very long to begin your science project.
3. I have only a vague ___memory___ (recollection) of when I was very little.
4. It is ___essential___ (important) for you to understand how to work these math problems.
5. King Artaxerxes sent ___Ezra___ (a priest) to set up civil and religious laws in Jerusalem.
6. Moses led the Israelites from Egypt in a grand ___Exodus___ (departure) after they had been held in slavery for a long time.
7. The king sent a ___messenger___ (courier) to tell the other armies the news of the battle.
8. There is an ___appendix___ (index) at the end of the book that tells the definitions of your words.
9. This beautiful woman, ___Esther___, (Mordecai's cousin) became the Queen of Persia.
10. This table looks so old, I am sure it must be a ___genuine___ (authentic) antique.
11. We like to visit the ___cemetery___ (graveyard) to read the names and dates on the tombstones.
12. You can easily peel the ___banana___ (yellow fruit) at lunch time.

Word Bank

appendix	essential	Ezra	memory
banana	Esther	Genesis	messenger
cemetery	Exodus	genuine	recommend

326

#	Word	Sentence
1.	weather	Laney watched the **weather** report to see the forecast for her birthday.
2.	heifer	Beth has not decided whether she will raise a **heifer** or a lamb for 4-H.
3.	New Mexico	Mr. Canfield gave the class a quiz about **New Mexico**.
4.	Texas	He also asked several questions about the state of **Texas**.
5.	credit	Laney got **credit** for the bonus question on the quiz.
6.	delta	During math, Mr. Canfield drew a triangle and wrote "**delta**" under it.
7.	Maryland	"She can move back to **Maryland**, or New York, or wherever," said Beth.
8.	weapon	Disinterest was her **weapon** to defend her hurt feelings.
9.	method	Laney wasn't sure of the best **method** to win Beth as a friend.
10.	shelter	Beth tried to **shelter** her hurt feelings by acting like she didn't care.
11.	attend	She acted as if she did not want to **attend** Laney's party.
12.	lever	Angrily, she twisted the **lever** on the water fountain.
13.	strength	God can give us **strength** to be kind to someone who has hurt us.
14.	tennis	Beth kicked off her school shoes and put on her **tennis** shoes.
15.	tense	She felt **tense** and angry and wanted to relax.
16.	denim	She plopped down on her **denim** floor pillow to write.
17.	selfish	"I think Laney is **selfish** and spoiled," she wrote in her diary.
18.	healthy	She knew she did not have a **healthy** attitude toward Laney.
19.	respect	God says we should **respect** others and care about their feelings.
20.	umbrella	After school, Beth offered to share her **umbrella** with Laney.

I Game

Name _____

Go with Laney as she takes the lost invitation to Beth. Move one space for each word you or your team spells correctly.

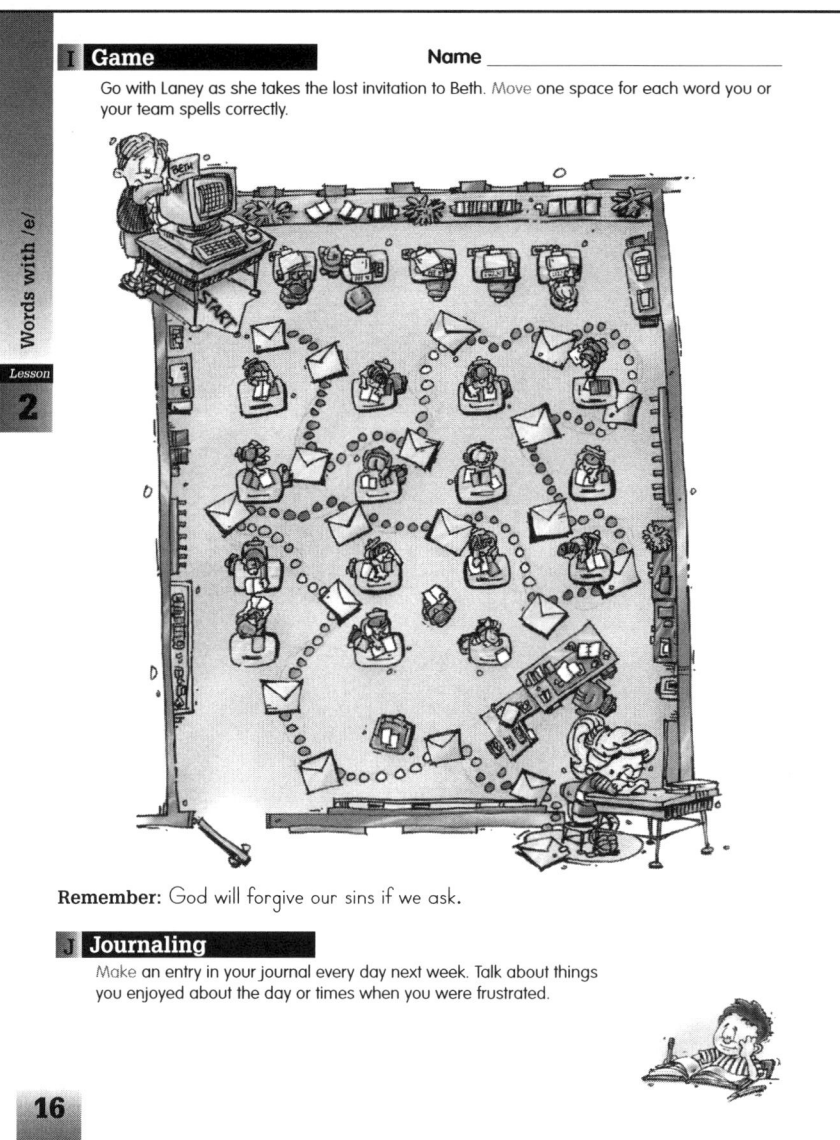

Remember: God will forgive our sins if we ask.

J Journaling

Make an entry in your journal every day next week. Talk about things you enjoyed about the day or times when you were frustrated.

16

How to Play:

- Divide the class into two teams.
- Have each student place his/her game piece on Start.
- Have a student from team A go to the board.
- Say the spelling word.
- Have the student write the word on the board.
- If correct, instruct each member of team A to move his/her game piece forward one space.
- Alternate between teams A and B.
- The team to reach Beth first is the winner.
- **Small Group Option**: Students may play this game without teacher direction in small groups of two or more.

---

2 Game

Reinforce spelling skills and provide motivation and interest.

Materials

- game page (from student text)
- game pieces (1 per child)
- game word list

Game Word List

1. **weapon**
2. **weather**
3. **credit**
4. **heifer**
5. **healthy**
6. **delta**
7. **selfish**
8. **shelter**
9. **umbrella**
10. **attend**
11. **denim**
12. **strength**
13. **tennis**
14. **tense**
15. **Maryland**
16. **respect**
17. **method**
18. **lever**
19. **New Mexico**
20. **Texas**

3 Journaling

Provide a meaningful reason for correct spelling through personal writing.

Review the story using discussion leads provided on the following page. Encourage students to apply the Scriptural value in their journaling.

21

(Say)
- Why did Laney start e-mailing Megan? (Laney's mom let her get her own e-mail account.)
- Why do you think Beth and Laney seem to always misunderstand each other? (They have different backgrounds. Beth has grown up on a farm. Laney grew up in New York City. Beth may be jealous of Laney, too.)
- Why did Beth decide not to tear pages out of her diary? (She wanted to remind herself to look for the good in people.)
- Has writing something down ever helped you discover something new or understand something better? Why or why not?

The word kayak is spelled the same forward and backward. It is a one-word palindrome.

Word-Wow!

Jeans, Juice, and a Jerk

When Kristin wears expensive new jeans to a messy outdoor party, she finds that more than the jeans need cleaning.

"Hurry up, Kristin." Nine-year-old Cathy grabbed her shoes and sat on the side of her bed to put them on. "You're not even dressed yet and the party starts in 15 minutes!"

"Okay, okay!" Kristin grabbed a shirt off the pile on her bed and slipped it over her head. "I'll be ready in a second, and the Hugheses only live a couple blocks away. We won't be late."

Mom opened the door to the room Cathy and Kristin shared and stuck her head in. "Dad said to let you girls know the car is leaving for the Hugheses' house in five minutes." She stepped all the way into the room and looked at the older girl. "Kristin, it may not be a good idea to wear those jeans to Carol's party. Don't you have an older pair?"

"But, M-o-m! These jeans are the brand everyone's wearing now." Kristin plopped down onto her bed.

"It seems I've heard that particular argument before, especially at the store when you were begging me to buy them." Mrs. Wright shook her head and added, "Just remember, Kristin, if they get ruined you won't have 'the brand everyone's wearing' anymore. They were much too expensive to replace. The party's in the backyard because some of the activities and games will be too messy for indoors."

"Maggy!" Dad called from further down the hall.

Mom glanced at her watch. "Three minutes left, girls!" She closed the door gently as she left to see what Dad wanted.

Kristin jumped up and pulled some socks out of a drawer.

"The party invitation even said something about wearing old clothes," Cathy reminded her as she threaded a belt through the loops of her old jeans. "Aren't you going to change?"

"No." Kristin reached for a shoe, "I'll just be really careful and not do any of the things that might mess up my jeans." She glanced up and noticed the look on her little sister's face. "Well, Mom didn't say I had to change!" She grabbed the other shoe. "Since Carol's in high school now, there'll be lots of older kids at this party. I want to look good tonight."

Colored lights were strung everywhere. The Hugheses' backyard was transformed into a mini-carnival with activities for kids of all ages, including a water balloon toss, bobbing for apples, a dart throw and even a pie-eating contest. Kristin stood around most of the evening, avoiding all the things that could ruin her expensive new jeans.

"Hey, Kristin!" Cathy hurried by with Jared, Carol's ten-year-old brother. "C'mon! They're bringing out homemade ice cream!"

"M-m-m-m. Sounds good, doesn't it?" The girl Kristin had been talking to turned to follow Cathy and Jared toward the table on the patio.

"Yes, it sure does! I love homemade ice cream." Kristin walked beside her new friend. She couldn't remember her name, but she was a seventh-grader and seemed really nice.

The long table was covered with a bright plastic tablecloth. On one end, two large freezers of homemade ice cream were surrounded by bowls, spoons and napkins. The other end was covered with clear plastic cups filled with juice. "Strawberry or vanilla?" Mrs. Hughes held the ice cream scoop poised over the freezers.

"Vanilla, please." Kristin accepted the loaded bowl and licked the ice cream that was running over on one side.

"Let's go sit on the brick wall over there," her new friend suggested. "I'll trade a little strawberry for some of your vanilla before we start eating. Want to?"

Before Kristin could reply, something or someone crashed into her, knocking her feet right out from under her. The bowl of ice cream dumped down the front of her shirt. She jumped up sputtering. "What...who... YOU!" She spotted Jared standing there with a sheepish look on his face—and an empty plastic cup in his hand. "Why don't you watch where you're going!" Kristin tried to wipe the dripping mess off her shirt with the crumpled paper napkin she still clutched in one hand.

"I'm sorry," Jared said as he held out his napkin to Kristin. It wasn't in much better shape than her own. "I didn't see you there."

"You...you WHAT?" Kristin exploded. "Are you blind or something?"

"Here." The seventh-grade girl handed Kristin her clean napkin and bent to pick up the empty bowl and spoon. "Let's go ask Mrs. Hughes for a damp towel or something. Okay?"

Kristin nodded and turned toward the house. "What a jerk! He can't put one foot in front of the other without causing a disaster! He's always been that way. Whenever there's a mess, you can be sure Jared caused it! Why, one time he...."

"Kristin, honey!" Mrs. Hughes handed the ice cream scoop to Carol when she spotted the soggy Kristin approaching. "Come on in the house and let's get you cleaned up." She ushered Kristin away while Kristin's new seventh-grade friend went to rejoin the party and eat her own melting ice cream.

"That's much better." Mrs. Hughes stood back and

23

looked at the wet, but clean, front of Kristin's shirt.

"Thanks, Mrs. Hughes." Kristin smiled at her mother's friend and started out of the kitchen to rejoin the party.

She stopped in her tracks when Mrs. Hughes said, "Kristin, honey, that looks like juice on the back of your jeans." Kristin craned her neck to check it out. Sure enough, Jared's plastic cup had been empty because all the juice had gotten dumped on the back of her legs!

"You'd better ask your mother to take care of that right away, honey. That's grape juice and it will stain." She glanced at the clock on the kitchen wall.

"Your dad should be here soon to pick you up. Otherwise I'd have you go ahead and change into something of Jared's so I could get those stains treated."

"I'll take care of it right away," Kristin assured the worried Mrs. Hughes. *But I'll do it myself,* she added in her own mind. *I don't want Mom to know that my new jeans got messed up at the party after all.*

Later that evening Kristin attempted to get the stains out. Bar soap from the bathtub didn't work well. Kristin squirted some liquid soap from the dispenser by the kitchen sink onto one of the larger spots and scrubbed some more. That didn't make the spots disappear either.

How are you supposed to get grape juice stains out, anyway? Kristin sat on the edge of the tub and stared at the dark spots on the jeans in the sink. *That Jared Hughes! He's an absolute pain! I can't stand him! He ruins everything! Why'd he have to go and ruin these jeans!*

When Kristin returned to her room Cathy was already in bed. "The party sure was fun, wasn't it?" Cathy yawned and turned on her side to talk to her big sister.

"It was until Jared decided to ruin it," Kristin

muttered.

"That's not fair, Kristin."

Cathy sat up in bed. "You know he didn't mean to run into you. It was an accident! And besides, Mrs. Hughes got all the ice cream off your shirt."

"Yeah, my shirt's fine." Kristin jerked the bedspread off her bed. "But my jeans aren't!"

"What are you talking about?" Cathy pulled her knees up and looped her arms around them. "I didn't see anything on your jeans."

"Of course not!" Kristin shook her head angrily. "I made sure no one saw the back of my jeans during the last of the party and all the way home! I didn't want Mom to know that they're ruined!" Kristin's voice rose. "I thought I could get out the grape juice that Jared dumped on me all by myself, but I can't! My jeans are RUINED and it's all Jared's fault! If he wasn't such a jerk it wouldn't have happened. Life would be a lot nicer if he just…didn't exist!"

Cathy stared quietly at her sister for so long that Kristin grew uncomfortable. Finally Cathy shook her head and laid back down. "Maybe Mom could get the grape juice out—or maybe your jeans are ruined, I don't know." She pulled her covers up. "But I think the stuff you're saying about Jared is worse than any old stain." Cathy turned over and closed her eyes.

"But…" Kristin began and then stopped. What could she say? Cathy was right. She sat on the side of her bed and stared at the back of her sister's head. She was still upset and mad, but perhaps, if she was really honest, she was mostly upset that her new jeans—the brand everyone was wearing now—were ruined. She was upset with herself for wearing her jeans when she probably shouldn't have. She was upset with herself for saying such mean things about Jared, too, especially to the seventh-grade girl she'd just met. After all, she'd known Jared all her life and they'd been good friends even though he was one grade behind her. Sure, he made her mad sometimes, but he really wasn't so bad. She really liked Jared.

She really liked those jeans, too—and now they were ruined. Kristin envisioned those ugly grape juice stains

on the back of her jeans. Then she was struck with an even more sobering thought, *Am I stained like that inside?*

Kristin jumped up and got her jeans out of the bathroom where she'd hidden them. She'd see if Mom could do anything about those stains.

"I already know Someone who can take care of the stains inside me, and I'll ask Him to give me a new, clean heart right now," she whispered to herself. "That's even more important than spots on my jeans."

Check understanding of the story and development of personal values.

- Why had Kristin begged her mother to get a certain brand of jeans even though they were expensive?
- Where were Kristin and her family going?
- Why did Kristin want to wear her new jeans?
- Why did Mrs. Wright suggest Kristin wear something else?
- What happened to Kristin's jeans?
- How did Kristin feel about Jared?
- Was it Jared's fault that the jeans were stained? Why or why not?
- How could Kristin get rid of the stains in her heart?
- Have you ever blamed someone for something that was really your fault?

A Preview

Write **each word as your teacher says it.**

Name _____

1. income
2. England
3. insist
4. Virginia
5. glitter
6. disk
7. glisten
8. Mississippi
9. Michigan
10. lizard
11. limit
12. assist
13. index
14. discuss

15. hymn
16. admit
17. infant
18. history
19. cliffs
20. kidnap

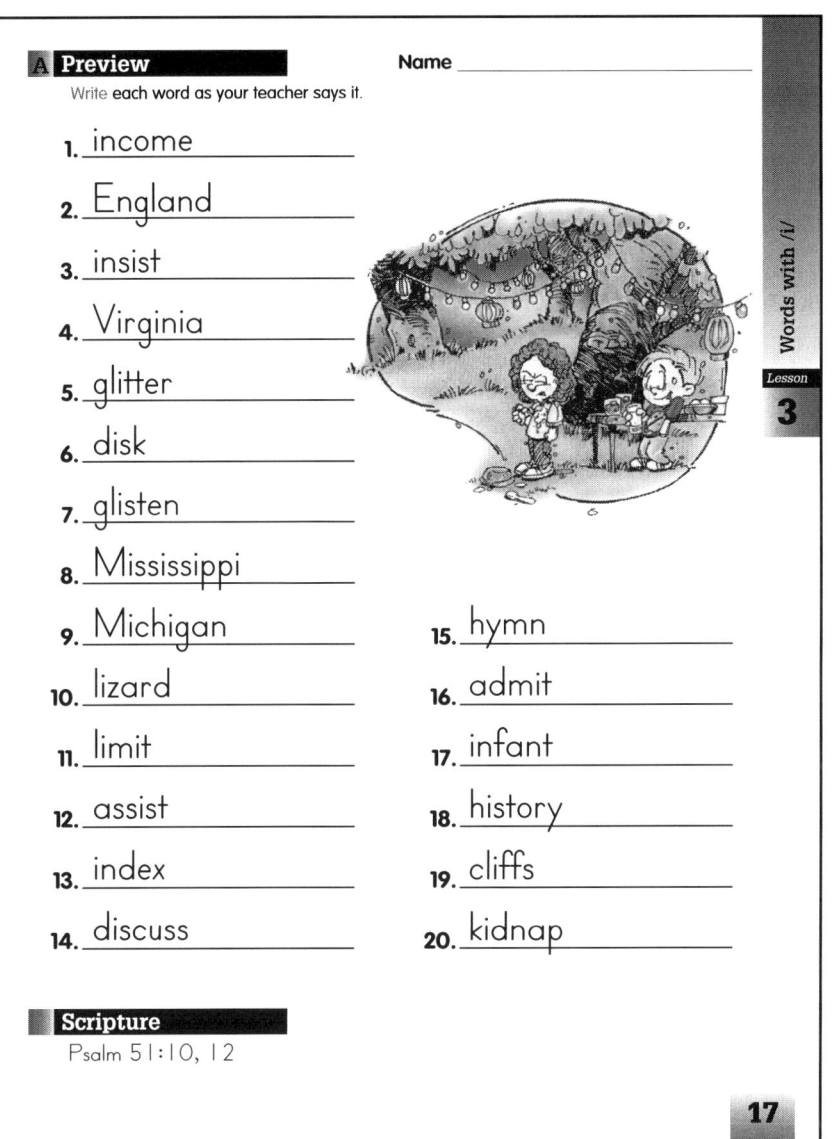

Words with /i/

Lesson **3**

Scripture
Psalm 51:10, 12

17

Preview
Test for knowledge of the correct spellings of these words.

Customize Your List
On a separate sheet of paper, additional words of your choice may be tested.

(Say) I will say each word once, use the word in a sentence, then say the word again. Write the words on the lines in your Worktext.

Correct Immediately!
(Say) Let's correct our Preview. I will spell each word out loud. If you spelled a word incorrectly, rewrite it correctly.

Progress Chart
Students may record scores. (Reproducible master provided in Appendix B.)

1.	income	"I don't intend to spend all of our **income** on clothes," Mom said.
2.	England	The jeans were designed in **England.**
3.	insist	Kristin did **insist** on wearing them even after her mom said she shouldn't.
4.	Virginia	The Hughes family had moved from **Virginia** three years before.
5.	glitter	Their backyard seemed to **glitter** with color.
6.	disk	The large, round table looked like a shimmering golden **disk.**
7.	glisten	She saw the ice cubes **glisten** in the punch bowl.
8.	Mississippi	In the "Name That State" game, Cathy guessed **Mississippi.**
9.	Michigan	Jared knew the answer to the next question was **Michigan.**
10.	lizard	A tiny **lizard** wriggled up the ivy near Kristin and her new friend.
11.	limit	There was almost no **limit** to the anger she felt towards Jared.
12.	assist	Mrs. Hughes tried to **assist** Kristin in getting the ice cream off her shirt.
13.	index	Kristin ran her **index** finger over the dark grape juice stain.
14.	discuss	She did not want to **discuss** her stained jeans with her mom.
15.	hymn	The words of a **hymn** they had sung at church went through her mind.
16.	admit	Kristin had to **admit** that the way she had treated Jared was wrong.
17.	infant	She realized she'd behaved like an **infant.**
18.	history	She did not want to have a **history** of treating others badly.
19.	cliffs	There are no **cliffs** in the Hugheses' backyard.
20.	kidnap	She had let Satan **kidnap**, or take control of, her thoughts and actions.

Word Shapes

4

Help students form a correct image of whole words.

Say

Look at each word and think about its shape. Now, write the word in the correct Word Shape Boxes. You may check off each word as you use it.

(Short vowels are usually found in syllables in which a vowel is immediately preceded and followed by a consonant, consonant cluster, or digraph.)

Say

In the Word Shape Boxes, fill in the boxes containing the letter or letters that spell the sound of /i/ in each word.

Take a minute to memorize...

Psalm 51:10,12

Words with /i/

Lesson 3

B Word Shapes

Name _____

Using the word bank below, write each word in the correct Word Shape Boxes. Next, in the Word Shape Boxes, fill in the boxes containing the letter or letters that spell the sound of /i/ in each word.

1. assist
2. index
3. discuss
4. income
5. hymn
6. limit
7. insist
8. glisten
9. Virginia
10. Mississippi

11. disk
12. kidnap
13. infant
14. Michigan
15. lizard
16. cliffs
17. admit
18. glitter
19. England
20. history

Word Bank

admit	disk	history	infant	lizard
assist	England	hymn	insist	Michigan
cliffs	glisten	income	kidnap	Mississippi
discuss	glitter	index	limit	Virginia

18

_____ Answers may vary for duplicate word shapes. _____

Be Prepared For Fun

Check these supply lists for **Fun Ways to Spell** - presented **Day 2**.
Purchase and/or gather these items ahead of time!

General
• Pencil
• 3 X 5 Cards cut in half (20 per child)
• Spelling List

Auditory
• Spelling List

Visual
• Pencil
• Notebook Paper
• Spelling List

Tactile
• Blackboard and Chalk
  -OR-
• White Board and Marker
• Spelling List

26

C Hide and Seek   Name _____

Play **Hide and Seek** with your words. Fill in a box on the bar graph (left to right) for each word you spell correctly.

LOOK   SAY   SPELL ALOUD   WRITE   SEEK   CHECK

D Other Word Forms

Using the words below, follow the instructions given by your teacher.

admittance	disking	incoming	limited
admitted	English	indexed	limitless
assistant	glistening	indexing	lizards
assisted	glistens	infantile	Michigander
cliff	glittered	infants	Mississippian
cliffy	glittering	insisted	Virginian
discussed	historical	insisting	
discussing	hymnal	kidnapped	
disked	hymns	kidnapping	

E Fun Ways to Spell

Initial the box of each activity you finish.

1. [ ] match match
Spell your words, then play "Concentration."

2. [ ] s_e_l_n w_r_s
Decode your spelling words.

3. [ ] Johnny has a puppy!
Spell your words in a sentence.

4. [ ] sp
Play the game "Spelling Backwards."

Words with /i/

Lesson **3**

19

---

1 Hide and Seek

Reinforce spelling by using multiple styles of learning.

On a white board, Teacher writes each word — one at a time. **Have students:**

• **Look** at the word.
• **Say** the word out loud.
• **Spell** the word out loud.
• **Hide** (teacher erases word.)
• **Write** the word on paper.
• **Seek** (teacher rewrites word.)
• **Check** spelling. If incorrect, rewrite word correctly.

2 Other Word Forms

This activity is optional. Have students find and circle the Other Word Forms that are most nearly synonyms of the following:

granted access
sparkled
demanded
boundless

3 Fun Ways to Spell

Four activities are provided. Use one, two, three, or all of the activities. Have students initial the box for each activity they complete.

Options:

• assign activities to students according to their learning styles
• set up the activities in learning centers for the students to do throughout the day
• divide students into four groups and assign one activity per group
• do one activity per day

General
Spell your words; then play "Concentration"...
• Write each spelling word on a card. Mix your cards and a classmate's cards together. Arrange them face down in five rows of eight. Pick up two cards. If the cards match, play again. If the cards do not match, turn them back over. It is your classmate's turn. Continue taking turns until all the cards are matched. The player with the most cards wins!

Auditory
To spell your words in a sentence...
• Ask a classmate to read a spelling word to you from the list.
• Spell the word aloud and use it in a sentence.
• Ask your classmate to check your spelling.
• Each correctly spelled word that is used properly in a sentence counts as one point.
• Switch with a classmate and continue taking turns.

Visual
To decode your spelling words...
• Look at the first word on your list.
• Write every other letter of the word on your paper, putting a blank where each missing letter belongs.
• Trade papers with a classmate and fill in the missing letters.
• Check your spelling.

Tactile
To play the game "Spelling Backwards"...
• Ask a classmate to stand behind you and draw the letters to spell a word from your list on your back.
• Write the spelling word on the board as your classmate traces the letters on your back.
• Ask your classmate to check your spelling.
• Trade places and take turns until you have each spelled all the words.

1 Working with Words

Familiarize students with word meaning and usage.

Clues

Write this incomplete sentence on the board:

To imagine events while you are asleep is to _____.

Guide the students in choosing the word **dream**.

Say) Read each sentence and choose a spelling word for each definition. You may use a dictionary to help you. Write the word in the blank.

Take a minute to memorize...

Psalm 51:10,12

Words with /i/ — Lesson 3

F Working with Words   Name _____

Clues

Write a spelling word for each clue.

1. Something that shines or sparkles is said to <u>glisten or glitter</u>.
2. To carry someone away against his will is to <u>kidnap</u> him.
3. The state that is abbreviated MI is <u>Michigan</u>.
4. Someone who is a baby is called an <u>infant</u>.
5. To <u>glisten or glitter</u> means to be sparkling, showy, or attractive.
6. To argue or consider carefully is to <u>discuss</u>.
7. A flat, thin, object with a circular shape is a <u>disk</u>.
8. A <u>hymn</u> is a song of praise to God.
9. To take a resolute stand is to <u>insist</u>.
10. <u>Virginia</u> was one of the original thirteen colonies.
11. High steep faces of rock, earth, or ice are called <u>cliffs</u>.
12. <u>History</u> is a record of significant events of the past.
13. A gain in money from labor, business, or property is <u>income</u>.
14. To help or aid people is to <u>assist</u> them.
15. <u>England</u> is a country in Europe.
16. An <u>index</u> is an alphabetical list with page numbers indicating where items can be found in a book.
17. To restrict in quantity or extent is to <u>limit</u>.
18. To allow someone to enter is to <u>admit</u> her.
19. Jackson is the capitol of <u>Mississippi</u>, a state of the Deep South.
20. A four-legged reptile with a long tapering tail is a <u>lizard</u>.

Word Bank

admit	disk	history	infant	lizard
assist	England	hymn	insist	Michigan
cliffs	glisten	income	kidnap	Mississippi
discuss	glitter	index	limit	Virginia

20

28

G Dictation

Name _____

Write **each sentence as your teacher dictates**. Use **correct punctuation.**

1. <u>If you insist on wearing those pants, you will</u>
   <u>just have to limit the games you play.</u>

2. Kristin <u>knows she is wrong, but she does not</u>
   <u>like to admit it.</u>

3. <u>Mom knows a lady who can follow her family</u>
   <u>history back to a small country in England.</u>

H Proofreading

If a word is misspelled, fill in the oval by that word. If all the words are spelled correctly, fill in the oval by **no mistake**.

1. ○ kidnap
   ○ weapon
   ○ heifer
   ● no mistake

2. ○ cliffs
   ● hym
   ○ healthy
   ○ no mistake

3. ○ selfish
   ○ limit
   ● england
   ○ no mistake

4. ○ income
   ○ umbrella
   ○ index
   ● no mistake

5. ● infent
   ○ Virginia
   ○ tennis
   ○ no mistake

6. ○ assist
   ● disck
   ○ shelter
   ○ no mistake

7. ○ New Mexico
   ○ discuss
   ○ glisten
   ● no mistake

8. ● histry
   ○ Texas
   ○ insist
   ○ no mistake

9. ○ strength
   ● Misissippi
   ○ weather
   ○ no mistake

10. ○ glitter
    ● lizerd
    ○ Maryland
    ○ no mistake

11. ○ denim
    ○ tense
    ○ admit
    ● no mistake

12. ○ attend
    ○ method
    ● michigen
    ○ no mistake

21

1 Dictation

Reinforce correct spelling by using current and previous words in context.

(Say) Listen as I read each sentence and then write it in your Worktext. Remember to use correct capitalization and punctuation. (Slowly read each sentence twice. Sentences are found in the Student Worktext to the left.)

2 Proofreading

Familiarize students with standardized test format and reinforce recognition of misspelled words.

(Say) Look at each set of words. If a word is misspelled, fill in the oval by that word. If all the words are spelled correctly, fill in the oval by **no mistake**.

Hide and Seek

Reinforce correct spelling of current spelling words.
Repeat this activity from Day 2.

Vocabulary Extension

Have your students complete this activity to strengthen spelling ability and expand vocabulary. The reproducible master is provided in Appendix A as shown on the inset page to the right.

Posttest

Visit the **A Reason For** website to download free, printable Posttest pages.

I will say the word once, use it in a sentence, then say it again. Write your words on a separate sheet of paper.

Progress Chart

Students may record scores. (Appendix B)

Personal Dictionary

Students may add any words they have misspelled to their personal dictionaries. (Appendix B)

Hide and Seek

Play Hide and Seek with your words. Fill in a bar graph (left to right) for each word you spell correctly.

LOOK. SAY. HIDE. WRITE. SEEK. CHECK.

Vocabulary Extension

Multiple Choice

Fill in the oval by the word(s) with the same or nearly the same meaning as the word in bold type.

1. consider
- ● ponder
- ○ babble
- ○ thoughtless
- ○ balance

2. Timothy
- ○ Old Testament book
- ● companion of Paul
- ○ first king of Israel
- ○ town in western Judah

3. convince
- ○ chosen one
- ○ lenses for your eyes
- ○ prisoner
- ● persuade

4. Corinthians
- ○ friends of Isaiah
- ○ Old Testament book
- ● people who lived in Corinth
- ○ Abraham's nephew

5. initials
- ● beginning letters of a name
- ○ first book of the Bible
- ○ important document
- ○ good judgment

6. political
- ○ ethical
- ● governmental
- ○ noticeable
- ○ license

7. friction
- ○ smoothness
- ● disagreement
- ○ roll carefully
- ○ flattering

8. grimace
- ● expression
- ○ enemy
- ○ lonely
- ○ frightening

9. minimum
- ○ receive
- ○ administer
- ● smallest
- ○ record

10. Kings
- ○ to take an oath
- ○ to persuade
- ○ prophet of Israel
- ● Old Testament books

327

1.	income	"Our **income** can't all be spent on clothes," said Mom.
2.	England	Kristin wanted a pair of the jeans designed in London, **England**.
3.	insist	Kristin did **insist** on going against her mom's wishes.
4.	Virginia	Three years earlier, the Hughes had moved from **Virginia**.
5.	glitter	The colored lights strung around the yard seemed to **glitter**.
6.	disk	Some kids played catch with a flying **disk** during the party.
7.	glisten	Kristin saw the flower-shaped ice cubes **glisten** in the punch bowl.
8.	Mississippi	Jared's answer in the "Name That State" game was **Mississippi**.
9.	Michigan	Cathy knew the answer to the third question was **Michigan**.
10.	lizard	Kristin did not want to touch the **lizard** on the ivy.
11.	limit	Kristin felt there was no **limit** to her anger toward Jared.
12.	assist	Mrs. Hughes was quick to **assist** Kristin in cleaning her shirt.
13.	index	Kristin rubbed soap into the stain with her **index** finger.
14.	discuss	Kristin knew it would be hard to **discuss** the accident with her mom.
15.	hymn	A verse from a **hymn** she had just learned ran through her head.
16.	admit	Kristin had to **admit** her attitude had been very bad.
17.	infant	She had behaved like an **infant** in front of all the guests.
18.	history	She did not want to have a **history** of saying mean things.
19.	cliffs	There aren't any **cliffs** in the Hugheses' backyard.
20.	kidnap	Kristin did not want to let Satan **kidnap** her thoughts.

I Game

Name _____

Complete the secret phrase by spelling the words from this week's word list.

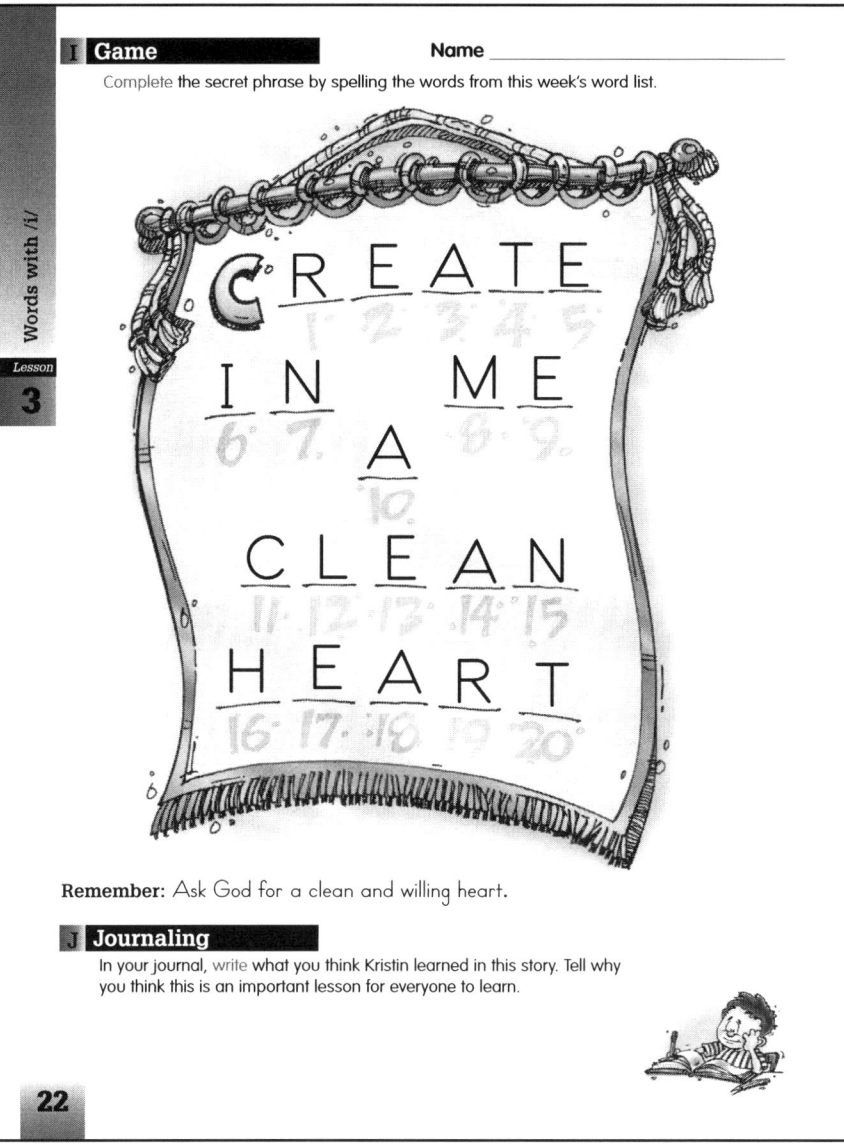

C R E A T E
1 2 3 4 5

I N   M E
6 7   8 9

A
10

C L E A N
11 12 13 14 15

H E A R T
16 17 18 19 20 !

Remember: Ask God for a clean and willing heart.

J Journaling

In your journal, write what you think Kristin learned in this story. Tell why you think this is an important lesson for everyone to learn.

22

How to Play:

- Divide the class into two teams, and decide which team will go first.
- Have a student from team A choose a number from 1 to 20.
- Say the word that matches that number from the team's word list.
- Have the student write the word on the board.
- If correct, have each member of team A write the given letter in the matching space on his/her game page.
- Alternate between teams A and B having the students choose a number of a blank space.
- The team to complete the secret phrase first is the winner.

2 Game

Reinforce spelling skills and provide motivation and interest.

Materials

- game page (from student text)
- pencils (1 per child)
- game word list

Game Word List

Team A	Team B
1. kidnap (R)	1. disk (R)
2. cliffs (E)	2. discuss (E)
3. hymn (A)	3. glisten (A)
4. limit (T)	4. history (T)
5. England (E)	5. insist (E)
6. income (I)	6. Mississippi (I)
7. index (N)	7. Michigan (N)
8. infant (M)	8. admit (M)
9. Virginia (E)	9. glitter (E)
10. assist (A)	10. lizard (A)
11. disk (C)	11. kidnap (C)
12. discuss (L)	12. cliffs (L)
13. glisten (E)	13. hymn (E)
14. history (A)	14. limit (A)
15. insist (N)	15. England (N)
16. Mississippi (H)	16. income (H)
17. Michigan (E)	17. index (E)
18. admit (A)	18. infant (A)
19. glitter (R)	19. Virginia (R)
20. lizard (T)	20. assist (T)

3 Journaling

Provide a meaningful reason for correct spelling through personal writing.

Review the story using discussion leads provided on the following page. Encourage students to apply the Scriptural value in their journaling.

31

Journaling (continued)

 Say

- Is there something you've wanted just because everyone else seemed to be getting it, like Kristin's jeans?

- Where was the party the Wright family attended? (In the backyard of the Hugheses' home.)

- What was the party like? (Lots of activities for all age levels including water balloon toss, bobbing for apples, a dart throw and pie-eating. Colored lights were strung and there was home made ice cream and juice.)

- Do you think Kristin enjoyed the party? Why or why not?

- What happened to Kristin's jeans? (Jared bumped into her and spilled his grape juice on the back of her jeans.)

- What kinds of things might "stain" our hearts like the jeans were stained? (Unkind thoughts about others, lying, selfishness, etc.)

- Why didn't Kristin ask her mom to get the stains out right away? (She didn't want her mom to know that the jeans were stained.)

- How did Kristin try to get the stains out and did it work? (She tried bar soap and hand soap. It didn't work.)

- Can we get the stains out of our own hearts by ourselves? (No.)

- How can we get rid of them? (By asking God to give us new, clean hearts.)

There are only
12 letters in the
Hawaiian alphabet —
5 vowels and 7 consonants.

Don't Call Me in the Morning

Tommy is a real grouch in the mornings. Can anything help him change?

"Good morning, Tommy! Time to get up. Breakfast will be ready when you get downstairs." Tommy groaned and rolled over, burying his head in the covers when he heard his dad's familiar wake-up call.

"Tommy!" Dad's voice was now closer to the bed, "You've got to get up, young man! You'll be late for school if you don't get moving." Tommy grabbed for the covers when his dad started to tug them off him.

"'Kay." Tommy mumbled, "I'm up."

"Well, I wouldn't say you're really up yet," Dad chuckled, "but at least you seem to be alive. See you downstairs!" Mr. Rawson tickled Tommy's ribs, then left to call Lisa. He didn't notice the frown on his son's face.

When Tommy finally dragged himself out of his cozy bed and across the upstairs landing to the bathroom door, it was shut. Tommy banged on it.

"Just a minute!" Lisa, his older sister, called cheerfully. "I'll be out soon."

Tommy sagged against the wall for what he thought was a minute and then banged louder. "Hurry up, Lisa! Other people live in this house besides you!"

"It's all yours," Lisa said as she held the door open for him with a smile. "Hey, look at that sunshine!" She pointed at the light streaming through the bathroom window. "Isn't it great? The weather man said it was going to rain today, but it looks like he was wrong!"

Tommy grunted and shuffled into the bathroom. "LISA!" he bellowed. "You left your curling iron right next to the sink! I could've burned myself! And look at all this other junk you left out."

He glowered at his sister when she came back to see what he was yelling about.

"Sorry, Tommy. I thought you wanted me to hurry after my shower, so I left this to put away later when you were through in the bathroom." Lisa picked up the offending curling iron and said lightly, "This wasn't even plugged in." She stuck it in her drawer and left.

"Yeah, yeah, yeah," Tommy muttered as he closed the door harder than he needed to.

He'd finished his shower and was back in his room searching for his shoes when his dad called again from downstairs. "Tommy! Time to eat!"

"I'm coming! I'm coming!" Tommy practically shouted. He frowned fiercely as he located a shoe and started to put it on only to discover a knot in the lace. He threw it across the room, and it thunked against the wall. He kicked the other shoe out of his way and went downstairs for breakfast in his socks, muttering all the way.

A few mornings later, the rest of the family was already gathered around the table when Tommy slid into the kitchen. "Good morning, Tommy." Mrs. Rawson smiled at her son as she poured orange juice for him. Tommy just grunted.

Dad's voice was stern when he said, "Tommy, you will treat your mother with the respect she deserves."

"Yes, sir." Tommy slipped into his chair. "I'm sorry, Mom. Good morning." Mom patted his shoulder when she placed the juice in front of him.

"What's the problem, Tommy?" Dad's voice was more relaxed. "Seems like you've had some rough mornings lately."

"He sure has!" Lisa agreed. "For the last couple of weeks he practically bites my head off whenever he sees me in the morning!"

"So what's going on?" Dad leaned back in his chair and waited for an answer.

"Well, I'm just so tired. It's hard to get up, and I feel angry when I wake up." Tommy picked up his napkin and tore off a little piece. "I just wish I could sleep as long as I wanted to and not have anybody telling me to get up and stuff!"

"Hmmm. I see." Dad changed the subject, "Lisa, will you ask the blessing on our food?"

"Dear God, thank You for the food we're about to eat. Help it make us strong to serve You today. And please help Tommy not to be so grumpy in the mornings. Amen."

Tommy frowned at Lisa, but she just grinned at him and took a sip of her orange juice.

"Mr. Canfield said that sometimes kids get really tired when they're growing fast," Tommy said, picking up his glass and taking a big swallow. "I'm growing a lot right now, don't you think?"

"Yes, that's pretty obvious from the clothes you keep outgrowing." Mom reached over to cut up Grandma's waffle.

"True." Dad dipped strawberries onto his waffle. "However, while I think that's something to be happy about, I don't think it's an acceptable excuse for bad behavior every morning."

Tommy dropped the conversation and turned his attention back to his own plate.

Several mornings later Tommy stirred and stretched in his bed. Something had awakened him. Blinking open blurry eyes, he looked around his room. Daylight, but Dad wasn't there calling him to get up for school or for breakfast or anything. Good. Tommy settled into a comfortable position and drifted back to sleep. When he woke up again, he looked

33

around and figured it must be time to get up, but since no one had called him yet, he closed his eyes and dozed off again.

When Tommy finally decided to get up, he headed for the bathroom. The door was open and Lisa was nowhere to be seen. After a quick shower, Tommy was more alert. When he returned to his room he glanced at the clock. 10:30! That couldn't be right, could it? Tommy was frightened until he reminded himself it must be the weekend.

He bounced down the stairs and into an empty kitchen. "Mom!" Tommy called. "Mom, where are you?" No answer. Tommy checked the living room and Grandma's room. Nobody there. He checked the laundry room and the dining room. No one. He ran back upstairs to check the bedrooms. "MOM! DAD!"

Tommy started to panic as he dashed back down the stairs and repeated his search through each room. Where was everyone? Mom, Dad, Lisa—even Grandma—had all vanished without a trace. Tommy flung open the door to the garage. No one there. There was no one anywhere! "DAD!" Tommy's throat hurt from yelling so loudly.

Suddenly he felt someone shaking him. "Huh, what?" Tommy's eyes flew open. Slowly his own room came into focus. Dad stood by the side of the bed, gently shaking his shoulder.

"Come on, lazy bones, better get up or you're going to miss breakfast," Mr. Rawson called as he left the room. "I'll save you a few of Mom's blueberry pancakes if you hurry!"

Tommy looked at the clock, then rubbed his eyes and checked again: 6:30. He propped himself up on his elbows and looked around, trying to get his bearings. His racing heart began to beat more normally as he realized he could hear voices from downstairs. A dream! Tommy flopped back down on the bed in relief. It had all been an awful dream! He

grinned at the sound of Lisa's voice warbling her favorite song in the bathroom.

Hmmm. Tommy tucked both hands behind his head and stretched his long legs. *Never thought I'd be so glad to hear Lisa's screeching!* He sat up and reached for his Bible. *Think I'll read for a minute since she beat me to the bathroom as usual.* He opened the Scriptures and flipped a few pages. *Let's see. This book is Psalms. Mr. Canfield said the Psalms were like songs.* Tommy chose a chapter and began to read silently to himself. *Psalm 92:2. "Every morning tell him, 'Thank you for your kindness,' and every evening rejoice in all his faithfulness…."*

Tommy stopped reading and stared out the window while he thought about that Scripture. *I sure haven't been doing a very good job of thanking God for His kindness every morning lately. I've been grumping and growling at everyone like I have nothing at all to be thankful for!*

Yummy smells drifted up from the kitchen. Tommy sniffed appreciatively. *Mom's good food is one thing I should be thankful for instead of taking it for granted. Family is another.* Tommy shivered. *Until my family all disappeared in my nightmare, I hadn't thought about how important our family is to me.*

"Troublesome Tommy!" Lisa called as she passed his open bedroom door. "Bathroom's free now."

"Thanks, Lisa." Tommy grinned when he caught the look of astonishment on his older sister's face. "See you at breakfast!"

Maybe I'm growing in more than one way! he thought. *At least I hope I am.*

2 Discussion Time

Check understanding of the story and development of personal values.

- How did Tommy react when Mr. Rawson woke him up in the morning?
- Why did Tommy yell at his sister Lisa?
- When his mom said "Good morning" and Tommy just grunted in reply, what did his dad say?
- Describe Tommy's dream.
- How did the dream change Tommy's feelings?
- What is it like around your house in the mornings?
- How could you make it better?

A Preview

Write **each word as your teacher says it.**

Name _____

1. automatic
2. crawl
3. astronaut
4. launch
5. somersault
6. laundry
7. exhaust
8. audience
9. precaution
10. clause
11. Australia
12. coffee
13. strawberry
14. Vermont
15. awkward
16. automobile
17. online
18. lawyers
19. Washington
20. alcohol

Words with /ô/ or /o/

Lesson 4

Scripture
Psalm 92:2, 4

23

Preview
3 Test for knowledge of the correct spellings of these words.

 Customize Your List
On a separate sheet of paper, additional words of your choice may be tested.

 I will say each word once, use the word in a sentence, then say the word again. Write the words on the lines in your Worktext.

 Correct Immediately!
Let's correct our Preview. I will spell each word out loud. If you spelled a word incorrectly, rewrite it correctly.

 Progress Chart
Students may record scores. (Reproducible master provided in Appendix B.)

1. automatic — It was almost **automatic** for Tommy to wake up grumpy.
2. crawl — Tommy's dad heard him finally **crawl** out of bed.
3. astronaut — Tommy had been dreaming that he was an **astronaut**.
4. launch — His shuttle had just experienced a successful **launch**.
5. somersault — He didn't exactly feel like doing a **somersault** now.
6. laundry — He grumbled as he looked for his favorite socks in the **laundry**.
7. exhaust — Tommy's foul moods were about to **exhaust** his family's patience.
8. audience — They did not enjoy being the **audience** for his bad morning moods.
9. precaution — Lisa took every **precaution** to stay out of Tommy's way.
10. clause — "We need a 'no-grumpiness' **clause** added to our family constitution," she said.
11. Australia — "Or we could just send him to **Australia** for a while," Lisa teased.
12. coffee — "Here, will some black **coffee** help any?" she joked.
13. strawberry — Tommy usually enjoys **strawberry** jam on his waffles.
14. Vermont — Lisa loves the maple syrup they get from **Vermont**.
15. awkward — Tommy felt **awkward** and embarrassed after being rude to his mom.
16. automobile — The Rawson family **automobile** is a red sedan.
17. online — Tommy enjoys getting **online** after he's done with his homework.
18. lawyers — Mr. Canfield told the class about several presidents that started out as **lawyers**.
19. Washington — Lincoln studied law, but **Washington** learned surveying skills.
20. alcohol — Tommy's mom cleans her pierced ears with **alcohol**.

4 Word Shapes

Help students form a correct image of whole words.

Say

Look at each word and think about its shape. Now, write the word in the correct Word Shape Boxes. You may check off each word as you use it.

(In some words /ô/ is spelled with **a**, and it is often spelled this way when it is followed by **l** or **ll**. In other words /ô/ is spelled with **aw**, **o**, or **au**. The sound of /o/ can be spelled with **o**. Sometimes /o/ is spelled with **a**, especially when it follows **w**.)

Say

In the Word Shape Boxes, fill in the boxes containing the letter or letters that spell the sound of /o/ or /ô/ in each word.

Take a minute to memorize...

Psalm 92:2,4

B Word Shapes   Name _____

Using the word bank below, write each word in the correct Word Shape Boxes. Next, in the Word Shape Boxes, fill in the boxes containing the letter or letters that spell the sound of /ô/ or /o/ in each word.

Words with /ô/ or /o/

Lesson **4**

1. astronaut
2. Vermont
3. lawyers
4. automobile
5. laundry
6. strawberry
7. online
8. clause
9. audience
10. launch

11. awkward
12. crawl
13. somersault
14. exhaust
15. precaution
16. coffee
17. automatic
18. alcohol
19. Australia
20. Washington

Word Bank

alcohol	automatic	coffee	laundry	somersault
astronaut	automobile	crawl	lawyers	strawberry
audience	awkward	exhaust	online	Vermont
Australia	clause	launch	precaution	Washington

24

Answers may vary for duplicate word shapes.

Be Prepared For Fun

Check these supply lists for **Fun Ways to Spell** - presented **Day 2**. Purchase and/or gather these items ahead of time!

General
- Pencil
- Notebook Paper
- Spelling List

Auditory
- Pencil
- 3 X 5 Cards Cut in half lengthwise (20 per child)
- Spelling List

Visual
- Colored Pencils
- Graph Paper (2 sheets per child)
- Spelling List

Tactile
- Clay
- Spelling List

C Hide and Seek Name _____

Play Hide and Seek with your words. Fill in a box on the bar graph (left to right) for each word you spell correctly.

LOOK. SAY SPELL ALOUD WRITE SEEK CHECK.

D Other Word Forms

Using the words below, follow the instructions given by your teacher.

alcoholic	automatically	exhausted	somersaulted
alcoholism	automobiles	exhausting	somersaulting
astronauts	awkwardly	launched	strawberries
astronomer	awkwardness	launching	Vermonter
audiences	coffeepot	laundries	Washingtonian
Australian	crawled	lawyerly	
automated	crawling	precautionary	

E Fun Ways to Spell

Initial the box of each activity you finish.

1. ☐
Classify your words according to syllables.

2. ☐
Spell your words on graph paper.

3. got a "fish"? NOPE! ☐
Spell your words and play "Match-It."

4. clay ☐
Spell your words with clay.

25

Words with /ô/ or /o/

Lesson 4

Day 2

Lesson 4

---

1 Hide and Seek

Reinforce spelling by using multiple styles of learning.

On a white board, Teacher writes each word — one at a time. **Have students:**

- **Look** at the word.
- **Say** the word out loud.
- **Spell** the word out loud.
- **Hide** (teacher erases word.)
- **Write** the word on paper.
- **Seek** (teacher rewrites word.)
- **Check** spelling. If incorrect, rewrite word correctly.

2 Other Word Forms

This activity is optional. Have students write original sentences using these Other Word Forms:

somersaulted
automated
precautionary
awkwardly

3 Fun Ways to Spell

Four activities are provided. Use one, two, three, or all of the activities. Have students initial the box for each activity they complete.

Options:

- assign activities to students according to their learning styles
- set up the activities in learning centers for the students to do throughout the day
- divide students into four groups and assign one activity per group
- do one activity per day

General

To classify your words according to syllables...
- Write three headings on your paper: One-syllable, Two-syllable, and Three-syllable.
- Write the first word on your list under the proper heading.
- Draw a line through the word to divide it into syllables.
- Do this with each word.

Visual

To spell your words on graph paper...
- Look at the first word on your list.
- Shade in squares to form the letters of each word.
- Check your spelling.
- Do this with each word.

Auditory

To spell your words and play "Match-It"...
- Write each word on a card. Mix your word-cards and a classmate's together. Deal six cards to each player; the rest face down between you. Ask your classmate for a word-card. If the word-card matches, take it and play again. If not, draw from the stack, and it is your classmate's turn. Take turns until all cards are matched.

Tactile

To spell your words with clay...
- Roll pieces of clay into ropes.
- Use the ropes to make the letters of each word.
- Put them in the right order to spell each word.
- Check your spelling.

Secret Words

The boxed letters in the acrostic are a phrase from the Scripture verse for this week.

(Say)

Use the clues to write the words in the puzzle. You may use a dictionary to help you. Then write the boxed letters on the lines below to find the secret words from this week's Scripture.

Take a minute to memorize...

Psalm 92:2,4

F **Working with Words**   Name _____

Secret Words

Use the clues to write the words in the puzzle. Then write the boxed letters on the lines below to find the secret words from this week's Scripture.

Words with /ô/ or /o/

Lesson **4**

1. a u t o m a t i c
2. e x h a u s t
3. c r a w l
4. a s t r o n a u t
5. l a u n d r y
6. a l c o h o l
7. l a u n c h
8. c o f f e e
9. a u t o m o b i l e
10. V e r m o n t
11. l a w y e r s
12. s o m e r s a u l t
13. p r e c a u t i o n
14. A u s t r a l i a
15. a w k w a r d
16. o n l i n e
17. W a s h i n g t o n
18. a u d i e n c e
19. s t r a w b e r r y
20. c l a u s e

1. instinctive
2. to fatigue or tire
3. creep about on all fours
4. space aviator
5. washing
6. colorless liquid used in making medicines and fuels
7. start
8. drink made by brewing ground beans in water
9. car

10. New England state
11. attorneys
12. flip
13. forethought
14. smallest continent
15. clumsy
16. using the Internet
17. only state named for a president
18. congregation
19. small red fruit
20. part of a sentence

Write the secret phrase:

T h a n k y o u f o r y o u r k i n d n e s s.

Word Bank

alcohol	automatic	coffee	laundry	somersault
astronaut	automobile	crawl	lawyers	strawberry
audience	awkward	exhaust	online	Vermont
Australia	clause	launch	precaution	Washington

26

C Dictation

Write **each sentence as your teacher dictates.** Use **correct punctuation.**

1. Tommy <u>crawled out of bed exhausted and</u>
   <u>cross every day.</u>

2. <u>"My best pants are in the laundry, so I have</u>
   <u>to wear old ones," he growled.</u>

3. <u>Doing somersaults felt awkward, so he</u>
   <u>practiced a lot.</u>

H Proofreading

If a word is misspelled, fill in the oval by that word. If all the words are spelled correctly, fill in the oval by **no mistake.**

1. ● audiunce
   ○ cliffs
   ○ kidnap
   ○ no mistake

2. ○ hymn
   ○ launch
   ● summersalt
   ○ no mistake

3. ○ limit
   ○ laundry
   ○ Australia
   ● no mistake

4. ● clauze
   ○ exhaust
   ○ England
   ○ no mistake

5. ● astrunot
   ○ automobile
   ○ income
   ○ no mistake

6. ○ infant
   ● precaushun
   ○ index
   ○ no mistake

7. ○ awkward
   ○ crawl
   ○ Virginia
   ● no mistake

8. ○ lawyers
   ● strawberrie
   ○ assist
   ○ no mistake

9. ○ disk
   ○ history
   ● cofee
   ○ no mistake

10. ● alcohaul
    ○ online
    ○ Vermont
    ○ no mistake

11. ○ insist
    ○ Mississippi
    ● washington
    ○ no mistake

12. ○ automatic
    ○ discuss
    ○ glisten
    ● no mistake

27

Dictation

Reinforce correct spelling by using current and previous words in context.

 Say

Listen as I read each sentence and then write it in your Worktext. Remember to use correct capitalization and punctuation. (Slowly read each sentence twice. Sentences are found in the Student Worktext to the left.)

Proofreading

Familiarize students with standardized test format and reinforce recognition of misspelled words.

 Say

Look at each set of words. If a word is misspelled, fill in the oval by that word. If all the words are spelled correctly, fill in the oval by **no mistake.**

3 Hide and Seek

Reinforce correct spelling of current spelling words.
Repeat this activity from Day 2.

4 Vocabulary Extension

Have your students complete this activity to strengthen spelling ability and expand vocabulary. The reproducible master is provided in Appendix A as shown on the inset page to the right.

1 Posttest

Visit the **A Reason For** website to download free, printable Posttest pages.

Say

I will say the word once, use it in a sentence, then say it again. Write your words on a separate sheet of paper.

Progress Chart
Students may record scores. (Appendix B)

Personal Dictionary
Students may add any words they have misspelled to their personal dictionaries. (Appendix B)

Hide and Seek

Play Hide and Seek with your words. Fill in a bar graph (left to right) for each word you spell correctly.

LOOK   SAY   HIDE   WRITE   SEEK   CHECK

Lesson 4 | Vocabulary Extension

Vocabulary Extension

Cause and Effect

Write a word from the word bank to complete each sentence.

1. If you are reading the fifth book of the Bible, you are reading ___Deuteronomy___ .
2. If a machine runs by mechanical or computerized means, it is an ___electronic___ device.
3. If you are reading a collection of sacred hymns from the Bible, you are reading the ___Psalms___ .
4. If someone brings something to completion, they were able to ___accomplish___ it.
5. If someone pretends to be very good but is not, he is guilty of ___hypocrisy___ .
6. If something is too small to see without using a special magnifying lens, it is ___microscopic___ .
7. If you are reading a poetical book of essays and practical statements, you are reading ___Proverbs___ .
8. If you live where there is government rule by the people, you live in a ___democracy___ .
9. If you want to learn about the reign of King David, you may read the books of ___Chronicles___ .
10. If you wanted to read about Jesus' cousin, you would read about ___John___ the Baptist.
11. If you wanted to read a letter written by Paul, you could read the book of ___Colossians___ .
12. If you wanted to learn more about the man who led the Israelites after Moses, you would learn about ___Joshua___ .

Word Bank

accomplish	democracy	hypocrisy	microscopic
Chronicles	Deuteronomy	John	Proverbs
Colossians	electronic	Joshua	Psalms

328

---

1. **automatic** — It seemed **automatic** for Tommy to wake up grumpy.
2. **astronaut** — He didn't want his dream of being an **astronaut** to end.
3. **launch** — His dream began with a successful **launch**.
4. **somersault** — Next he was doing a **somersault** in outer space.
5. **laundry** — He complained as he looked through his clean, folded **laundry**.
6. **precaution** — Lisa took an extra **precaution** to avoid Tommy in the bathroom.
7. **audience** — Tommy's family did not enjoy being the **audience** for his morning moods.
8. **online** — Mr. Wright may take away Tommy's **online** privileges.
9. **Australia** — "Let's buy him a one-way ticket to **Australia**," Lisa teased.
10. **coffee** — "I'll get you some **coffee** if it'll help you get out of this mood," she offered.
11. **Vermont** — Lisa smothered her waffle in butter and **Vermont** maple syrup.
12. **strawberry** — Mom had put the **strawberry** jam on the table just for Tommy.
13. **awkward** — Tommy felt **awkward** and ashamed under his dad's reproach.
14. **clause** — "Let's add a 'no-grumpiness' **clause** to our family constitution," said Lisa.
15. **automobile** — In Tommy's nightmare their **automobile** wasn't even in the garage.
16. **crawl** — It was awful to **crawl** out of bed and find everyone gone!
17. **exhaust** — "A nightmare can **exhaust** you and make you thankful!" Tommy said.
18. **alcohol** — The prescription cough medicine contains **alcohol**.
19. **Washington** — Mr. Canfield told his class that **Washington** had been a surveyor.
20. **lawyers** — He said some presidents were **lawyers** before they took office.

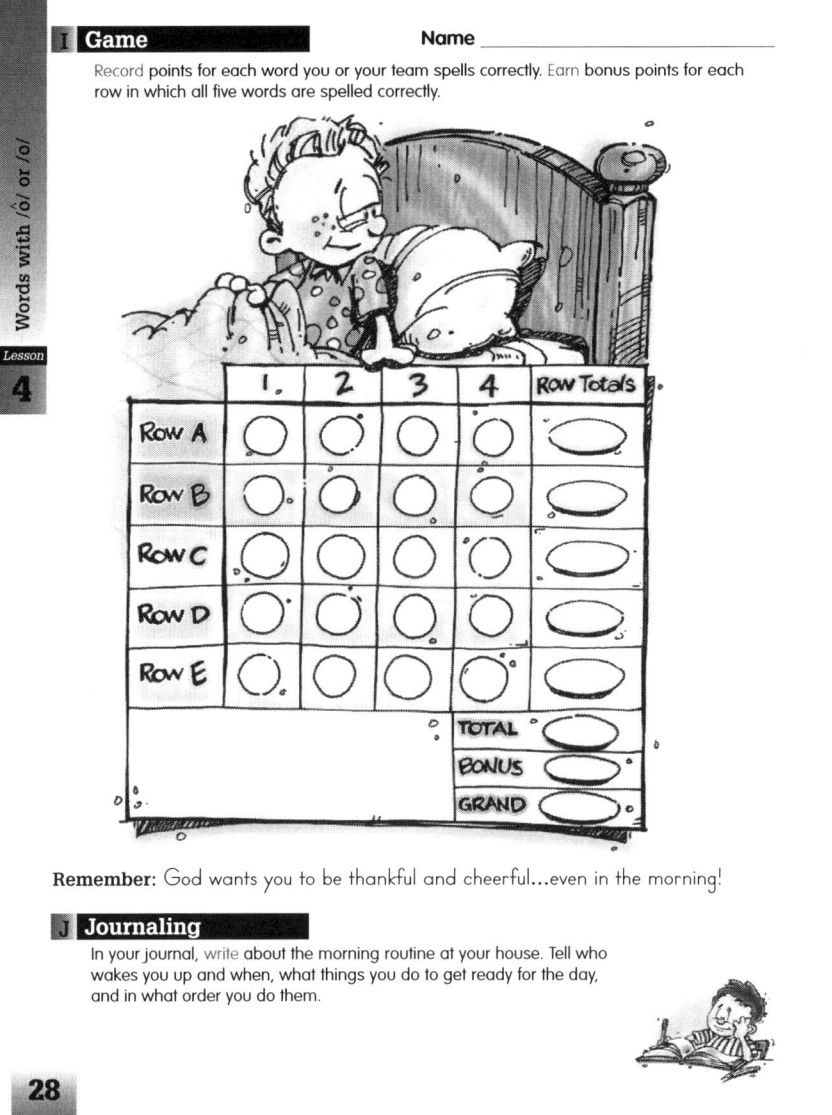

I Game

Name _____

Record points for each word you or your team spells correctly. Earn bonus points for each row in which all five words are spelled correctly.

Remember: God wants you to be thankful and cheerful...even in the morning!

J Journaling

In your journal, write about the morning routine at your house. Tell who wakes you up and when, what things you do to get ready for the day, and in what order you do them.

28

How to Play:

- Divide the class into two teams.
- Have a student from team A choose a square on the grid by indicating the row letter and number.
- Say the word that matches that row letter and number from the team's word list.
- Have the student write the word on the board.
- If correct, have each member of that team record the awarded points (in parentheses by the word) in the circle in that box. If the word is misspelled, have him/her put an **X** in that circle. That square may not be chosen again.
- Repeat this process with the second team.
- When all the words have been spelled by both teams, have each team tally its score. Award a bonus of 5 points for each row in which all four words were spelled correctly.
- Have the teams record their grand totals. The team with the highest score is the winner.

2 Game

Reinforce spelling skills and provide motivation and interest.

Materials

- game page (from student text)
- pencils (1 per child)
- game word list

Game Word List

Team A			Team B
E4	**audience (2)**		A1
E3	**somersault (3)**		A2
E2	**launch (1)**		A3
E1	**laundry (4)**		A4
D4	**Australia (1)**		B1
D3	**clause (3)**		B2
D2	**exhaust (4)**		B3
D1	**astronaut (2)**		B4
C4	**automobile (3)**		C1
C3	**automatic (4)**		C2
C2	**precaution (1)**		C3
C1	**awkward (2)**		C4
B4	**crawl (4)**		D1
B3	**lawyers (3)**		D2
B2	**strawberry (2)**		D3
B1	**Washington (1)**		D4
A4	**coffee (4)**		E1
A3	**alcohol (2)**		E2
A2	**on-line (1)**		E3
A1	**Vermont (3)**		E4

3 Journaling

Provide a meaningful reason for correct spelling through personal writing.

Review the story using discussion leads provided on the following page. Encourage students to apply the Scriptural value in their journaling.

Day 5 | Lesson 4

41

(Say)

- What kinds of nicknames did Lisa use for her brother? (Troublesome Tommy, Terrible Tommy, Tommy the Terror, etc.)

- How did these names fit the way Tommy was acting in the mornings? (He was being a real grouch every morning to his whole family.)

- What did Tommy tell his family Mr. Canfield had said about being tired? (That kids who are growing fast sometimes get really tired.)

- Is it okay to be grumpy and grouchy if we're really tired? Why or why not? (No. Even when we feel bad we shouldn't be unkind to those around us—including our families.)

- How did Tommy's dream help him change? (When everyone disappeared in his dream he realized how important his family was to him and how badly he'd been treating them.)

- How do you feel and act when it's time to get up in the morning?

- Try thanking God for something the first thing each morning and let Him help you be joyful instead of grouchy.

Upper and lower case letters are named 'upper' and 'lower,' because in the time when all original print had to be set in individual letters, the 'upper case' letters were stored in the top or upper part of the case and the 'lower case' letters were stored in the bottom or lower part of the case.

Word Wow!

Casing the Jump

Tony learns about good friends, BMX racing, and being content with his height.

"Mama! Where's my helmet? Stephen and I want to ride bikes in Mr. Sample's empty lot." Tony stood in the doorway to the garage.

"On the shelf in your closet, Tony-O." Maria Vanetti continued to stir the gravy she was making for dinner. "Be back by 5:00. Your papa is coming at 6:00 to pick you up for the weekend—remember?"

"He'll be late," Tony said as he passed by the kitchen. He grabbed the stool out of the bathroom and carried it into his bedroom. He pushed his shoes aside so the legs would rest evenly on his closet floor. *I think I'll be short forever!* He stepped onto the stool and slid his blue helmet off the top shelf.

In the garage Tony jumped onto his blue six-speed mountain bike. He fastened the strap securely beneath his chin before peddling out to the sidewalk.

Stephen met him in front of his duplex. "What took you so long? I think Laney's coming too."

Tony squirmed. *Laney's always fun; but she's a girl and towers over me,* he thought. *She never teases me about my size—or calls me Little Italy, Tiny Tony, or Cut Spaghetti Vanetti. Maybe that's why I like being around her. I wonder if I'll still be this short in eighth grade. Mama keeps saying I'll have a growth spurt. I hope it's soon.* Tony quit thinking about Laney as he slammed on his brakes and skidded to keep from hitting Stephen's bike at the intersection.

"You trying to T-bone me, Tony? Save some tread for the trail."

"T-bone?" Tony wrinkled his forehead.

"Yeah, that's what Laney calls it when you slam into another biker from the side."

The three friends had a good time in the empty lot. They made some ramps for jumping and worked on the berm for one of the track's corners. Before they parted, they promised to meet the next Monday after school.

"I've got a surprise for you!" Mr. Vanetti headed around to the back of the truck. "Give me your bag."

Tony handed the green duffel bag to his papa and turned to wave to the smiling woman standing on the front porch. "See you Sunday night, Mama!" He crawled up into the truck and buckled his seat belt. "Where were you, Papa? You were supposed to be here at 6:00."

"Merilee needed some help with the baby. Hey, take a look at this." Marcus Vanetti tossed an issue of *Bicycles Today* onto Tony's lap. "It's the latest issue of the NBL's newsletter. It's loaded with pictures, stories of big races, news from state and local tracks, and, of course, the standings of all NBL members. Whatdaya think?"

Tony squirmed and looked at the floor. "Are you talking about baseball?"

Papa grinned, "National Bicycle League, Tony-O. I've signed you up! Here's your membership card and NBL number." Mr. Vanetti reached behind his seat to retrieve the membership card and number for his son. "With this number, the NBL tabulates and posts the points you earn on ANY of their tracks. You can compete in local, state and national events and will be eligible for year-end awards."

"What are you talking about? There aren't any tracks around here, so how could I earn points?"

"We're going to your first BMX race this weekend! They've built a track near Fayetteville. You've been cruisin' around the neighborhood rompin' and stompin' with your buddies and racing on homemade tracks in the backyard long enough. That's how BMX racing got started, but now we've got a competitive track in Fayetteville. Whatdaya think?"

Tony arched his eyebrows, "I don't have a BMX bike."

"BMX isn't a kind of bike. It stands for bicycle motocross. It's the type of racing you and Stephen do on your bikes all the time. You're already a great BMXer. You do jumps, make dirt berms, and create tricks. That girl from New York rides with you guys, too, doesn't she? What's her name?" Mr. Vanetti pulled out on the highway leading to his home in Fayetteville.

"Laney Ausherman. We have a great time, but I don't have the right stuff for real racing. We just have fun with our mountain bikes. Don't you have to have a special helmet and a bike that costs a lot of money? Laney said that bikes for real racing cost anywhere from $300 to $3000."

"Check out that box back there, Tony-O." Papa pointed over his shoulder to a large cardboard carton on the floor behind his seat.

Tony discovered a new helmet with mouth protection and a pair of gloves. "Thanks, Papa, but I didn't bring my bike. Even if I did, it's not a bike for moto-whatever. I don't know much about them, but I know I don't want to race with mine. Everyone would laugh."

Papa just smiled. "I have something in the garage at home that might work for you. You'll have to make the final decision. No matter what you decide, Stephen and his dad are going to meet us at the new track tomorrow evening and you're going to see a real BMX race. It's sponsored by the NBL. Sound fun?"

Tony nodded and tried on his new gloves.

He couldn't believe his good fortune when he saw the new 20-inch BMX bike in the

43

garage. It was shiny black. There were no chain guard, reflectors, kickstand, or other gadgets. The crossbars and handle bars were padded, as well as the frame and gooseneck. "Is this really mine?" was all he could say.

Tony was embarrassed when Papa had to adjust the seat as low as it would go. But he got over it after he hopped on and felt how easy it was to maneuver and ride. He pinched himself to make sure he wasn't dreaming.

The next evening Tony sat between Laney and Stephen to watch their first BMX race. Coach Larkin and Laney had come with Stephen and his dad. The three friends were really excited.

"Ewww! That guy did a face plant." Laney pointed to a kid who'd flipped over his handlebars and landed on his face. "Look at that ramp. I don't think I'm ready for that."

The group watched the bikers head for the starting gate below them.

"Oh! Did you see her case that jump? She flattened her rim. I hope she has a spare or she won't be racing today." Coach Larkin nodded toward a girl who was leaning back to check out her rear wheel.

Laney leaned over toward Tony. "Stephen said you might race in the open class today with the new bike your dad got you."

Tony shrugged, "We haven't had time to look at the whole track or practice, but it looks pretty easy."

"I dare you, Tony," Stephen grinned.

Tony looked over at Laney. *Maybe she'll be impressed if I do well in the race,* he thought. *Maybe she'll forget that she towers over me. It really shouldn't be too hard on my new bike.*

"Sure. Why not?" he said aloud.

Laney frowned. "I think you should practice, Tony. This track is harder than it looks. The ramps are high and there're some double jumps, too. The Skatepark in New York had some of this stuff. It's

tricky."

Tony shrugged. "I think I can do it. There are no points in the open class, so it'll be good practice."

"It may not feel like good practice if you fall or someone T-bones you from the side," Laney warned.

Tony balanced his front wheel against the gate, which kept it from crossing the starting line. A gun went off, and the starting gate dropped. The race was on!

Tony shot out in front of the pack. "Go for it, Tony!" Coach Larkin yelled. "This is his first race—and he's in the lead!"

Tony rounded the curve and came up to the first set of doubles. It looked like two humps of dirt. From Tony's new perspective, the humps looked bigger than they had from the stands. As soon as he was airborne, he knew he was in trouble.

"That's a dead sailor," someone in the stands yelled.

Stephen turned to Laney, "What's a 'dead sailor?'"

"Tony," she said as she closed her eyes. "He's all stiff and out of control."

"The little kid out front is gonna case the jump!" a man shouted.

Laney heard a sickening thud and opened her eyes. "His bike's broken in now!"

"The rear wheel has a flat spot." Stephen grimaced, "I shouldn't have dared him. He's got this complex about being short. I knew if I dared him he'd do it."

Somehow Tony managed not to get smashed by the other racers. When they had all passed him, he wheeled his bike off the track and over to where Laney and Stephen were standing. Their fathers waited in the stands.

Stephen playfully punched his friend on the shoulder. "What happened, Tony? Were you thinking about Laney?"

Tony smiled sheepishly. "I was thinking about how I wanted to prove I could do this—but all I proved is how much more practice I need." Tony swept his hand in the direction of the spectators in the stands. "I should've concentrated on what I was doing,

instead of who was watching."

"We like you, Tony. You don't have to prove anything to us." Laney bent down to look at the bent rim. "Maybe you should think of the Lord, like in the Scripture verse Mr. Canfield taught us. You fell because you were tense and nervous. Relax. Just be happy with who you are. You'll race better. You'll do everything better."

"Preach on!" Stephen teased.

Laney stood up and smiled, "I can't believe I said that."

"Neither can I." Tony grinned. "But you're okay. Thanks."

2 Discussion Time

Discussion Time

Check understanding of the story and development of personal values.

- Raise your hand if you've ever watched a BMX race or have been to a track.
- What was it like?
- What did Tony's dad give him?
- How did Tony feel when his dad had to lower the seat all the way?
- Why did Tony decide to race with his new bike without practicing?
- What happened?
- How did Laney react when Tony cased the jump?

A Preview

Write each word as your teacher says it.

Name _____

1. minutes
2. construct
3. circuit
4. freedom
5. summary
6. shrug
7. District of Columbia
8. opossum
9. umpire
10. pulse
11. adult
12. numb
13. crumb
14. gruffly
15. museum
16. hungry
17. wisdom
18. album
19. tundra
20. suffix

Scripture

Psalm 16:8, 9

29

3 Preview

Test for knowledge of the correct spellings of these words.

Customize Your List

On a separate sheet of paper, additional words of your choice may be tested.

(Say) I will say each word once, use the word in a sentence, then say the word again. Write the words on the lines in your Worktext.

Correct Immediately!

(Say) Let's correct our Preview. I will spell each word out loud. If you spelled a word incorrectly, rewrite it correctly.

Progress Chart

Students may record scores. (Reproducible master provided in Appendix B.)

1.	minutes	Laney arrived at the empty lot within **minutes** of Stephen and Tony.
2.	construct	They discussed how to **construct** a berm for one corner of the track.
3.	circuit	A diagram of an electric **circuit** ran across Tony's old blue helmet.
4.	freedom	Tony's papa has the **freedom** to buy very expensive gifts.
5.	summary	He gave Tony a **summary** of BMX racing.
6.	shrug	Tony gave a **shrug** when his dad asked him what the NBL was.
7.	District of Columbia	Do they print the BMX magazine in the **District of Columbia**?
8.	opossum	An **opossum** waddled across the road as they drove to the race.
9.	umpire	There is no **umpire** at a BMX race.
10.	pulse	Tony felt his **pulse** race as he put the front wheel of his bike in the gate.
11.	adult	Another **adult** shouted, "He's gonna case the jump!"
12.	numb	He felt **numb** for a few seconds after his crash on the track.
13.	crumb	He felt small and unimportant, like a **crumb** under the table.
14.	gruffly	Stephen and Laney did not speak **gruffly** to Tony.
15.	museum	"Hey, you should donate your bike to a BMX **museum**," Stephen teased.
16.	hungry	"Don't be so **hungry** to be different. Be happy with who you are."
17.	wisdom	There was a lot of **wisdom** in Laney's advice.
18.	album	He will put the picture from the race in his photo **album** at home.
19.	tundra	Mr. Canfield defined and showed pictures of the **tundra**.
20.	suffix	Tony is getting better at spelling a word correctly when adding a **suffix**.

4 Word Shapes

Help students form a correct image of whole words.

Say

Look at each word and think about its shape. Now, write the word in the correct Word Shape Boxes. You may check off each word as you use it.

(The sound of **/u/** or **/ə/** is often spelled with **a**, **o**, or **u**. The sound of **/i/** is usually spelled with **i**.)

Say

In the Word Shape Boxes, fill in the boxes containing the letter or letters that spell the sound of **/u/**, **/ə/**, or **/i/** in each word.

Take a minute to memorize...

Psalm 16:8,9

B Word Shapes Name _____

Using the word bank below, write each word in the correct Word Shape Boxes. Next, in the Word Shape Boxes, fill in the boxes containing the letter or letters that spell the sound of /u/, /ə/, or /i/ in each word.

Words with /u/, /ə/, or /i/
Lesson 5

1. adult
2. minutes
3. suffix
4. shrug
5. crumb
6. album
7. circuit
8. construct
9. opossum
10. District of Columbia

11. museum
12. numb
13. umpire
14. wisdom
15. hungry
16. gruffly
17. pulse
18. freedom
19. summary
20. tundra

Word Bank

adult	crumb	hungry	opossum	summary
album	District of Columbia	minutes	pulse	tundra
circuit	freedom	museum	shrug	umpire
construct	gruffly	numb	suffix	wisdom

30

Answers may vary for duplicate word shapes.

Be Prepared For Fun

Check these supply lists for **Fun Ways to Spell** - presented **Day 2**.
Purchase and/or gather these items ahead of time!

General
- Pencil
- Graph Paper (1 sheet per child)
- Spelling List

Auditory
- Pencil
- Notebook Paper
- Spelling List

Visual
- Colored Pencils
- Alphabet Stencils
- Paper

Tactile
- Uncooked Rice
- Art Paper (1 sheet per child)
- Glue
- Spelling List

C ▸ Hide and Seek

Name _____

Play Hide and Seek with your words. Fill in a box on the bar graph (left to right) for each word you spell correctly.

LOOK   SAY   SPELL ALOUD   WRITE   SEEK   CHECK

D ▸ Other Word Forms

Using the words below, follow the instructions given by your teacher.

(adulthood)	D.C.	numbly	suffixing
albums	(free)	numbness	summaries
circuited	gruff	opossums	(summarize)
circuitous	gruffness	pulsed	umpired
constructing	hunger	pulsing	umpiring
construction	hungering	shrugged	
crumbling	minute	shrugging	
crumbly	(minutely)	suffixes	

E ▸ Fun Ways to Spell

Initial the box of each activity you finish.

1. ☐
Spell your words in a "Word Find."

2. ☐
Spell your words with stencils.

3. ☐
Play "Spelling Tic-Tac-Toe."

4. ☐
Spell your words with rice.

31

Words with /u/, /ə/, or /i/

Lesson **5**

---

1 ▸ # Hide and Seek

Reinforce spelling by using multiple styles of learning.

On a white board, Teacher writes each word — one at a time. **Have students:**

- **Look** at the word.
- **Say** the word out loud.
- **Spell** the word out loud.
- **Hide** (teacher erases word.)
- **Write** the word on paper.
- **Seek** (teacher rewrites word.)
- **Check** spelling. If incorrect, rewrite word correctly.

2 ▸ # Other Word Forms

This activity is optional. Have students find and circle the Other Word Forms that are most nearly antonyms of the following:

elongate
enormously
restrained
childhood

3 ▸ # Fun Ways to Spell

Four activities are provided. Use one, two, three, or all of the activities. Have students initial the box for each activity they complete.

Day 2   **Lesson 5**

Options:

- assign activities to students according to their learning styles
- set up the activities in learning centers for the students to do throughout the day
- divide students into four groups and assign one activity per group
- do one activity per day

General
To spell your words in a "Word Find"...
- Arrange your words on a piece of graph paper.
- Put one letter of each word in a square.
- Words may be written backwards, forwards, or diagonally.
- Outline your puzzle.
- Hide your words by filling in all the spaces inside the puzzle with random letters.
- Trade grids with a classmate and find the hidden words.

Auditory
To play "Spelling Tic-Tac-Toe"...
- Draw a Tic-Tac-Toe grid.
- Ask a classmate to read a spelling word.
- Spell the word aloud.
- If the word is spelled correctly, place your mark on the grid.
- Take turns with your classmate.

Visual
To spell your words with stencils...
- Look at the first letter of a word on your list.
- Place the stencil for the proper letter over your paper.
- Shade inside the stencil.
- Choose the proper stencil for the next letter of the word and shade it in next to the first letter.
- Finish the word in this way.
- Do this with each word.

Tactile
To spell your words with rice...
- Choose a word from your spelling list.
- Shape the letters of your word with rice.
- Glue the rice to art paper.
- Do this for each word on your list.

1 Working with Words

Familiarize students with word meaning and usage.

Drawing Conclusions

Explain that to figure something out using logic is to draw a conclusion. On the board write:

This area is hot, dry, and barren. It is a _____ region.

Have a volunteer supply the word **desert**.

Complete each conclusion by writing a word from the word bank. You may use a dictionary to help you.

Take a minute to memorize...

Psalm 16:8,9

F Working with Words

Name _____

Drawing Conclusions

Complete each conclusion by writing a word from the word bank.

1. My raccoon doesn't like its cage. Most likely it wants its ___freedom___.
2. I feel a rhythmical beat in my wrist. This is my ___pulse___.
3. We are going to see some paintings. We will go to a ___museum___.
4. I dropped the plate of cookies. I had to clean up every ___crumb___.
5. My stomach is rumbling. I am probably ___hungry___.
6. We have a book of pictures. It is a photo ___album___.
7. He is 24 years old. He is considered an ___adult___.
8. He will come soon. It will only be a few ___minutes___.
9. Washington, D.C. is the United States capitol. D.C. stands for ___District of Columbia___.
10. This short statement gives the main ideas. It is a ___summary___ of the story.
11. He found a gray, furry marsupial that was playing dead. It is probably an ___opossum___.
12. He felt grouchy. He probably spoke to her ___gruffly___.
13. If you have knowledge, experience, and good judgment you have ___wisdom___.
14. He is ruling on the plays in the ball game. He is the ___umpire___.
15. He is building a house. He will ___construct___ it.
16. She doesn't seem to care. She shows this with a ___shrug___.
17. The soil under the surface is permanently frozen. This area is a ___tundra___.
18. We can add "**ing**" to some words. We can add a ___suffix___.
19. You can't turn on the light. There may be a break in the ___circuit___.
20. My toes are so cold I can't move them. They are ___numb___.

Word Bank

adult	crumb	hungry	opossum	summary
album	District of Columbia	minutes	pulse	tundra
circuit	freedom	museum	shrug	umpire
construct	gruffly	numb	suffix	wisdom

32

G Dictation

Name _____

Write **each sentence as your teacher dictates**. Use **correct punctuation**.

1. Tony's pulse raced as he headed for the first jump in the track.

2. The three kids worked hard to construct a track on which to ride their bicycles.

3. Laney had an album of pictures showing a museum she had visited in the District of Columbia.

H Proofreading

If a word is misspelled, fill in the oval by that word. If all the words are spelled correctly, fill in the oval by **no mistake**.

1.
- ○ gruffly
- ● sufix
- ○ strawberry
- ○ no mistake

2.
- ○ shrug
- ○ lawyers
- ○ Washington
- ● no mistake

3.
- ○ adult
- ○ alcohol
- ○ pulse
- ● no mistake

4.
- ○ album
- ○ Vermont
- ● district of Columbia
- ○ no mistake

5.
- ● crum
- ○ precaution
- ○ awkward
- ○ no mistake

6.
- ● freedum
- ○ coffee
- ○ numb
- ○ no mistake

7.
- ○ crawl
- ● muzeum
- ○ construct
- ○ no mistake

8.
- ○ umpire
- ○ somersault
- ● opposum
- ○ no mistake

9.
- ○ audience
- ○ launch
- ● sumary
- ○ no mistake

10.
- ○ laundry
- ○ wisdom
- ○ hungry
- ● no mistake

11.
- ○ Australia
- ● circut
- ○ tundra
- ○ no mistake

12.
- ○ clause
- ○ exhaust
- ● minites
- ○ no mistake

33

Dictation

Reinforce correct spelling by using current and previous words in context.

(Say)

Listen as I read each sentence and then write it in your Worktext. Remember to use correct capitalization and punctuation. (Slowly read each sentence twice. Sentences are found in the Student Worktext to the left.)

Proofreading

Familiarize students with standardized test format and reinforce recognition of misspelled words.

(Say)

Look at each set of words. If a word is misspelled, fill in the oval by that word. If all the words are spelled correctly, fill in the oval by **no mistake**.

3 Hide and Seek

Reinforce correct spelling of current spelling words. Repeat this activity from Day 2.

4 Vocabulary Extension

Have your students complete this activity to strengthen spelling ability and expand vocabulary. The reproducible master is provided in Appendix A as shown on the inset page to the right.

1 Posttest

Visit the **A Reason For** website to download free, printable Posttest pages.

I will say the word once, use it in a sentence, then say it again. Write your words on a separate sheet of paper.

Progress Chart
Students may record scores. (Appendix B)

Personal Dictionary
Students may add any words they have misspelled to their personal dictionaries. (Appendix B)

Hide and Seek

Play Hide and Seek with your words. Fill in a bar graph (left to right) for each word you spell correctly.

LOOK   SAY   HIDE   WRITE   SEEK   CHECK

Vocabulary Extension

Fill in the Blanks

Choose a word from the word bank that best fits each sentence clue.

1. If you want the cookies to turn out well, you must follow the ___instructions___.
2. The seventh book of the Bible, ___Judges___, is named for the way Israel was ruled during this time.
3. I had to ___struggle___ to get the saddle on the huge horse, but I finally was successful.
4. ___Numbers___, the fourth book of the Bible, begins with a census taken at Sinai.
5. The art class I want to sign up for allows a ___maximum___ of twenty students.
6. When our sink developed a leak underneath, we called a ___plumber___.
7. It felt absolutely ___wonderful___ to go swimming in the middle of the hot day.
8. Someday she would like to travel to several other ___countries___ for a visit.
9. The stray cat soon became a ___regular___ visitor to our dog's bowl on the back porch.
10. The hotel where we stayed provided ___shuttle___ service to the nearby attractions.
11. Several ___companies___ sent me their catalogs of outdoor gear when I subscribed to a ski magazine.
12. Mom is looking forward to the ___luxury___ of a long soak in the whirlpool.

Word Bank

companies	Judges	Numbers	shuttle
countries	luxury	plumber	struggle
instructions	maximum	regular	wonderful

329

1.	minutes	Only a few **minutes** passed before Laney met the boys at the lot.
2.	construct	The three friends helped each other **construct** a berm for the track.
3.	circuit	A bright electrical **circuit** decorated Tony's blue helmet.
4.	freedom	Tony's mom doesn't have the **freedom** to buy expensive gifts like his dad.
5.	summary	Tony's papa gave him a brief but exciting **summary** of BMX racing.
6.	shrug	By Tony's **shrug**, his dad knew he needed to explain more about the sport.
7.	District of Columbia	Was the BMX newsletter printed in the **District of Columbia**?
8.	opossum	Tony saw an **opossum** as they drove to the race.
9.	umpire	There is no **umpire** to make calls during a BMX race.
10.	pulse	Tony's **pulse** began to race as he neared the starting gate.
11.	adult	An **adult** high in the stands shouted, "That's a dead sailor!"
12.	numb	Tony's mind went **numb** as he realized he was going to crash.
13.	crumb	He wanted to crawl under a table like a **crumb**.
14.	gruffly	None of his friends or their parents spoke **gruffly** to Tony.
15.	museum	"Wanna donate your bike to the BMX **museum**?" teased Stephen.
16.	album	Tony will put the picture of him before the race in his **album** at home.
17.	hungry	"Don't be too **hungry** to be different than you are," encouraged Laney.
18.	wisdom	"You've got a lot of **wisdom** for a girl," joked Tony with a grin.
19.	suffix	Tony is learning how a **suffix** can change the meaning of a word.
20.	tundra	Mr. Canfield showed slides of plant life that thrives in the **tundra**.

Game

Name _____

Take the ramp with Tony. Move one space for each word you or your team spells correctly.

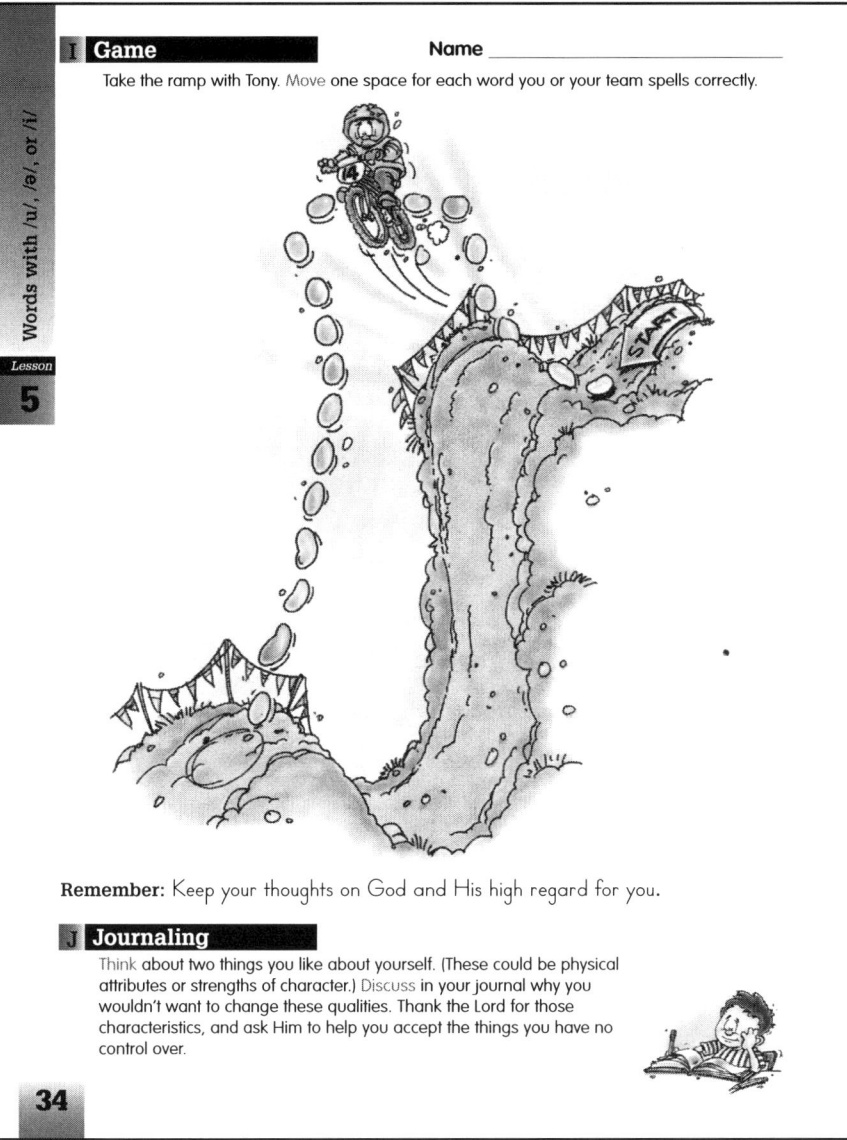

Remember: Keep your thoughts on God and His high regard for you.

Journaling

Think about two things you like about yourself. (These could be physical attributes or strengths of character.) Discuss in your journal why you wouldn't want to change these qualities. Thank the Lord for those characteristics, and ask Him to help you accept the things you have no control over.

34

How to Play:

- Divide the class into two teams.
- Have each student place his/her game piece on Start.
- Have a student from team A go to the board.
- Say the spelling word.
- Have the student write the word on the board.
- If correct, instruct each member of team A to move his/her game piece forward one space.
- Alternate between teams A and B.
- The team to complete the jump first is the winner.
- **Small Group Option**: Students may play this game without teacher direction in small groups of two or more.

2 Game

Reinforce spelling skills and provide motivation and interest.

Materials

- game page (from student text)
- game pieces (1 per child)
- game word list

Game Word List

1. **construct**
2. **gruffly**
3. **suffix**
4. **shrug**
5. **adult**
6. **pulse**
7. **album**
8. **District of Columbia**
9. **crumb**
10. **freedom**
11. **museum**
12. **numb**
13. **opossum**
14. **summary**
15. **umpire**
16. **wisdom**
17. **hungry**
18. **tundra**
19. **circuit**
20. **minutes**

3 Journaling

Provide a meaningful reason for correct spelling through personal writing.

Review the story using discussion leads provided on the following page. Encourage students to apply the Scriptural value in their journaling.

51

Journaling (continued)

(Say)

- How did Tony reach the helmet high on his closet shelf? (A stool)
- What names did Tony's classmates sometimes call him? (Little Italy, Tiny Tony, Cut Spaghetti Vanetti)
- How did Tony feel about Laney towering over him? (He didn't like it.)
- Was Tony's dad on time to pick him up? (No.)
- What did Tony's dad get for him? (A helmet, gloves, and racing bike)
- What did Stephen do to get Tony to race? (Dared him to.)
- How did Laney feel about Tony racing without practicing? (She didn't think it was a good idea.)
- What happened to Tony on the first jump of the race? (He cased the jump.)
- What did Laney say to Tony after he crashed on the jump? ("Maybe you should think of the Lord. You fell because you were tense and nervous. Relax. Just be happy with who you are. You'll race better. You'll do everything better.")

In English, "four" is the only digit that has the same number of letters as its value.

Word-Wow!

Invisible Instructor

When Christopher gets an opportunity to fly in a small plane, he learns what it means to depend on God's guidance.

Christopher was so excited he was speechless—for a change. Dad pulled the green SUV into a parking spot and opened his door. "You coming, Son?"

Christopher nodded and jumped out of the car as if it were on fire. He soaked in the smells and sounds around him as he walked beside his dad across the tarmac and into an air-conditioned terminal. His eyes darted this way and that way, trying to see as much as he could. With each step, he lagged a little further behind his dad as he tried to take everything in.

Halfway down the corridor he cannoned into his father, who'd suddenly stopped. "Good afternoon, Mr. Wright." Christopher stuck his head around his dad to see who was talking. "And you must be Christopher!" The man was tall and lean. His blond hair and mustache were neatly trimmed. He shook Mr. Wright's hand and then stuck out his hand to Christopher. "Glad you could join us today."

"Christopher, this is Paul McInley." Dad nudged Christopher forward to shake the man's hand.

"H-hello, sir." Christopher managed to greet the man in uniform.

"It sure was kind of you to let my son come along, Paul." Mr. Wright rested a hand on Christopher's shoulder as the three of them walked toward a glass door. "But I should probably warn you that once he gets started he's likely to talk your ear off asking questions. Airplanes are his favorite subject—and this is his first flight in a small plane."

"Nothing I like to talk about more!" Mr. McInley laughed and held open the door for Christopher and his dad before leading the way across the tarmac to a

blue and white airplane. A *beautiful* blue and white airplane. Christopher could hardly believe his good fortune. Dad had to make a brief business trip. It was a great opportunity for Christopher to tag along since it would be only a two-hour flight each way, with a short stop for business.

"You sit up here by me," Mr. McInley motioned Christopher into the seat across from his right, in front of the instruments. "After I get the preflight inspection complete and get this thing in the air, you just ask any questions you like. I'm always happy to meet someone who loves airplanes as much as I do."

Christopher absorbed details about the instrument panel while the pilot went through the preflight checklist. After the thrill of takeoff, Christopher began firing questions. "What's that thing for? Why did you do that? What do these gauges tell you? How do you control the altitude?"

Paul McInley patiently answered each question. He explained that they were flying a Cessna Skylane 182T that was built in 2017. He explained that the Skylane is one of the most widely produced airplanes in history—more than 23,000 of them had rolled out of the Cessna plant, to date. Christopher learned that the Skylane featured a constant speed propeller and had a wingspan of 36 feet.

"How high can we go?" Christopher peered out at the patchwork earth far below.

"From sea level, this baby can climb to 18,000 feet. Normal cruising altitude is about half that, though." Mr. McInley tapped a gauge on the instrument panel. "This is the altimeter. It indicates our altitude, or height."

Christopher pointed at a gauge in the middle, "What's that instrument for—that one that looks like a plane sitting on a runway?"

"It's called an attitude indicator. Watch this." Mr. McInley moved a control and suddenly the tiny plane on the attitude indicator flipped sideways at the same time that Christopher felt the plane tip to the right. One instant there was clear blue sky out Christopher's window; the next instant his window was pointed at the ground and he was gazing in fascination at the tiny hills far below. Just as quickly, Mr. McInley righted the plane again and the tiny plane on the attitude indicator faithfully reflected the change—its wings leveling out even with the horizontal lines across it once again.

"ALL RIGHT!" Christopher grinned across at the pilot. "Do some more stuff like that, please?"

Mr. McInley chuckled. "How about a quick course in landing this beauty instead? We're approaching the airport in a couple of minutes."

"Already?" Christopher peered out his window in dismay. Sure enough, way down there more roads converged and a bunch of tiny buildings appeared. Christopher listened intently as Mr. McInley spoke over the radio and prepared to land. He consoled himself with the thought that they still got to fly back home that night.

By the time Mr. Wright finished his business and he and Christopher arrived back at the airport, it was getting dark and cloudy. "We may be in for a bit of a rough ride on the return trip," Mr. McInley commented as they climbed in the Cessna. "That storm they've predicted for tomorrow morning is blowing in sooner than expected. Shouldn't cause a real problem—just be a little bumpy."

Christopher sat quietly in his seat as the pilot put the small plane into motion. As they taxied down the runway gaining

53

speed, the aircraft worked extra hard dragging itself up into the wind. The lights on the ground winked and then disappeared as the Cessna rose into the gathering darkness of the clouds. The three of them in the small airplane seemed to be the only things that existed anymore. By the light from the instrument panel, Christopher watched Paul McInley maneuver the plane.

"Mr. McInley, how do you know where you're going?" Christopher waved a hand at the blackness surrounding all the windows. "How do you find the airport?"

"The instruments, Christopher." Mr. McInley smiled and explained, "I don't have to be able to see where I'm going, because these instruments tell me."

"Do they tell you where other airplanes are?" Christopher stared out his window toward the light on the wing tip. Wisps of cloud often obscured its blinking glow. "There were a whole bunch of planes landing and taking off back at the airport. How do you keep from crashing into each other in the air when you can't see anything?"

"That's why I talk to the guy in the tower, the one who knows where everyone's headed." The pilot checked his airspeed and altitude. "That person is called an air traffic controller. At larger airports, like the one we just left, air traffic controllers keep track of every airplane in the area. If I follow the directions they give me, I'll stay out of trouble by keeping clear of the flight path of other…"

His voice trailed off as the plane lurched wildly. The turbulence required all of Mr. McInley's attention and skill. Christopher was happy to be quiet and let the pilot concentrate on flying the plane—especially when it continued to buck and drop in the currents of air.

Christopher assured himself that he wasn't really scared. After all, anyone would feel a little strange when their airplane was acting more like a roller-coaster!

Christopher was glad he was wearing a seat belt and he was glad Mr. McInley knew what he was doing. The thin aluminum walls shuddered and seemed pretty fragile when the wind buffeted the Skylane around. Well, maybe he was scared. Just a little bit.

"So, here's my aspiring young pilot!" Mom met Christopher and his dad at the door later that night. "Was it fun? Did you learn a lot?"

"Sure did!" Christopher grinned. "Especially how important it is to pay attention to your instruments and to obey the…the…, you know, that person who knows what's best for everyone."

"You're talking about air traffic controllers, aren't you?" Mom ruffled Christopher's hair like she used to when he was little and laughed at the look on his face. "Since the air traffic controllers know what all the planes around an airport are doing, pilots who obey their instructions stay on the right course."

"That's it! Air traffic controllers," Christopher repeated. He ran a hand through his wavy brown hair to smooth it back down.

"Well, I was sure glad to know someone out there could tell Mr. McInley where to go tonight." Mr. Wright laid his briefcase on the table and stretched. He thought aloud for a moment, "Someone who can keep us safely on the right course even when we're not flying…Hmmm. You know, that's a lot like life."

He grinned at his wife and son and finished his thought. "We obey God because He knows everything about us—even where we're headed. Obeying His instructions keeps us on the right track. See what I mean?"

His son returned the grin. "Gonna keep us flyin' straight, Dad."

Check understanding of the story and development of personal values.

- Where did Christopher go with his dad?
- Why was he so excited about it?
- In what kind of plane were they flying?
- Did the pilot mind having Christopher come along?
- What happened on the flight back home?
- How did Christopher feel when the storm made the flight rough?
- How did Mr. McInley know how to fly the plane when he couldn't see anything?
- How can you keep on the right track when life is rough?

A Test-Words

Name _____

Write each spelling word on the line as your teacher says it.

1. lizard
2. glitter
3. income
4. index
5. discuss
6. assist
7. history
8. camera
9. album
10. limit
11. England
12. cliffs
13. Mississippi
14. infant
15. glisten
16. online

Review

Lesson **6**

B Test-Sentences

Write the sentences on the lines below, correcting each misspelled word, as well as all capitalization and punctuation errors. Two words are misspelled in each sentence.

with great skill the astronot began the lawnch

1. With great skill, the astronaut began the launch.

the dentist grufly told the boy that he had a cavitie?

2. The dentist gruffly told the boy that he had a cavity.

do you have friends in virginya and michigin.

3. Do you have friends in Virginia and Michigan?

Our teacher gave us freadum at the muzeam

4. Our teacher gave us freedom at the museum.

35

Test-Sentences

Reinforce recognizing misspelled words.

 Say

Read each sentence carefully. Write the sentences on the lines in your Worktext. There are two misspelled words in each sentence. Correct each misspelled word, as well as all capitalization and punctuation errors.

 Take a minute to memorize...

Psalm 119:33,34

3 Test-Words

Test for knowledge of the correct spellings of these words.

Say I will say each word once, use the word in a sentence, then say the word again. Write the words on the lines in your Worktext.

1. lizard — Christopher saw a **lizard** sunning himself on the tarmac.
2. glitter — The **glitter** in the stripes on the plane made it sparkle in the sun.
3. income — Mr. McInley earns an **income** flying people in his plane.
4. index — Christopher ran his **index** finger along the instrument panel.
5. discuss — Mr. McInley was very eager to **discuss** airplanes and flying.
6. assist — "These instruments **assist** me in knowing my altitude or height."
7. history — He explained the **history** of the Cessna Skylanes.
8. camera — Christopher's dad pulled his **camera** out of his briefcase.
9. album — He took a picture of Christopher and the pilot for his son's photo **album**.
10. limit — There was no **limit** to the questions Christopher wanted to ask.
11. England — "Have you ever flown to **England**?" he asked Mr. McInley.
12. cliffs — "Yes, I flew over some gorgeous **cliffs** over there!" he exclaimed.
13. Mississippi — "I've flown across the **Mississippi** River too many times to count."
14. infant — It seemed that Christopher had loved planes since he was an **infant**.
15. glisten — He loved to see a plane **glisten** in the sunlight as it landed.
16. online — He could hardly wait to get **online** and learn more about the Cessna Skylane.

55

1 Test-Dictation

Reinforce correct spelling by using current and previous words in context.

Say

Listen as I read each sentence, then write it in your worktext. Remember to use correct capitalization and punctuation. (Slowly read each sentence twice. Sentences are found in the student text to the right. The words **banana, lawyers, construct,** and **Washington** are found in this unit.)

2 Test-Proofreading

Familiarize students with standardized test format and reinforce recognizing misspelled words.

Say

Look at each set of words. If a word is misspelled, fill in the oval by that word. If all the words are spelled correctly, fill in the oval by **no mistake**.

Review Lesson **6**

C Test-Dictation   Name _____

Write **each sentence as your teacher dictates.** Use **correct punctuation.**

1. There is a yellow banana on the sidewalk.
2. Both of those lawyers are in my employ.
3. They plan to construct a wide gate here.
4. When in Washington, I saw my grandmother.

D Test-Proofreading

If a word is misspelled, fill in the oval by that word. If all the words are spelled correctly, fill in the oval by **no mistake**.

1. ● sufix
   ○ lizard
   ○ glitter
   ○ no mistake

2. ○ income
   ○ automobile
   ○ index
   ● no mistake

3. ○ discuss
   ○ assist
   ● austraila
   ○ no mistake

4. ○ history
   ● opposum
   ○ limit
   ○ no mistake

5. ● wepon
   ○ album
   ○ England
   ○ no mistake

6. ○ cliffs
   ○ Mississippi
   ● minites
   ○ no mistake

7. ● strawberrie
   ○ infant
   ○ glisten
   ○ no mistake

8. ○ online
   ○ disk
   ● hymm
   ○ no mistake

9. ○ somersault
   ● acsent
   ○ pulse
   ○ no mistake

10. ○ exhaust
    ○ camera
    ○ weather
    ● no mistake

11. ○ automatic
    ○ insist
    ○ strength
    ● no mistake

12. ○ admit
    ● circut
    ○ adapt
    ○ no mistake

36

E Test-Table

Name _____

If a word is misspelled, fill in the space on the grid.

Montanna	assid	lacth	alcohaul
crumb	method	aspekt	vermont
denim	kiddnap	credit	tundra
planit	clause	selfish	cavern

Lesson 6

F Writing Assessment

Write about a flight you have taken. Tell all about the experience including when you flew, where you were going, and what the plane was like. If you haven't flown, write about how you would feel if you were in the plane with Christopher when the airplane felt more like a roller coaster than a plane.

_____

_____

_____

_____

_____

_____

Scripture

Psalm 119:33, 34

37

A rubric for scoring is provided in Appendix B.

"I am"
is the shortest sentence
in the English language.

Test-Table

1 Test mastery of words in this unit.

Say: If a word is misspelled, fill in the space on the grid.

Writing Assessment

2 Assess student's spelling, grammar, and composition skills through personal writing.

Say:
- Have you ever flown in an airplane? (Allow time to share experiences.)
- Why did Christopher get to go on the trip with his dad? (It was a two hour flight each way with a short stop for business at the other end and there was room in the plane.)
- What kinds of questions did Christopher have for Mr. McInley, the pilot? (What's that? What do these gauges tell you? How do you control the altitude? How high can we go? etc.)
- How did Mr. McInley show Christopher what the attitude indicator was for? (He tipped the plane on it's side so Christopher's window was facing the ground.)
- Why was the flight rough on the way back? (A storm had moved into the area.)
- How was Mr. McInley able to keep the plane on the right track even in the thick clouds? (By using his instruments and paying attention to and doing what the air traffic controller said to do.)
- How can you keep on the right track? (By paying attention to and doing what God says to do.)

1 Test-Sentences

Reinforce recognizing misspelled words.

Say

Read each sentence carefully. Write the sentences on the lines in your Worktext, correcting each misspelled word, as well as all capitalization and punctuation errors.

G Test-Sentences   Name _____

Write the sentences on the lines below. Correct each misspelled word, as well as all capitalization and punctuation errors. Two words are misspelled in each sentence.

the audiunse can often read a sumery of the play!

1. The audience can often read a summary of the play.

feeling awkwerd she swung at the tinnis ball,

2. Feeling awkward, she swung at the tennis ball.

they hung a baner to welcome the athleat

3. They hung a banner to welcome the athlete.

is the heffer helthy enough to show at the state fair.

4. Is the heifer healthy enough to show at the state fair?

H Test-Words

Write each spelling word on the line as your teacher says it.

1. disk
2. somersault
3. pulse
4. weather
5. insist
6. admit
7. strength
8. adapt
9. precaution
10. panic
11. lever
12. wisdom
13. respect
14. batch
15. hungry
16. coffee

38

2 Test-Words

Test for knowledge of the correct spellings of these words.

Say

I will say the word once, use the word in a sentence, then say the word again. Write the word on the lines in your Worktext.

1. disk   The center of the Cessna's propeller looked like a perfectly round **disk**.
2. somersault   During the storm, he felt like the plane might do a **somersault**.
3. pulse   He could feel his **pulse** pounding in his temples.
4. weather   It was a relief to everyone to be out of the rough **weather**.
5. insist   "I **insist** you let us buy you some dinner," said Mr. Wright to Paul.
6. admit   Christopher had to **admit** he was a little scared during the storm.
7. strength   His legs were shaking, so he wasn't sure he had the **strength** to stand.
8. adapt   Mr. McInley will **adapt** his course if instructed to do so.
9. precaution   "The tower informs me of each **precaution** I need to take to land safely."
10. panic   Storm clouds and dense fog can cause pilots to **panic**.
11. lever   "He always knew just which **lever** to move," said Christopher in awe.
12. wisdom   "I saw the **wisdom** in listening to the tower," he told his mom.
13. respect   It is clear to see that Christopher has great **respect** for the pilot.
14. batch   Mom had a **batch** of oatmeal cookies hot out of the oven.
15. hungry   "Hope you're **hungry** for some cookies and milk," she said.
16. coffee   "I'd love a cup of **coffee** myself," said Mr. Wright.

Test-Editing

Name _____

If a word is spelled correctly, fill in the oval under **Correct**. If the word is misspelled, fill in the oval under **Incorrect**, and spell the word correctly on the blank.

		Correct	Incorrect	
1.	gram	●	○	_____
2.	cannada	○	●	Canada
3.	mass	●	○	_____
4.	California	●	○	_____
5.	atlus	○	●	atlas
6.	delta	●	○	_____
7.	shellter	○	●	shelter
8.	attend	●	○	_____
9.	tinse	○	●	tense
10.	Marylund	○	●	Maryland
11.	New Mexico	●	○	_____
12.	laundry	●	○	_____
13.	umbrela	○	●	umbrella
14.	crawl	●	○	_____
15.	texas	○	●	Texas
16.	shrugg	○	●	shrug
17.	adult	●	○	_____
18.	District of Columbia	●	○	_____
19.	numm	○	●	numb
20.	umpire	●	○	_____

39

3 Test-Editing

Reinforce recognizing and correcting misspelled words.

4 Action Game

Reinforce spelling skills and provide motivation and interest.

Materials

- masking tape
- four square ball
- word list on certificate at end of unit

BOUNCE BACK

Use tape to mark a two-square game grid on the classroom floor. Divide the class into two teams. Line up the two teams on opposite sides of the two-square court. The first player from each team steps into the court, one player holding a ball. Call out the first spelling word to be reviewed. The player with the ball says the first letter of the word as he or she hits the ball into the opposite square. The player in that square says the second letter of the word as he or she hits the ball back. This continues until the word has been spelled. If a player misspells a word by saying an incorrect letter, play stops and the other team gets a point. If the word is spelled correctly, both teams get a point. Give a new word to the next two players and continue in this pattern. The team with the most points wins!

1 Game

Reinforce spelling skills and provide motivation and interest.

Materials
- game page (from student text)
- colored pencils (1 per child)
- game word list

Game Word List
Check off each word lightly in pencil as it is used.

The Pipers
1. automobile
2. Australia
3. opossum
4. weapon
5. minutes
6. strawberry
7. hymn
8. denim
9. planet

The Bonanzas
1. acid
2. method
3. kidnap
4. clause
5. latch
6. aspect
7. credit
8. selfish
9. alcohol

The Cessnas
1. Vermont
2. tundra
3. cavern
4. accent
5. exhaust
6. automatic
7. circuit
8. Montana
9. crumb

J Game   Name _____

Score points for each review word or Other Word Form you or your team spells correctly.

Review Lesson 6

Remember: Let God be the "air traffic controller" of your life.

40

How to Play:
- Divide the class into three teams. Name one team **The Pipers**, one **The Cessnas**, and one **The Bonanzas**. (Option: You may wish to seat students in groups of three, each student from a different team. They should share one game page.)
- Have a student from the first team go to the board.
- Say the spelling word.
- Have the student write the word on the board.
- If the word is spelled correctly, have each team member color a point symbol by his/her team name. If the word is misspelled, have him/her put an **X** through one point symbol. That word may not be given again.
- Repeat this process with the second team and then the third.
- When the words from all three lists have been used, the team with the most points is the winner.
- Play another round using Other Word Forms.

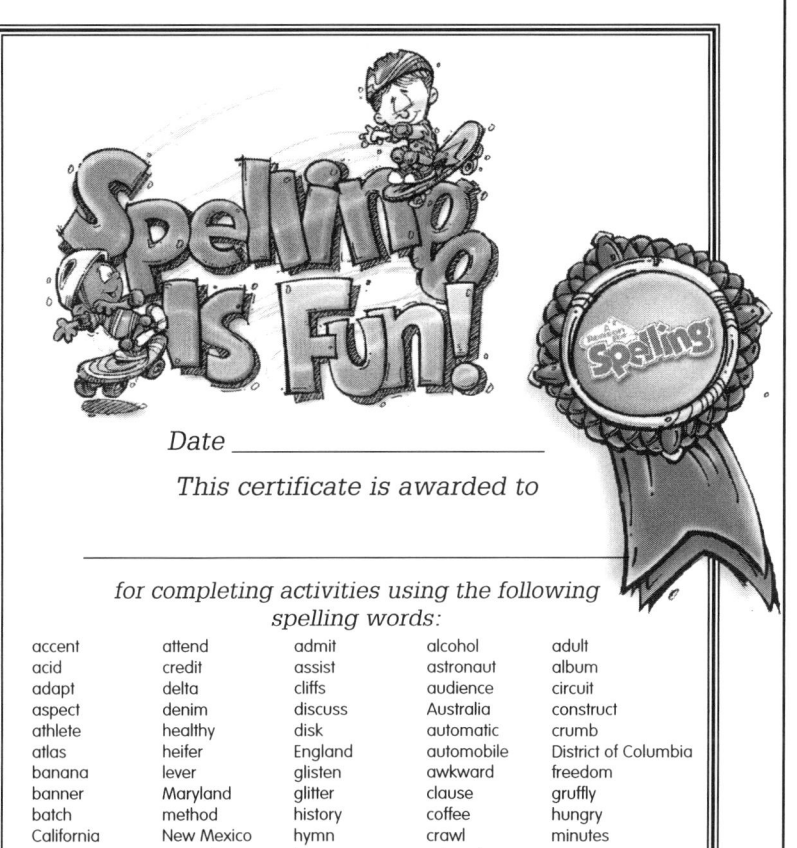

Date _____

This certificate is awarded to

_____

for completing activities using the following spelling words:

accent	attend	admit	alcohol	adult
acid	credit	assist	astronaut	album
adapt	delta	cliffs	audience	circuit
aspect	denim	discuss	Australia	construct
athlete	healthy	disk	automatic	crumb
atlas	heifer	England	automobile	District of Columbia
banana	lever	glisten	awkward	freedom
banner	Maryland	glitter	clause	gruffly
batch	method	history	coffee	hungry
California	New Mexico	hymn	crawl	minutes
camera	respect	income	exhaust	museum
Canada	selfish	index	launch	numb
cavern	shelter	infant	laundry	opossum
cavity	strength	insist	lawyers	pulse
gram	tennis	kidnap	online	shrug
latch	tense	limit	precaution	suffix
mass	Texas	lizard	somersault	summary
Montana	umbrella	Michigan	strawberry	tundra
panic	weapon	Mississippi	Vermont	umpire
planet	weather	Virginia	Washington	wisdom

2 Certificate

Provide an opportunity for parents or guardians to encourage and assess their child's progress.

 Fill in today's date and your name on your certificate.

 Take a minute to memorize...

Psalm 119:33,34

Review **6** | Day 5

61

3 **Letter**

Provide the parent or guardian with the spelling word lists for the next unit.

Say

Give your parents or guardian this letter that lists your spelling words for the next unit. Put it where you will remember to practice the words together.

Dear Parent,

We are about to begin a new spelling unit containing five weekly lessons. A set of twenty words will be studied each week. All the words will be reviewed in the sixth week. Values based on the Scriptures listed below will be taught in each lesson.

Lesson 7	Lesson 8	Lesson 9	Lesson 10	Lesson 11
Asia	appeal	admire	banjo	accuse
chase	brief	alibi	boldly	canoe
contain	creep	arrive	buffalo	confuse
crater	deceit	byte	cargo	crew
debate	eager	diary	control	cue
decade	Hawaii	diet	dome	dune
decay	idea	geyser	donate	flu
detail	liter	guide	enroll	foolish
escape	Louisiana	guys	flamingo	funeral
estate	meter	height	macro	future
flavor	piece	Idaho	Minnesota	igloo
labor	Puerto Rico	Iowa	Oklahoma	include
Maine	relief	isle	patrol	Massachusetts
mesa	reveal	liar	portfolio	raccoon
Pennsylvania	shield	minor	soldier	tomb
prey	shriek	Ohio	sole	truly
ratio	skiing	recital	stereo	tulip
stray	Tennessee	riot	studio	useless
veil	vetoes	silence	voltage	Utah
vein	wield	wife	Wyoming	view
Psalm 37:4,5	Psalm 62:8	Psalm 89:14	Psalm 62:7	Psalm 119:96-98

Funny Money

Matthew's little sister reminds him to trust the Lord, who is able to give him his heart's desire.

(Note: Your class might enjoy looking at a real $100 bill. Lower denominations have also been updated. It might be fun for them to find all the things found in this story that make counterfeiting more difficult.)

"*B*elieve me, I'd rather play Monopoly than practice this report." Matthew spread the book open on the floor in front of him. "I'd rather do 'most anything," he mumbled under his breath.

"Can't you just play with us for a little while? We don't have to finish the game." Alex took the game board out of the box and put it on the table.

Matthew tried to hide his discomfort. "Did you know…" His voice cracked. He paused to lick his lips. His tongue felt thick and dry. "…U.S. currency is used more than any other kind of money in the world?"

"No," nine-year-old Alex answered. "I thought our money was only good here. Don't all countries make their own?"

Matthew rubbed his clammy hands across the carpet. "Yeah, but I guess our money is safer because its value doesn't make extreme changes all the time. Our economy is stable relative to other countries." He hesitated again to wipe the beads of perspiration off his upper lip. "Here's another trivia question for you two." He took a deep breath and let it out slowly—trying to control his rising anxiety. "The one dollar bill is most used. But what bill comes in second?"

"The ten dollar bill," Alex guessed, tucking his allotment of Monopoly money under the edge of the game board.

Matthew shook his head. "Nope, try again."

Alex looked down at Matthew. "Are you okay?"

Matthew ignored the question and wrote something down on a piece of notebook paper.

"Hundreds," his first-grade sister guessed.

Matthew's eyebrows shot up. "How did you know that, Em?"

Emily shrugged. "I doe know—just do."

Matthew smiled at his little sister. "You're right."

"Are you sick? I thought you couldn't play Monopoly because you had homework." Alex put three game pieces on "Go."

"I do. I need to practice this report. I have to read it in front the class." Matthew felt a lump in his throat, and his stomach felt funny, too. "The best ones have to do theirs again for the whole school."

I can't even imagine doing that, Matthew thought. *My hands shake so much I can't read my paper in front of my own class. My tongue feels thick and dry, and I stumble over the words. I feel so stupid. I wish Mrs. Burton was still our teacher. She never made us do stuff like this.* Matthew's heart started to pound just thinking about the coming ordeal.

"Is youah wepoaht about money?" Emily rolled the dice and moved the silver dog to Baltic.

Matthew didn't even notice how his sister still mispronounced her r's. He focused on what she said and tried not to think about giving the report. He knew his fear was unreasonable, but he couldn't stop it. Getting up in front of

the whole class just terrified him. Finally he answered, "Yeah, my report's about money."

"Well, wead it to us. I like money." Emily got up from the table and came over to sit beside her brother. She picked up the book and examined the picture on the cover. It was of a girl peeking around the edge of a huge sheet of $100 bills hot off the press. Then she looked up at Matthew's face. "What's the mattah, Matt?"

Matthew ignored her question and started to read from his notebook. "The old Presidents look better than ever! The Treasury decided in the mid-1990's to make new currency because of 'funny money'—those fake bills counterfeiters try to pass off as real. A counterfeiter once needed special engraving skills—but with the rise of scanners and high-quality color copies, counterfeiting became too easy."

Emily moved closer to Matthew and put her hand on his back.

Matthew stopped reading and looked up at her before he continued. "The $100 bill has two pictures of Ben Franklin. One shows up only when the bill is held up to a light. It's called a watermark; a scanner or copier can't see it. Details in the bigger, off-center picture of Ben make the face easier to recognize and the bill harder to copy. On the left side, the ink is raised in the printing on his shoulder. Tiny letters spelling 'The United States of America' are hidden in his jacket collar, and the edge of the blank space around the watermark is printed with 'USA 100' in letters so small you might need a magnifying glass to see them." Matthew stopped reading and pointed to a picture of the magnified words in the book.

Alex got up from the table and came over to look at the pictures, too.

Matthew continued, "To the right of Ben's face, there's a blue 3-D security ribbon that is woven into the paper. If you tilt the $100 bill, you'll see the images on the ribbon shift between a picture of a bell and the number 100. Tilt the bill up and down, and the images shift side to

Story (continued)

side, but if you tilt the bill side to side, the bells and 100s shift up and down. To the right of the security ribbon, there is an outline of an old-fashioned inkwell with a bell inside, and in the lower-right corner, the number 100. Both of these are printed in color-changing ink, that shifts from green to copper as you move the bill. Also, every authentic United States bill is printed on special paper created from a secret formula. It's not only extra durable, but no other paper feels quite the same."

"This is cool." Alex bent down to take a look at the bill in the book. "Why is the '100' on the back so big?"

Matthew could feel the tension leaving his body. His brother and sister liked his report—even more than playing Monopoly. He smiled. "I'm not going to tell. You have to figure it out. You want to hear the rest of this?"

Both kids nodded, so Matthew began to read the last paragraphs. "Don't get any ideas about copying your own money. The United States Secret Service was formed in 1865, during the presidency of Abraham Lincoln, to fight counterfeiting. (Now it has other jobs, too, including protecting the President.) It investigates every counterfeit case immediately, and the penalties are very stiff, including up to 15 years in prison, high fines and restitution, and seizure of equipment used to create or spend the fake money. It is also a federal felony conviction, which makes life far more difficult, even after prison."

Matthew glanced over at his siblings, who were listening with obvious interest, then continued, "Unless your copy of paper money is one-sided and less than three-fourths the bill's actual size, or at least 1.5 times larger than the real currency, you're counterfeiting — and counterfeiting is a serious crime. When in doubt, stick with Monopoly money!"

Emily clapped her hands.

"That's good, Matthew. I want to look at a weal $100 bill now." She bent down and looked at Matthew's face. "You feeling bettah?"

Matthew nodded.

"Aah you scaaahed? You don't want to say youah wepoaht to youah class?"

Alex returned to the game table. "That's a good report. Yours will be one of the best. I think you should play Monopoly with us now and quit worrying."

Matthew's eyes got big.

Emily patted his hand. "Pway, Matt. Twust Jesus to help you do it. He will." A smile spread across the little girl's face.

The words blurred on the report in his hand. "I sure need your help, God. But it's okay if You help me just enough to do it in front of my own class," he prayed silently.

Matthew closed his notebook. "Thanks for listening to my report, guys. I think I can play Monopoly now. Pass me some of that real 'funny money!'"

2 Discussion Time

Check understanding of the story and development of personal values.

- How many of you have ever saved one hundred dollars?
- Raise your hand if you've held a one hundred dollar bill recently?
- What are some of the things Matthew talked about that make the one hundred dollar bill harder to counterfeit?
- Why do you think Matthew was afraid to give his report in front of the class?
- What did Emily do to encourage her older brother?
- Tell about a time you learned something or were reminded of it by someone younger.

A Preview

Name _____

Write each word as your teacher says it.

1. labor
2. detail
3. estate
4. Pennsylvania
5. Asia
6. Maine
7. decay
8. escape
9. crater
10. stray
11. decade
12. mesa
13. prey
14. ratio
15. flavor
16. vein
17. contain
18. debate
19. chase
20. veil

Words with /ā/

Lesson 7

Scripture
Psalm 37:4, 5

43

3 Preview
Test for knowledge of the correct spellings of these words.

Customize Your List
On a separate sheet of paper, additional words of your choice may be tested.

Say

I will say each word once, use the word in a sentence, then say the word again. Write the words on the lines in your Worktext.

Correct Immediately!

Say

Let's correct our Preview. I will spell each word out loud. If you spelled a word incorrectly, rewrite it correctly.

Progress Chart
Students may record scores. (Reproducible master provided in Appendix B.)

1.	labor	It was a great **labor** for Matthew to prepare to speak publicly.
2.	detail	He carefully researched every **detail** of how money is printed.
3.	estate	Ben Franklin, pictured on the hundred dollar bill, did not live on an **estate**.
4.	Pennsylvania	A United States mint is located in Philadelphia, **Pennsylvania**.
5.	Asia	Our money is not printed on the continent of **Asia**, but in North America.
6.	Maine	There are no mints in **Maine**.
7.	decay	Matthew's enthusiasm about his report began to **decay** as fear overcame him.
8.	escape	He wished there was a way to **escape** this assignment.
9.	crater	Matthew thought a **crater** on the moon would be a good place to hide!
10.	stray	He tried not to allow his thoughts to **stray**.
11.	decade	To Matthew, every minute in front of the class felt like a **decade**.
12.	mesa	The platform at the front of the room felt like a huge **mesa**.
13.	prey	Matthew's nerves fell **prey** to his fears.
14.	ratio	His **ratio** of confidence to fear was very low.
15.	flavor	Em's favorite **flavor** of ice cream is mint chocolate chip.
16.	vein	"Why is the **vein** on your forehead popping out?" asked Alex.
17.	contain	Matthew's siblings could not **contain** their excitement about his report.
18.	debate	Em said there was no **debate**; he just needed to trust God to help him.
19.	chase	God can **chase** away our fears and replace them with strength and peace.
20.	veil	He lifted the **veil** of fear in front of Matthew's eyes.

4 Word Shapes

Help students form a correct image of whole words.

(Say) Look at each word and think about its shape. Now, write the word in the correct Word Shape Boxes. You may check off each word as you use it.

(In many words, the sound of /ā/ is spelled with **a** at the end of a syllable, or with **a-consonant-e**, **ai**, **ay**, **ey**, and occasionally **ei**.)

(Say) In the Word Shape Boxes, fill in the boxes containing the letter or letters that spell the sound of /ā/ in each word.

Take a minute to memorize...
Psalm 37:4,5

B Word Shapes   Name _____

Using the word bank below, write each word in the correct Word Shape Boxes. Next, in the Word Shape Boxes, fill in the boxes containing the letter or letters that spell the sound of /ā/ in each word.

Words with /ā/
Lesson **7**

1. ratio
2. Maine
3. escape
4. prey
5. stray
6. labor
7. decade
8. detail
9. decay
10. Asia

11. crater
12. veil
13. debate
14. Pennsylvania
15. estate
16. vein
17. chase
18. flavor
19. mesa
20. contain

Word Bank

Asia	debate	escape	Maine	ratio
chase	decade	estate	mesa	stray
contain	decay	flavor	Pennsylvania	veil
crater	detail	labor	prey	vein

44

Answers may vary for duplicate word shapes.

Be Prepared For Fun

Check these supply lists for **Fun Ways to Spell** - presented **Day 2**.
Purchase and/or gather these items ahead of time!

General
- Pencil
- Graph Paper (1 sheet per child)
- Spelling List

Auditory
- Voice Recorder
- Spelling List

Visual
- American Sign Language reproducible master (provided in Appendix B)
- Spelling List

Tactile
- Soccer Ball, Basketball, Tennis Ball, or 4-Square Ball
- Spelling List

C **Hide and Seek**

Name _____

Play **Hide and Seek** with your words. Fill in a box on the bar graph (left to right) for each word you spell correctly.

LOOK   SAY   SPELL ALOUD   WRITE   SEEK   CHECK

D **Other Word Forms**

Using the words below, follow the instructions given by your teacher.

Asian	debating	estates	preys
chased	decades	flavored	ration
chasing	decayed	flavoring	ratios
contained	decaying	labored	strayed
container	detailing	laboring	straying
cratered	details	mesas	veiled
cratering	escapee	Pennsylvanian	veins
debated	escaping	preying	unveiling

E **Fun Ways to Spell**

Initial the box of each activity you finish.

1. ☐
Create a crossword puzzle with clues.

2. ☐
w·o·r·d
Spell your words with sign language.

3. ☐
W·O·R·D
Spell your words on a voice recorder.

4. ☐
B·A·T·C·H
Bounce a ball as you spell your words.

45

---

1 **Hide and Seek**

Reinforce spelling by using multiple styles of learning.

On a white board, Teacher writes each word — one at a time. **Have students:**

• **Look** at the word.
• **Say** the word out loud.
• **Spell** the word out loud.
• **Hide** (teacher erases word.)
• **Write** the word on paper.
• **Seek** (teacher rewrites word.)
• **Check** spelling. If incorrect, rewrite word correctly.

2 **Other Word Forms**

This activity is optional. Have students find and circle the Other Word Forms that are most nearly synonyms of the following:

arguing
toiled
rotten
covered

3 **Fun Ways to Spell**

Four activities are provided. Use one, two, three, or all of the activities. Have students initial the box for each activity they complete.

Options:

• assign activities to students according to their learning styles
• set up the activities in learning centers for the students to do throughout the day
• divide students into four groups and assign one activity per group
• do one activity per day

General

To create a crossword puzzle...
• Use a pencil to arrange your words on graph paper.
• Overlap words where letters are shared.
• Don't create any new words.
• Outline each word with a marker and number it.
• Write a clue for each word.
• Erase your words.
• Trade with a classmate and work each other's puzzles.

Auditory

To spell your words using a voice recorder...
• Record yourself as you say and spell each word on your spelling list.
• Listen to your recording and check your spelling.

Visual

To spell your words with sign language...
• Have a classmate read a spelling word to you from the list.
• Spell the word using the American Sign Language alphabet.
• Do this with each word on your list.

Tactile

To bounce a ball as you spell your words...
• Look at the first word on your list.
• Bounce the ball as you say each letter of the word aloud.
• Do this with each word on your list.

1 | Working with Words

Familiarize students with word meaning and usage.

Word Building

Write the endings **s**, **ed**, and **ing**, and the word **glisten** on the board. Have a volunteer add each suffix to the word until you have **glistens**, **glistened**, and **glistening**.

You will be adding each suffix to these spelling words to make other word forms.

The A's Have It

Answer each question with an /ā/ word from the word bank. You may use a dictionary to help you. Write the word in the blank.

Take a minute to memorize...

Psalm 37:4,5

F | Working with Words   Name _____

Word Building

Add each suffix to the word in each row to make a new word. Remember, when words have the consonant-vowel-consonant-**e** pattern, drop the **e** when adding an ending that begins with a vowel.

		+s or es	+d or ed	+ing
1.	debate	debates	debated	debating
2.	stray	strays	strayed	straying
3.	labor	labors	labored	laboring
4.	detail	details	detailed	detailing
5.	veil	veils	veiled	veiling
6.	prey	preys	preyed	preying
7.	chase	chases	chased	chasing
8.	flavor	flavors	flavored	flavoring
9.	vein	veins	veined	veining
10.	decay	decays	decayed	decaying
11.	contain	contains	contained	containing
12.	escape	escapes	escaped	escaping

The A's Have It

Answer each question with an /ā/ word from the word bank. Write the word in the blank.

1. What /ā/ word means flat-topped hill with steep sides? __mesa__
2. What /ā/ word is the name of the world's largest continent? __Asia__
3. What /ā/ word means a number relationship between two things? __ratio__
4. What /ā/ word is a state whose capitol is Augusta? __Maine__
5. What /ā/ word means a period of ten years? __decade__
6. What /ā/ word is a state whose southern boundary is part of the Mason-Dixon line? __Pennsylvania__
7. What /ā/ word means a depression formed by an explosion? __crater__
8. What /ā/ word means a person's land and property? __estate__

Word Bank

Asia	debate	escape	Maine	ratio
chase	decade	estate	mesa	stray
contain	decay	flavor	Pennsylvania	veil
crater	detail	labor	prey	vein

46

G Dictation

Name _____

Write **each sentence as your teacher dictates.** Use **correct punctuation.**

1. "The money has many details so people can not copy it," he said.

2. He wanted to escape and not have to speak in front of class.

3. We read about children in parts of Asia who have to labor all day in a factory.

H Proofreading

If a word is misspelled, fill in the oval by that word. If all the words are spelled correctly, fill in the oval by **no mistake**.

1. ○ decay
   ○ prey
   ○ wisdom
   ● no mistake

2. ○ stray
   ● laber
   ○ minutes
   ○ no mistake

3. ○ umpire
   ○ circuit
   ● dekade
   ○ no mistake

4. ○ hungry
   ● detale
   ○ veil
   ○ no mistake

5. ○ contain
   ○ summary
   ○ Maine
   ● no mistake

6. ● Pensylvania
   ○ opossum
   ○ tundra
   ○ no mistake

7. ○ vein
   ○ escape
   ○ crumb
   ● no mistake

8. ○ chase
   ● messa
   ○ numb
   ○ no mistake

9. ● rashio
   ○ crater
   ○ construct
   ○ no mistake

10. ○ gruffly
    ○ suffix
    ● debait
    ○ no mistake

11. ○ pulse
    ○ estate
    ● flaver
    ○ no mistake

12. ○ shrug
    ○ adult
    ● asia
    ○ no mistake

47

Dictation

Reinforce correct spelling by using current and previous words in context.

Say

Listen as I read each sentence and then write it in your Worktext. Remember to use correct capitalization and punctuation. (Slowly read each sentence twice. Sentences are found in the Student Worktext to the left.)

Proofreading

Familiarize students with standardized test format and reinforce recognition of misspelled words.

Say

Look at each set of words. If a word is misspelled, fill in the oval by that word. If all the words are spelled correctly, fill in the oval by **no mistake**.

3 Hide and Seek

Reinforce correct spelling of current spelling words. Repeat this activity from Day 2.

4 Vocabulary Extension

Have your students complete this activity to strengthen spelling ability and expand vocabulary. The reproducible master is provided in Appendix A as shown on the inset page to the right.

1 Posttest

Visit the **A Reason For** website to download free, printable Posttest pages.

 (Say) I will say the word once, use it in a sentence, then say it again. Write your words on a separate sheet of paper.

Progress Chart

Students may record scores. (Appendix B)

Personal Dictionary

Students may add any words they have misspelled to their personal dictionaries. (Appendix B)

Hide and Seek

Play Hide and Seek with your words. Fill in a bar graph (left to right) for each word you spell correctly.

Vocabulary Extension

Crossword Puzzle

Use the clues below to complete the puzzle.

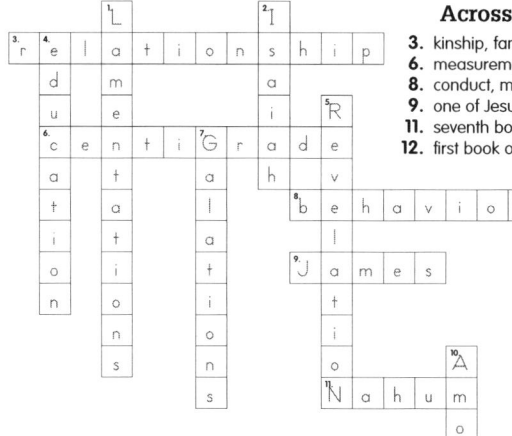

Across
3. kinship, family tie
6. measurement of temperature
8. conduct, manners
9. one of Jesus' disciples
11. seventh book of the Minor Prophets
12. first book of the Minor Prophets

Down
1. Old Testament book following Jeremiah
2. Old Testament book before Jeremiah
4. instruction, schooling
5. last book of the Bible
7. letter written by Paul
10. third book of the Minor Prophets

Word Bank

Amos	education	Isaiah	Nahum
behavior	Galatians	James	relationship
centigrade	Hosea	Lamentations	Revelation

330

---

1. **labor** — Matthew did not mind the **labor** of preparing the written report.
2. **detail** — He went over his report in **detail**, checking spelling and grammar.
3. **estate** — Ben Franklin, the man on the hundred dollar bill, did not own a large **estate**.
4. **Pennsylvania** — One of our nation's mints is in Philadelphia, **Pennsylvania**.
5. **Asia** — We do not have our money printed in **Asia**.
6. **Maine** — There is not a mint in **Maine**, but there is one in Colorado.
7. **decay** — Matthew felt his excitement over his report **decay**.
8. **prey** — His mind fell **prey** to the fear of public speaking.
9. **decade** — When he spoke in front of his class, a minute felt like a **decade** to him.
10. **mesa** — The platform seemed like an enormous **mesa**!
11. **stray** — Matthew allowed his thoughts to **stray** from reality for a moment.
12. **escape** — He thought of wild ways to **escape** his oral report.
13. **crater** — "I could fly to the moon and hide in a **crater**!" he said.
14. **ratio** — His **ratio** of fear to confidence was not good.
15. **flavor** — The **flavor** of ice cream Em served to the boys was chocolate chip.
16. **vein** — "Relax so that **vein** in your neck doesn't bulge," said Alex.
17. **contain** — "Your report sure does **contain** interesting facts!" he continued.
18. **debate** — Em knew there was no **debate**; Matthew needed to trust God for His help.
19. **chase** — God can and will **chase** away your fears.
20. **veil** — He removed the **veil** of fear from Matthew's eyes and gave him strength.

I Game

Name _____

Support Matthew as he gives his oral report to the class. Move one space for each word you or your team spells correctly.

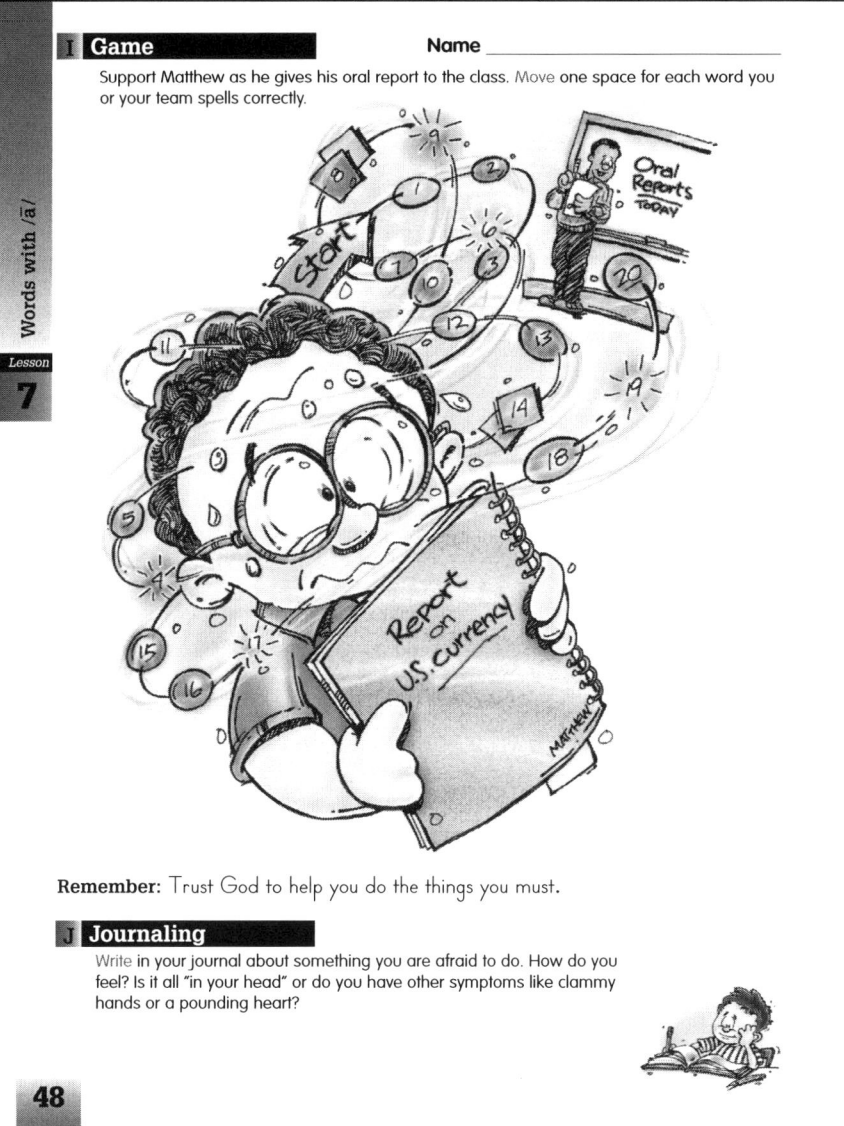

Remember: Trust God to help you do the things you must.

J Journaling

Write in your journal about something you are afraid to do. How do you feel? Is it all "in your head" or do you have other symptoms like clammy hands or a pounding heart?

48

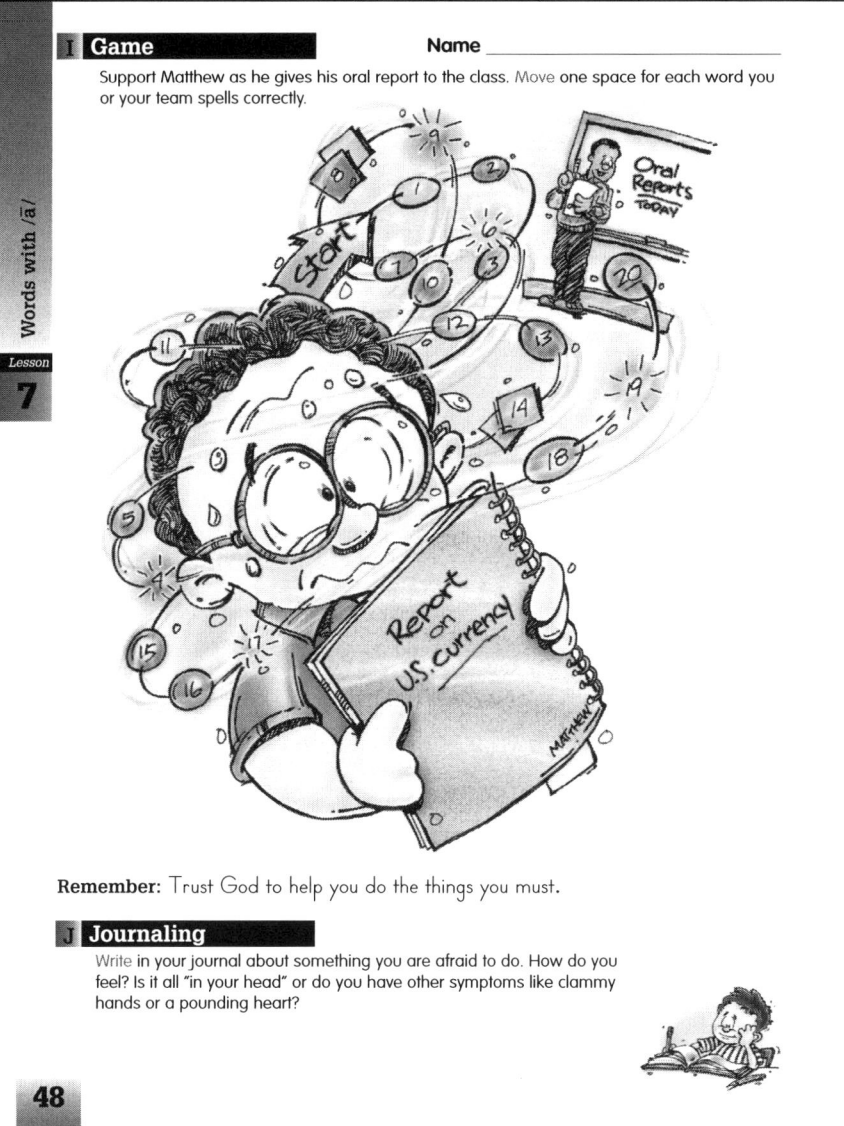

How to Play:

- Divide the class into two teams.
- Have each student place his/her game piece on Start.
- Have a student from team A go to the board.
- Say the spelling word.
- Have the student write the word on the board.
- If correct, instruct each member of team A to move his/her game piece forward one space.
- Alternate between teams A and B.
- The team to reach the platform first is the winner.
- **Small Group Option**: Students may play this game without teacher direction in small groups of two or more.

2 Game

Reinforce spelling skills and provide motivation and interest.

Materials
- game page (from student text)
- game pieces (1 per child)
- game word list

Game Word List

1. **decay**
2. **prey**
3. **stray**
4. **labor**
5. **decade**
6. **detail**
7. **veil**
8. **contain**
9. **Maine**
10. **Pennsylvania**
11. **vein**
12. **escape**
13. **chase**
14. **mesa**
15. **ratio**
16. **crater**
17. **debate**
18. **estate**
19. **flavor**
20. **Asia**

3 Journaling

Provide a meaningful reason for correct spelling through personal writing.

Review the story using discussion leads provided on the following page. Encourage students to apply the Scriptural value in their journaling.

Journaling (continued)

(Say)
- What game did Alex and Emily want Matthew to play? (Monopoly)
- Why couldn't Matthew play with his brother and sister? (He was practicing a report he had to present.)
- Why did Matthew's voice crack, his lips and tongue feel dry, his stomach feel queasy, and his palms feel clammy? (He was very anxious even thinking about reading the report in front of his class.)
- Why was Matthew afraid to give such an interesting report? (It was an unreasonable fear. He just didn't want to do it.)
- What did Emily suggest he do? ("Pway, Matt. Twust Jesus to help you do it. He will.")
- What are some things you are afraid to do?

Have you ever wondered. . .

Why do we park on driveways and drive on parkways?

Why is "abbreviation" such a long word?

What's another word for Thesaurus?

Under the Influence

While her mother's alcoholism causes more and more difficulties, Sarah chooses to keep trusting God.

"Now, don't forget to give these notes to your parents!" Mr. Canfield picked up a sheaf of papers and began passing them out. "Over the next few weeks we want as many parents as possible to come tell us about their jobs. I'll be getting in touch with each of them later by phone or e-mail, but I want to give them some time to think about this project." He reached over Tony's head to hand a note to Stephen. "And don't forget your science assignment!"

"Mr. Canfield!" Katelynn caught the teacher's attention as he handed out the last few notes. "Both of my parents work. Are they both supposed to come?"

"Sure, if it's possible," Mr. Canfield replied as he handed the last note to Sarah and the kids began to stream toward the door. "The more the merrier!"

Setsuko rested her denim backpack on the corner of Sarah's desk. "Maybe my father can bring some X-rays to show everyone."

"Just a second." Sarah reached for her library book and stuffed it into her tattered book bag along with her science book. "Are you done with your science assignment?"

"No, but I think I can finish it tonight." Setsuko swung her backpack over one shoulder and fell into step with Sarah as the girls left the classroom. "I wonder if there's anything my mother could bring to show. Probably not, but she sure could tell some stories."

Setsuko held the glass door open for Sarah and then followed her out. "There was a lady that tried on everything in her size in the whole store. She was there for hours, and after all that she left without buying a single thing! Then there's the lady who…" Her voice trailed off when she noticed her friend's face. "What's wrong, Sarah?"

"Nothing, really." Sarah shrugged. "It's just that your dad's an X-ray technician and your mom's in charge of the women's department at a big store. Those are interesting, important jobs all the kids will like hearing about." She kicked at a small pebble on the sidewalk and mumbled, "My momma cleans hotel rooms."

"Well, that's important, too." Setsuko shifted her backpack. "But I see what you mean. It might not be the most interesting of jobs. There's my mother. See you tomorrow!"

Sarah waved and dropped to the curb in her usual spot. A steady stream of cars came and went. Not all were new, but most were shiny and well kept. Those people were probably secretaries and doctors and lawyers and clerks and interesting things like that. She held Mr. Canfield's note between two fingers and let it flap in the light wind.

"Oh, no!" Her sister Nellie's exclamation jerked Sarah's attention from the note in her hand. "Just look!" Nellie pointed toward a car turning into the school drive. "Momma's wrecked the car!"

The battered old car had once been red. Long ago it had lost its shine and shape, but today it looked much worse for the wear. Both passenger-side doors were smashed in and the glass was broken out. The right front wheel was turned a bit outwards so that it looked like the car was trying to go two ways at once. A headlight was missing and the fender was crumpled. The girls rushed over when the car shuddered to a stop.

"What happened?" Nellie demanded as she opened the back door on the driver's side and slid across the back seat. Sarah followed and pulled the door closed.

Mrs. Johansen's voice was strained. "Watch out for glass. I think it's all cleaned up, but be careful anyway." Sarah caught a glimpse of her mother's eyes in the mirror. They were puffy and red, as if she'd been crying. Mrs. Johansen finally spoke. "There was an accident. A car hit me from the left side and knocked my car into a telephone pole. No one was injured."

Nobody spoke as the car rattled down the street. Mrs. Johansen didn't add any details, and Nellie and Sarah didn't ask any questions. Sarah was sure Nellie was thinking pretty much the same thoughts that were spinning through her own head. *Momma's probably been drinking.* A number of the sedan's bumps and scrapes were a result of their mother's drinking habit, but this time the damage was severe.

Later that evening, Sarah yawned and closed her library book. When she replaced it in her backpack, the note from Mr. Canfield caught her attention. *Back to reality, Sarah Johansen,* she thought to herself. *From the wonderful adventures of the Barton twins in my library book to real-life problems.*

Sarah flopped on her bed. *I really, really, really don't want Momma to come talk to my class about cleaning hotel rooms. But Mr. Canfield's going to talk to her about it, so I've got to give the note to her.* Sarah dragged herself off the bed and toward the kitchen. *Maybe she'll forget to show up at the right time.* That thought was comforting for a second until she realized her mother might show up at the right time after she was drinking. *Talk about embarrassing!*

"Momma, Mr. Canfield said to give you this note." Mrs. Johansen leaned against the kitchen counter and read it. When she was finished, she folded it carefully in half and laid it on the table where Nellie was working on her homework.

"Nellie. Sarah." Mrs.

73

Johansen cleared her throat. "There's something you should know. I won't be coming to your classroom for this, Sarah, because I don't have a job anymore. I lost my job today." She sank into a chair. "A few days ago my boss told me if I was late again he'd fire me. Because of the accident this morning, I was late to work."

Sarah's ears were buzzing. She felt like screaming. From what seemed like far away she heard Nellie ask, "Was the accident your fault, Momma? Had you been drinking?" She didn't really need to see her mother nod her head to know the truth. Of course her mother had been drinking again. And now instead of a low-paying job, she had no job at all!

Sarah rushed away as Nellie asked something else. She locked herself in the bathroom. Her hand shook a little when she squirted toothpaste on her toothbrush. *Better not use very much toothpaste. It was bad enough before, when Momma spent so much of her pay on liquor. Now we won't have any money at all.* She brushed her teeth with jerky strokes. *I've prayed and prayed and asked God for help. I'm so tired of Momma's drinking! When she's drunk she's not like my mom at all. I miss the mom I used to have. I'm tired of keeping this secret. I'm tired of never having nice clothes and food and all the stuff most kids have.*

A single tear trickled down Sarah's cheek, quickly followed by a torrent. She was so tired of it all! "God, why aren't you helping? We need help so bad. Please, please help us." Sarah whispered as she rinsed her mouth and then stared into the small mirror above the sink. "I know you don't promise to take away all the bad things in this world. And I know you don't force people to do right, but I wish you would do something to make Momma want to quit drinking!" Sarah leaned over the sink and splashed cold water on her face. "You do promise to be with me always and

help me through whatever happens. So, even though things are getting worse and worse, I'll keep trusting you. But, God, I'd really, really, really, really appreciate it if you would help Momma."

Sarah dried her face and unlocked the bathroom door. Squaring her shoulders, she walked back into the kitchen. Nellie sat alone at the kitchen table. "Where's Momma?" Sarah reached into the cupboard for a glass.

Nellie laid down her pencil and grinned. "You'll never guess!"

Sarah set the glass down on the counter, forgetting all about getting a drink of water. She stared at her obviously elated sister. "I don't have a clue, so just tell me!"

"Okay. Listen to this!" Nellie leaned forward. "Our mother, Mrs. Johansen, is... at..." Nellie drew out the suspense, "... a meeting for people who want to quit drinking!"

Sarah's mouth dropped open. "Told you you'd never guess!" Nellie bounced around the small kitchen in excitement. "After you left, she told me she knew we were upset about her drinking and that we were praying for her, but she'd always thought it wasn't really such a big deal. She thought she kinda deserved to forget her problems since our father left when we were so little and all."

Nellie picked up Sarah's abandoned glass and filled it with water. "Anyway, she said when she met Setsuko's mom she started realizing how her drinking was out of control, and how really bad it was for us." Nellie handed the glass of water to her sister. "She wanted to be more like Mrs. Noma, but she couldn't seem to make a change—till today when she lost her job, smashed the car, and was arrested for driving under the influence. She knows now that she is an alcoholic, and needs help."

A few weeks later, Sarah sat with her class and listened to her mother tell about her new job in the hospital kitchen. The kids were interested and asked a lot of questions. Sarah wasn't embarrassed at all—in fact, she could hardly quit smiling.

She found herself smiling again

when it was time for handwriting. The Scripture for the week was "Oh my people, trust him all the time. Pour out your longings before him, for he can help!" Psalm 62:8.

Sarah thoroughly enjoyed writing that verse, because she knew from experience that He can and does help those who trust Him.

2 Discussion Time

Check understanding of the story and development of personal values.

- Why was Mr. Canfield inviting all the parents to come to the classroom?
- How did Sarah feel about having her mother come talk to the class? Why?
- What happened to Mrs. Johansen's car?
- Why did Mrs. Johansen lose her job?
- How did Sarah feel about her mother's alcoholism?
- Where did Mrs. Johansen go to get help to stop drinking?
- What new job did Mrs. Johansen get?

A Preview
Write **each word** as your teacher says it.

Name _____

1. piece
2. idea
3. brief
4. eager
5. appeal
6. creep
7. shriek
8. deceit
9. reveal
10. shield
11. wield
12. Puerto Rico
13. skiing
14. liter
15. vetoes
16. Hawaii
17. meter
18. Tennessee
19. Louisiana
20. relief

Words with /ē/

Lesson **8**

Scripture
Psalm 62:8

49

3 **Preview**
Test for knowledge of the correct spellings of these words.

Customize Your List
On a separate sheet of paper, additional words of your choice may be tested.

Say
I will say each word once, use the word in a sentence, then say the word again. Write the words on the lines in your Worktext.

Correct Immediately!
Say
Let's correct our Preview. I will spell each word out loud. If you spelled a word incorrectly, rewrite it correctly.

Progress Chart
Students may record scores. (Reproducible master provided in Appendix B.)

1.	piece	Mr. Canfield gave a **piece** of paper to each student.
2.	idea	He had a great **idea** to inform the class of a variety of jobs.
3.	brief	His note to the parents was a **brief** description of his plan.
4.	eager	He was **eager** to have parents tell the class about their jobs.
5.	appeal	The idea of having her mom come to her class did not **appeal** to Sarah.
6.	creep	She wanted to **creep** out of the classroom without taking a note.
7.	shriek	She felt like letting out a **shriek** and a groan when she saw the battered car.
8.	deceit	Sarah knew the **deceit** her mom sometimes used to hide her alcoholism.
9.	reveal	Slowly, Mrs. Johansen began to **reveal** the story of her wreck.
10.	shield	Their mother did not try to **shield** the girls from the effects of her drinking.
11.	wield	"What does **wield** mean?" asked Sarah.
12.	Puerto Rico	Sarah enjoyed reading about the Barton twins' trip to **Puerto Rico**.
13.	skiing	Sarah and Nellie have never been **skiing** in the mountains.
14.	liter	They think just buying a **liter** of pop and some ice cream would be fun!
15.	vetoes	Lack of money often **vetoes** their plans.
16.	Hawaii	Sarah didn't even allow herself to dream of vacationing in **Hawaii**.
17.	meter	Mr. Canfield defined the measurement called a **meter**.
18.	Tennessee	He also read the first chapter in a book by a man from **Tennessee**.
19.	Louisiana	The man journaled his travels through Mississippi and **Louisiana**.
20.	relief	Sarah and Nellie felt a great **relief** at the good news about their mom.

4

Word Shapes

Help students form a correct image of whole words.

Look at each word and think about its shape. Now, write the word in the correct Word Shape Boxes. You may check off each word as you use it.

(In many words, the sound of /ē/ is spelled with **e** at the end of a syllable, or with **ea**, **ee**, **ei**, **ie**, and occasionally **i**. The spelling **y** can be used at the end of a word.)

In the Word Shape Boxes, fill in the boxes containing the letter or letters that spell the sound of /ē/ in each word.

Take a minute to memorize...

Psalm 62:8

Lesson 8 | **Day 1**

B Word Shapes

Name _____

Using the word bank below, write each word in the correct Word Shape Boxes. Next, in the Word Shape Boxes, fill in the boxes containing the letter or letters that spell the sound of /ē/ in each word.

Words with /ē/
Lesson 8

1. reveal
2. skiing
3. appeal
4. creep
5. eager
6. Louisiana
7. shield
8. wield
9. relief
10. brief
11. shriek
12. idea
13. liter
14. Tennessee
15. deceit
16. Hawaii
17. meter
18. vetoes
19. Puerto Rico
20. piece

Word Bank

appeal	eager	Louisiana	relief	skiing
brief	Hawaii	meter	reveal	Tennessee
creep	idea	piece	shield	vetoes
deceit	liter	Puerto Rico	shriek	wield

50

Answers may vary for duplicate word shapes.

Be Prepared For Fun

Check these supply lists for **Fun Ways to Spell** - presented **Day 2**. Purchase and/or gather these items ahead of time!

General
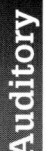
- Pencil
- Notebook Paper
- Spelling List

Auditory
- Pencil
- Notebook Paper
- Dictionary
- Spelling List

Visual

- Pencil
- Notebook Paper
- Spelling List

Tactile
- Clay
- Spelling List

76

C **Hide and Seek**

Name _____

Play Hide and Seek with your words. Fill in a box on the bar graph (left to right) for each word you spell correctly.

LOOK   SAY   SPELL ALOUD   WRITE   SEEK   CHECK

D **Other Word Forms**

Using the words below, follow the instructions given by your teacher.

appealed	eagerness	relieved	skied
appealing	Hawaiian	relieving	skier
briefest	ideal	revealed	Tennessean
briefly	idealistic	reveals	vetoed
creeping	liters	shielded	vetoing
creepy	meters	shielding	wielded
deceitful	pieced	shrieking	wielding
deceive	piecing	shrieks	
eagerly	Puerto Rican	ski	

E **Fun Ways to Spell**

Initial the box of each activity you finish.

1. ☐

Code
A B C D E F G H
26 25 24 23 22 21 30 10
8 11 22 15 15
S P E L L

Encode your spelling words.

2. ☐

Word or row do rod

Find hidden words in your spelling words.

3. ☐

Define your spelling words.

4. ☐

clay

Spell your words with clay.

51

---

1 **Hide and Seek**

Reinforce spelling by using multiple styles of learning.

On a white board, Teacher writes each word — one at a time. **Have students:**

- **Look** at the word.
- **Say** the word out loud.
- **Spell** the word out loud.
- **Hide** (teacher erases word.)
- **Write** the word on paper.
- **Seek** (teacher rewrites word.)
- **Check** spelling. If incorrect, rewrite word correctly.

2 **Other Word Forms**

This activity is optional. Have students write original sentences using these Other Word Forms:

eagerness
appealed
wielded
liters

3 **Fun Ways to Spell**

Four activities are provided. Use one, two, three, or all of the activities. Have students initial the box for each activity they complete.

Options:

- assign activities to students according to their learning styles
- set up the activities in learning centers for the students to do throughout the day
- divide students into four groups and assign one activity per group
- do one activity per day

General

To encode your spelling words...
- Write the alphabet on your paper.
- Write your own code for each letter underneath it.
- Write your spelling words in your code.
- Trade papers with a classmate and decode the words.
- Check to make sure your classmate spelled the words correctly.

Auditory

To define your spelling words...
- Ask a classmate to look up a word from the spelling list in the dictionary and read the definition to you, but not the spelling word.
- Decide which word on your list matches this definition and write the word.
- Ask your classmate to check your spelling.
- Switch and continue taking turns.

Visual

To find hidden words in your spelling words...
- Choose a word from your spelling list.
- Write it on your paper.
- Find and write as many smaller words as you can that are contained within your spelling word.
- Do this with each word.

Tactile

To spell your words with clay...
- Roll pieces of clay into ropes.
- Use the ropes to make the letters of each word.
- Put them in the right order to spell each word.
- Check your spelling.

1 Working with Words

Familiarize students with word meaning and usage.

Scrambled Words

(Say)

Write the letters **acehs** on the board. Have a student unscramble the letters to make the word **chase**.

Unscramble each spelling word. Write the word correctly on the line. Remember to use capital letters where they are needed.

Word Clues

(Say)

Use your word bank to help you match the spelling words to the clues. Some of the clues are synonyms, words that have the same meaning as the spelling word. You may use a dictionary or thesaurus to help you.

Take a minute to memorize...

Psalm 62:8

F Working with Words   Name _____

Words with /ē/   Lesson 8

Scrambled Words

Unscramble each word. Write the unscrambled word on the line. Use capital letters and a space where they are needed.

1.	aeegr	eager	11.	ceeip	piece
2.	aahiiw	Hawaii	12.	aaelpp	appeal
3.	aaiilnosu	Louisiana	13.	eeeennsst	Tennessee
4.	cdeeit	deceit	14.	eilrt	liter
5.	adei	idea	15.	eefilr	relief
6.	befir	brief	16.	giikns	skiing
7.	eemrt	meter	17.	eoprtu cior	Puerto Rico
8.	deilw	wield	18.	dehils	shield
9.	ceepr	creep	19.	aeelrv	reveal
10.	eeostv	vetoes	20.	ehikrs	shriek

Word Clues

Match the spelling words to the clues. You may use a dictionary or thesaurus to help you.

1.	sneak, prowl	creep	11.	request, plead	appeal
2.	cheating, trickery	deceit	12.	assistance, comfort	relief
3.	disclose, make known	reveal	13.	protect, conceal	shield
4.	the island state	Hawaii	14.	scream, yell	shriek
5.	liquid measure	liter	15.	momentary, fleeting	brief
6.	southeastern state	Tennessee	16.	sliding, gliding	skiing
7.	enthusiastic, zealous	eager	17.	belief, thought	idea
8.	rhythm, measure	meter	18.	southern state	Louisiana
9.	fragment, part	piece	19.	prohibits, denies	vetoes
10.	Caribbean island	Puerto Rico	20.	raise, brandish	wield

Word Bank

appeal	eager	Louisiana	relief	skiing
brief	Hawaii	meter	reveal	Tennessee
creep	idea	piece	shield	vetoes
deceit	liter	Puerto Rico	shriek	wield

52

G Dictation

Name _____

Write **each sentence as your teacher dictates.** Use **correct punctuation.**

1. Setsuko is eager for her dad to visit her classroom to tell about the work he does.

2. Sarah had no idea why her sister would look so happy, or where Mom could be.

3. What a relief it was to the girls when Mom was able to get some help and find work.

H Proofreading

If a word is misspelled, fill in the oval by that word. If all the words are spelled correctly, fill in the oval by **no mistake**.

1. ○ idea
   ○ crater
   ● peice
   ○ no mistake

2. ○ debate
   ○ estate
   ● sking
   ○ no mistake

3. ● breef
   ○ relief
   ○ Asia
   ○ no mistake

4. ○ ratio
   ● eeger
   ○ shriek
   ○ no mistake

5. ○ chase
   ● appiel
   ○ reveal
   ○ no mistake

6. ● weild
   ○ shield
   ○ flavor
   ○ no mistake

7. ○ Puerto Rico
   ● kreep
   ○ decay
   ○ no mistake

8. ● Hawai
   ○ Tennessee
   ○ prey
   ○ no mistake

9. ○ deceit
   ○ contain
   ● lieter
   ○ no mistake

10. ○ meter
    ○ labor
    ○ veil
    ● no mistake

11. ○ Maine
    ○ stray
    ○ vetoes
    ● no mistake

12. ● Louiziana
    ○ decade
    ○ detail
    ○ no mistake

53

Dictation

Reinforce correct spelling by using current and previous words in context.

Say Listen as I read each sentence and then write it in your Worktext. Remember to use correct capitalization and punctuation. (Slowly read each sentence twice. Sentences are found in the Student Worktext to the left.)

Proofreading

Familiarize students with standardized test format and reinforce recognition of misspelled words.

Say Look at each set of words. If a word is misspelled, fill in the oval by that word. If all the words are spelled correctly, fill in the oval by **no mistake**.

3 Hide and Seek

Reinforce correct spelling of current spelling words.
Repeat this activity from Day 2.

4 Vocabulary Extension

Have your students complete this activity to strengthen spelling ability and expand vocabulary. The reproducible master is provided in Appendix A as shown on the inset page to the right.

1 Posttest

Visit the **A Reason For** website to download free, printable Posttest pages.

(Say)

I will say the word once, use it in a sentence, then say it again. Write your words on a separate sheet of paper.

Progress Chart
Students may record scores. (Appendix B)

Personal Dictionary
Students may add any words they have misspelled to their personal dictionaries. (Appendix B)

Hide and Seek

Play Hide and Seek with your words. Fill in a bar graph (left to right) for each word you spell correctly.

LOOK. SAY. HIDE. WRITE. SEEK. CHECK.

Vocabulary Extension

Trade-off

Choose a word from the word bank to replace the word(s) in parentheses. Write the word in the blank.

1. Descendants of Jacob became known as ___Hebrews___ (Israelites).
2. Levers, screws, pulleys, and gears are all simple ___machines___ (devices).
3. Anne has always done very well. She will ___succeed___ (triumph) now.
4. Dad ___yielded___ (surrendered) to the other car so we would not have an accident.
5. When we go out in the ___extreme___ (excessive) cold, we dress in many layers of clothes.
6. Paul wrote a letter to ___Philemon___ (Onesimus' master) asking him to treat the slave as a brother in Christ.
7. Brushing your teeth every morning and night is an example of good ___hygiene___ (health habits).
8. ___Peter___ (Simon) was an eager, earnest, and courageous disciple of Jesus Christ.
9. We quickly called the police and hoped they would catch the ___thieves___ (burglars) who had robbed us.
10. I am teaching my dog how to ___retrieve___ (fetch) a stick when I throw it for him.
11. ___Ecclesiastes___ (Old Testament book) was written by King Solomon and tells his view of life.
12. She has the gift of ___leadership___ (administration), so she is the yearbook editor.

Word Bank

Ecclesiastes	hygiene	Peter	succeed
extreme	leadership	Philemon	thieves
Hebrews	machines	retrieve	yielded

331

---

1. piece	The **piece** of paper Mr. Canfield handed out was a note to the parents.
2. idea	Most of the students were excited about their teacher's **idea**.
3. eager	Setsuko was **eager** for her dad to show the class some X-rays.
4. brief	The **brief** note told the parents to expect a phone call from Mr. Canfield.
5. relief	Sarah let out a sigh of **relief** because her mom did not have a cell phone.
6. appeal	"I'll make my **appeal** to your mom after school one day," smiled her teacher.
7. Puerto Rico	Sarah wished she could move to **Puerto Rico** that very moment.
8. creep	She wanted to **creep** out of the room without the note from Mr. Canfield.
9. shriek	A **shriek** slipped out of her mouth when she saw the battered car.
10. reveal	As she drove, Mrs. Johansen began to **reveal** the details of her accident.
11. shield	She could not **shield** her daughters from the ill effects of her drinking.
12. deceit	Mrs. Johansen often practiced **deceit** to hide her alcoholism.
13. skiing	The girls have a picture of their mom snow **skiing** when she was young.
14. vetoes	Lack of money always **vetoes** their plans to learn to ski.
15. liter	There was not even a **liter** of cheap soda in the refrigerator.
16. wield	Sarah did not know what "**wield**" meant.
17. Hawaii	Nellie and Sarah didn't even daydream about traveling to **Hawaii**.
18. Tennessee	Mr. Canfield read the first chapter in a book by a man from **Tennessee**.
19. Louisiana	The book chronicled his explorations through the state of **Louisiana**.
20. meter	During math, Mr. Canfield defined the measurement called a **meter**.

80

I Game

Name _____

Complete the secret phrase by spelling the words from this week's word list.

Words with /ē/
Lesson 8

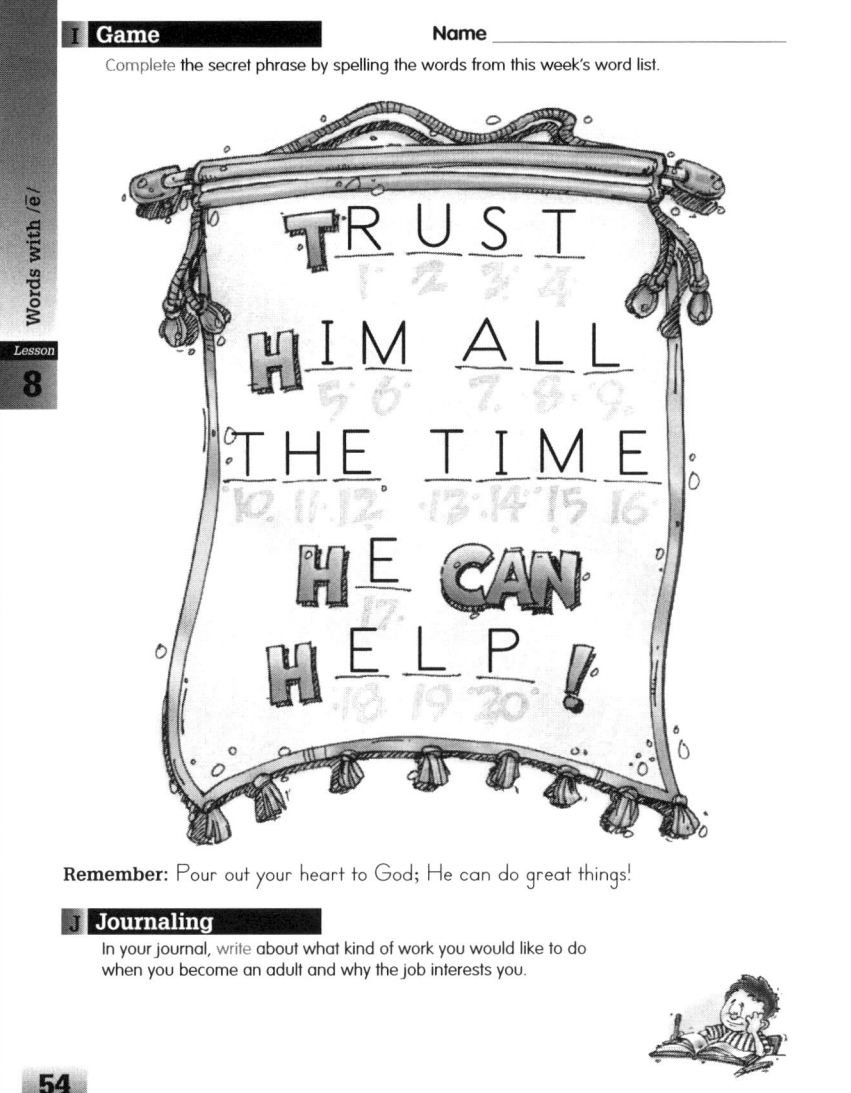

```
T R U S T
  1  2  3  4
H I M  A L L
  5  6    7  8  9.
T H E   T I M E
 10. 11. 12.  13. 14. 15. 16
H E   C A N
     17.
H E L P !
 18. 19. 20.
```

Remember: Pour out your heart to God; He can do great things!

J Journaling

In your journal, write about what kind of work you would like to do when you become an adult and why the job interests you.

54

How to Play:

- Divide the class into two teams, and decide which team will go first.
- Have a student from team A choose a number from 1 to 20.
- Say the word that matches that number from the team's word list.
- Have the student write the word on the board.
- If correct, have each member of team A write the given letter in the matching space on his/her game page.
- Alternate between teams A and B having the students choose a number of a blank space.
- The team to complete the secret phrase first is the winner.

2 Game

Reinforce spelling skills and provide motivation and interest.

Materials

- game page (from student text)
- pencils (1 per child)
- game word list

Game Word List

Team A	Team B
1. **idea** (R)	1. **wield** (R)
2. **piece** (U)	2. **Puerto Rico** (U)
3. **skiing** (S)	3. **creep** (S)
4. **brief** (T)	4. **Hawaii** (T)
5. **relief** (I)	5. **Tennessee** (I)
6. **eager** (M)	6. **deceit** (M)
7. **shriek** (A)	7. **liter** (A)
8. **appeal** (L)	8. **meter** (L)
9. **reveal** (L)	9. **vetoes** (L)
10. **shield** (T)	10. **Louisiana** (T)
11. **wield** (H)	11. **idea** (H)
12. **Puerto Rico** (E)	12. **piece** (E)
13. **creep** (T)	13. **skiing** (T)
14. **Hawaii** (I)	14. **brief** (I)
15. **Tennessee** (M)	15. **relief** (M)
16. **deceit** (E)	16. **eager** (E)
17. **liter** (E)	17. **shriek** (E)
18. **meter** (E)	18. **appeal** (E)
19. **vetoes** (L)	19. **reveal** (L)
20. **Louisiana** (P)	20. **shield** (P)

3 Journaling

Provide a meaningful reason for correct spelling through personal writing.

Review the story using discussion leads provided on the following page. Encourage students to apply the Scriptural value in their journaling.

81

Journaling (continued)

(Say)

- What kind of work do your parents do? (Allow time to share information.)

- Why was Sarah embarrassed to have her mother come tell the class about her job? (Her mother cleaned hotel rooms. Sarah felt that it wasn't an interesting or important job, and she was afraid her mother would drink before she came to the school.)

- Is cleaning hotel rooms a less important job than others? Explain. (No. Any job is important and should be done to the best of our abilities.)

- What caused Mrs. Johansen to have a wreck? (She had been drinking.)

- What other bad things happened because of her drinking? (She lost her job and had to go to court for driving under the influence. She didn't act the same towards her children, and didn't provide them with enough food or clothes.)

- Could God make Mrs. Johansen quit drinking? (He could, but He doesn't force anyone to make good choices.)

- Why did Sarah decide to keep trusting God even though things just kept getting worse? (She knew that when we tell God about our troubles He promises to help us through them.)

"Beijing" has three dotted letters in a row (in lower case), as do "Fiji" and "hijinks." Four dotted letters in a row occur in "Ujiji," the town where Stanley found Livingstone in 1871.

A High Price to Pay

Katelynn discovers that unpleasant justice may come with God's unconditional forgiveness.

"Katelynn, you wore that shirt yesterday!" Jennifer ran a brush through her long hair. "Why are you wearing it again?"

"I like it—everybody does."

"That's disgusting! It can't be clean after you wore it all day long. Mom just did the laundry, so wear something else—everything's clean."

"Including this," Katelynn muttered, looking down at her favorite shirt. "Remember we have chapel this morning, and I want to look good." Katelynn examined her reflection in the bathroom mirror.

"Your hair is really getting long. I like it." Katelynn's older sister reached in front of her to get the toothpaste. "I like your shirt, too—just not every day. I hope Grandma sends me one for my birthday."

"So you don't think I should wear it today?" Katelynn sought the reflection of her sister's dark eyes in the mirror.

"I guess if it's clean…." Jennifer sighed.

"Let's go, girls or you'll be late for school." Mr. Hatasaki called from the living room.

"Coming," the girls chorused.

Later that afternoon, Mrs. Hatasaki trudged up the apartment stairs. She stopped in front of the red door marked 308-B and unlocked it. The big gold chain kept her from completely opening the door. "Katie, I'm home."

Katelynn ran to let her mother in. Mrs. Hatasaki gave her daughter a hug. "Let's hurry and get supper ready so we can eat as soon as your dad and Jennifer get home. I need to go to the mall and look for some new shoes. These black ones are really worn, and

there are some good sales at several of the stores this week. You want to come?"

Katelynn nodded.

On their way through the mall, Jennifer saw a classmate from school trying on jackets in one of the trendier stores.

"Hi, Jen!" Sandra St. Clair gushed, "Look at these jackets. They're just what I've been looking for. Everyone has them. Which do you like better?" The girl held up two she liked.

Jennifer shrugged. "I don't know—they're both nice." She picked up the nearest jacket and gasped when she saw the price. Their family never spent that much money on clothes—ever!

"You don't like them?"

"Sure. I just think…."

"I can't make up my mind," Sandra interrupted as she turned back and forth in front of the three-way mirror.

Mrs. Hatasaki and Sandra's mother were soon engaged in a serious discussion about the pros and cons of the new school dress code.

Katelynn and Jennifer watched silently as Sandra admired her reflection. After a while, they tired of waiting for her to try on all the different styles and colors. They began to examine the other beautifully displayed clothes. "Here's a shirt just like Grandma got you." Jennifer held it up for her sister to see.

"Did you girls find something?" Mom and Mrs. St. Clair walked up behind the girls.

"Sandra can't decide what jacket she likes, but we like these shirts. They're like the one Grandma sent Katelynn. Look! They're on sale." Jennifer held up the shirt.

Mom raised her eyebrows when she checked the price tag. Mrs. St. Clair excused herself and went over to look at jackets with Sandra.

"Do you girls have enough money for these? They are quite pricey even when they're on sale," Mrs. Hatasaki whispered. "We'll go to the outlet mall later this week."

"I have babysitting money." Jennifer picked a shirt to try on and headed to the dressing room. Mrs. St. Clair chose some more clothes for Sandra to try and followed Jennifer.

Sandra paused and looked over the pile of clothes in her arms. "Wait just a minute. I want you to tell me which one of these looks best with my blond hair."

Katelynn glanced up at her mom, who nodded and smiled. Sandra and Jennifer finally came out. "That's my favorite." Katelynn smiled and looked at Jennifer. "I think you should definitely get that one."

"Why don't you get one?" Sandra pulled a shirt off the rack for Katelynn to try on.

"Oh. I like this one," Katelynn said as she held up a different color.

"Try it on, Katelynn," Mrs. St. Clair suggested as she walked up beside the trio with more clothes on her arm. "It's the perfect color for your dark hair and eyes."

Katelynn shook her head. "I don't think so."

Sandra eventually chose a jacket, as well as several other new outfits. Katelynn leaned against the counter, waiting for Jennifer to pay for her shirt. Sandra stood beside her—arms loaded with clothes "Aren't you going to get that shirt you tried on? It looks so great on you."

"I didn't try it on—and no." Katelynn stood on the side of her feet. "I don't have enough money."

"There are other ways to get what you want," whispered Sandra. "My friend Elizabeth and I do this all the time. Watch."

Katelynn wrinkled her forehead.

83

Sandra glanced at the clerk, who was now busy ringing up all the St. Clairs' purchases. The blond girl casually took the shirt Katelynn liked off the rack and walked back into the dressing room. She returned minutes later—patting a bag from another store in the mall.

As the three girls walked down the mall behind their mothers (who were still discussing Knowlton Elementary), Sandra pulled out the stolen shirt from the bag. When Jennifer stopped to examine some purses, Sandra quietly stuffed it into one of Katelynn's bags.

"Consider it a gift," Sandra said, smiling sweetly.

Katelynn jumped when Jennifer turned around to show her a purse. Her stomach didn't feel so good.

Mom was already at work the next morning when Katelynn cut the tags off the stolen shirt. When she put it on and looked in the mirror, there was an unexpected pit in the bottom of her stomach. *Jennifer will know it's the shirt from the mall and Mom will wonder where it came from when she sees it in the wash. What am I going to do? If I take it back, Sandra will get in trouble. If I don't tell on Sandra, how will I explain to the store that I didn't steal it, but want to bring it back?* Katelynn slowly took off the shirt and tucked the tags in her notebook.

When Dad dropped the girls off in front of Knowlton Elementary, Katelynn lingered in the car until Jennifer was out of earshot. Big tears slipped down her cheeks. "My stomach really hurts. I have to tell you something really bad. Will you help me make it right?"

After school, Katelynn and her dad returned to the mall for a much-less-fun excursion than the one the previous evening. An hour later they left the mall security office—minus one shirt. Katelynn took a deep breath of the fresh fall air. She slowly exhaled as she leaned up against a big cement pillar at the arched entrance to the mall. She fumbled with the zipper of her jacket. Dad looked solemn. Neither spoke for a while.

Katelynn finally broke the silence. "I can't believe they put my name in their computer when I brought the shirt back. I didn't steal it."

Mr. Hatasaki wiped his hand across his upper lip. "You carried it out of the mall without paying for it, Katie. God's plan for creation rests on two important principles — kind of like that pillar behind you helps support this archway." Dad patted the huge cement column. "One of God's traits is grace, which means He loves us and forgives our sins. But God is also righteous. Scripture tells us that He loves justice and hates wickedness."

When Katelynn looked puzzled, her father explained, "God's grace will cover your sins. He forgives you no matter how badly you mess up. But don't forget that other pillar. Yes, He will forgive you, but He doesn't erase the pain your mistakes cause. If mall security ever catches you shoplifting, you'll be in serious trouble because your name is already in the computer system. That's justice, Katie."

Katelynn smiled weakly. "I think I like the grace part of God's nature better than the justice. And I wouldn't even dream of shoplifting. This experience was bad enough," she shuddered.

Her dad agreed. "I'm sorry they entered your name into their database today, but I can see why they want it. Stores lose millions of dollars a year from shoplifting. It's honest people who pay for the stolen items, because the stores raise their prices to cover their losses and still make a profit. Every time a shoplifter is caught, it helps keep prices down."

Dad squeezed Katelynn's shoulder as they headed toward the parking lot. "Just remember, 'Character is made by what you stand for; reputation, by what you fall for.' I'm proud of the stand you took today."

"Thanks," Katelynn said as she climbed into the car.

Discussion Time

2

Check understanding of the story and development of personal values.

- Who is the nicest person you know in school?
- What made you think of that person?
- Who is someone you know that always dresses well?
- Why did you choose that particular person?
- Which is more important—character or appearance?
- How did Katelynn get her priorities out of balance?
- Who can help you keep things in the proper perspective?

Lesson **9** | Day 1

A Preview

Write each word as your teacher says it.

Name _____

1. riot
2. guys
3. guide
4. Ohio
5. admire
6. recital
7. diet
8. isle
9. geyser
10. silence
11. arrive
12. alibi
13. minor
14. byte
15. height
16. wife
17. diary
18. liar
19. Idaho
20. Iowa

Words with /ī/

Lesson **9**

Scripture
Psalm 89:14

55

3 Preview

Test for knowledge of the correct spellings of these words.

Customize Your List
On a separate sheet of paper, additional words of your choice may be tested.

(Say) I will say each word once, use the word in a sentence, then say the word again. Write the words on the lines in your Worktext.

Correct Immediately!

(Say) Let's correct our Preview. I will spell each word out loud. If you spelled a word incorrectly, rewrite it correctly.

Progress Chart
Students may record scores. (Reproducible master provided in Appendix B.)

1.	riot	It looked like there was a small **riot** outside in the mall parking lot.
2.	guys	Several **guys** were gathered around a minor car accident.
3.	guide	"I can be your personal fashion **guide**," Sandra teased Katelynn.
4.	Ohio	"Our mall in **Ohio** was three times the size of this one," she bragged.
5.	admire	Katelynn watched Sandra **admire** herself in the dressing room mirror.
6.	recital	"I think I'll wear this at my piano **recital**," she told Katelynn.
7.	diet	Sarah already talks about going on a **diet** to stay thin.
8.	isle	The St. Clairs spent the summer vacationing on an **isle** in the Mediterranean.
9.	geyser	Sandra hoped to see a huge **geyser** on the island.
10.	silence	There was a long **silence** after Katelynn confessed to her dad.
11.	arrive	She was dreading the moment they would **arrive** at the mall office.
12.	alibi	Katelynn did not have an **alibi**.
13.	minor	Since Katelynn is a **minor** and returned the shirt, the mall did not press charges.
14.	byte	She wished she could erase every **byte** of memory in the mall computer system!
15.	height	She was sure that this was the **height** of embarrassment and shame!
16.	wife	Mr. Hatasaki called his **wife** at work to tell her about Katelynn.
17.	diary	Katelynn recorded the awful event in her **diary**.
18.	liar	She realized that she did not want to be a thief and a **liar**.
19.	Idaho	The state of **Idaho** is famous for its hardy crops of delicious potatoes.
20.	Iowa	Many of us associate the growing of corn with the state of **Iowa**.

Word Shapes

Help students form a correct image of whole words.

 (Say) Look at each word and think about its shape. Now, write the word in the correct Word Shape Boxes. You may check off each word as you use it.

(In many words, the sound of /ī/ is spelled with **i** at the end of a syllable, or with **ie**, or **i-consonant-e**. It is sometimes spelled with **y**.)

 (Say) In the Word Shape Boxes, fill in the boxes containing the letter or letters that spell the sound of /ī/ in each word.

 Take a minute to memorize...
Psalm 89:14

Day 1

Lesson 9

B Word Shapes

Name _____

Using the word bank below, write each word in the correct Word Shape Boxes. Next, in the Word Shape Boxes, fill in the boxes containing the letter or letters that spell the sound of /ī/ in each word.

Words with /ī/

Lesson **9**

1. r e c i t a l
2. d i e t
3. g e y s e r
4. a l i b i
5. d i a r y
6. g u y s
7. w i f e
8. g u i d e
9. a r r i v e
10. h e i g h t

11. I o w a
12. s i l e n c e
13. m i n o r
14. i s l e
15. a d m i r e
16. b y t e
17. r i o t
18. O h i o
19. I d a h o
20. l i a r

Word Bank

admire	diary	guys	isle	recital
alibi	diet	height	liar	riot
arrive	geyser	Idaho	minor	silence
byte	guide	Iowa	Ohio	wife

56

Answers may vary for duplicate word shapes.

 Be Prepared For Fun

Check these supply lists for **Fun Ways to Spell** - presented **Day 2**. Purchase and/or gather these items ahead of time!

General
- Pencil
- 3 X 5 Cards cut in half (20 per child)
- Spelling List

Auditory
- Spelling List

Visual
- Pencil
- Notebook Paper
- Spelling List

Tactile
- Blackboard and Chalk
  -OR-
- White Board and Marker
- Spelling List

C Hide and Seek

Name _____

Play Hide and Seek with your words. Fill in a box on the bar graph (left to right) for each word you spell correctly.

LOOK. SAY. SPELL ALOUD. WRITE. SEEK. CHECK.

D Other Word Forms

Using the words below, follow the instructions given by your teacher.

(admirable)	diaries	heightened	Ohioan
admiration	dieted	Idahoan	recitalist
alibied	dieting	Iowan	recitation
alibis	geysers	island	rioted
(arrival)	(guided)	islet	riots
arriving	guiding	lied	silenced
bytes	guyed	lying	silent
gigabytes	guying	minored	wifehood
megabytes	heighten	(minority)	wifely

E Fun Ways to Spell

Initial the box of each activity you finish.

1. ☐
Spell your words, then play "Concentration."

2. ☐
Decode your spelling words.

3. ☐
Johnny has a puppy!
Spell your words in a sentence.

4. ☐
Play the game "Spelling Backwards."

57

---

1 Hide and Seek

Reinforce spelling by using multiple styles of learning.

On a white board, Teacher writes each word — one at a time. **Have students:**

- **Look** at the word.
- **Say** the word out loud.
- **Spell** the word out loud.
- **Hide** (teacher erases word.)
- **Write** the word on paper.
- **Seek** (teacher rewrites word.)
- **Check** spelling. If incorrect, rewrite word correctly.

2 Other Word Forms

This activity is optional. Have students find and circle the Other Word Forms that are most nearly antonyms of the following:

despicable
unassisted
departure
bulk

3 Fun Ways to Spell

Four activities are provided. Use one, two, three, or all of the activities. Have students initial the box for each activity they complete.

Options:

- assign activities to students according to their learning styles
- set up the activities in learning centers for the students to do throughout the day
- divide students into four groups and assign one activity per group
- do one activity per day

General
Spell your words; then play "Concentration"...
- Write each spelling word on a card. Mix your cards and a classmate's cards together. Arrange them face down in five rows of eight. Pick up two cards. If the cards match, play again. If the cards do not match, turn them back over. It is your classmate's turn. Continue taking turns until all the cards are matched. The player with the most cards wins!

Auditory
To spell your words in a sentence...
- Ask a classmate to read a spelling word to you from the list.
- Spell the word aloud and use it in a sentence.
- Ask your classmate to check your spelling.
- Each correctly spelled word that is used properly in a sentence counts as one point.
- Switch and continue taking turns.

Visual
To decode your spelling words...
- Look at the first word on your list.
- Write every other letter of the word on your paper, putting a blank where each missing letter belongs.
- Trade papers with a classmate and fill in the missing letters.
- Check your spelling.

Tactile
To play the game "Spelling Backwards"...
- Ask a classmate to stand behind you and draw the letters to spell a word from the list on your back.
- Write the spelling word on the board as your classmate traces the letters on your back.
- Ask your classmate to check your spelling.
- Trade places and take turns until you have each spelled all the words.

1 Working with Words

Familiarize students with word meaning and usage.

Hidden Words

Explain that the spelling words for this week are hidden in the puzzle. After finding each word, the student should write the word under the correct heading.

Say Use the word bank to help you find each of the words in the puzzle. Words may go across, down, or diagonally. Circle, then write the words.

Take a minute to memorize...

Psalm 89:14

F **Working with Words**

Name _____

Hidden Words

Use the word bank to help you find each of the words in the puzzle. Words may go across, down, or diagonally. Circle and write the words.

Words with /ī/

Lesson **9**

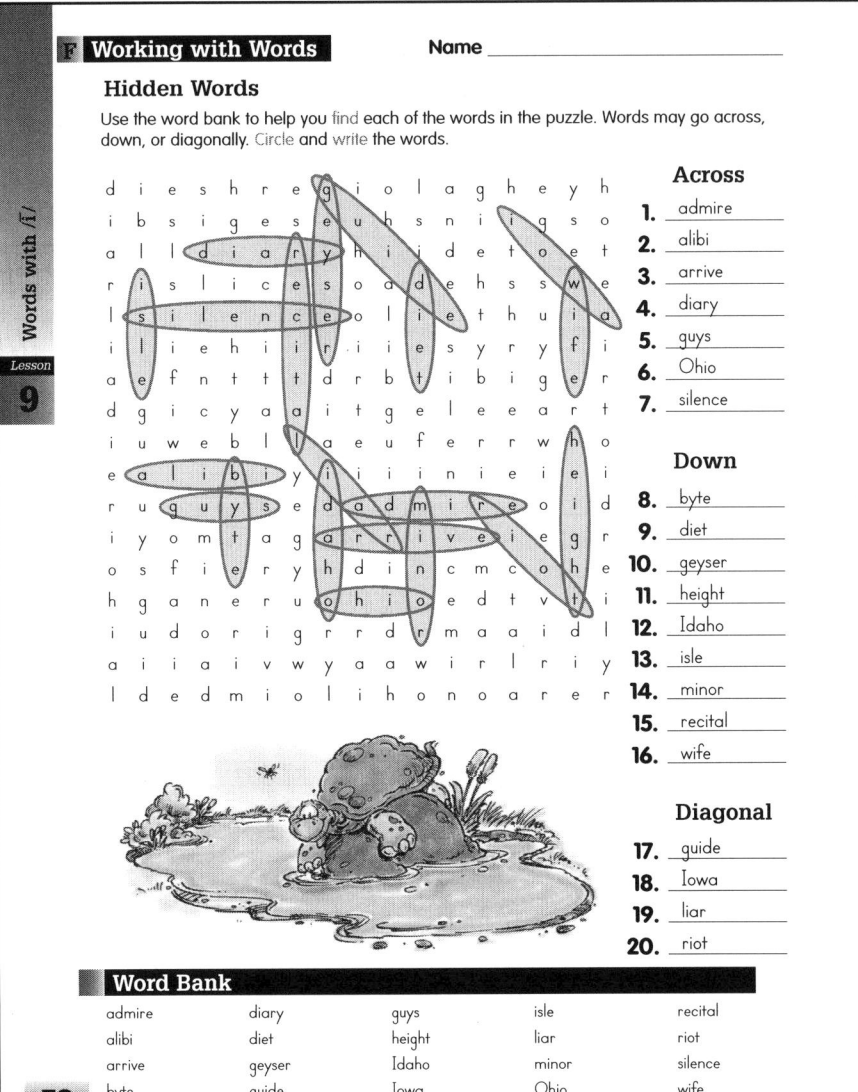

```
d i e s h r e g i o l a g h e y h
i b s i g e s e u h s n i i g s o
a l l d i a r y h i j d e t o e t
r i s l i c e s o a d e h s s w e
l s i l e n c e o l i e t h u i a
i l i e h i i r i i e s y r y f i
a e f n t t d r b t i b i g e e r
d g i c y a a i t g e l e e a r t
i u w e b l a e u f e r r w h o i
e a l i b i y i i i n i e i e i d
r u g u y s e d a d m i r e o i d
i y o m t a g a r r i v e i e g r
o s f i e r y h d i n c m c o h e
h g a n e r u o h i o e d t v t i
i u d o r i g r r d r m a a i d l
a i i a i v w y a a w i r l r i y
l d e d m i o l i h o n o a r e r
```

Across

1. admire
2. alibi
3. arrive
4. diary
5. guys
6. Ohio
7. silence

Down

8. byte
9. diet
10. geyser
11. height
12. Idaho
13. isle
14. minor
15. recital
16. wife

Diagonal

17. guide
18. Iowa
19. liar
20. riot

Word Bank

admire	diary	guys	isle	recital
alibi	diet	height	liar	riot
arrive	geyser	Idaho	minor	silence
byte	guide	Iowa	Ohio	wife

58

G Dictation

Name _____

Write **each sentence as your teacher dictates**. Use correct punctuation.

1. Sandra <u>looked in the mirror to admire</u>
<u>the clothes.</u>

2. Katelynn <u>did not want to take clothes from the</u>
<u>store, but she looked on in silence.</u>

3. <u>Dad guided her back to the car, and they</u>
<u>soon arrived at school.</u>

H Proofreading

If a word is misspelled, fill in the oval by that word. If all the words are spelled correctly, fill in the oval by **no mistake**.

1. ○ diary
   ○ Tennessee
   ○ deceit
   ● no mistake

2. ○ liar
   ○ diet
   ○ Louisiana
   ● no mistake

3. ○ creep
   ○ Hawaii
   ● riut
   ○ no mistake

4. ● ohio
   ○ alibi
   ○ shield
   ○ no mistake

5. ○ guide
   ● Idahoe
   ○ vetoes
   ○ no mistake

6. ○ wife
   ○ isle
   ○ liter
   ● no mistake

7. ● silense
   ○ Puerto Rico
   ○ eager
   ○ no mistake

8. ○ admire
   ○ idea
   ● minnor
   ○ no mistake

9. ○ byte
   ● heit
   ○ piece
   ○ no mistake

10. ○ recital
    ● arive
    ○ skiing
    ○ no mistake

11. ● iowa
    ○ guys
    ○ reveal
    ○ no mistake

12. ○ brief
    ○ relief
    ● gyser
    ○ no mistake

59

Dictation

Reinforce correct spelling by using current and previous words in context.

Say — Listen as I read each sentence and then write it in your Worktext. Remember to use correct capitalization and punctuation. (Slowly read each sentence twice. Sentences are found in the Student Worktext to the left.)

Proofreading

Familiarize students with standardized test format and reinforce recognition of misspelled words.

Say — Look at each set of words. If a word is misspelled, fill in the oval by that word. If all the words are spelled correctly, fill in the oval by **no mistake**.

89

3 Hide and Seek

Reinforce correct spelling of current spelling words. Repeat this activity from Day 2.

4 Vocabulary Extension

Have your students complete this activity to strengthen spelling ability and expand vocabulary. The reproducible master is provided in Appendix A as shown on the inset page to the right.

1 Posttest

Visit the **A Reason For** website to download free, printable Posttest pages.

Say

I will say the word once, use it in a sentence, then say it again. Write your words on a separate sheet of paper.

Progress Chart

Students may record scores. (Appendix B)

Personal Dictionary

Students may add any words they have misspelled to their personal dictionaries. (Appendix B)

Lesson 9 | Vocabulary Extension

Hide and Seek

Play Hide and Seek with your words. Fill in a bar graph (left to right) for each word you spell correctly.

LOOK   SAY   HIDE   WRITE   SEEK   CHECK

Vocabulary Extension

Multiple Choice

Fill in the oval by the word(s) with the same or nearly the same meaning as the word in bold type.

1. Obadiah
- ○ New Testament prophet
- ○ son of Ruth and Boaz
- ● the shortest book in the Old Testament
- ○ the longest book in the Old Testament

2. sacrifice
- ○ to commandeer an airplane
- ● an offering
- ○ to communicate
- ○ resemblance

3. satellite
- ○ to soak thoroughly
- ○ uncivilized
- ● an object that orbits a heavenly body
- ○ sixth planet from the sun

4. Nehemiah
- ● Old Testament book before Esther
- ○ Old Testament book after Esther
- ○ New Testament book after Ezra
- ○ follower of Jesus who called Peter

5. Jeremiah
- ○ important city in the Jordan Valley
- ○ city where the temple stood
- ○ first king of Israel
- ● the "weeping prophet"

6. Micah
- ○ an archangel
- ○ a town near Bethel
- ● book of the minor prophets
- ○ last Old Testament book

7. Zephaniah
- ○ prophet in the days of King Josiah
- ○ ninth book of the Bible
- ○ last book of the Old Testament
- ● son of Zilpah

8. Zechariah
- ○ next to the last book of the Bible
- ● Old Testament book following Haggai
- ○ a man who climbed a tree to see Jesus
- ○ a town in Shephelah in Judah

9. variety
- ○ undue pride in oneself
- ○ an animal considered a pest
- ● assortment of different things
- ○ fine particles floating in the air

10. Titus
- ○ the 10th part of one's increase
- ○ letter written by Peter
- ○ a covenant
- ● New Testament book before Philemon

332

1.	guys	Some high school **guys** were hanging around the mall entrance.
2.	diet	Even though Sandra does not need to **diet**, she talks about it a lot.
3.	riot	Katelynn hoped they would not start a **riot**.
4.	Ohio	"This mall is tiny compared to the one we shopped at in **Ohio**," Sandra said.
5.	guide	"I read the fashion **guide** in every magazine my mom gets."
6.	admire	Sandra likes people to **admire** her hair and clothes.
7.	recital	"This would look terrific for my piano **recital**," Sandra bragged.
8.	isle	"We spent the summer on an **isle** in the Mediterranean," said Sandra's mom.
9.	geyser	"We all hoped to see a **geyser**," said Mrs. St. Clair.
10.	silence	There was a long, awkward **silence** after she told her dad what she had done.
11.	alibi	She had no **alibi**.
12.	minor	Katelynn is a **minor** and, so, was not charged with shoplifting.
13.	byte	"My name is in every **byte** of their computer's memory," groaned Katelynn.
14.	height	"This has to be the **height** of embarrassment," she told her dad.
15.	arrive	She dreaded the moment they would **arrive** at the mall office.
16.	wife	Mr. Hatasaki sadly told his **wife** about Katelynn's bad choice.
17.	diary	Katelynn cried as she recorded the terrible events of the day in her **diary**.
18.	liar	She had no desire to be a thief or a **liar**.
19.	Idaho	Katelynn loves baked **Idaho** potatoes with butter and sour cream.
20.	Iowa	Some of the corn grown in **Iowa** is used for animal feed.

I Game

Name _____

Go with Katelynn and her dad to return the shirt. Move one space for each word you or your team spells correctly.

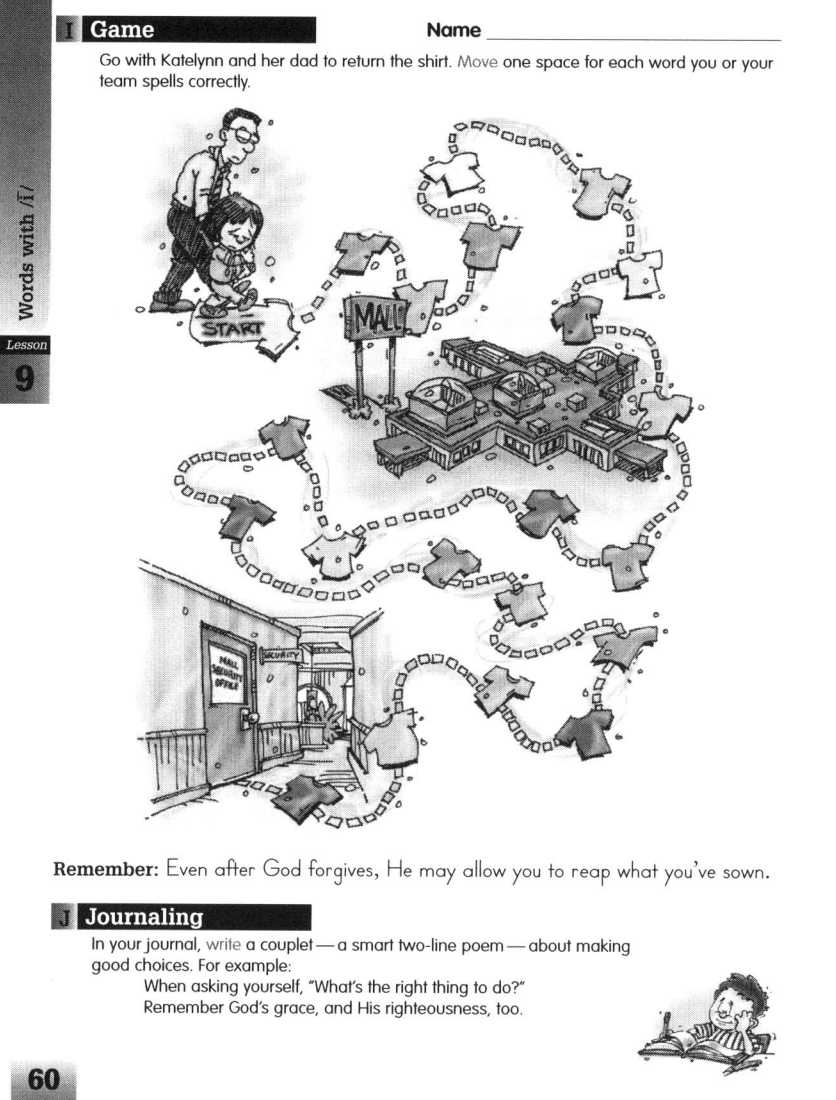

Remember: Even after God forgives, He may allow you to reap what you've sown.

J Journaling

In your journal, write a couplet — a smart two-line poem — about making good choices. For example:

When asking yourself, "What's the right thing to do?"
Remember God's grace, and His righteousness, too.

60

How to Play:

- Divide the class into two teams.
- Have each student place his/her game piece on Start.
- Have a student from team A go to the board.
- Say the spelling word.
- Have the student write the word on the board.
- If correct, instruct each member of team A to move his/her game piece forward one space.
- Alternate between teams A and B.
- The team to reach the mall security office first is the winner.
- **Small Group Option**: Students may play this game without teacher direction in small groups of two or more.

---

2 Game

Reinforce spelling skills and provide motivation and interest.

Materials

- game page (from student text)
- game pieces (1 per child)
- game word list

Game Word List

1. **diary**
2. **liar**
3. **diet**
4. **riot**
5. **Ohio**
6. **alibi**
7. **guide**
8. **Idaho**
9. **wife**
10. **isle**
11. **silence**
12. **minor**
13. **admire**
14. **byte**
15. **height**
16. **recital**
17. **arrive**
18. **Iowa**
19. **guys**
20. **geyser**

3 Journaling

Provide a meaningful reason for correct spelling through personal writing.

Review the story using discussion leads provided on the following page. Encourage students to apply the Scriptural value in their journaling.

Journaling (continued)

 (Say)

- What do you think Mr. Hatasaki meant when he said, "Character is made by what you stand for; reputation, by what you fall for?" (When you make wise choices you are strengthening a good character. When you make a mistake people often hear about it and your reputation can be damaged.)

- How did Katelynn damage her reputation? (She took the shirt Sandra handed her even though she knew it hadn't been paid for.)

- What did Katelynn do that showed her strength of character? (She went to the mall and returned the shirt.)

- Why was Katelynn's dad proud of her? (Katelynn had recognized her mistake, asked forgiveness, and made it right.)

- In poetry a couplet is a two-line verse. Usually the last words of each line rhyme. Couplets can be sophisticated, simple, silly, or fun. Some examples are:

  There are times when two together,

  Add up to one—one thing that's better!

  —Leah Knowlton

  But if the while I think on thee, dear friend,

  All losses are restored and sorrows end.

  —Shakespeare

- Write the first line of a possible couplet on the board: **When asking yourself, "What's the right thing to do?"** Help students think of words that rhyme with do. Together, compile a list of possible rhyming words.

"CATERCORNER" has eight spellings in the third edition of Webster's Dictionary: catercorner, cater-cornered, cata-corner, cata-cornered, catty-corner, catty-cornered, kitty-corner, and kitty-cornered.

Word-Wow!

The Suspect

Stephen learns about drug abuse, and where he can always turn for help.

"**B**eth!" Tony skidded to a stop beside his friend. "Have you noticed all the awesome clothes Brutus has been wearing?"

Beth looked across the playground at the big eighth grader talking to a younger child. "Yeah. He's changed since he flunked eighth grade last year."

"Who're you talkin' about? Rudest Brutus?" Stephen said as he joined his friends.

Beth nodded. "Who else?"

"I'm just thankful he's been leaving us alone; and I, for one, am going to keep out of his way," Stephen said.

"I still wonder where he gets such expensive clothes. He used to wear old hand-me-downs." Tony took the comb out of his back pocket and ran it through his hair.

"No one's big enough to give him hand-me-downs anymore," Beth observed.

"No, that's just it. The clothes he wore last year didn't look like kid-clothes. They looked like stuff even grown-ups didn't want to wear any more. And I'd wear what he has on today—if it were a little smaller," Tony grinned. "It just doesn't make sense."

"Maybe his dad got a new job or something?" Beth suggested.

"No," Tony bent down to tie his shoe. "He lives with his mom. I think his dad's in jail or something."

"I'm not getting close enough to ask him." Stephen watched the big boy as he put his hand on the shoulder of a seventh-grade girl and bent over to say something into her ear.

"We could be detectives!" suggested Beth.

"Later!" Tony said. "Looks like Mr. Canfield is ready to play soccer. Race you to the goal!"

After recess, Mr. Canfield walked to the front of the class and waited for them to settle down before he spoke. "We're going to have a guest every Monday afternoon for a while. He'll be here for about an hour. His name is Officer Klein and he's going to dare you to do something."

A brisk knock sounded at the door, and Mr. Canfield went to answer it. A blue-clad police officer entered, followed by a very big German shepherd. "Kelly, sit," the officer commanded. The dog obeyed instantly. "Kelly, stay," Officer Klein made eye contact with his dog, then turned his attention to the class.

"How many of you have ever been told no?" Every hand in the class shot up in the air. "Is it hard for you to tell a friend no?" Heads nodded around the room. "Your school has invited me to come to your classroom to teach you how to say no! Raise your hand if you believe me." Everyone looked around to see how everyone else was voting. Thorny raised his hand first. Matthew followed. Everyone else wasn't sure. The officer continued. "I want to teach you about a program called D.A.R.E. D.A.R.E. is an acronym. Does anyone know what an acronym is?" Thorny and Matthew raised their hands. Mr. Klein pointed to Thorny.

"An acronym is a word formed from the initial letter or letters of a series of words."

"I think what Thorny's trying to say is an acronym comes from the beginning letters of words to make a new word. You know, like 'SWAK' for 'Sealed With A Kiss,'" Matthew interpreted. The class burst out laughing. Matthew's face turned red. "That's what my grandma always writes on the back of the envelope when she sends me a letter," he explained.

"Good job, boys! Have any of you heard of the acronym D.A.R.E.?" Officer Klein reached down and patted his dog on the head.

No one raised a hand.

He wrote on the board while he spoke, "D.A.R.E. stands for Drug Abuse Resistance Education." When he was finished he underlined the first letter of each word he had written. "So what's the acronym for drug abuse resistance education?"

"D.A.R.E.!" Kristin blurted.

"Great," Officer Klein nodded. "I'm here today because I don't want drugs to be the *last* thing you do! I dare you to say no to drug abuse!"

"My dog Kelly is trained to smell illegal drugs. If I were to give her the command, she would use her sensitive nose to detect if there were any drugs in a car, a locker, or even on a person. She's rarely wrong!" The big dog wopped her tail on the carpet as if she understood what her master was saying about her.

"Over the next few weeks we're going to be role-playing eight different ways to say no to drugs. I would hate for Kelly to find drugs on you—ever!"

"I need a volunteer." Laney waved her hand in the air and Officer Klein motioned her to the front of the room. "What would you say if one of your friends came up to you and said, 'Wanna try some oxycodone? It's a prescription painkiller, so you know it has to be safe. It stays in your bloodstream less than 24 hours. Come on—it's harmless. It's a great feeling and everyone's doing it!'"

Laney looked over at the dog. "No?"

"Great job," Officer Klein shook Laney's hand. "Next time try to say it more forcefully—like you really mean it."

The class continued to role-play different situations. They divided into small groups and did some cooperative learning activities

93

before Officer Klein and Kelly went on to the eighth-grade classroom.

Later that evening Tony and Stephen collapsed on the ground after their fifth run through a soccer drill they'd set up in Mason Springs Park. "I wonder if Kelly could smell drugs in someone's desk or locker after they took them out," Tony said thoughtfully.

"Worried?" Stephen teased.

"No. I was thinking about Brutus. On the way home from school today I saw him talking to some guys from the high school—older, like maybe juniors or seniors. They were in a new Corvette. It kinda looked like they handed him something. Maybe he's into drugs. That would explain all his new clothes."

"Just because we don't like Brutus doesn't mean he deals drugs," Stephen reasoned. "I know he's mean and everything, but I don't think he's dumb enough to do drugs."

"Maybe he just sells them—to get what he wants, ya know."

"We could watch him like Beth said today. If we don't catch him, I'm sure Kelly could." The two boys stood up.

During lunch break the next day, Beth, Tony, and Stephen halfheartedly kicked the soccer ball back and forth. They kept watching for the suspect, Brutus. "I think we should talk to that seventh-grade girl we saw him with yesterday. What's her name? Sandra?" Beth picked up the soccer ball.

"Well, that would be a start," Tony agreed. "He probably doesn't bring the drugs to school, especially now that Officer Klein and Kelly are here every day."

"Sandra's right over there. Maybe she'll know something about the suspect's new clothes." Beth headed off across the playground.

Tony and Stephen followed at a distance. Brutus almost ran them down as he rushed around the corner of the school. "Get out of my way, you little rug rats. Who gave you permission to live? I want

you and your little friends to stay away from my girl—or I'll bounce you across that cement over there like I did your little cars last year! Any questions?" Both boys shook their heads and looked down submissively at the toes of the eighth grader's shoes. "Here, let me give you a sample of what I mean." Brutus grabbed each boy by the coat and lifted them a foot off the ground.

Stephen knew his head was going to be smashed against the brick wall beside them, and he shut his eyes. "Save us, God," he breathed.

"What'd you say?" Brutus glared at Stephen as he lifted the boys higher.

A booming voice answered, "I said put them down and come with me, Brutus!"

Brutus let go of their coats, and Stephen opened his eyes a crack as he crumpled to the ground.

He watched Mr. Canfield sling his big arm over the bully's shoulder.

"'Your protection and success come from God alone. He is your refuge, a Rock where no enemy can reach you,'" was the Scripture stated by Mr. Canfield as he guided the eighth grader toward the front of the building.

"Was he talking to us or Brutus?" Tony asked.

"I don't know. I prayed for protection. I think Brutus may need it now, though. He even looks small compared to Mr. Canfield." Stephen laughed. "And Mr. Canfield doesn't look too happy."

"Do you think he believes in God?" Tony dusted off his clothes and took the comb out of his pocket.

"Who—Brutus?" Stephen stood up slowly.

Tony nodded.

"He sure doesn't act like it." Stephen frowned. "And Mr. Canfield can't be everywhere...."

"But God can." Tony remembered what his Grandma had told him. "All we have to do is ask."

(To be continued...)

2 Discussion Time

Check understanding of the story and development of personal values.

- Tell about a time God protected you.
- How did you feel as you asked God for help?
- What is a refuge?
- Why do you think David compared God to a rock in Psalm 62:7?
- How did God answer Stephen's prayer for protection?
- Do you think Mr. Canfield can always successfully protect Stephen and Tony?
- How do you think God might continue to protect them?

1. banjo
2. Wyoming
3. buffalo
4. soldier
5. cargo
6. stereo
7. boldly
8. studio
9. flamingo
10. enroll
11. patrol
12. sole
13. macro
14. control

15. portfolio
16. voltage
17. dome
18. Oklahoma
19. Minnesota
20. donate

Words with /ō/

Lesson 10

Scripture

Psalm 62:7

61

Preview 3

Test for knowledge of the correct spellings of these words.

Customize Your List
On a separate sheet of paper, additional words of your choice may be tested.

Say I will say each word once, use the word in a sentence, then say the word again. Write the words on the lines in your Worktext.

Correct Immediately!
Say Let's correct our Preview. I will spell each word out loud. If you spelled a word incorrectly, rewrite it correctly.

Progress Chart
Students may record scores. (Reproducible master provided in Appendix B.)

Lesson 10 | Day 1

1. banjo — None of the students in Mr. Canfield's class plays the **banjo**.
2. Wyoming — Mr. Canfield read a terrific story set in **Wyoming** in the early 1800's.
3. buffalo — It described the huge herds of mighty **buffalo** that roamed the land.
4. soldier — The story told about a **soldier** that settled his family there.
5. cargo — Mr. Canfield read about enormous steam engines that hauled **cargo** to the west.
6. stereo — After the story, he played music by a famous composer on the **stereo** speakers.
7. boldly — The music of the tuba **boldly** represented trains in the first piece.
8. studio — Mr. Canfield has one corner of the room set up like an art **studio**.
9. flamingo — Sarah's painting of a **flamingo** is hanging on the wall.
10. enroll — Knowlton Elementary was eager to **enroll** in Officer Klein's program.
11. patrol — Officer Klein takes his dog Kelly on **patrol** with him every day.
12. sole — He can tap a signal to Kelly with the **sole** of his shoe.
13. macro — When Stephen said Kelly was a **macro** dog, Officer Klein laughed.
14. control — His work is invaluable to the **control** of illegal drug distribution.
15. portfolio — At his office he keeps a file or **portfolio** of cases he has solved.
16. voltage — He carries a stun gun that shocks a fleeing criminal with low **voltage**.
17. dome — The lights on top of a squad car are no longer **dome** shaped, but rectangular.
18. Oklahoma — Officer Klein said he grew up in the state of **Oklahoma**.
19. Minnesota — He has a good friend on the police force in **Minnesota**.
20. donate — Some parents **donate** their time and money to promote the D.A.R.E. program.

95

4 Word Shapes

Help students form a correct image of whole words.

 Say Look at each word and think about its shape. Now, write the word in the correct Word Shape Boxes. You may check off each word as you use it.

(In many words, the sound of /ō/ is spelled with **o** or **o-consonant-e**.)

 Say In the Word Shape Boxes, fill in the boxes containing the letter or letters that spell the sound of /ō/ in each word.

 Take a minute to memorize...

Psalm 62:7

B Word Shapes

Name _____

Using the word bank below, write each word in the correct Word Shape Boxes. Next, in the Word Shape Boxes, fill in the boxes containing the letter or letters that spell the sound of /ō/ in each word.

Words with /ō/

Lesson **10**

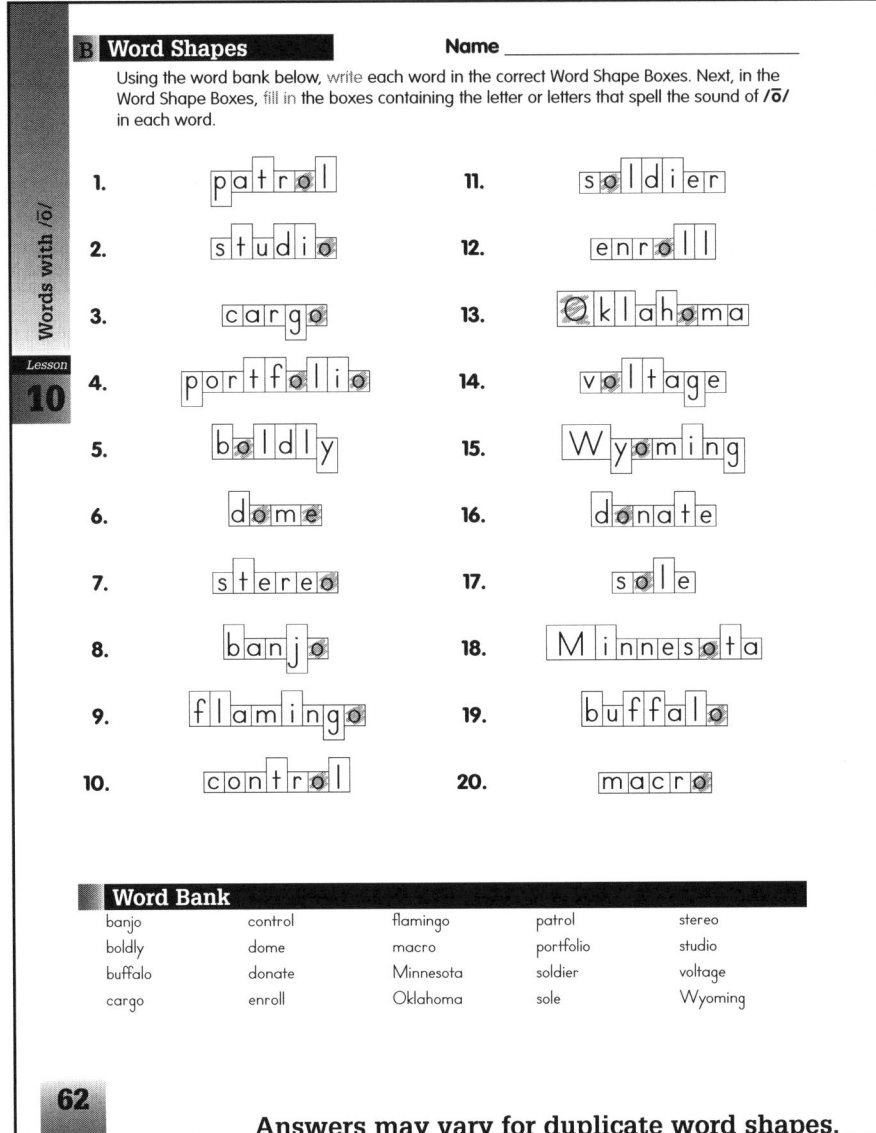

1. patrol
2. studio
3. cargo
4. portfolio
5. boldly
6. dome
7. stereo
8. banjo
9. flamingo
10. control
11. soldier
12. enroll
13. Oklahoma
14. voltage
15. Wyoming
16. donate
17. sole
18. Minnesota
19. buffalo
20. macro

Word Bank

banjo	control	flamingo	patrol	stereo
boldly	dome	macro	portfolio	studio
buffalo	donate	Minnesota	soldier	voltage
cargo	enroll	Oklahoma	sole	Wyoming

62

Answers may vary for duplicate word shapes.

 Be Prepared For Fun

Check these supply lists for **Fun Ways to Spell** - presented **Day 2**.
Purchase and/or gather these items ahead of time!

General
- Pencil
- Notebook Paper
- Spelling List

Auditory
- Pencil
- 3 X 5 Cards Cut in half lengthwise (20 per child)
- Spelling List

Visual
- Colored Pencils
- Graph Paper (2 sheets per child)
- Spelling List

Tactile
- Clay
- Spelling List

Lesson 10 | **Day 1**

96

C Hide and Seek

Name _____

Play Hide and Seek with your words. Fill in a box on the bar graph (left to right) for each word you spell correctly.

LOOK   SAY   SPELL ALOUD   WRITE   SEEK   CHECK

D Other Word Forms

Using the words below, follow the instructions given by your teacher.

banjoist	controlling	macros	solely
banjos	domed	Minnesotan	stereophonic
bold	domes	Oklahoman	stereos
bolded	donated	patrolled	studios
buffaloed	donating	patrolling	volt
buffaloes	enrolled	portfolios	voltaic
cargoes	enrolling	soldiered	
controllable	flamingos	soldiering	

E Fun Ways to Spell

Initial the box of each activity you finish.

1. ☐ Classify your words according to syllables.

3. got a "fish? nope! ☐ Spell your words and play "Match-It."

2. Gryph ☐ Spell your words on graph paper.

4. clay ☐ Spell your words with clay.

63

Hide and Seek

1

Reinforce spelling by using multiple styles of learning.

On a white board, Teacher writes each word — one at a time. **Have students:**

- **Look** at the word.
- **Say** the word out loud.
- **Spell** the word out loud.
- **Hide** (teacher erases word.)
- **Write** the word on paper.
- **Seek** (teacher rewrites word.)
- **Check** spelling. If incorrect, rewrite word correctly.

Other Word Forms

2

This activity is optional. Have students find and circle the Other Word Forms that are synonyms of the following:

brazen
bamboozled
singularly
manipulating

Fun Ways to Spell

3

Four activities are provided. Use one, two, three, or all of the activities. Have students initial the box for each activity they complete.

Options:

- assign activities to students according to their learning styles
- set up the activities in learning centers for the students to do throughout the day
- divide students into four groups and assign one activity per group
- do one activity per day

General

To classify your words according to syllables...
- Write three headings on your paper: One-syllable, Two-syllable, and Three-syllable.
- Write the first word on your list under the proper heading.
- Draw a line through the word to divide it into syllables.
- Do this with each word.

Visual

To spell your words on graph paper...
- Look at the first word on your list.
- Shade in squares to form the letters of each word.
- Check your spelling.
- Do this with each word.

Auditory

To spell your words and play "Match-It"...
- Write each word on a card. Mix your word-cards and a classmate's together. Deal six cards to each player; the rest face down between you. Ask your classmate for a word-card. If the word-card matches, take it and play again. If not, draw from the stack, and it is your classmate's turn. Take turns until all cards are matched.

Tactile

To spell your words with clay...
- Roll pieces of clay into ropes.
- Use the ropes to make the letters of each word.
- Put them in the right order to spell each word.
- Check your spelling.

Working with Words

Familiarize students with word meaning and usage.

Clues

Write this incomplete sentence on the board:

An underground prison is called a _____.

Guide the students in choosing the word **dungeon**.

Read each sentence and choose a spelling word for each definition. You may use a dictionary to help you. Write the word in the blank.

Take a minute to memorize...

Psalm 62:7

Lesson **10** | Day 3

Words with /ō/

Lesson **10**

F Working with Words

Name _____

Clues

Write a spelling word for each clue.

1. The force of electrical current is called ___voltage___.
2. A large shaggy-maned mammal with a big muscular hump is a ___buffalo___.
3. The bottom of your foot is called the ___sole___.
4. A ___banjo___ is a musical instrument with a long neck and usually five strings.
5. A person who is in the army is called a ___soldier___.
6. To ___donate___ is to make a contribution or gift.
7. ___Macro___ relates to something with very large quantities.
8. To have direct influence over something is to ___control___ it.
9. A ___patrol___ checks an area for maintenance or security.
10. The freight carried in a ship, airplane, or vehicle is called ___cargo___.
11. A ___studio___ is the place where an artist works.
12. Saint Paul is the capitol of ___Minnesota___.
13. A ___flamingo___ is a long-legged long-necked tropical water bird with scarlet wings.
14. A sports building with a roof is known as a ___dome___.
15. One of the mountain states of the United States is ___Wyoming___.
16. A portable case for papers and drawings is called a ___portfolio___.
17. The state bordered by Colorado, Kansas, Missouri, and Arkansas is ___Oklahoma___.
18. To do something courageously and valiantly is to do it ___boldly___.
19. To put your name on a list to join a club or class is to ___enroll___.
20. A ___stereo___ is a sound system that uses two or more channels of sound.

Word Bank

banjo	control	flamingo	patrol	stereo
boldly	dome	macro	portfolio	studio
buffalo	donate	Minnesota	soldier	voltage
cargo	enroll	Oklahoma	sole	Wyoming

64

G Dictation

Name _____

Write **each sentence as your teacher dictates.** Use **correct punctuation.**

1. Kelly, <u>the patrol dog, was the picture of</u> <u>control since she had been well trained.</u>

2. Stephen <u>looked in his portfolio to find his</u> <u>report on buffalo.</u>

3. <u>People used to donate clothes to the older boy,</u> <u>but now he dressed in style.</u>

H Proofreading

If a word is misspelled, fill in the oval by that word. If all the words are spelled correctly, fill in the oval by **no mistake**.

1. ● banjoe
   ○ arrive
   ○ Iowa
   ○ no mistake

2. ○ guys
   ○ flamingo
   ● cargoe
   ○ no mistake

3. ○ admire
   ● buffaloe
   ○ byte
   ○ no mistake

4. ○ geyser
   ○ macro
   ○ stereo
   ● no mistake

5. ○ boldly
   ● enrole
   ○ recital
   ○ no mistake

6. ○ control
   ○ alibi
   ● patroll
   ○ no mistake

7. ○ donate
   ○ Minnesota
   ○ diary
   ● no mistake

8. ○ portfolio
   ● soldyer
   ○ guide
   ○ no mistake

9. ○ sole
   ● voltige
   ○ height
   ○ no mistake

10. ● doam
    ○ studio
    ○ liar
    ○ no mistake

11. ○ Oklahoma
    ○ Ohio
    ○ diet
    ● no mistake

12. ● Wyomng
    ○ riot
    ○ Idaho
    ○ no mistake

65

Dictation

Reinforce correct spelling by using current and previous words in context.

Say — Listen as I read each sentence and then write it in your Worktext. Remember to use correct capitalization and punctuation. (Slowly read each sentence twice. Sentences are found in the Student Worktext to the left.)

Proofreading

Familiarize students with standardized test format and reinforce recognition of misspelled words.

Say — Look at each set of words. If a word is misspelled, fill in the oval by that word. If all the words are spelled correctly, fill in the oval by **no mistake**.

Day 4

Lesson 10

99

3 Hide and Seek

Reinforce correct spelling of current spelling words.
Repeat this activity from Day 2.

4 Vocabulary Extension

Have your students complete this activity to strengthen spelling ability and expand vocabulary. The reproducible master is provided in Appendix A as shown on the inset page to the right.

1 Posttest

Visit the **A Reason For** website to download free, printable Posttest pages.

I will say the word once, use it in a sentence, then say it again. Write your words on a separate sheet of paper.

Progress Chart
Students may record scores. (Appendix B)

Personal Dictionary
Students may add any words they have misspelled to their personal dictionaries. (Appendix B)

Hide and Seek

Play Hide and Seek with your words. Fill in a bar graph (left to right) for each word you spell correctly.

LOOK   SAY   HIDE   WRITE   SEEK   CHECK

Vocabulary Extension
Cause and Effect
Write a word from the word bank to complete each sentence.

1. If you wanted to ___approach___ someone, you would go up and talk to them.
2. If a family had lived in the city of Thessalonica, they would be known as ___Thessalonians___.
3. If you want to look at something that is very small, you would use a ___microscope___.
4. If you want to read the book of the Bible between Hosea and Amos, you would read the book of ___Joel___.
5. If you wanted to describe the brilliance that radiates from a heavenly angel, you might use the word ___glory___.
6. If a carpenter wanted to hold up the roof of a porch, he might use pillars to ___support___ it.
7. If you wanted to describe someone who had suffered a lot, you might compare them to a man in the Bible named ___Job___.
8. If you want to go into a cave to discover what it is like, you will ___explore___ it.
9. If you were telling a story about a man who had been swallowed by a large fish, you would be telling the story of ___Jonah___.
10. If you had written a letter to a friend and needed to mail it, you would write the address on an ___envelope___.
11. If you challenged a friend to a game of tennis, you would play at a tennis ___court___.
12. If your family were citizens of Rome, they would be known as ___Romans___.

Word Bank

approach	explore	Joel	Romans
court	glory	Jonah	support
envelope	Job	microscope	Thessalonians

333

1.	banjo	Mr. Canfield brought a **banjo**, guitar, and violin for the class to see.
2.	stereo	He also set up a **stereo** speakers in the classroom for the best sound.
3.	donate	Many parents were willing to **donate** CD's of music by famous composers.
4.	Wyoming	One composer wrote a piece to describe the beauty he saw in **Wyoming**.
5.	studio	The kind officer admired the students' paintings in the **studio** area.
6.	buffalo	Using a charcoal pencil, Thorny sketched a very realistic **buffalo**.
7.	flamingo	He complimented Sarah on her beautiful **flamingo**.
8.	Oklahoma	The officer moved from **Oklahoma** when he was twenty-one.
9.	soldier	He had thought about being a **soldier** in the armed forces.
10.	enroll	He said that God wanted him to **enroll** in the police academy instead.
11.	boldly	In his training, he had to learn to **boldly** face danger.
12.	control	His teachers also trained him to exercise self-**control**.
13.	voltage	He has a stun gun that can shock a fleeing criminal with low **voltage**.
14.	patrol	Officer Klein is glad to have Kelly as his partner on **patrol**.
15.	sole	He tapped the floor twice with the **sole** of his shoe and Kelly sat down.
16.	macro	"You'd probably laugh again if I said the dog has **macro** teeth."
17.	cargo	He and Kelly often check the **cargo** of vehicles for illegal drugs.
18.	portfolio	Officer Klein showed the class a **portfolio** of drug seizure photos.
19.	dome	Newer patrol cars do not have **dome** lights; they are rectangular instead.
20.	Minnesota	His best friend from school is an officer in **Minnesota**.

I Game

Name _____

Record points for each word you or your team spells correctly. Earn bonus points for each row in which all five words are spelled correctly.

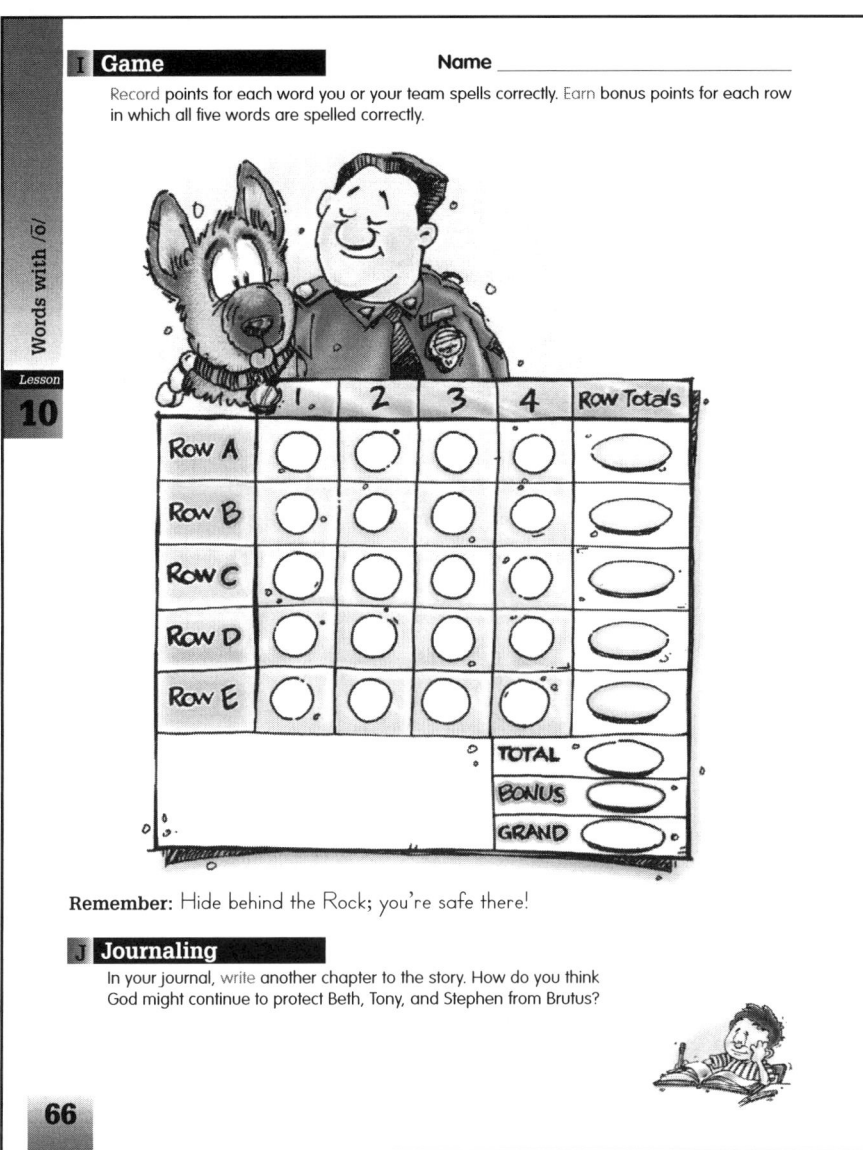

Remember: Hide behind the Rock; you're safe there!

J Journaling

In your journal, write another chapter to the story. How do you think God might continue to protect Beth, Tony, and Stephen from Brutus?

66

How to Play:

- Divide the class into two teams.
- Have a student from team A choose a square on the grid by indicating the row letter and number.
- Say the word that matches that row letter and number from the team's word list.
- Have the student write the word on the board.
- If correct, have each member of that team record the awarded points (in parentheses by the word) in the circle in that box. If the word is misspelled, have him/her put an **X** in that circle. That square may not be chosen again.
- Repeat this process with the second team.
- When all the words have been spelled by both teams, have each team tally its score. Award a bonus of 5 points for each row in which all four words were spelled correctly.
- Have the teams record their grand totals. The team with the highest score is the winner.

2 Game

Reinforce spelling skills and provide motivation and interest.

Materials

- game page (from student text)
- pencils (1 per child)
- game word list

Game Word List

Team A		Team B
E4	banjo (4)	A1
E3	buffalo (3)	A2
E2	cargo (2)	A3
E1	flamingo (1)	A4
D4	macro (2)	B1
D3	stereo (4)	B2
D2	studio (1)	B3
D1	boldly (3)	B4
C4	control (2)	C1
C3	enroll (1)	C2
C2	patrol (3)	C3
C1	portfolio (4)	C4
B4	soldier (1)	D1
B3	sole (4)	D2
B2	voltage (3)	D3
B1	dome (2)	D4
A4	Oklahoma (4)	E1
A3	Wyoming (3)	E2
A2	donate (1)	E3
A1	Minnesota (2)	E4

3 Journaling

Provide a meaningful reason for correct spelling through personal writing.

Review the story using discussion leads provided on the following page. Encourage students to apply the Scriptural value in their journaling.

101

Journaling (continued)

(Say)

- Whom is Brutus still being mean to? (Stephen and Tony)
- Why does Beth suggest they should be detectives? (Brutus is wearing nice clothes this year and they can't figure out how he affords them.)
- Whom did Tony see Brutus talking to on the way home from school? (Some high school boys in a Corvette.)
- What do Stephen, Beth, and Tony suspect Brutus is doing? (Making money from illegal drugs.)
- Do you think Brutus is selling drugs?
- Do you think Tony and Stephen will need protection again?

The words "erroneousnesses" and "verrucosenesses" are the longest words consisting of only letters that do not extend below or above any other letters.

Smart Mouths

When they have a substitute teacher, Rosa and her classmates learn to be careful what they say about people.

Carlos walked into the kitchen, head down, pawing through his backpack. "Have you guys seen my history paper? I finished it last night. It's gotta be here somewhere!" He pulled his history book out and frantically flipped through it.

"Well, don't panic." Maria glanced up from her place at the breakfast table. "Where'd you leave it, anyway?"

"Right here on the table where I was working!" 16-year-old Carlos stuffed the book back in his pack before dropping the whole thing on the floor and slumping into his seat at the table.

"That's strange," said their father, turning from the refrigerator with a jar of jam. "Did you see anything when you set the table for breakfast, Rosa?"

"Jisss bum unch fapers." Rosa answered around a mouthful of cereal.

Mr. Vasquez frowned across the table at her. "Try that again, please, without the food in your mouth."

Rosa nodded and swallowed rapidly. "I said, just a bunch of papers." She spooned another bite into her mouth.

"Rosa, would you quit stuffing yourself for just a minute?" Carlos demanded. "Where's my history paper?!"

Rosa washed down the cereal with orange juice. She shrugged. "I don't know if it was your history paper, Carlos. There was a stack of papers on the table when I was supposed to set it for breakfast, so I moved them." Rosa took another bite of cereal.

"Moved them where?" Carlos clunked his spoon down on the table and glared at his little sister. When she pointed to her full mouth instead of answering immediately, Carlos exploded. "Are you deaf and dumb—or just dumb?!"

Mr. Vasquez spoke sternly, "Carlos, you may leave the table or make a sincere apology to your sister. You will not use words that belittle others."

For a moment it was so quiet that Rosa's chewing sounded loud. Then Carlos sighed. "I'm sorry, Rosa. That report's real important and it's due today."

Rosa fumed as she picked up her glass of orange juice. "I put the papers on the coffee table in the living room, but I'm so dumb I didn't look to see if your history report was with them." She glared across the table at her older brother.

"Why don't you go check right now, Carlos?" Mr. Vasquez shook his head at Rosa. "I'm sure we'll all enjoy our breakfast more once that report is found."

Later that morning, Carlos slowed the car to a stop in front of Knowlton Elementary School. "I'll pick you up here right after school," he said as his sisters got out.

"Okay!" Rosa scrambled out after Maria. "Do you still have your history paper, Carlos? I really don't think someone who can't keep track of their work should be driving! See you!" She grinned impishly and slammed the door, drowning out her brother's reply.

"Hey, Rosa, hurry up!" Rosa's friend, Kristin, motioned from halfway up the sidewalk. When Rosa caught up with her, Kristin wiped the back of her hand across her forehead. "Whew! I'm sure glad you got here safely. It takes years off my life just thinking about Carlos driving a car!"

"I just close my eyes and hold on!"

Rosa laughed as the girls walked into the building. "Hey, you think Mr. Canfield will let us sit together for art today like he did last week?"

"Probably. Let's ask…. Who's that?" Kristin stopped just inside the classroom door and pointed at someone writing on the board.

"That is our substitute teacher," Beth whispered as she walked by. "Can you believe that hair?"

Kristin whispered back, "It, um, it's certainly a long, straight ponytail. And thick. Like a horse's tail!"

"Just wait till she turns around!" Beth moved on to her desk.

Kristin snickered when the substitute teacher turned around. Her face was long and thin, with large brown eyes—just like a horse's face. Kristin cleared her throat to keep from laughing when she read the name written on the board: Miss Horace.

"Good morning, children. I'm Miss Horace, your teacher for today. Now, please stand and repeat the pledge of allegiance."

Rosa stood with her class and faced the flag, but she rolled her eyes to study the substitute teacher. Miss Horace didn't appear to be very old, although her mane of hair was streaked with gray. Her face was smooth and unlined, not a smile, wrinkle or a laugh line to be found. "…with liberty and justice for all." Rosa finished the pledge with her classmates and started to sit back down.

"Young man!" The substitute teacher's voice snapped across the room. "Yes, you in the black shirt." Everyone turned to see who she was talking to. Christopher Wright, Kristin's twin brother, stood in the aisle clutching his pencil with the jet eraser on the end. "Sit down."

"I was just going to sharpen my pencil, Miss Horace." Christopher held up the red pencil so the teacher could see its dull point.

Miss Horace frowned and barked, "I said, sit down."

"Um, Miss Horace?"

103

Christopher tried once more to explain. "I need my pencil for this first class and Mr. Canfield lets us sharpen our pencils whenever we need to."

Miss Horace stared at Christopher without saying a word before walking across the room to stand directly in front of him. "I said, SIT DOWN." Christopher turned quickly and bolted to his desk.

Miss Horace returned to the front of the room. "I am your teacher today and I am not Mr. Canfield. Now get out your books and turn to page 79."

"She can sure say that again!" Tommy whispered to a red-faced Christopher as he handed a sharp pencil across the aisle to him.

"Yep, this day is gonna be as much fun as a paper cut!" Daniel whispered from the back row.

The day dragged on minute by minute. By art time, Rosa knew better than to ask Miss Horace if she could sit with Kristin. Usually art class was noisy and fun. Mr. Canfield encouraged them to talk about ideas and to try new things. Today the room was much quieter. Miss Horace was busy at the front of the room writing on the board.

"Psst, Katelynn." Rosa nudged the girl in front of her. "Look at my sculpture."

Katelynn studied the lump of clay balanced on four wobbly clay legs. "What is it?"

Rosa leaned forward and whispered, "I call it Miss Horse." Katelynn slapped her hand over her mouth to hold her giggles in. Nearby, Beth choked on her laughter and went into a fit of coughing.

Beth poked Stephen and pointed at Rosa's sculpture. "That's Miss Horse." She tossed her own short ponytail and raised her eyebrows at the substitute teacher's long one.

Stephen grinned and caught Tommy's attention. "Miss Horse," he mouthed and nodded at Rosa's lopsided clay horse.

"Miss Horse looks like what my grandma used to call 'one brick short of a load.'" Tommy whispered back.

Christopher jabbed at his own lump of clay and muttered, "I'd say more like two or three bricks short."

Rosa wiggled her eyebrows. "Maybe she's a donut short of a dozen."

"I believe the expression 'a bubble off plumb' is used by those in the building profession to represent the same idea you are suggesting." Thorny divided his clay precisely into equal parts.

Stephen rolled his eyes. "You mean, like, she's a throwback from the gene pool?"

Daniel held up his hand to get the attention of everyone around him. He motioned toward the woman writing on the board at the front of the room, her long ponytail swishing back and forth down her back. "I can't figure out if Miss Horse is deaf and dumb—or just dumb."

At that exact moment, Miss Horace turned around. "Daniel, did you have a question?"

"Nay." Daniel grinned as his classmates almost burst trying to hold in their laughter. "I mean, no, Miss Horace."

Miss Horace frowned around the room and turned back to finish what she was writing.

Tommy read the words the substitute teacher had written. "Oops," he whispered. "Check that out, guys." He pointed his pencil at the board.

"At your service, sir!" Daniel leaned over in his seat and bowed to Tommy. "'Nothing is perfect except your words. Oh, how I love them. I think about them all day long.'" Daniel's whisper lost it's cocky tone as he read, "'They make me wiser than my enemies, because....'" His voice trailed off. Then he turned to his classmates and added, "'Oops' is right."

At last Thorny broke the silence in the classroom. He chose his words even more carefully than usual. "Our words have been anything but perfect," Thorny said, frowning at the neat clay birdhouse on his desk. "We appear to have given little thought to what is right and thus have made a significant error."

"Thorny, what are you talking about?" Christopher rubbed his face and left a streak of clay.

Stephen's eyes rolled again. "He means we blew it."

Rosa nodded, "Blew it big time."

I knew how bad it felt when Carlos said mean things to me this morning. But I did the same thing to somebody else. I think I need a fresh start—in more ways than one. Rosa smiled, then wadded the clay horse into a ball and started her art project over again.

2 | **Discussion Time**

Check understanding of the story and development of personal values.

- What was Carlos looking for at breakfast time?
- Why was he upset with Rosa?
- When Carlos called Rosa "dumb," how did Mr. Vasquez respond?
- Describe the substitute teacher Rosa's class had that day.
- What did Miss Horace do when Christopher got up to sharpen his pencil?
- What did Rosa make during art time?
- What made Rosa and her classmates realize that they were doing wrong?

A Preview

Write **each word as your teacher says it.**

Name _____

1. flu
2. useless
3. foolish
4. view
5. cue
6. include
7. funeral
8. confuse
9. canoe
10. dune
11. tulip
12. tomb
13. raccoon
14. crew
15. accuse
16. igloo
17. truly
18. future
19. Utah
20. Massachusetts

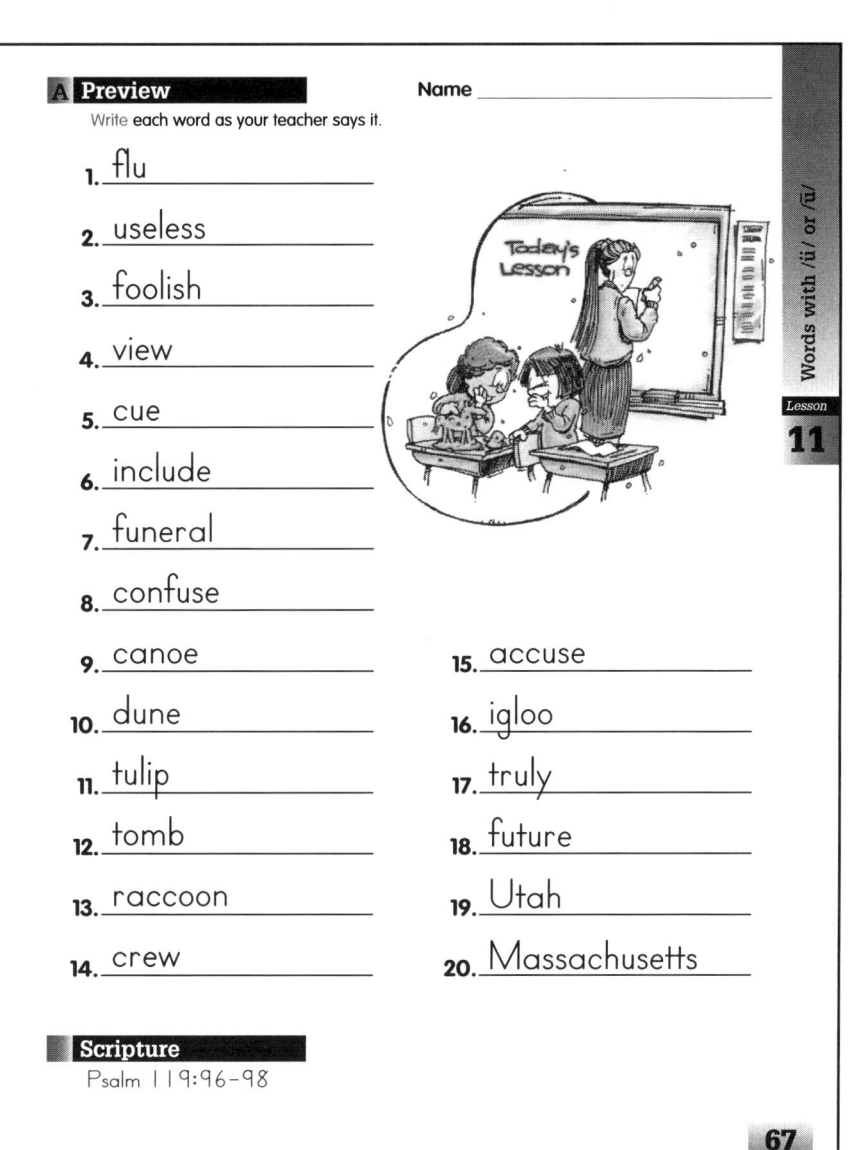

Scripture
Psalm 119:96-98

67

Customize Your List
On a separate sheet of paper, additional words of your choice may be tested.

 I will say each word once, use the word in a sentence, then say the word again. Write the words on the lines in your Worktext.

Correct Immediately!
 Let's correct our Preview. I will spell each word out loud. If you spelled a word incorrectly, rewrite it correctly.

Progress Chart
 Students may record scores. (Reproducible master provided in Appendix B.)

1.	flu	The whole class thought having Miss Horace for a teacher was as bad as having the **flu.**
2.	useless	They felt like trying to please Miss Horace was **useless.**
3.	foolish	Christopher felt **foolish** when she would not let him sharpen his pencil.
4.	view	Rosa got Katelynn's attention so she could **view** her sculpture.
5.	cue	Her classmate began to snicker right on **cue.**
6.	include	Mr. Canfield always tried to **include** everyone in interesting discussions.
7.	funeral	Miss Horace looked like she had just come from a **funeral.**
8.	confuse	It was impossible to **confuse** the two teachers' methods, as they are opposite.
9.	canoe	Talking to her was like paddling a **canoe** upstream.
10.	dune	Daniel compared being in her class to climbing a **dune** without any water!
11.	tulip	Setsuko carefully shaped a small piece of clay into a **tulip.**
12.	tomb	Thorny made a realistic Egyptian **tomb** out of his lump of clay.
13.	raccoon	Beth made an adorable **raccoon** family sitting on a log.
14.	crew	A road **crew** was repairing a portion of the school parking lot.
15.	accuse	"Did she **accuse** you of talking during the test?" Daniel asked Tommy.
16.	igloo	Sarah made a miniature **igloo** out of clay.
17.	truly	They were **truly** sorry they had made fun of Miss Horace.
18.	future	"In the **future,** we need to let God's words be in our mouths," said Tommy.
19.	Utah	Miss Horace's parents live in **Utah,** where she used to teach.
20.	Massachusetts	She is hoping to get a job in **Massachusetts.**

4 Word Shapes

Help students form a correct image of whole words.

Say Look at each word and think about its shape. Now, write the word in the correct Word Shape Boxes. You may check off each word as you use it.

(In most words, the sound of /ü/ is spelled with **oo**, or **u**. However, the sound of /ü/ can also be spelled with **o**, **oe**, **ew**, or **u-consonant-e**.) The sound of /ū/ can be spelled with **ue**, **ew**, **eu**, or **ie**.

Say In the Word Shape Boxes, fill in the boxes containing the letter or letters that spell the sound of /ū/ or /ü/ in each word.

Take a minute to memorize...
Psalm 119:96-98

B Word Shapes

Name _____

Using the word bank below, write each word in the correct Word Shape Boxes. Next, in the Word Shape Boxes, fill in the boxes containing the letter or letters that spell the sound of /ü/ or /ū/ in each word.

Words with /ü/ or /ū/ — Lesson **11**

1. foolish
2. igloo
3. dune
4. cue
5. truly
6. tulip
7. canoe
8. view
9. Massachusetts
10. confuse
11. include
12. crew
13. funeral
14. Utah
15. future
16. flu
17. useless
18. tomb
19. accuse
20. raccoon

Word Bank

accuse	cue	funeral	Massachusetts	tulip
canoe	dune	future	raccoon	useless
confuse	flu	igloo	tomb	Utah
crew	foolish	include	truly	view

68

Answers may vary for duplicate word shapes.

Be Prepared For Fun

Check these supply lists for **Fun Ways to Spell** - presented **Day 2**. Purchase and/or gather these items ahead of time!

General
- Pencil
- Graph Paper (1 sheet per child)
- Spelling List

Auditory
- Pencil
- Notebook Paper
- Spelling List

Visual
- Colored Pencils
- Alphabet Stencils
- Paper

Tactile
- Uncooked Rice
- Art Paper (1 sheet per child)
- Glue
- Spelling List

C **Hide and Seek**

Name _____

Play **Hide and Seek** with your words. Fill in a box on the bar graph (left to right) for each word you spell correctly.

LOOK   SAY   SPELL ALOUD   WRITE   SEEK   CHECK

D **Other Word Forms**

Using the words below, follow the instructions given by your teacher.

accusation	crewed	futurity	tulips
accused	cueing	igloos	useful
canoed	cues	included	uselessness
canoeing	dunes	including	Utahan
confusing	foolishly	influenza	viewed
confusion	foolishness	raccoons	viewing
crewcut	funerals	tombs	

E **Fun Ways to Spell**

Initial the box of each activity you finish.

1.

Spell your words in a "Word Find."

2.

Spell your words with stencils.

3.

M·i·s·s·i·s·s·i·p·p·i

Play "Spelling Tic-Tac-Toe."

4.

Spell your words with rice.

69

1 **Hide and Seek**

Reinforce spelling by using multiple styles of learning.

On a white board, Teacher writes each word — one at a time. **Have students:**

- **Look** at the word.
- **Say** the word out loud.
- **Spell** the word out loud.
- **Hide** (teacher erases word.)
- **Write** the word on paper.
- **Seek** (teacher rewrites word.)
- **Check** spelling. If incorrect, rewrite word correctly.

2 **Other Word Forms**

This activity is optional. Have students write original sentences using these Other Word Forms:

viewed
dunes
uselessness
confusion

3 **Fun Ways to Spell**

Four activities are provided. Use one, two, three, or all of the activities. Have students initial the box for each activity they complete.

Options:

- assign activities to students according to their learning styles
- set up the activities in learning centers for the students to do throughout the day
- divide students into four groups and assign one activity per group
- do one activity per day

General

To spell your words in a "Word Find"...
- Arrange your words on a piece of graph paper.
- Put one letter of each word in a square.
- Words may be written backwards, forwards, or diagonally.
- Outline your puzzle.
- Hide your words by filling in all the spaces inside the puzzle with random letters.
- Trade grids with a classmate and find the hidden words.

Auditory

To play "Spelling Tic-Tac-Toe"...
- Draw a Tic-Tac-Toe grid.
- Ask a classmate to read a word from the list.
- Spell the word aloud.
- If the word is spelled correctly, place your mark on the grid.
- Take turns with your classmate.

Visual

To spell your words with stencils...
- Look at the first letter of a word on your list.
- Place the stencil for the proper letter over your paper.
- Shade inside the stencil.
- Choose the proper stencil for the next letter of the word and shade it in next to the first letter.
- Finish the word in this way.
- Do this with each word.

Tactile

To spell your words with rice...
- Choose a word from your spelling list.
- Shape the letters of your word with rice.
- Glue the rice to art paper.
- Do this for each word on your list.

107

Working with Words

Familiarize students with word meaning and usage.

Secret Words

The boxed letters in the acrostic are a phrase from the Scripture verse for this week.

Say

Use the clues to write the words in the puzzle. You may use a dictionary to help you. Then write the boxed letters on the lines below to find the secret words from this week's Scripture.

Take a minute to memorize...

Psalm 119:96-98

Lesson 11 | Day 3

F Working with Words

Name _____

Secret Words

Use the clues to write the words in the puzzle. Then write the boxed letters on the lines below to find the secret words from this week's Scripture.

Words with /ü/ or /ū/

Lesson 11

1. t r u l y
2. c o n f u s e
3. c u e
4. f u t u r e
5. c r e w
6. c a n o e
7. r a c c o o n
8. i n c l u d e
9. M a s s a c h u s e t t s
10. U t a h
11. f u n e r a l
12. v i e w
13. t o m b
14. y
15. i g l o o
16. a c c u s e
17. t u l i p
18. d u n e
19. u s e l e s s

1. absolutely, really
2. bewilder, baffle
3. suggestion, hint
4. afterward, by-and-by
5. group, gang
6. dugout, kayak
7. masked animal
8. involve, comprise
9. New England state
10. mountain state north of Arizona
11. burial ceremony
12. scene, vista
13. grave, memorial
14. 25th letter of the alphabet
15. ice house
16. blame, reproach
17. spring flower
18. small round hill
19. futile, hopeless

Write the secret phrase:

Y o u r   w o r d s   a r e   m y   g u i d e .

Word Bank

accuse	cue	funeral	Massachusetts	tulip
canoe	dune	future	raccoon	useless
confuse	flu	igloo	tomb	Utah
crew	foolish	include	truly	view

70

G Dictation

Name _____

Write each sentence as your teacher dictates. Use correct punctuation.

1. Carlos read his paper about how native tribes built canoes and igloos.

2. Christopher found that it was useless to argue with the teacher.

3. Once the children read the words, they quit saying foolish and unkind things.

H Proofreading

If a word is misspelled, fill in the oval by that word. If all the words are spelled correctly, fill in the oval by **no mistake**.

1. ○ banjo
    ○ crew
    ● canoo
    ○ no mistake

2. ● confuze
    ○ studio
    ○ boldly
    ○ no mistake

3. ○ igloo
    ○ voltage
    ○ stereo
    ● no mistake

4. ● veiw
    ○ include
    ○ cargo
    ○ no mistake

5. ○ foolish
    ○ truly
    ○ flamingo
    ● no mistake

6. ○ tomb
    ● tullip
    ○ dome
    ○ no mistake

7. ○ dune
    ● funneral
    ○ macro
    ○ no mistake

8. ○ control
    ○ enroll
    ● Massachusitts
    ○ no mistake

9. ○ patrol
    ○ raccoon
    ○ useless
    ● no mistake

10. ○ portfolio
    ○ future
    ● Utaw
    ○ no mistake

11. ○ cue
    ○ flu
    ○ buffalo
    ● no mistake

12. ● accuze
    ○ soldier
    ○ sole
    ○ no mistake

71

---

1 Dictation

Reinforce correct spelling by using current and previous words in context.

(Say)

Listen as I read each sentence and then write it in your Worktext. Remember to use correct capitalization and punctuation. (Slowly read each sentence twice. Sentences are found in the Student Worktext to the left.)

2 Proofreading

Familiarize students with standardized test format and reinforce recognition of misspelled words.

(Say)

Look at each set of words. If a word is misspelled, fill in the oval by that word. If all the words are spelled correctly, fill in the oval by **no mistake**.

109

3 Hide and Seek

Reinforce correct spelling of current spelling words. Repeat this activity from Day 2.

4 Vocabulary Extension

Have your students complete this activity to strengthen spelling ability and expand vocabulary. The reproducible master is provided in Appendix A as shown on the inset page to the right.

1 Posttest

Visit the **A Reason For** website to download free, printable Posttest pages.

I will say the word once, use it in a sentence, then say it again. Write your words on a separate sheet of paper.

Progress Chart

Students may record scores. (Appendix B)

Personal Dictionary

Students may add any words they have misspelled to their personal dictionaries. (Appendix B)

Hide and Seek

Play Hide and Seek with your words. Fill in a bar graph (left to right) for each word you spell correctly.

LOOK SAY HIDE WRITE SEEK CHECK

Vocabulary Extension
Fill in the Blanks
Choose a word from the word bank that best fits each sentence clue.

1. When I saw my brother playing with my yo-yo, I had to ____conclude____ that he had taken it.

2. We did not mean to ____exclude____ you; we accidentally left you out of the game.

3. Grandma always smells like a rose garden. I like the ____perfume____ she wears.

4. When my sister broke her leg, lots of people sent flowers to her. Their kindness was abundant and ____profuse____.

5. I am memorizing a verse in the 26th book of the New Testament. I am learning a verse in the book of ____Jude____.

6. My grandfather thinks I look very young. He comments on how ____youthful____ I seem.

7. I have good opinions and feelings about school. I have a positive ____attitude____.

8. My mother-in-law's name was Naomi. I was kind to her. I later married Boaz. My name was ____Ruth____.

9. The round black part of your eye that lets light travel through it is called the ____pupil____.

10. I was a doctor and wrote the third gospel. I also traveled with Paul. My name was ____Luke____.

11. The earth, the planets, the stars and everything in space make up the ____universe____.

12. My brother likes to make funny little drawings. He likes to draw ____cartoon____s.

Word Bank

attitude	exclude	perfume	Ruth
cartoon	Jude	profuse	universe
conclude	Luke	pupil	youthful

334

---

1. crew — The class saw the road **crew** working to repair the school parking lot.
2. funeral — Miss Horace looked as cheerful as if she'd just come from a **funeral**.
3. canoe — "Talking to her is like paddling your **canoe** upstream," exclaimed Beth.
4. useless — "Pleasing her is **useless**, I'd say," replied Rosa.
5. view — Daniel thought he was out of her **view** as he made his silly faces.
6. flu — "I'd rather have the **flu** than have her for a teacher," he said with a groan.
7. cue — As if on **cue**, Miss Horace turned around to see what Daniel was doing.
8. include — She did not make an attempt to **include** the class in any exciting discussions.
9. foolish — Her harshness made Christopher feel **foolish**.
10. accuse — "I don't want her to **accuse** me of anything," worried Tony.
11. confuse — On the quiz, Matthew found it easy to **confuse** adjectives and adverbs.
12. tulip — Setsuko made more than one **tulip** and arranged them in a clay vase.
13. tomb — Thorny scored the sides of his Egyptian **tomb** to look like stone.
14. raccoon — "Do you like my **raccoon**, Laney?" Beth asked.
15. igloo — Sarah shaped several little figures to stand outside her **igloo**.
16. dune — At lunch, Thorny said Miss Horace's teaching delivery was as dry as a desert **dune**.
17. truly — When the class saw the verse on the board they were **truly** sorry.
18. future — "Our words should be more carefully chosen in the **future**," commented Thorny.
19. Massachusetts — Miss Horace is looking for a teaching position in **Massachusetts**.
20. Utah — She recently visited her parents in **Utah**.

I Game

Name _____

Follow along with Mr. Canfield's class to meet their substitute teacher. Move one space for each word you or your team spells correctly.

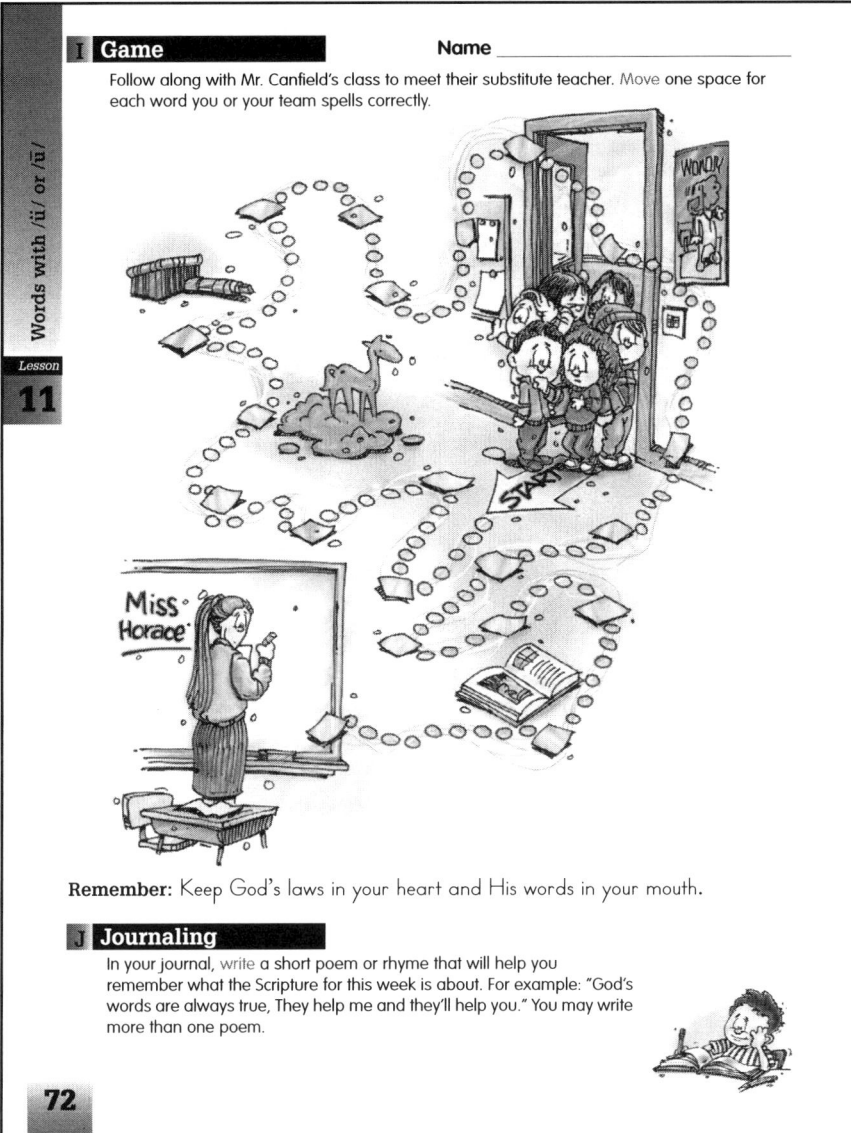

Remember: Keep God's laws in your heart and His words in your mouth.

J Journaling

In your journal, write a short poem or rhyme that will help you remember what the Scripture for this week is about. For example: "God's words are always true, They help me and they'll help you." You may write more than one poem.

72

How to Play:

- Divide the class into two teams.
- Have each student place his/her game piece on Start.
- Have a student from team A go to the board.
- Say the spelling word.
- Have the student write the word on the board.
- If correct, instruct each member of team A to move his/her game piece forward one space.
- Alternate between teams A and B.
- The team to reach Miss Horace first is the winner.
- **Small Group Option**: Students may play this game without teacher direction in small groups of two or more.

2 Game

Reinforce spelling skills and provide motivation and interest.

Materials

- game page (from student text)
- game pieces (1 per child)
- game word list

Game Word List

1. canoe
2. crew
3. cue
4. flu
5. igloo
6. view
7. include
8. foolish
9. truly
10. tulip
11. tomb
12. dune
13. funeral
14. raccoon
15. Massachusetts
16. useless
17. accuse
18. confuse
19. future
20. Utah

3 Journaling

Provide a meaningful reason for correct spelling through personal writing.

Review the story using discussion leads provided on the following page. Encourage students to apply the Scriptural value in their journaling.

Journaling (continued)

Say

- Do you sometimes have disagreements with your brother or sister like Rosa and Carlos did? (Allow time to share experiences.)

- What things gave Rosa the idea of calling her substitute "Miss Horse?" (The teacher had a long straight brown pony tail, a long thin face, and her name was Miss Horace.)

- Why do you think the class made fun of Miss Horace? (They didn't like her because she was different from Mr. Canfield. She was strict and she didn't smile much.)

- Is it okay to make fun of people? Why or why not? (No. It is never okay to say things that belittle others.)

- How do you feel when people make fun of you or say unkind things about you?

- How can we be sure we never belittle others? (By making God's words our constant guide.)

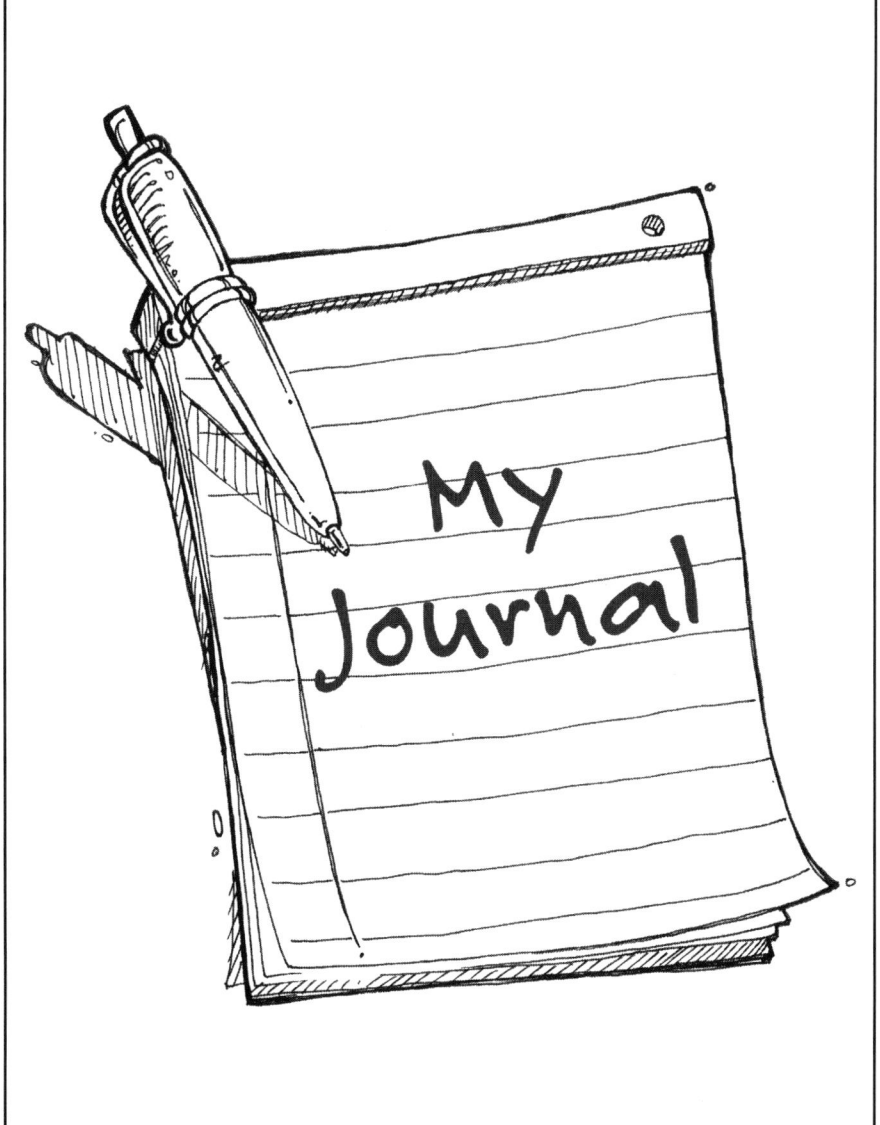

My Journal

A GOOGOL is the figure 1 followed by 100 zeros. Mathematician Edward Kasner supposedly asked his nephew, Milton, to suggest a name for the number. Milton came up with this word, which is now found in many dictionaries. The million, billion, trillion, quadrillion system skips over this number.

Word-Wow!

A Satisfying Solution

Stephen learns to be satisfied with God's answers to his prayer in God's time.

"Hey, Wimp!"

Stephen quickened his pace at the sound of the voice behind him. His hands shook as he grabbed the handle on the glass door.

A big hand reached out and seized his arm; a gruff voice snarled in his ear, "Watch yourself! Mr. Canfield can't be everywhere!" The big eighth grader glared down at Stephen before the younger boy darted into the gym behind his classmates.

"I want you to line up behind the free-throw line," Mr. Canfield was saying as Stephen joined his classmates. The big teacher spun the basketball in his hand, dribbled it under his right leg, then arched it effortlessly toward the basket. The ball swished through the net before it bounced toward the group of kids lining up.

Tony darted out of line, grabbed the orange ball, and passed it back to his teacher. Mr. Canfield dribbled the ball all around himself as he walked to the head of the line. He easily made 10 shots in a row before one bounced off the rim without swishing through the net. "Everyone gets 10 free-throws today," he said. "After the tenth, try a layup, then go to the end of the line."

Mr. Canfield grinned and threw the ball to Beth before he took another one out of the equipment bag and positioned himself underneath the backboard. When Beth's ball arched through the air toward the basket, Mr. Canfield threw her the next one.

"He's amazing!" Tony looked at his teacher in awe. "If he can't help us improve our game, nobody can. Laney says they pay him to ref at Mason Springs Park, so we can't complain about him not knowing the rules." Tony watched Beth continue to shoot.

Stephen ignored his friend's comments and absently rubbed his arm where Brutus had grabbed him. He shook his head as if to rid his brain of the bully's warning.

After her layup, Beth joined her friends at the end of the line. "I got four. Do you think you can beat that?"

"No one can beat Mr. Canfield!" Tony declared. "Even Brutus!"

Tony noticed Stephen wasn't joining in the conversation. "What's wrong with you, Stephen? You in trouble?"

"Brutus," Stephen whispered. "He caught me in the hall as I was coming in here. No one else was around. I don't know how he does that."

"Wha'd he say?" Beth asked.

"He said, 'Watch yourself! Mr. Canfield can't be everywhere!'"

"I think we should tell Mr. Canfield," declared Beth.

"I think if Brutus finds out we told, we'll be dead." Stephen rubbed his arm again. "He's right, you know—Mr. Canfield can't be everywhere."

After school that afternoon, Stephen didn't linger in the hall. He rushed to the curb when he saw the family car pull up.

"Surprise!" Mom said as he slipped in the back seat and slammed the door. "Look who's here!" Stephen peered around the headrest and grinned when he saw his grandma.

"When did you get here? How long can you stay? Did you drive? Is Grandpa here too? Why didn't you tell me you were coming? Can you come to my basketball game?"

"Just a minute, Stephen, my boy. One question at a time. We got here about noon. We drove…." The three chatted happily all the way home. Stephen almost forgot about his trouble with Brutus.

After supper, Mom and Dad were in deep discussion with Grandpa about a church issue. They'd gone into the living room to look something up in the Scriptures.

Grandma joined Stephen at the sink. "How 'bout I wash and you dry, my boy?" The older woman smiled down at her grandson. "How's your problem with Brutus goin'? You haven't mentioned him lately." Grandma filled the sink with hot water. Stephen didn't answer immediately.

"I guess he graduated since he was in eighth grade last year," Grandma continued. "Praise the Lord! He never gives us more than we can bear. Did you ever tell your teacher about what he did last year?" The gray-haired woman squirted soap into the steamy water.

"Nope," Stephen finally answered. "We just tried to keep out of his way. I don't know what Mrs. Burton could have done anyway. Brutus is a lot bigger than she is."

"The Lord answers prayer, Stephen. In His own time." Grandma plunged her hands into the soapy dishwater and tackled the dinner plates. "When I look back, I'm always satisfied."

"You sound like the Scripture we're learning in school this week, Grandma." Stephen picked up a plate from the dish rack. "It goes something like this, 'I will bless you as long as I live, lifting up my hands to you in prayer. At last I shall be fully satisfied.'"

After a short pause Stephen said thoughtfully, "I'm glad He answers your prayers, but he doesn't seem to do that for me. Brutus flunked last year! He's back and he's worse than ever. I think he might be dealing drugs, but we can't prove it. A few weeks ago he grabbed me and Tony, and was about to slam us into the wall when our teacher caught him. He got in trouble, and now he's really out

113

to get me. For some reason he always picks on me. Today he grabbed my arm and said, 'Watch yourself! Mr. Canfield can't be everywhere.'" Stephen lifted his shirt sleeve to reveal the black-and-blue handprint, "Look what he did to my arm, Grandma."

Grandma sucked in her breath and carefully controlled her facial features. "My boy, this is soundin' serious. I think it's 'bout time you should be tellin' someone, like your teacher. You want me to go with you?"

"No, Grandma." Stephen put the clean plate in the cupboard. "I can tell Mr. Canfield. He's bigger than Brutus. You should see him play basketball! But if Brutus ever found out I told on him, I'd be dead. And he always seems to find me."

"Maybe you could telephone your teacher. Brutus can't see you do that. You should always stick with a friend, too. Never go anywhere at school alone. That way if Brutus ever did anything to you, it wouldn't just be your word against his. If Mr. Canfield understands what's happenin'—I'm sure he'll help you."

Stephen nodded thoughtfully and picked up another plate to dry.

"I'll be prayin' for you, Stephen. I'll ask the good Lord to surround you with angels that excel in strength. I'll be prayin' that you'll be fully satisfied when this is over. I'll finish the dishes here. You better be makin' that phone call."

At lunch recess the next day, no one paid much attention when a police car parked in front of Knowlton Elementary. Everyone was used to seeing Officer Klein and Kelly coming to the school for D.A.R.E. classes. They were surprised, though, when he came out a few minutes later, followed by Brutus and an officer they didn't recognize. Brutus tried to jerk away from the officer, and kicked at his shins. The officers put Brutus into the back seat of the police car, and drove away.

All kinds of rumors flew around the school. Some eighth graders said Brutus had been caught selling drugs. Sandra was telling everyone he'd been framed by older high school guys who drove a Corvette. Some younger kids thought he'd flunked a drug test. One kid thought Officer Klein's dog had found drugs in his desk. None of the teachers at Knowlton Elementary would say why Brutus was taken away by the police.

The next day it was spread across the front page of the local newspaper for everyone to see. "Local Youth Arrested on Drug Charges," screamed the bold, black headline.

"It doesn't look like Brutus will be back to school," Grandma said as she showed Stephen the newspaper that evening. "I think we can praise the Lord with great joy for solving your problem."

"I know, but I'm kinda in the habit of praying for him now, Grandma."

"I don't think you have to stop just because you're satisfied he won't be botherin' you any more. I'm sure he needs your prayers more than ever now. Poor boy, it says here his mama works nights and his daddy is already servin' time for armed robbery up north somewhere. Why don't you come in here to my room and we'll praise the Lord for solving your problem—and ask Him to keep workin' on Brutus?" The older woman put her arm around Stephen's broadening shoulders and gave her grandson a tight squeeze. "There is tremendous power in prayer, my boy—tremendous power."

2 Discussion Time

Check understanding of the story and development of personal values.

- How did Stephen feel when he saw his grandma in the car?
- What did Grandma ask him about when they were finally alone?
- What are some things you might pray about over an extended period of time?
- Talk about how long it has taken God to answer some of your prayers.
- How does Stephen feel now that he doesn't have to worry anymore about Brutus?
- What are some ways you can praise God?

A Test-Words

Name _____

Write each spelling word on the line as your teacher says it.

1. escape
2. chase
3. prey
4. arrive
5. shriek
6. brief
7. silence
8. foolish
9. accuse
10. height
11. admire
12. include
13. guys
14. sole
15. useless
16. soldier

Review

Lesson 12

B Test-Sentences

Write the sentences on the lines below, correcting each misspelled word, as well as all capitalization and punctuation errors. Two words are misspelled in each sentence.

it has been a deckade since we have been to maine?

1. It has been a decade since we have been to Maine.

everyone is eeger to leave on the skying trip:

2. Everyone is eager to leave on the skiing trip.

he painted the bufaloe on the plains of whyoming

3. He painted the buffalo on the plains of Wyoming.

the racoon jumped into the canoo

4. The raccoon jumped into the canoe.

73

4 Test-Sentences

Reinforce recognizing misspelled words.

Say Read each sentence carefully. Write the sentences on the lines in your Worktext. There are two misspelled words in each sentence. Correct each misspelled word, as well as all capitalization and punctuation errors.

Take a minute to memorize...

Psalm 63:3-5

Review **12** | Day 1

3 Test-Words

Test for knowledge of the correct spellings of these words.

Say I will say each word once, use the word in a sentence, then say the word again. Write the words on the lines in your Worktext.

1. escape — Stephen thought there might be no **escape** from Brutus.
2. chase — He knew Brutus could **chase** him down easily.
3. prey — Stephen felt like Brutus was a lion and he was his **prey**!
4. arrive — Stephen was afraid and eager to **arrive** safely in the gym.
5. shriek — He stifled a **shriek** when Brutus grabbed him by the arm.
6. brief — For one **brief** moment, Stephen thought Brutus might hit him.
7. silence — There was an awkward **silence** after Brutus made his threat.
8. foolish — Stephen felt **foolish** and shaken after his meeting with the bully.
9. accuse — Stephen knew that Brutus would **accuse** him of telling.
10. height — Mr. Canfield suggested that Matthew put some **height** on the ball.
11. admire — The class does greatly **admire** Mr. Canfield.
12. include — Mr. Canfield is always eager to **include** all his students.
13. guys — All the **guys** would like to be tall and athletic like their teacher.
14. sole — Sometimes he is the **sole** referee at the games in the park.
15. useless — "Are my prayers **useless**?" he asked himself.
16. soldier — Stephen's grandmother is a faithful **soldier** in the Lord's army.

115

Test-Dictation

Reinforce correct spelling by using current and previous words in context.

 Say

Listen as I read each sentence, then write it in your worktext. Remember to use correct capitalization and punctuation. (Slowly read each sentence twice. Sentences are found in the student text to the right. The words **diary**, **idea**, **vein**, and **Pennsylvania** are found in this unit.)

Test-Proofreading

Familiarize students with standardized test format and reinforce recognizing misspelled words.

 Say

Look at each set of words. If a word is misspelled, fill in the oval by that word. If all the words are spelled correctly, fill in the oval by **no mistake**.

C Test-Dictation   Name _____

Write **each sentence as your teacher dictates**. Use correct punctuation.

1. She will write everything in her diary.
2. It was a good idea to have our neighbor over.
3. Can you see the vein carrying the blood?
4. Take your camera to beautiful Pennsylvania.

Review
Lesson 12

D Test-Proofreading

If a word is misspelled, fill in the oval by that word. If all the words are spelled correctly, fill in the oval by **no mistake**.

1. ○ escape
   ● meater
   ○ chase
   ○ no mistake

2. ● Huwaii
   ○ prey
   ○ arrive
   ○ no mistake

3. ○ shriek
   ○ brief
   ● viel
   ○ no mistake

4. ○ silence
   ● aliby
   ○ foolish
   ○ no mistake

5. ○ accuse
   ○ height
   ● beyte
   ○ no mistake

6. ○ flamingo
   ○ admire
   ○ include
   ● no mistake

7. ○ guys
   ● doughnate
   ○ sole
   ○ no mistake

8. ● leeter
   ○ useless
   ○ soldier
   ○ no mistake

9. ● appeel
   ○ boldly
   ○ patrol
   ○ no mistake

10. ○ crater
    ○ view
    ○ relief
    ● no mistake

11. ○ detail
    ○ rashio
    ○ contain
    ○ no mistake

12. ○ stereo
    ○ decay
    ● maysa
    ○ no mistake

74

E Test-Table

Name _____

If a word is misspelled, fill in the space on the grid.

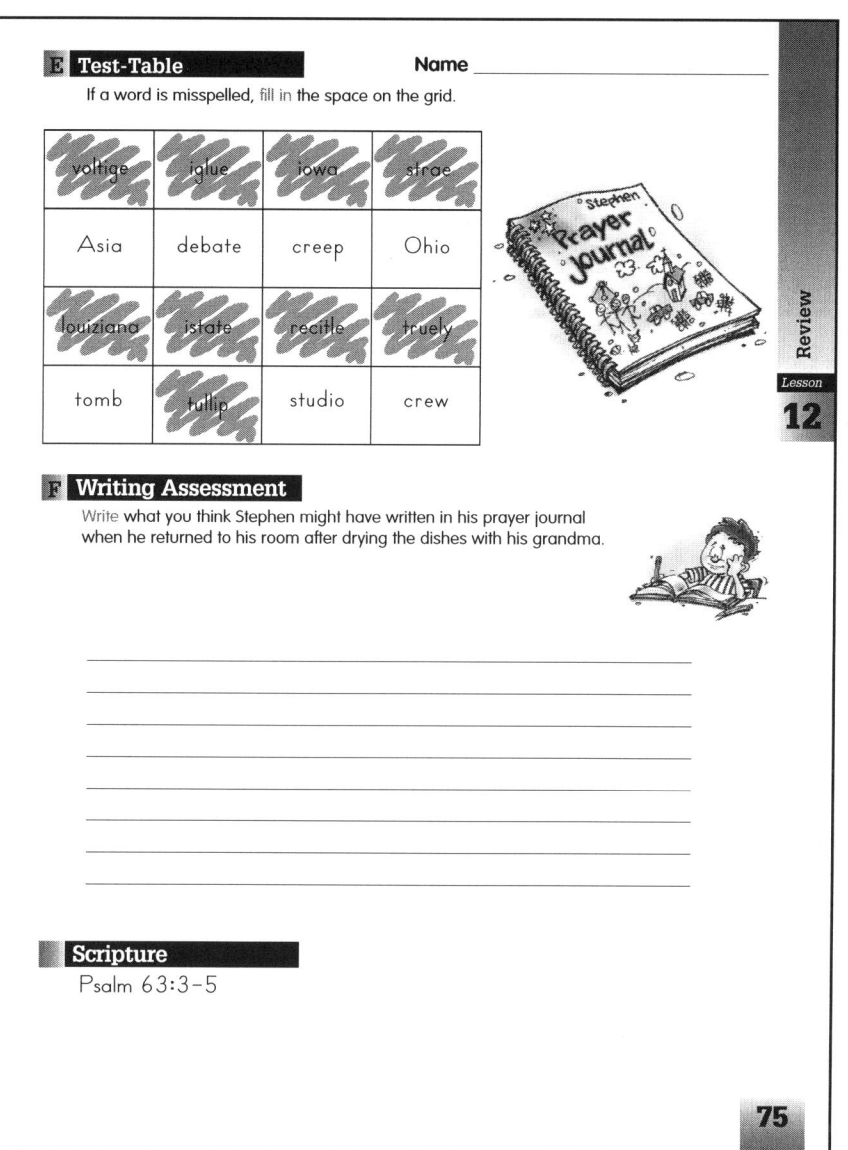

~~voltige~~	~~iglue~~	~~iowa~~	~~strae~~
Asia	debate	creep	Ohio
~~louiziana~~	~~istate~~	~~recitle~~	~~truely~~
tomb	~~tullip~~	studio	crew

F Writing Assessment

Write what you think Stephen might have written in his prayer journal when he returned to his room after drying the dishes with his grandma.

_____

_____

_____

_____

_____

_____

_____

Scripture

Psalm 63:3–5

75

A rubric for scoring is provided in Appendix B.

Test-Table
1

Test mastery of words in this unit.

(Say) If a word is misspelled, fill in the space on the grid.

Writing Assessment
2

Assess student's spelling, grammar, and composition skills through personal writing.

(Say)
- What do you think would cause someone to be a bully? (Students may suggest: home environment, lack of good role models, dissatisfaction with size, low self-esteem, desire to dominate, wish to have own way, or perception of unfairness)
- What did Grandma think Stephen should do about Brutus? (Call and tell Mr. Canfield what was happening.)
- When Grandma told Stephen why Brutus had been arrested, how did Stephen feel? (He was relieved, but also thought he'd keep praying for him.)

Review 12 | **Day 3**

"I" is the most commonly spoken word in English, followed by "you," "the," and "a."

Word-Wow!

1 Test-Sentences

Reinforce recognizing
misspelled words.

Say

Read each sentence
carefully. Write the
sentences on the lines in
your Worktext, correcting
each misspelled word, as
well as all capitalization
and punctuation errors.

G Test-Sentences   Name _____

Write the sentences on the lines below, correcting each misspelled word, as well as all
capitalization and punctuation errors. Two words are misspelled in each sentence.

Review

Lesson
12

we plan to visit a mackro gyser in this state park?

1. We plan to visit a macro geyser in this state park.

he held up his sheald and began to weild his sword

2. He held up his shield and began to wield his sword.

the peice of cake was moist and had great flaver

3. The piece of cake was moist and had great flavor!

the ship took the cargoe to a small ile nearby

4. The ship took the cargo to a small isle nearby.

H Test-Words

Write each spelling word on the line as your teacher says it.

1. boldly   9. deceit

2. patrol   10. minor

3. view   11. liar

4. relief   12. wife

5. detail   13. guide

6. contain   14. control

7. stereo   15. confuse

8. decay   16. future

76

---

2 Test-Words

Test for knowledge of the correct spellings of these words.

Say

I will say the word once, use the word in a sentence, then say
the word again. Write the word on the lines in your Worktext.

1. boldly   "You've got to keep comin' **boldly** before the Lord," said Grandma.

2. patrol   No one was surprised to see the **patrol** car parked in front of the school.

3. view   The kids looked outside to get a **view** of Brutus.

4. relief   Stephen felt a great **relief** when the officer took Brutus away.

5. detail   The next morning's newspaper told every **detail** of the arrest.

6. contain   The story did **contain** a lot of details Stephen didn't know.

7. stereo   The police found a **stereo** and other expensive things in the eighth grader's house.

8. decay   Brutus had shown an even greater **decay** in his attitude.

9. deceit   He regularly practiced **deceit** with his mom and his teachers.

10. minor   Since Brutus is a **minor**, it was not clear what charges would be pressed.

11. liar   The newspaper described his dad as a **liar** and a thief.

12. wife   It said his **wife** worked nights at a factory.

13. guide   Neither of his parents had been a good **guide** for Brutus.

14. control   Brutus has never given God **control** of his life.

15. confuse   It was easy for Brutus to **confuse** having money with having security.

16. future   "We need to be prayin' for Brutus and his **future**," encouraged Grandma.

I Test-Editing

Name _____

If a word is spelled correctly, fill in the oval under **Correct**. If the word is misspelled, fill in the oval under **Incorrect**, and spell the word correctly on the blank.

		Correct	Incorrect	
1.	labor	●	○	
2.	reveel	○	●	reveal
3.	porto reeco	○	●	Puerto Rico
4.	Tennessee	●	○	
5.	vetoes	●	○	
6.	diet	●	○	
7.	reiut	○	●	riot
8.	idahoe	○	●	Idaho
9.	banjo	●	○	
10.	inrole	○	●	enroll
11.	portfolio	●	○	
12.	cue	●	○	
13.	flu	●	○	
14.	doone	○	●	dune
15.	funral	○	●	funeral
16.	massechusettes	○	●	Massachusetts
17.	Utah	●	○	
18.	dome	●	○	
19.	Oklahoma	●	○	
20.	Minnisoda	○	●	Minnesota

77

4 Action Game

Reinforce spelling skills and provide motivation and interest.

Materials

- masking tape
- two 9 x 13 inch pans of damp sand
- word list on certificate at end of unit

SAND RELAY

Divide the class into two teams. Mark a line on the floor and line each team up behind that line. Place two containers of sand a few yards on the other side of the line. Choose a team leader for each team. Each team leader holds a list of spelling words to be reviewed and stands by his or her team's sand. When you give the signal to begin, the first player from each team runs to the sand where his or her team leader will say a spelling word. The player will write the word in the sand while the team leader checks the spelling. If the word is misspelled the player is given a different word to spell. If the word is spelled correctly, the player runs back to the line. When the player crosses the line, the next player runs to the sand to spell a word. The first team to finish wins!

119

1 Game

Reinforce spelling skills and provide motivation and interest.

Materials
- game page (from student text)
- colored pencils (1 per child)
- game word list

Game Word List
Check off each word lightly in pencil as it is used.

Stephen's Team

1. meter
2. Hawaii
3. veil
4. alibi
5. byte
6. flamingo
7. donate
8. liter
9. appeal

Officer Klein's Team

1. crater
2. ratio
3. mesa
4. voltage
5. Asia
6. Louisiana
7. tomb
8. igloo
9. debate

Mr. Canfield's Team

1. estate
2. tulip
3. Iowa
4. creep
5. recital
6. studio
7. stray
8. Ohio
9. truly

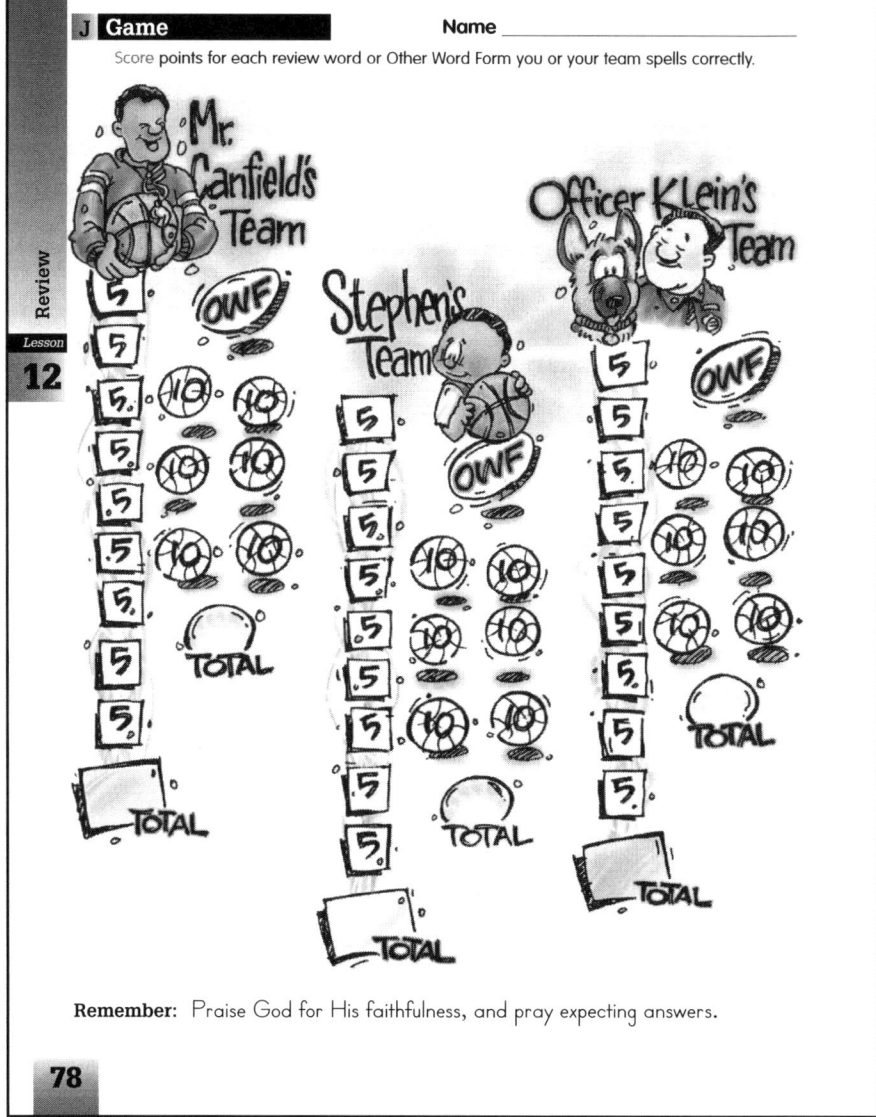

J Game   Name _____

Score points for each review word or Other Word Form you or your team spells correctly.

Review Lesson **12**

Remember: Praise God for His faithfulness, and pray expecting answers.

78

How to Play:
- Divide the class into three teams. Name one team **Stephen's Team**, one **Officer Klein's Team**, and one **Mr. Canfield's Team**. (Option: You may wish to seat students in groups of three, each student from a different team. They should share one game page.)
- Have a student from the first team go to the board.
- Say the spelling word.
- Have the student write the word on the board.
- If the word is spelled correctly, have each team member color a point symbol by his/her team name. If the word is misspelled, have him/her put an **X** through one point symbol. That word may not be given again.
- Repeat this process with the second team and then the third.
- When the words from all three lists have been used, the team with the most points is the winner.
- Play another round using Other Word Forms.

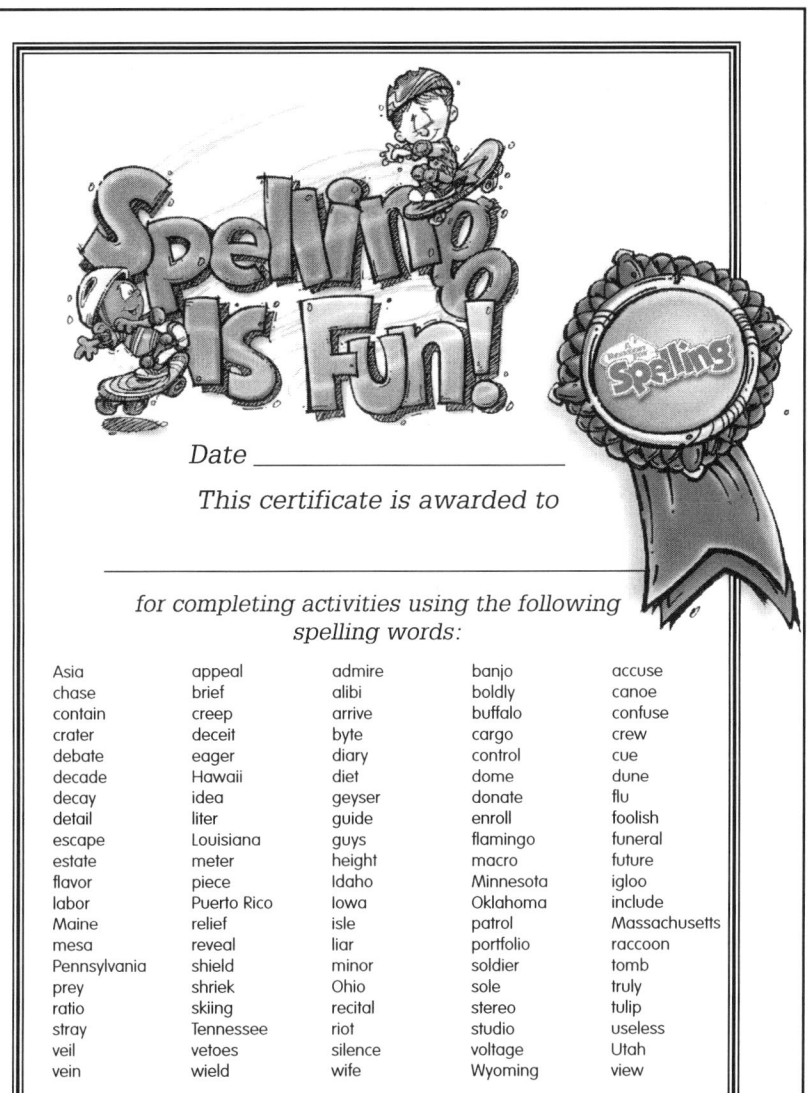

Date _____

This certificate is awarded to

_____

for completing activities using the following spelling words:

Asia	appeal	admire	banjo	accuse
chase	brief	alibi	boldly	canoe
contain	creep	arrive	buffalo	confuse
crater	deceit	byte	cargo	crew
debate	eager	diary	control	cue
decade	Hawaii	diet	dome	dune
decay	idea	geyser	donate	flu
detail	liter	guide	enroll	foolish
escape	Louisiana	guys	flamingo	funeral
estate	meter	height	macro	future
flavor	piece	Idaho	Minnesota	igloo
labor	Puerto Rico	Iowa	Oklahoma	include
Maine	relief	isle	patrol	Massachusetts
mesa	reveal	liar	portfolio	raccoon
Pennsylvania	shield	minor	soldier	tomb
prey	shriek	Ohio	sole	truly
ratio	skiing	recital	stereo	tulip
stray	Tennessee	riot	studio	useless
veil	vetoes	silence	voltage	Utah
vein	wield	wife	Wyoming	view

Certificate

Provide an opportunity for parents or guardians to encourage and assess their child's progress.

Say

Fill in today's date and your name on your certificate.

Take a minute to memorize...

Psalm 63:3-5

3 Letter

Provide the parent or guardian with the spelling word lists for the next unit.

(Say) Give your parents or guardian this letter that lists your spelling words for the next unit. Put it where you will remember to practice the words together.

Dear Parent,

We are about to begin a new spelling unit containing five weekly lessons. A set of twenty words will be studied each week. All the words will be reviewed in the sixth week. Values based on the Scriptures listed below will be taught in each lesson.

Lesson 13	Lesson 14	Lesson 15	Lesson 16	Lesson 17
Alabama	adopt	Antarctica	aerobics	aisle
Colorado	atomic	argument	area	aspire
combat	borrow	Arkansas	Arizona	biceps
gallon	bottom	artery	aware	climate
gallop	college	artichoke	barracks	combine
gather	colonies	bargain	barren	compile
Indiana	comment	cardiac	barrier	coyote
inhabit	commerce	cartilage	caramel	crime
mammal	compost	carton	compare	crisis
Nevada	concentrate	chart	Delaware	decline
New Hampshire	contact	compartment	embarrassed	device
perhaps	continent	dart	librarian	dining
random	conversation	department	marriage	entice
rascal	crocodile	harbor	narrate	eyeing
savanna	demolish	hardship	narrow	fiery
scallop	deposit	harmony	Ontario	haiku
soprano	doctor	hearty	parakeet	iceberg
static	geometry	partner	parallel	imply
valley	glossary	radar	prepare	migrant
valve	Wisconsin	snarl	software	pride
Psalm 119:29,30	Psalm 127:1	Psalm 98:7	Psalm 57:10	Psalm 18:30

Lost in Space

Christopher gets a new computer game and finds out that doing right may not mean just avoiding wrong.

Mr. Wright caught the sales clerk's attention. "Excuse me, sir. Do you carry the latest version of Tax Manager?"

"I believe that's in. Just a moment, please, and I'll check."

Christopher wandered over to a display of computer games while his dad rested an elbow on the checkout counter to wait for the clerk. Some of the learning games looked familiar. Some of the other games looked kind of creepy.

Then he spotted it. Christopher grabbed the shiny black box with the gleaming, streamlined space vehicle in 3-D on the front. "Dad, the Hugheses have this game. It's fantastic! Jared and I played when we were over at their house last week. May I buy it?"

"Let's see that." Mr. Wright turned the box over and read the description of the game. "Hmmm. Choose from six spaceships or design your own...32 missions...Unexpected challenges...."

"I apologize for the wait, sir." The sales clerk rushed back over. "Is this the program you needed?" He placed a box on the counter in front of Mr. Wright.

"That's it." Mr. Wright tapped the box.

"Will that be all, sir?" The clerk began ringing up the sale.

"No, we'll take this as well." Dad handed Christopher's game to the clerk and turned to his son, "You'll have to teach me how to play it sometime."

"All right!" Christopher raised a hand and gave his dad a high five. "It's a really great game! You'll see."

"Christopher, come play with me." Six-year-old Cory leaned on the back of Christopher's computer chair. Christopher's eyes never left the screen in front of him. "Not now, Cory." He shrugged his little brother's hands off his shoulders.

"But I haven't had anyone to play with all day while you guys were at school." Cory leaned over the chair to look up into his big brother's face.

"Cory! Get out of the way! I'm right in the middle of this mission!" Christopher's fingers worked the controls rapidly. He didn't notice when Cory finally gave up and left the room.

One afternoon later that week, Mrs. Wright called to her son, "Christopher, we're going for a walk since it's such nice weather. Want to go with us?"

"Not right now, Mom." Christopher took evasive action to avoid having his ship pulled into a gravitational field. "I'm busy!"

A few days later, Cathy, Christopher's nine-year-old sister, popped her head around the door. "Christopher, come play with us."

Christopher just shook his head while he checked fuel levels and judged the distance to the next planetary settlement.

"Christopher, come on!" Cathy persisted, "Cory and Kristin and I all want to play a board game, and it's a lot more fun with four people. Pleeeeeze?"

"Sorry, but I said no!" Christopher changed his speed and watched carefully for enemy craft in this sector. "Can't you see I'm already playing a game?"

"Of course!" Cathy tossed her head. "That's hard to miss. You've been playing that computer game constantly for two weeks!"

"Christopher, it's for you!" Mrs.

Wright handed the phone to her son where he sat at the computer, then walked toward the laundry room with a load of wash.

"Hello?" Christopher paused the game. "Hey, Jared!" He greeted his friend with enthusiasm. "Guess what? I'm already on level 12!...Yeah, the graphics are great!... Really?... Awesome!... Just a minute, let me ask my mom." Christopher hopped up to find his mother, taking the phone with him. "Yeah, that one almost caught me off guard on level 5...Did you manage to make it through sector seven-zero?... Oh, just a sec!"

Christopher dropped the phone from his ear when he arrived in the laundry room. "Mom, can I go shopping with the Hughes family this afternoon?"

Mrs. Wright scooped the last few fresh-smelling items out of the dryer and stood up. "Probably. Let me talk to Jared's mom for a minute and we'll see."

"Hey, Jared!" Christopher spoke into the phone. "Did you hear that?... Yeah, she wants to talk to your mom first, but I can probably go...Okay! See you soon." Christopher handed the phone over to his mom and rushed back to finish his game before Jared's family came to pick him up.

"Check this out, Chris." Jared and Christopher stopped in front of an eye-catching display in the store. "The expansion is out!"

"Amazing! Look at this," Christopher pointed to the list of capabilities and new challenges the add-on provided. "Awesome! I'm gonna get this."

"Dad said he'd take us to the food court as soon as he was done looking here. Why don't you wait till afterwards to get it?" Jared suggested. "That way you won't have to worry about hanging on to a package while you're eating."

Christopher was ready for a snack. "Let's go!"

"Let's see if Dad's done!"

123

Story (continued)

The next evening, Kristin frowned at the wrong answer she'd just written in her spelling book. "Christopher, let me use your eraser."

"Use your own." Christopher propped his elbow on the kitchen table and rested his chin in his hand.

"The eraser is worn off this pencil." Kristin held it up for her twin to see.

"Well, go get another one." Christopher waved his sister away with one hand. "I'm busy and I shouldn't have to do everything for you."

"That's it!" Kristin slapped the pencil down on the table. "You're always busy, and you never do anything for anyone anymore!"

Christopher frowned. "What're you talking about?"

"This!" Kristin thumped the spelling book in front of her. "Remember this Scripture?"

"Yeah," Christopher shrugged. "So?"

"Then you know it says you should obey and not do anything wrong. Don't you think spending your life playing computer games is wrong?" Kristin demanded.

"Of course not!" Christopher shook his head and rolled his eyes. "The game I'm playing isn't bloody and gross or satanic or anything! It's just a really great game!"

"Well, this Scripture says to 'keep me far from every wrong' not just 'keep me from doing wrong.'" Kristin stood up and brushed her hair back behind her ear. "It seems to me you're not far from being addicted to those games. You've spent every spare minute for the last two weeks playing that space exploration game, then you spent all your money on an expansion! That was what—$50?"

Kristin shook her head, still fuming at her twin. "You don't play with Cory, or Cathy, or me. You rush through your homework

and chores. You barely answer when someone talks to you." Kristin ticked each item off on her fingers. "You didn't even want to take time to talk to Dad when he called from LA during his business trip! Seems to me that computer game is all you care about. Maybe it's not violent or evil, but it's sure taken over your whole life."

Kristin walked a few steps toward the door, then turned back. "It may not be wrong—but it can't be far from it."

"Sisters!" Christopher muttered as she disappeared down the hall. "Now, where was I?" He ran his finger down the page of his book till he found where he'd been. "The desert was so still," Christopher read aloud. "Silence. Silence all around. Johnny could hear himself breathing. But what was that? A soft hiss…."

Christopher lapsed into silent reading when Kristin came back with an eraser. When he finished the story, Christopher picked up his pencil to write the report Mr. Canfield had assigned, but he couldn't remember what the story was about! Instead of the desert adventure he'd been reading about, his head was filled with scenes from his computer game.

Christopher shook his head, trying to clear it of space vehicles. "Uh, Kristin?" He grinned sheepishly when his twin looked up. "Maybe you had a good point. When this homework's done, you want to go shoot some baskets or something before dark?"

2 Discussion Time

Check understanding of the story and development of personal values.

- What was Christopher's dad looking for at the store?
- What kind of game did he get for Christopher?
- What did Christopher do when Cory wanted to play with him?
- What did Christopher do when the family went for a walk?
- What did Christopher do when Cathy, Kristin, and Cory wanted him to play a board game?
- Is it wrong to spend all your time doing one thing, even if that thing isn't a bad thing?

Name _____

1. soprano
2. Nevada
3. scallop
4. Alabama
5. gather
6. Colorado
7. random
8. valve
9. inhabit
10. gallon
11. combat
12. Indiana
13. valley
14. mammal
15. New Hampshire
16. savanna
17. static
18. perhaps
19. rascal
20. gallop

Words with /a/

Lesson **13**

81

3 **Preview**
Test for knowledge of the correct spellings of these words.

Customize Your List
On a separate sheet of paper, additional words of your choice may be tested.

Say I will say each word once, use the word in a sentence, then say the word again. Write the words on the lines in your Worktext.

Correct Immediately!
Say Let's correct our Preview. I will spell each word out loud. If you spelled a word incorrectly, rewrite it correctly.

Progress Chart
Students may record scores. (Reproducible master provided in Appendix B.)

Lesson **13** | Day 1

1.	soprano	Kristin practices the **soprano** part of the choral arrangement.
2.	Nevada	The new choir director from **Nevada** thinks Kristin has a real talent.
3.	scallop	She plans to take a **scallop** shell to school when they discuss marine life.
4.	Alabama	She found it on a beach in **Alabama** while they were on vacation last summer.
5.	gather	Kristin was able to **gather** many beautiful shells that day.
6.	Colorado	Christopher's cousin in **Colorado** e-mailed him about the new computer game.
7.	random	Selecting the game was not a **random** choice.
8.	valve	"I need to go by the auto supply store for a new **valve**," said his dad.
9.	inhabit	"Earn extra fuel if you **inhabit** Mars within 48 hours," Christopher read.
10.	gallon	He celebrated each **gallon** of fuel he conserved on a mission.
11.	combat	The **combat** mode of the game was really exciting!
12.	Indiana	He'd love to go to **Indiana** to meet the software designers who wrote the game.
13.	valley	The goal of the mission was to capture a station in a **valley** on Venus.
14.	mammal	"Which **mammal** did you decide to research for your paper?" she asked.
15.	New Hampshire	"Something that lives in **New Hampshire**," was his rude remark.
16.	savanna	"Or maybe something that lives on a **savanna** on Pluto," he snickered.
17.	static	"Can I talk to you on a channel that's not all **static**?" asked Kristin.
18.	perhaps	"**Perhaps** you shouldn't spend all your spare time in front of the computer!"
19.	rascal	Cory was being a **rascal** when he hid Christopher's mouse.
20.	gallop	Kristin laughed when Christopher began to **gallop** around the driveway.

125

Word Shapes

Help students form a correct image of whole words.

Say Look at each word and think about its shape. Now, write the word in the correct Word Shape Boxes. You may check off each word as you use it.

(Short vowels are usually found in syllables in which a vowel is immediately preceded and followed by a consonant, consonant cluster, or digraph.)

Say In the Word Shape Boxes, fill in the boxes containing the letter or letters that spell the sound of **/a/** in each word.

Take a minute to memorize...

Psalm 119: 29,30

B Word Shapes   **Name** _____

Using the word bank below, write each word in the correct Word Shape Boxes. Next, in the Word Shape Boxes, fill in the boxes containing the letter or letters that spell the sound of /a/ in each word.

Words with /a/

Lesson **13**

1. New Hampshire
2. Colorado
3. Nevada
4. mammal
5. savanna
6. static
7. Indiana
8. scallop
9. Alabama
10. gallon

11. gallop
12. valley
13. valve
14. soprano
15. combat
16. rascal
17. gather
18. inhabit
19. random
20. perhaps

Word Bank

Alabama	gallop	mammal	random	soprano
Colorado	gather	Nevada	rascal	static
combat	Indiana	New Hampshire	savanna	valley
gallon	inhabit	perhaps	scallop	valve

82

Answers may vary for duplicate word shapes.

Be Prepared For Fun

Check these supply lists for **Fun Ways to Spell** - presented **Day 2**.
Purchase and/or gather these items ahead of time!

General
- Pencil
- Graph Paper (1 sheet per child)
- Spelling List

Auditory
- Voice Recorder
- Spelling List

Visual
- American Sign Language reproducible master (provided in Appendix B)
- Spelling List

Tactile
- Soccer Ball, Basketball, Tennis Ball, or 4-Square Ball
- Spelling List

C Hide and Seek   Name _____

Play Hide and Seek with your words. Fill in a box on the bar graph (left to right) for each word you spell correctly.

LOOK   SAY   SPELL ALOUD   WRITE   SEEK   CHECK

D Other Word Forms

Using the words below, follow the instructions given by your teacher.

Alabaman	galloping	mammals	savannas
Coloradan	gathered	Nevadan	scalloped
combatant	gathering	New Hampshirite	sopranos
combative	Indianan	randomize	statically
gallons	inhabitant	randomly	valleys
galloped	inhabited	rascally	valves

E Fun Ways to Spell

Initial the box of each activity you finish.

1. ☐ Create a crossword puzzle with clues.

2. ☐ Spell your words with sign language.

3. W·O·R·D ☐ Spell your words on voice recorder.

4. B·A·T·C·H ☐ Bounce a ball as you spell your words.

83

---

1 Hide and Seek

Reinforce spelling by using multiple styles of learning.

On a white board, Teacher writes each word — one at a time. **Have students:**

- **Look** at the word.
- **Say** the word out loud.
- **Spell** the word out loud.
- **Hide** (teacher erases word.)
- **Write** the word on paper.
- **Seek** (teacher rewrites word.)
- **Check** spelling. If incorrect, rewrite word correctly.

2 Other Word Forms

This activity is optional. Have students find and circle the Other Word Forms that are antonyms of the following:

peaceful
dispersed
intentionally
deserted

3 Fun Ways to Spell

Four activities are provided. Use one, two, three, or all of the activities. Have students initial the box for each activity they complete.

Options:

- assign activities to students according to their learning styles
- set up the activities in learning centers for the students to do throughout the day
- divide students into four groups and assign one activity per group
- do one activity per day

General

To create a crossword puzzle...
- Use a pencil to arrange your words on graph paper.
- Overlap words where letters are shared.
- Don't create any new words.
- Outline each word with a marker and number it.
- Write a clue for each word.
- Erase your words.
- Trade with a classmate and work each other's puzzles.

Auditory

To spell your words using a voice recorder...
- Record yourself as you say and spell each word on your spelling list.
- Listen to your recording and check your spelling.

Visual

To spell your words with sign language...
- Have a classmate read a spelling word to you from the list.
- Spell the word using the American Sign Language alphabet.
- Do this with each word on your list.

Tactile

To bounce a ball as you spell your words...
- Look at the first word on your list.
- Bounce the ball as you say each letter of the word aloud.
- Do this with each word on your list.

Working with Words

Familiarize students with word meaning and usage.

Drawing Conclusions

Explain that to figure something out using logic is to draw a conclusion. On the board write:

You are using a tool to make holes in wood. You are probably using a _____.

Have a volunteer supply the word **drill**.

Complete each conclusion by writing a word from the word bank. You may use a dictionary to help you.

Take a minute to memorize...

Psalm 119: 29,30

F **Working with Words**　　　　Name _____

Drawing Conclusions

Complete each conclusion by writing a word from the word bank.

1. You choose by saying "Eeny, Meeny, Miny, Moe." You choose at __random__.
2. You hear noise on your phone. You may have __static__.
3. A singer has a high voice. She probably sings __soprano__.
4. You are moving to Concord. You may be going to __New Hampshire__.
5. You live in a house. This means you __inhabit__ it.
6. You are in a state whose name means "reddish-colored." You are in __Colorado__.
7. A farm girl has gone out to collect eggs. She will __gather__ them.
8. That baby animal is drinking milk from its mother. It is a __mammal__.
9. Your dad brought home a jug of milk. He probably bought a __gallon__.
10. A gazelle is grazing on grass. It is probably on the __savanna__.
11. The soldiers are digging trenches. They are about to enter __combat__.
12. One student is very mischievous. He could be considered a __rascal__.
13. We camped in a low place between two mountains. We were in a __valley__.
14. One state is called "The Heart of Dixie." It is the state of __Alabama__.
15. You think you possibly might do something. You think __perhaps__ you might.
16. Your horse is running fast. He is probably going at a __gallop__.
17. You may want to visit the midwest state nicknamed "The Hoosier State." You may want to visit __Indiana__.
18. He closed something to keep the liquid flowing in the right direction. He closed a __valve__.
19. You will be driving through Las Vegas to get to Hoover Dam. You will be in the state of __Nevada__.
20. You cut a fancy rounded edge on your Valentine. You may have cut a __scallop__.

Word Bank

Alabama	gallop	mammal	random	soprano
Colorado	gather	Nevada	rascal	static
combat	Indiana	New Hampshire	savanna	valley
gallon	inhabit	perhaps	scallop	valve

84

G Dictation

Name _____

Write **each sentence as your teacher dictates.** Use **correct punctuation.**

1. Christopher <u>set the controls as his astronaut</u> <u>flew over the combat field.</u>

2. Christopher <u>read about several kinds of</u> <u>mammals that inhabit Colorado.</u>

3. <u>Perhaps Dad will take us to the store</u> <u>to buy a used game.</u>

H Proofreading

If a word is misspelled, fill in the oval by that word. If all the words are spelled correctly, fill in the oval by **no mistake**.

1. ○ inhabit
   ● Colarado
   ○ igloo
   ○ no mistake

2. ● nevada
   ○ include
   ○ foolish
   ○ no mistake

3. ● gallun
   ○ gallop
   ○ tulip
   ○ no mistake

4. ○ valley
   ○ valve
   ○ raccoon
   ● no mistake

5. ○ Alabama
   ○ useless
   ● scallup
   ○ no mistake

6. ● mammel
   ○ New Hampshire
   ○ accuse
   ○ no mistake

7. ○ Indiana
   ● randum
   ○ Utah
   ○ no mistake

8. ● sevanna
   ○ gather
   ○ crew
   ○ no mistake

9. ○ perhaps
   ○ cue
   ● sopranoe
   ○ no mistake

10. ● rasckal
    ○ flu
    ○ view
    ○ no mistake

11. ● combatt
    ○ truly
    ○ tomb
    ○ no mistake

12. ○ future
    ● statick
    ○ confuse
    ○ no mistake

85

---

1 Dictation

Reinforce correct spelling by using current and previous words in context.

(Say) Listen as I read each sentence and then write it in your Worktext. Remember to use correct capitalization and punctuation. (Slowly read each sentence twice. Sentences are found in the Student Worktext to the left.)

2 Proofreading

Familiarize students with standardized test format and reinforce recognition of misspelled words.

(Say) Look at each set of words. If a word is misspelled, fill in the oval by that word. If all the words are spelled correctly, fill in the oval by **no mistake**.

129

3 Hide and Seek

Reinforce correct spelling of current spelling words. Repeat this activity from Day 2.

4 Vocabulary Extension

Have your students complete this activity to strengthen spelling ability and expand vocabulary. The reproducible master is provided in Appendix A as shown on the inset page to the right.

1 Posttest

Visit the **A Reason For** website to download free, printable Posttest pages.

Say I will say the word once, use it in a sentence, then say it again. Write your words on a separate sheet of paper.

Progress Chart

Students may record scores. (Appendix B)

Personal Dictionary

Students may add any words they have misspelled to their personal dictionaries. (Appendix B)

Hide and Seek

Play Hide and Seek with your words. Fill in a bar graph (left to right) for each word you spell correctly.

Vocabulary Extension

Crossword Puzzle

Use the clues below to complete the puzzle.

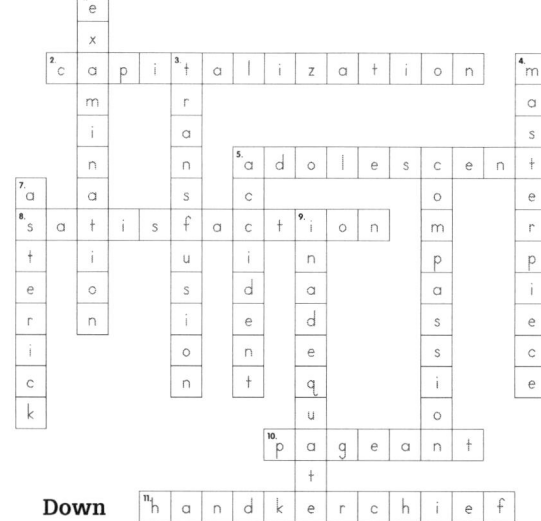

Down
1. questionnaire, test
3. add blood through a vein
4. done with extraordinary skill
5. catastrophe, misfortune
6. tenderness, mercy
7. six-pointed star
9. insufficient, imperfect

Across
2. writing or printing in uppercase letters
5. a person between childhood and adulthood
8. contentment, happiness
10. display, show
11. scarf, tissue

Word Bank

accident	capitalization	handkerchief	pageant
adolescent	compassion	inadequate	satisfaction
asterisk	examination	masterpiece	transfusion

335

1.	soprano	Kristin is learning to sing **soprano** in the school choir.
2.	Nevada	The new music director is from **Nevada**.
3.	New Hampshire	The choir may compete in a choral competition in **New Hampshire**.
4.	mammal	Kristin and Christopher each have a report to prepare about a **mammal**.
5.	gather	"Did you **gather** any of the information you need for your paper?" she asked.
6.	random	Christopher did not choose his new game at **random**.
7.	combat	He had heard the **combat** mode was awesome.
8.	Colorado	Even Christopher's cousin in **Colorado** said the game was terrific.
9.	Alabama	The sales clerk had recently moved to town from **Alabama**.
10.	inhabit	The instructions for the mission read, "Conquer and **inhabit** Mars."
11.	valley	He felt as if he were really guiding his spaceship through a **valley** on Venus.
12.	savanna	Finding the hidden base in a **savanna** on Saturn was the next mission.
13.	Indiana	The team that wrote the computer game is located in **Indiana**.
14.	scallop	Kristin has a **scallop** shell she found on the beach during vacation.
15.	valve	This marine mollusk has not one **valve**, but two.
16.	static	"Talking to you is like being on a phone with a lot of **static**," Kristin frowned.
17.	rascal	After Kristin's reprimand, Christopher realized he had been a **rascal**.
18.	perhaps	"I have, **perhaps**, been a little consumed with the game," he said.
19.	gallop	He liked to **gallop** around the driveway to make his sister laugh.
20.	gallon	After a game of one-on-one, he felt like he could drink a **gallon** of water.

130

I Game

Name _____

Follow along with Christopher to shoot some hoops with Kristin. Move one space for each word you or your team spells correctly.

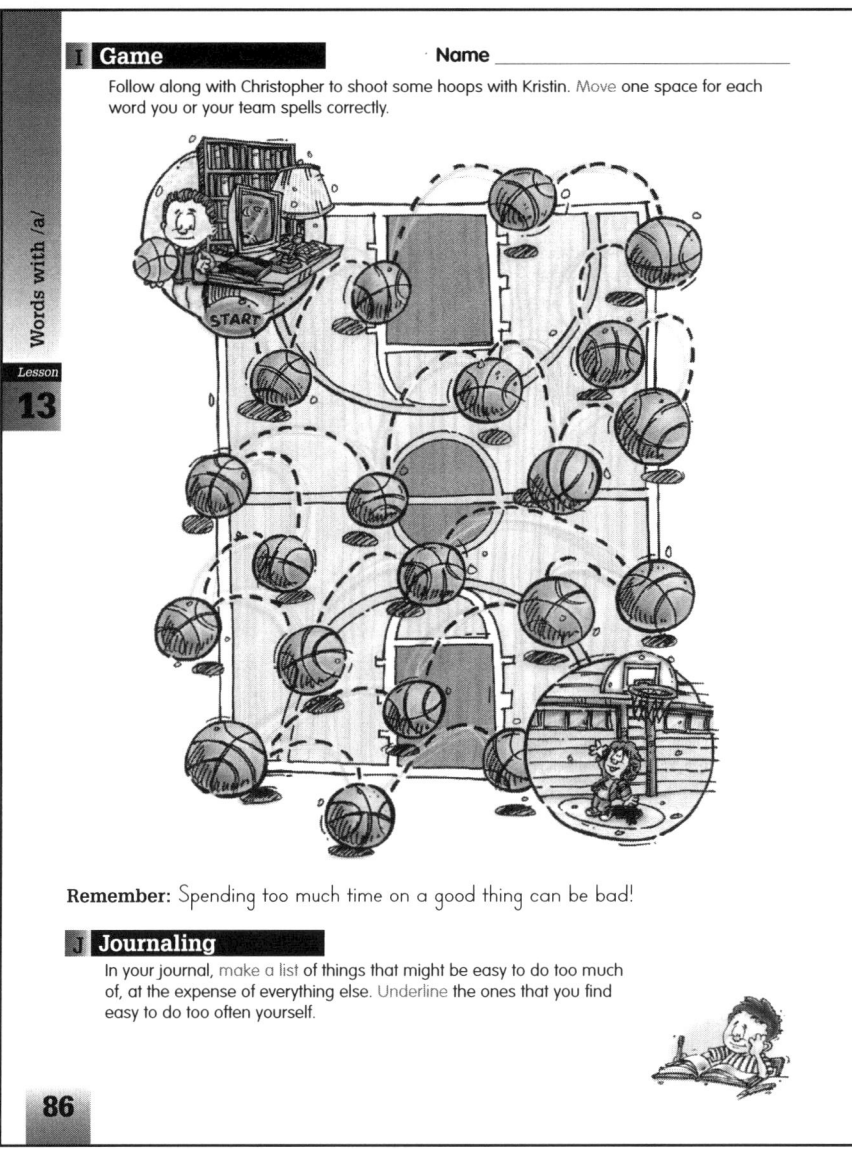

Remember: Spending too much time on a good thing can be bad!

J Journaling

In your journal, make a list of things that might be easy to do too much of, at the expense of everything else. Underline the ones that you find easy to do too often yourself.

86

How to Play:

- Divide the class into two teams.
- Have each student place his/her game piece on Start.
- Have a student from team A go to the board.
- Say the spelling word.
- Have the student write the word on the board.
- If correct, instruct each member of team A to move his/her game piece forward one space.
- Alternate between teams A and B.
- The team to reach Kristin at the basketball goal first is the winner.
- **Small Group Option**: Students may play this game without teacher direction in small groups of two or more.

---

2 Game

Reinforce spelling skills and provide motivation and interest.

Materials
- game page (from student text)
- game pieces (1 per child)
- game word list

Game Word List
1. inhabit
2. Colorado
3. Nevada
4. gallon
5. gallop
6. valley
7. valve
8. scallop
9. Alabama
10. mammal
11. New Hampshire
12. Indiana
13. random
14. savanna
15. soprano
16. perhaps
17. rascal
18. gather
19. combat
20. static

3 Journaling

Provide a meaningful reason for correct spelling through personal writing.

Review the story using discussion leads provided on the following page. Encourage students to apply the Scriptural value in their journaling.

131

Journaling (continued)

- Do you regularly play console or computer games? (Allow time to share experiences.)
- What kind of things did Christopher's new game include? (Choosing or designing space ships and flying them through challenging missions.)
- Was it a bad game, violent or evil? (No.)
- What was the problem with Christopher playing it, then? (He played it all the time and didn't do anything else.)
- Can you think of some other things that might be easy to do too much? (Sports, TV, reading, etc.— even talking on the phone!)

The ten most used words in the English language, according to publishers of the Oxford English Dictionary, are (in order): the, be, to, of, and, a, in, that, have, I.

Tony in Training

Tony painfully determines to learn more about people with limitations and resolves to work on his prejudice.

"Mr. Canfield is unbelievable! Is there any sport he isn't good at?" Tony watched his teacher sprint down the track. "He's fast! So far this year, he's been good at everything. Do you think he plays baseball, too?"

"Probably," Stephen smiled. "He's awesome."

"Let's stretch before you do any running," Mr. Canfield said as he stood in front of the class and jogged in place. "Toe touches! Everybody reach for your right toe. No bouncing. Hold it right there. One, two, three, four, five, six, seven, eight, nine and ten. Now reach for your left toe. Hold it! One, two...."

"Are you going to run in the Turkey Trot to help raise money for the Sunshine School?" Stephen looked through his legs at Tony.

"Yeah!" Stephen smirked.

Tony touched the top of his running shoes with the palms of his hands. "I've been practicing. Five miles is long way to run for charity, but Grandma wants me to enter. She's already paid the registration fee."

"I bet Mr. Canfield wins!" Stephen stretched toward the ground between his toes.

"Is he entering?"

"That's what I heard him telling Mrs. Bently in the office this morning."

"No wonder he's been running every night at Mason Springs Park! He must be getting ready for the Turkey Trot." Tony straightened his back and reached for the sky. "Maybe he'd give me some training tips."

Tony fell in step beside Mr. Canfield as they returned to the classroom after PE. "What are you doing to get ready for the Turkey Trot, Mr. Canfield?"

The teacher looked down and smiled at Tony's eagerness. "Well I'm drinking lots of water, getting plenty of sleep, and eating a balanced diet. I've been running a couple miles every night, too." He playfully punched Tony's shoulder. "You gonna run?"

"Aren't the kids at the Sunshine School, like … a brick short of a load?" Tommy interrupted.

"Or as Thorny would say, a bubble off plumb," Daniel laughed.

Tommy nodded. "Yeah. And I don't know if I can run the whole five miles. My grandma thinks it's a good idea to help raise money for the school, although I don't really know why. She's been helping me line up sponsors."

"Why? You have something you want to tell us, Tony?" Stephen joked.

"No! She says serving others is the only way to happiness."

Mr. Canfield smiled, "Smart lady."

"Winning would make me happy," Tony declared.

Tommy laughed and gave the smaller boy a playful shove.

After supper that evening Tony put on his jacket. "I'm going to wait for Mr. Canfield on the front steps, Grandma." He whispered to himself, "I hope he runs tonight."

"Don't you want some ice cream, Tony?" Grandma asked.

"No, 'cause I'm in training for the Turkey Trot. Ice cream will clog my system," Tony said as he ran out the door. He sat down on the grass in the front yard to do warm-up stretches while he watched for Mr. Canfield. He'd just about given up when he saw his teacher's black compact car round the corner. He sprinted across the street and

skidded to a stop as the car pulled to the curb.

Mr. Canfield kissed his wife, then hopped out of the car. He stuck his head back inside, "Get me in half an hour, Hon? I'll meet you here." He slammed the car door and waved to the two kids in the back seat as his wife pulled away from the curb. "I love you," he mouthed.

"Well, hi, Tony." The big man looked down at his student and slung an arm across his shoulders. "Are you here to train with me?"

Tony looked over his shoulder at the little car. "I didn't know you had two kids."

"Yup! J.J. will be seven this year and Jessica is five. You ready?"

"I've seen Jessica at school, but J.J. doesn't go to Knowlton Elementary does he?"

"Nope." Jason Canfield sprinted down the trail.

Tony ran to catch up. All his energy focused on matching his teacher's pace, and soon he was breathing too hard to ask any of the questions popping into his head.

After the first mile Tony was dragging. "I gotta quit. You're fast," he panted.

"Why don't you walk a lap and then see how you feel? If you're up to it, jog the third mile at your own pace. Then walk until you cool down. Jogging up a hill would help build your leg muscles and increase your endurance, too. Relax, do your best, and leave it with the Lord!" Mr. Canfield waved as he took off on his second lap around the park.

After finishing the third mile, Tony trudged up the steps of the duplex and gulped down three tall glasses of water. "Grandma, does Mama still have some of those high-protein drinks?"

"I don't think so, unless they're in the pantry. I'll check."

"Grandma, where are those ankle weights Mama used in her aerobics class?"

"Probably out in the garage somewhere,

133

Tony-O." Grandma wiped her hands on her apron and closed the pantry door. "No drinks. I'll get some when I go grocery shopping."

Tony rummaged around in the garage without success. "I can't find them. Maybe Mama knows where they are. I think I'll run up to Stephen's. They have some of those little dumbbells you hold in your hands when you exercise. Maybe I can borrow them."

Grandma Miller smiled and shook her head as she watched Tony run out the door. *I'm glad he's interested in bodybuilding and training, but I hope it's for the right reasons.* She began a silent prayer. "Lord, help my grandson. He's short and wants so badly to prove himself to his peers. Help him realize the builder's work is useless without You, Lord." The gray-haired woman wiped the corner of her eye with a wrinkled hand and sat down on the couch.

Tony trained faithfully every day after school—with or without Mr. Canfield. Friday afternoon he strapped on his ankle weights and took the blue plastic dumbbells he'd borrowed from Stephen and headed out the door. "I'm going to run up to Stephen's, Grandma," he yelled.

The run to Stephen's was getting easier, but his friend wasn't home. Tony jogged up and down the hill until his legs ached. He finally collapsed on his front lawn. He absently watched a woman and two children coming toward him across Mason Springs Park. The little girl's hair was braided in tiny braids that swung around her face as she danced around a bigger boy. The boy's head was tilted at an odd angle and he was walking with a peculiar gait.

Tony kept watching. He jumped up and waved wildly when he saw Mr. Canfield zip around the corner and park his black car at the curb. Tony recognized the woman first. It was Mrs. Canfield! And

the little girl was Jessica. She ran to meet her daddy and jumped up into his arms. Tony could hear her laughing. He still didn't recognize the boy and was surprised when he walked around the car and fumbled with the door handle. Mr. Canfield came over and watched him slowly get into the car, then buckled the boy's seat belt and kissed him on the forehead.

Suddenly Tony understood! *That's J.J.! He doesn't go to Knowlton Elementary because … oh, wow … Mr. Canfield's son has a disability. And we all joked about those Sunshine School kids with Down Syndrome and stuff … in front of him!* Tony was mortified.

I'm running in the Turkey Trot because I want to win and look good. Mr. Canfield is running because he wants to help his own kid and others like him. Tony didn't feel like talking to his teacher anymore. He turned and rushed into the house. He wanted to hide.

He sat on the edge of his bed in the darkening room. "I'm so sorry, Lord," he prayed. "I've been a fool."

Grandma Miller came in quietly and sat down beside him. After looking at his face she said, "I see you found out."

Tony nodded. "I sure made a fool out of myself, Grandma. Mr. Canfield probably thinks I'm awful—but he's been nice. He's helping me train for the race even after he heard us joke about the Sunshine School kids."

"Body building and winning are useless without the Lord, Tony-O." Grandma put her arm around her dejected grandson and squeezed. "Ask Him to be with you and do your best."

"But Grandma, how do the Canfields stand it? I mean, it's so hard to even think about the things we said," Tony whispered.

"The Canfields have been dealing with their son's limitations for seven years now. The Lord has helped them accept his condition, and they're handling people's ignorance and prejudice. I'm sure your teacher is proud of you for training hard and participating in a fund-raising project to help the kids at J.J.'s school."

Tony looked at his Grandma

out of the corner of his eye. "I'm so embarrassed!"

"You should be!" The older woman got up slowly from the bed. "The Lord loves building projects, Tony-O, but I think you might want to let Him work on tearing down that prejudice you have."

"I see that now. Hey, Grandma, would you make me a T-shirt that says, 'Proudly Running for the Sunshine School?' I'd like to wear a special shirt when I run in the Turkey Trot!"

Check understanding of the story and development of personal values.

- Have you ever participated in a race to raise money for a good cause?
- When and what for?
- Why was Tony participating in the Turkey Trot?
- Why was he training so hard?
- Was that a good reason to train so diligently?
- What does it mean when someone says you "put your foot in your mouth?"
- How did Tony put his foot in his mouth?
- How did he feel when he realized Mr. Canfield's son had special needs?
- How did Tony's reason for running change?

1. glossary
2. colonies
3. college
4. geometry
5. contact
6. doctor
7. conversation
8. continent
9. borrow
10. crocodile
11. Wisconsin
12. commerce
13. concentrate
14. atomic
15. deposit
16. adopt
17. comment
18. compost
19. bottom
20. demolish

Words with /o/

Lesson 14

Scripture

Psalm 127:1

87

Preview

Test for knowledge of the correct spellings of these words.

Customize Your List
On a separate sheet of paper, additional words of your choice may be tested.

Say) I will say each word once, use the word in a sentence, then say the word again. Write the words on the lines in your Worktext.

Correct Immediately!
Say) Let's correct our Preview. I will spell each word out loud. If you spelled a word incorrectly, rewrite it correctly.

Progress Chart
Students may record scores. (Reproducible master provided in Appendix B.)

Lesson **14** Day 1

1.	glossary	"Use the **glossary** to complete the assignment," instructed Mr. Canfield.
2.	colonies	"They may have had Turkey Trots in the **colonies**," he teased.
3.	college	"Did you run track in **college**, Mr. Canfield?" Tony asked.
4.	geometry	"Yes, and in high school I ran laps while I memorized **geometry** theorems."
5.	contact	"I never played a **contact** sport like football, though."
6.	doctor	"I was afraid I'd spend more time going to the **doctor** than playing the game."
7.	conversation	The boys really enjoyed having a **conversation** with their teacher.
8.	continent	"I think you could win a race on any **continent**!" exclaimed Stephen.
9.	borrow	"Can I **borrow** some of your energy?" Tony asked with admiration.
10.	crocodile	He sprawled out on the grass like a lazy **crocodile**.
11.	Wisconsin	"My brother recently won a 3-mile run in **Wisconsin**," he told the boys.
12.	commerce	During history, Mr. Canfield discussed international **commerce**.
13.	concentrate	"Some countries wanted to **concentrate** their resources on gaining power."
14.	atomic	"The power of an **atomic** weapon is potentially devastating," he explained
15.	deposit	"America had no plans to allow Russia to **deposit** a nuclear weapon here!"
16.	adopt	Senators urged Congress to **adopt** new policies and increase the defense budget.
17.	comment	Tony regretted the **comment** about special needs kids.
18.	compost	"I'm so embarrassed I could hide in the **compost** pile," Tony told Gram.
19.	bottom	"From the **bottom** of my heart, I apologize for the things I said," Tony explained.
20.	demolish	"God, please **demolish** the prejudice in my heart," Tony prayed.

135

Word Shapes

4

Help students form a correct image of whole words.

Say Look at each word and think about its shape. Now, write the word in the correct Word Shape Boxes. You may check off each word as you use it.

(Short vowels are usually found in syllables in which a vowel is immediately preceded and followed by a consonant, consonant cluster, or digraph. The sound of /o/ is usually spelled with **o** or **a**.)

Say In the Word Shape Boxes, fill in the boxes containing the letter or letters that spell the sound of /o/ in each word.

Take a minute to memorize...
Psalm 127:1

B Word Shapes   Name _____

Using the word bank below, write each word in the correct Word Shape Boxes. Next, in the Word Shape Boxes, fill in the boxes containing the letter or letters that spell the sound of /o/ in each word.

Words with /o/
Lesson **14**

1. college
2. comment
3. geometry
4. atomic
5. crocodile
6. doctor
7. adopt
8. conversation
9. borrow
10. concentrate

11. demolish
12. contact
13. continent
14. glossary
15. commerce
16. deposit
17. compost
18. Wisconsin
19. colonies
20. bottom

Word Bank

adopt	college	compost	conversation	doctor
atomic	colonies	concentrate	crocodile	geometry
borrow	comment	contact	demolish	glossary
bottom	commerce	continent	deposit	Wisconsin

88

Answers may vary for duplicate word shapes.

Be Prepared For Fun

Check these supply lists for **Fun Ways to Spell** - presented **Day 2**.
Purchase and/or gather these items ahead of time!

General
- Pencil
- Notebook Paper
- Spelling List

Auditory
- Pencil
- Notebook Paper
- Dictionary
- Spelling List

Visual
- Pencil
- Notebook Paper
- Spelling List

Tactile
- Clay
- Spelling List

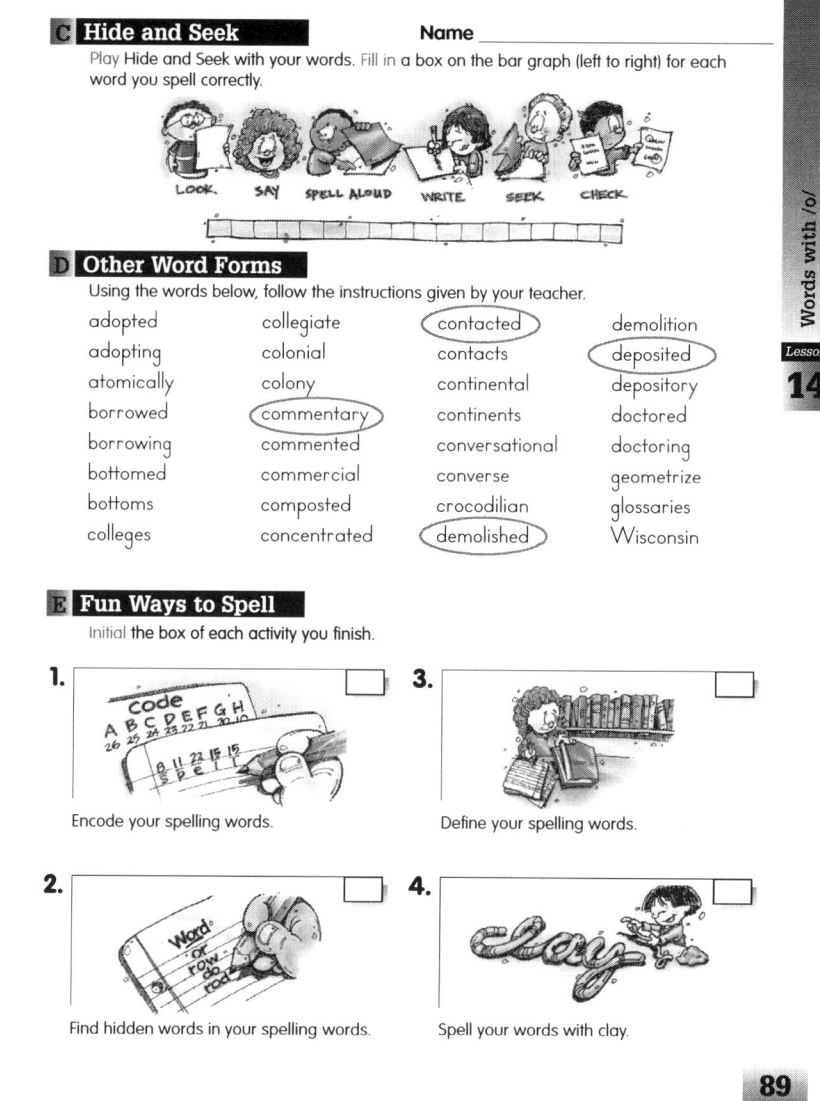

C Hide and Seek

Name _____

Play Hide and Seek with your words. Fill in a box on the bar graph (left to right) for each word you spell correctly.

LOOK. SAY SPELL ALOUD WRITE SEEK CHECK

D Other Word Forms

Using the words below, follow the instructions given by your teacher.

adopted	collegiate	contacted	demolition
adopting	colonial	contacts	deposited
atomically	colony	continental	depository
borrowed	commentary	continents	doctored
borrowing	commented	conversational	doctoring
bottomed	commercial	converse	geometrize
bottoms	composted	crocodilian	glossaries
colleges	concentrated	demolished	Wisconsin

E Fun Ways to Spell

Initial the box of each activity you finish.

1.
Code
A B C D E F G H
Spell
Encode your spelling words.

3.
Define your spelling words.

2.
Word or Row do root
Find hidden words in your spelling words.

4.
clay
Spell your words with clay.

89

---

1 Hide and Seek

Reinforce spelling by using multiple styles of learning.

On a white board, Teacher writes each word — one at a time. **Have students:**

- **Look** at the word.
- **Say** the word out loud.
- **Spell** the word out loud.
- **Hide** (teacher erases word.)
- **Write** the word on paper.
- **Seek** (teacher rewrites word.)
- **Check** spelling. If incorrect, rewrite word correctly.

2 Other Word Forms

This activity is optional. Have students find and circle the Other Word Forms that are synonyms of the following:

laid waste
reached
dropped
critique

3 Fun Ways to Spell

Four activities are provided. Use one, two, three, or all of the activities. Have students initial the box for each activity they complete.

Options:

- assign activities to students according to their learning styles
- set up the activities in learning centers for the students to do throughout the day
- divide students into four groups and assign one activity per group
- do one activity per day

General
To encode your spelling words...
- Write the alphabet on your paper.
- Write your own code for each letter underneath it.
- Write your spelling words in your code.
- Trade papers with a classmate and decode the words.
- Check to make sure your classmate spelled the words correctly.

Auditory
To define your spelling words...
- Ask a classmate to look up a word from your spelling list in the dictionary and read the definition to you, but not the spelling word.
- Decide which word on your list matches this definition and write the word.
- Ask your classmate to check your spelling.
- Switch and continue taking turns.

Visual
To find hidden words in your spelling words...
- Choose a word from your spelling list.
- Write it on your paper.
- Find and write as many smaller words as you can that are contained within your spelling word.
- Do this with each word.

Tactile
To spell your words with clay...
- Roll pieces of clay into ropes.
- Use the ropes to make the letters of each word.
- Put them in the right order to spell each word.
- Check your spelling.

Working with Words

Familiarize students with word meaning and usage.

Scrambled Words

Write the letters **aeghrt** on the board. Have a student unscramble the letters to make the word **gather**.

Unscramble each spelling word. Write the word correctly on the line. Remember to use capital letters where they are needed.

Word Clues

Use your word bank to help you match the spelling words to the clues. Some of the clues are synonyms, words that have the same meaning as the spelling word. You may use a dictionary or thesaurus to help you.

Take a minute to memorize...

Psalm 127:1

F **Working with Words**   Name _____

Scrambled Words

Unscramble each word. Write the unscrambled word on the line. Use capital letters where they are needed.

1. cdoort — doctor
2. aceinnoorstv — conversation
3. ccdeiloor — crocodile
4. acimot — atomic
5. deiopst — deposit
6. accnott — contact
7. ciinnossw — Wisconsin
8. wororb — borrow
9. ceilnoos — colonies
10. cemmnot — comment
11. ceeglo — college
12. eegmorty — geometry
13. ceinnnott — continent
14. aglorssy — glossary
15. bmoott — bottom
16. podat — adopt
17. acceennortt — concentrate
18. cmoopst — compost
19. cceemmor — commerce
20. dehilmos — demolish

Word Clues

Match the spelling words to the clues. You may use a dictionary or thesaurus to help you.

1. microscopic, smallest — atomic
2. observation, remark — comment
3. get temporary use of — borrow
4. lowest part, base — bottom
5. communities, settlements — colonies
6. business, trading — commerce
7. decayed organic matter — compost
8. pay attention, focus — concentrate
9. connection, touch — contact
10. land mass — continent
11. reptilian, alligator — crocodile
12. destroy, wreck — demolish
13. sediment, silt — deposit
14. physician, M. D. — doctor
15. take into one's family — adopt
16. math about angles — geometry
17. educational institution — college
18. list of terms, dictionary — glossary
19. talking together — conversation
20. north–central state — Wisconsin

Word Bank

adopt	college	compost	conversation	doctor
atomic	colonies	concentrate	crocodile	geometry
borrow	comment	contact	demolish	glossary
bottom	commerce	continent	deposit	Wisconsin

90

138

G Dictation

Name _____

Write **each sentence as your teacher dictates.** Use **correct punctuation.**

1. Mr. Canfield did not say much as the boys laughed and made unkind comments.

2. Tony concentrated on eating healthy foods as he built his strength.

3. He looked in the glossary to find more about the commerce of the early colonies.

H Proofreading

If a word is misspelled, fill in the oval by that word. If all the words are spelled correctly, fill in the oval by **no mistake.**

1. ● convirsation
    ○ inhabit
    ○ Colorado
    ○ no mistake

2. ○ gallop
    ○ gallon
    ● crocadial
    ○ no mistake

3. ● docter
    ○ Nevada
    ○ valley
    ○ no mistake

4. ○ valve
    ● collige
    ○ scallop
    ○ no mistake

5. ● colonys
    ○ demolish
    ○ Alabama
    ○ no mistake

6. ● mammal
    ○ New Hampshire
    ● attomic
    ○ no mistake

7. ● coment
    ○ Indiana
    ○ random
    ○ no mistake

8. ○ compost
    ● comerce
    ○ savanna
    ○ no mistake

9. ○ concentrate
    ● geometrey
    ○ perhaps
    ○ no mistake

10. ○ contact
    ○ Wisconsin
    ● continint
    ○ no mistake

11. ● addopt
    ○ bottom
    ○ borrow
    ○ no mistake

12. ○ soprano
    ○ deposit
    ● glossry
    ○ no mistake

91

Dictation

Reinforce correct spelling by using current and previous words in context.

Say

Listen as I read each sentence and then write it in your Worktext. Remember to use correct capitalization and punctuation. (Slowly read each sentence twice. Sentences are found in the Student Worktext to the left.)

Proofreading

Familiarize students with standardized test format and reinforce recognition of misspelled words.

Say

Look at each set of words. If a word is misspelled, fill in the oval by that word. If all the words are spelled correctly, fill in the oval by **no mistake.**

3 Hide and Seek

Reinforce correct spelling of current spelling words.
Repeat this activity from Day 2.

4 Vocabulary Extension

Have your students complete this activity to strengthen spelling ability and expand vocabulary. The reproducible master is provided in Appendix A as shown on the inset page to the right.

1 Posttest

Visit the **A Reason For** website to download free, printable Posttest pages.

(Say)

I will say the word once, use it in a sentence, then say it again. Write your words on a separate sheet of paper.

Graph

Progress Chart

Students may record scores. (Appendix B)

My Personal Dictionary

Personal Dictionary

Students may add any words they have misspelled to their personal dictionaries. (Appendix B)

Hide and Seek

Play Hide and Seek with your words. Fill in a bar graph (left to right) for each word you spell correctly.

LOOK   SAY   HIDE   WRITE   SEEK   CHECK

Vocabulary Extension

Trade-off

Choose a word from the word bank to replace the word(s) in parentheses. Write the word in the blank.

1. My teacher said that the ____composition____ (essay) I wrote was really good.
2. There was a lot of ____opposition____ (conflict) to the plans for the new gymnasium.
3. The lawyer for the ____prosecution____ (accuser) had plenty of evidence to convict the thief.
4. She was so upset that her arguments became very ____illogical____ (unreasonable).
5. The boys finally gave up on the go-cart they were trying to build. They decided it was ____impossible____ (hopeless).
6. The laws in our country that state the rights of the people and the powers of the government are known as the ____constitution____ (written laws).
7. The fraction 13/7 is an ____improper____ (incorrect) fraction because the numerator is greater than its denominator.
8. I love to look at the ____constellation____ (pattern of stars) Orion in the sky on a dark night.
9. Jeans are the most ____dominant____ (most common) kind of clothes in my closet.
10. We need to be ____tolerant____ (accepting) of others by showing respect for their customs, beliefs, or opinions.
11. I want to protect valuable things such as forests, wildlife, and natural resources. I believe in ____conservation____ (preservation).
12. If you have a ____conversation____ (discourse) with someone, you talk to them for a while.

Word Bank

composition	constitution	illogical	opposition
conservation	conversation	impossible	prosecution
constellation	dominant	improper	tolerant

336

---

1. glossary — "Use the **glossary** at the back of your book," instructed Mr. Canfield.
2. concentrate — "Please, **concentrate** on completing the first two pages," he continued.
3. geometry — Mr. Canfield introduced his class to several principles of **geometry**.
4. crocodile — Tony dropped to the grass, his mouth open like a giant **crocodile**.
5. borrow — "I'd like to **borrow** some of his talent and ability!" exclaimed Tony.
6. conversation — The boys thought it was neat to share **conversation** with their teacher.
7. contact — "Did you play any **contact** sports?" inquired Stephen.
8. doctor — "No, I thought I'd have to see the **doctor** too often," he laughed.
9. college — "I ran track in high school and in **college**," said Mr. Canfield.
10. colonies — "Think they used to have a Turkey Trot in the **colonies** way back when?"
11. Wisconsin — "My brother who lives in **Wisconsin** recently won a race," he told the boys.
12. bottom — Tony was sorry from the **bottom** of his heart.
13. atomic — "How did the knowledge of **atomic** power change the world?" he asked the students.
14. commerce — "Tony, what effect did that have on international **commerce**?"
15. compost — Tony felt low enough to crawl in the **compost** pile!
16. continent — "What changes affected our **continent** specifically, Kristin?"
17. deposit — He saw Mr. Canfield scoop up his son and **deposit** him safely in the car.
18. adopt — Tony wanted to **adopt** a more kind attitude.
19. comment — Tony was so sorry for his unkind **comment** in front of his teacher.
20. demolish — Tony wanted God to **demolish** any prejudice in his heart.

I Game

Name _____

Go with Tony as he apologizes to Mr. Canfield. Move one space for each word you or your team spells correctly.

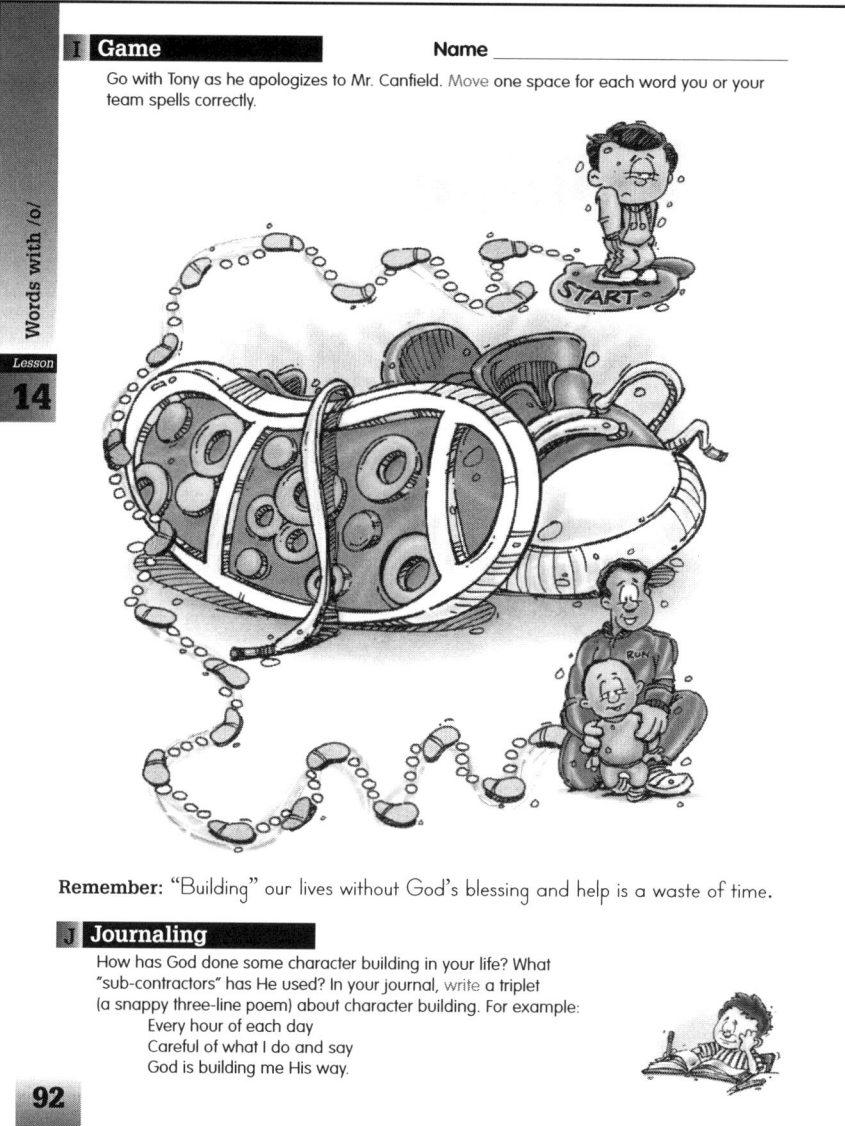

Words with /o/

Lesson **14**

Remember: "Building" our lives without God's blessing and help is a waste of time.

J Journaling

How has God done some character building in your life? What "sub-contractors" has He used? In your journal, write a triplet (a snappy three-line poem) about character building. For example:

Every hour of each day
Careful of what I do and say
God is building me His way.

92

How to Play:

- Divide the class into two teams.
- Have each student place his/her game piece on Start.
- Have a student from team A go to the board.
- Say the spelling word.
- Have the student write the word on the board.
- If correct, instruct each member of team A to move his/her game piece forward one space.
- Alternate between teams A and B.
- The team to reach Mr. Canfield first is the winner.
- **Small Group Option**: Students may play this game without teacher direction in small groups of two or more.

2 Game

Reinforce spelling skills and provide motivation and interest.

Materials

- game page (from student text)
- game pieces (1 per child)
- game word list

Game Word List

1. **conversation**
2. **crocodile**
3. **doctor**
4. **college**
5. **colonies**
6. **demolish**
7. **atomic**
8. **comment**
9. **commerce**
10. **compost**
11. **geometry**
12. **concentrate**
13. **contact**
14. **continent**
15. **Wisconsin**
16. **adopt**
17. **borrow**
18. **bottom**
19. **deposit**
20. **glossary**

3 Journaling

Provide a meaningful reason for correct spelling through personal writing.

Review the story using discussion leads provided on the following page. Encourage students to apply the Scriptural value in their journaling.

(Say) • Why did Tony want to win the Turkey Trot? (To look good.)

• Why do you think Grandma Miller told Tony that body building and winning were useless without the Lord? (She knew serving others is the only way to happiness.)

• What does it mean when someone says you "just put your foot in your mouth"? (You've said something to embarrass yourself.)

• How did Tony put his foot in his mouth? (While Mr. Canfield was listening, he laughed at jokes about children with disabilities and said winning was what would make him happy.)

• What character traits do you think the Lord helped Tony build? (Compassion, empathy, humility)

• Triplets are three-line poems. They're not as common as couplets (two-line poems) and quatrains (four-line poems). Sometimes triplets rhyme— sometimes they don't. When a triplet rhymes, all three lines may rhyme (aaa), the first and last lines may rhyme (aba), the first two lines can rhyme (aab), or just the last two may rhyme (abb).

• Write these incomplete triplets on the board. Ask students to complete them. Share results.

• **aaa** pattern (all three lines rhyme)

Running is a lot of fun

_____

But it feels great when I am done

• **abb** pattern (the last two lines rhyme)

Tony always combs his hair!

He thinks it's out of place

_____

ICEBOX is a word with horizontal symmetry when written in capital letters (it reflects itself across a horizontal line); some others are DECIDED, EXCEEDED, CHECK-BOOK, OKEECHOBEE, HIDE, CHOICE, DIOXIDE, CEBID (a type of monkey), and OBOE.

Protection in Paradise

Laney spends Christmas vacation in the Bahamas with her dad, his new wife, and daughter.

Dear Megan,

I have so much to tell you, but it's hard to get it out of my fingers and into the computer. Guess what? Two exciting things! First, my dad is taking me to the Bahamas for Christmas vacation! I'll get out of this place for a while! He's already sent my tickets, so I know he won't forget our plans this time. I've been reading about the Bahamas on the Internet. Did you know there are 700 islands in the Bahamas? (I didn't either until yesterday.) The closest islands are only 50 miles off the Florida coast. I get to spend a day in New York on the way back. So the second exciting thing is—I'll get to see you!! ☺ Are you going to be home December 30?

Love,
Laney

Dear Laney,

I'll be here! I can hardly wait till you are! It seems like forever since you lived here and we went to school together. Your dad must be trying to make up for forgetting about your plans with him last spring. Glad you have your tickets! Lucky bird (as our friend Brittany would say)! I've always wanted to go snorkeling and sailing in the Bahamas. All that warm, blue water, those coral reefs, and crashing waves! Which of the 700 islands are you going to visit?
See ya!
Megan

Dear Megan,

I'm going to Paradise Island! We're flying into Nassau, the capital city of the Bahamas. Apparently it was founded in 1670. Over half the people in the Bahamas live there. I don't know where we're going after that. The only reason I know we're going to Nassau is because of my ticket. You know how busy Dad always is. He probably won't tell me until we're in the air exactly what we're going to do. Maybe we'll stay in Paradise the whole time. Who knows? (Hopefully Dad.)

Love,
Laney

Dear Laney,

Brittany wants to know if she can come with you. You know how she loves birds. She said 60,000 West Indian flamingos live in the Bahamas. Flamingos are the national bird. Her brother said the exotic Abaco parrots live in one of the national parks. Do you get to sail and learn to scuba dive?
Megan

Dear Megan,

Tell Brittany I'd love for her to come. Which island do the flamingos live on? My stepdad gave me a whole list of things to take with me today! He says I need to wear lots of sunscreen. I told him Dad and Suzanne would bring stuff like that. He said nothing could ruin a trip to the beach more than a sunburn. He wants me to take some aloe vera and a hat. He says I need a jacket, too. I don't think I'll miss his hovering over me all the time trying to protect me. It gets kind of irritating. I'll be with my own dad. Mom says we get to go shopping tomorrow. I don't think it will do much good. Where will I get summer clothes in December?

Love,
Laney

Dear Laney,

Just tell Coach Larkin your real dad can take care of you in Paradise. Brittany said the flamingos are on the island that is farthest away—Iguana, I think she said. When do you leave? Can you e-mail on your trip?
Megan

Dear Megan,

I'm sure Dad will bring his laptop and cell phone. He couldn't stand to stay away from his law practice for more than a day. Maybe he'll let me e-mail. Tell Brittany the island with the Flamingos is Great Inagua—I looked it up. Same letters as Iguana, just a different order.

Love,
Laney

Dear Laney,

My Mom saw your dad's wife today in town. She said you were going on a cruise. You lucky duck! Are you sure you have an airline ticket?
Megan

Dear Megan,

You're right. I am going on a cruise! We'll leave from New York and sail all the way! Then we island hop. My stepdad says I need more than one swimming suit, and I should take some books to read on rainy days. He told me they drive on the wrong side of the road down there too. (He wants me to wear my seat belt because tourists aren't used to driving on the left side of the road.) Can you believe him? Gotta go.
Laney

Dear Megan,

I leave tomorrow. I'll miss Wicker. I really love that dog. Mom even lets him sleep on a big pillow bed in my room now—if I brush him before I let him in. He'll howl if they make him sleep out in his kennel again. Poor boy. It'll seem funny to have a warm Christmas. I'm used to snow. Mom and my stepdad gave me a Christmas present today. It's two swimming suits, a mask, and snorkel.

143

(Mom found the swimming suits online.) They said 5 percent of the world's coral reefs are in Bermuda and they want me to get a good look at them. Is this for real? Matthew gave me money to buy him some stamps. (He collects them.) Heather wants me to take pictures of insects. Everyone else in my class wants shells from the endless sandy beaches. I can hardly wait.

Love,
Laney

P.S. My friend Rachel said she would come over and play catch with Wicker every day, so at least the poor dog won't get so lonely.

Dear Laney,
Have fun. I'm looking forward to seeing you.
Megan

Dear Megan,
I got here late last night. I don't know why I'm e-mailing. I can call you on the phone!
Love,
Laney

Dear Laney,
Good to hear your voice three days ago. Where are you? E-mail me.
Megan

Dear Megan,
We're here—on Paradise Island! We came into port last night. I couldn't e-mail you on the ship. Dad said we were taking a break from "civilization." It was good to actually talk to you last week. I'm looking forward to seeing you when we get back. Suzanne and Dad were seasick all the way here, but I wasn't, so I got to babysit Suzette. Too exciting. I think we go to the beach tomorrow. I'm not sure yet. Dad still doesn't feel well.
Laney

Dear Megan,
You won't believe this. I'm the only one in this

family that's not sunburned. Dad Larkin was right. (I hate to put that in writing.) I'm glad he sent me my own sunscreen. It was waterproof. The stuff Suzanne brought wasn't. My dad was pretty mad at her. I let them use some of my aloe vera stuff. It helped. I didn't tell them Dad Larkin made me bring it.
Laney

Dear Megan,
I never thought I'd say this but I miss home—my new home. I miss Mom, I miss Wicker, and I hate to admit it, but I even miss my stepdad. We've started having family worship every night—Dad Larkin, Mom, and me. Rachel's family does that. I told Mom I thought we should start. She told Dad, and now we do it. Sometimes it isn't very interesting or comes at a bad time, but usually I like it because we do it together. Nobody here gets into having family anything. We're so busy on this cruise we don't see each other some days! Dad goes off deep-sea fishing or scuba diving with Suzanne. I take Suzette and we go on some kids' trip with a tour guide. It's fun, but I wish Dad and Suzanne would do things with us. When Dad and Suzanne get back, Dad works, or falls asleep because he's so tired.

The warm ocean is endless. I praise God for it—but I'll be glad to be home. I guess I'm learning that home is where your family is, and my real family now is Mom, Dad Larkin, and Wicker.
Love,
Laney

Discussion Time

Check understanding of the story and development of personal values.

- What two things was Laney so excited about?
- Raise your hand if you've ever been on a tropical island vacation.
- What are some things you like most about the ocean?
- What do you think this Scripture verse means? "Let the sea in all its vastness roar with praise! Let the earth and all those living on it shout, 'Glory to the Lord.'"
- What did Laney miss about being away from home?

1. Antarctica
2. Arkansas
3. hardship
4. artery
5. radar
6. argument
7. bargain
8. department
9. snarl
10. chart
11. partner
12. harbor
13. compartment
14. hearty

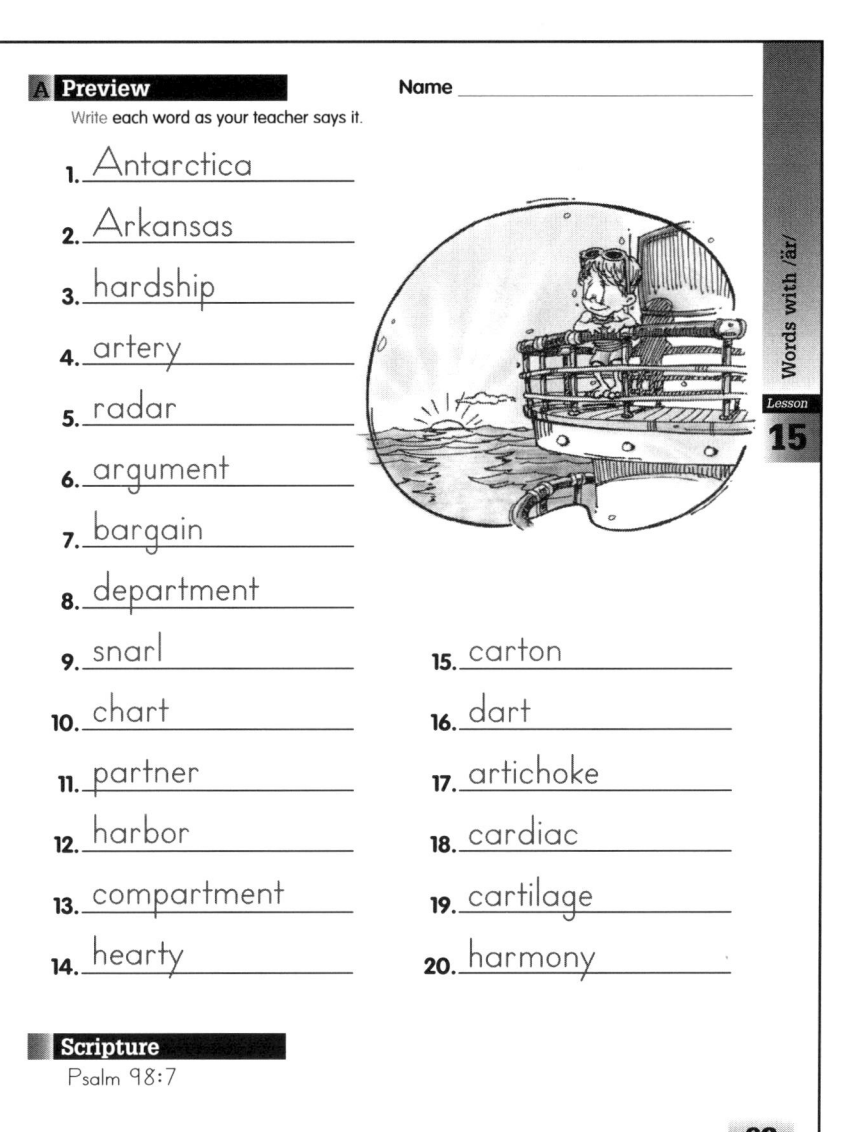

Words with /är/

Lesson 15

15. carton
16. dart
17. artichoke
18. cardiac
19. cartilage
20. harmony

Scripture

Psalm 98:7

93

3 **Preview**

Test for knowledge of the correct spellings of these words.

Customize Your List
On a separate sheet of paper, additional words of your choice may be tested.

 Say

I will say each word once, use the word in a sentence, then say the word again. Write the words on the lines in your Worktext.

 Say

Correct Immediately!
Let's correct our Preview. I will spell each word out loud. If you spelled a word incorrectly, rewrite it correctly.

Progress Chart
Students may record scores. (Reproducible master provided in Appendix B.)

Lesson **15** | Day 1

1.	Antarctica	Laney is going to the Bahamas, not **Antarctica**.
2.	Arkansas	Her dad lives in New York, but he grew up in **Arkansas**.
3.	hardship	"It will be such a **hardship** to spend a week in the Bahamas," her mom teased.
4.	artery	"Dad's going to clog an **artery** worrying about what I pack," she said disrespectfully.
5.	radar	"He has a built-in safety **radar**," said Laney with a groan.
6.	argument	Laney knew she should not get into an **argument** with Dad Larkin.
7.	bargain	Her mom found a **bargain** on swimsuits when she looked online.
8.	department	The girls' **department** at the stores in town had none.
9.	snarl	Laney heard Wicker **snarl** at a squirrel that stole a piece of his dog food.
10.	chart	The captain and his crew carefully **chart** the course for their voyage.
11.	partner	Laney's real dad has a **partner** that will see to business while he is away.
12.	harbor	The captain gave the orders to take the cruise ship slowly out of **harbor**.
13.	compartment	Laney liked her little sleeping **compartment**.
14.	hearty	They served a **hearty** breakfast each morning of the cruise.
15.	carton	She chose a small **carton** of milk to share with Suzette.
16.	dart	Laney threw a **dart** at the board on the upper deck.
17.	artichoke	At dinner, she sampled steamed **artichoke** and really liked it.
18.	cardiac	Laney's dad has had some **cardiac** trouble due to stress.
19.	cartilage	Even the **cartilage** in her dad's and Suzanne's ears felt sunburned!
20.	harmony	After the trip, Laney appreciated the **harmony** in her home.

145

4 Word Shapes

Help students form a correct image of whole words.

Say Look at each word and think about its shape. Now, write the word in the correct Word Shape Boxes. You may check off each word as you use it.

(In most words, the letters **ar** spell the sound of /är/, whether it is at the beginning, middle, or end of a word. There are a few exceptions.)

Say In the Word Shape Boxes, fill in the boxes containing the letters that spell the sound of /är/ in each word.

Take a minute to memorize...

Psalm 98:7

Words with /är/ · Lesson 15

B Word Shapes   Name _____

Using the word bank below, write each word in the correct Word Shape Boxes. Next, in the Word Shape Boxes, fill in the boxes containing the letter or letters that spell the sound of /är/ in each word.

1. artichoke
2. compartment
3. snarl
4. partner
5. Antarctica
6. harbor
7. hardship
8. radar
9. argument
10. cardiac
11. harmony
12. chart
13. hearty
14. dart
15. Arkansas
16. carton
17. bargain
18. artery
19. department
20. cartilage

Word Bank

Antarctica	artichoke	carton	department	hearty
argument	bargain	chart	harbor	partner
Arkansas	cardiac	compartment	hardship	radar
artery	cartilage	dart	harmony	snarl

94

Answers may vary for duplicate word shapes.

Be Prepared For Fun

Check these supply lists for **Fun Ways to Spell** - presented **Day 2**. Purchase and/or gather these items ahead of time!

General
- Pencil
- 3 X 5 Cards cut in half (20 per child)
- Spelling List

Auditory
- Spelling List

Visual
- Pencil
- Notebook Paper
- Spelling List

Tactile
- Blackboard and Chalk
  -OR-
- White Board and Marker
- Spelling List

146

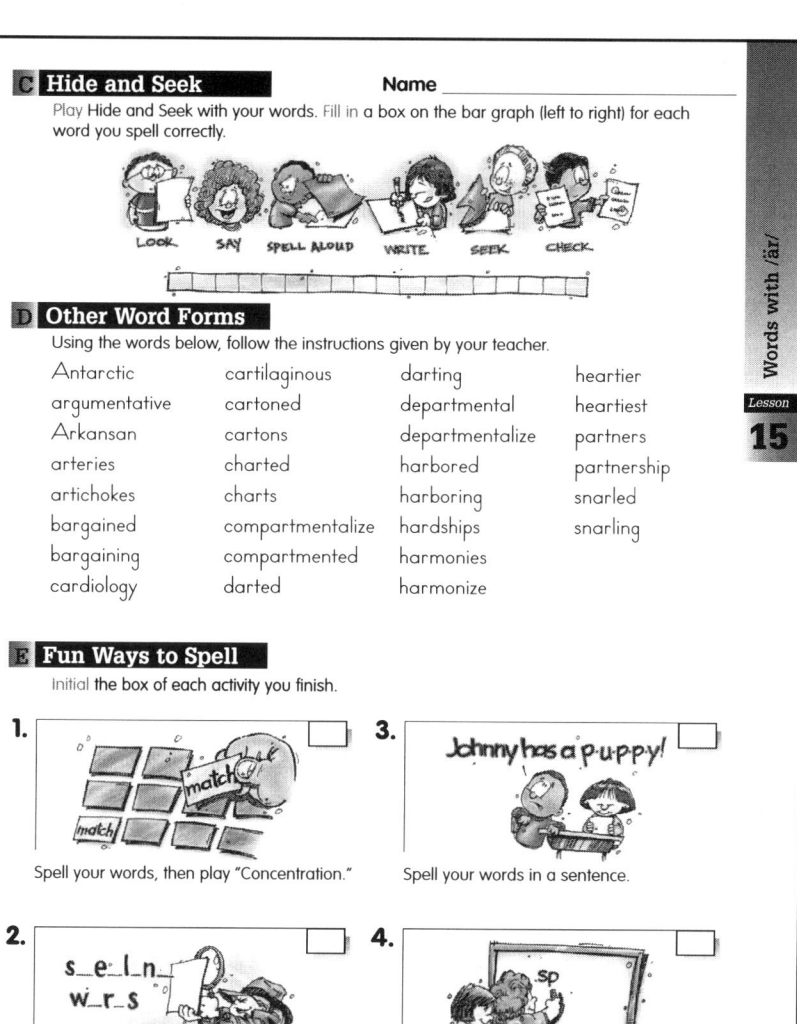

C Hide and Seek

Name _____

Play Hide and Seek with your words. Fill in a box on the bar graph (left to right) for each word you spell correctly.

LOOK SAY SPELL ALOUD WRITE SEEK CHECK

D Other Word Forms

Using the words below, follow the instructions given by your teacher.

Antarctic	cartilaginous	darting	heartier
argumentative	cartoned	departmental	heartiest
Arkansan	cartons	departmentalize	partners
arteries	charted	harbored	partnership
artichokes	charts	harboring	snarled
bargained	compartmentalize	hardships	snarling
bargaining	compartmented	harmonies	
cardiology	darted	harmonize	

E Fun Ways to Spell

Initial the box of each activity you finish.

1. [ ] Spell your words, then play "Concentration."

3. [ ] Johnny has a puppy! Spell your words in a sentence.

2. [ ] s_e_l_n_ w_r_s Decode your spelling words.

4. [ ] Play the game "Spelling Backwards."

95

---

1 Hide and Seek

Reinforce spelling by using multiple styles of learning.

On a white board, Teacher writes each word — one at a time. **Have students:**

- **Look** at the word.
- **Say** the word out loud.
- **Spell** the word out loud.
- **Hide** (teacher erases word.)
- **Write** the word on paper.
- **Seek** (teacher rewrites word.)
- **Check** spelling. If incorrect, rewrite word correctly.

2 Other Word Forms

This activity is optional. Have students write original sentences using these Other Word Forms:

**snarled
cartoned
departmental
partnership**

3 Fun Ways to Spell

Four activities are provided. Use one, two, three, or all of the activities. Have students initial the box for each activity they complete.

Options:

- assign activities to students according to their learning styles
- set up the activities in learning centers for the students to do throughout the day
- divide students into four groups and assign one activity per group
- do one activity per day

General

Spell your words; then play "Concentration"...
- Write each spelling word on a card. Mix your cards and a classmate's cards together. Arrange them face down in five rows of eight. Pick up two cards. If the cards match, play again. If the cards do not match, turn them back over. It is your classmate's turn. Continue taking turns until all the cards are matched. The player with the most cards wins!

Auditory

To spell your words in a sentence...
- Ask a classmate to read a spelling word to you from the list.
- Spell the word aloud and use it in a sentence.
- Ask your classmate to check your spelling.
- Each correctly spelled word that is used properly in a sentence counts as one point.
- Switch and continue taking turns.

Visual

To decode your spelling words...
- Look at the first word on your list.
- Write every other letter of the word on your paper, putting a blank where each missing letter belongs.
- Trade papers with a classmate and fill in the missing letters.
- Check your spelling.

Tactile

To play the game "Spelling Backwards"...
- Ask a classmate to stand behind you and draw the letters to spell a word from your list on your back.
- Write the spelling word on the board as your classmate traces the letters on your back.
- Ask your classmate to check your spelling.
- Trade places and take turns until you have each spelled all the words.

Working with Words

Familiarize students with word meaning and usage.

Rhyming Clues

Write the words **farmstead**, **freewheeler**, **forehead**, and **cartwheel** on the board. Have a volunteer underline the two words that rhyme (**farmstead**, **forehead**). Tell students that, for this exercise, words need to rhyme on at least the last syllable to be considered rhyming words. Explain that students will be matching some of their spelling words to a rhyming word.

Write the spelling word that rhymes with each word below.

The AR's Have It

Each spelling word in this lesson has the **/är/** sound. Answer each question with a word from the word bank. You may use a dictionary to help you. Write the word in the blank.

Take a minute to memorize...

Psalm 98:7

Similar Sounds

Write the spelling word that rhymes with the last syllable of each word below.

1. message — cartilage
2. kindergartner — partner
3. battery — artery
4. horsewhip — hardship
5. tailspin — bargain
6. start — dart or chart
7. tartan — carton

8. replica — Antarctica
9. smart — chart or dart
10. maniac — cardiac
11. barber — harbor
12. womenfolk — artichoke
13. symphony — harmony
14. party — hearty
15. overdraw — Arkansas
16. bizarre — radar
17. gnarl — snarl
18. confident — argument, compartment, or department

The AR's Have It

Answer each question with an **/är/** word from the word bank. Write the word in the blank.

1. What /är/ word means a pleasing blend of sounds? __harmony__
2. What /är/ word means to strike an agreement? __bargain__
3. What /är/ word means vigorously healthy? __hearty__
4. What /är/ word means a quarrel or disagreement? __argument__
5. What /är/ word is a continent centered on the South Pole? __Antarctica__
6. What /är/ word means relating to the heart? __cardiac__
7. What /är/ word means a place to safely anchor boats? __harbor__
8. What /är/ word is what your outer ear is made of? __cartilage__
9. What /är/ word means a tube that carries blood from the heart? __artery__
10. What /är/ word means a section of enclosed space? __compartment__
11. What /är/ word is a state whose eastern border is the Mississippi River? __Arkansas__

Word Bank

Antarctica	artichoke	carton	department	hearty
argument	bargain	chart	harbor	partner
Arkansas	cardiac	compartment	hardship	radar
artery	cartilage	dart	harmony	snarl

G Dictation

Name _____

Write each sentence as your teacher dictates. Use correct punctuation.

1. Mom and I went to a big department store to shop for clothes to take with me.

2. Suzanne and Dad had an argument over the sunscreen she had brought.

3. As the huge ship sailed into the harbor, we saw people selling many things.

H Proofreading

If a word is misspelled, fill in the oval by that word. If all the words are spelled correctly, fill in the oval by **no mistake**.

1. ○ crocodile
   ○ doctor
   ● harber
   ○ no mistake

2. ● cardiack
   ○ hardship
   ○ comment
   ○ no mistake

3. ● antarctica
   ○ compost
   ○ contact
   ○ no mistake

4. ○ Hawaii
   ● Arkansaw
   ○ college
   ○ no mistake

5. ○ deposit
   ○ glossary
   ● argumint
   ○ no mistake

6. ● bargin
   ○ snarl
   ○ bottom
   ○ no mistake

7. ○ radar
   ○ colonies
   ● harmonie
   ○ no mistake

8. ● arttery
   ○ artichoke
   ○ demolish
   ○ no mistake

9. ○ atomic
   ○ commerce
   ● cartillage
   ○ no mistake

10. ● cartin
    ○ geometry
    ○ chart
    ○ no mistake

11. ○ dart
    ● compartmint
    ○ partner
    ○ no mistake

12. ● departmint
    ○ hearty
    ○ concentrate
    ○ no mistake

97

149

3 Hide and Seek

Reinforce correct spelling of current spelling words. Repeat this activity from Day 2.

4 Vocabulary Extension

Have your students complete this activity to strengthen spelling ability and expand vocabulary. The reproducible master is provided in Appendix A as shown on the inset page to the right.

1 Posttest

Visit the **A Reason For** website to download free, printable Posttest pages.

I will say the word once, use it in a sentence, then say it again. Write your words on a separate sheet of paper.

Progress Chart
Students may record scores. (Appendix B)

Personal Dictionary
Students may add any words they have misspelled to their personal dictionaries. (Appendix B)

Hide and Seek

Play Hide and Seek with your words. Fill in a bar graph (left to right) for each word you spell correctly.

Vocabulary Extension

Multiple Choice

Fill in the oval by the word(s) with the same or nearly the same meaning as the word in bold type.

1. pharmacist
- ○ large, brightly colored bird
- ● person who prepares and sells medicines
- ○ one who grows crops
- ○ machine that reproduces sounds

2. carpenter
- ○ thick floor covering made of fabric
- ○ vehicle pulled by horses
- ○ part of the engine in a car
- ● someone who works with wood

3. bargain
- ● discuss the price of something
- ○ to trade food for other goods
- ○ land where crops will not grow
- ○ common cereal plant

4. margin
- ○ something made of stone or cement
- ○ dark reddish brown color
- ○ place where people buy and sell food
- ● blank space down the edge of a page

5. article
- ○ disease that makes people's joints swell
- ○ false, not real or natural
- ● piece of writing published in a newspaper
- ○ conceited and proud

6. charming
- ● enchanting and appealing
- ○ document that states the rights of people
- ○ raising money to help people in need
- ○ deep crack in the surface of the earth

7. regard
- ○ in spite of everything
- ● opinion; esteem
- ○ to give money back to someone
- ○ person who is forced to leave their home

8. darkened
- ○ room with photography equipment
- ○ someone who is dearly loved
- ○ unpleasantly wet and damp
- ● caused something to be without light

9. enlarged
- ● made bigger or increased
- ○ gave something all your attention
- ○ mystery or puzzle
- ○ made something better or greater

10. guardian
- ○ person who is dirty or sloppy
- ○ musical instrument with strings
- ● person legally responsible for a child
- ○ direction or supervision

337

1.	argument	Laney did not want to get into an **argument** with Dad Larkin.
2.	department	There weren't any swimsuits for sale in the girls' **department**.
3.	bargain	Shopping online yielded a **bargain** or two on summer clothing.
4.	snarl	Wicker began to **snarl** when the squirrel got too close to his dog food.
5.	cardiac	Laney hoped her dad's **cardiac** trouble would not flare up.
6.	hardship	The stress of his job is a real **hardship** on his heart.
7.	artery	He had a clogged **artery** and high blood pressure.
8.	partner	His law-firm **partner** will be in charge while Laney's dad is gone on vacation.
9.	Arkansas	Her dad grew up in **Arkansas**, but has not been there in years.
10.	Antarctica	They will not pass close to **Antarctica** on their way to the Bahamas.
11.	artichoke	At dinner, the waiter brought a platter of steamed **artichoke**.
12.	hearty	She enjoyed the **hearty** breakfast they served each morning.
13.	harbor	The ship docked safely in the **harbor**.
14.	carton	Laney opened a small **carton** of milk for Suzette as they relaxed on the deck.
15.	radar	A ship uses sonar rather than **radar** to detect objects in its path.
16.	cartilage	Laney's dad said even the **cartilage** inside his nose felt sunburned.
17.	chart	The captain and his crew carefully **chart** their course before the voyage.
18.	compartment	Laney's sleeping **compartment** was small but very comfortable.
19.	dart	Laney expertly threw a **dart** at the bull's-eye on the board.
20.	harmony	Laney realized she should thank God for the **harmony** in her home.

I **Game**   Name _____

Help Laney pack the things Coach Larkin suggested. Move one space for each word you or your team spells correctly.

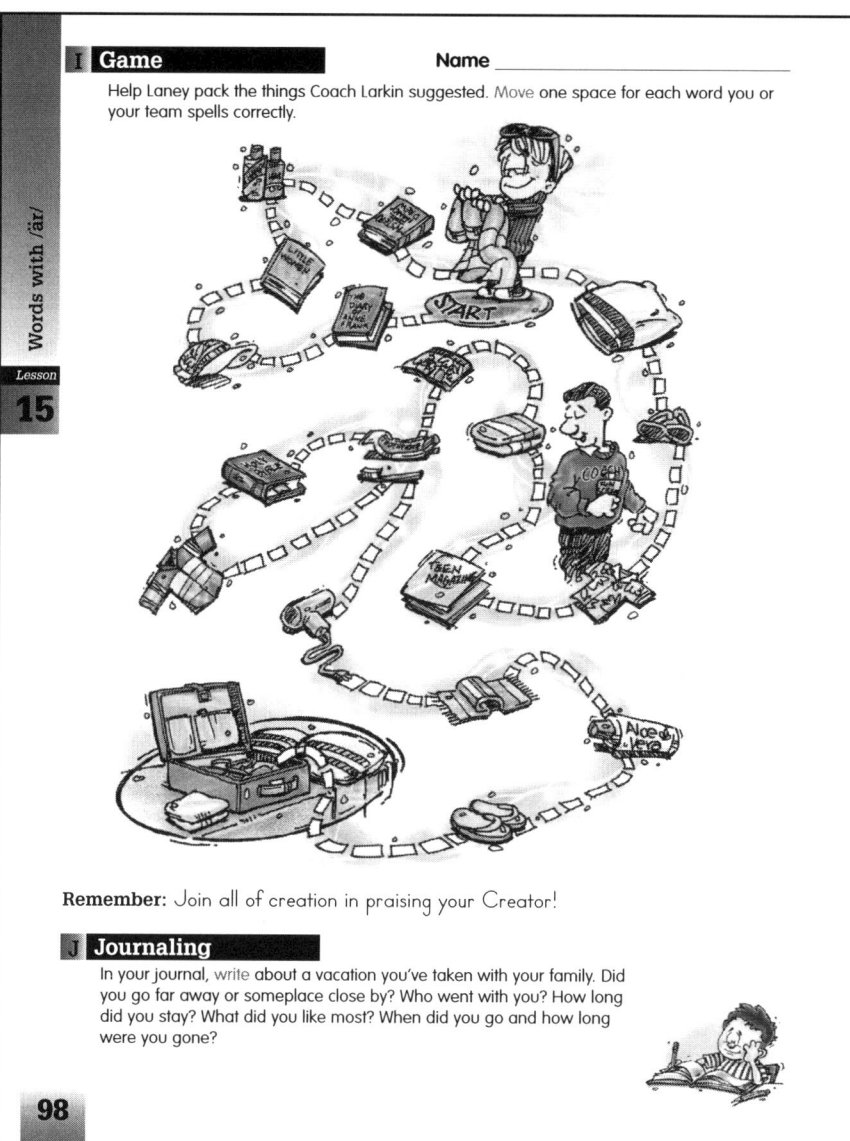

Remember: Join all of creation in praising your Creator!

J **Journaling**

In your journal, write about a vacation you've taken with your family. Did you go far away or someplace close by? Who went with you? How long did you stay? What did you like most? When did you go and how long were you gone?

98

How to Play:

- Divide the class into two teams.
- Have each student place his/her game piece on Start.
- Have a student from team A go to the board.
- Say the spelling word.
- Have the student write the word on the board.
- If correct, instruct each member of team A to move his/her game piece forward one space.
- Alternate between teams A and B.
- The team to reach Laney's suitcase first is the winner.
- **Small Group Option**: Students may play this game without teacher direction in small groups of two or more.

Game

2 Reinforce spelling skills and provide motivation and interest.

Materials

- game page (from student text)
- game pieces (1 per child)
- game word list

Game Word List

1. **harbor**
2. **cardiac**
3. **hardship**
4. **Antarctica**
5. **Arkansas**
6. **argument**
7. **bargain**
8. **snarl**
9. **harmony**
10. **radar**
11. **artery**
12. **artichoke**
13. **cartilage**
14. **carton**
15. **chart**
16. **compartment**
17. **department**
18. **dart**
19. **hearty**
20. **partner**

Journaling

3 Provide a meaningful reason for correct spelling through personal writing.

Review the story using discussion leads provided on the following page. Encourage students to apply the Scriptural value in their journaling.

151

(Say)
- Where did Laney go for Christmas vacation? (The Bahamas.)
- Where are some places you've been for Christmas vacation?
- How did Laney feel about leaving the small town where she lives with her mom and stepdad? (She was happy to get out of there for a while.)
- What were some of the things Laney was looking forward to seeing or doing in the Bahamas? (Coral reefs, sailing, snorkeling, clear blue water, crashing waves)
- Whom did Laney miss while she was gone? (Her mom, stepdad, and Wicker.)
- Why do you think she missed them so much?

IRAQ is one of the very few words ending in Q.

Word Wow!

Fujiyama

When Setsuko and her parents climb Mount Fuji, she gets an idea of how truly incredible God is.

Setsuko checked the classroom clock. She had a few minutes free. Maybe she'd work on her spelling journal assignment. Pulling the worktext out of her desk, she flipped a few pages till she found the right spot. Silently she read the directions. "Read Psalm 57:10. Think about the words this Scripture uses to describe God's love. In your journal, write about something you think of when you read these descriptive words."

Setsuko turned the page and read the Scripture. "Vast as the heavens. Higher than the skies." She stared out the window as the words triggered a memory from last summer....

"Aren't we ready yet?" Setsuko tugged at her father's sleeve. "Look, those people are leaving."

Mr. Noma tucked a full water bottle in his small pack. "What's the hurry, Suzy-Q? You've been rushing from one thing to the next ever since we got to Japan. Afraid you'll miss something? You know, we'll be on Fujiyama all night."

"I want to be sure we get to the top before the sun comes up." Setsuko stepped behind her father to get out of the way of a group of boisterous young men.

Mrs. Noma worked her way through another group of climbers to reach her husband and daughter. "What a crowd!" She shook her head, "I think there are more climbers tonight than when we climbed Fuji-san before."

"Well, you know, Sweetheart, that was a long, long time ago," Mr. Noma teased. "Hey!" He barely caught the jacket she tossed at him. "When you and I climbed as teenagers, the weather was

lousy. Since the climbing season only lasts from July 1 to August 31, whenever the weather's decent, the mountain's crowded. And tonight it's almost perfect."

"So let's climb!" Setsuko urged.

"Put this on, Setsuko-chan." Mrs. Noma handed a jacket to her daughter. "Then we'll go." She glanced at her watch. "We'll have plenty of time to make it for the tradition of watching sunrise from the summit, especially since we're starting from the fifth station."

"How many stations are there?" Setsuko almost stepped on her father's heels as she eagerly followed him from the hut.

"Ten, dividing the climb into stages." Mr. Noma led his family onto the trail. "At each one we can pay to get another stamp burned into our climbing sticks."

"All right!" Setsuko admired the octagonal walking stick in her hand. "Do all the stamps look like this one?" She ran her hand over the rectangles filled with Japanese characters.

"No, they're all different." Mrs. Noma stopped and flicked her flashlight off for an instant to look into the sky. "Isn't the moon beautiful now that we're away from the lights?"

"Yeah." Setsuko glanced up. "But we could see it even better if some people weren't carrying those lanterns. Why do they do that, Otosan?"

"Pilgrimage." Mr. Noma moved at a steady pace, following the stream of people in front of him. "Climbing Mount Fuji began as a religious practice, and some people in Japan still consider the mountain to be sacred. See those climbers in grass sandals?"

Setsuko kicked a rock with the toe of her sturdy hiking boot. "I bet they're going to have really sore feet by the time they get to the top!" She walked in silence for a few moments. "How far is it to the top?"

"Well, the volcano is 12,395 feet high, the highest peak in Japan, and the path switches back and forth as it goes up the side." Mr. Noma shifted the pack on his back. "We'll be covering a lot of ground in the next few hours."

"What do we do if we get to the top before the sun comes up?" Setsuko's eyes followed a man with a red and white handkerchief tied around his head. He passed the Nomas and trotted on.

"We probably won't get there too early," Mother chuckled. "The path is almost level right here at station 5, but that won't last for long!"

The trail turned steeply up the mountain. Mr. Noma called over his shoulder, "Watch your step."

Soon Setsuko was struggling to get enough air. "Is it...pff...pff...like this...pff...pff...all the way?"

Mr. Noma paused by a tall wooden sign and waited for Setsuko to catch up. "Some parts of the path are dirt, some gravel, some cobblestone. It's not a technical climb, but it certainly is a grueling hike, and lots of people that start out don't make it to the top." He motioned to the sign. "Look at these rules."

Setsuko read the list aloud, "'Avoid climbing during bad weather. Take refuge at nearby shelters when lightning, strong wind, or heavy rain occurs. Do not stray from the route. Do not run when descending. Beware of falling rocks. Do not climb when tired. Be careful and enjoy a safe climb.' But, I'm already tired!" she wailed.

"Come on, Suzy-Q! Where's all that energy we've seen while you've been dragging your mother and me all over Tokyo?" Mr. Noma teased.

"Gone," Setsuko sighed as they rejoined the stream of climbers. She concentrated on placing one foot in front of the other and was

153

surprised when they reached the sixth station. Setsuko revived a bit when she ate some crackers and watched in fascination as the station stamp was burned onto her stick with a small branding iron heated in an open fire. Then, back to the climb.

"Okasan, my feet slide back a step for every two steps forward!" Setsuko complained.

"That's because this part of the trail is volcanic ash." Mrs. Noma swept the light from her flashlight along the trail. "We take a different trail down the mountain. It's almost entirely an ash slide. One step down and you can slide for yards! It makes a quick trip down that you'll be glad for then, but I'll admit this is hard stuff to climb." Setsuko's mother used both hands and feet to make it up a particularly steep place.

Suddenly a young woman almost bowled over some climbers as she raced down the trail. Setsuko slipped and sat down hard on the trail when the girl flew past the Noma family. The woman's laughter rang out as she ran swiftly down the ash slide. Setsuko stared in horror when the young woman's laughter turned to screams of terror. She was going too fast and she couldn't stop! In seconds she would go over the sheer drop along the edge of the trail.

In an instant, two men on the trail below launched themselves toward her, knocking her off her feet. Everyone along that stretch of trail held their breath as the three climbers slid in a tangle of arms and legs toward the edge. Inches away from thin air, they halted.

Setsuko took the hand her father offered and pulled herself up. "I guess that's why the rule says 'Do not run when descending.'" She shook her head and started carefully climbing once more.

It didn't get easier. Just before the seventh station they scaled a rock face. It was kind of scary finding handholds and pulling yourself up the chains that had been firmly placed along the rock face, especially since the weather had changed and occasional drops of freezing rain pelted the climbers. The crowded station was warm and the fire wonderful.

"Otosan, are we even going to be able to see the sunrise at all in this weather?" Setsuko shrugged into a thick sweatshirt. "I thought it would stay nice like it was when we started."

"Fuji-san is tall enough to create its own weather, Suzy-Q." Mr. Noma sipped hot tea gratefully. "But it could be clear on top. Somewhere around station eight the mountain usually breaks through the clouds. Ready?"

"I'm tired and sleepy and cold." Setsuko rubbed her gritty eyes. "I don't think I can make it," she grumbled.

"Sure you can." Mrs. Noma gave her daughter a hug. "We'll just keep up a slow, steady pace and be there before you know it."

But when they reached station eight, Setsuko was still ready to quit. Parts of the shelter were occupied by hikers sleeping on mats. Effects of high altitude, stiff winds, and the hard night climb tempted Setsuko to join them.

"This should revive you, Setsuko-chan." Father handed her a bowl of deliciously warm, fragrant soup.

The soup helped. Setsuko even found the energy to write a short message on a couple of postcards and to drop them in the mailbox at station eight, Mount Fuji Post Office. Then it was back to putting one foot in front of the other, trying to ignore the cold and her tired muscles.

"Seven hours—not bad." Setsuko bumped into her father when he suddenly stopped. "Whoa, there! Don't you want to stay a minute or two after working so hard to get here?"

"Here?" Setsuko squeaked. "This is it?" She looked around in dismay. A shrine, several mountain huts and a crowd of weary hikers. True, the sign on the shrine said "SUMMIT," but could this really be it? It seemed anti-climactic—that is until a few minutes later when the sun began to rise!

Mrs. Noma slipped her arm around her weary daughter and whispered the well known verse as they watched the sunrise, "The heavens declare the glory of God."

"Everything in heaven and earth is Yours, oh Lord," Mr. Noma added quietly, wrapping his arms around mother and daughter. Setsuko leaned back against her father, tiredness forgotten. The light and color were breathtaking, the view awesome as the sun slipped slowly into the heavens.

A bell rang. Setsuko blinked and looked around. She was at school, and her free time was up. Oh, well, at least she knew what she would write about in her journal this week!

2 Discussion Time

Check understanding of the story and development of personal values.

- Of what did Psalm 57:10 remind Setsuko?
- What mountain did Setsuko and her parents climb last summer in Japan?
- Why do most people climb the mountain at night?
- Why were there so many people climbing the mountain that night?
- At which station did the Noma family start their climb?
- What happened to the woman that ran down the trail?
- What did Setsuko think when they reached the summit?
- How did her thoughts change when the sun began to rise?

A Preview

Write each word as your teacher says it.

Name _____

1. Arizona
2. librarian
3. prepare
4. software
5. narrate
6. marriage
7. Ontario
8. narrow
9. area
10. aware
11. caramel
12. parakeet
13. barracks
14. embarrassed

15. barrier
16. aerobics
17. Delaware
18. barren
19. compare
20. parallel

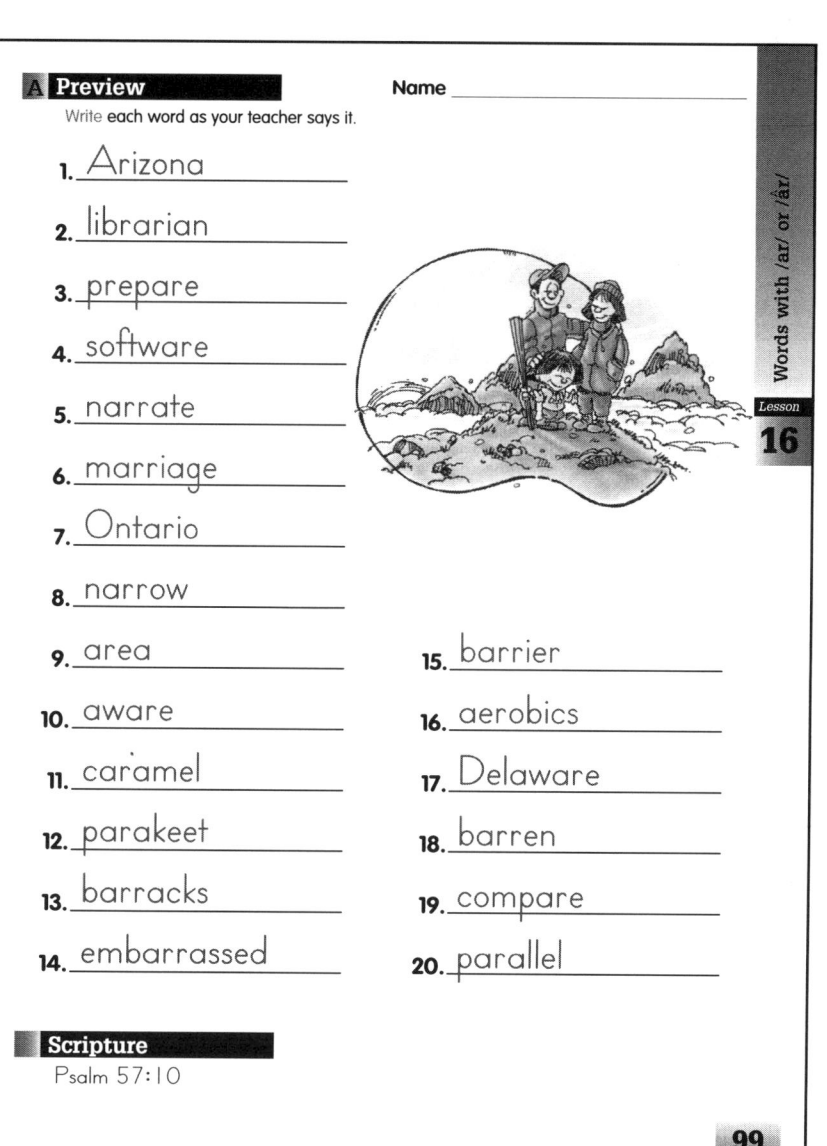

Scripture
Psalm 57:10

99

3 Preview

Test for knowledge of the correct spellings of these words.

Customize Your List
On a separate sheet of paper, additional words of your choice may be tested.

 Say

I will say each word once, use the word in a sentence, then say the word again. Write the words on the lines in your Worktext.

Correct Immediately!

 Say

Let's correct our Preview. I will spell each word out loud. If you spelled a word incorrectly, rewrite it correctly.

 Graph

Progress Chart
Students may record scores. (Reproducible master provided in Appendix B.)

1.	Arizona	Mt. Fuji is not in **Arizona**.
2.	librarian	Before the trip, the **librarian** helped Setsuko find information on travel in Japan.
3.	prepare	She wanted to **prepare** for the trip in every way possible.
4.	software	The Nomas purchased **software** that helped them plan their trip.
5.	narrate	Setsuko listened to her father **narrate** an ancient tale about Mt. Fuji.
6.	marriage	This was the first time since their **marriage** that the Nomas had been to Japan.
7.	Ontario	A scientist from **Ontario** was there to make the climb.
8.	narrow	The trail quickly became **narrow** and steep.
9.	area	There was more than one rest **area** along the trail.
10.	aware	Setsuko wasn't **aware** the climb would be so exhausting.
11.	caramel	She chewed a sticky **caramel** as she rested.
12.	parakeet	One woman carried her caged **parakeet** on the climb.
13.	barracks	There are **barracks** or bunk houses at the foot of Mt. Fuji.
14.	embarrassed	The woman was **embarrassed** about nearly falling off the mountain.
15.	barrier	Two men made a **barrier** with their bodies, to stop her fall.
16.	aerobics	Setsuko felt sure she would not feel like doing **aerobics** after this climb.
17.	Delaware	Their friends from **Delaware** had made the long trip with them.
18.	barren	The summit seemed like a dismal, **barren** place till the sun rose.
19.	compare	Setsuko thought no sight could **compare** with this.
20.	parallel	"Nothing can **parallel** God's majesty," said Mr. Noma.

4 Word Shapes

Help students form a correct image of whole words.

Say Look at each word and think about its shape. Now, write the word in the correct Word Shape Boxes. You may check off each word as you use it.

(In many words, the sounds of **/ar/** and **/âr/** are spelled with **are** or **ar**. Because spellers cannot rely on a phonetic way of remembering the various spellings, this sound is often difficult.)

Say In the Word Shape Boxes, fill in the boxes containing the letters that spell the sound of **/ar/** or **/âr/** in each word.

Take a minute to memorize...

Psalm 57:10

B Word Shapes Name _____

Using the word bank below, write each word in the correct Word Shape Boxes. Next, in the Word Shape Boxes, fill in the boxes containing the letter or letters that spell the sound of /ar/ or /âr/ in each word.

1. Delaware
2. barren
3. narrow
4. Arizona
5. librarian
6. compare
7. narrate
8. marriage
9. aerobics
10. barrier

11. barracks
12. aware
13. caramel
14. embarrassed
15. area
16. parakeet
17. software
18. parallel
19. prepare
20. Ontario

Word Bank

aerobics	barracks	compare	marriage	parakeet
area	barren	Delaware	narrate	parallel
Arizona	barrier	embarrassed	narrow	prepare
aware	caramel	librarian	Ontario	software

100

Answers may vary for duplicate word shapes.

Be Prepared For Fun

Check these supply lists for **Fun Ways to Spell** - presented **Day 2**. Purchase and/or gather these items ahead of time!

General
• Pencil
• Notebook Paper
• Spelling List

Auditory
• Pencil
• 3 X 5 Cards Cut in half lengthwise (20 per child)
• Spelling List

Visual
• Colored Pencils
• Graph Paper (2 sheets per child)
• Spelling List

Tactile
• Clay
• Spelling List

C Hide and Seek Name _____

Play Hide and Seek with your words. Fill in a box on the bar graph (left to right) for each word you spell correctly.

LOOK SAY SPELL ALOUD WRITE SEEK CHECK

D Other Word Forms

Using the words below, follow the instructions given by your teacher.

areaway	caramels	library	parakeets
Arizonan	compared	marriageable	paralleled
awareness	comparison	narration	paralleling
barrenly	Delawarean	narrator	preparation
barrenness	embarrass	narrower	prepared
barriers	embarrassing	narrowest	unprepared

E Fun Ways to Spell

initial the box of each activity you finish.

1.
Classify your words according to syllables.

3.
got a "fish"? nope!
Spell your words and play "Match-It."

2.
Spell your words on graph paper.

4.
clay
Spell your words with clay.

101

Options:

- assign activities to students according to their learning styles
- set up the activities in learning centers for the students to do throughout the day
- divide students into four groups and assign one activity per group
- do one activity per day

General

To classify your words according to syllables...
- Write three headings on your paper: One-syllable, Two-syllable, and Three-syllable.
- Write the first word on your list under the proper heading.
- Draw a line through the word to divide it into syllables.
- Do this with each word.

Auditory

To spell your words and play "Match-It"...
- Write each word on a card. Mix your word-cards and a classmate's together. Deal six cards to each player; the rest face down between you. Ask your classmate for a word-card. If the word-card matches, take it and play again. If not, draw from the stack, and it is your classmate's turn. Take turns until all cards are matched.

Visual

To spell your words on graph paper...
- Look at the first word on your list.
- Shade in squares to form the letters of each word.
- Check your spelling.
- Do this with each word.

Tactile

To spell your words with clay...
- Roll pieces of clay into ropes.
- Use the ropes to make the letters of each word.
- Put them in the right order to spell each word.
- Check your spelling.

---

1 Hide and Seek

Reinforce spelling by using multiple styles of learning.

On a white board, Teacher writes each word — one at a time. **Have students:**

- **Look** at the word.
- **Say** the word out loud.
- **Spell** the word out loud.
- **Hide** (teacher erases word.)
- **Write** the word on paper.
- **Seek** (teacher rewrites word.)
- **Check** spelling. If incorrect, rewrite word correctly.

2 Other Word Forms

This activity is optional. Have students find and circle the Other Word Forms that are most nearly antonyms of the following:

ready
fruitfulness
ignorance
dissimilar

3 Fun Ways to Spell

Four activities are provided. Use one, two, three, or all of the activities. Have students initial the box for each activity they complete.

1 Working with Words

Familiarize students with word meaning and usage.

Hidden Words

Explain that the spelling words for this week are hidden in the puzzle. After finding each word, the student should write the word under the correct heading.

(Say) Use the word bank to help you find each of the words in the puzzle. Words may go across, down, or diagonally. Circle, then write the words.

Take a minute to memorize...

Psalm 57:10

F Working with Words

Name _____

Hidden Words

Use the word bank to help you find each of the words in the puzzle. Words may go across, down, or diagonally. Circle and write the words.

Words with /ar/ or /âr/

Lesson 16

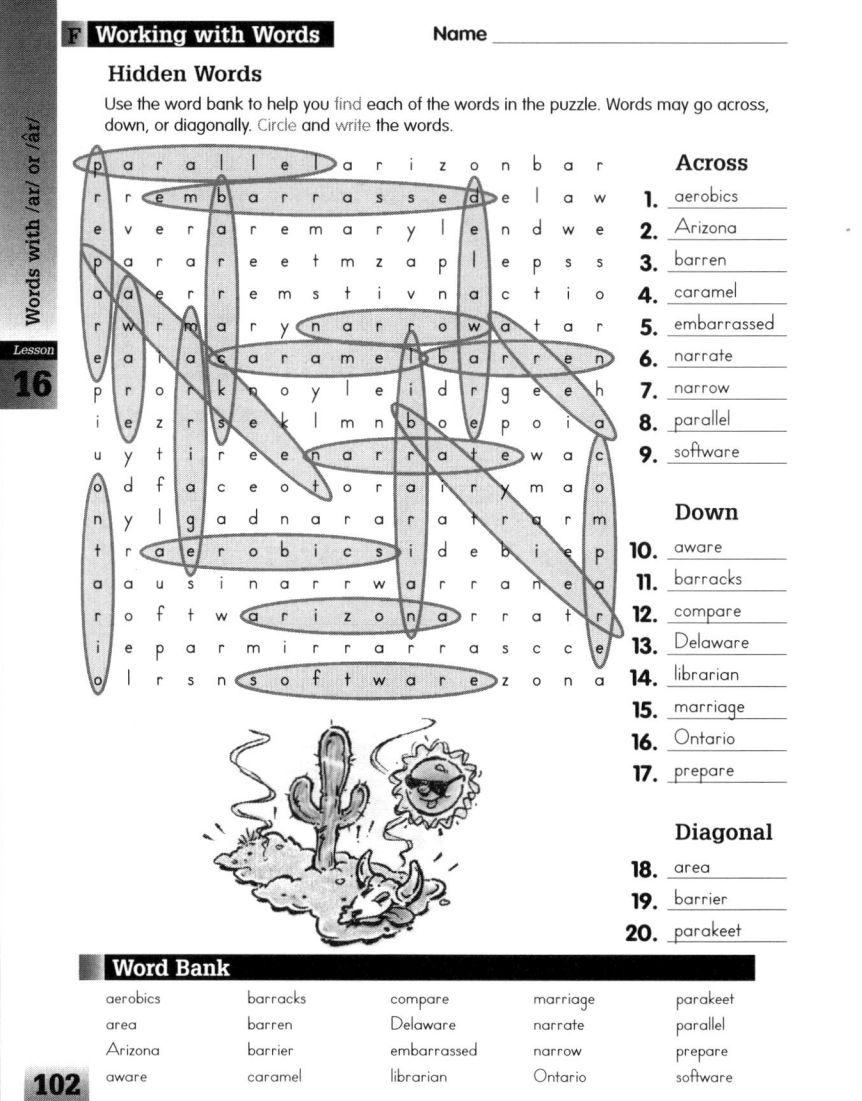

Across
1. aerobics
2. Arizona
3. barren
4. caramel
5. embarrassed
6. narrate
7. narrow
8. parallel
9. software

Down
10. aware
11. barracks
12. compare
13. Delaware
14. librarian
15. marriage
16. Ontario
17. prepare

Diagonal
18. area
19. barrier
20. parakeet

Word Bank

aerobics	barracks	compare	marriage	parakeet
area	barren	Delaware	narrate	parallel
Arizona	barrier	embarrassed	narrow	prepare
aware	caramel	librarian	Ontario	software

102

158

G Dictation

Name _____

Write **each sentence as your teacher dictates**. Use **correct punctuation**.

1. Setsuko was so weary, she found it hard to climb up the narrow, slippery track.

2. Looking around the area, she became aware of the beautiful things God had made.

3. Setsuko asked the librarian to help her find books about famous places.

H Proofreading

If a word is misspelled, fill in the oval by that word. If all the words are spelled correctly, fill in the oval by **no mistake**.

1.
- ○ area
- ● arizona
- ○ argument
- ○ no mistake

2.
- ● awair
- ○ radar
- ○ snarl
- ○ no mistake

3.
- ● baracks
- ○ barren
- ○ harmony
- ○ no mistake

4.
- ○ caramel
- ○ artichoke
- ● barryer
- ○ no mistake

5.
- ○ bargain
- ● compair
- ○ Delaware
- ○ no mistake

6.
- ● embarassed
- ○ hardship
- ○ Arkansas
- ○ no mistake

7.
- ○ cartilage
- ○ department
- ● librarien
- ○ no mistake

8.
- ○ cardiac
- ○ Antarctica
- ● marrige
- ○ no mistake

9.
- ● airobics
- ○ narrate
- ○ narrow
- ○ no mistake

10.
- ○ Ontario
- ● parakeat
- ○ chart
- ○ no mistake

11.
- ● parralel
- ○ carton
- ○ compartment
- ○ no mistake

12.
- ○ prepare
- ● softwair
- ○ harbor
- ○ no mistake

103

1 Dictation

Reinforce correct spelling by using current and previous words in context.

Say

Listen as I read each sentence and then write it in your Worktext. Remember to use correct capitalization and punctuation. (Slowly read each sentence twice. Sentences are found in the Student Worktext to the left.)

2 Proofreading

Familiarize students with standardized test format and reinforce recognition of misspelled words.

Say

Look at each set of words. If a word is misspelled, fill in the oval by that word. If all the words are spelled correctly, fill in the oval by **no mistake**.

3 Hide and Seek

Reinforce correct spelling of current spelling words. Repeat this activity from Day 2.

4 Vocabulary Extension

Have your students complete this activity to strengthen spelling ability and expand vocabulary. The reproducible master is provided in Appendix A as shown on the inset page to the right.

1 Posttest

Visit the **A Reason For** website to download free, printable Posttest pages.

I will say the word once, use it in a sentence, then say it again. Write your words on a separate sheet of paper.

Progress Chart
Students may record scores. (Appendix B)

Personal Dictionary
Students may add any words they have misspelled to their personal dictionaries. (Appendix B)

Lesson 16 | Vocabulary Extension

Hide and Seek

Play Hide and Seek with your words. Fill in a bar graph (left to right) for each word you spell correctly.

LOOK   SAY   HIDE   WRITE   SEEK   CHECK

Vocabulary Extension
Cause and Effect
Write a word from the word bank to complete each sentence.

1. If you promise that something will work, you ___guarantee___ it.
2. If you study about the tubes that carry blood throughout your body, you are learning about arteries, veins, and ___capillaries___.
3. If you want to write a letter to someone, you may write on some pretty ___stationery___.
4. If you do not know what a word means, you can look it up in a ___dictionary___.
5. If you are riding an exercise bike, it does not take you anywhere because it is ___stationary___.
6. If you are sent to teach people about Jesus, you are being a ___missionary___.
7. If you recite the details of something that has happened, you are being a ___narrator___.
8. If you have a glass tank in which you keep fish, you have an ___aquarium___.
9. If your mom says you must clean your room, it is ___necessary___ for you to do it.
10. If a country has a group of soldiers in the navy, air force, or army, they are known as a country's ___military___.
11. If you are hired to handle records, mail, and routine work for another person, you are their ___secretary___.
12. If you own a store that sells tools, bolts, nails, knobs, and other such things, you own a ___hardware___ store.

Word Bank

aquarium	guarantee	missionary	secretary
capillaries	hardware	narrator	stationary
dictionary	military	necessary	stationery

338

---

1. **librarian**   Setsuko asked the **librarian** for books about travel in Japan.
2. **prepare**   She and her family wanted to properly **prepare** for the trip.
3. **software**   There was a lot of **software** available for travel planning.
4. **marriage**   Since the beginning of their **marriage**, the Nomas had been planning a trip to Japan.
5. **Arizona**   Mt. Fuji is not in **Arizona**, but rather in Japan.
6. **narrow**   The path turned sharply and became **narrow** and steep.
7. **area**   Setsuko plopped down in the rest **area**, exhausted.
8. **caramel**   She pulled a **caramel** from her backpack and unwrapped it.
9. **aware**   She was not **aware** the climb would be so tiring.
10. **narrate**   While she rested, an elderly man began to **narrate** some of his childhood memories.
11. **parakeet**   One woman actually carried her **parakeet** in a cage as she climbed.
12. **barracks**   There were **barracks** at the foot of the mountain for spending the night.
13. **embarrassed**   The woman who fell was **embarrassed**, but very thankful.
14. **barrier**   She was very glad the two men formed a **barrier** to stop her fall.
15. **aerobics**   Setsuko knew she would not feel like attending **aerobics** after this climb.
16. **Delaware**   They met people from **Delaware** who had three young boys.
17. **Ontario**   The scientist from **Ontario** was a very strong climber.
18. **barren**   The summit looked **barren** and uninteresting at first.
19. **parallel**   Setsuko believed there was no **parallel** to the beauty before her.
20. **compare**   Nothing could **compare** with the majestic sunrise!

160

I Game

Name _____

Record points for each word you or your team spells correctly. Earn bonus points for each row in which all five words are spelled correctly.

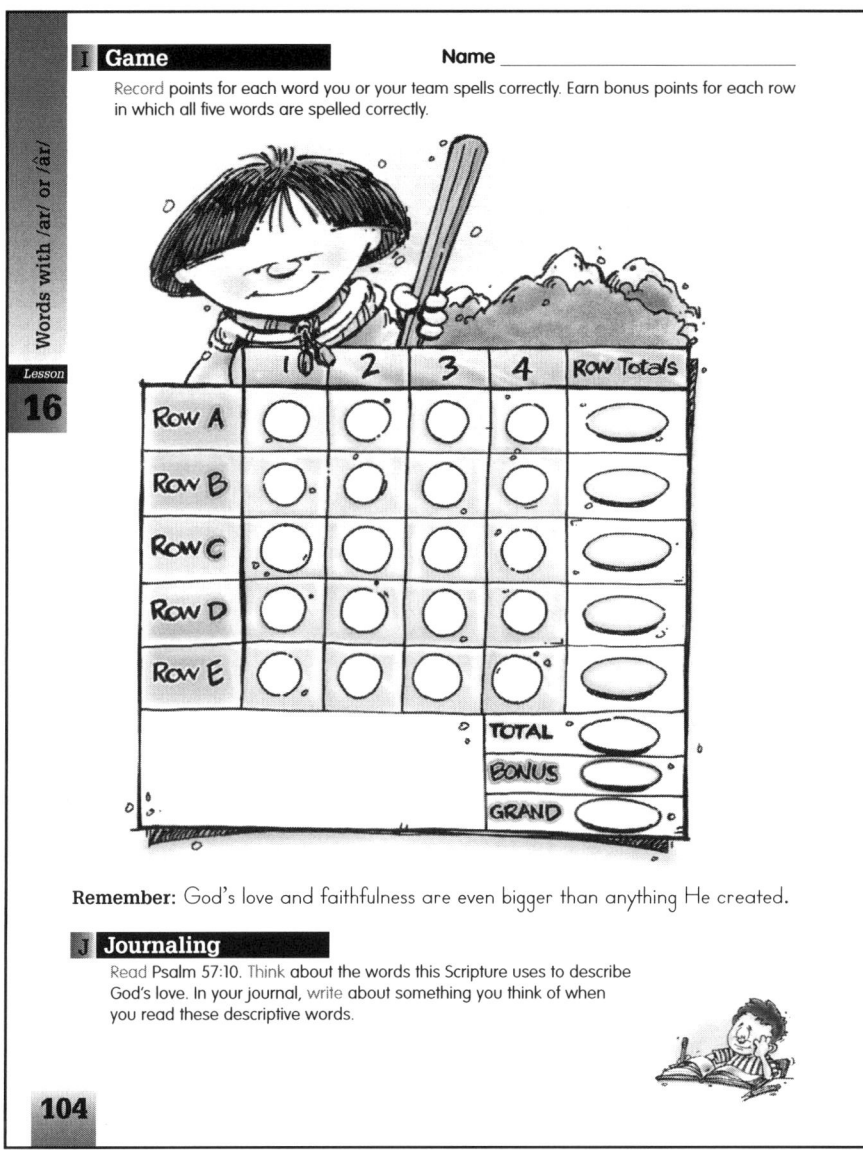

	1	2	3	4	Row Totals
Row A	○	○	○	○	⬭
Row B	○	○	○	○	⬭
Row C	○	○	○	○	⬭
Row D	○	○	○	○	⬭
Row E	○	○	○	○	⬭
				TOTAL	⬭
				BONUS	⬭
				GRAND	⬭

Remember: God's love and faithfulness are even bigger than anything He created.

J Journaling

Read Psalm 57:10. Think about the words this Scripture uses to describe God's love. In your journal, write about something you think of when you read these descriptive words.

104

How to Play:

- Divide the class into two teams.
- Have a student from team A choose a square on the grid by indicating the row letter and number.
- Say the word that matches that row letter and number from the team's word list.
- Have the student write the word on the board.
- If correct, have each member of that team record the awarded points (in parentheses by the word) in the circle in that box. If the word is misspelled, have him/her put an **X** in that circle. That square may not be chosen again.
- Repeat this process with the second team.
- When all the words have been spelled by both teams, have each team tally its score. Award a bonus of 5 points for each row in which all four words were spelled correctly.
- Have the teams record their grand totals. The team with the highest score is the winner.

2 Game

Reinforce spelling skills and provide motivation and interest.

Materials

- game page (from student text)
- pencils (1 per child)
- game word list

Game Word List

Team A			Team B
E4	**aerobics (4)**		A1
E3	**area (2)**		A2
E2	**Arizona (3)**		A3
E1	**aware (1)**		A4
D4	**barracks (4)**		B1
D3	**barren (1)**		B2
D2	**barrier (3)**		B3
D1	**caramel (2)**		B4
C4	**compare (2)**		C1
C3	**Delaware (1)**		C2
C2	**embarrassed (3)**		C3
C1	**librarian (4)**		C4
B4	**marriage (3)**		D1
B3	**narrate (1)**		D2
B2	**narrow (4)**		D3
B1	**Ontario (2)**		D4
A4	**parakeet (1)**		E1
A3	**parallel (4)**		E2
A2	**prepare (2)**		E3
A1	**software (3)**		E4

3 Journaling

Provide a meaningful reason for correct spelling through personal writing.

Review the story using discussion leads provided on the following page. Encourage students to apply the Scriptural value in their journaling.

Journaling (continued)

Say

- Have you ever climbed a mountain? (Allow time to share experiences.)

- Why is Mount Fuji special to the Japanese people? (It is the highest peak in Japan. Climbing the mountain began as a religious practice and many still consider the mountain to be sacred.)

- What were some of the rules for climbing Mount Fuji? (Avoid climbing during bad weather. Take refuge at nearby huts when lightning, strong wind, or heavy rain occurs. Do not stray from the route. Do not run when descending. Beware of falling rocks. Do not climb when tired. Be careful.)

- Why were so many people climbing that night? (The climbing season only lasts from July 1 to August 31, so many people climb whenever the weather is good during that time.)

- Why did Setsuko get so tired? (It got cold, they were climbing at a high altitude on steep trails, and they climbed all night.)

- What could you pay to have done to your walking stick at each station? (You could have a souvenir stamp from that station burned into the wooden walking stick.)

- What was different about Station 8? (There was a post office there on the mountain.)

- Do you think Setsuko was glad she made it to the top? Why or why not? (Yes. The view of the sunrise was awesome.)

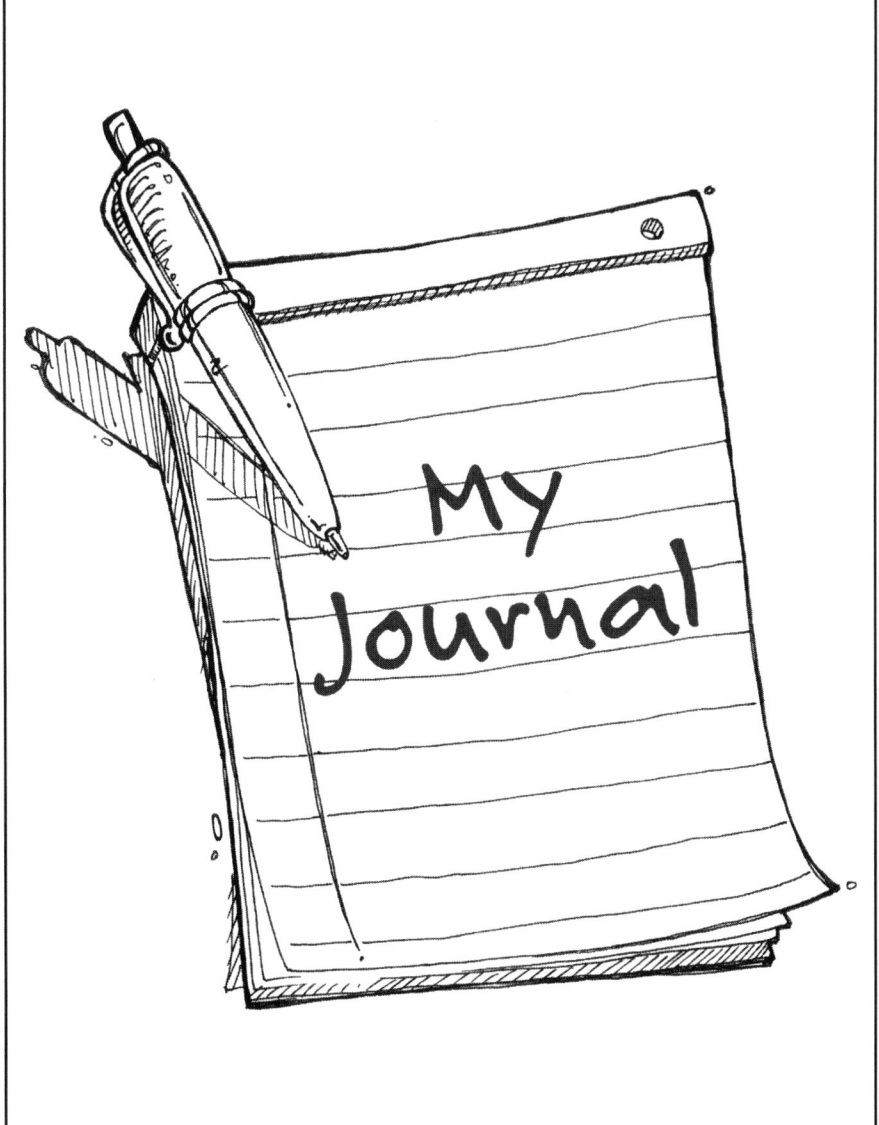

"OF" is apparently the only word in which an "F" is pronounced like a "V."

The Promise of Peace

Setsuko learns that, although horrible things happen in this world, God always keeps his promises to be with us.

"Look, Okasan!" Setsuko pointed out the window of the train. "There's a river. I wonder if it's the Ota River. Aren't there six rivers here?"

"That's right." Mrs. Noma watched the changing scenes flash by. "Hiroshima means 'Wide Island' and its nickname is the 'City of Water' because it grew from five different villages that were settled on the river deltas. Now we usually remember it as the city destroyed by the first atomic bomb."

"Our stop is next—have you got everything together?" Mr. Noma asked Setsuko.

Setsuko grabbed her backpack, "Right here—camera, wallet, comb. Are we going to the museum first?"

"I think so." Father led the way toward the door. "Stick close, you two."

The triangular-shaped park was a peaceful island in the city between two rivers. Once an area filled with fashionable shops, it was demolished by the atomic bomb on August 6, 1945. Now there are flowers and more than 1,600 trees shading the various peace memorials in the area.

Walking into the park from the south, the Nomas passed a statue of a mother bending over to shield a small child she held in her arms, while reaching behind to protect her older child. Next, the massive Fountain of Peace sprayed constantly into the sky.

The Peace Memorial Hall was a long rectangular cement-and-glass building built on 10 cement columns. It was quiet inside the museum. Setsuko gazed in horrified fascination at the displays. She couldn't stop looking at the lunch boxes blackened by the blast, wristwatches stopped at the instant of the explosion, glass bottles melted

together from the intense heat, and stone columns on which human shadows are permanently etched.

After a couple of hours, it was nice to get out in the sun again, to hear birds singing and children laughing in the park. Setsuko pointed out an object at the end of a wide cement walkway. "What's that thing that looks kind of like the top part of a covered wagon?"

"A cenotaph. This booklet says that it's the shape of an ancient Japanese clay house and is there to keep the souls of those who died in the bombing out of the rain." Mr. Noma scanned the brochure while leading his family toward the strange monument.

Mrs. Noma read the inscription on the stone coffin under the arched shelter. "Let all the souls here rest in peace; For we shall not repeat the evil." She stepped back to let someone carrying flowers get close.

"Because of the bomb that was dropped here, almost 200 thousand people died," Mother told Setsuko quietly while they watched another person light incense. "A register of all their names is kept inside that stone coffin. Over the years the list has grown as people continue to die from illnesses caused by exposure to the radiation."

"Look at that building over there." Setsuko pointed at a ruined building that they could see by looking through the arch of the cenotaph. "Was that here when the atomic bomb hit?"

"Yes, it was." Mr. Noma explained while the three strolled around the large reflecting pool, "Nearly everything within a radius of two kilometers of ground zero was destroyed. After the blast only a few shells of reinforced

concrete buildings were still standing. The one with the iron dome was the Hiroshima Prefecture Industrial Promotion Hall. Now it's called the A-Bomb Dome and is still standing as a sort of memorial."

They walked past the Fire of Peace at the far end of the pool and wandered through the rest of the park. Under a concrete arch, a huge gong that could be struck for peace hung quietly.

A tall concrete monument by a covered rose garden caught Setsuko's attention. It was topped by a metal statue of a girl holding a giant origami crane. Inside the monument, shaped like an upside down cup with three large spaces cut out, hung thousands—maybe millions—of paper cranes.

Setsuko touched a bright red origami crane and asked her father, "What's this monument about?"

"Let's sit over there on that bench and I'll tell you about it," Mr. Noma suggested. "A two-year-old girl survived the bombing. At least she seemed to be okay until about 10 years later. In the fall of her twelfth year, Sadako Sasaki got leukemia, a kind of cancer, from the radiation of the A-bomb. She had one hope. She believed that if she could fold 1,000 paper cranes, she'd be cured. She didn't live long enough. Her classmates were so sad and upset by her death, they started a project which grew into a national one to build this monument, called the Children's Peace Monument. Now there are always new paper cranes symbolizing prayers for peace."

"That's so sad." Setsuko stared at the monument and thought of the girl, so close to her own age, who had fought so hard to live.

"Yes, it certainly is," Mrs. Noma agreed. "It's all so sad. When that atomic bomb exploded, people within a one-kilometer circle died. People as far away as three and one-half kilometers got terrible burns. Many suffer still from keloids or massive scars. In fact, your grandmother's cousins lived here then. Why don't you ask her to tell you about that when we get back to her house?"

163

The next day Setsuko sat on the floor of her grandmother's small house in Yokohama and flipped through the postcards she'd purchased in Hiroshima. "Grandmother, look at this." She held up one of the cards for her grandmother to see. "Okasan told me about the girl who made origami cranes. Did you know her?"

Grandmother shook her head. She took the postcard and gazed at it for a long moment before handing it back. "So many people—so many dead and hurt."

"What was it like?" Setsuko placed the cards back in their folder. "Did you see it?"

Setsuko's grandmother shook her head again. "My cousin told me how it was." Setsuko moved closer and listened intently. "The day before had been a holiday, and she and her sister had gone swimming. They had had a wonderful time, but when she woke up on August 6, my cousin Keiko had a fever, so her mother kept her home from school. It was a beautiful, clear day. She watched her older sister go off to work at the factory."

Without pause, the small woman moved across the room to make tea, while continuing her story. Her hands moved through each task with the sure ease of much practice. "It was still early when Keiko stepped outside to get the newspaper out of the letter box for her mother. The sun was shining so brightly she almost didn't notice the plane flying very high, but its silver wings reflected the light and caught her attention. She thought she saw a parachute coming down from the plane, and then the whole sky flashed. She thought a fire had been set in her eyes—a purple-like spark a billion times stronger than anything she'd seen before. The explosion knocked her to the ground as buildings and their contents crashed all around.

"The beautiful day had vanished. It was like evening, and everything appeared vague and hazy. The house was gone—

flattened—as were all the other houses in the area. Keiko managed to move some boards and other debris to help her mother out. When fires broke out soon after the explosion, the two of them struggled to a nearby river. They saw incredible suffering and devastation. My cousin Keiko now has keloid scars on her back and right arm from severe burns, but she and her mother survived. Many people did not. They never saw her father or sister again."

Grandmother handed a steaming cup of tea to her granddaughter. Setsuko sniffed the fragrant tea appreciatively, but looked up with a frown. "I don't see how God could let something so awful happen."

Grandmother took a sip of her own tea before replying. "It was awful, but many other awful, horrible things have happened—and will happen—in this world. We just have to remember that God has promised to help us through whatever happens to us, even the awful, horrible things. And you know, Setsuko-chan, that God always keeps his promises."

Setsuko carefully set down her teacup before giving her grandmother a tight hug. "I love you, Grandmother. I wish we could always be together."

The old woman smiled and held her granddaughter close. "I love you." She wiped away a tear. "This visit has been much too short, and you're growing so very fast. Soon you will be a young lady and I will be an even older one." She chuckled. "Already you are almost as tall as your grandmother." She stroked Setsuko's smooth hair. "It is sad that we can't always be together, but remember the promise?" With one finger under Setsuko's chin, she tipped her granddaughter's face up towards her own.

"You mean that God will help us through whatever happens to us?"

"Yes!" Grandmother reached for a piece of paper on the small table nearby and began to fold it expertly. "Do you trust God to keep that promise, Setsuko-chan?"

Setsuko nodded. She watched her grandmother's quick fingers shape the red paper. "Perhaps this will remind you

that no matter how far apart we are, you are in my heart and that God is keeping His promises." Grandmother gave Setsuko a squeeze and handed her a tiny red origami crane.

2 Discussion Time

Check understanding of the story and development of personal values.

- On their trip to Japan, Setsuko and her parents visited a city that had been destroyed by an atomic bomb during World War II. What was its name?
- What things did Setsuko see in the Peace Memorial Hall museum?
- Why was one ruined building left standing at the park?
- Why did the little girl, Sadako Sasaki, try to make one thousand paper cranes?
- Who did Setsuko's grandmother know that had been in Hiroshima when the bomb fell?
- What did grandmother make and give to Setsuko?

A Preview

Write each word as your teacher says it.

1. haiku
2. biceps
3. coyote
4. migrant
5. crisis
6. device
7. entice
8. iceberg
9. fiery
10. aisle
11. eyeing
12. compile
13. crime
14. climate
15. dining
16. combine
17. decline
18. pride
19. aspire
20. imply

Name _____

Words with /ī/

Lesson **17**

Scripture

Psalm 18:30

105

3 Preview

Test for knowledge of the correct spellings of these words.

Customize Your List
On a separate sheet of paper, additional words of your choice may be tested.

 (Say) I will say each word once, use the word in a sentence, then say the word again. Write the words on the lines in your Worktext.

Correct Immediately!
 (Say) Let's correct our Preview. I will spell each word out loud. If you spelled a word incorrectly, rewrite it correctly.

 Progress Chart
Students may record scores. (Reproducible master provided in Appendix B.)

1.	haiku	A **haiku** is a Japanese lyric poem that often points to something in nature.
2.	biceps	The man who loaded their luggage on the train had large **biceps**.
3.	coyote	There is not a single **coyote** in Japan.
4.	migrant	Setsuko's grandfather was a **migrant** worker when he first arrived in America.
5.	crisis	The bombing of Hiroshima was no little **crisis** for the people of Japan.
6.	device	There was no **device** on the ground that could save the inhabitants.
7.	entice	The bombing did **entice** the people away from war and toward peace.
8.	iceberg	The largest **iceberg** in the world could not have withstood the heat of the bomb.
9.	fiery	There was more than one **fiery** explosion after the bomb fell.
10.	aisle	In one memorial, there was an **aisle** running between two rows of flowers.
11.	eyeing	Setsuko stood for a long while **eyeing** the monument filled with red paper cranes.
12.	compile	Historians have tried to **compile** photos and documentation of the bombing.
13.	crime	It is a **crime** to deface a war monument in Hiroshima.
14.	climate	The **climate** in Hiroshima was favorable during their visit.
15.	dining	After **dining** at an outdoor cafe, the Nomas continued their tour.
16.	combine	Most people in Japan do not **combine** sugar with their tea, but rather drink it plain.
17.	decline	Setsuko did not **decline** the tea, but drank it gratefully.
18.	pride	Setsuko felt a warm **pride** at her grandmother's ability to fold the paper.
19.	aspire	She will **aspire** to learn origami as well as her grandmother has.
20.	imply	Setsuko's grandmother did more than **imply** that God is faithful!

165

Help students form a correct image of whole words.

Say

Look at each word and think about its shape. Now, write the word in the correct Word Shape Boxes. You may check off each word as you use it.

(In many words, the sound of /ī/ is spelled with **i** at the end of a syllable, or with **ie**, or **i-consonant-e**. It is sometimes spelled with **y** at the end of a word.)

Say

In the Word Shape Boxes, fill in the boxes containing the letter or letters that spell the sound of /ī/ in each word.

Take a minute to memorize...

Psalm 18:30

Lesson 17 | **Day 1**

B Word Shapes

Name _____

Using the word bank below, write each word in the correct Word Shape Boxes. Next, in the Word Shape Boxes, fill in the boxes containing the letter or letters that spell the sound of /ī/ in each word.

Words with /ī/

Lesson **17**

1. a i s l e
2. h a i k u
3. c r i s i s
4. c l i m a t e
5. a s p i r e
6. d i n i n g
7. p r i d e
8. f i e r y
9. d e c l i n e
10. e y e i n g

11. c o m b i n e
12. b i c e p s
13. i c e b e r g
14. c o m p i l e
15. c r i m e
16. d e v i c e
17. m i g r a n t
18. c o y o t e
19. i m p l y
20. e n t i c e

Word Bank

aisle	combine	crisis	entice	iceberg
aspire	compile	decline	eyeing	imply
biceps	coyote	device	fiery	migrant
climate	crime	dining	haiku	pride

106

Answers may vary for duplicate word shapes.

Be Prepared For Fun

Check these supply lists for **Fun Ways to Spell** - presented **Day 2**. Purchase and/or gather these items ahead of time!

General
- Pencil
- Graph Paper (1 sheet per child)
- Spelling List

Auditory
- Pencil
- Notebook Paper
- Spelling List

Visual
- Colored Pencils
- Alphabet Stencils
- Paper

Tactile
- Uncooked Rice
- Art Paper (1 sheet per child)
- Glue
- Spelling List

C Hide and Seek   Name _____

Play Hide and Seek with your words. Fill in a box on the bar graph (left to right) for each word you spell correctly.

LOOK   SAY   SPELL ALOUD   WRITE   SEEK   CHECK

D Other Word Forms

Using the words below, follow the instructions given by your teacher.

aisles	compiling	devices	icebergs
(aspiration)	coyotes	(devise)	implication
aspiring	crimes	dined	implied
climatic	criminal	enticed	migration
combination	crises	eyed	(proud)
combining	(declined)	fierier	
compilation	declining	fieriest	

E Fun Ways to Spell

Initial the box of each activity you finish.

1. ☐
   acknnjes
   bcwordos
   lnfindinr
   btmhxdrg
   rmncsdrb

   Spell your words in a "Word Find."

2. ☐
   Spell your words with stencils.

3. ☐
   t o k
   x
   M·is·si·
   s·si·ppi
   Play "Spelling Tic-Tac-Toe."

4. ☐
   Spell your words with rice.

107

Words with /ī/

Lesson **17**

---

Right sidebar:

1 Hide and Seek

Reinforce spelling by using multiple styles of learning.

On a white board, Teacher writes each word — one at a time. **Have students:**

- **Look** at the word.
- **Say** the word out loud.
- **Spell** the word out loud.
- **Hide** (teacher erases word.)
- **Write** the word on paper.
- **Seek** (teacher rewrites word.)
- **Check** spelling. If incorrect, rewrite word correctly.

2 Other Word Forms

This activity is optional. Have students find and circle the Other Word Forms that are synonyms of the following:

ambition
contrive
haughty
rejected

3 Fun Ways to Spell

Four activities are provided. Use one, two, three, or all of the activities. Have students initial the box for each activity they complete.

Day 2 | Lesson **17**

Options:

- assign activities to students according to their learning styles
- set up the activities in learning centers for the students to do throughout the day
- divide students into four groups and assign one activity per group
- do one activity per day

General

To spell your words in a "Word Find"...
- Arrange your words on a piece of graph paper.
- Put one letter of each word in a square.
- Words may be written backwards, forwards, or diagonally.
- Outline your puzzle.
- Hide your words by filling in all the spaces inside the puzzle with random letters.
- Trade grids with a classmate and find the hidden words.

Auditory

To play "Spelling Tic-Tac-Toe"...
- Draw a Tic-Tac-Toe grid.
- Ask a classmate to read a word from the list.
- Spell the word aloud.
- If the word is spelled correctly, place your mark on the grid.
- Take turns with your classmate.

Visual

To spell your words with stencils...
- Look at the first letter of a word on your list.
- Place the stencil for the proper letter over your paper.
- Shade inside the stencil.
- Choose the proper stencil for the next letter of the word and shade it in next to the first letter.
- Finish the word in this way.
- Do this with each word.

Tactile

To spell your words with rice...
- Choose a word from your spelling list.
- Shape the letters of your word with rice.
- Glue the rice to art paper.
- Do this for each word on your list.

Working with Words

Familiarize students with word meaning and usage.

Clues

Write this incomplete sentence on the board:

A larva that changes into a butterfly or moth is a _____.

Guide the students in choosing the word **caterpillar**.

Read each sentence and choose a spelling word for each definition. You may use a dictionary to help you. Write the word in the blank.

Take a minute to memorize...

Psalm 18:30

F **Working with Words**

Name _____

Clues

Write a spelling word for each clue.

1. A _____coyote_____ is a North American mammal related to a wolf.
2. A person who moves around doing seasonal work is a _____migrant_____.
3. To express indirectly, or hint at, is to _____imply_____.
4. An unrhymed Japanese poem of three lines is called _____haiku_____.
5. _____Dining_____ means to be eating a meal.
6. The muscles in the front of the upper arm are called _____biceps_____.
7. Something that is burning or blazing is _____fiery_____.
8. To allure or tempt someone is to _____entice_____ them.
9. To _____aspire_____ is to try to attain or accomplish a certain goal.
10. Elation over an act or possession is called _____pride_____.
11. A _____crisis_____ is a decisive or critical moment.
12. A piece of equipment for a special purpose is a _____device_____.
13. _____Combine_____ means to put some things together to become one.
14. To collect and edit writings to make a book is to _____compile_____.
15. The _____climate_____ is the average weather condition of a place.
16. To be looking at something or watching it is to be _____eyeing_____ it.
17. A large floating mass of ice broken from a glacier is an _____iceberg_____.
18. A _____crime_____ is a serious offense against the public law.
19. _____Decline_____ is a gradual sinking and wasting away.
20. A passage between sections of seats is an _____aisle_____.

Word Bank

aisle	combine	crisis	entice	iceberg
aspire	compile	decline	eyeing	imply
biceps	coyote	device	fiery	migrant
climate	crime	dining	haiku	pride

108

G Dictation

Name _____

Write **each sentence as your teacher dictates.** Use **correct punctuation.**

1. Setsuko listened as Grandmother told of the fiery atomic crisis.

2. Setsuko walked down the aisle of the museum, eyeing things without comment.

3. She began to compile a book of haiku to remind her of her family.

H Proofreading

If a word is misspelled, fill in the oval by that word. If all the words are spelled correctly, fill in the oval by **no mistake.**

1. ○ imply
    ● biseps
    ○ area
    ○ no mistake

2. ○ crisis
    ○ device
    ○ Arizona
    ● no mistake

3. ● entise
    ○ parakeet
    ○ parallel
    ○ no mistake

4. ● iceburg
    ○ pride
    ○ software
    ○ no mistake

5. ○ migrant
    ● hiku
    ○ prepare
    ○ no mistake

6. ○ aisle
    ○ compile
    ○ crime
    ● no mistake

7. ● climit
    ○ combine
    ○ dining
    ○ no mistake

8. ○ narrow
    ○ Ontario
    ● dekline
    ○ no mistake

9. ● firey
    ○ aware
    ○ barracks
    ○ no mistake

10. ○ barrier
    ● cyote
    ○ barren
    ○ no mistake

11. ○ caramel
    ● aspier
    ○ compare
    ○ no mistake

12. ○ eyeing
    ○ embarrassed
    ○ librarian
    ● no mistake

109

1 Dictation

Reinforce correct spelling by using current and previous words in context.

(Say) Listen as I read each sentence and then write it in your Worktext. Remember to use correct capitalization and punctuation. (Slowly read each sentence twice. Sentences are found in the Student Worktext to the left.)

2 Proofreading

Familiarize students with standardized test format and reinforce recognition of misspelled words.

(Say) Look at each set of words. If a word is misspelled, fill in the oval by that word. If all the words are spelled correctly, fill in the oval by **no mistake.**

3 Hide and Seek

Reinforce correct spelling of current spelling words. Repeat this activity from Day 2.

4 Vocabulary Extension

Have your students complete this activity to strengthen spelling ability and expand vocabulary. The reproducible master is provided in Appendix A as shown on the inset page to the right.

1 Posttest

Visit the **A Reason For** website to download free, printable Posttest pages.

(Say) I will say the word once, use it in a sentence, then say it again. Write your words on a separate sheet of paper.

Progress Chart
Students may record scores. (Appendix B)

Personal Dictionary
Students may add any words they have misspelled to their personal dictionaries. (Appendix B)

Hide and Seek

Play Hide and Seek with your words. Fill in a bar graph (left to right) for each word you spell correctly.

LOOK   SAY   HIDE   WRITE   SEEK   CHECK

Vocabulary Extension
Fill in the Blanks

Choose a word from the word bank that best fits each sentence clue.

1. I spoke to my mom in a rude manner. I'm afraid I was being ___impolite___.
2. I have learned to ride my mountain bike well. I am a good ___bicyclist___.
3. My dad had to get new glasses that have two sections in the lenses. He can see up close and far away with his new ___bifocals___.
4. We had to change the plans for our tree house; however, we only needed to ___modify___ them a little.
5. We visited a ___refinery___, a factory where raw materials are purified and made into finished products.
6. Your body needs foods that give you energy. Eat plenty of ___carbohydrates___, such as bread, pasta, and potatoes.
7. We needed lightweight foods to take on our backpack trip, so Mom helped us ___dehydrate___ some in the food dryer.
8. Uncle Paul sure can eat a lot. He has a huge ___appetite___ because he works so hard.
9. My nephews play in the community orchestra. They are both good ___violinist___s.
10. I like to study about nature and the physical world. I really enjoy ___scientific___ experiments.
11. Some drivers travel too fast. This is a ___violation___ of the speed limit laws.
12. We watched a play in which the story was told through gestures, body movements, and facial expressions instead of words. It was called a ___pantomime___.

Word Bank

appetite	carbohydrates	modify	scientific
bicyclist	dehydrate	pantomime	violation
bifocals	impolite	refinery	violinist

339

---

1. **biceps** — The man on the train used his strong **biceps** to lift the heavy luggage.
2. **crisis** — God is able to help us through any **crisis**, large or small.
3. **device** — There was a special **device** used to detonate the atomic bomb.
4. **fiery** — Many people in Hiroshima saw a **fiery** purple explosion in the sky.
5. **entice** — It seemed that nothing could **entice** the Axis powers to peace.
6. **iceberg** — No **iceberg** of any size could withstand the heat of that blast.
7. **dining** — The Nomas knew they would be **dining** with Grandmother later that day.
8. **eyeing** — "I know it is hard to understand," Grandmother said, **eyeing** Setsuko's face.
9. **pride** — "We must never have the **pride** that says we know more than God," she said.
10. **imply** — The Bible does not **imply**, but states boldly, that God keeps his promises.
11. **compile** — Setsuko has tried to **compile**, or collect, many family stories.
12. **migrant** — She knew that her dad's father was a **migrant** worker his first years in America.
13. **aisle** — Setsuko quietly walked down the **aisle** of the huge peace memorial.
14. **crime** — It is a serious **crime** to deface any peace memorial in Hiroshima.
15. **climate** — The **climate** in Japan is much like that of the continental United States.
16. **combine** — She plans to **combine** information she reads with stories from her relatives.
17. **decline** — Setsuko would never **decline** her grandmother's offer to tell her a story.
18. **aspire** — Setsuko will **aspire** to be like her godly grandmother in many ways.
19. **haiku** — A **haiku** is a short 17-syllable Japanese poem.
20. **coyote** — There is not even one **coyote** in Japan.

I Game

Name _____

Complete the secret phrase by spelling the words from this week's word list.

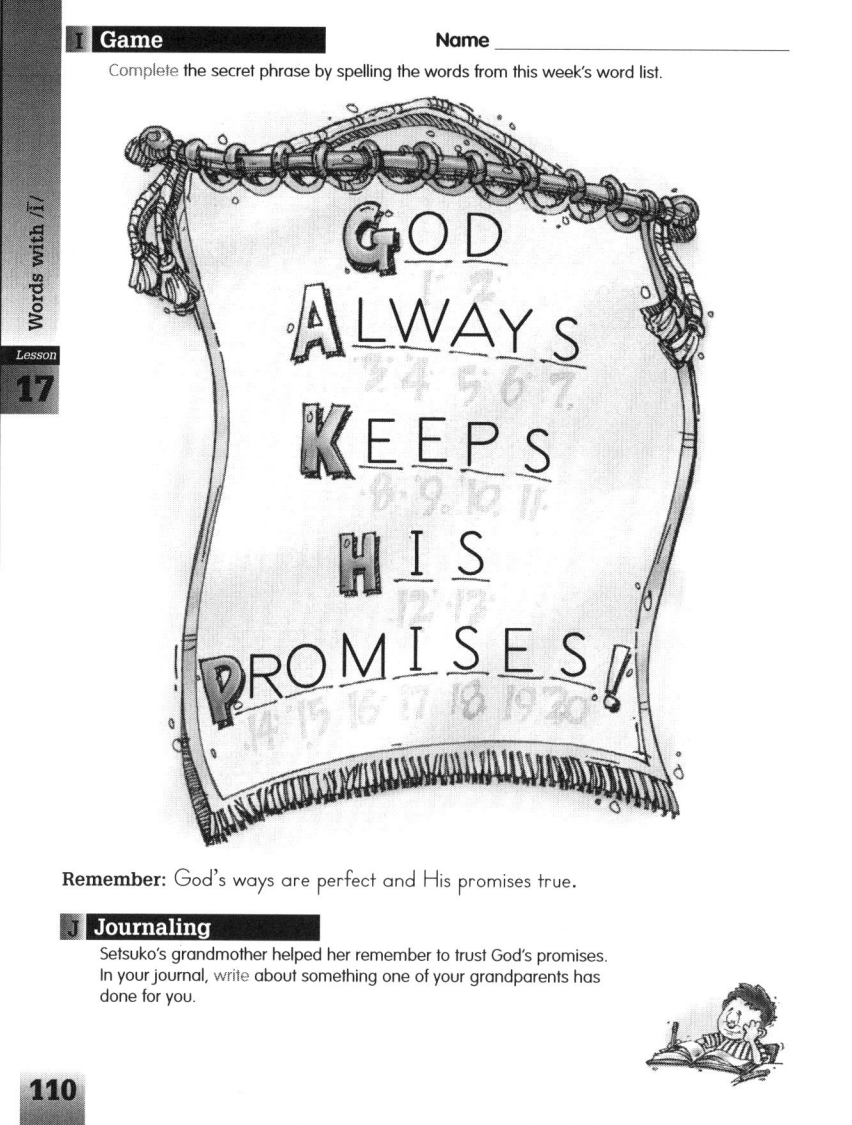

GOD
ALWAYS
KEEPS
HIS
PROMISES!

Remember: God's ways are perfect and His promises true.

J Journaling

Setsuko's grandmother helped her remember to trust God's promises. In your journal, write about something one of your grandparents has done for you.

110

How to Play:

- Divide the class into two teams, and decide which team will go first.
- Have a student from team A choose a number from 1 to 20.
- Say the word that matches that number from the team's word list.
- Have the student write the word on the board.
- If correct, have each member of team A write the given letter in the matching space on his/her game page.
- Alternate between teams A and B having the students choose a number of a blank space.
- The team to complete the secret phrase first is the winner.

2 Game

Reinforce spelling skills and provide motivation and interest.

Materials

- game page (from student text)
- pencils (1 per child)
- game word list

Game Word List

Team A	Team B
1. imply (O)	1. compile (O)
2. biceps (D)	2. crime (D)
3. crisis (L)	3. climate (L)
4. device (W)	4. combine (W)
5. entice (A)	5. dining (A)
6. iceberg (Y)	6. decline (Y)
7. pride (S)	7. fiery (S)
8. migrant (E)	8. aspire (E)
9. haiku (E)	9. eyeing (E)
10. aisle (P)	10. coyote (P)
11. compile (S)	11. imply (S)
12. crime (I)	12. biceps (I)
13. climate (S)	13. crisis (S)
14. combine (R)	14. device (R)
15. dining (O)	15. entice (O)
16. decline (M)	16. iceberg (M)
17. fiery (I)	17. pride (I)
18. aspire (S)	18. migrant (S)
19. eyeing (E)	19. haiku (E)
20. coyote (S)	20. aisle (S)

3 Journaling

Provide a meaningful reason for correct spelling through personal writing.

Review the story using discussion leads provided on the following page. Encourage students to apply the Scriptural value in their journaling.

Journaling (continued)

(Say) • Hiroshima means "Wide Island." How did it get its name? (Because the city grew from five different villages that were settled on six river deltas.)

• What was inside the cenotaph? (The names of the one hundred and ninety thousand people who died because of the atomic bomb.)

• Who makes the origami cranes that hang from the Children's Peace Monument? (School children all across Japan still make the cranes symbolizing prayers for peace.)

• What happened to grandmother's cousin, Keiko, when the bomb fell? (She was home from school because she had a fever. She was outside and saw the plane very high in the sky and then a purple light. She was badly burned, but managed to get her mother out of the rubble that used to be their house. Keiko survived, but never saw her father or sister again.)

• Why do such horrible, awful things happen in this world? (Because God doesn't force people to be good.)

• Why did grandmother make and give Setsuko the tiny origami crane? (To remind Setsuko that her grandmother loves her, that God loves her and has promised to be with her through whatever happens, and that God always keeps his promises.)

PIKES PEAK is spelled without an apostrophe by law. The Colorado legislature established the correct spelling in 1978. There are other cases in which spelling was established by law.

Federation of Praise

Heather looks at participating in the Piano Federation Competition.

"**J**ennifer is playing superbly," Beth whispered.

Heather nodded, absently adjusted her headband, and smoothed her skirt as she watched Jennifer Hatasaki's fingers fly up and down the keyboard.

Beth leaned over and said, "This judge should give her another superior plus."

"You and Tony did well this morning. I liked your duet," Heather said softly. The music from the baby grand piano floated around her as her thoughts drifted back to the beginning of the school year when she and Beth had first talked about the Piano Federation.

"Aren't you done eating yet?" Beth squeezed the Velcro strips of her lunch bag together as she stood in front of Heather's desk.

"Mmmmm." Heather held up one finger while she chewed a mouthful of Fritos.

Beth waited impatiently for Heather to swallow. "Did Miss Paula talk to you about the Piano Federation?"

Heather nodded.

"Well, what are you going to play?" Beth arched her ball of trash into the wastebasket. "Your cousin Tony and I are going to do the duets together. Miss Paula is helping me pick the two solos to memorize. I'm entering in the 'easy three' category. Mom said I could get a new dress, and Dad said he'd get our piano tuned. So are you going to tell me what you're playing—or keep chewing all afternoon?"

Heather held up her finger again and slowly wiped her mouth with her napkin before she answered, "Miss Paula wants me to enter, but this is the first year I've taken lessons."

"You play better than anyone else in our class," Beth encouraged. "I thought you'd taken lessons for years."

"I play by ear. Reading music and playing it the way it's written is new for me. And in front of a judge!" Heather laughed, "I'd probably forget what I memorized and start making it up as I went along. The judges would love that!" She looked down at her bag of chips and then put another into her mouth.

"Does Miss Paula want you to enter the medium or difficult category?"

"Mmmmm." Heather pointed to her mouth again.

"Well, I think you should enter." Beth walked toward the door. "You'd earn one of those gold certificates for sure."

Heather watched Beth put her lunch sack away and get a basketball. *I don't know how I'd practice,* she thought to herself. *We don't have a full keyboard. It works for lessons, but its too small to play a duet on. How would I learn my part? And being in front of so many people...I'm just not sure.*

She avoided Beth the rest of the day. She didn't really feel like telling her all the reasons she couldn't perform for the Piano Federation judges. Even if she found a way to practice a duet with someone, she was very nervous about being judged on her performance. Heather tried to put the Piano Federation out of her mind, but it kept sneaking back in.

That afternoon Grandma Miller drove Heather and her brother, Collin, home after school. "The Jensen children are still asleep," the older woman explained, "so your mom called and asked me to bring you home today."

"Do you know the spelling Scripture?" Tony twisted around in the front seat to look at Heather.

Heather arched her eyebrows and recited, "'There I will go to the altar of God my exceeding joy, and praise him with my harp. Oh God— my God!'"

"Yeah, I guess you do. So who are you playing your duets with?" Tony asked.

"I'm not sure I'm going to do Federation." Heather looked out the car window.

"I'm playing with Beth. We both started lessons in first grade and are still at about the same level. Miss Paula will have the music ready at my lesson tomorrow. Papa promised to be there to hear me. I'm getting some new shoes and a tie with musical notes all over it."

The car stopped and Heather jumped out without answering Tony.

The Stark children thanked Grandma Miller before they hurried up the sidewalk. Heather turned and waved to Tony and Grandma before she quietly opened the front door. She didn't want to wake up the children her mom baby-sat. Collin went on into the kitchen to talk to their mother about an upcoming field trip.

Heather unlocked her bedroom door and plopped down on the bed. Next to Heather's three favorite insect identification guides, the postcards Laney had mailed her from the Bahamas were sitting on the little table. Heather picked them up and thumbed through the colorful pictures. There were pictures of flamingos, white sandy beaches, lots of blue water, and sailboats. Laney must have liked sailing. There was a picture of the cruise ship she had sailed on from New York and then some of smaller sailboats. One card said, "Ships are safe in port, but that's not why they were built." Heather flopped back on her bed and studied the ceiling. "I guess it's safer not to play at the Piano Federation, but I don't see how I could do it even if I wanted to," she said out loud.

Two days later

Day 1 | **Review 18**

173

Grandma Miller took Heather home again. Collin had gone over to a friend's and Tony was at basketball practice, so the two were alone in the car. Grandma pulled the car to the curb in front of the Starks' small house. "Heather, why aren't you going to enter the Piano Federation competition?"

"Well, I've never played for judges. They're going to grade us on how accurately we play, smoothness, rhythm, and how it sounds. I'm not sure I'm ready for that. Just the thought makes my hands sweaty and my stomach hurt."

"What does Miss Paula say?" The older woman prodded gently.

"She wants me to enter the difficult category."

"Then you should! God has blessed you with remarkable musical ability. You shouldn't keep it hidden. That's not why God gave you the talent. Your gift will never fully mature to bless others if you don't use it."

Heather thought about the postcard beside her bed. *Ships are safe in port, but that's not why they were built.*

"I never thought of Piano Federation as being a way to praise God," she said aloud.

"What was that Scripture verse you recited for Tony the other day?"

"'There I will go to the altar of God my exceeding joy, and praise him with my harp. Oh God—my God!'"

"That's the one. A harp has a lot in common with the piano," Grandma Miller pointed out.

"I never thought of that, either," Heather admitted.

The two were quiet for a while, Heather with her own thoughts, Grandma Miller praying to her God. Finally Heather broke the silence. "But I don't have a piano to practice the duets on."

"You can use mine."

"Well, that takes care of two problems." Heather looked at the floorboard of the car.

"What else?" the perceptive woman asked.

"I don't have a dress to wear. Miss Paula said we were supposed to wear church clothes. By Federation time, it will be the middle of winter. I don't have a winter church dress, and I can't ask Mom to get me one, because she and dad are already paying for piano lessons."

"I see," Grandma said. "How about letting me worry about the dress, and you concentrate on practicing the pieces Miss Paula helps you pick out?"

A smile crept across Heather's face. "This is amazing!"

The noise of the applauding audience brought Heather back to reality. She watched Jennifer curtsy and exit the stage. Her hands felt damp, and her heart was beating loudly. She looked at the folded program in her hand. Maria was next. Then it would be her turn at the keyboard.

Grandma Miller came up behind her and touched her gently on the shoulder. "You'll do fine, Heather," the older woman encouraged. A warm smile crinkled her leathery face. "You look lovely, and I've heard you sail effortlessly through this hymn many times."

Sail! Heather thought of the words on the postcard Laney had sent. *Ships are safe in port, but that's not why they were built.* Grandma Miller squeezed her shoulders, "Go out there and praise God with your music!"

Heather rubbed the blue velvet of her new skirt between her fingers. "Thanks, Grandma Miller, thanks for everything. I hope I sail through again!"

Discussion Time

Check understanding of the story and development of personal values.

- What are the reasons Heather doesn't think she will play at the Piano Federation?
- Why does Beth think Heather should play?
- What did Tony ask that tells us he thought she was playing for the Federation?
- Who helps Heather decide to perform for the Piano Federation?
- What did Grandma Miller tell Heather about using her talent of musical ability?
- How did Grandma Miller help Heather be able to play for the Piano Federation?
- What talent has God given you to praise Him with?

A Test-Words

Name _____

Write **each spelling word on the line as your teacher says it.**

1. college
2. carton
3. caramel
4. combine
5. New Hampshire
6. random
7. librarian
8. barrier

9. parallel
10. crime
11. crisis
12. compartment
13. eyeing
14. aspire
15. pride
16. soprano

Review
Lesson
18

B Test-Sentences

Write **the sentences on the lines below, correcting each misspelled word, as well as all capitalization and punctuation errors. Two words are misspelled in each sentence.**

in what climit does the artichoak plant grow.

1. In what climate does the artichoke plant grow?

the soldier heard the cyotee outside the bearicks

2. The soldier heard the coyote outside the barracks.

a crockidile will usually inhabitt the swamps

3. A crocodile will usually inhabit the swamps.

the ship will dock at a harber on Delewear's coast.

4. The ship will dock at the harbor on Delaware's coast.

111

---

4 Test-Sentences

Reinforce recognizing misspelled words.

 (Say)

Read each sentence carefully. Write the sentences on the lines in your Worktext. There are two misspelled words in each sentence. Correct each misspelled word, as well as all capitalization and punctuation errors.

Take a minute to memorize...

Psalm 43:4

---

3 Test-Words

Test for knowledge of the correct spellings of these words.

(Say) I will say each word once, use the word in a sentence, then say the word again. Write the words on the lines in your Worktext.

1. college — "You're good enough to study music in **college**," complimented Beth.
2. carton — She drank the last bit of milk from the small **carton**.
3. caramel — Heather pulled a **caramel** candy out of her lunch bag.
4. combine — Beth and Tony will **combine** their talents in a piano duet.
5. New Hampshire — Miss Paula, their piano teacher, is originally from **New Hampshire**.
6. random — She does not choose the competition pieces at **random**.
7. librarian — Heather thanked the **librarian** for finding the book on famous musicians.
8. barrier — Heather's fears were a **barrier** to her wanting to perform.
9. parallel — She was not sure her talents could **parallel** that of the other contestants.
10. crime — "It's not a **crime** not to play at Piano Federation, is it?" she asked.
11. crisis — Just thinking about the judges at the competition felt like a **crisis**.
12. compartment — Grandma Miller put a box of tissues in the glove **compartment**.
13. eyeing — She was **eyeing** Heather in the mirror when she did not answer Tony.
14. aspire — When she practices, Heather does **aspire** to do her very best.
15. pride — It is good to take **pride** in your work and do it well.
16. soprano — Heather's mom has a lovely **soprano** singing voice.

175

1 Test-Dictation

Reinforce correct spelling by using current and previous words in context.

Say

Listen as I read each sentence, then write it in your worktext. Remember to use correct capitalization and punctuation. (Slowly read each sentence twice. Sentences are found in the student text to the right. The words **adopt**, **parakeet**, **Ontario**, and **snarl** are found in this unit.)

2 Test-Proofreading

Familiarize students with standardized test format and reinforce recognizing misspelled words.

Say

Look at each set of words. If a word is misspelled, fill in the oval by that word. If all the words are spelled correctly, fill in the oval by **no mistake**.

Review
Lesson
18

C Test-Dictation

Name _____

Write **each sentence as your teacher dictates**. Use correct punctuation.

1. Do they plan to adopt a baby?
2. The big, green parakeet was very near our table.
3. My cousin lives in Ontario, Canada.
4. With a snarl, the dog rose to his feet.

D Test-Proofreading

If a word is misspelled, fill in the oval by that word. If all the words are spelled correctly, fill in the oval by **no mistake**.

1. ● wisconson
   ○ decline
   ○ carton
   ○ no mistake

2. ○ soprano
   ● mygrant
   ○ combine
   ○ no mistake

3. ○ barrier
   ○ compartment
   ○ atomic
   ● no mistake

4. ○ gather
   ● glossery
   ○ parallel
   ○ no mistake

5. ● raskal
   ○ crisis
   ○ pride
   ○ no mistake

6. ○ caramel
   ● continint
   ○ aspire
   ○ no mistake

7. ○ fiery
   ○ compare
   ○ eyeing
   ● no mistake

8. ○ aisle
   ○ random
   ● cartliage
   ○ no mistake

9. ○ department
   ○ aware
   ● statick
   ○ no mistake

10. ○ borrow
    ● cardiack
    ○ bottom
    ○ no mistake

11. ● commurse
    ○ deposit
    ○ Colorado
    ○ no mistake

12. ○ embarrassed
    ○ college
    ● harty
    ○ no mistake

112

176

E Test-Table

Name _____

If a word is misspelled, fill in the space on the grid.

~~airea~~	dart	~~geometrey~~	~~arobics~~
~~arizona~~	device	imply	narrow
~~compiel~~	dining	~~Indyana~~	Nevada
contact	~~convirsation~~	~~mammel~~	radar

F Writing Assessment

Imagine you are Heather or Tony. Write a letter to your Uncle Mark about the Piano Federation and how Heather performed.

_____
_____
_____
_____
_____
_____
_____

Scripture

Psalm 43:4

113

A rubric for scoring is provided in Appendix B.

Test-Table

Test mastery of words in this unit.

(Say) If a word is misspelled, fill in the space on the grid.

Writing Assessment

Assess student's spelling, grammar, and composition skills through personal writing.

(Say)
- Who thought Heather should play for the judges at the Piano Federation (Miss Paula her piano teacher, Beth, Tony, and Grandma Miller.)
- Why do you think Heather decided to play at the Piano Federation? (Grandma Miller provided a piano to practice the duet on, bought a special dress for her to wear, and encouraged her to use her talents for the Lord.)
- What are some ways you can praise God with exceeding joy like Psalm 43:4 talks about? (Students may suggest: By what I say. By how I act. By developing and using my talents.)
- How do you think Heather will play for the Piano Federation judges?

Review **18** | Day 3

RAISE/RAZE are homophones with approximately opposite meanings.

177

1 Test-Sentences

Reinforce recognizing misspelled words.

Say

Read each sentence carefully. Write the sentences on the lines in your Worktext, correcting each misspelled word, as well as all capitalization and punctuation errors.

G Test-Sentences   Name _____

Write the sentences on the lines below, correcting each misspelled word, as well as all capitalization and punctuation errors. Two words are misspelled in each sentence.

dad carried the gallin bucket to the composte pile

1. Dad carried the gallon bucket to the compost pile.

my uncle lives in a beautiful vallee in arkansaw

2. My uncle lives in a beautiful valley in Arkansas.

an arguemint can easily disturb the group harmoney

3. An argument can easily disturb the group harmony.

our family docter pointed to a charte on the wall

4. Our family doctor pointed to a chart on the wall.

Review • Lesson 18

H Test-Words

Write each spelling word on the line as your teacher says it.

1. decline
2. bottom
3. aware
4. comment
5. embarrassed
6. perhaps
7. concentrate
8. compare
9. prepare
10. borrow
11. deposit
12. department
13. gather
14. aisle
15. marriage
16. Colorado

114

---

2 Test-Words

Test for knowledge of the correct spellings of these words.

Say

I will say the word once, use the word in a sentence, then say the word again. Write the word on the lines in your Worktext.

1. decline — Heather planned to **decline** the invitation to play at Federation.
2. bottom — "Let's talk and get to the **bottom** of those fears," Grandma Miller teased.
3. aware — Heather wasn't **aware** Mrs. Miller knew there was a problem.
4. comment — At first, Heather didn't want to **comment** on her feelings.
5. embarrassed — "I'd be **embarrassed** to make a mistake in front of so many people," she admitted.
6. perhaps — "Would you, **perhaps**, let me pick out a new dress?" Grandma Miller asked.
7. concentrate — "You only need to **concentrate** on your piano piece."
8. compare — "My talents might not **compare** with the other students," said Heather.
9. prepare — "I can't **prepare** properly without a piano, either," she continued.
10. borrow — Since pianos are hard to **borrow**, Grandma Miller let Heather use hers.
11. deposit — "Just **deposit** your books on the table and start practicing!" she said.
12. department — Grandma Miller bought Heather a new outfit at a **department** store.
13. gather — Heather tried to **gather** her thoughts before going on stage.
14. aisle — She was glad to be in the front row and not have to walk down an **aisle**.
15. marriage — Heather was thankful for her parents' strong, happy **marriage**.
16. Colorado — Heather's dad had just returned from driving his truck to **Colorado**.

I Test-Editing

Name _____

If a word is spelled correctly, fill in the oval under **Correct**. If the word is misspelled, fill in the oval under **Incorrect**, and spell the word correctly on the blank.

		Correct	Incorrect	
1.	Alabama	●	○	
2.	barrin	○	●	barren
3.	combatt	○	●	combat
4.	iceburg	○	●	iceberg
5.	suvannah	○	●	savanna
6.	valve	●	○	
7.	demolish	●	○	
8.	artiry	○	●	artery
9.	partner	●	○	
10.	bargin	○	●	bargain
11.	narate	○	●	narrate
12.	byseps	○	●	biceps
13.	collinies	○	●	colonies
14.	intise	○	●	entice
15.	hikuu	○	●	haiku
16.	scalopp	○	●	scallop
17.	gallup	○	●	gallop
18.	anartica	○	●	Antarctica
19.	softwear	○	●	software
20.	hardship	●	○	

Review
Lesson
18

115

3 Test-Editing
Reinforce recognizing and correcting misspelled words.

4 Action Game
Reinforce spelling skills and provide motivation and interest.

Materials
- whiteboard or chalkboard
- markers or chalk
- word list on certificate at end of unit

PICTOSPELL

Divide the class into two teams. Have each team sit on the floor as far away from each other as possible, but where they can see the board. Call a player up from one team and show him or her a spelling word to be reviewed. When you say "go" the player begins drawing a picture of the word. That player's team must guess the word in one minute or the other team has a chance to guess. When a word is guessed, it must be spelled correctly by the team member who guessed it in order for that team to get a point. When that word has been guessed, a player from the other team will be given a word to draw. Continue to alternate between teams. The team with the most points wins!

Game

Reinforce spelling skills and provide motivation and interest.

Materials
- game page (from student text)
- colored pencils (1 per child)
- game word list

Game Word List
Check off each word lightly in pencil as it is used.

The Musicians

1. **Wisconsin**
2. **migrant**
3. **atomic**
4. **glossary**
5. **rascal**
6. **continent**
7. **fiery**
8. **cartilage**
9. **static**

The Audience

1. **cardiac**
2. **commerce**
3. **hearty**
4. **area**
5. **Arizona**
6. **compile**
7. **contact**
8. **device**
9. **dining**

The Judges

1. **Delaware**
2. **geometry**
3. **imply**
4. **Indiana**
5. **mammal**
6. **aerobics**
7. **narrow**
8. **Nevada**
9. **radar**

J Game   Name _____

Score points for each review word or Other Word Form you or your team spells correctly.

Review Lesson 18

Remember: Use your gifts and talents to praise God.

116

How to Play:
- Divide the class into three teams. Name one team **The Musicians**, one **The Audience**, and one **The Judges**. (Option: You may wish to seat students in groups of three, each student from a different team. They should share one game page.)
- Have a student from the first team go to the board.
- Say the spelling word.
- Have the student write the word on the board.
- If the word is spelled correctly, have each team member color a point symbol by his/her team name. If the word is misspelled, have him/her put an **X** through one point symbol. That word may not be given again.
- Repeat this process with the second team and then the third.
- When the words from all three lists have been used, the team with the most points is the winner.
- Play another round using Other Word Forms.

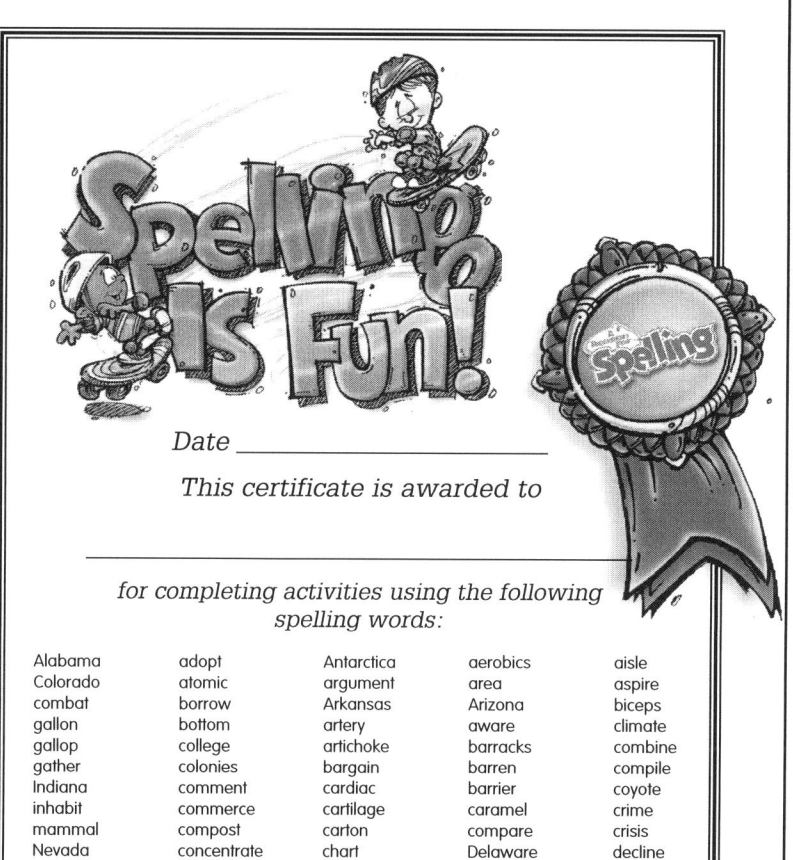

Date _____

This certificate is awarded to

_____

for completing activities using the following spelling words:

Alabama	adopt	Antarctica	aerobics	aisle
Colorado	atomic	argument	area	aspire
combat	borrow	Arkansas	Arizona	biceps
gallon	bottom	artery	aware	climate
gallop	college	artichoke	barracks	combine
gather	colonies	bargain	barren	compile
Indiana	comment	cardiac	barrier	coyote
inhabit	commerce	cartilage	caramel	crime
mammal	compost	carton	compare	crisis
Nevada	concentrate	chart	Delaware	decline
New Hampshire	contact	compartment	embarrassed	device
perhaps	continent	dart	librarian	dining
random	conversation	department	marriage	entice
rascal	crocodile	harbor	narrate	eyeing
savanna	demolish	hardship	narrow	fiery
scallop	deposit	harmony	Ontario	haiku
soprano	doctor	hearty	parakeet	iceberg
static	geometry	partner	parallel	imply
valley	glossary	radar	prepare	migrant
valve	Wisconsin	snarl	software	pride

2 Certificate

Provide an opportunity for parents or guardians to encourage and assess their child's progress.

 Say Fill in today's date and your name on your certificate.

 Take a minute to memorize...

Psalm 43:4

Letter

3

Provide the parent or guardian with the spelling word lists for the next unit.

(Say)

Give your parents or guardian this letter that lists your spelling words for the next unit. Put it where you will remember to practice the words together.

Dear Parent,

We are about to begin a new spelling unit containing five weekly lessons. A set of twenty words will be studied each week. All the words will be reviewed in the sixth week. Values based on the Scriptures listed below will be taught in each lesson.

Lesson 19	Lesson 20	Lesson 21	Lesson 22	Lesson 23
Africa	average	Alaska	Amazon	afternoon
autograph	badge	backup	blaze	basketball
difference	cringe	banquet	blizzard	broadcast
difficult	dungeon	chaos	bruise	brother-in-law
dolphin	gadget	chorus	citizen	candlestick
effort	heritage	earthquake	closet	driveway
fiber	hinges	echoes	design	evergreen
forecast	jacket	equal	desire	foolproof
forth	jaguar	equator	despise	footnote
fossil	jogging	inquire	enclose	grasshopper
funds	junior	Kentucky	freezing	grassland
hyphen	jury	liquid	graze	greenhouse
nephew	justice	Nebraska	horizon	greyhound
paragraph	legend	o'clock	Kansas	livestock
photos	manage	preschool	laser	newborn
phrase	merge	quality	Missouri	Newfoundland
sheriff	pledge	Quebec	plaza	old-fashioned
siphon	plunge	quicksand	raise	password
sphere	refuge	squall	stanza	peppermint
trophy	rigid	squid	surprise	runaway
Psalm 27:14	Psalm 66:8,9	Psalm 19:9,10	Psalm 25:4,5	Psalm 141:1

Extraordinary Adventure

Thorny goes cross-country skiing for the first time and has to be brave and wait patiently for help.

"A-h-h-h-h. Pristine air such as this is incredibly invigorating!" Thorny took a deep breath and exhaled, his breath forming a white cloud. "One might even call such an unpolluted atmosphere intoxicating."

"No one but you would." Tommy shook his head. "I don't know about the 'intoxicating' bit, but if you keep huffing and puffing like that, you'll probably get light-headed before we even get started skiing."

"Ah, yes. The molecules are significantly more widely dispersed at higher altitudes." Thorny pulled a bulging day pack out of the trunk.

"What on earth have you got in that?" Tommy reached up to unload the cross-country skis from the roof rack. "You didn't bring a bunch of books like you did when we went canoeing, did you?"

"Of course not." Hubert Thornton Remington III looked down his nose at the shorter Tommy. "One must not endeavor to carry more than is reasonable, particularly when not accustomed to the extreme physical challenge provided by cross-country skiing. One of the first rules of safety for cross-country skiing is—'Know your own physical limits.'"

"I see." Tommy stuck a long, thin pair of skis upright in the snow. "You didn't bring a bunch of books 'cause you've already researched everything there is to know about cross-country skiing."

"And found it to be truly fascinating." Thorny dropped a pile of poles on the snow beside the skis. "The sport's origins can be traced back about 5,000 years to people in Scandinavia who strapped the bones of large animals to shoes with leather thongs."

"These beauties sure beat bones." Tommy ran his hand along the sleek blue skis.

Thorny laced his ski boots. "Along with the much-improved runners of fiberglass, wood, and plastics, these bindings that keep the heel free have revolutionized the sport of cross-country skiing."

"Well, then, let's see what all these improvements do for you." Tommy handed Thorny a pair of green skis with a fish-scale pattern on the bottom. "These are the ones Dad rented for you. They're waxless. The pattern on the bottom of the skis grabs the snow but also makes you glide faster." When Thorny had attached the skis, Tommy handed him poles. "I'm sure you know all about these, too."

"Of course." Thorny stood and shoved off with the poles. "I kno-o-o-o-o-o-O-O-O-W!" SPLAT! Thorny sat up and looked at Tommy, snow plastering his face. "Well, I do know—in theory, that is." He struggled around in the snow trying to get up, enlarging the hole in the drift. Finally Tommy stopped laughing long enough to give Thorny a hand.

"I know something else, too. The snow conditions are ideal for cross-country skiing today, with at least a two-foot base," Thorny announced, brushing the snow off his head. "I just checked it myself." Both boys laughed so hard they almost ended up back in the snow.

"You guys ready?" Mr. Rawson and Steve Simmons trudged through the snow from the ranger outpost.

"Looks like we'd better get these two on the trail before they get into any more trouble," Mr. Simmons teased as he swiped more snow off Thorny's backside.

Mr. Rawson clipped his skis on expertly. "We're going only about two and one-half miles to this warm-up shelter." He pointed to a spot on a small map with green, blue and black lines weaving around on it. He traced the routes with a gloved finger, "We'll stop for lunch there and decide if we want to take this longer loop back to the car or this shorter one. Remember, watch for the green trail blazes. We're sticking to those today since it's the first time out for some of us." He winked at Thorny. "I'll lead and Steve will bring up the rear. That way you boys will always be between us, so even if we get spread out we can keep track of you." He folded the map and stuck it in his windbreaker pocket. "Let's hit the trail!"

"YIPPEE!" Tommy yelled as he shoved off down the trail. "Come on, Thorny, I'll show you a few things you may not have learned in your research. This is the diagonal stride." Tommy demonstrated and Thorny tried. "No, no, no, no!" Tommy covered his eyes with his hand when Thorny took another dive into the snow.

But before long Thorny was getting the hang of it. He stopped for a break and wiped the sweat off his forehead, "Now I begin to comprehend why the articles I read indicated that one of the most common mistakes of novice cross-country skiers is to wear more clothing than they need."

"It's a workout!" Tommy swished to a stop beside his friend. "I bet we're almost to the warm-up shelter. I'm starved!" On cue his stomach growled loudly.

"If I should lose sight of you I'll simply follow the sound of your stomach." Thorny laughed.

A few minutes later the skiers gathered in the shelter and passed around sandwiches and hot cocoa. "M-mmm, I needed that." Tommy licked the chocolate off his lips.

Thorny helped himself to another sandwich, "At

183

Story (continued)

800 calories an hour, we've burned a considerable number this morning."

Mr. Rawson stretched his arms above his head. "I can sure tell I've worked all the muscle groups in my body. Guess I need to get out here more often. Well, which way back to the car?"

They decided on the longer route. In the still afternoon the only sounds were the swish of the skis against the packed snow. Thorny considered what the right word would be to describe the experience. It was calming, peaceful, beautiful. Extraordinary. That was it!

"Hello!" A lone skier came toward them. Following the rules of cross-country skiing, they moved to the right of the trail. The man nodded as he passed, then stopped and asked Mr. Simmons a question.

"You all go on," Mr. Simmons called to the rest of the group, "I'm just going to show this guy where we are on the trail; then I'll catch up."

Mr. Rawson waved his understanding and they headed up the rise. As they skied down the other side, Thorny felt something give on his left boot. He snowplowed to a stop and bent to tie the lace. By the time he was finished, Tommy and his dad were out of sight.

"A perfect opportunity to test my newly acquired skating skills," Thorny muttered to himself as he eyed the upward slope. "With proper weight shift, a skier can easily skate or scale even the steepest hill." He took a deep breath, "Here goes!"

After struggling up the hill, Thorny stopped to catch his breath. There was no sign of Tommy and his dad other than their tracks in the snow. "Perhaps I'll overtake them on this downhill stretch." Thorny started to shove off when he noticed the trail forked. The green trail blaze was on a tree between two sets of tracks—and it appeared there were a similar number of ski tracks going each way.

Thorny finally decided

the blaze looked a little closer to one of the trails and headed that way. He watched carefully for green blazes, but didn't see any. Other ski tracks cut across the trail he was following several times, but he didn't pay any attention to them until he decided he was going the wrong way. When he tried to retrace his way back to the fork, those tracks were a real problem. He suddenly realized he didn't know which way he'd come!

"Perhaps the wisest course of action is to remain in this location." Thorny leaned on his poles and looked around. "It is highly likely that I'm becoming more disoriented with each turn I make. If I just stay still, the others will notice I'm missing and endeavor to locate me."

Thorny took off his skis and stood them beside the trail. Brushing the snow off a fallen log, he sat down to wait. And wait. When his teeth began to chatter from sitting still, he shrugged on another layer of clothes from his day pack.

He occupied himself with reviewing everything he'd researched about cross-country skiing—especially what to do in emergencies. Then he began repeating all the Scriptures he could remember learning since he'd come to live with the Simmons and attend Knowlton Elementary School. The most recent one, Psalm 27:14, seemed particularly fitting. "Don't be impatient. Wait for the Lord, and he will come and save you! Be brave, stouthearted and courageous. Yes, wait and he will help you."

Although it seemed like he'd been waiting on the frozen log forever, he kept telling himself it hadn't been all that long—until the sun started going down. Then he knew he'd been waiting for hours, and the panic started to rise in his throat. Shadows lengthened across the wooded valley around him. Moonlight on the snow made the shadows more obvious. Why hadn't they found him? He wanted to scream! He wanted to get up and ski out—but where?

"Get a grip, Thorny!" He spoke aloud in the silence. "You know what to do. Remember, be brave and courageous!" He clipped on his skis

and began gathering twigs and small logs. Using one of the larger sticks, he cleared a small area of most of the snow and arranged the wood on it. From his day pack he took matches, toilet paper, an insulated blanket and a candy bar.

When his friends found him an hour after sundown, the fire was burning and the candy bar was gone!

"Well, what did you think of your first cross-country skiing trip?" Tommy joked in the car on the way home.

"Upon due consideration," Thorny answered thoughtfully, "I'd say it was… extraordinary!"

Discussion Time

Check understanding of the story and development of personal values.

- Had Thorny ever gone cross-country skiing before?
- What happened when Thorny first stood on his rented skis?
- Why did Mr. Rawson ski in front and Mr. Simmons in the back?
- What kind of trail markers were they following?
- How did Thorny become separated from the group?
- Why couldn't he find his way back to the original trail?
- How did Thorny keep from panicking as more and more time passed?
- What did Thorny do while he waited for someone to find him?

A Preview

Write **each word as your teacher says it.**

Name _____

1. autograph
2. paragraph
3. phrase
4. hyphen
5. difference
6. effort
7. difficult
8. nephew
9. forecast
10. sheriff
11. siphon
12. dolphin
13. funds
14. Africa
15. forth
16. sphere
17. fiber
18. fossil
19. trophy
20. photos

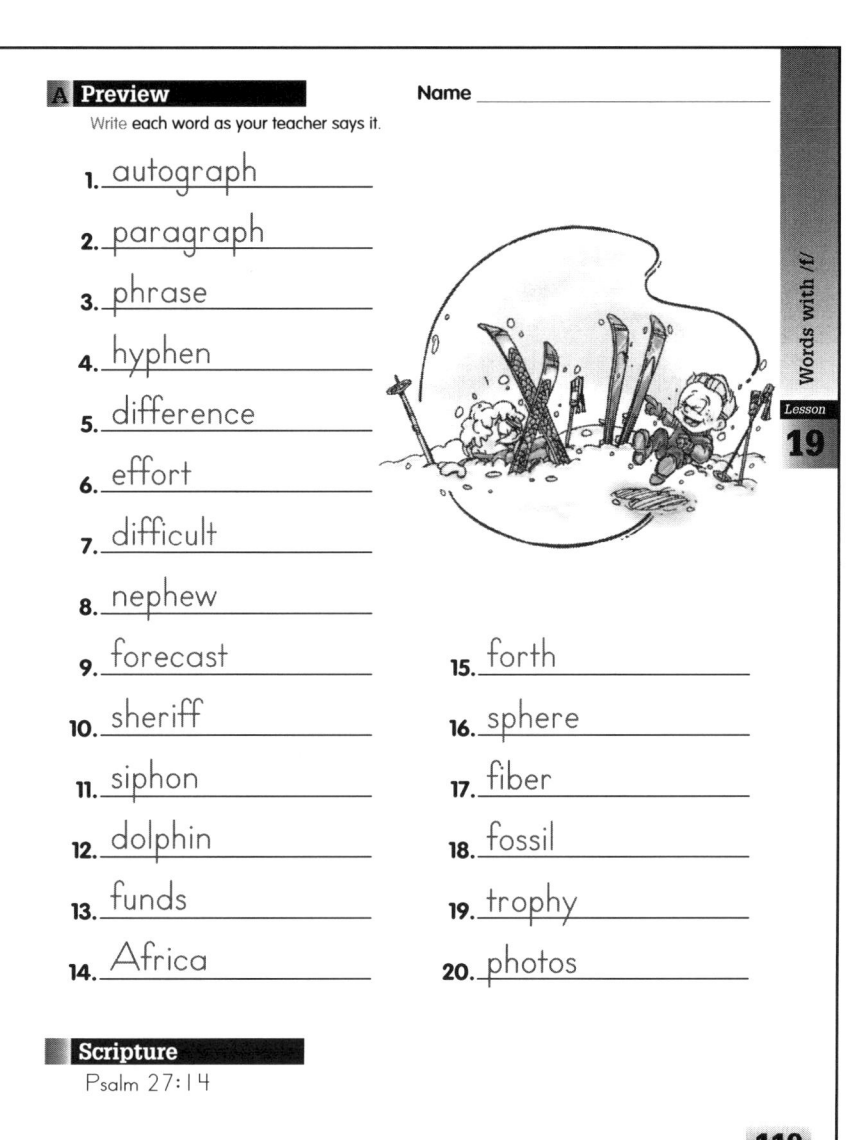

Words with /f/

Lesson **19**

Scripture

Psalm 27:14

119

3 **Preview**
Test for knowledge of
the correct spellings
of these words.

Customize Your List
On a separate sheet of
paper, additional words of
your choice may be tested.

I will say each word once,
use the word in a sentence,
then say the word again.
Write the words on the lines
in your Worktext.

Correct Immediately!
Let's correct our Preview.
I will spell each word
out loud. If you spelled a
word incorrectly, rewrite it
correctly.

Progress Chart
Students may record scores.
(Reproducible master
provided in Appendix B.)

1.	autograph	Tommy's skis had a famous skier's **autograph** along the bottom.
2.	paragraph	Thorny quoted an entire **paragraph** from a book he'd read.
3.	phrase	"Could you translate a **phrase** or two into layman's terms?" teased Tommy.
4.	hyphen	"Is there a **hyphen** anywhere in that long word you just used?" he queried.
5.	difference	They noticed a **difference** in their breathing in the higher altitude.
6.	effort	Thorny made every **effort** to stay upright on his skis.
7.	difficult	He found skiing a little more **difficult** than he'd expected.
8.	nephew	Mr. Simmons has a **nephew** that is an exceptionally good skier.
9.	forecast	"The **forecast** showed today as favorable for our outing," commented Thorny.
10.	sheriff	The county **sheriff** and his men patrol the mountain roads routinely.
11.	siphon	The sheriff helped one stranded man to **siphon** gas into his empty tank.
12.	dolphin	Thorny looked wistfully at the **dolphin** on the candy wrapper.
13.	funds	"Perhaps we will use our vacation **funds** to visit a warmer climate."
14.	Africa	"At the moment, **Africa** sounds incredibly appealing!" he shivered.
15.	forth	He reached in his pack and brought **forth** the necessary matches for a fire.
16.	sphere	"Forming a large **sphere** of snow will block the wind from this side."
17.	fiber	The **fiber** content of his blanket was wool, which would help him keep warm.
18.	fossil	To pass the time, Thorny examined surrounding rocks for a **fossil**.
19.	trophy	"You deserve a **trophy** for bravery," smiled Tommy.
20.	photos	After the trip, the boys enjoyed looking at the **photos** they had taken.

185

4 Word Shapes

Help students form a correct image of whole words.

Lesson 19 | Day 1

Say Look at each word and think about its shape. Now, write the word in the correct Word Shape Boxes. You may check off each word as you use it.

(In many words, the sound of **/f/** is spelled with **f, ff, gh,** or **ph**. The **ff** and **gh** spellings are never found at the beginning of a word.)

Say In the Word Shape Boxes, fill in the boxes containing the letter or letters that spell the **/f/** sound in each word.

Take a minute to memorize...

Psalm 27:14

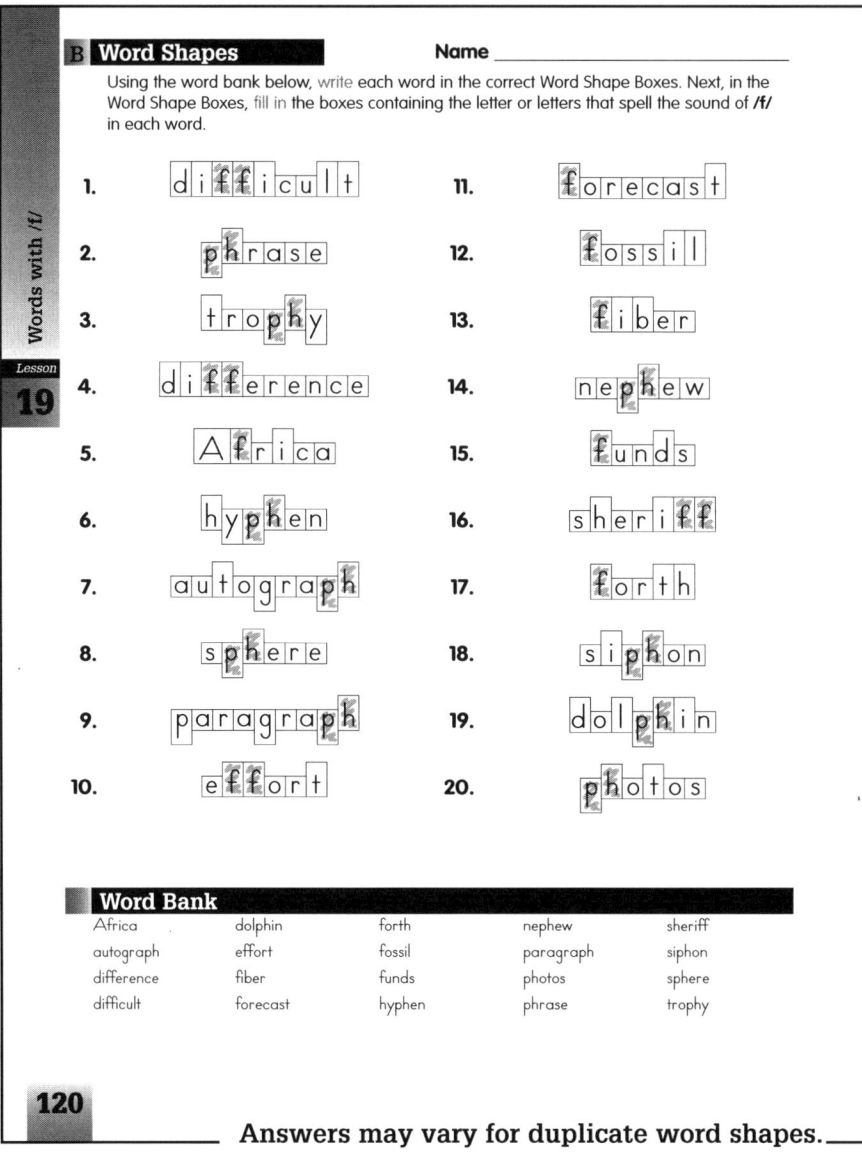

B Word Shapes Name _____

Using the word bank below, write each word in the correct Word Shape Boxes. Next, in the Word Shape Boxes, fill in the boxes containing the letter or letters that spell the sound of **/f/** in each word.

Words with /f/ — Lesson 19

1. difficult
2. phrase
3. trophy
4. difference
5. Africa
6. hyphen
7. autograph
8. sphere
9. paragraph
10. effort
11. forecast
12. fossil
13. fiber
14. nephew
15. funds
16. sheriff
17. forth
18. siphon
19. dolphin
20. photos

Word Bank

Africa	dolphin	forth	nephew	sheriff
autograph	effort	fossil	paragraph	siphon
difference	fiber	funds	photos	sphere
difficult	forecast	hyphen	phrase	trophy

120

Answers may vary for duplicate word shapes.

Be Prepared For Fun

Check these supply lists for **Fun Ways to Spell** - presented **Day 2**.
Purchase and/or gather these items ahead of time!

General
- Pencil
- Graph Paper (1 sheet per child)
- Spelling List

Auditory
- Voice Recorder
- Spelling List

Visual
- American Sign Language reproducible master (provided in Appendix B)
- Spelling List

Tactile
- Soccer Ball, Basketball, Tennis Ball, or 4-Square Ball
- Spelling List

186

C **Hide and Seek**　　　Name _____

Play Hide and Seek with your words. Fill in a box on the bar graph (left to right) for each word you spell correctly.

LOOK.　SAY　SPELL ALOUD　WRITE　SEEK　CHECK

D **Other Word Forms**

Using the words below, follow the instructions given by your teacher.

African	fibrous	funding	photography
autographed	forecasted	hyphenated	phraseology
autographs	forecasting	hyphens	phrases
different	forthright	nephew's	sheriffs
difficulty	forthwith	nephews	siphoned
dolphins	fossilize	paragraphing	spheres
effortless	fossils	paragraphs	spherical
fibers	funded	photographs	trophies

E **Fun Ways to Spell**

Initial the box of each activity you finish.

1. ☐
Create a crossword puzzle with clues.

3. W·O·R·D ☐
Spell your words on a voice recorder.

2. w·o·r·d ☐
Spell your words with sign language.

4. B·A·T·C·H ☐
Bounce a ball as you spell your words.

121

1 **Hide and Seek**

Reinforce spelling by using multiple styles of learning.

On a white board, Teacher writes each word — one at a time. **Have students:**

- **Look** at the word.
- **Say** the word out loud.
- **Spell** the word out loud.
- **Hide** (teacher erases word.)
- **Write** the word on paper.
- **Seek** (teacher rewrites word.)
- **Check** spelling. If incorrect, rewrite word correctly.

2 **Other Word Forms**

This activity is optional. Have students write original sentences using these Other Word Forms:

effortless
spherical
forecasted
funded

3 **Fun Ways to Spell**

Four activities are provided. Use one, two, three, or all of the activities. Have students initial the box for each activity they complete.

Options:

- assign activities to students according to their learning styles
- set up the activities in learning centers for the students to do throughout the day
- divide students into four groups and assign one activity per group
- do one activity per day

General

To create a crossword puzzle...
- Use a pencil to arrange your words on graph paper.
- Overlap words where letters are shared.
- Don't create any new words.
- Outline each word with a marker and number it.
- Write a clue for each word.
- Erase your words.
- Trade with a classmate and work each other's puzzles.

Auditory

To spell your words using a voice recorder...
- Record yourself as you say and spell each word on your spelling list.
- Listen to your recording and check your spelling.

Visual

To spell your words with sign language...
- Have a classmate read a spelling word to you from the list.
- Spell the word using the American Sign Language alphabet.
- Do this with each word on your list.

Tactile

To bounce a ball as you spell your words...
- Look at the first word on your list.
- Bounce the ball as you say each letter of the word aloud.
- Do this with each word on your list.

1 Working with Words

Familiarize students with word meaning and usage.

Secret Words

The boxed letters in the acrostic are a phrase from the Scripture verse for this week.

(Say)

Use the clues to write the words in the puzzle. You may use a dictionary to help you. Then write the boxed letters on the lines below to find the secret words from this week's Scripture.

Take a minute to memorize...

Psalm 27:14

F Working with Words

Name _____

Secret Words

Use the clues to write the words in the puzzle. Then write the boxed letters on the lines below to find the secret words from this week's Scripture.

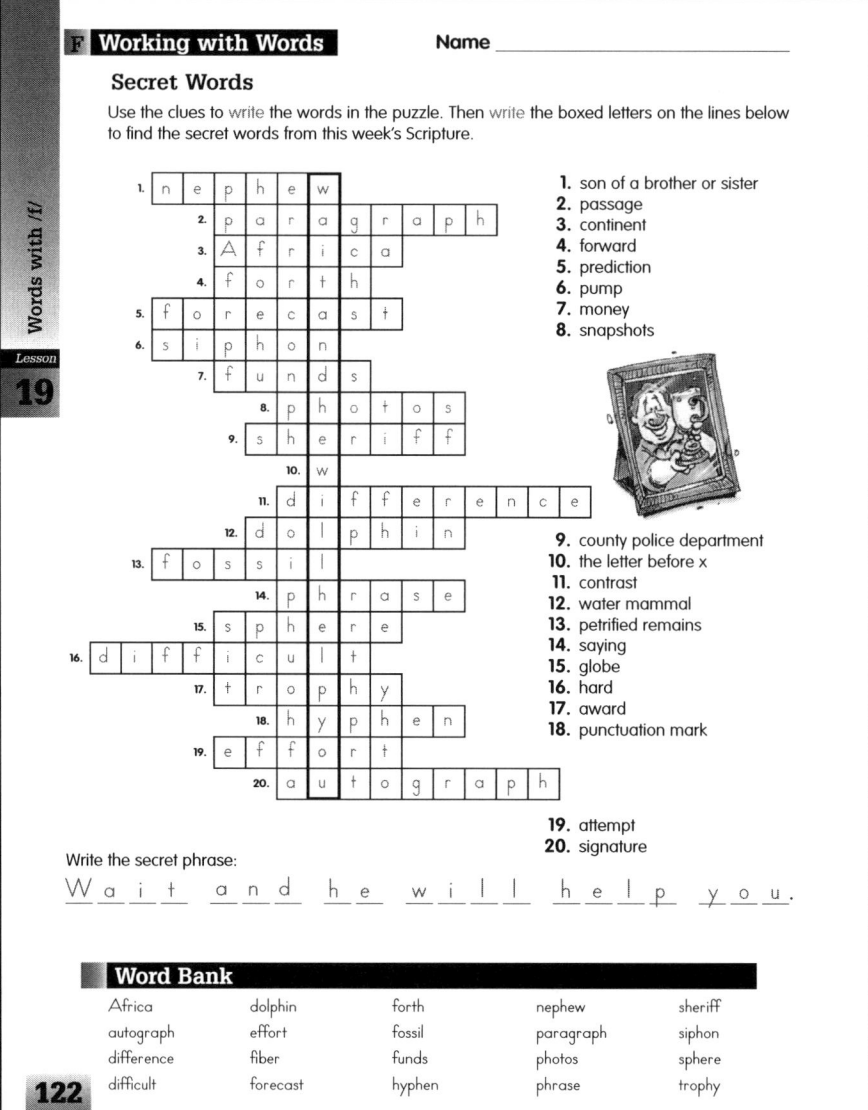

1. n e p h e w
2. p a r a g r a p h
3. A f r i c a
4. f o r t h
5. f o r e c a s t
6. s i p h o n
7. f u n d s
8. p h o t o s
9. s h e r i f f
10. w
11. d i f f e r e n c e
12. d o l p h i n
13. f o s s i l
14. p h r a s e
15. s p h e r e
16. d i f f i c u l t
17. t r o p h y
18. h y p h e n
19. e f f o r t
20. a u t o g r a p h

1. son of a brother or sister
2. passage
3. continent
4. forward
5. prediction
6. pump
7. money
8. snapshots
9. county police department
10. the letter before x
11. contrast
12. water mammal
13. petrified remains
14. saying
15. globe
16. hard
17. award
18. punctuation mark
19. attempt
20. signature

Write the secret phrase:

W a i t   a n d   h e   w i l l   h e l p   y o u .

Word Bank

Africa	dolphin	forth	nephew	sheriff
autograph	effort	fossil	paragraph	siphon
difference	fiber	funds	photos	sphere
difficult	forecast	hyphen	phrase	trophy

122

G Dictation

Name _____

Write **each sentence as your teacher dictates.** Use **correct punctuation.**

1. <u>It took some effort, but he was soon able to</u> <u>get up and begin skiing across the snow.</u>

2. Thorny <u>found it to be more difficult than he</u> <u>had thought.</u>

3. <u>He had read several paragraphs about the history</u> <u>of skiing and had listened to the weather forecast.</u>

H Proofreading

If a word is misspelled, fill in the oval by that word. If all the words are spelled correctly, fill in the oval by **no mistake.**

1. ○ Africa
   ● autograff
   ○ imply
   ○ no mistake

2. ○ paragraph
   ● frase
   ○ biceps
   ○ no mistake

3. ● ephort
   ○ crisis
   ○ nephew
   ○ no mistake

4. ○ sphere
   ● diference
   ○ device
   ○ no mistake

5. ○ difficult
   ○ pride
   ○ migrant
   ● no mistake

6. ○ sheriff
   ○ coyote
   ● hyfen
   ○ no mistake

7. ○ fiber
   ● syphon
   ○ eyeing
   ○ no mistake

8. ○ crime
   ○ forth
   ○ entice
   ● no mistake

9. ○ photos
   ● dolfin
   ○ trophy
   ○ no mistake

10. ○ aisle
    ● fossel
    ○ compile
    ○ no mistake

11. ○ funds
    ○ iceberg
    ○ haiku
    ● no mistake

12. ○ forecast
    ○ combine
    ○ dining
    ● no mistake

123

1 Dictation

Reinforce correct spelling by using current and previous words in context.

Say

Listen as I read each sentence and then write it in your Worktext. Remember to use correct capitalization and punctuation. (Slowly read each sentence twice. Sentences are found in the Student Worktext to the left.)

Day 4

2 Proofreading

Familiarize students with standardized test format and reinforce recognition of misspelled words.

Say

Look at each set of words. If a word is misspelled, fill in the oval by that word. If all the words are spelled correctly, fill in the oval by **no mistake.**

Lesson **19**

3 Hide and Seek

Reinforce correct spelling of current spelling words. Repeat this activity from Day 2.

4 Vocabulary Extension

Have your students complete this activity to strengthen spelling ability and expand vocabulary. The reproducible master is provided in Appendix A as shown on the inset page to the right.

1 Posttest

Visit the **A Reason For** website to download free, printable Posttest pages.

I will say the word once, use it in a sentence, then say it again. Write your words on a separate sheet of paper.

Progress Chart
Students may record scores. (Appendix B)

Personal Dictionary
Students may add any words they have misspelled to their personal dictionaries. (Appendix B)

Hide and Seek

Play Hide and Seek with your words. Fill in a bar graph (left to right) for each word you spell correctly.

Vocabulary Extension
Crossword Puzzle
Use the clues below to complete the puzzle.

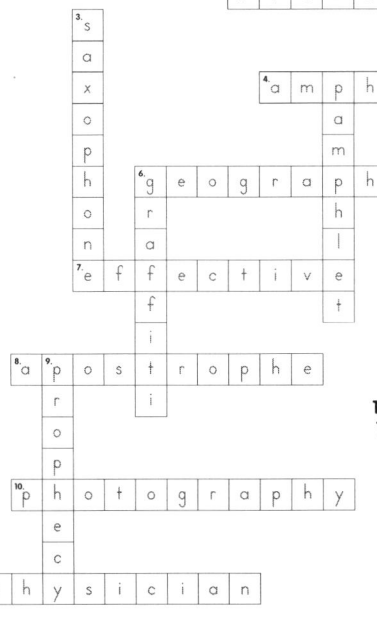

Across
1. changes sound into electric current
4. cold-blooded animal that lives in water when young and on land as an adult
6. study of the earth
7. working well
8. punctuation for possessive nouns
10. making pictures with a camera
11. doctor

Down
2. director, leader
3. musical instrument
5. booklet, brochure
6. wall writing, scribbling
9. prediction

Word Bank

amphibian	geography	official	physician
apostrophe	graffiti	pamphlet	prophecy
effective	microphone	photography	saxophone

340

1.	sheriff	The **sheriff** and his deputies carry extra gasoline for stranded drivers.
2.	siphon	The man was thankful the sheriff could **siphon** gas into his empty tank.
3.	paragraph	Thorny effortlessly quoted a **paragraph** from a skiers guide book.
4.	hyphen	"I believe there is a **hyphen** in that technical term," stated Thorny.
5.	phrase	"Repeat that last **phrase** in English, please," teased Tommy.
6.	forecast	"The **forecast** is most favorable for a cross–country ski trip!" Thorny reported.
7.	difficult	He found skiing much more **difficult** than he'd expected.
8.	forth	"An adequate amount of practice should bring **forth** the desired results!"
9.	nephew	"Your foster dad's **nephew** is a professional skier, right?" asked Tommy.
10.	photos	Tommy took several **photos** of Thorny sprawled in the snow.
11.	trophy	"I expect I will not receive a **trophy** for my skiing skills today," joked Thorny.
12.	difference	The setting sun made a **difference** in the appearance of his surroundings.
13.	sphere	As the giant **sphere** dropped behind the hills, the temperature dropped.
14.	fossil	To occupy his time, he tried to find a **fossil** in a nearby rock.
15.	dolphin	The **dolphin** on the candy bar wrapper made him think of a tropical island.
16.	fiber	He was thankful for the high wool **fiber** content of his blanket.
17.	funds	"Perhaps our vacation **funds** would be better spent on a summer retreat."
18.	Africa	"The climate in **Africa** sounds quite appealing to me at the moment!"
19.	effort	"I made an **effort** to have courage, like the verse said to do!" said Thorny.
20.	autograph	"Can I have your **autograph**, Thorny?" smiled Tommy.

190

I Game

Name _____

Ski down the slope with Thorny. Move one space for each word you or your team spells correctly.

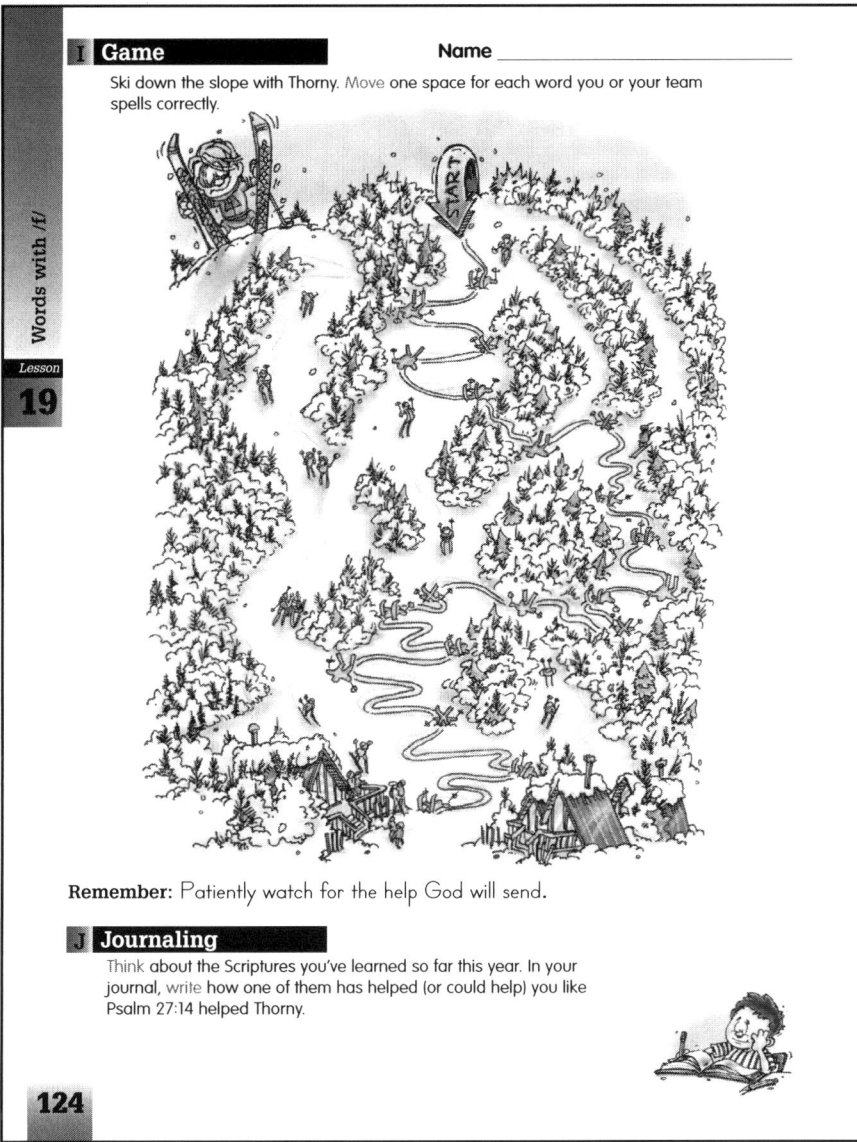

Remember: Patiently watch for the help God will send.

J Journaling

Think about the Scriptures you've learned so far this year. In your journal, write how one of them has helped (or could help) you like Psalm 27:14 helped Thorny.

How to Play:

- Divide the class into two teams.
- Have each student place his/her game piece on Start.
- Have a student from team A go to the board.
- Say the spelling word.
- Have the student write the word on the board.
- If correct, instruct each member of team A to move his/her game piece forward one space.
- Alternate between teams A and B.
- The team to reach the bottom of the slope first is the winner.
- **Small Group Option**: Students may play this game without teacher direction in small groups of two or more.

2 Game

Reinforce spelling skills and provide motivation and interest.

Materials

- game page (from student text)
- game pieces (1 per child)
- game word list

Game Word List

1. **Africa**
2. **autograph**
3. **paragraph**
4. **phrase**
5. **effort**
6. **nephew**
7. **sphere**
8. **difference**
9. **difficult**
10. **sheriff**
11. **hyphen**
12. **fiber**
13. **siphon**
14. **forecast**
15. **forth**
16. **photos**
17. **trophy**
18. **dolphin**
19. **fossil**
20. **funds**

3 Journaling

Provide a meaningful reason for correct spelling through personal writing.

Review the story using discussion leads provided on the following page. Encourage students to apply the Scriptural value in their journaling.

Journaling (continued)

(Say)

- Have you ever been cross-country skiing or down-hill skiing? (Allow time to share experiences.)

- Why didn't Thorny bring any books about skiing along on the trip? (He'd already read everything he could find about the subject.)

- What did Thorny say the first skis were made of? (Animal bones.)

- Did Thorny know how to ski because of all the research he'd done? (No. He had to try skiing to learn.)

- What wise choice did Thorny make when he realized he was lost? (He decided to stay put and wait for someone to come find him.)

- What did Thorny do to pass the time? (Repeated all the Scriptures he could remember learning since he'd come to live in the Simmons foster home.)

- How did that help him? (He remembered the verse that said to be patient, brave, and courageous, waiting for the Lord to save you.)

- Why do you think it was a good thing Thorny had done all that reading about cross-country skiing? (He had packed extra clothes, matches, toilet paper in a plastic bag, an insulated blanket, and a candy bar.)

'E' is the most frequently occurring letter in English, as well as in French, Spanish, and German.

Socially Acceptable

Daniel attends a fancy dinner party with his parents and has a hard choice to make.

"Well, how do I look, Milli?" Daniel struck a pose, hands held palm up to the side.

Milli, the DeVore's live-in maid, slowly circled the boy, eyeing him critically. Then she stopped in front of him, her hand tucked under her chin and her head cocked to one side. Finally, she winked. "Sure'n you be a-lookin' right smart tonight! 'Twould be surprisin' if you weren't the best lookin' lad attendin' that fancy shindig."

"Aw, Milli," Daniel grinned in embarrassment. "Of course that's not true, but you really think I look okay? I'm just so glad Dad and Mom want me to go tonight. They don't usually take me anywhere with them, and they've never taken me with them to anything like this. I want to be sure I do everything right!"

"Now that sounds a right-fine goal to be a-aimin' for, young Daniel." Milli straightened his tie a bit. "And you be a-lookin' more than okay."

"Milli! Send Daniel down, please," Mr. DeVore called from the bottom of the stairs. "We should be leaving for the Hopewell's right away."

Daniel wiped suddenly damp palms on his dressy slacks. Milli grinned. "Now I can't be a-figurin' out any reason for you to be nervous, lad. You know more about which fork to be a-usin' first than most of us." She gave him a quick hug, then straightened his suit coat. "Just have a grand time, m'lad."

"See you later, Milli." Daniel offered a crooked grin and started down the broad, curved staircase.

"There you are." Mrs. DeVore looked her only son over with a critical eye. "By all means, stand up straight, Daniel. You hardly look impressive all hunched over like that. Now, remember to greet Mrs. Hopewell first, like I showed you, with a small bow over her hand. Then, greet Mr. Hopewell, but be sure to call him 'Sir.' After all, he's from England and that is his title. It simply wouldn't do for you to call him 'mister.' Now...."

The steady stream of instructions continued as the three DeVores took their places in the car. They kept coming as Mr. DeVore eased the luxurious sedan out onto Stoneridge Court and headed toward the Hopewell's home. When Mrs. DeVore finally fell silent, Mr. DeVore spoke up. "Are you sure you want to take Daniel with us, Sandra? You're just going to be worrying all evening about how he behaves."

"I will not!" Daniel's mother snapped. "You know very well that we have to take Daniel tonight to make a good impression on the Hopewells. They dote on their boy, Carson. Especially Cynthia. Why, she acts as if that child is absolutely perfect. They center their lives around him." She shook her perfectly groomed head. "They'd think us very strange if we didn't bring Daniel."

Daniel didn't hear the rest of the discussion. He stared out the window without seeing anything, but his thoughts were resentful. *It shouldn't surprise me, really. They've never cared enough about me to want to be with me. I don't know why I thought this was any different, but somehow I did. I thought they wanted to take me to this fancy party because they were proud of me. I'm such a stupid jerk, I never learn!*

The hurt inside Daniel churned up familiar feelings of helpless anger. Parents are supposed to love and care for their kids! Why couldn't his parents get the message?

When they arrived at the Hopewell's sprawling estate, Daniel performed perfectly. The introductions, the pre-dinner chitchat, the formal dinner with three forks and two spoons—Daniel dealt with each flawlessly. He even kept his cool when he tripped slightly on the edge of a thick Persian carpet and the Hopewell's "perfect" son, Carson, asked him when he learned to walk. But inside, his feelings continued to boil. After dinner, the adults drifted around in small groups visiting and gossiping. Daniel found an inconspicuous spot in a corner and flopped into a soft chair.

A boy about Daniel's own age spotted him. "Hey, aren't you the DeVore kid?"

Daniel nodded.

"Daniel, isn't it? Well, I'm Jonathan Hightower, but you can call me Rusty." The boy tugged a reddish brown curl and shrugged. "Hey, you guys, come here!" He motioned two other boys over to Daniel's corner. "This is Peter and that's Randall, Randy for short. We've got a plan. You want to hear it?"

Daniel shrugged. The three boys moved in closer. "It's like this," Rusty began. "It's that Carson Hopewell. We've got to do something about him."

"Why?" Daniel was confused.

"Haven't you met him?" Rusty demanded, as if that was enough of an explanation. When Daniel nodded, Rusty went on, "Then you know. His parents think he can't do anything wrong and he believes it! He thinks he's better than anyone else and treats everyone like dirt. When Peter's family arrived tonight Carson ignored him—looked through him like he wasn't even there. Randy said 'Yo' instead of 'Hello,' and this Carson guy looked at Randy like he was insane and asked him why he didn't learn to speak proper English."

Judging from his flashing green eyes, Rusty

193

was working himself into quite a temper. "Why, I heard his mother telling someone he didn't want to eat with us, so she let him eat in a private dining room. Well, our dads are rich, too. Maybe they aren't 'Sirs,' but we're just as important as he is—and we've got a plan to show him just that!"

Daniel's own feelings of hurt and anger grew. Maybe he couldn't do anything about his own parents not thinking he was good enough for them to spend time with, but he could sure do something about this Carson character not thinking he was good enough! He leaned forward in the chair. "What's the plan?" The other three boys huddled around and explained.

"So," Rusty finished. "Are you in?"

Daniel started to reply, but another voice interrupted.

"What kind of drinks have you got there?" Peter had spotted a server passing through the hallway. The young woman, looking official in a black dress and crisp white apron, carried a silver tray of frosty crystal glasses.

"White grape juice, apple juice, strawberry-kiwi and raspberry lemonade, sir," she answered Peter's question respectfully.

Randy and Peter made their selections. Rusty frowned. "Don't you have any pop?"

"No, sir." The girl answered respectfully. "I can be a-checkin' in the kitchen if you be a-wishin' it."

"No, this is fine." Rusty took apple juice. Daniel picked up a glass, too, not even sure what he was getting. The girl didn't look anything like Milli, but she sounded so much like her!

Just hearing that lilting voice made Daniel think about Milli and their earlier conversation. *Milli is proud of me. Milli thinks I look better than okay—and she expects me to do what is right.*

As the waitress walked away, Rusty repeated the question. "So, DeVore, are you in?"

Daniel shook his head

and calmly said, "No."

"NO!?" The three echoed. "Why ever not?" Peter demanded.

Daniel rubbed the moisture off the outside of his glass. "Well, I want to, but I can't."

Randy looked puzzled. "What's the problem?"

"Well, even though he made fun of me and was a real jerk to you guys, it just wouldn't be right, that's all." Daniel took a sip of raspberry lemonade.

"Well, well." Rusty shook his head and stared at Daniel as if he had sprouted another head or something. "I'd heard you were a pretty tough guy, that you could handle yourself in things like this, that you'd even gotten into major trouble over some stuff you'd done. You must have changed." He turned away. "C'mon guys."

"Uh, see ya." Randy and Peter seemed embarrassed.

"Yeah, see you later." Peter half-waved and the two sauntered off.

Later that evening, Daniel told Milli all about it. "So, if that maid hadn't sounded so much like you, I probably would have gotten in big trouble. As it was, the other guys didn't follow through with their plan, and Carson Hopewell got away with his meanness." Daniel sighed and rested his chin on his hands where he sat at the kitchen work table watching Milli make up a tray for his parents, who'd gone straight to their room.

"That's where you be a-thinkin' wrong." Milli placed two fine china cups and saucers on the tray.

"Where?" Daniel rubbed the bridge of his nose, trying to ease the headache building behind his eyes.

"Everyone must be a-payin' for their actions sooner or later, lad. Carson Hopewell will be a-payin' for his as surely as you will pay for yours." Milli reached for the delicate sugar bowl and put it on the tray. "I be a-thinkin' your payments will be vastly different, though!" She winked. "Sure'n you have changed, m'lad, and I be a-praisin' God for a-holdin' you tight in His hand and a-keepin' your feet on the right path this night."

"Whether I wanted to stay there or

not!" Daniel chuckled.

Milli walked over and shook her finger under Daniel's nose. "You made the choice, lad. The right choice." She squeezed his shoulder, then stepped back to study him, tucking one hand under her chin and cocking her head to one side in thought. Finally, she winked. "Sure'n you be a-lookin' right smart tonight!"

2 Discussion Time

Check understanding of the story and development of personal values.

- Where were Daniel's parents taking him?
- What did Daniel's mother say to him on the way?
- What did Rusty, Peter, and Randy ask Daniel to help them do?
- Why did the boys want to "do something" about Carson Hopewell?
- What happened just as Daniel was about to answer the boys?
- What choice did Daniel make?
- What did Milli say about the choice Daniel made?

A Preview

Write each word as your teacher says it.

Name _____

1. average
2. jacket
3. merge
4. cringe
5. jury
6. manage
7. heritage
8. badge
9. junior
10. legend
11. jaguar
12. dungeon
13. jogging
14. gadget

15. hinges
16. rigid
17. justice
18. plunge
19. refuge
20. pledge

Words with /j/

Lesson
20

Scripture

Psalm 66:8, 9

125

Preview

3

Test for knowledge of the correct spellings of these words.

Customize Your List
On a separate sheet of paper, additional words of your choice may be tested.

(Say) I will say each word once, use the word in a sentence, then say the word again. Write the words on the lines in your Worktext.

Correct Immediately!
(Say) Let's correct our Preview. I will spell each word out loud. If you spelled a word incorrectly, rewrite it correctly.

Progress Chart
Students may record scores. (Reproducible master provided in Appendix B.)

1.	average	"You be lookin' a might above **average** tonight!" complemented Milli.
2.	jacket	The **jacket** Daniel wore complemented his slacks and tie.
3.	merge	Mr. DeVore began to carefully **merge** the expensive sedan into the next lane.
4.	cringe	Daniel's mother's constant instructions made him **cringe** and feel more nervous.
5.	jury	He felt as if he were standing before a judge and **jury**.
6.	manage	"I do hope you can **manage** to do right!" worried Mrs. DeVore.
7.	heritage	"The Hopewell family has a rich family **heritage**," she commented.
8.	badge	"They wear their son Carson like a **badge** or something!" she sneered.
9.	junior	"They act as if he's **junior** partner in the firm already!"
10.	legend	"This is the only known copy of this ancient English **legend**," bragged Carson.
11.	jaguar	Daniel thought the porcelain **jaguar** in the dining room looked fierce.
12.	dungeon	"I'll bet there's a creepy **dungeon** under this huge house," joked Randy.
13.	jogging	"Your dad goes **jogging** with Sir Hopewell, doesn't he?" asked Rusty.
14.	gadget	While the boys talked in the kitchen, Daniel noticed many a fancy **gadget**.
15.	hinges	The metal door to the kitchen had **hinges** that swung both ways.
16.	rigid	At first Daniel felt **rigid** with anger and wanted to join the boys.
17.	justice	"Let's serve a little **justice** on Conceited Carson!" laughed Rusty.
18.	plunge	"Are you too scared to take the **plunge** with us?" Rusty mocked Daniel.
19.	refuge	When he got home, he hurried to take **refuge** in the kitchen with Milli.
20.	pledge	"I remembered my **pledge** to God to follow His path," he told her.

195

4 Word Shapes

Help students form a correct image of whole words.

 Say
Look at each word and think about its shape. Now, write the word in the correct Word Shape Boxes. You may check off each word as you use it.

(In many words, the sound of /j/ is spelled with **j**, and it is often spelled this way when it is at the beginning of a word. The /j/ sound can also be spelled with **g** when followed by **i**, **y**, or **e**. The spelling **dge** is used at the end of a word.)

Say
In the Word Shape Boxes, color the letter or letters that spell the sound of /j/ in each word.

Take a minute to memorize...
Psalm 66:8,9

Words with /j/

Lesson 20

B Word Shapes

Name _____

Using the word bank below, write each word in the correct Word Shape Boxes. Next, in the Word Shape Boxes, fill in the boxes containing the letter or letters that spell the sound of /j/ in each word.

1. gadget
2. heritage
3. merge
4. legend
5. jaguar
6. jury
7. rigid
8. jacket
9. refuge
10. badge
11. pledge
12. average
13. cringe
14. justice
15. manage
16. jogging
17. dungeon
18. junior
19. plunge
20. hinges

Word Bank

average	gadget	jaguar	justice	pledge
badge	heritage	jogging	legend	plunge
cringe	hinges	junior	manage	refuge
dungeon	jacket	jury	merge	rigid

126

Answers may vary for duplicate word shapes.

Be Prepared For Fun

Check these supply lists for **Fun Ways to Spell** - presented **Day 2**.
Purchase and/or gather these items ahead of time!

General
- Pencil
- Notebook Paper
- Spelling List

Auditory
- Pencil
- Notebook Paper
- Dictionary
- Spelling List

Visual
- Pencil
- Notebook Paper
- Spelling List

Tactile
- Clay
- Spelling List

C Hide and Seek

Name _____

Play **Hide and Seek** with your words. Fill in a box on the bar graph (left to right) for each word you spell correctly.

LOOK   SAY   SPELL ALOUD   WRITE   SEEK   CHECK

D Other Word Forms

Using the words below, follow the instructions given by your teacher.

averaged	hinged	legendary	(plunged)
averaging	inheritance	manageability	plunging
badges	jacketed	(manageable)	refugee
(cringed)	jaguars	merged	refuges
cringing	jogger	merging	rigidity
dungeons	jogs	pledged	(rigidly)
gadgets	juries	pledging	

E Fun Ways to Spell

Initial the box of each activity you finish.

1. ☐

Encode your spelling words.

2. ☐

Find hidden words in your spelling words.

3. ☐

Define your spelling words.

4. ☐

Spell your words with clay.

127

Words with /j/

Lesson **20**

Day 2

Lesson **20**

Hide and Seek

1 Reinforce spelling by using multiple styles of learning.

On a white board, Teacher writes each word — one at a time. **Have students:**

- **Look** at the word.
- **Say** the word out loud.
- **Spell** the word out loud.
- **Hide** (teacher erases word.)
- **Write** the word on paper.
- **Seek** (teacher rewrites word.)
- **Check** spelling. If incorrect, rewrite word correctly.

Other Word Forms

2 This activity is optional. Have students find and circle the Other Word Forms that are most nearly synonyms of the following:

recoiled
unyieldingly
doable
dived

Fun Ways to Spell

3 Four activities are provided. Use one, two, three, or all of the activities. Have students initial the box for each activity they complete.

Options:

- assign activities to students according to their learning styles
- set up the activities in learning centers for the students to do throughout the day
- divide students into four groups and assign one activity per group
- do one activity per day

General

To encode your spelling words...
- Write the alphabet on your paper.
- Write your own code for each letter underneath it.
- Write your spelling words in your code.
- Trade papers with a classmate and decode the words.
- Check to make sure your classmate spelled the words correctly.

Auditory

To define your spelling words...
- Ask a classmate to look up a word from your spelling list in the dictionary and read the definition to you, but not the spelling word.
- Decide which word on your list matches this definition and write the word.
- Ask your classmate to check your spelling.
- Switch and continue taking turns.

Visual

To find hidden words in your spelling words...
- Choose a word from your spelling list.
- Write it on your paper.
- Find and write as many smaller words as you can that are contained within your spelling word.
- Do this with each word.

Tactile

To spell your words with clay...
- Roll pieces of clay into ropes.
- Use the ropes to make the letters of each word.
- Put them in the right order to spell each word.
- Check your spelling.

Working with Words

Familiarize students with word meaning and usage.

Drawing Conclusions

Explain that to figure something out using logic is to draw a conclusion. On the board write:

You are riding a large, strong animal with hoofs. You are probably riding a _____.

Have a volunteer supply the word **horse**.

Complete each conclusion by writing a word from the word bank. You may use a dictionary to help you.

Take a minute to memorize...

Psalm 66:8,9

F Working with Words

Name _____

Drawing Conclusions

Complete each conclusion by writing a word from the word bank.

1. The weather is chilly. You should probably wear a ____jacket____.
2. You are standing, facing the flag. You are about to say the ____pledge____.
3. The door squeaks when it is opened. It needs oil on the ____hinges____.
4. If something is usual and ordinary, it is said to be ____average____.
5. You are running at a slow, steady pace. You are ____jogging____.
6. A sheriff is wearing a silver star on his uniform. He is wearing a ____badge____.
7. You decided to jump off the high dive. You will ____plunge____ into the water.
8. Twelve men and women sit listening to the lawyers. They are probably the ____jury____.
9. The verdict sounds fair. ____Justice____ has been done.
10. The old castle has a room for prisoners. This room is called the ____dungeon____.
11. Mom has a small tool for slicing eggs. She says it is a new ____gadget____.
12. You have good self-control. You are able to ____manage____ yourself.
13. Dad needs to change lanes into a line of cars. He needs to ____merge____.
14. Our teacher is pretty strict. Her rules are very ____rigid____.
15. We needed to find shelter from the storm. We looked for a place of ____refuge____.
16. I am an American. Freedom is my ____heritage____.
17. I shrank in fear when I heard the thunder. It made me ____cringe____.
18. We read a story about a blue ox named Babe. The story is a ____legend____.
19. My brother will graduate next year. He is a ____junior____ in high school.
20. At the zoo, I saw a cat that looked like a big leopard. It must be a ____jaguar____.

Word Bank

average	gadget	jaguar	justice	pledge
badge	heritage	jogging	legend	plunge
cringe	hinges	junior	manage	refuge
dungeon	jacket	jury	merge	rigid

Words with /j/

Lesson **20**

128

Lesson **20** | Day 3

198

G Dictation

Name _____

Write **each sentence as your teacher dictates.** Use **correct punctuation.**

1. Daniel looked sharp in his new suit jacket, although he felt tense.

2. It made him cringe as he thought of the plan to get even.

3. Daniel managed to stay out of trouble, although his choice embarrassed the boys.

H Proofreading

If a word is misspelled, fill in the oval by that word. If all the words are spelled correctly, fill in the oval by **no mistake.**

1. ● avrige
   ○ badge
   ○ Africa
   ○ no mistake

2. ○ gadget
   ○ autograph
   ○ effort
   ● no mistake

3. ● jackit
   ○ paragraph
   ○ jaguar
   ○ no mistake

4. ○ sphere
   ● manige
   ○ pledge
   ○ no mistake

5. ○ forth
   ○ refuge
   ● legind
   ○ no mistake

6. ○ cringe
   ○ difference
   ○ sheriff
   ● no mistake

7. ○ dolphin
   ● junor
   ○ funds
   ○ no mistake

8. ○ justice
   ● merje
   ○ hyphen
   ○ no mistake

9. ○ hinges
   ○ rigid
   ○ fossil
   ● no mistake

10. ○ jogging
    ○ phrase
    ○ nephew
    ● no mistake

11. ● heritige
    ○ plunge
    ○ difficult
    ○ no mistake

12. ○ fiber
    ○ jury
    ● dunjon
    ○ no mistake

129

Dictation

Reinforce correct spelling by using current and previous words in context.

(Say) Listen as I read each sentence and then write it in your Worktext. Remember to use correct capitalization and punctuation. (Slowly read each sentence twice. Sentences are found in the Student Worktext to the left.)

Proofreading

Familiarize students with standardized test format and reinforce recognition of misspelled words.

(Say) Look at each set of words. If a word is misspelled, fill in the oval by that word. If all the words are spelled correctly, fill in the oval by **no mistake.**

3 Hide and Seek

Reinforce correct spelling of current spelling words. Repeat this activity from Day 2.

4 Vocabulary Extension

Have your students complete this activity to strengthen spelling ability and expand vocabulary. The reproducible master is provided in Appendix A as shown on the inset page to the right.

1 Posttest

Visit the **A Reason For** website to download free, printable Posttest pages.

Say I will say the word once, use it in a sentence, then say it again. Write your words on a separate sheet of paper.

Progress Chart
Students may record scores. (Appendix B)

Personal Dictionary
Students may add any words they have misspelled to their personal dictionaries. (Appendix B)

Hide and Seek

Play Hide and Seek with your words. Fill in a bar graph (left to right) for each word you spell correctly.

LOOK   SAY   HIDE   WRITE   SEEK   CHECK

Vocabulary Extension

Trade-off

Choose a word from the word bank to replace the word(s) in parentheses. Write the word in the blank.

1. Dad bought Mom a ___corsage___ (small bouquet) to wear to the formal event.
2. The hungry deer had to ___forage___ (search) for food during the harsh winter.
3. Medics are trained to act quickly and carefully in an ___emergency___ (crisis).
4. Michael forgot to put the milk back in the ___refrigerator___ (cooling appliance), so it soured.
5. Measles, chicken pox, and the flu are all ___contagious___ (infectious) diseases that can spread to other people.
6. A ___generation___ (span of time) is said to be around 30 years between the births of parents and that of their children.
7. A ___sergeant___ (member of the armed forces) was waiting at the train station.
8. Mom and Dad had made an ___arrangement___ (agreement) for me to stay at a neighbor's house until they got home.
9. Getting used to his new school took some ___adjustment___ (adaptation), but he soon made new friends.
10. We say a pledge to our country's flag to show ___allegiance___ (loyalty) to the country we live in.
11. People train dogs with high ___intelligence___ (aptitude) to serve as police dogs and seeing-eye dogs.
12. The traffic accident occurred because of the ___negligence___ (carelessness) of the driver who ran the stop sign.

Word Bank

adjustment	contagious	forage	negligence
allegiance	corsage	generation	refrigerator
arrangement	emergency	intelligence	sergeant

341

---

1. **average** — "This is no **average** party," Daniel told Milli.
2. **badge** — Sometimes people with lots of wealth wear their success like a **badge**.
3. **jogging** — Mrs. DeVore and Mrs. Hopewell go **jogging** together sometimes.
4. **jacket** — Milli dusted some lint off the back of Daniel's dinner **jacket**.
5. **merge** — Mr. DeVore began to slowly **merge** the sedan into the flow of traffic.
6. **manage** — "Can you **manage** to behave like a gentleman tonight?" asked his mother.
7. **cringe** — His mother's sharp remarks made Daniel **cringe**.
8. **heritage** — "The Hopewells are extremely proud of their family **heritage**," she continued.
9. **junior** — "Carson will be the **junior** partner in his father's firm one day," said Mrs. DeVore.
10. **legend** — An antique book of an ancient English **legend** sat on the table in the foyer.
11. **jaguar** — A large porcelain **jaguar** stood in the corner of the Hopewell's dining room.
12. **hinges** — The **hinges** on the kitchen door allowed it to swing freely both ways.
13. **gadget** — There was more than one fancy **gadget** in the huge kitchen.
14. **dungeon** — "Think there's a **dungeon** underneath this castle?" joked Randy.
15. **justice** — "Let's serve some **justice** on that old Carson Hopewell," suggested Rusty.
16. **rigid** — At first, the boys' comments made Daniel feel **rigid** with anger.
17. **pledge** — Daniel thought for a moment and said, "I made a **pledge** to follow the right path."
18. **jury** — "You're acting like a judge and **jury**, Daniel," mocked Rusty.
19. **plunge** — "We thought you were tough enough to take the **plunge**," they sneered.
20. **refuge** — After he got home, Daniel took **refuge** in the kitchen with Milli.

Lesson 20 — Day 4 / Day 5

I Game

Name _____

Complete the secret phrase by spelling the words from this week's word list.

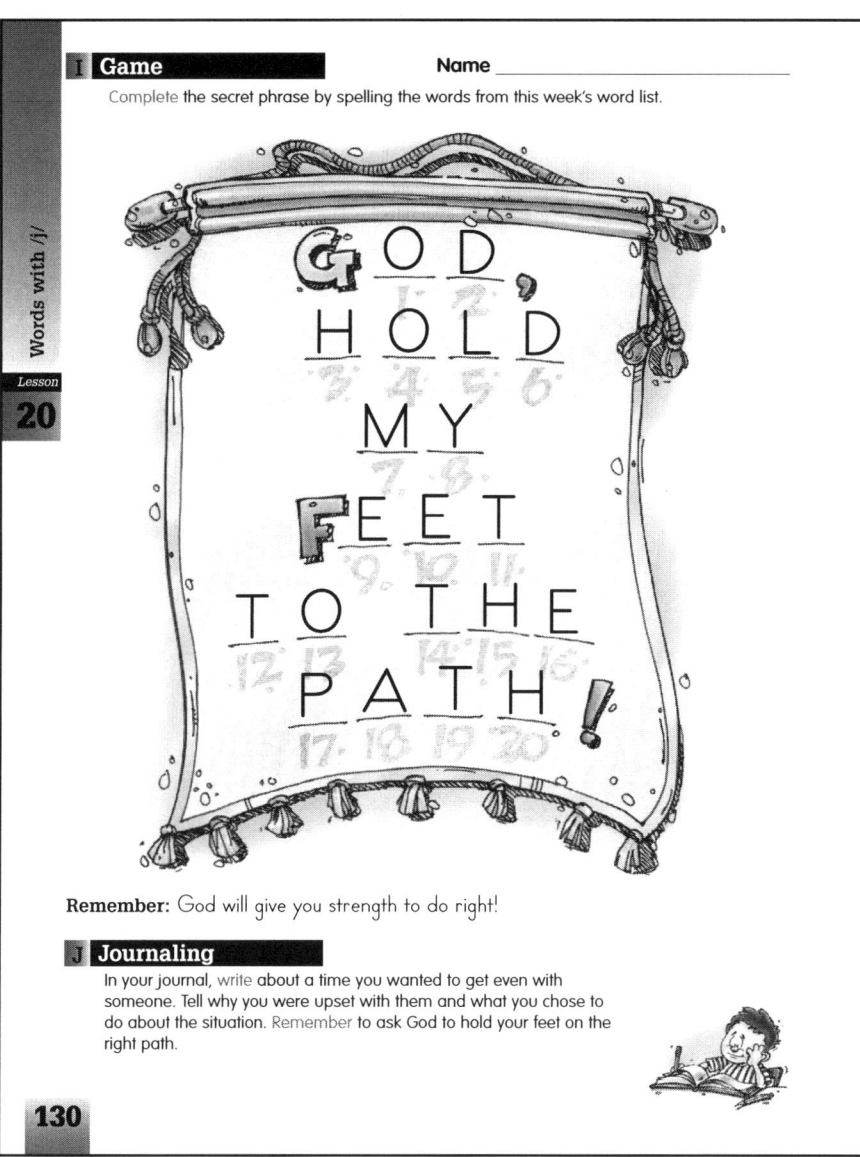

Remember: God will give you strength to do right!

J Journaling

In your journal, write about a time you wanted to get even with someone. Tell why you were upset with them and what you chose to do about the situation. Remember to ask God to hold your feet on the right path.

130

How to Play:

- Divide the class into two teams, and decide which team will go first.
- Have a student from team A choose a number from 1 to 20.
- Say the word that matches that number from the team's word list.
- Have the student write the word on the board.
- If correct, have each member of team A write the given letter in the matching space on his/her game page.
- Alternate between teams A and B having the students choose a number of a blank space.
- The team to complete the secret phrase first is the winner.

2 Game

Reinforce spelling skills and provide motivation and interest.

Materials

- game page (from student text)
- pencils (1 per child)
- game word list

Game Word List

Team A	Team B
1. average (O)	1. cringe (O)
2. badge (D)	2. hinges (D)
3. gadget (H)	3. rigid (H)
4. jacket (O)	4. jogging (O)
5. jaguar (L)	5. junior (L)
6. manage (D)	6. jury (D)
7. pledge (M)	7. merge (M)
8. legend (Y)	8. justice (Y)
9. refuge (E)	9. dungeon (E)
10. heritage (E)	10. plunge (E)
11. cringe (T)	11. average (T)
12. hinges (T)	12. badge (T)
13. rigid (O)	13. gadget (O)
14. jogging (T)	14. jacket (T)
15. junior (H)	15. jaguar (H)
16. jury (E)	16. manage (E)
17. merge (P)	17. pledge (P)
18. justice (A)	18. legend (A)
19. dungeon (T)	19. refuge (T)
20. plunge (H)	20. heritage (H)

3 Journaling

Provide a meaningful reason for correct spelling through personal writing.

Review the story using discussion leads provided on the following page. Encourage students to apply the Scriptural value in their journaling.

Journaling (continued)

- Why was Daniel so happy that his parents were taking him to the fancy dinner party? (He wanted to be with them and thought that they were taking him because they were proud of him and wanted to be with him, too.)

- What made him realize that they weren't taking him because they wanted to? (His mother said they had to take him to make a good impression on the Hopewells.)

- How did Daniel react to knowing his parents didn't really want him with them? (He felt very angry and upset.)

- What was Carson Hopewell like? (He was a spoiled brat. His parents thought he couldn't do anything wrong, but he was selfish and mean to the other boys.)

- How did the serving girl stop Daniel from choosing to go along with the boys' plan to do something to Carson? (Her accent sounded like Milli's, and thinking of Milli reminded Daniel to do what was right.)

The longest word with one vowel is STRENGTHS.

Word Wow!

Over the Limit

Carlos learns how important it is to obey all laws
— including traffic laws.

"Carlos, that sign says the speed limit is 40 miles an hour!" Rosa waved at the sign they'd just sped by. "You know, f-o-r-t-y, FORTY!"

"Yeah, yeah, yeah." Carlos flipped on the radio. "I'm only going a little over that. Relax already, would ya?" When he located a station he liked, he turned up the volume. Music throbbed through the yellow car and put a halt to any further discussion.

Soon Carlos braked to a stop in the Wrights' driveway. He spoke loudly to be heard over the radio. "See, little sister? Here you are, safe and sound. I'll be back to pick you up when basketball practice is over at 8:00."

Rosa gathered up her stuff and climbed out of the little car. She waved as her older brother backed out of the driveway and turned down Appleby Road. True to form, he didn't come to a stop at the corner—just a pause and then off down the road again.

"Hi, Rosa!" Kristin opened the front door. "Come on in. Burrrr. It's cold out there!"

The Wrights' house was warm and smelled delicious. "Mom's baking cinnamon rolls," Kristin informed her friend when she saw her sniffing the air. "They should be out in time for supper. Let's work in my room." She led the way to the room she shared with her younger sister, Cathy. "Did you bring everything?"

When Rosa upended her tote bag a variety of objects rolled out onto the carpet—Popsicle sticks, a Ziploc bag of hay, small pieces of wood, and a couple of metal pop-bottle lids.

"Dad said we could use this box." Kristin sank down on the floor and began adding her contributions to the pile, "Here are glue, paints, wire, cotton balls, and pipe cleaners." Kristin set the box on its side. "Well, let's get started."

Rosa picked up the wire and some Popsicle sticks. "I'll start the fence and you can paint the background, okay?"

Kristin jumped up, "Just a second. I'll get some plastic to put down so we don't mess up the carpet."

Gradually the diorama began to take shape. By the time Cathy came to call them to supper, she could tell that the scene was a horse barn and pasture.

After a yummy supper of vegetable soup and warm cinnamon rolls, the two friends went back to work. "Do you think this hay looks all right by the barn like this?" Rosa leaned back to study the effect.

"Uh-huh." Kristin placed a fluff of cotton on the background and glued the cloud in place. "Looks GREAT to me!" She stretched and looked at the mess around them. "What time is Carlos coming to get you?"

Rosa began picking up leftover bits and pieces. "He said basketball practice would be over at 8:00, so he'll probably get here two minutes after that." She shook her head. "He drives so fast!"

"Does his driving scare you?" Kristin held open a plastic bag and Rosa dropped the leftovers inside.

"No, not really." Rosa leaned back against the side of Cathy's bed. "He always says he's in control and that he doesn't go faster than is safe, but I say speed limits are posted for a reason and he should pay attention to them."

"What does your dad say about it?"

Rosa shrugged. "I haven't said anything to Dad about it. Carlos worked so hard to get the money to buy that car, and he's spent so much time and effort

fixing it up. It's like a person to him. I'm pretty sure Dad wouldn't let him drive if he knew he was breaking some rules, so I've just been trying to get Carlos to slow down and stuff on my own." She sighed. "Maria just ignores the whole situation. She doesn't care how he drives as long as he'll take her places."

"Well, I think you should tell your dad." Kristin looked at her friend seriously.

"Carlos would never forgive me if I did that and Dad took away his car!" Rosa protested.

"Maybe not," Kristin admitted. "But like you said, those speed limits and stop signs are there for a reason. He'll get a ticket or, worse yet, have an accident if he keeps on ignoring them—and then your dad will find out for sure."

Rosa got up and changed the subject. "Since we're done with this project, let's do something fun till Carlos gets here. How about that new game you got for Christmas?"

Kristin plopped onto her stomach and helped Rosa set up the game on the floor. Kristin was winning when the doorbell chimed. She helped Rosa carry the diorama out and settle it safely in the back seat. "Don't forget to bring it to school tomorrow!" she reminded as Rosa climbed in the front seat by her brother. "See you later!"

Rosa waved as Carlos backed out of the driveway.

"That thing you guys made looks good, Rosita." Carlos slowed at the stop sign, and, after glancing around, accelerated again.

"Thanks, Carlos." Rosa gulped, then went on, "You didn't stop at that stop sign. Don't you think you should have?"

"Naaa!" Carlos changed his headlights to low beam as a car came toward them. "You could see as well as I could that there weren't any cars at the intersection! It was totally safe to keep going. What's the big deal?"

"Well, the sign said to stop. That's the law." Rosa took a deep breath. "What if you get so used to ignoring traffic signs that you ignore them when it isn't safe?"

"Give me a break, Rosa!" Carlos shifted into a higher gear. "I think I know a bit more about driving than you do. After all, I have a license and you don't!" The yellow car picked up speed rapidly.

"Carlos, you're going too fast!" Rosa insisted. "The speed limit here is 55!"

"Nag, nag, nag!" Carlos exploded. "You're always complaining and carrying on! Well, I'm a good driver! Besides, this is my car and I'll drive it the way I want! You just be quiet and be glad you have a ride! Just because I don't stop and wait an hour at every stop sign doesn't mean that...."

Suddenly, everything seemed to slide into slow motion. Carlos stomped on the brake pedal. The tires shrieked against the pavement, but couldn't cling to it. The road quietly curved around the bend as it always did—but the shiny yellow car didn't make the turn. Rosa screamed! The little car launched into space. There was the sound of an impact; everything went dark.

When Rosa woke up she hurt all over. It took a major effort to open her eyes. "Well, hello, young lady." A pleasant stranger leaned over her and peered into her eyes.

"Wh-what happened?" Rosa didn't recognize her own scratchy voice.

"What do you remember?" The woman began writing on a clipboard.

Slowly Rosa's thoughts became less muddled. She realized she was in a hospital room and this must be a nurse. "We," her voice squeaked. She cleared her throat and tried again. "We had a wreck. Is Carlos okay?"

"Yes, he'll be just fine." The woman checked the IV hanging by the bed. "He's been very anxious to see you." She smiled down at Rosa. "And your father and sister are here, too, along with several

other people. They'll be very glad you decided to wake up!"

Rosa started to raise her head to look around the room. "OUCH!"

"Now, don't try to move, young lady." The woman rested a hand lightly on her forehead. "You're going to be pretty sore for a few days. The best thing is just to lie still and let your body mend itself."

"What's wrong with me?" The nurse could hear the fear in Rosa's voice.

"Nothing that won't heal up just fine," she reassured the injured girl. "You have three broken ribs, a punctured lung, and lots of scrapes and cuts, as well as a bump on the head. None of those injuries are fun, but you'll soon be as good as new. Now, are you ready to let your family— especially that brother of yours—in to see you before they break the door down?"

"Okay." Rosa smiled a little at the woman's exaggeration. She closed her eyes for a moment and listened to the voices in the hallway. When the door opened, her dad rushed in with Maria on his heels. Carlos hung back near the door.

Rosa could see tears in Dad's eyes when he leaned over the hospital bed and wordlessly stroked the hair off her forehead.

Maria circled around to the other side of the bed and pulled a chair close. "You look awful, but I'm sure glad you're in one piece! You should see your diorama—it's totally smashed! And Carlos's car will never be the same."

"Is Carlos really okay?" Rosa tried to look over by the door, but it hurt too much to turn her head.

"I'm fine." Carlos stood at the foot of the bed so she could see him. He had a couple of stitches on his chin and a long white bandage on one arm. "I'm sorry, Rosa." His voice broke and he paused and stared down at his hands, twisting them nervously. "Since it was all my fault, I wish I'd been the one hurt worse. I know I can't ever make this up to you, but I'll try." He took a deep breath. "Little sister, I promise I'll obey all the traffic laws from now on."

Rosa smiled up at her big brother, looking so worried and upset. "Maybe redoing my diorama would make it up to me!"

A big grin creased Carlos' face. "You got it, Rosa! You got it!"

2 Discussion Time

Check understanding of the story and development of personal values.

- Why was Rosa concerned about her brother's driving?
- On what school project were Kristin and Rosa working?
- Why hadn't Rosa told her father about Carlos not obeying all the traffic rules?
- How did Carlos react when Rosa reminded him that he hadn't really stopped at the stop sign?
- What happened to the little yellow car?
- How badly was Rosa hurt?
- How did Carlos feel about Rosa being hurt so badly?

A Preview

Write each word as your teacher says it.

Name _____

1. squid
2. Quebec
3. equator
4. chorus
5. banquet
6. Nebraska
7. Alaska
8. Kentucky
9. squall
10. earthquake
11. equal
12. chaos
13. backup
14. o'clock
15. quicksand
16. echoes
17. preschool
18. inquire
19. liquid
20. quality

Words with /k/ or /kw/

Lesson 21

Scripture
Psalm 19:9, 10

131

3 Preview
Test for knowledge of the correct spellings of these words.

Customize Your List
On a separate sheet of paper, additional words of your choice may be tested.

(Say) I will say each word once, use the word in a sentence, then say the word again. Write the words on the lines in your Worktext.

Correct Immediately!
(Say) Let's correct our Preview. I will spell each word out loud. If you spelled a word incorrectly, rewrite it correctly.

Progress Chart
Students may record scores. (Reproducible master provided in Appendix B.)

1.	squid	"Have any of you ever seen a live **squid**?" Mr. Canfield asked.
2.	Quebec	"A fisherman from **Quebec** caught this one last year."
3.	equator	Mr. Canfield pointed to the **equator** on the large map.
4.	chorus	The class practiced a **chorus** for morning assembly.
5.	banquet	They also made plans for the spring **banquet**.
6.	Nebraska	The speed limit is clearly marked on the **Nebraska** interstate.
7.	Alaska	**Alaska** also requires all drivers to wear seatbelts.
8.	Kentucky	The **Kentucky** Highway Patrol enforces the speed limits.
9.	squall	Storm clouds in the distance forecasted a coming **squall**.
10.	earthquake	Rosa suddenly felt like she was in the middle of an **earthquake**.
11.	equal	She had never felt any pain to **equal** this.
12.	chaos	To the untrained eye, the busyness in the ER can look like **chaos**.
13.	backup	The nurse switched the machine to the **backup** oxygen supply.
14.	o'clock	Visiting hours at the hospital began at 4 **o'clock**.
15.	quicksand	Carlos's legs felt weak, like he was in the middle of **quicksand**.
16.	echoes	He could still hear **echoes** of the squeal of his brakes.
17.	preschool	Some of the children in the **preschool** sent Rosa pictures.
18.	inquire	Mr. Canfield called Mr. Vasquez to **inquire** about Rosa.
19.	liquid	The **liquid** in the clear pack dripped slowly through the IV tube.
20.	quality	The **quality** of Rosa's handwriting will be poor till she fully recovers.

4 Word Shapes

Help students form a correct image of whole words.

Say

Look at each word and think about its shape. Now, write the word in the correct Word Shape Boxes. You may check off each word as you use it.

(In many words, the sound of **/k/** is spelled with **k**, and it is often spelled this way when it is at the beginning or middle of a word. The **/k/** sound can also be spelled with **c** when followed by **a**, **o**, or **u**. The spelling **ck** occurs in the middle or at the end of a word. The letter **q** is always followed by **u** and usually has the sound of **/kw/**.)

Say

In the Word Shape Boxes, color the letter or letters that spell the sound of **/k/** or **/kw/** in each word.

Take a minute to memorize...

Psalm 19:9,10

B Word Shapes

Name _____

Using the word bank below, write each word in the correct Word Shape Boxes. Next, in the Word Shape Boxes, fill in the boxes containing the letter or letters that spell the sound of /k/ or /kw/ in each word.

Words with /k/ or /kw/

Lesson 21

1. preschool
2. o'clock
3. squid
4. liquid
5. chorus
6. earthquake
7. quality
8. Quebec
9. equal
10. backup

11. squall
12. Kentucky
13. Alaska
14. Nebraska
15. echoes
16. chaos
17. equator
18. inquire
19. quicksand
20. banquet

Word Bank

Alaska	chorus	equator	Nebraska	Quebec
backup	earthquake	inquire	o'clock	quicksand
banquet	echoes	Kentucky	preschool	squall
chaos	equal	liquid	quality	squid

132

Answers may vary for duplicate word shapes.

Be Prepared For Fun

Check these supply lists for **Fun Ways to Spell** - presented **Day 2**. Purchase and/or gather these items ahead of time!

General
- Pencil
- 3 X 5 Cards cut in half (20 per child)
- Spelling List

Auditory
- Spelling List

Visual
- Pencil
- Notebook Paper
- Spelling List

Tactile
- Blackboard and Chalk
  -OR-
- White Board and Marker
- Spelling List

C Hide and Seek   Name _____

Play Hide and Seek with your words. Fill in a box on the bar graph (left to right) for each word you spell correctly.

LOOK   SAY   SPELL ALOUD   WRITE   SEEK   CHECK

D Other Word Forms

Using the words below, follow the instructions given by your teacher.

Alaskan	echoed	Kentuckian	qualities
banqueted	echoing	liquefy	Quebecker
banqueting	equaled	liquidation	squalled
chaotic	equaling	Nebraskan	squids
chorused	equators	preschooler	
chorusing	inquired	preschooling	
earthquakes	inquiring	qualitative	

E Fun Ways to Spell

Initial the box of each activity you finish.

1. [ ]
Spell your words, then play "Concentration."

2. s_e_l_n_
   w_r_s
   [ ]
Decode your spelling words.

3. Johnny has a puppy!
   [ ]
Spell your words in a sentence.

4. sp
   [ ]
Play the game "Spelling Backwards."

133

---

1 Hide and Seek

Reinforce spelling by using multiple styles of learning.

On a white board, Teacher writes each word — one at a time. **Have students:**

- **Look** at the word.
- **Say** the word out loud.
- **Spell** the word out loud.
- **Hide** (teacher erases word.)
- **Write** the word on paper.
- **Seek** (teacher rewrites word.)
- **Check** spelling. If incorrect, rewrite word correctly.

2 Other Word Forms

This activity is optional. Have students find and circle the Other Word Forms that are most nearly antonyms of the following:

**differed
orderly
reporting**

3 Fun Ways to Spell

Four activities are provided. Use one, two, three, or all of the activities. Have students initial the box for each activity they complete.

Options:

- assign activities to students according to their learning styles
- set up the activities in learning centers for the students to do throughout the day
- divide students into four groups and assign one activity per group
- do one activity per day

General

Spell your words; then play "Concentration"...
- Write each spelling word on a card. Mix your cards and a classmate's cards together. Arrange them face down in five rows of eight. Pick up two cards. If the cards match, play again. If the cards do not match, turn them back over. It is your classmate's turn. Continue taking turns until all the cards are matched. The player with the most cards wins!

Visual

To decode your spelling words...
- Look at the first word on your list.
- Write every other letter of the word on your paper, putting a blank where each missing letter belongs.
- Trade papers with a classmate and fill in the missing letters.
- Check your spelling.

Auditory

To spell your words in a sentence...
- Ask a classmate to read a spelling word to you from the list.
- Spell the word aloud and use it in a sentence.
- Ask your classmate to check your spelling.
- Each correctly spelled word that is used properly in a sentence counts as one point.
- Switch and continue taking turns.

Tactile

To play the game "Spelling Backwards"...
- Ask a classmate to stand behind you and draw the letters to spell a word from your list on your back.
- Write the spelling word on the board as your classmate traces the letters on your back.
- Ask your classmate to check your spelling.
- Trade places and take turns until you have each spelled all the words.

207

Working with Words

Familiarize students with word meaning and usage.

Rhyming Clues

Write the words **girlfriend**, **surrender**, **pretend**, and **endurance** on the board. Have a volunteer underline the two words that rhyme (**girlfriend**, **pretend**). Tell students that, for this exercise, words need to rhyme on at least the last syllable to be considered rhyming words. Explain that students will be matching some of their spelling words to a rhyming word.

Say Write the spelling word that rhymes with each word below.

The K's and KW's Have It

Say Each spelling word in this lesson has the **/k/** or **/kw/** sound. Answer each question with a word from the word bank. You may use a dictionary to help you. Write the word in the blank.

Take a minute to memorize...

Psalm 19:9,10

208

F **Working with Words**   Name _____

Similar Sounds

Write the spelling word that rhymes with the last syllable of each word below.

1. cheesecake	earthquake	7. wrap-up	backup
2. moonlit	banquet	8. grid	squid
3. wall	squall	9. forbid	liquid
4. watchband	quicksand	10. emboss	chaos
5. unlucky	Kentucky	11. paycheck	Quebec
6. padlock	o'clock	12. frivolity	quality
		13. perspire	inquire
		14. translator	equator
		15. sequel	equal
		16. porous	chorus
		17. compose	echoes
		18. whirlpool	preschool

The K's and KW's Have It

Answer each question with a /k/ or /kw/ word from the word bank. Write the word in the blank.

1. What /kw/ word means degree of excellence? _____ quality
2. What /k/ word is a state in the Great Plains? _____ Nebraska
3. What /kw/ word means to ask about? _____ inquire
4. What /k/ word relates to a child's life from infancy to the age of five or six? _____ preschool
5. What /k/ word means one that serves as a substitute or alternative? _____ backup
6. What /kw/ word is a province of eastern Canada? _____ Quebec
7. What /kw/ word is a long-bodied sea mollusk with eight arms? _____ squid
8. What /kw/ word means a deep mass of loose sand mixed with water? _____ quicksand
9. What /k/ word means complete disorder, confusion, and disarray? _____ chaos
10. What /k/ word was explored by Daniel Boone? _____ Kentucky

134

Word Bank				
Alaska	chorus	equator	Nebraska	Quebec
backup	earthquake	inquire	o'clock	quicksand
banquet	echoes	Kentucky	preschool	squall
chaos	equal	liquid	quality	squid

G Dictation

Name _____

Write **each sentence as your teacher dictates.** Use **correct punctuation.**

1. The girls did good quality work on their farm scene.

2. Carlos said he would pick up his sister at eight o'clock.

3. After the crash, everything was in chaos.

H Proofreading

If a word is misspelled, fill in the oval by that word. If all the words are spelled correctly, fill in the oval by **no mistake.**

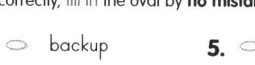

1.
○ backup
○ average
● kaoss
○ no mistake

2.
○ rigid
● korus
○ echoes
○ no mistake

3.
○ Kentucky
● oclock
○ preschool
○ no mistake

4.
○ legend
○ heritage
○ Alaska
● no mistake

5.
○ jogging
○ junior
○ Nebraska
● no mistake

6.
○ jury
● erthquake
○ pledge
○ no mistake

7.
○ equal
○ jaguar
● equater
○ no mistake

8.
○ refuge
○ inquire
○ liquid
● no mistake

9.
● banquit
○ hinges
○ quality
○ no mistake

10.
● Kwebec
○ quicksand
○ dungeon
○ no mistake

11.
○ jacket
● squal
○ plunge
○ no mistake

12.
○ cringe
○ gadget
○ squid
● no mistake

135

Dictation

Reinforce correct spelling by using current and previous words in context.

Say

Listen as I read each sentence and then write it in your Worktext. Remember to use correct capitalization and punctuation. (Slowly read each sentence twice. Sentences are found in the Student Worktext to the left.)

Proofreading

Familiarize students with standardized test format and reinforce recognition of misspelled words.

Say

Look at each set of words. If a word is misspelled, fill in the oval by that word. If all the words are spelled correctly, fill in the oval by **no mistake.**

3 Hide and Seek

Reinforce correct spelling of current spelling words. Repeat this activity from Day 2.

4 Vocabulary Extension

Have your students complete this activity to strengthen spelling ability and expand vocabulary. The reproducible master is provided in Appendix A as shown on the inset page to the right.

1 Posttest

Visit the **A Reason For** website to download free, printable Posttest pages.

Say

I will say the word once, use it in a sentence, then say it again. Write your words on a separate sheet of paper.

Progress Chart
Students may record scores. (Appendix B)

Personal Dictionary
Students may add any words they have misspelled to their personal dictionaries. (Appendix B)

Hide and Seek

Play Hide and Seek with your words. Fill in a bar graph (left to right) for each word you spell correctly.

LOOK   SAY   HIDE   WRITE   SEEK   CHECK

Vocabulary Extension
Multiple Choice
Fill in the oval by the word(s) with the same or nearly the same meaning as the word in bold type.

Lesson 21

1. comedian
○ process of catching fire and burning
○ punctuation used to split a sentence
○ booklet with cartoon stories
● entertainer who tells funny stories

2. custodian
● person who cleans a large building
○ dessert made of milk, eggs, and sugar
○ something you do regularly
○ arrested by the police

3. reflection
○ automatic action such as blinking
● an image on a shiny surface
○ shelter from danger or trouble
○ to happen again

4. confidence
○ organize something and carry it out
○ to ask someone's advice
● strong belief in your own abilities
○ say that something is definitely true

5. circumference
● distance around something
○ cautious or careful
○ conditions of an event
○ move in a circle or pattern

6. conference
○ a famous Chinese philosopher
○ mistake one thing for another
○ doing what the law requires
● meeting for discussing ideas

7. creature
● living thing
○ something that has been made
○ using your imagination
○ model of the baby Jesus

8. culture
○ guilty of doing wrong
○ to develop by studying
● way of life, ideas, customs, traditions
○ used to make sofas more comfortable

9. sculpture
○ confused and disorderly fight
● figure made of wood, metal, or stone
○ to examine something closely
○ strong feelings about right and wrong

10. accuracy
○ performs gymnastic acts
○ skin condition from clogged pores
○ to admit something
● precision, exactness

342

---

1. inquire — "Could I **inquire** about your speed?" Rosa asked worriedly.
2. preschool — "I'm not in **preschool**, you know!" Carlos snapped back.
3. quality — He knew the **quality** of his safety habits was questionable.
4. chaos — There was instant **chaos** as Carlos slammed on his brakes.
5. earthquake — Everything around them blurred as if they were in an **earthquake.**
6. echoes — The **echoes** of the accident would haunt Carlos for a long time.
7. Kentucky — **Kentucky** is proud of its clean, safe highways and interstates.
8. backup — The **backup** surgeon came quickly to the hospital.
9. Alaska — The speed limit laws are no less strict in **Alaska.**
10. Nebraska — The **Nebraska** Highway Patrol enforces safe driving.
11. o'clock — Visiting hours at the hospital end at 7 **o'clock** sharp.
12. liquid — Rosa awoke to see a nurse replacing the IV **liquid** pack.
13. equal — She could not remember feeling any pain **equal** to this!
14. quicksand — Even when lying down, Rosa felt like there was **quicksand** under her feet.
15. squall — Right before the accident, Rosa remembered seeing signs of a **squall** to the north.
16. equator — Kristin listed the continents north of the **equator.**
17. Quebec — She loaned Rosa her notes from social studies about the province of **Quebec.**
18. squid — She sketched a **squid** in her science notes so Rosa could understand the lesson better.
19. banquet — "I hope Rosa will be able to come to the Spring **banquet**," Kristin said.
20. chorus — The class recorded more than one funny **chorus** to send to Rosa.

210

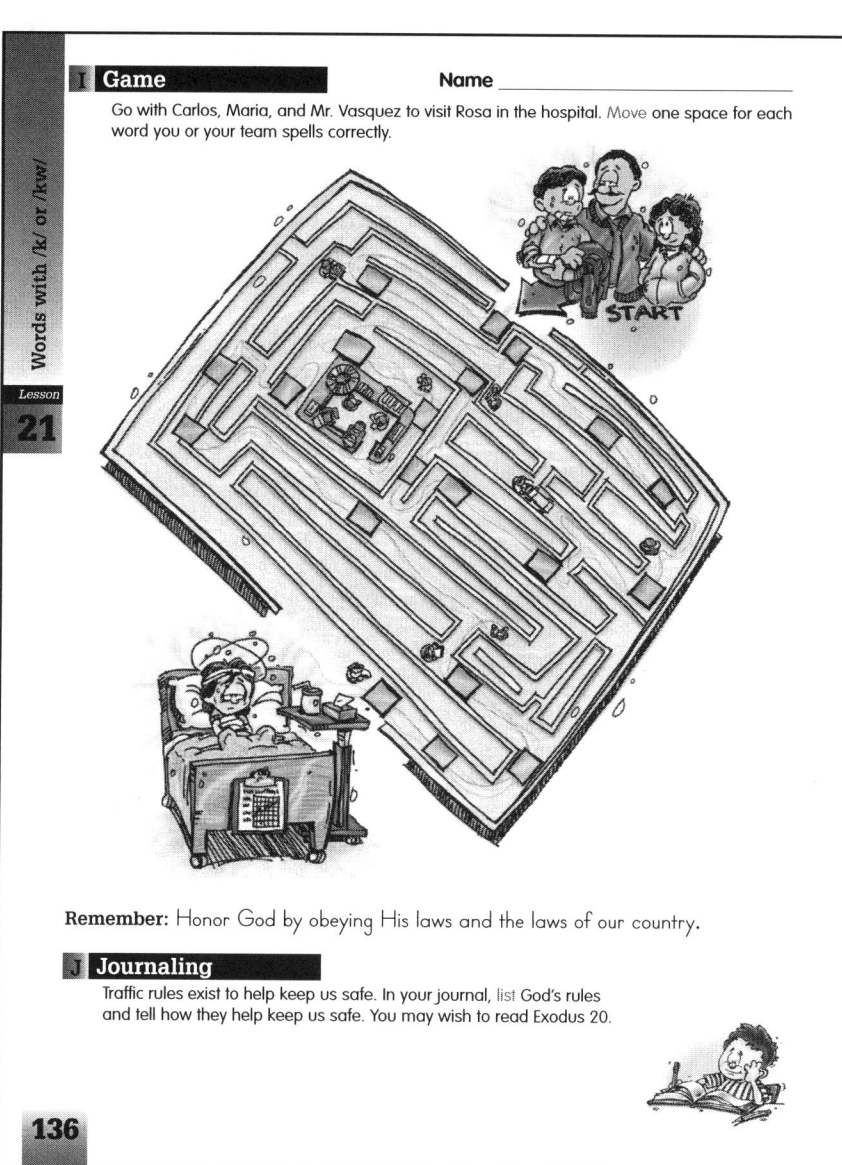

Go with Carlos, Maria, and Mr. Vasquez to visit Rosa in the hospital. Move one space for each word you or your team spells correctly.

START

Remember: Honor God by obeying His laws and the laws of our country.

J Journaling

Traffic rules exist to help keep us safe. In your journal, list God's rules and tell how they help keep us safe. You may wish to read Exodus 20.

Words with /k/ or /kw/

Lesson 21

2 Game

Reinforce spelling skills and provide motivation and interest.

Materials

- game page (from student text)
- game pieces (1 per child)
- game word list

Game Word List

1. **backup**
2. **chaos**
3. **chorus**
4. **echoes**
5. **Kentucky**
6. **o'clock**
7. **preschool**
8. **Alaska**
9. **Nebraska**
10. **banquet**
11. **earthquake**
12. **equal**
13. **equator**
14. **inquire**
15. **liquid**
16. **quality**
17. **Quebec**
18. **quicksand**
19. **squall**
20. **squid**

Lesson 21 | Day 5

How to Play:

- Divide the class into two teams.
- Have each student place his/her game piece on Start.
- Have a student from team A go to the board.
- Say the spelling word.
- Have the student write the word on the board.
- If correct, instruct each member of team A to move his/her game piece forward one space.
- Alternate between teams A and B.
- The team to reach Rosa first is the winner.
- **Small Group Option**: Students may play this game without teacher direction in small groups of two or more.

3 Journaling

Provide a meaningful reason for correct spelling through personal writing.

Review the story using discussion leads provided on the following page. Encourage students to apply the Scriptural value in their journaling.

Journaling (continued)

 Say

- Why did Rosa need a ride to Kristin's house? (The two girls were supposed to work together on a school project, a diorama of a horse barn and pasture.)

- Why was Carlos so proud of his car? (He'd worked very hard to earn the money to buy it and spent a lot of time and effort fixing it up.)

- What did Kristin advise Rosa to do about her brother's poor driving habits? (To tell her dad.)

- What caused the wreck? (Carlos got angry when Rosa said something about him not stopping at the stop sign and he sped up too fast to make the turn.)

- Where did Rosa wake up? (In the hospital.)

- What injuries did Rosa and Carlos have? (Rosa had three broken ribs, a punctured lung, and lots of scrapes and cuts along with a bump on the head. Carlos had a cut on his chin and a gash on one arm.)

- Do you think Carlos learned something from the accident? Why or why not? (Yes. He realized he'd caused the wreck by going too fast and was very sorry. He wished he'd been the one hurt worse instead of Rosa. He promised to obey traffic rules in the future.)

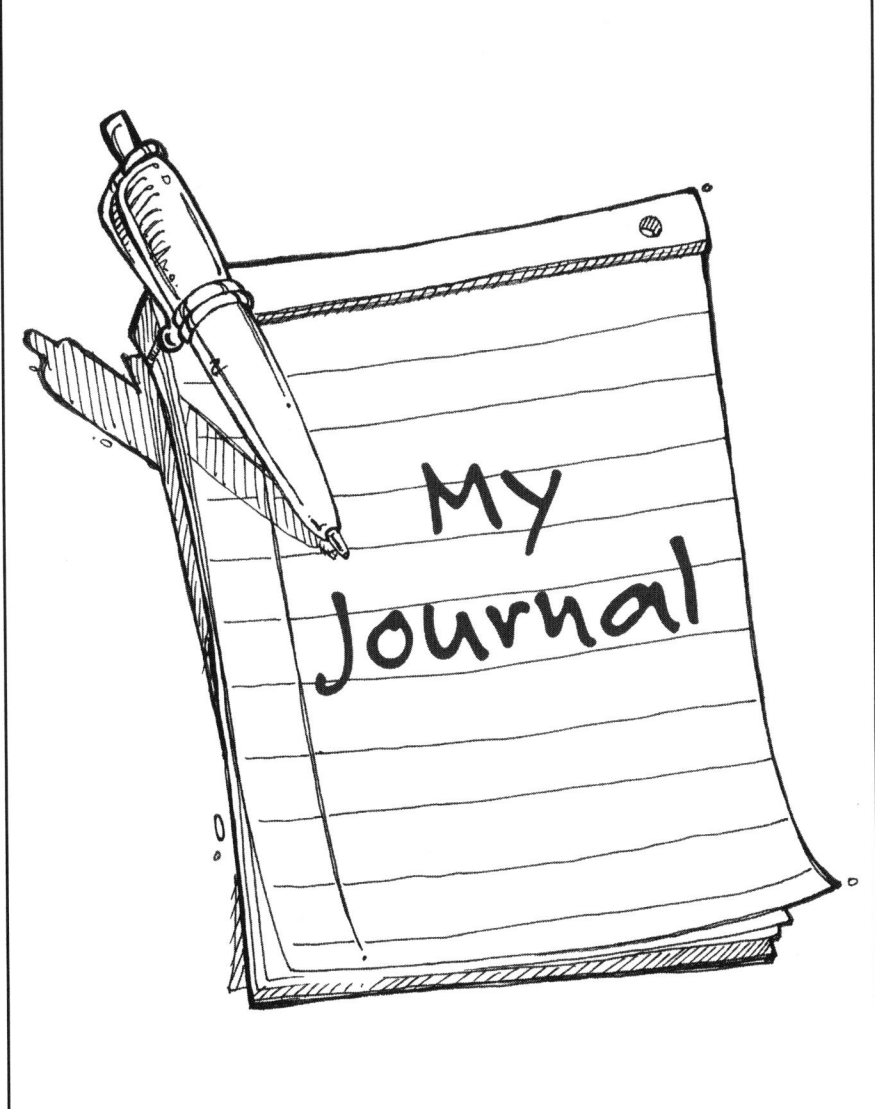

"SUPERCALIFRAGILISTICEXPIALIDO-CIOUS" (from the Mary Poppins movie) is not the longest word in English, nor is "floccinaucinihilipilification" with 28 letters. It is enough to give you hippopotomonstrosesquipedaliophobia or a "fear of long words."

Word-Wow!

Way to Go!

Rachel and her family contemplate moving.

"Come on, Rach. Father wants all of us in the living room. It's family council time."

Rachel Jacobson groaned, "I wonder what we need to decide now?"

"Who knows? I just hope democracy works fast tonight. I have a math test I need to study for." Rebecca led the way downstairs.

Helen Jacobson was already in the living room designing a huge zoo with brightly colored blocks. The 18-month-old twins were "helping" her. Leah held up a white polar bear, "He needs cold."

"That's right, Leah. Polar bears live where it's cold. Benj, help Mommy find some white blocks to build an icy home for this ferocious bear." Helen smiled as she watched the toddlers search through the pile for white blocks.

Vanessa came into the living room and joined the construction crew on the floor. "I think this seal and her pup need a place to swim." The seventh grader nudged a black seal with her toe and started collecting blue blocks.

"Me hep." Benjamin handed his sister a handful of blocks.

"Just the blue ones, Benj," eight-year-old Natalie instructed as she peered down from her perch on the edge of the couch.

"Now that we're all here...." David Jacobson looked up and smiled at Rachel and Rebecca as they walked into the room. "Your mother and I have something we'd like to discuss with you."

Vanessa stopped building. Rachel and Rebecca exchanged a quick glance, then gave David Jacobson their undivided attention.

"I got a call yesterday from a fellow I went to law school with, an old friend named Tyler. He lives in a remote area out west. He's started a program at Shadow Creek Ranch for troubled kids. The program's been up and running for a few years, and it's doing quite well. To get right to the point, he needs help running the ranch. The program is growing, and they'd like to be able to accommodate more kids—which means more help. And that's where we come in." Mr. Jacobson paused and made eye contact with each of his girls. Even the twins stopped building and watched him intently.

Rachel was the first to find her voice, "They want us to—like move out there? We just moved here from Dallas."

"It's been over three years, Rach," Rebecca corrected.

"What would you do?...Where out west?...When would we have to leave?...Can we finish school?...Do we sell our house first?...Would we home school?...Is there electricity?...What about running water?" The girls paused in their questioning when Father raised his hand.

"Hold on. One at a time. Shadow Creek Ranch is in Montana. They would like us in the spring or early summer. You would have to be homeschooled because school buses can't always make it out to the ranch through all the snow. There is electricity, running water and indoor plumbing. Because of her teaching background, your mom would help with homeschooling all the staff children. Since I grew up on a ranch, I'd be involved with general upkeep of the place and also teach the guests who come basic ranching skills." Father leaned back in his chair and folded his arms across his broad chest.

"It sounds like you've already made up your mind." Vanessa frowned.

"On the contrary, I'm very happy here—just as all of you seem to be. I don't miss Dallas at all and I'm not anxious to leave. But I have been praying recently for God to show me how I can effectively share His love. I've also asked to be open to His will—and willing to do whatever that is. Frankly, I'm not sure what He has in mind here. I don't know if this is God's invitation or not. I'd simply like each of you to pray and ask the Lord to lead our family." Father uncrossed his arms and leaned back in his chair.

The room was absolutely quiet. Even the twins did not resume playing with the blocks.

"Let's pray," Mrs. Jacobson suggested.

Mr. Jacobson smiled at his wife and motioned with his arms for his family to gather in a prayer circle. He picked up Benjamin, and the little boy snuggled against his father's neck and gave him a damp kiss on the cheek. "Lord, help us as we make this decision. Show us the path where we should go. Lead us. Teach us. Enable us to understand Your will for our lives. Give us the courage to follow no matter where You lead. In your name, Amen."

Rachel followed her older sister back up to the bedroom they shared. Rebecca sat down at her desk and took out her math book, but she had a hard time concentrating. "How do you figure out God's will, Rach? How do you know what God wants?"

Rachel looked up from the book she'd been staring at. "I don't remember a lot about our mommy. I was only four when she died. But I do remember her pulling me into her lap on one of her good days sometime in that last year she was alive. It's like a framed picture in my mind. She had on a green baseball cap because her hair had all fallen out from the chemo. She cupped my face between her hands and looked me right in the eye. She said, 'Rach, you can always talk to Jesus about any problem, any time. He's always willing to help you.' You know, I don't even remember why she

213

Story (continued)

thought I needed to talk to Jesus—just that I could and should. I guess that's the best way to figure it out. What I don't get is—how does He talk to us?"

Rebecca leaned back in her chair. "The Bible?...Parents, teachers, Christian friends?...Nature?..." She looked her sister in the eye and said slowly, "Those answers we've heard in Bible class don't seem very realistic tonight. I guess I don't know how He'll speak to us."

"The Bible isn't going to say, 'The Jacobsons should move to Shadow Creek Ranch next spring!' And I'm sure my friend Laney Ausherman won't tell me to go. Father just said he wasn't sure, and how in the world is Mr. Canfield supposed to know if we should leave?" Rachel picked up her Bible, closed her eyes, and then opened it in her lap. With her eyes still closed, she pointed to a verse on the left page, then opened her eyes. "'Be still and know that I am God,'" she read. "There's our answer. 'Be still,' it says. We can't go anywhere if we're still."

Rebecca laughed at her sister's suggestion. "Yeah, but what about the text that says, 'Do unto others as you would have them do unto you'? If you were a kid in trouble, wouldn't you want someone to take you out to a ranch and teach you about God's love?"

Rachel stood up and headed out the door. "That's not the one that I read." She smiled, "My text says, 'Be still.'"

Rebecca looked up at her younger sister. "I think what Mommy said so long ago makes sense. Let's just pray. Maybe He'll surprise us with an answer!"

The next morning when Rachel went out to the garage to feed the cat, she met Vanessa coming in the garage door carrying her new navy wool sweater. It was covered with frost. "Vanessa, what are you doing with that? Did you leave it outside?"

The younger girl nodded. "I was putting out a fleece, like Gideon. I didn't have a sheepskin, but this sweater is wool." She smiled sheepishly, "I asked God to make the sweater dry if we should go, and have the ground wet, just like Gideon in the Bible. I forgot about it being winter. That complicates things. The ground is frozen and the sweater is dry now. I guess when this frost melts, it'll be wet then; but I don't know if that counts. Maybe I should pray for the sweater to be wet. That would be hard to do in the middle of winter. Maybe the ground should be wet and the sweater dry." Vanessa headed on into the house muttering to herself.

Rachel stared at Vanessa's back, then finished giving the yellow cat its breakfast. She paused for a moment and prayed, "Lord, I think our family's a little mixed up right now. Please hurry up and point us in the right direction, Amen."

(to be continued. . .)

2 Discussion Time

Check understanding of the story and development of personal values.

- How do you figure out what God wants you to do?
- What were the Jacobson family's two choices?
- How do you feel about Rachel's way of finding God's will in the Bible?
- How did Vanessa try to discover what God wanted them to do?
- What did Rachel's father suggest the children do while they "contemplate this invitation?"
- What would you do?
- Do you think the Jacobsons will move? (You may want to take a vote. Remind your students how they voted before you find out the answer in lesson 25.)

A Preview

Write each word as your teacher says it.

Name _____

1. plaza
2. bruise
3. enclose
4. laser
5. surprise
6. Missouri
7. raise
8. despise
9. Amazon
10. graze
11. citizen
12. blizzard
13. Kansas
14. blaze
15. stanza
16. closet
17. desire
18. freezing
19. design
20. horizon

Words with /z/

Lesson
22

Scripture
Psalm 25:4, 5

137

3 Preview
Test for knowledge of the correct spellings of these words.

Customize Your List
On a separate sheet of paper, additional words of your choice may be tested.

(Say) I will say each word once, use the word in a sentence, then say the word again. Write the words on the lines in your Worktext.

Correct Immediately!
(Say) Let's correct our Preview. I will spell each word out loud. If you spelled a word incorrectly, rewrite it correctly.

Progress Chart
Students may record scores. (Reproducible master provided in Appendix B.)

1.	plaza	Dad drove home from his office on the downtown **plaza**.
2.	bruise	Benjamin had a **bruise** on his forehead from a recent tumble.
3.	enclose	His mom helped him build a block fence to **enclose** his zoo animals.
4.	laser	"I need to finish reading an article about **laser** surgery," Vanessa told her dad.
5.	surprise	The announcement came as a **surprise** to the entire family.
6.	Missouri	"Did you say **Missouri** or Montana, Dad?" asked Rebecca.
7.	raise	"I knew this announcement would **raise** a lot of questions," chuckled Dad.
8.	despise	Rachel felt sure she would **despise** living out west.
9.	Amazon	"We might as well move to the **Amazon**," she muttered.
10.	graze	"I don't want to live where cattle **graze** in your front yard," she continued.
11.	citizen	"Will I still be considered an American **citizen**?" she asked sarcastically.
12.	blizzard	"Don't they have a **blizzard** or two every winter?" she asked.
13.	Kansas	Rachel thought Montana might look like **Kansas**.
14.	blaze	"I wish God would just **blaze** the answer across the sky!" said Rachel.
15.	stanza	A **stanza** of an old hymn ran through Vanessa's mind.
16.	closet	Vanessa pulled her navy blue sweater from her **closet**.
17.	desire	She had a real **desire** to know God's will for their family.
18.	freezing	She laid her sweater on the **freezing** ground.
19.	design	Rachel doodled a **design** on her prayer journal.
20.	horizon	There was too much potential change on the **horizon** for her liking.

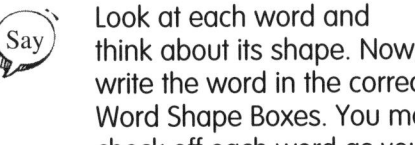

Word Shapes

Help students form a correct image of whole words.

(Say) Look at each word and think about its shape. Now, write the word in the correct Word Shape Boxes. You may check off each word as you use it.

(The sound of **/z/** can be spelled with **s**, **z**, or **zz**. The **/z/** sound can also be spelled **ss** in the middle of a word.)

(Say) In the Word Shape Boxes, color the letter or letters that spell the sound of **/z/** in each word.

Take a minute to memorize...

Psalm 25:4,5

B Word Shapes

Name _____

Using the word bank below, write each word in the correct Word Shape Boxes. Next, in the Word Shape Boxes, fill in the boxes containing the letter or letters that spell the sound of /z/ in each word.

Words with /z/

Lesson **22**

1. laser
2. blaze
3. raise
4. plaza
5. design
6. stanza
7. graze
8. Amazon
9. Missouri
10. Kansas

11. despise
12. horizon
13. enclose
14. freezing
15. blizzard
16. citizen
17. bruise
18. desire
19. surprise
20. closet

Word Bank

Amazon	citizen	despise	horizon	plaza
blaze	closet	enclose	Kansas	raise
blizzard	design	freezing	laser	stanza
bruise	desire	graze	Missouri	surprise

138

Answers may vary for duplicate word shapes.

Be Prepared For Fun

Check these supply lists for **Fun Ways to Spell** - presented **Day 2**. Purchase and/or gather these items ahead of time!

General
• Pencil
• Notebook Paper
• Spelling List

Auditory
• Pencil
• 3 X 5 Cards Cut in half lengthwise (20 per child)
• Spelling List

Visual
• Colored Pencils
• Graph Paper (2 sheets per child)
• Spelling List

Tactile
• Clay
• Spelling List

C Hide and Seek　　Name _____

Play Hide and Seek with your words. Fill in a box on the bar graph (left to right) for each word you spell correctly.

LOOK　SAY　SPELL ALOUD　WRITE　SEEK　CHECK

D Other Word Forms

Using the words below, follow the instructions given by your teacher.

Amazonia	citizenship	despising	Kansan
Amazonian	closeted	enclosing	Missourian
blazed	closeting	enclosure	raised
blazing	designed	freezes	raising
blizzards	designing	frozen	stanzas
bruised	desired	grazes	surprised
bruises	desirous	grazing	surprising
citizens	despises	horizons	

E Fun Ways to Spell

Initial the box of each activity you finish.

1. ☐ Classify your words according to syllables.

2. ☐ Spell your words on graph paper.

3. got a "fish"? NOPE! ☐ Spell your words and play "Match-It."

4. clay ☐ Spell your words with clay.

139

Hide and Seek

1 Reinforce spelling by using multiple styles of learning.

On a white board, Teacher writes each word — one at a time. **Have students:**

- **Look** at the word.
- **Say** the word out loud.
- **Spell** the word out loud.
- **Hide** (teacher erases word.)
- **Write** the word on paper.
- **Seek** (teacher rewrites word.)
- **Check** spelling. If incorrect, rewrite word correctly.

Other Word Forms

2 This activity is optional. Have students write original sentences using these Other Word Forms:

blazing
citizens
enclosure
blizzards

Fun Ways to Spell

3 Four activities are provided. Use one, two, three, or all of the activities. Have students initial the box for each activity they complete.

Options:

- assign activities to students according to their learning styles
- set up the activities in learning centers for the students to do throughout the day
- divide students into four groups and assign one activity per group
- do one activity per day

General

To classify your words according to syllables...
- Write three headings on your paper: One-syllable, Two-syllable, and Three-syllable.
- Write the first word on your list under the proper heading.
- Draw a line through the word to divide it into syllables.
- Do this with each word.

Visual

To spell your words on graph paper...
- Look at the first word on your list.
- Shade in squares to form the letters of each word.
- Check your spelling.
- Do this with each word.

Auditory

To spell your words and play "Match-It"...
- Write each word on a card. Mix your word-cards and a classmate's together. Deal six cards to each player; the rest face down between you. Ask your classmate for a word-card. If the word-card matches, take it and play again. If not, draw from the stack, and it is your classmate's turn. Take turns until all cards are matched.

Tactile

To spell your words with clay...
- Roll pieces of clay into ropes.
- Use the ropes to make the letters of each word.
- Put them in the right order to spell each word.
- Check your spelling.

Working with Words

Familiarize students with word meaning and usage.

Scrambled Words

Write the letters **abneqtu** on the board. Have a student unscramble the letters to make the word **banquet**.

Unscramble each spelling word. Write the word correctly on the line. Remember to use capital letters where they are needed.

Word Clues

Use your word bank to help you match the spelling words to the clues. Some of the clues are synonyms, words that have the same meaning as the spelling word. You may use a dictionary or thesaurus to help you.

Take a minute to memorize...

Psalm 25:4,5

F **Working with Words**

Name _____

Scrambled Words

Unscramble each word. Write the unscrambled word on the line. Use capital letters where they are needed.

#	scramble	answer	#	scramble	answer
1.	aeirs	raise	13.	aanstz	stanza
2.	deeirs	desire	14.	iimorssu	Missouri
3.	eefignrz	freezing	15.	ceiintz	citizen
4.	abdilrzz	blizzard	16.	deeipss	despise
5.	aalpz	plaza	17.	eiprrssu	surprise
6.	aaknss	Kansas	18.	aelrs	laser
7.	abelz	blaze	19.	celost	closet
8.	beirsu	bruise	20.	aegrz	graze
9.	degins	design			
10.	ceelnos	enclose			
11.	hinoorz	horizon			
12.	aamnoz	Amazon			

Word Clues

Match the spelling words to the clues. You may use a dictionary or thesaurus to help you.

1. inhabitant of a city — citizen
2. public square — plaza
3. wardrobe, locker — closet
4. 2nd longest river in the world — Amazon
5. arrangement, plan — design
6. verse, refrain — stanza
7. long for, crave — desire
8. central state whose capitol is Topeka — Kansas
9. hate, scorn — despise
10. flame, burn — blaze
11. central state whose capitol is Jefferson City — Missouri
12. astonishment, shock — surprise
13. brush against — graze
14. surround, encircle — enclose
15. light beam — laser
16. frigid, icy — freezing
17. elevate, lift — raise

Word Bank

Amazon	citizen	despise	horizon	plaza
blaze	closet	enclose	Kansas	raise
blizzard	design	freezing	laser	stanza
bruise	desire	graze	Missouri	surprise

Name _____

Write **each sentence as your teacher dictates.** Use **correct punctuation.**

1. After breakfast, the whole family helped to design Antarctica.

2. Some of Dad's comments about the ranch surprised the family.

3. Vanessa had a desire to know God's will, but was not sure how to find it.

H Proofreading

If a word is misspelled, fill in the oval by that word. If all the words are spelled correctly, fill in the oval by **no mistake.**

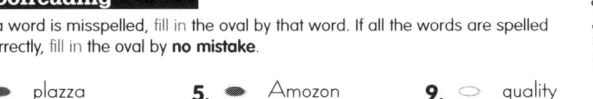

1. ● plazza
   ○ equator
   ○ earthquake
   ○ no mistake

2. ○ stanza
   ● Misouri
   ○ backup
   ○ no mistake

3. ○ chaos
   ○ blaze
   ○ graze
   ● no mistake

4. ● lazer
   ○ o'clock
   ○ squall
   ○ no mistake

5. ● Amozon
   ○ raise
   ○ echoes
   ○ no mistake

6. ○ citizen
   ○ Alaska
   ● clozit
   ○ no mistake

7. ● dezine
   ○ desire
   ○ banquet
   ○ no mistake

8. ● Kansus
   ○ liquid
   ○ despise
   ○ no mistake

9. ○ quality
   ● surprize
   ○ Nebraska
   ○ no mistake

10. ○ enclose
    ○ Quebec
    ● bruse
    ○ no mistake

11. ○ freezing
    ○ horizon
    ○ equal
    ● no mistake

12. ○ inquire
    ● blizard
    ○ chorus
    ○ no mistake

141

Reinforce correct spelling by using current and previous words in context.

 Say

Listen as I read each sentence and then write it in your Worktext. Remember to use correct capitalization and punctuation. (Slowly read each sentence twice. Sentences are found in the Student Worktext to the left.)

Day 4

Familiarize students with standardized test format and reinforce recognition of misspelled words.

Say

Look at each set of words. If a word is misspelled, fill in the oval by that word. If all the words are spelled correctly, fill in the oval by **no mistake.**

Lesson **22**

3 Hide and Seek

Reinforce correct spelling of current spelling words. Repeat this activity from Day 2.

4 Vocabulary Extension

Have your students complete this activity to strengthen spelling ability and expand vocabulary. The reproducible master is provided in Appendix A as shown on the inset page to the right.

1 Posttest

Visit the **A Reason For** website to download free, printable Posttest pages.

I will say the word once, use it in a sentence, then say it again. Write your words on a separate sheet of paper.

Progress Chart

Students may record scores. (Appendix B)

Personal Dictionary

Students may add any words they have misspelled to their personal dictionaries. (Appendix B)

Hide and Seek

Play Hide and Seek with your words. Fill in a bar graph (left to right) for each word you spell correctly.

LOOK, SAY, HIDE, WRITE, SEEK, CHECK.

Vocabulary Extension

Cause and Effect

Write a word from the word bank to complete each sentence.

1. If you are using a piece of clear, triangular glass that breaks light up into colors, you are looking through a ___prism___.
2. If you want to measure something very precisely, you want it to be ___exact___.
3. If you are reading the book of the Bible that comes before Daniel, you are reading the book of ___Ezekiel___.
4. If you ___exaggerate___, you try to make something seem bigger, better, or more important than it really is.
5. If you are reading a booklet that has news, articles, photographs, and advertisements, you are reading a ___magazine___.
6. If you are a detective, you will ___examine___ the evidence carefully.
7. If a company makes, sells or provides a service, it is known as a ___business___.
8. If you have painted some pictures that you want to show to the public, you would set up an ___exhibit___.
9. If were reading Paul's letter to the people who lived in Ephesus, you would be reading the Bible book of ___Ephesians___.
10. If you were living in a war zone and heard the sounds of guns and bombings, you would be hearing ___explosion___s.
11. If you are about to dive into a lake that you know is cold, you may pause or ___hesitate___ before jumping in.
12. If you live in a neighborhood, you are considered a ___resident___.

Word Bank

business	exaggerate	explosion	magazine
Ephesians	examine	Ezekiel	prism
exact	exhibit	hesitate	resident

343

1.	laser	"I just need to finish that article on **laser** surgery," said Vanessa.
2.	bruise	She kissed a little **bruise** on her baby brother's head.
3.	enclose	She helped Benjamin and Leah **enclose** their zoo with a block fence.
4.	surprise	The whole family listened in **surprise** to their dad's announcement.
5.	plaza	"Don't you like your new office on the **plaza** downtown, Dad?" queried Rebecca.
6.	desire	"Yes, but I **desire** to go where the Lord wants me," he replied.
7.	raise	"I know this will **raise** a lot of questions in your minds," Dad continued.
8.	blaze	"God may not **blaze** the answer across the sky, but He will show us somehow!" Dad said.
9.	Amazon	"Montana! It might as well be the **Amazon**!" cried Rebecca.
10.	Kansas	"I'd rather move to a shanty in the middle of **Kansas**," she groaned.
11.	Missouri	"Did I misunderstand? Did you really say **Missouri**?" she asked.
12.	graze	"Yuk! I don't want cows to **graze** in my front yard!" muttered Rachel.
13.	citizen	"Can I still be an American **citizen**?" she said grouchily.
14.	blizzard	"I can do without a **blizzard** every winter!" continued Rachel.
15.	closet	Vanessa went quietly to her **closet** to get her wool sweater.
16.	freezing	She tiptoed outside and laid it on the **freezing** ground.
17.	stanza	She hummed a **stanza** of a hymn that encouraged her to trust God.
18.	design	She was excited about the **design** God had in mind for their future.
19.	despise	Rachel, on the other hand, knew she would **despise** having to move.
20.	horizon	She was not keen on the idea of so much change on the **horizon**.

I Game

Name _____

Record points for each word you or your team spells correctly. Earn bonus points for each row in which all five words are spelled correctly.

Words with /z/

Lesson 22

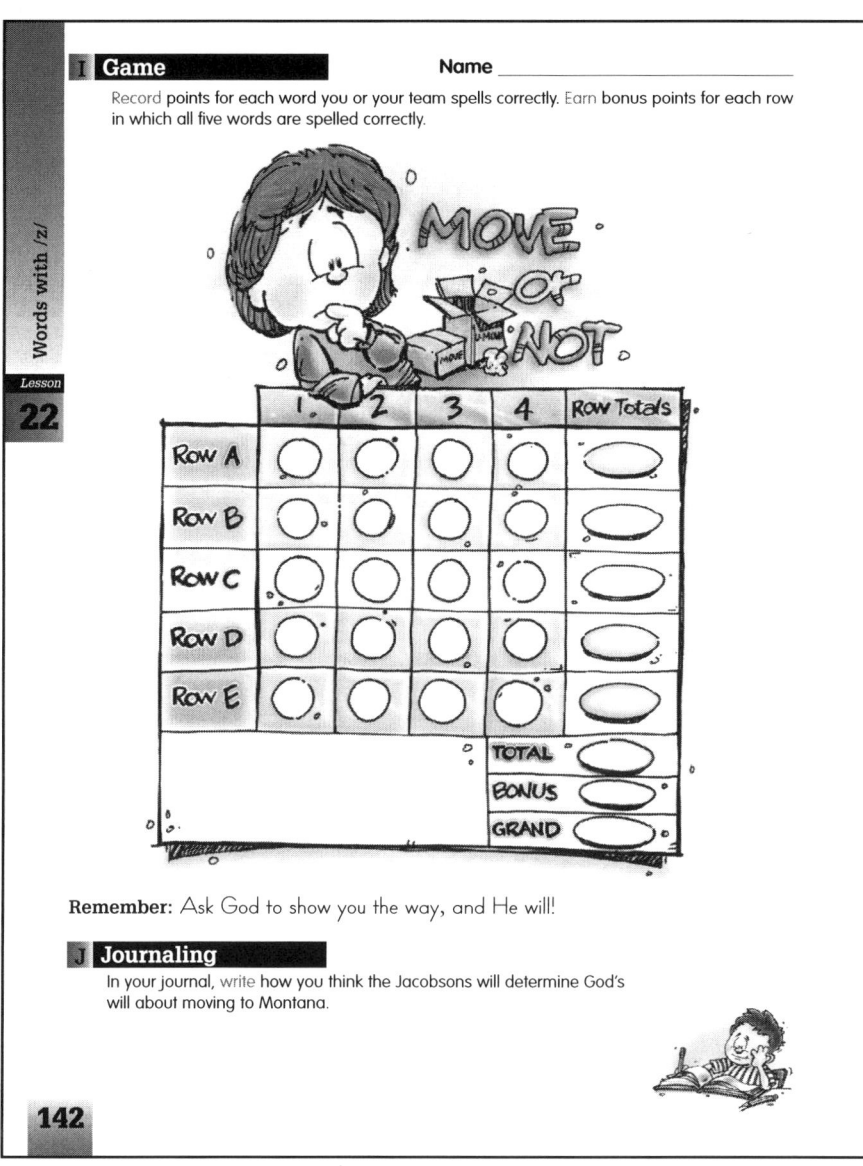

Remember: Ask God to show you the way, and He will!

J Journaling

In your journal, write how you think the Jacobsons will determine God's will about moving to Montana.

142

How to Play:

- Divide the class into two teams.
- Have a student from team A choose a square on the grid by indicating the row letter and number.
- Say the word that matches that row letter and number from the team's word list.
- Have the student write the word on the board.
- If correct, have each member of that team record the awarded points (in parentheses by the word) in the circle in that box. If the word is misspelled, have him/her put an **X** in that circle. That square may not be chosen again.
- Repeat this process with the second team.
- When all the words have been spelled by both teams, have each team tally its score. Award a bonus of 5 points for each row in which all four words were spelled correctly.
- Have the teams record their grand totals. The team with the highest score is the winner.

2 Game

Reinforce spelling skills and provide motivation and interest.

Materials

- game page (from student text)
- pencils (1 per child)
- game word list

Game Word List

Team A		Team B
E4	plaza (1)	A1
E3	Amazon (4)	A2
E2	Kansas (3)	A3
E1	stanza (2)	A4
D4	Missouri (1)	B1
D3	blaze (4)	B2
D2	graze (2)	B3
D1	laser (3)	B4
C4	raise (4)	C1
C3	bruise (2)	C2
C2	citizen (3)	C3
C1	closet (1)	C4
B4	design (2)	D1
B3	desire (3)	D2
B2	despise (4)	D3
B1	surprise (1)	D4
A4	enclose (4)	E1
A3	freezing (3)	E2
A2	horizon (1)	E3
A1	blizzard (2)	E4

3 Journaling

Provide a meaningful reason for correct spelling through personal writing.

Review the story using discussion leads provided on the following page. Encourage students to apply the Scriptural value in their journaling.

Journaling (continued)

- Why did Mr. Jacobson call a family council? (He wanted to tell them about a job offer he had. He asked them to pray about the invitation to move.)

- How did Rachel feel about moving? (She didn't want to go.)

- How did Vanessa feel about moving? (She wanted to stay.)

- Before she died what had Rachel's mommy told her about problem solving? ("You can always talk to Jesus about any problem, any time. He's always willing to help you.")

- How did Rachel's older sister Rebecca think God might talk to them? (Through teachers, Christian friends, parents, Bible, nature.)

- Tell about a time God helped you make a decision.

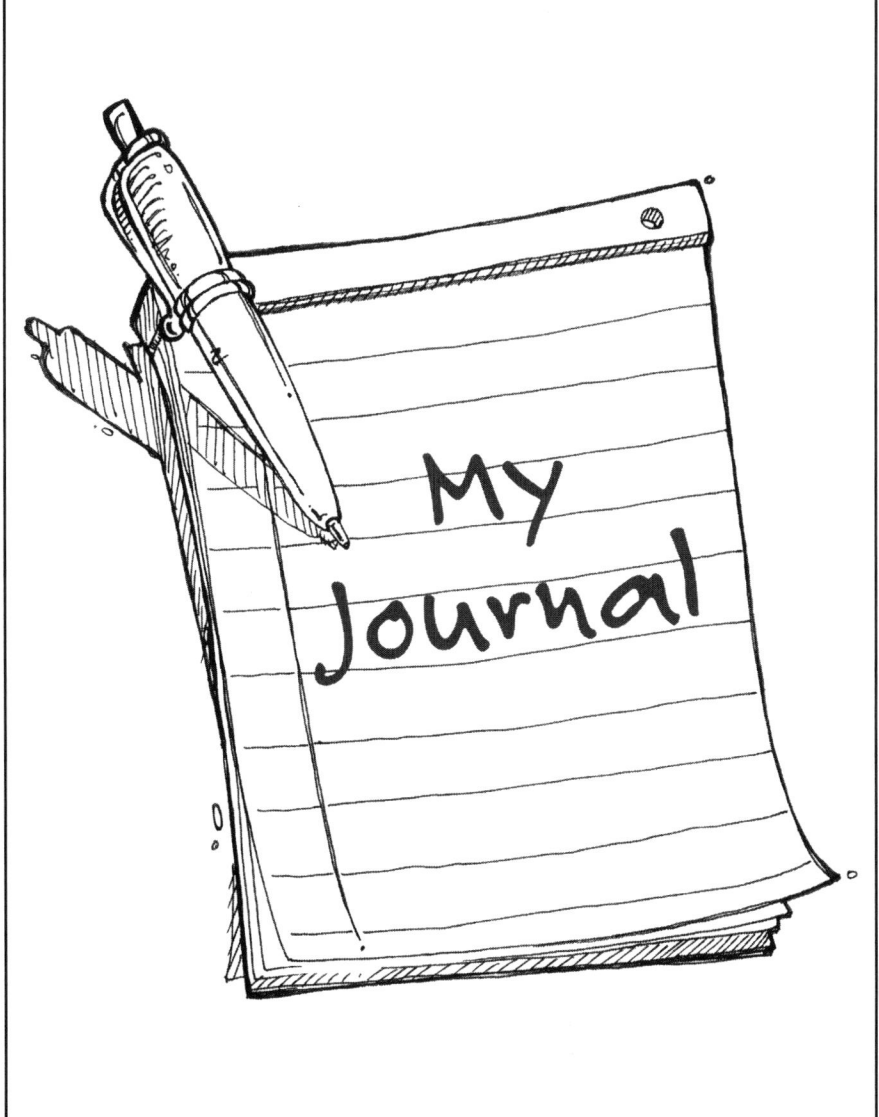

"SMILES" is sometimes said to be the longest word in the dictionary because "there's a <u>mile</u> between the two S's."

Tired of Sleeping

Katelynn prays for a quick resolution to her mom's constant fatigue.

Katelynn unhooked the safety chain on the front door to let her mother in. "Hi Mom," the dark-haired girl smiled in greeting. "I'm almost done with the list of stuff you left for me to do. I just need to finish vacuuming my room. You'll never guess what I did on the spelling preview today. I got all 20 right! Let me finish vacuuming and then I'll show you."

Katelynn stopped chattering and started down the hall toward her room. She paused when she remembered the phone call. "Someone from the church called—Lin Chow." Katelynn saw a shadow fall across her mother's face. "I know I'm not supposed to answer the phone when I'm home by myself." She hurried to explain, "The message is on the answering machine. It sounded important." Mrs. Hatasaki just nodded and headed toward the answering machine on the kitchen counter.

Katelynn finished vacuuming her room. She returned the vacuum cleaner to its place in the hall closet, then hurried back to her room for the spelling paper. She looked at the bright sticker and the red 100% at the top of the page and smiled in anticipation. Doing well in school was important to both her parents. She knew her mom would be proud of her high score, especially on a preview.

"See, check this out!" Katelynn said as she walked into the kitchen. When there was no response, the girl realized she was alone. "I wonder where Mom went?" she murmured.

Katelynn stopped short in the doorway of her parents' bedroom. "Asleep again," she muttered. She glanced at the form of her mother curled under a quilt on the queen-sized bed. A book lay unopened beside the sleeping woman. Katelynn noticed the red bookmark was near the beginning of the book.

"She's tired all the time."

Katelynn jumped at the sound of her older sister's voice. "When did you get home?"

"Just now," the older girl whispered.

"Why isn't Dad home?" Katelynn moved back down the hall toward the kitchen.

"He said he'd be late today—remember?" Jennifer sat down on a high stool and scooted up to the counter. "He needed to go by the bank."

"He usually comes home early on Tuesdays." Katelynn looked out the window by the front door.

"That was when Mom was playing racquetball with Mrs. Hill. She doesn't do that any more."

"Yeah, she doesn't do a lot of things anymore. I think something's wrong with her. Nothing used to keep her from racquetball night."

"I know," the older girl agreed. "Why don't we make tacos and let her sleep? She might feel better when she wakes up."

But Mrs. Hatasaki didn't wake up for the meal; in fact, she slept the entire evening. She got up for a few minutes to wish the girls good night, then went back into the bedroom. Her husband came in a few minutes later with the phone in his hand.

He held the phone out to his wife, "It's for you, My Sweet."

"Ask if I can call them back or just take a message," she whispered.

Mr. Hatasaki nodded and said, "Janette, can I take a message or have her call you tomorrow? She's already in bed." He walked back into the kitchen while he continued to talk to his wife's friend. "I'll tell her. She loves to go to the spring craft fairs. I don't think she'll want to miss it. I'll have her call. Bye now." After Mr. Hatasaki hung up the phone, he went back to the bedroom to talk to his wife. But he found her asleep—again.

Early the next morning, as he watched her prepare for work, he told his wife about Janette Hill's invitation. "You should go. You'd have fun."

"I don't really feel like it," the petite woman responded in a dull voice. "I'll call her on my first break this morning and let her know."

Greg Hatasaki looked back down at the open Bible in his lap and sent a quick prayer heavenward before he responded to his wife's lack of enthusiasm.

"You love craft fairs! I'll come home early and be here for Katelynn so she won't be alone until 5:00. Or maybe she could go over to a friend's house or something. You always go to the craft fairs. Why don't you want to go this year?"

Mrs. Hatasaki shrugged, picked up her ID card, and shoved it into the pocket of her white pants. "I'm just too tired. I don't have the energy to wander around craft fairs all day Friday. We need to save all the money we can, anyway."

She walked out of the room before her husband had time to add anything to the conversation.

"Lord, help her," he prayed. "She's been to the doctor and there doesn't seem to be anything physically wrong with her. But she's losing weight and interest in life itself. She's so tired all the time. She moves in slow motion and just isn't the same person she was six months ago. Help me know what to do, Lord. Amen."

Katelynn's head jerked up when Mr. Decker walked into her classroom later that morning and called her name. She couldn't imagine what the principal of Knowlton Elementary would want with her. As soon as they were in the hall, her eyebrows shot up and furrows appeared in her forehead. "Is my mother all right?"

Mr. Decker turned around and looked into Katelynn's dark eyes. "Your mother is fine, as far as I know. I just called you out for the testing your parents requested at the last parent/teacher conference. They want to know exactly where your weak areas in math are. Your mother plans to work with you at home but needs to pinpoint what you need help with. It's really no big deal." The principal headed toward his office and motioned for her to follow.

"It would be a miracle if Mom kept her eyes open for an evening," the girl muttered.

"Excuse me?" The principal turned and looked at Katelynn again.

"Nothing important. Where am I going to take the test and how long will it take?"

"Right in my office." Mr. Decker continued down the hall, adding, "It will take you about half an hour today. You'll be coming every day this week in order to complete the test. Some sections will take more time than others." Mr. Decker paused to answer a question for the school secretary.

Katelynn groaned. *I'm going to miss PE. It's not fair. Mom will probably never help me anyway. She isn't even keeping up with all the stuff she used to do for us. She hasn't been cooking or washing as often—and now she isn't even making the evening meal anymore.* Katelynn was so engrossed in her melancholy thoughts she didn't hear the principal invite her into his office.

"Katelynn," Mr. Decker repeated.

When Katelynn just stood in front of Mrs. Bentley's desk staring out the window, the principal noticed the clouded look on the girl's face and gently touched her shoulder. "Katelynn, you look a thousand miles away. Are you okay?"

Katelynn nodded and followed Mr. Decker into his spacious office.

Friday morning Katelynn and Beth were headed out the door for morning recess.

"What's that verse we need to know for spelling this week? Our test is right after we come back in." Beth returned to her desk and took out her spelling worktext.

Katelynn waited impatiently. "I think this is only the second recess I've had this week because of those tests Mr. Decker is making me take. It's a waste of time. Mom doesn't even notice when we're out of groceries any more. She just sleeps all the time. I don't know how she'll stay awake long enough to help me with math…."

Beth ignored her friend's complaints and read from the spelling worktext. "'Quick, Lord, answer me—for I have prayed. Listen when I cry to you for help! Psalm 141:1'" Beth shut the book and headed back out the door. "Quick, Lord, answer me!" Beth chanted.

"No, you answer me!" Katelynn interrupted.

Beth turned to look at her friend and noticed for the first time the look of desperation in her eyes. "How long has your mom been acting this way? Has she been working weekends or an extra shift or something?"

"No, but I'd say more than a month now. It started before parent/teacher conferences. But it wasn't so bad then. She isn't even going to the craft fairs with your mom today."

"I know. Mom said something about it this morning."

"She's been to Dr. Weaver, our family doctor. He says she's fine; but I say she isn't. I could've been the one who wrote our Scripture this week instead of David. 'Quick, Lord, answer me—for I have prayed. Listen when I cry to you for help!'"

"Well, you don't need to study the verse anymore. You know it—but don't forget to do it."

Katelynn wrinkled her brow. "Do what?"

Beth looked intently at her friend. "Pray for help. The Lord knows what's wrong with your mom."

"I have." Katelynn scuffed the toe of her shoe on the gray carpet. "I feel like the guy who wrote that Psalm. I wish the Lord would be quicker with His answers. I'm tired of Mom being tired."

Beth tossed Katelynn her glove. "Quick! Let's play ball while you can. You may have to take another math test this afternoon."

Katelynn caught the glove and smiled in spite of herself as she followed Beth to the ball diamond.

Discussion Time

Check understanding of the story and development of personal values.

- How does Katelynn feel when her mom walks in the door?
- Why is she excited?
- When does Mrs. Hatasaki take a nap?
- How long does she sleep?
- What are some of the things Katelynn's mom has quit doing?
- What would you do if your mom started acting like Katelynn's mom?

A Preview

Write each word as your teacher says it.

Name _____

1. candlestick
2. brother-in-law
3. basketball
4. afternoon
5. runaway
6. footnote
7. password
8. foolproof
9. peppermint
10. old-fashioned
11. driveway
12. grassland
13. greenhouse
14. greyhound
15. newborn
16. broadcast
17. grasshopper
18. evergreen
19. livestock
20. Newfoundland

Compound Words

Lesson 23

Scripture

Psalm 141:1

143

3 Preview

Test for knowledge of the correct spellings of these words.

Customize Your List
On a separate sheet of paper, additional words of your choice may be tested.

(Say) I will say each word once, use the word in a sentence, then say the word again. Write the words on the lines in your Worktext.

Correct Immediately!
(Say) Let's correct our Preview. I will spell each word out loud. If you spelled a word incorrectly, rewrite it correctly.

Progress Chart
Students may record scores. (Reproducible master provided in Appendix B.)

1.	candlestick	Katelynn put the **candlestick** back on the shelf after she dusted.
2.	brother-in-law	"Mr. Canfield's **brother-in-law** may come to our class," she said.
3.	basketball	"He has played professional **basketball** for six years!" she continued.
4.	afternoon	Mrs. Hatasaki seemed not to hear and went to take her **afternoon** nap.
5.	runaway	She noticed a **runaway** ball rolling down the sidewalk.
6.	footnote	Katelynn felt like everything she said was no more important than a **footnote**.
7.	password	She wondered wryly if she needed a **password** to talk to her mom.
8.	foolproof	There seemed to be no **foolproof** way to keep her mom awake lately.
9.	peppermint	Katelynn planned to buy a **peppermint** plant for her mom.
10.	old-fashioned	Katelynn missed her mom's **old-fashioned** chocolate cake.
11.	driveway	A short **driveway** leads to the apartment parking lot.
12.	grassland	Katelynn read over a paragraph in her geography book about **grassland**.
13.	greenhouse	From her window, she could see through the roof of the nearby **greenhouse**.
14.	greyhound	She watched a man walk by with a **greyhound** on a leash.
15.	newborn	She heard the small cry of the neighbor's **newborn** in the next apartment.
16.	broadcast	She did not want to **broadcast** their family problems to Beth.
17.	grasshopper	Katelynn didn't even smile at the antics of a nearby **grasshopper**.
18.	evergreen	Katelynn braided three needles together from the **evergreen** tree on the playground.
19.	livestock	No one keeps **livestock** in the city; it's against city ordinance.
20.	Newfoundland	Mr. Canfield read an interesting article about the people of **Newfoundland**.

4 Word Shapes

Help students form a correct image of whole words.

Say Look at each word and think about its shape. Now, write the word in the correct Word Shape Boxes. You may check off each word as you use it.

(Compound words are words that are made up of two or more words. In some words, a hyphen separates the words.)

Say In the Word Shape Boxes, circle each word in the compound words.

Take a minute to memorize...

Psalm 141:1

B Word Shapes   Name _____

Using the word bank below, write each word in the correct Word Shape Boxes. Next, in the Word Shape Boxes, circle each word in the compound words.

1. driveway
2. evergreen
3. basketball
4. broadcast
5. runaway
6. foolproof
7. newborn
8. afternoon
9. candlestick
10. grassland

11. peppermint
12. old-fashioned
13. brother-in-law
14. Newfoundland
15. greyhound
16. livestock
17. footnote
18. greenhouse
19. password
20. grasshopper

Word Bank

afternoon	candlestick	footnote	greyhound	old-fashioned
basketball	driveway	grasshopper	livestock	password
broadcast	evergreen	grassland	newborn	peppermint
brother-in-law	foolproof	greenhouse	Newfoundland	runaway

144

Answers may vary for duplicate word shapes.

Be Prepared For Fun

Check these supply lists for **Fun Ways to Spell** - presented **Day 2**. Purchase and/or gather these items ahead of time!

General
- Pencil
- Graph Paper (1 sheet per child)
- Spelling List

Auditory
- Pencil
- Notebook Paper
- Spelling List

Visual
- Colored Pencils
- Alphabet Stencils
- Paper

Tactile
- Uncooked Rice
- Art Paper (1 sheet per child)
- Glue
- Spelling List

226

C **Hide and Seek**

Name _____

Play Hide and Seek with your words. Fill in a box on the bar graph (left to right) for each word you spell correctly.

LOOK SAY SPELL ALOUD WRITE SEEK CHECK.

D **Other Word Forms**

Using the words below, follow the instructions given by your teacher.

afternoons	candlesticks	grasshoppers	Newfoundlander
basketballs	driveways	grasslands	passwords
broadcasting	evergreens	greenhouses	peppermints
brothers-in-law	footnoted	greyhounds	runaways

E **Fun Ways to Spell**

Initial the box of each activity you finish.

1.

acknnjes
bcwordos
Infindmr
btmhxdrg
rmnosdrb

Spell your words in a "Word Find."

3.

M·i·s·s·i-
s·s·i·p·p·i

Play "Spelling Tic-Tac-Toe."

2.

Spell your words with stencils.

4.

Spell your words with rice.

145

 Hide and Seek

Reinforce spelling by using multiple styles of learning.

On a white board, Teacher writes each word — one at a time. **Have students:**

- **Look** at the word.
- **Say** the word out loud.
- **Spell** the word out loud.
- **Hide** (teacher erases word.)
- **Write** the word on paper.
- **Seek** (teacher rewrites word.)
- **Check** spelling. If incorrect, rewrite word correctly.

 Other Word Forms

This activity is optional. Have students find and circle the Other Word Forms that are most nearly synonyms of the following:

keys
announcing
prairies

Fun Ways to Spell

Four activities are provided. Use one, two, three, or all of the activities. Have students initial the box for each activity they complete.

Day 2

Lesson 23

Options:

- assign activities to students according to their learning styles
- set up the activities in learning centers for the students to do throughout the day
- divide students into four groups and assign one activity per group
- do one activity per day

General

To spell your words in a "Word Find"...
- Arrange your words on a piece of graph paper.
- Put one letter of each word in a square.
- Words may be written backwards, forwards, or diagonally.
- Outline your puzzle.
- Hide your words by filling in all the spaces inside the puzzle with random letters.
- Trade grids with a classmate and find the hidden words.

Auditory

To play "Spelling Tic-Tac-Toe"...
- Draw a Tic-Tac-Toe grid.
- Ask a classmate to read a word from the list.
- Spell the word aloud.
- If the word is spelled correctly, place your mark on the grid.
- Take turns with your classmate.

Visual

To spell your words with stencils...
- Look at the first letter of a word on your list.
- Place the stencil for the proper letter over your paper.
- Shade inside the stencil.
- Choose the proper stencil for the next letter of the word and shade it in next to the first letter.
- Finish the word in this way.
- Do this with each word.

Tactile

To spell your words with rice...
- Choose a word from your spelling list.
- Shape the letters of your word with rice.
- Glue the rice to art paper.
- Do this for each word on your list.

227

Working with Words

Familiarize students with word meaning and usage.

Hidden Words

Explain that the spelling words for this week are hidden in the puzzle. After finding each word, the student should write the word under the correct heading.

Say Use the word bank to help you find each of the words in the puzzle. Words may go across, down, or diagonally. Circle, then write the words.

Take a minute to memorize...

Psalm 141:1

Name _____

Hidden Words

Use the word bank to help you find each of the words in the puzzle. Words may go across, down, or diagonally. Circle and write the words.

Compound Words

Lesson **23**

Across		Down	Diagonal
1. afternoon	7. grassland	12. candlestick	18. brother-in-law
2. basketball	8. greyhound	13. greenhouse	19. evergreen
3. broadcast	9. livestock	14. Newfoundland	20. footnote
4. driveway	10. newborn	15. old-fashioned	
5. foolproof	11. password	16. peppermint	
6. grasshopper		17. runaway	

Word Bank

afternoon	candlestick	footnote	greyhound	old-fashioned
basketball	driveway	grasshopper	livestock	password
broadcast	evergreen	grassland	newborn	peppermint
brother-in-law	foolproof	greenhouse	Newfoundland	runaway

146

228

G Dictation

Name _____

Write **each sentence as your teacher dictates. Use correct punctuation.**

1. Mrs. Hatasaki was asleep all afternoon.

_____

2. Katelynn noticed the neighbor playing basketball in his driveway.

3. My brother-in-law saw a broadcast about how someone built a greenhouse.

H Proofreading

If a word is misspelled, fill in the oval by that word. If all the words are spelled correctly, fill in the oval by **no mistake**.

1. ○ afternoon
   ○ plaza
   ● basketbal
   ○ no mistake

2. ○ broadcast
   ● brother in law
   ○ Missouri
   ○ no mistake

3. ● candelstick
   ○ driveway
   ○ laser
   ○ no mistake

4. ○ foolproof
   ○ enclose
   ○ citizen
   ● no mistake

5. ○ footnote
   ● grashopper
   ○ despise
   ○ no mistake

6. ○ grassland
   ● greenhous
   ○ surprise
   ○ no mistake

7. ○ evergreen
   ○ Amazon
   ○ Kansas
   ● no mistake

8. ● grayhound
   ○ stanza
   ○ livestock
   ○ no mistake

9. ○ horizon
   ● newborne
   ○ graze
   ○ no mistake

10. ● oldfashioned
    ○ blaze
    ○ password
    ○ no mistake

11. ● newfoundland
    ○ closet
    ○ design
    ○ no mistake

12. ○ peppermint
    ○ desire
    ○ runaway
    ● no mistake

147

Dictation

Reinforce correct spelling by using current and previous words in context.

(Say)

Listen as I read each sentence and then write it in your Worktext. Remember to use correct capitalization and punctuation. (Slowly read each sentence twice. Sentences are found in the Student Worktext to the left.)

Proofreading

Familiarize students with standardized test format and reinforce recognition of misspelled words.

(Say)

Look at each set of words. If a word is misspelled, fill in the oval by that word. If all the words are spelled correctly, fill in the oval by **no mistake**.

Day 4

Lesson 23

229

3 Hide and Seek

Reinforce correct spelling of current spelling words. Repeat this activity from Day 2.

4 Vocabulary Extension

Have your students complete this activity to strengthen spelling ability and expand vocabulary. The reproducible master is provided in Appendix A as shown on the inset page to the right.

1 Posttest

Visit the **A Reason For** website to download free, printable Posttest pages.

I will say the word once, use it in a sentence, then say it again. Write your words on a separate sheet of paper.

Progress Chart
Students may record scores. (Appendix B)

Personal Dictionary
Students may add any words they have misspelled to their personal dictionaries. (Appendix B)

Hide and Seek

Play Hide and Seek with your words. Fill in a bar graph (left to right) for each word you spell correctly.

LOOK   SAY   HIDE   WRITE   SEEK   CHECK

Lesson **23** | Vocabulary Extension

Vocabulary Extension

Fill in the Blanks

Choose a word from the word bank that best fits each sentence clue.

1. Someone who is attractive in appearance is said to be ___handsome___.

2. This book of the Bible, _Song of Solomon_, comes just before the book of Isaiah.

3. This pancake recipe calls for three teaspoons of baking powder. This is the same as one ___tablespoon___.

4. A beautiful flower is blooming in the garden. Dad took a ___close-up___ shot of it to get all the details.

5. The sauce didn't taste quite right, so Mom added a ___teaspoon___ of salt.

6. When the factory workers went on strike, many people formed a ___picket line___ to keep anyone from entering the building.

7. My older brothers both married, so I have two ___sisters-in-law___.

8. The team captain organized his ___teammates___ for the ice hockey game.

9. We have a computer lab at school. We are learning to type faster on the ___keyboard___.

10. The new boy in our class likes to draw pictures of airplanes and ___spacecraft___.

11. One of my favorite classes is physical education. We are learning how to play ___volleyball___.

12. We are going camping when school gets out on Friday. It will be a great ___weekend___.

Word Bank

close-up	picket line	spacecraft	teaspoon
handsome	sisters-in-law	tablespoon	volleyball
keyboard	Song of Solomon	teammates	weekend

344

---

1. brother-in-law — Mr. Canfield said his **brother-in-law** was coming the next day.
2. basketball — They all were looking forward to a professional **basketball** player visiting their class.
3. afternoon — Katelynn was eager to tell her mom about it that **afternoon**.
4. old-fashioned — She thought she might make her mom an **old-fashioned** chocolate cake.
5. newborn — She heard the tiny cry of the **newborn** baby in the apartment next door.
6. runaway — She noticed a **runaway** baseball rolling down the sidewalk.
7. greyhound — A **greyhound** on a leash seemed to be leading his master.
8. greenhouse — Katelynn liked looking through the nearby **greenhouse** roof.
9. driveway — She saw Mom turn the car into the short **driveway** and into a parking space.
10. Newfoundland — "**Newfoundland** was the easiest word on our preview," she told her mom.
11. peppermint — Mrs. Hatasaki absently unwrapped a **peppermint**, then laid it on the counter.
12. candlestick — She didn't even straighten the candle in the **candlestick** on the hall shelf.
13. password — "Is there a special **password** to get your attention?" Katelynn muttered.
14. evergreen — Katelynn pulled several more needles from the nearby **evergreen** tree.
15. foolproof — "There's no **foolproof** way to take care of this," she told Beth.
16. broadcast — "I feel silly having **broadcast** my family's problems to you," she admitted.
17. footnote — "I just don't like feeling like an insignificant **footnote** in my mom's life."
18. grasshopper — She scooped up a **grasshopper** sunning on the sidewalk.
19. grassland — "Find which animals inhabit the American **grassland**, or prairie," said Mr. Canfield.
20. livestock — No **livestock** are allowed within the city limits.

I Game

Name _____

Follow Katelynn out to the ball diamond to play catch with Beth. Move one space for each word you or your team spells correctly.

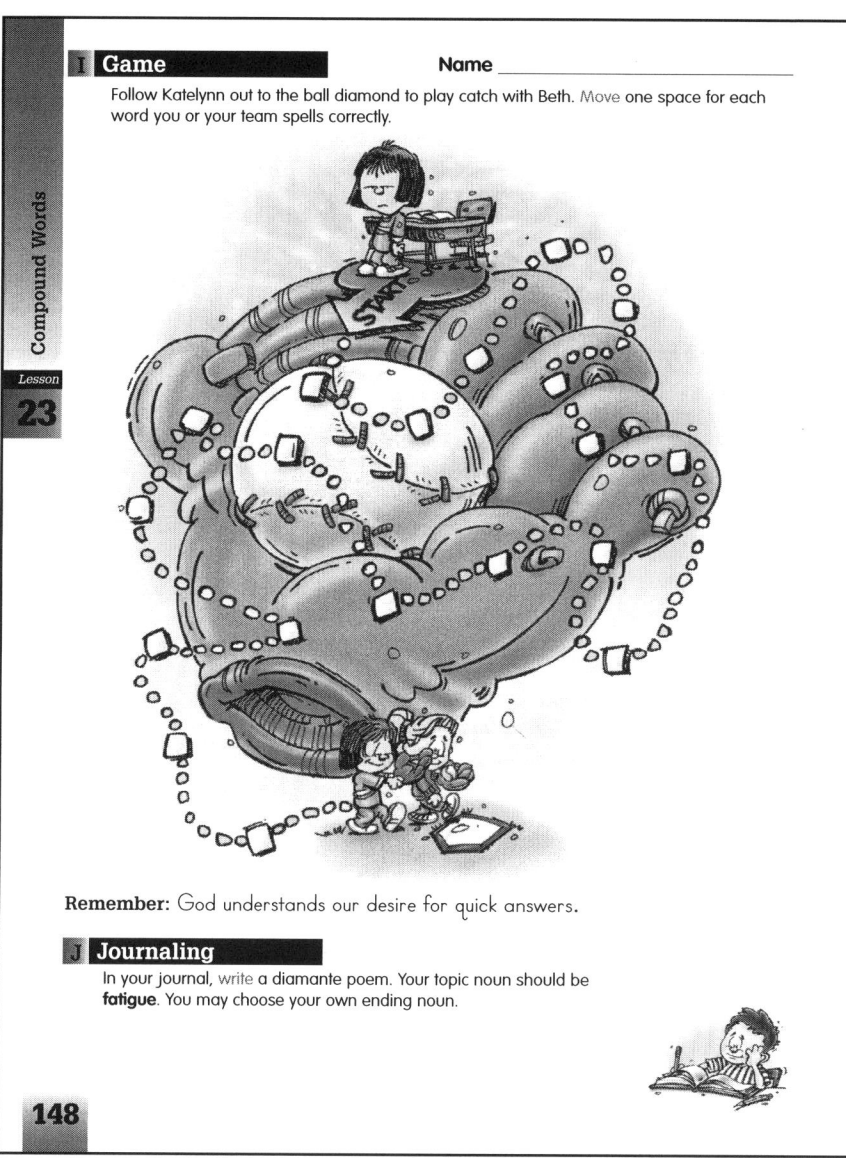

Remember: God understands our desire for quick answers.

J Journaling

In your journal, write a diamante poem. Your topic noun should be **fatigue**. You may choose your own ending noun.

148

---

2 Game

Reinforce spelling skills and provide motivation and interest.

Materials

- game page (from student text)
- game pieces (1 per child)
- game word list

Game Word List

1. **afternoon**
2. **basketball**
3. **broadcast**
4. **brother-in-law**
5. **candlestick**
6. **driveway**
7. **evergreen**
8. **foolproof**
9. **footnote**
10. **grasshopper**
11. **grassland**
12. **greenhouse**
13. **greyhound**
14. **livestock**
15. **newborn**
16. **Newfoundland**
17. **old-fashioned**
18. **password**
19. **peppermint**
20. **runaway**

How to Play:

- Divide the class into two teams.
- Have each student place his/her game piece on Start.
- Have a student from team A go to the board.
- Say the spelling word.
- Have the student write the word on the board.
- If correct, instruct each member of team A to move his/her game piece forward one space.
- Alternate between teams A and B.
- The team to reach Beth first is the winner.
- **Small Group Option**: Students may play this game without teacher direction in small groups of two or more.

3 Journaling

Provide a meaningful reason for correct spelling through personal writing.

Review the story using discussion leads provided on the following page. Encourage students to apply the Scriptural value in their journaling.

231

Journaling (continued)

(Say)
- Why did Mr. Decker want Katelynn? (To give her some math tests.)

- How did Katelynn feel about taking the tests? (She thought it would be a waste of time because her mom couldn't even keep up with what she was doing.)

- What did Beth want to check before she went out to recess? (She wanted to look at the Scripture in spelling.)

- What did Beth say Katelynn should do? (Pray for help like the Scripture said.)

- Diamante is the Italian word for diamond. A diamante poem is written in the shape of a diamond. Diamantes don't rhyme but there is a formula for writing each of the seven lines.

China
Vast, distant
Creating, expanding, exporting
Ancient, ambitious—Young, patriotic
Technologizing, changing, succeeding
Diverse, near
United States

1. First you choose a topic noun (first line): **China**

2. Then pick an antonym (for the last line): **United States**

3. Next select two describing words for the topic noun (second line): **Vast, distant**

4. Then select two describing words for the antonym (sixth line): **Diverse, near**

5. Think of three action words ("ing" words) for the topic noun (third line): **Creating, expanding, exporting**

6. Think of three action words ("ing" words) for the antonym too (fifth line): **Technologizing, changing, succeeding**

7. Last decide on four words — two for the topic noun and two that go with the ending noun (fourth line): **Ancient, ambitious — Young, patriotic**

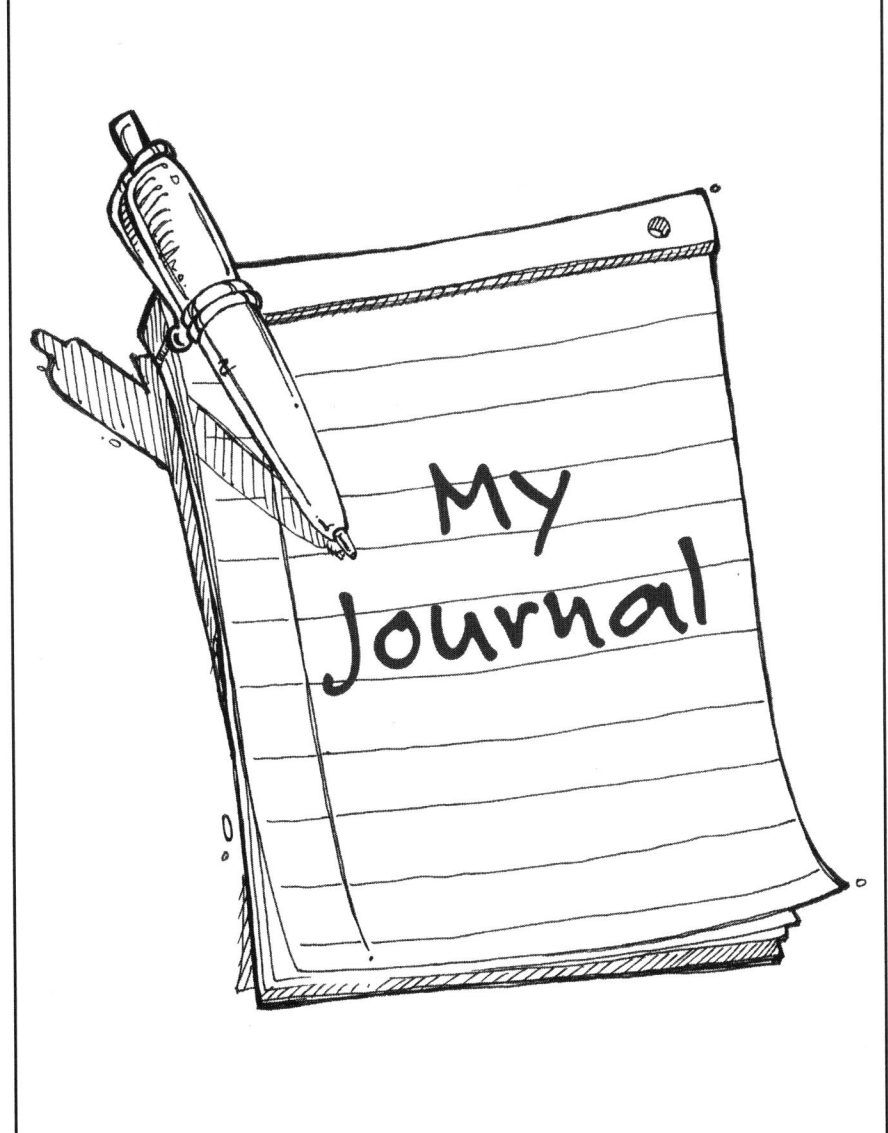

The longest place name is *"TAUMATAWHAKATANGIHAN-GAKOAUAUTAMATEATURIPU-KAKAPIKIMAUNGAHORONUKU-POKAIWHENUAKITANATAHU"* in New Zealand. It is usually called *"Taumata."*

What a Pain!

Rosa faces more health problems and becomes discouraged.

"Hello? Oh, hi, Kristin." Rosa Vasquez lowered herself gingerly onto the couch, careful not to jostle her mending ribs. "Yeah, thanks for sending it. Maria brought it home with all my schoolwork from today. It looks like a really good book, but I haven't read any of it yet." She rested her head against the back of the overstuffed sofa and listened to her best friend's chatter.

"Really? What a great field trip that'll be! Next Wednesday, huh? Well, I hope I'll be back by then." Rosa closed her eyes for a moment. "I have another checkup with Dr. Harrington tomorrow afternoon. Maybe she'll say I'm ready to go back to school." She scratched under Chipper's chin when the red squirrel crawled up her jeans and settled in her lap. "What? Yes, I'm okay. I don't hurt so much anymore. I guess it's just that I'm really tired or something." The dark-haired girl sighed. "So, tell me everything that's going on. It seems like I've been away forever!"

"Rosa? Rosa!" She awoke with a start a while later when her older sister, Maria, plopped down on the couch beside her. "Oops, sorry," Maria grimaced. "Did I hurt you?"

"No." Rosa rubbed her eyes. "What time is it, anyway?"

"Nearly 5:00." Maria's forehead wrinkled with concern as she peered into her sister's face. "Are you all right? You've been asleep ever since you got off the phone."

"I'm fine." Rosa shoved the hair out of her face and sat up carefully.

"Well, okay." Maria didn't look convinced. "Dad and Carlos are working outside and I'm going to plant some pansies. You want to come out with us?"

"Sure." Rosa relocated the snoozing Chipper to a throw pillow and got up. "What's Dad doing?"

"I don't know." Maria fastened her hair into a ponytail as she led the way to the front porch. "He's messing around with the mower. You know how he works it over every spring as soon the grass starts to turn green." She pulled a pair of gardening gloves out of her back jeans pocket. "Should I mix up all three colors or separate them in groups?" She pointed at the flats of delicate purple, yellow, and white pansies lined up along the edge of the porch.

But Rosa was too tired to care how Maria arranged the pansies.

Carlos was working in the shade of the huge oak tree, busily repainting the wooden swing that usually hung on the front porch. He waved his paintbrush in the air and called, "Rosa! Just a sec and I'll fetch you a lawn chair to sit in!"

"That's okay. I don't need...." Rosa shrugged as Carlos jogged into the garage. He reappeared moments later and set up the chair with a flourish.

"From here you can boss all of us around, m'lady." He bowed low, holding one arm out toward the chair like a royal servant. "Hey, are you okay? You don't look too good." Carlos dropped his banter and knelt on one paint-splattered knee in front of the lawn chair. "Are you feeling worse?"

"Everyone keeps asking that! I'm FINE!" Rosa rolled her eyes. "You better finish painting the swing before all the paint on you dries and you can't move."

"Yeah, yeah, yeah," Carlos groaned. "Everyone's a critic. Just wait, it will be a perfect job when I'm finished painting."

"What? You or the swing?" Maria dodged the acorn Carlos tossed her way as he returned to his painting. She took a deep breath, filling her lungs with the fresh air. "I just love spring, don't you, Rosa? Take a look at all the wildflowers in that field across the road. Then there are the daffodils, the wild plum thickets, the dogwood blossoms, all the tiny new green leaves." She turned in a circle as she spoke. "Everything is just bursting out in this warm spring weather! Doesn't the air smell wonderful?"

Rosa nodded and breathed in, but she couldn't seem to get enough air, couldn't breathe deeply at all. And it sure didn't feel like "warm spring weather" to her! She shivered. "Are you sure it's not too early to plant flowers, Maria?"

"Not at all." Maria bent and picked up a pansy with velvety purple blossoms. "We shouldn't have any more freezing weather, but even if we did, these guys could handle it." She gently patted the soil down around the transplanted pansy.

"Well, not me, I guess." Rosa stood up and wrapped her arms around herself. "I'm freezing! I guess I'll go back inside and read that book Kristin sent."

A couple of hours later Carlos went in search of her. "Rosa, where are you? Time to eat! Dad's got supper ready, so come and get it." He paused in the doorway of her bedroom. "Rosa, are you in here?" He flipped on the light.

"Uh-huh." Rosa groaned from beneath a pile of covers topped with a heavy quilt. "B-but I d-don't th-think I'm all right anymore." She shook with chills, and her teeth chattered so hard she could barely speak. "I'm s-so c-c-cold." She tugged the blankets tighter around her flushed face. She coughed and winced at the pain ripping through her chest.

"I'll get Dad!" Carlos darted out of the room and was back in a flash with Dad and Maria. Over the phone, Dr. Harrington listened carefully to Mr.

233

Story Continued

Vasquez's description of Rosa's condition. The evening meal was abandoned on the table when the doctor advised him to bring Rosa to the hospital right away.

"Well, young lady, it seems you were awfully anxious to see me again," Dr. Harrington teased when she checked Rosa over in the emergency room. "Couldn't even wait till tomorrow, could you?" The doctor monitored Rosa's symptoms as she spoke. "It looks like you'll be spending some more time with us here in the hospital." After completing her examination, she turned to Mr. Vasquez. "Your daughter's developed pneumonia. She'll need to be admitted to the hospital for…"

Rosa broke into a fit of painful coughing. When it was over, she struggled to catch her breath. Dad gripped her hand tightly and leaned over to drop a kiss on her forehead. "It'll be better soon, Rosita. I'm going to get you checked into the hospital right now and they'll give you something to help real soon. Hang in there, little one."

By the next afternoon Rosa imagined she felt a tiny bit better. The antibiotics dripping through the IV tube were beginning to take effect. The oxygen tube in her nose certainly made it easier to breath. But Rosa was discouraged. She stared unseeingly at the images flickering on the wall-mounted television, a fierce expression on her face. Back in the hospital again! Following the accident, she'd been hospitalized for a couple of weeks. Doctors had inserted a chest tube and reinflated her punctured lung, as well as caring for her other injuries. Even after being released to go home, she'd been bedridden for several more days. And now, here she was again, right when everything was supposed to be healed! Was she ever going to be well again?

"Hi, Rosa!" Maria breezed through the door, followed by Carlos.

"Shhhh. Dad's asleep," Rosa whispered. Mr. Vasquez was draped on the vinyl visitor's chair in the most uncomfortable-looking position imaginable, head back, mouth open in sleep.

"Was asleep." Mr. Vasquez stretched and yawned. He checked his watch. "4:30 already! Well, how are you doing, Rosita?" He got up stiffly and walked over to the bed.

"Okay, I guess." Rosa mumbled.

"Come on, Dad." Carlos took his dad's arm. "Let's walk down to the snack bar and get a cold drink. You look like you could use a break."

Dad hesitated. "Well…"

"You go on; I'll stay with Rosa," Maria insisted as she wheeled the bedside table closer to her sister. "I brought a bunch of stuff from school to show her." Maria punched a button on the side of Rosa's bed that turned the TV off, then pressed another one to move the hospital bed into an upright position. Rosa started to protest, but couldn't seem to find the energy. "Just wait till you see what's in here!" Maria reached into the bag and pulled out a bunch of cards and pictures. "Everyone made get-well cards for you. See?" She fanned them out in front of Rosa. "Want me to put them up on the wall like I did last time?"

"No." Rosa leaned her head back on the pillow.

Maria laid the cards on the table and reached into the bag again. "And we brought you this. TA DA!" She pulled out a pot with three blooming pansy plants. "Since you're stuck in here, we thought we'd bring spring inside to you!" Maria turned toward the window. "I'll put them right here in the windowsill so they can grow and you can still see them."

While Maria gave the flowers a drink, Rosa picked up the top card without much enthusiasm. A large yellow smiley face was drawn on the front of the card. Inside the card, the smiley face was drawn broken in two—but STILL smiling. Beneath the picture the card read, "'Those who trust in the Lord are steady as Mount Zion, unmoved by any circumstance.' Psalm 125:1. In your circumstances, aren't you

glad you can trust in Him? Your friend, Kristin."

Rosa felt tears prick her eyelids. She'd forgotten. True, she'd had a rough time lately with the accident—and now pneumonia—but she didn't have to let it discourage her. Her dad had spent the night by her bedside. Her friends were sending her encouraging messages. Her brother and sister did everything they could think of for her. But most of all, she had God on her side.

"Hey, are you okay?" Maria looked worried. "Should I call the nurse?"

"I'm fine." Rosa grinned through the tears. "I really am fine."

Discussion Time

Check understanding of the story and development of personal values.

- How did Rosa get her assignments while she was at home recovering from the accident?
- What were Maria, Carlos, and Mr. Vasquez doing outside?
- What question did everyone keep asking Rosa?
- Why did Mr. Vasquez have to take Rosa back to the hospital that evening?
- What did Dr. Harrington say was wrong with Rosa?
- What did Maria bring Rosa from her classmates the next day?
- Describe the card that Kristin made.

A Test-Words

Name _____

Write each spelling word on the line as your teacher says it.

1. photos
2. o'clock
3. forecast
4. desire
5. effort
6. jogging
7. grasshopper
8. freezing
9. jacket
10. afternoon
11. manage
12. cringe
13. hinges
14. difficult
15. raise
16. echoes

B Test-Sentences

Write the sentences on the lines below, correcting each misspelled word, as well as all capitalization and punctuation errors. Two words are misspelled in each sentence.

the baskitbal game was brodcast on the radio:

1. The basketball game was broadcast on the radio.

The Sheriff gave him a trophey for his act of bravery

2. The sheriff gave him a trophy for his act of bravery.

my parents are going to a banquitt in Kintuckey

3. My parents are going to a banquet in Kentucky.

in the brush the jagaur took reffuge from the hunter

4. In the brush, the jaguar took refuge from the hunter.

149

---

4 Test-Sentences

Reinforce recognizing misspelled words.

 Read each sentence carefully. Write the sentences on the lines in your Worktext. There are two misspelled words in each sentence. Correct each misspelled word, as well as all capitalization and punctuation errors.

 Take a minute to memorize...

Psalm 125:1

---

3 Test-Words

Test for knowledge of the correct spellings of these words.

 I will say each word once, use the word in a sentence, then say the word again. Write the words on the lines in your Worktext.

1. photos — She aimlessly looked at some **photos** while she rested on the couch.
2. o'clock — "It's five **o'clock**; want to come outside with us?" Maria asked Rosa.
3. forecast — "The **forecast** says SPRING!" quipped Maria cheerfully.
4. desire — "Does the lady **desire** a chair? I shall be happy to get her one!" said Carlos.
5. effort — Rosa made an **effort** to smile at Carlos, although she did not feel well.
6. jogging — Carlos went **jogging** into the garage for a lawn chair for Rosa.
7. grasshopper — She smiled weakly as a **grasshopper** landed right in his fresh paint job.
8. freezing — "I'm **freezing**," Rosa told Maria with a shiver.
9. jacket — "Do you want a **jacket**?" Maria asked.
10. afternoon — "I didn't read any of that book this **afternoon**," she replied.
11. manage — "If I can **manage** to stay awake, I'll read that for a while," she continued.
12. cringe — Rosa tried not to **cringe** as she stood up to go inside.
13. hinges — Even the **hinges** on the front screen door seemed to squeak much more loudly.
14. difficult — Rosa found it **difficult** to breathe, and very painful, too!
15. raise — She tried to **raise** up on her elbow when Carlos called, but she could not.
16. echoes — "Every noise **echoes** in my head," Rosa told her dad.

235

1 Test-Dictation

Reinforce correct spelling by using current and previous words in context.

Say

Listen as I read each sentence, then write it in your worktext. Remember to use correct capitalization and punctuation. (Slowly read each sentence twice. Sentences are found in the student text to the right. The words **blaze**, **candlestick**, **quicksand**, and **Amazon** are found in this unit.)

2 Test-Proofreading

Familiarize students with standardized test format and reinforce recognizing misspelled words.

Say

Look at each set of words. If a word is misspelled, fill in the oval by that word. If all the words are spelled correctly, fill in the oval by **no mistake**.

C Test-Dictation

Name _____

Write **each sentence as your teacher dictates.** Use correct punctuation.

1. The blaze swept quickly across the plain.

2. The boy put a candlestick in the front window.

3. He threw a rope to the man in the quicksand!

4. There are a few towns on the Amazon River.

Review
Lesson
24

D Test-Proofreading

If a word is misspelled, fill in the oval by that word. If all the words are spelled correctly, fill in the oval by **no mistake**.

1. ○ forecast
   ● mirge
   ○ photos
   ○ no mistake

2. ● autograff
   ○ funds
   ○ effort
   ○ no mistake

3. ○ desire
   ● syphon
   ○ jogging
   ○ no mistake

4. ○ squall
   ○ grasshopper
   ○ freezing
   ● no mistake

5. ● cittizen
   ○ jacket
   ○ afternoon
   ○ no mistake

6. ○ grassland
   ○ cringe
   ○ manage
   ● no mistake

7. ○ o'clock
   ● fosill
   ○ hinges
   ○ no mistake

8. ○ echoes
   ○ difficult
   ● old fashioned
   ○ no mistake

9. ○ raise
   ○ inquire
   ● pre-school
   ○ no mistake

10. ● incloase
    ○ closet
    ○ newborn
    ○ no mistake

11. ○ driveway
    ● Misourri
    ○ plaza
    ○ no mistake

12. ○ heritage
    ○ surprise
    ○ average
    ● no mistake

150

236

E **Test-Table**

Name _____

If a word is misspelled, fill in the space on the grid.

~~Kansis~~	~~pasword~~	~~dispise~~	quality
~~phraze~~	junior	~~Nufounland~~	equator
~~sphear~~	chaos	~~gadgit~~	badge
stanza	earthquake	livestock	~~Quibec~~

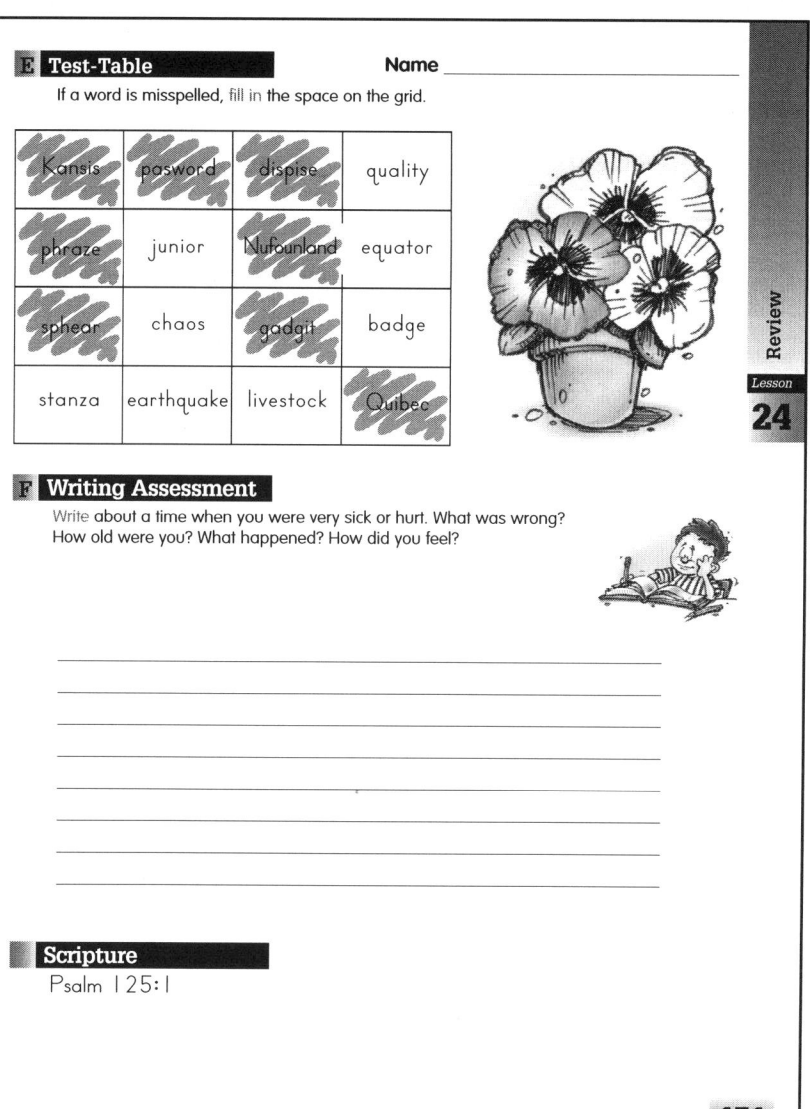

F **Writing Assessment**

Write about a time when you were very sick or hurt. What was wrong? How old were you? What happened? How did you feel?

_____

_____

_____

_____

_____

_____

Scripture
Psalm 125:1

151

A rubric for scoring is provided in Appendix B.

The most common word in the King James Bible is "THE."

Word Wow!

Test-Table

Test mastery of words in this unit.

Say

If a word is misspelled, fill in the space on the grid.

Writing Assessment

Assess student's spelling, grammar, and composition skills through personal writing.

Say

• Have you ever been very sick or had to stay in the hospital? (Allow time to share experiences.)

• Why was Rosa anxious to get back to school? (She'd been in the hospital and then at home for several weeks.)

• Why do you think Rosa got tired of people asking her if she was okay? (She'd been asked that so much since the accident.)

• What did Rosa do after she talked on the phone with Kristin? (She fell asleep on the couch.)

• Why didn't Rosa stay outside with the rest of her family? (She was too cold.)

• Where was Rosa when Carlos went to tell her supper was ready? (She was huddled beneath a pile of covers on her bed.)

• Why was Rosa discouraged about getting pneumonia? (She felt horrible and had to stay in the hospital again.)

• What did Maria bring Rosa from home? (Pansies like the ones planted in the front yard.)

• How did Kristin's card help Rosa feel better? (It reminded her to trust in God even in circumstances like this.)

237

1 Test-Sentences

Reinforce recognizing misspelled words.

Say

Read each sentence carefully. Write the sentences on the lines in your Worktext, correcting each misspelled word, as well as all capitalization and punctuation errors.

G **Test-Sentences**   Name _____

Write the sentences on the lines below, correcting each misspelled word, as well as all capitalization and punctuation errors. Two words are misspelled in each sentence.

Review Lesson 24

her brother in law has plants in his greanhuose

1. Her brother-in-law has plants in his greenhouse.

on the horrizon angry clouds foretold a blizard

2. On the horizon, angry clouds foretold a blizzard.

Write a paragraff about the dolfin's habitat

3. Write a paragraph about the dolphin's habitat.

the lawyer pleaded with the jurrey to choose justise

4. The lawyer pleaded with the jury to choose justice.

H **Test-Words**

Write each spelling word on the line as your teacher says it.

1. inquire
2. closet
3. newborn
4. driveway
5. plaza
6. surprise
7. average
8. bruise

9. difference
10. forth
11. liquid
12. peppermint
13. Africa
14. funds
15. chorus
16. pledge

152

---

2 Test-Words

Test for knowledge of the correct spellings of these words.

Say

I will say the word once, use the word in a sentence, then say the word again. Write the word on the lines in your Worktext.

1. inquire — Mr. Vasquez called the doctor to **inquire** about what to do for Rosa.
2. closet — Maria grabbed Rosa's backpack from the **closet.**
3. newborn — Mr. Vasquez carried Rosa as gently as if she were a **newborn.**
4. driveway — He quickly backed out of the garage and into the **driveway.**
5. plaza — Maria and Carlos waited in the beautiful hospital **plaza.**
6. surprise — "It's a **surprise** to find a miniature park inside a building," commented Maria.
7. average — "Are you're feeling a little below **average,** Rosa?" smiled Dr. Harrington.
8. bruise — "That **bruise** and scrape on your head have healed nicely though," she noted.
9. difference — "The **difference** in your energy level is caused by pneumonia," she continued.
10. forth — The nurse came back and **forth** in to Rosa's room to check on her.
11. liquid — She administered a **liquid** antibiotic through the IV.
12. peppermint — Kristin sent a small bag of soft **peppermint** candies for Rosa.
13. Africa — Thorny sent Rosa a very interesting article about animals in **Africa.**
14. funds — Sometimes Rosa worried if her dad had the **funds** for all the doctor bills.
15. chorus — God brought a **chorus** to Rosa's mind that encouraged her.
16. pledge — God has given us His **pledge,** or promise, to help us through everything!

238

Test-Editing

Name _____

If a word is spelled correctly, fill in the oval under **Correct**. If the word is misspelled, fill in the oval under **Incorrect**, and spell the word correctly on the blank.

		Correct	Incorrect	
1.	dungeon	●	○	
2.	design	●	○	
3.	legind	○	●	legend
4.	equall	○	●	equal
5.	back–up	○	●	backup
6.	grayhound	○	●	greyhound
7.	nephew	●	○	
8.	hyphen	●	○	
9.	fiber	●	○	
10.	rijid	○	●	rigid
11.	footnote	●	○	
12.	plunge	●	○	
13.	Allaska	○	●	Alaska
14.	evergreen	●	○	
15.	Nebraska	●	○	
16.	squid	●	○	
17.	graze	●	○	
18.	lazer	○	●	laser
19.	foolproof	●	○	
20.	runaway	●	○	

Review Lesson **24**

153

---

3 Test-Editing

Reinforce recognizing and correcting misspelled words.

4 Action Game

Reinforce spelling skills and provide motivation and interest.

Materials

- music
- beanbag
- word list on certificate at end of unit

BEANBAG SPELLING

Seat students in a large circle. As music is played, the students toss a beanbag randomly around or across the circle. When the music stops, whoever has the beanbag is given a spelling word to be reviewed. If the student misspells the word he or she passes the beanbag to the right and that student must spell the word. If the student spells the word correctly the music starts again and the game continues.

1 Game

Reinforce spelling skills and provide motivation and interest.

Materials
- game page (from student text)
- colored pencils (1 per child)
- game word list

Game Word List
Check off each word lightly in pencil as it is used.

The Nurses

1. merge
2. autograph
3. siphon
4. citizen
5. grassland
6. fossil
7. old-fashioned
8. preschool
9. enclose

The Doctors

1. Missouri
2. heritage
3. Kansas
4. phrase
5. sphere
6. stanza
7. password
8. junior
9. earthquake

The Lab Techs

1. despise
2. chaos
3. Newfoundland
4. gadget
5. livestock
6. quality
7. equator
8. liquid
9. Quebec

Score points for each review word or Other Word Form you or your team spells correctly.

Review Lesson 24

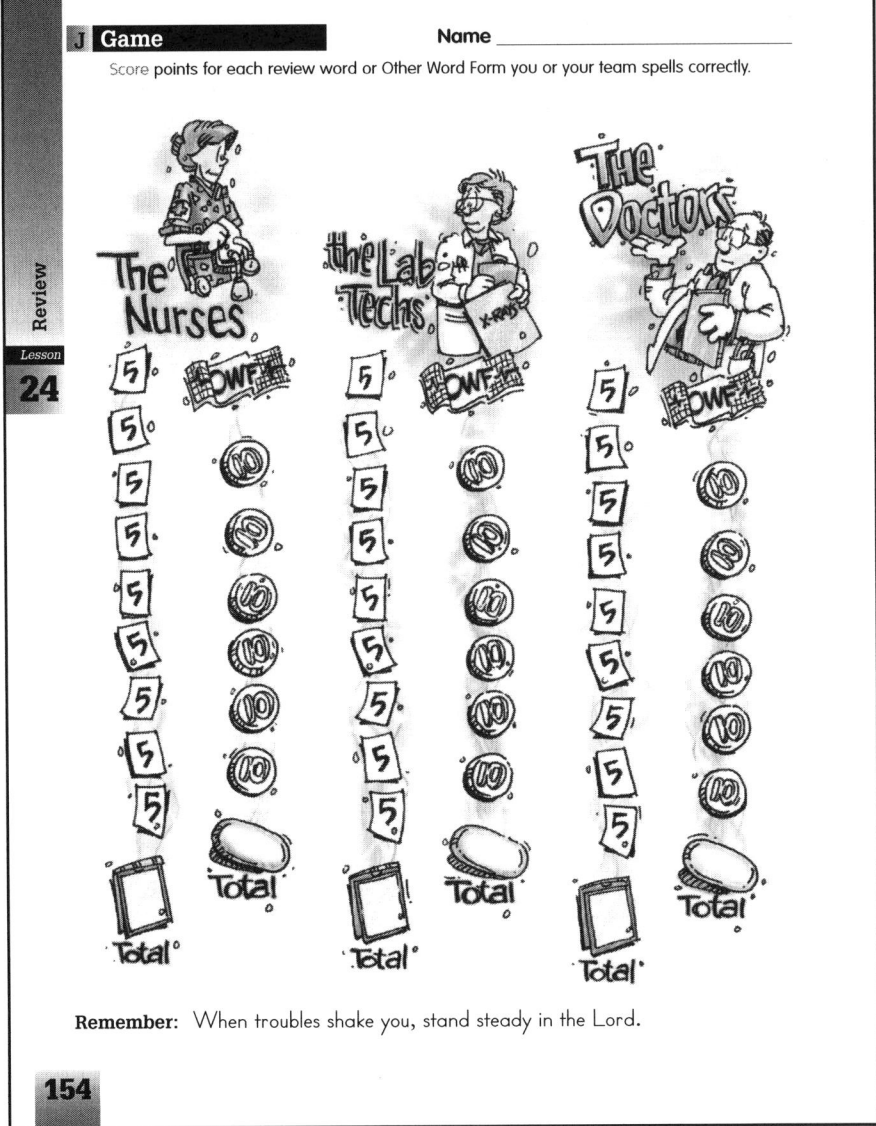

Remember: When troubles shake you, stand steady in the Lord.

154

How to Play:

- Divide the class into three teams. Name one team **The Nurses**, one **The Doctors**, and one **The Lab Techs**. (Option: You may wish to seat students in groups of three, each student from a different team. They should share one game page.)
- Have a student from the first team go to the board.
- Say the spelling word.
- Have the student write the word on the board.
- If the word is spelled correctly, have each team member color a point symbol by his/her team name. If the word is misspelled, have him/her put an **X** through one point symbol. That word may not be given again.
- Repeat this process with the second team and then the third.
- When the words from all three lists have been used, the team with the most points is the winner.
- Play another round using Other Word Forms.

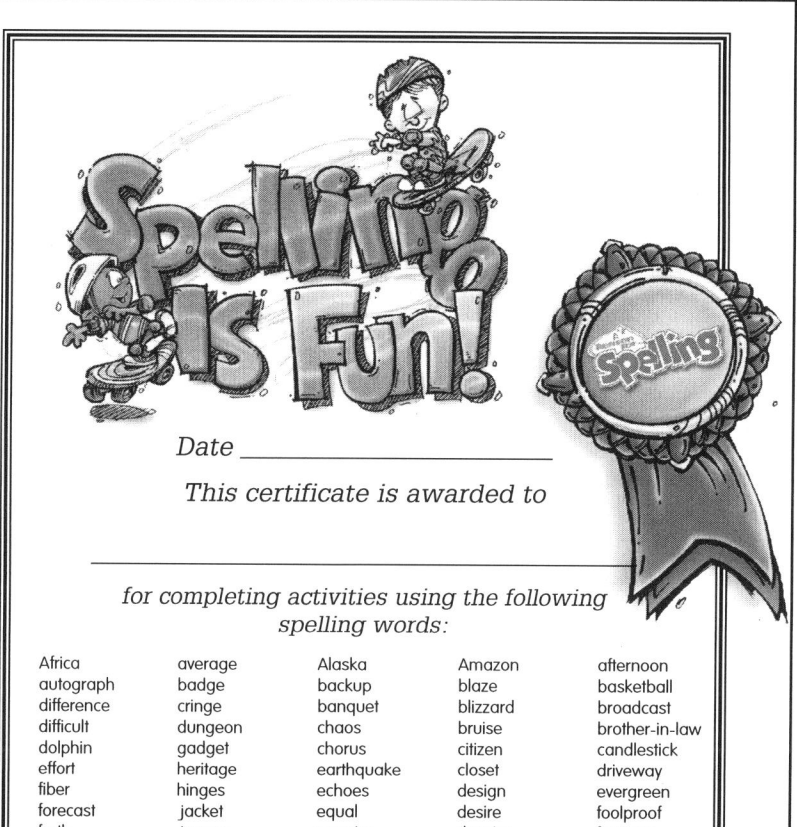

Date _____

This certificate is awarded to

_____

for completing activities using the following spelling words:

Africa	average	Alaska	Amazon	afternoon
autograph	badge	backup	blaze	basketball
difference	cringe	banquet	blizzard	broadcast
difficult	dungeon	chaos	bruise	brother-in-law
dolphin	gadget	chorus	citizen	candlestick
effort	heritage	earthquake	closet	driveway
fiber	hinges	echoes	design	evergreen
forecast	jacket	equal	desire	foolproof
forth	jaguar	equator	despise	footnote
fossil	jogging	inquire	enclose	grasshopper
funds	junior	Kentucky	freezing	grassland
hyphen	jury	liquid	graze	greenhouse
nephew	justice	Nebraska	horizon	greyhound
paragraph	legend	o'clock	Kansas	livestock
photos	manage	preschool	laser	newborn
phrase	merge	quality	Missouri	Newfoundland
sheriff	pledge	Quebec	plaza	old-fashioned
siphon	plunge	quicksand	raise	password
sphere	refuge	squall	stanza	peppermint
trophy	rigid	squid	surprise	runaway

2 Certificate

Provide an opportunity for parents or guardians to encourage and assess their child's progress.

 Fill in today's date and your name on your certificate.

 Take a minute to memorize...

Psalm 125:1

3 | Letter

Provide the parent or guardian with the spelling word lists for the next unit.

Say Give your parents or guardian this letter that lists your spelling words for the next unit. Put it where you will remember to practice the words together.

Dear Parent,

We are about to begin a new spelling unit containing five weekly lessons. A set of twenty words will be studied each week. All the words will be reviewed in the sixth week. Values based on the Scriptures listed below will be taught in each lesson.

Lesson 25	Lesson 26	Lesson 27	Lesson 28	Lesson 29
angle	adverb	aimless	border	account
bundle	anchor	cirrus	cornea	announcer
burial	burden	citrus	cornerstone	boundary
central	chapter	closeness	corridor	browse
crumple	charter	congress	dinosaur	clout
crystal	clerk	cumulus	dormitory	compound
decimal	clever	fungus	Florida	counterfeit
double	courage	interest	forehead	coward
dribble	deliver	mollusk	foreign	crouch
entitle	desert	nucleus	format	drought
example	deserve	obvious	formula	foul
fragile	energy	octopus	Georgia	mountains
humble	error	radius	horror	pronounce
mingle	journey	reckless	New York	scoundrel
miracle	major	restless	normal	scowl
missile	molar	services	North Carolina	snout
multiple	New Jersey	stillness	North Dakota	South Carolina
mumble	solar	virus	orbit	South Dakota
particle	version	walrus	ordeal	whereabouts
riddle	West Virginia	witness	Oregon	willpower
Psalm 25:14	Psalm 37:3	Psalm 59:16	Psalm 121:5-7	Psalm 47:1,2

Moving Right Along

Rachel and her family try to determine if it is God's plan for them to move.

Laney put her hands on her waist and looked intently at her friend. "Well, I say you shouldn't!"

"But what if God wants our family to move to Montana?" Rachel picked up the bright yellow tennis ball Wicker was nudging toward her feet and threw it for the dog.

"How can you possibly hear God telling you what to do? I think that's what He gave us brains for. If your family is happy here, why should you move to some ranch in the middle of nowhere?" Laney watched her Gordon Setter drop the tennis ball at her best friend's feet again; then she looked up into her eyes. "You do like it here—don't you?"

Rachel frowned, deliberately teasing her friend. "Sometimes I miss Dallas. But I suppose I'm getting used to this small-town life." When she saw Laney's shocked reaction, she couldn't keep the sparkle out of her eyes. "Of course I like it here, silly."

"Then why would you move? We moved here from New York because my mom married Coach Larkin. But your dad barely knows that family out there in Montana. How do you know you'll even like them?"

"We don't. And we haven't decided to move. My dad explained how he's been praying for God to open his eyes and show him how to share the love of Jesus. He also asked God to help him be willing to do whatever His will is. Then out of nowhere he gets this phone call from someone he went to school with! All Father wants us to do is pray. We haven't decided to go yet."

When Elisa Larkin came out on the back porch and called the girls in for supper, they hurried to put Wicker

back in his kennel. "Laney tells me your family is thinking of moving," Laney's mom said as the girls followed her into the house.

Rachel nodded. "I can't see why God would want us to leave. Nothing has happened since our father told us about the idea a few weeks ago to make me think we should go."

Laney didn't think about her conversation with Rachel until she was in bed that night. *How will God let the Jacobsons know what to do?* She pondered until she drifted off to sleep.

David Jacobson sat on the couch beside his wife. The house was quiet. It wasn't that way very often—not with six energetic children. He turned to Helen. "Are they all asleep?"

She leaned her head against his shoulder. "In bed, but not asleep. Natalie should be calling for a drink about now."

"Mom. Mom?"

David Jacobson smiled at his wife. "How did you know?"

"Because I know Natalie. I think she needs an extra kiss more than the drink." Helen shifted and started to get up. "She wants reassurance. The thought of moving and leaving everything that's familiar makes her feel insecure. She probably doesn't remember much about living in the apartment with just me and Vanessa. This is the only home she knows."

Mr. Jacobson put a hand on his wife's knee. "I'll get it for her, Love. But don't go away. I want to talk to you."

David Jacobson returned to the couch and pulled his wife close. "Well,

Natalie should feel loved and secure now. And now I want to share an idea with you. What would you think about putting our house up for sale?" He paused to let the words sink in. "I've been doing a little figuring, and I don't see how we could possibly afford to move without selling this place. We'd need to build in Montana, and that won't be cheap because of the remote location."

He squeezed his wife's shoulder as he continued, "If the house doesn't sell before Tyler needs an answer, maybe that's a way to determine God's will in this situation. Moving so far will cost a lot of money. We haven't saved much since we got married four years ago and moved here. With four girls in a private school and you staying home with the twins, we go through what I earn pretty quickly. I don't make the money I made in Dallas, either. Of course, I have time to spend with my family—and a lot less stress—but money is not something we have a surplus of."

The dark-haired man smiled down at his wife. "How does this idea sound to you?"

Helen didn't say anything for a while. "I love this home. It's our first." She reached for her husband's hand. "We brought the twins here from the hospital after they were born. I enjoy our church, and Knowlton Elementary has been such a blessing for the girls. But your idea is good. Do we have to put a sign in the front yard, or can we just let the Lord send a buyer?"

David laughed. "Now you sound like Vanessa and her wool sweater. You really want to make it hard for the Lord, don't you?"

Helen frowned. "I just want to make sure God wants us to move, because I'm not sure I do. It would be nice to visit Shadow Creek; I think that might help us make a decision."

"Let's just keep praying. I think the Lord will share His plan for us in His own time." Mr. Jacobson gave his wife a squeeze, and the two headed toward the master bedroom for some much-needed rest.

243

Story (continued)

The next evening David Jacobson took his place at the head of the table. All conversations ceased as he scooted his chair in. Even the twins were too engrossed in the Cheerios they were eating off the trays of their highchairs to chatter.

Father glanced around the table and cleared his throat. "Since we're all together, I want to tell you about something that happened today at work. One of the owners of the design studio next to my law office stopped by for a few minutes. He mentioned how much they're growing because of development and design work they're doing for local Christian publishers."

He paused a moment to let the drama build before continuing, "The bottom line is they'd like to buy my office. Todd said they need room for more workstations. They'd like to hire a couple more graphic designers, but just don't have the space to set them up with computers. They'd rather not relocate."

Mr. Jacobson studied the faces around the table. "Last night your mother and I discussed putting the house up for sale, but we haven't discussed selling the office. If our house would sell quickly, we'd be free to move to Montana. Real estate is not moving very fast right now, which is one reason I'd be hesitant to move without selling."

Rebecca asked the first question. "Aren't we at least going to go look at the ranch and meet the people? What if we sell everything and don't like Montana at all?"

"That's a good point, Rebecca." Father picked up his napkin and spread it across his lap. "Which brings me to the next thing I want to discuss. How would you four older girls like to fly out with your mother and me to visit the ranch? Mrs. Hill has offered to watch the twins for us. I called the ranch today and Tyler says the end of this week will work well for them. I made reservations today."

Everyone started talking at once. Rachel didn't think she ever wanted to move. Natalie agreed wholeheartedly. Rebecca, as the oldest, tried to be mature and said she wanted to see the place first. Vanessa didn't say much as she rubbed the wool of the navy sweater she was wearing. "Maybe the house won't sell," she finally added. Helen caught the eye of her husband at the far end of the table, smiled, and shrugged her shoulders.

The next weekend, the Jacobson family stopped on the steps as they were leaving church to chat with the Larkin family.

Coach pulled Mr. Jacobson aside. "So how was the trip, David?" he asked.

The dark-haired man got right to the point. "We're moving. We decided on the plane coming home."

"How do your kids feel?" Coach glanced over at the women and girls.

"They all agree."

"Amazing! Your house sell, too?"

"We have an offer. Someone called about buying my law practice, and came to look at both it and the house before we flew out Thursday morning. My head's still spinning. God has opened every door. We believe He wants us to move."

"What convinced the girls?"

"Tyler Hansan and his family. They were wonderful. The girls immediately saw how they could be a part of God's work. They'll miss their friends here, but they can't help but see the needs out West as well as God's guidance in this move."

"Well, isn't that what God promises?" Coach Larkin slapped his friend on the back. "'Trust in the Lord with all your heart; and lean not unto your own understanding. In all your ways acknowledge Him, and He will direct your paths.'"

David Jacobson smiled. "That's quite a promise, Edward! But so true. When we reverence the Lord, He shares the secrets of His promises. But hold on tight—you never know what'll happen!"

2 Discussion Time

Check understanding of the story and development of personal values.

- Tell about a friend of yours who has moved away.
- What are some ways you can still keep in touch with your distant friend?
- How do you feel about it?
- How did Laney feel about her friend Rachel moving?
- How did the Jacobsons decide God's will was for them to move?
- How do you think Laney will feel when Rachel tells her they are moving?
- Is it always hard to follow God's will?

A Preview

Write each word as your teacher says it.

Name _____

1. crystal
2. dribble
3. missile
4. angle
5. miracle
6. riddle
7. fragile
8. mingle
9. burial
10. humble
11. mumble
12. particle
13. decimal
14. crumple
15. example
16. multiple
17. entitle
18. double
19. bundle
20. central

Scripture
Psalm 25:14

157

3 Preview
Test for knowledge of the correct spellings of these words.

Customize Your List
On a separate sheet of paper, additional words of your choice may be tested.

Say — I will say each word once, use the word in a sentence, then say the word again. Write the words on the lines in your Worktext.

Correct Immediately!
Say — Let's correct our Preview. I will spell each word out loud. If you spelled a word incorrectly, rewrite it correctly.

Progress Chart
Students may record scores. (Reproducible master provided in Appendix B.)

Lesson 25 | Day 1

1.	crystal	Mrs. Larkin served the girls juice in **crystal** punch cups.
2.	dribble	When Rachel would **dribble** the ball, Wicker would bark loudly.
3.	missile	Wicker tossed his head and the ball flew like a **missile**.
4.	angle	He could jump and catch the ball at any **angle**.
5.	miracle	"It will be a **miracle** if God makes me want to move," exclaimed Rachel.
6.	riddle	God's will sometimes seems like a **riddle** to us.
7.	fragile	We like feeling strong, not **fragile** and helpless.
8.	mingle	Rachel felt a little excitement begin to **mingle** with her worries.
9.	burial	"Dad says there is an ancient Native American **burial** ground near the ranch."
10.	humble	"Dad also says we need to **humble** ourselves and listen to the Holy Spirit."
11.	mumble	"Why does God's will mean my best friend has to move?" she heard Laney **mumble**.
12.	particle	"Not one **particle** of my being will be happy if you leave!" Laney said dramatically.
13.	decimal	Getting the **decimal** in the right place really frustrated her today!
14.	crumple	She felt the urge to **crumple** her worksheet up and toss it into the trash.
15.	example	She looked absently at the **example** at the top of her worksheet.
16.	multiple	She could think of **multiple** reasons why Rachel shouldn't move.
17.	entitle	"Doesn't being your best friend **entitle** me to be upset?" Laney exclaimed.
18.	double	Helen packed **double** of everything for the twins' stay with the Hills.
19.	bundle	Leah and Benjamin are a **bundle** of energy and then some!
20.	central	In the **central** part of the airport, the Jacobsons looked at their itinerary.

245

4 Word Shapes

Help students form a correct image of whole words.

 Say
Look at each word and think about its shape. Now, write the word in the correct Word Shape Boxes. You may check off each word as you use it.

(In many words, the sound of /əl/ is spelled with **le**, **al**, **el**, or **il**. Because spellers cannot rely on a phonetic way of remembering the various spellings, this sound is often difficult.)

 Say
In the Word Shape Boxes, fill in the boxes containing the letters that spell the sound of /əl/ in each word.

 Take a minute to memorize...

Psalm 25:14

Words with /əl/
Lesson **25**

B Word Shapes

Name _____

Using the word bank below, write each word in the correct Word Shape Boxes. Next, in the Word Shape Boxes, fill in the boxes containing the letter or letters that spell the sound of /əl/ in each word.

1. decimal
2. particle
3. bundle
4. central
5. angle
6. fragile
7. crumple
8. entitle
9. missile
10. mumble

11. mingle
12. double
13. riddle
14. humble
15. crystal
16. example
17. multiple
18. burial
19. dribble
20. miracle

Word Bank

angle	crumple	dribble	humble	multiple
bundle	crystal	entitle	mingle	mumble
burial	decimal	example	miracle	particle
central	double	fragile	missile	riddle

158

Answers may vary for duplicate word shapes.

 Be Prepared For Fun

Check these supply lists for **Fun Ways to Spell** - presented **Day 2**. Purchase and/or gather these items ahead of time!

General
• Pencil
• Graph Paper (1 sheet per child)
• Spelling List

Auditory
• Voice Recorder
• Spelling List

Visual
• American Sign Language reproducible master (provided in Appendix B)
• Spelling List

Tactile
• Soccer Ball, Basketball, Tennis Ball, or 4-Square Ball
• Spelling List

246

C Hide and Seek

Name _____

Play Hide and Seek with your words. Fill in a box on the bar graph (left to right) for each word you spell correctly.

LOOK. SAY. SPELL ALOUD. WRITE. SEEK. CHECK.

D Other Word Forms

Using the words below, follow the instructions given by your teacher.

angled	crystallize	fragility	multiply
angles	decimals	humbleness	mumbled
bundled	doubling	humbly	mumbling
bundling	redoubled	mingled	particles
burials	dribbled	mingling	riddled
centrally	dribbling	miracles	riddles
crumpled	entitled	miraculous	
crumpling	entitling	missiles	
crystalline	examples	multiplication	

E Fun Ways to Spell

Initial the box of each activity you finish.

1. Create a crossword puzzle with clues.

3. W·O·R·D Spell your words on a voice recorder.

2. w·o·r·d Spell your words with sign language.

4. B·A·T·C·H Bounce a ball as you spell your words.

Words with /əl/

Lesson 25

159

---

1 Hide and Seek

Reinforce spelling by using multiple styles of learning.

On a white board, Teacher writes each word — one at a time. **Have students:**

- **Look** at the word.
- **Say** the word out loud.
- **Spell** the word out loud.
- **Hide** (teacher erases word.)
- **Write** the word on paper.
- **Seek** (teacher rewrites word.)
- **Check** spelling. If incorrect, rewrite word correctly.

Day 2

2 Other Word Forms

This activity is optional. Have students find and circle the Other Word Forms that are most nearly antonyms of the following:

articulating
unauthorized
strength
smoothed

Lesson 25

3 Fun Ways to Spell

Four activities are provided. Use one, two, three, or all of the activities. Have students initial the box for each activity they complete.

Options:

- assign activities to students according to their learning styles
- set up the activities in learning centers for the students to do throughout the day
- divide students into four groups and assign one activity per group
- do one activity per day

General

To create a crossword puzzle...
- Use a pencil to arrange your words on graph paper.
- Overlap words where letters are shared.
- Don't create any new words.
- Outline each word with a marker and number it.
- Write a clue for each word.
- Erase your words.
- Trade with a classmate and work each other's puzzles.

Auditory

To spell your words using a voice recorder...
- Record yourself as you say and spell each word on your spelling list.
- Listen to your recording and check your spelling.

Visual

To spell your words with sign language...
- Have a classmate read a spelling word to you from the list.
- Spell the word using the American Sign Language alphabet.
- Do this with each word on your list.

Tactile

To bounce a ball as you spell your words...
- Look at the first word on your list.
- Bounce the ball as you say each letter of the word aloud.
- Do this with each word on your list.

1 Working with Words

Familiarize students with word meaning and usage.

Clues

Write this incomplete sentence on the board:

The upper surface inside a room is called a _____.

Guide the students in choosing the word **ceiling**.

(Say) Read each sentence and choose a spelling word for each definition. You may use a dictionary to help you. Write the word in the blank.

Take a minute to memorize...
Psalm 25:14

F Working with Words

Name _____

Clues

Write a spelling word for each clue.

1. _____Central_____ means situated at, in, or near the middle.
2. An object or weapon that is fired or thrown at a target is a _____missile_____.
3. The dot between dollars and cents is called a _____decimal_____ point.
4. Something that is easily broken, damaged, or destroyed is _____fragile_____.
5. A number divided by another number with no remainder is a _____multiple_____.
6. To _____double_____ means to make twice as much in size, strength, or amount.
7. To move a ball or puck with repeated light bounces or kicks is to _____dribble_____ it.
8. A _____particle_____ is a very small piece or part; a tiny portion or speck.
9. Something wrapped or tied up for carrying is called a _____bundle_____.
10. To _____mumble_____ is to talk indistinctly by lowering the voice.
11. To mix or bring together in combination, usually without loss of individual characteristics, is to _____mingle_____.
12. The figure formed by two lines diverging from a common point is called an _____angle_____.
13. A _____miracle_____ is an event that appears unexplained by the laws of nature and so is held to be an act of God.
14. To crush together or press into wrinkles is to _____crumple_____.
15. The act of placing something in a grave or a tomb is a _____burial_____.
16. A _____riddle_____ is a question or statement requiring thought to understand.
17. To be _____humble_____ is to be meek or modest in behavior and attitude.
18. A _____crystal_____ is a glass-like mineral, especially a transparent form of quartz.
19. One thing that is representative of a group as a whole is an _____example_____.
20. To furnish with a right or claim to something is to _____entitle_____.

Word Bank

angle	crumple	dribble	humble	multiple
bundle	crystal	entitle	mingle	mumble
burial	decimal	example	miracle	particle
central	double	fragile	missile	riddle

160

248

G Dictation

Name _____

Write **each sentence as your teacher dictates.** Use correct punctuation.

1. Selling the house and the law practice was like a double miracle.

2. The girls saw examples of how they could be part of God's work.

3. She mumbled as she swept up multiple particles of crystal from the broken glass.

H Proofreading

If a word is misspelled, fill in the oval by that word. If all the words are spelled correctly, fill in the oval by **no mistake**.

1. ● dribbel
   ○ double
   ○ afternoon
   ○ no mistake

2. ○ humble
   ○ brother-in-law
   ○ basketball
   ● no mistake

3. ○ mumble
   ● particel
   ○ driveway
   ○ no mistake

4. ○ miracle
   ○ candlestick
   ○ evergreen
   ● no mistake

5. ○ bundle
   ○ riddle
   ○ grasshopper
   ● no mistake

6. ○ fragile
   ○ foolproof
   ● missill
   ○ no mistake

7. ● angul
   ○ grassland
   ○ greenhouse
   ○ no mistake

8. ● mingel
   ○ broadcast
   ○ footnote
   ○ no mistake

9. ○ crumple
   ○ old-fashioned
   ● decimel
   ○ no mistake

10. ○ example
    ○ multiple
    ○ peppermint
    ● no mistake

11. ● buriul
    ○ entitle
    ○ password
    ○ no mistake

12. ○ crystal
    ● centrel
    ○ newborn
    ○ no mistake

161

1 Dictation

Reinforce correct spelling by using current and previous words in context.

(Say) Listen as I read each sentence and then write it in your Worktext. Remember to use correct capitalization and punctuation. (Slowly read each sentence twice. Sentences are found in the Student Worktext to the left.)

2 Proofreading

Familiarize students with standardized test format and reinforce recognition of misspelled words.

(Say) Look at each set of words. If a word is misspelled, fill in the oval by that word. If all the words are spelled correctly, fill in the oval by **no mistake**.

249

3 Hide and Seek

Reinforce correct spelling of current spelling words. Repeat this activity from Day 2.

4 Vocabulary Extension

Have your students complete this activity to strengthen spelling ability and expand vocabulary. The reproducible master is provided in Appendix A as shown on the inset page to the right.

1 Posttest

Visit the **A Reason For** website to download free, printable Posttest pages.

I will say the word once, use it in a sentence, then say it again. Write your words on a separate sheet of paper.

Progress Chart

Students may record scores. (Appendix B)

Personal Dictionary

Students may add any words they have misspelled to their personal dictionaries. (Appendix B)

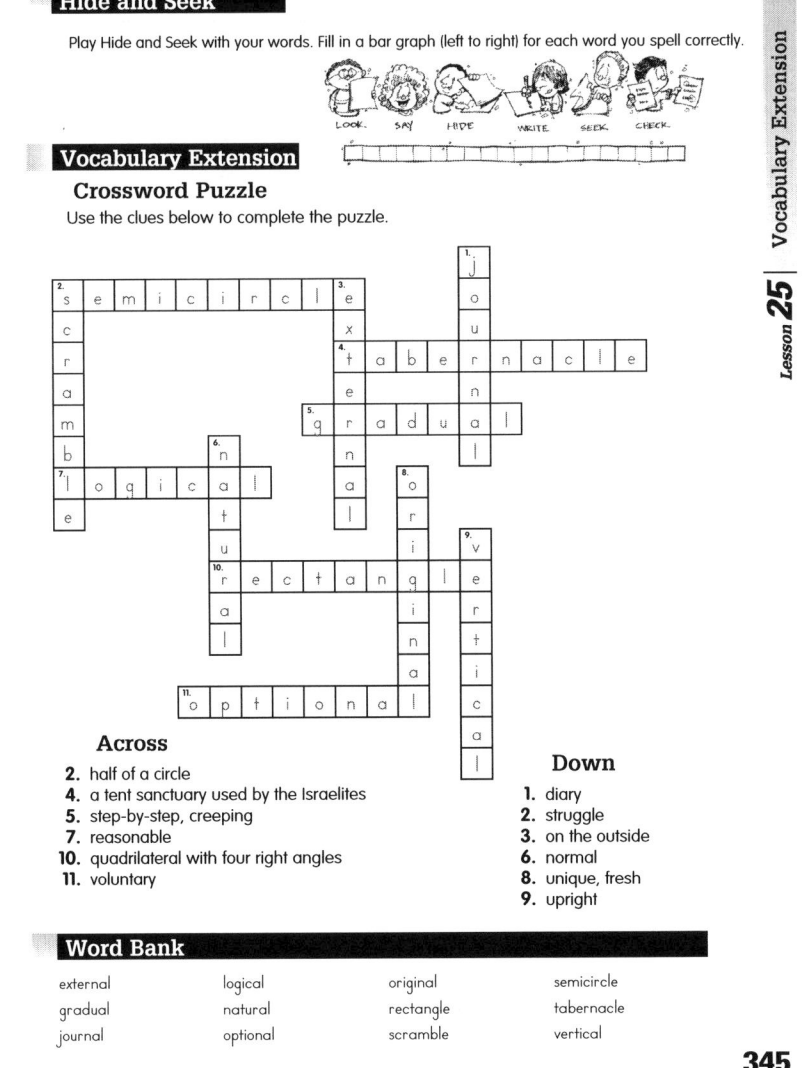

Hide and Seek

Play Hide and Seek with your words. Fill in a bar graph (left to right) for each word you spell correctly.

LOOK. SAY. HIDE. WRITE. SEEK. CHECK.

Vocabulary Extension

Crossword Puzzle

Use the clues below to complete the puzzle.

Across

2. half of a circle
4. a tent sanctuary used by the Israelites
5. step-by-step, creeping
7. reasonable
10. quadrilateral with four right angles
11. voluntary

Down

1. diary
2. struggle
3. on the outside
6. normal
8. unique, fresh
9. upright

Word Bank

external	logical	original	semicircle
gradual	natural	rectangle	tabernacle
journal	optional	scramble	vertical

345

#	Word	Sentence
1.	dribble	"If you **dribble** the ball, Wicker goes absolutely nuts!" laughed Laney.
2.	angle	"Watch him; Wicker can catch this tennis ball from any **angle**," Laney said.
3.	missile	Wicker lunged through the air like a **missile** to catch the tennis ball.
4.	double	"When we mix up the cookies, let's make a **double** batch," said Laney.
5.	particle	The girls scraped the last **particle** of cookie dough from the bowl.
6.	crystal	They thought it was fun to drink out of **crystal** cups at dinner time.
7.	mumble	"I know it's wrong to **mumble** and grumble," confessed Laney.
8.	example	"You've been a good **example** to me and a great friend!" Laney said.
9.	entitle	"Doesn't that **entitle** me to feel upset that you're leaving?" she questioned.
10.	humble	"I'm learning to **humble** myself—more listening, less talking," Rachel told her.
11.	mingle	"I actually feel some excitement starting to **mingle** with my anxiousness."
12.	burial	"There's a Native American **burial** ground near the ranch," she told Laney.
13.	fragile	"I don't really enjoy feeling **fragile** and not in control," confessed Rachel.
14.	decimal	Laney couldn't concentrate enough to put the **decimal** in the right place.
15.	crumple	She wanted to **crumple** up her math homework and throw it away!
16.	multiple	It was easy to think of **multiple** reasons Rachel should stay.
17.	bundle	"Here's another **bundle** of diapers for the twins," said Mrs. Jacobson.
18.	central	"Let's stay in a **central** location till they call our flight number," said Dad.
19.	riddle	God does not want His will for us to be a giant **riddle**.
20.	miracle	"I know it's a **miracle**, but I want to move now," said Rachel amazed.

I Game

Name _____

Board the plane with the Jacobsons to visit the ranch. Move one space for each word you or your team spells correctly.

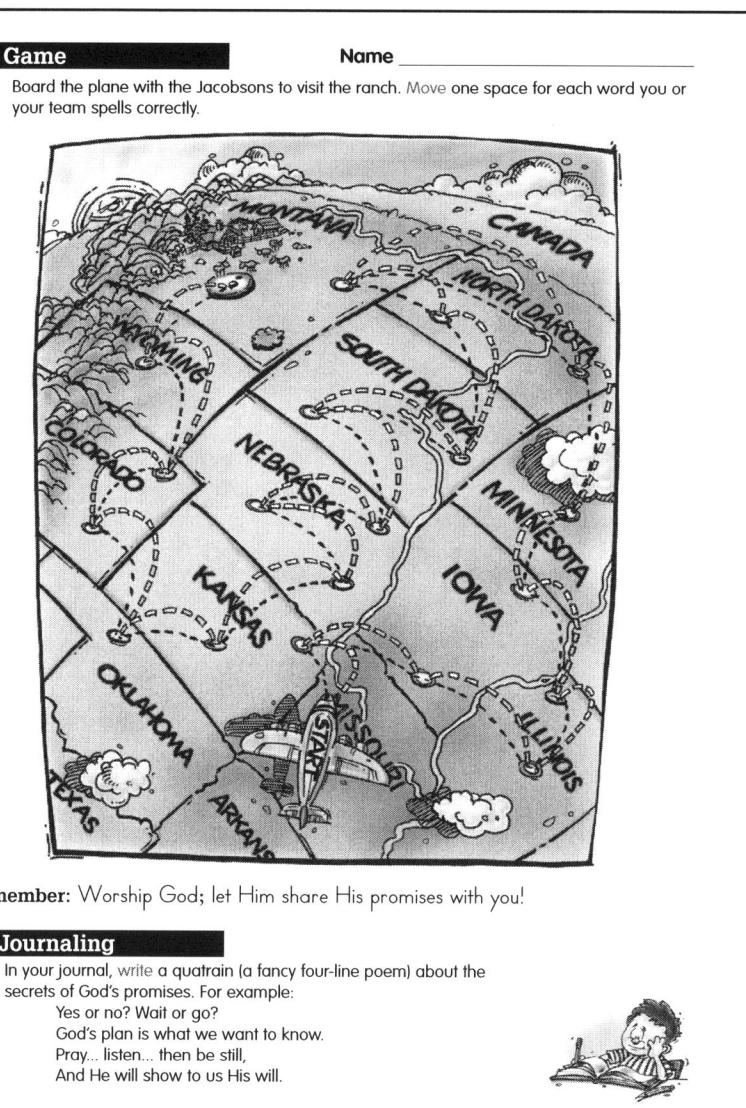

Remember: Worship God; let Him share His promises with you!

J Journaling

In your journal, write a quatrain (a fancy four-line poem) about the secrets of God's promises. For example:

Yes or no? Wait or go?
God's plan is what we want to know.
Pray... listen... then be still,
And He will show to us His will.

162

How to Play:

- Divide the class into two teams.
- Have each student place his/her game piece on Start.
- Have a student from team A go to the board.
- Say the spelling word.
- Have the student write the word on the board.
- If correct, instruct each member of team A to move his/her game piece forward one space.
- Alternate between teams A and B.
- The team to reach the ranch first is the winner.
- **Small Group Option**: Students may play this game without teacher direction in small groups of two or more.

2 Game

Reinforce spelling skills and provide motivation and interest.

Materials

- game page (from student text)
- game pieces (1 per child)
- game word list

Game Word List

1. double
2. dribble
3. humble
4. mumble
5. particle
6. miracle
7. bundle
8. riddle
9. fragile
10. missile
11. angle
12. mingle
13. decimal
14. crumple
15. example
16. multiple
17. burial
18. entitle
19. central
20. crystal

3 Journaling

Provide a meaningful reason for correct spelling through personal writing.

Review the story using discussion leads provided on the following page. Encourage students to apply the Scriptural value in their journaling.

251

(Say) • What are ways God reveals His will to us? (Brainstorm. You may want to write students' ideas on the board. The Bible, parents, teachers, nature…Christian friends could be included.)

• What did the Jacobsons do to prepare themselves for God's answer? (Prayed together and individually)

• How did God reveal the "secret of his promises" to the Jacobson family? (The business and house have a buyer. The whole family loved Shadow Creek Ranch. All the girls saw how they could be a part of God's work and agreed the family should move.)

• Does God always quickly and clearly reveal His will for your life?

• Tell about a time you asked God to help you make a decision.

• There are four quarters in a dollar. There are four cups in a quart. A quadrangle has four angles. What do you think a quatrain is? A quatrain is a four-line poem—rhymed or unrhymed. Like a triplet, it can have a lot of different rhyming patterns. All four lines can rhyme (aaaa). The first two lines can rhyme and then the last two (aabb). Sometimes the first line rhymes with the third and the second with the fourth (abab). The second and fourth lines may be the only ones that rhyme (abac). Quatrains are a common form of poetry.

• When you write a quatrain, you may choose whatever rhyming pattern you like best.

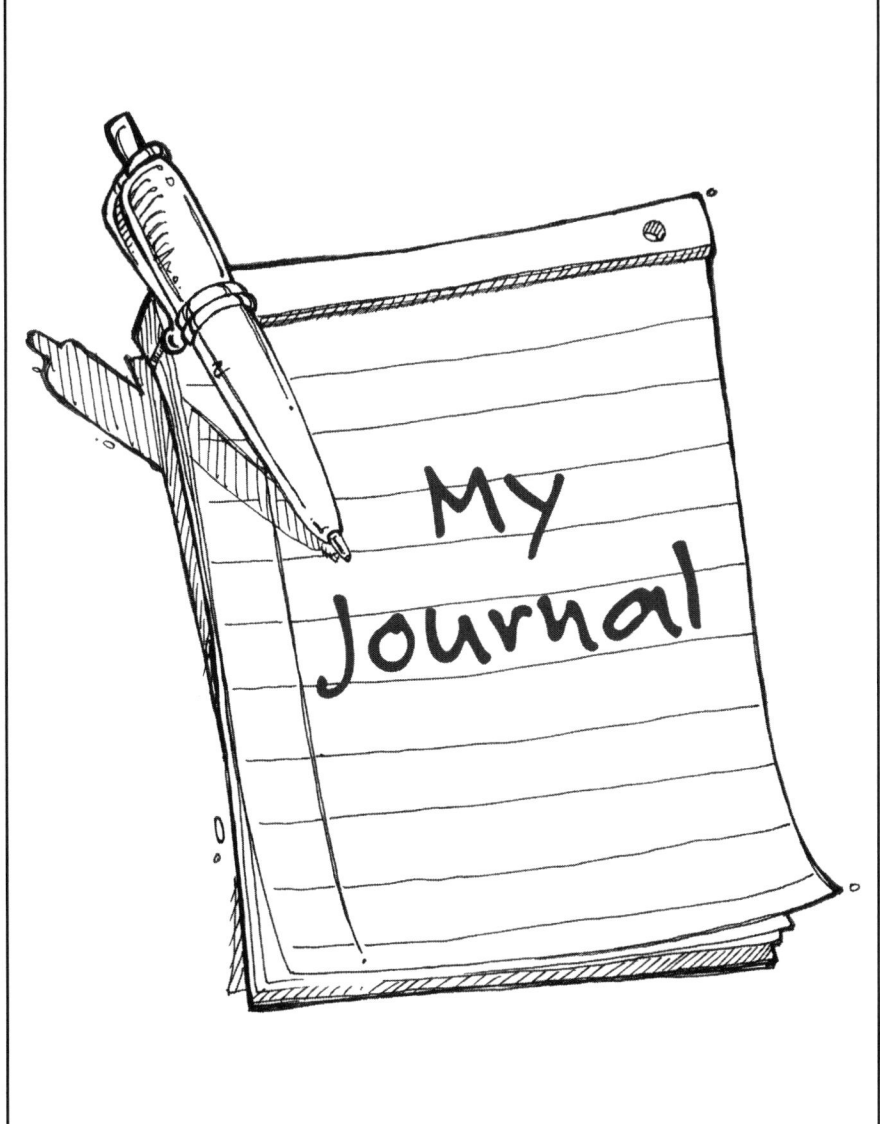

Here are a few words named for people.

BEGONIA	*Michel Bégon*
BOYSENBERRY	*Rudolph Boysen*
MAVERICK	*Samuel A. Maverick*
SANDWICH	*John Montagu,*
	the Fourth Earl of Sandwich
DUNCE	*John Duns Scotus*
	(who was actually very smart)
SAXOPHONE	*Antoine Joseph Sax*
SIDEBURNS	*Gen. Ambrose Everett Burnside*
TEDDY BEAR	*Theodore Roosevelt*

Home Plans and Helping

Just when Setsuko's family has saved enough to build a home of their own, the Johansen's car won't run anymore. What will the Nomas do?

"**O**kasan! Come here please!" Setsuko sat on her bedroom floor surrounded by various-sized wooden boxes.

"What happened here, Hurricane Suzy-Q?" Mrs. Noma stopped in the doorway, wiping her hands on a kitchen towel.

Setsuko held up one of the wooden boxes. "I can't find anywhere to put these. My dresser's full, my closet's full, even the storage boxes under my bed are full! What am I going to do with all these boxes? They've got to go someplace safe, but every place was already crammed before Grandmother sent me these beautiful dolls!"

Mrs. Noma stepped carefully over the boxes to open the closet. "Hmmm. I see what you mean." She tried unsuccessfully to rearrange the shelf and gain more space.

"Maybe I should just leave the display up all year." Setsuko removed the ornate empress doll from her box. The doll was dressed in an elaborate imperial silk wedding kimono, complete with a phoenix coronet and flowering tassels of coral beads. "When they were all in the dining room I didn't have to worry about storing them."

"That would never do!" Mrs. Noma lifted the edge of the bedspread and searched in vain for storage space under the bed. "Who knows what might happen to you if we left them displayed after March 3?"

"What do you mean, something might happen to me?"

"Well, you know that these dolls are made for Girls' Day, which is March 3. It's a spring celebration for girls, just when the ornamental peach trees are in bloom." Mrs. Noma sat down on

Setsuko's bed and picked up one of the wooden boxes. "Traditionally, the dolls are given to a girl on her first Girls' Day by relatives and close friends. They're often passed from mother to daughter as family heirlooms."

"I know all that." Setsuko smoothed the empress's shiny silk kimono. "What does that have to do with something happening to me?"

"It has to do with timing, Setsuko. About 10 days before the festival, a seven-tiered stand—seven is thought to be a lucky number—is set up in the best room of the house. It's draped with red, which also stands for good luck. The 15 special dolls are carefully unwrapped and arranged on the stand, with the emperor and empress on the top."

"We did all that—so what does it have to do with me?" Setsuko replaced the empress in her box.

"On Girls' Day, girls eat rice cakes and crackers." Mrs. Noma stroked the emperor's smooth black lacquered hat and continued, "Although people display these dolls from the middle of February, it is necessary to put them away on the day of the festival, March 3. The tradition is that while the set of dolls is displayed, bad luck is transferred from girls to the dolls. So you have to put them away as soon as the festival is over. Otherwise, bad luck may return and they may be doomed."

"Doomed!" Setsuko squeaked in alarm.

"Of course, the real reason we took the display down on the third was that I needed the space in the dining room." Mrs. Noma laughed as she put the lid back on the emperor's box. "Now, if we just had a place to store them." She stood up and moved toward the door.

"Why don't you stack the boxes in that corner for now."

Setsuko stacked the boxes carefully, remembering that dolls like this could cost between $1,000 and $10,000. Surely she wouldn't be doomed just because the doll boxes weren't really put away. After all, they weren't being displayed!

Setsuko wandered into the small duplex kitchen where her mother was fixing supper. "Okasan, where did this come from?" She picked up a Home Plan Ideas book from the counter.

"I picked that up when I went to the store yesterday." Mrs. Noma turned to her daughter with a sparkle in her eye, "We have enough money saved to start looking for land and choosing the house we want to build."

"ALL RIGHT!" Setsuko twirled herself completely around on the stool three times. "YES!" Then she opened the book and began to flip through it, studying each floor plan.

"I like the way this one looks outside with the porch all across the front, but it's not brick. And I like the way this one has a huge utility room near the back door—a great place to keep Chimi's stuff and boots and snowsuits and everything." She turned pages in silence for a few moments.

"I found it! Look, Okasan, it's perfect!" Mrs. Noma leaned over the counter while Setsuko pointed out the merits of the Open Country plan. "See, it's brick with a big porch and lots of windows. It's got a big utility room by the back door and a workshop area in the garage." Her index finger pointed out each item on the floor plan as she spoke. "And look here—this bedroom has a bay window and a huge walk-in closet! I'd have plenty room for the dolls and all my other stuff if we built this house!"

"Which house, Suzy-Q?" Mr. Noma came through the door from the carport.

"Otosan!" Setsuko launched herself at her father. "Can we really start looking for a place to build our house? Are you sure we have enough money? When can we look? How long will it take to build? Can I choose all the paint and carpet and stuff for my room?"

"Let's see now," Mr. Noma held up fingers as he counted off answers to Setsuko's questions, "Yes. I think so. Maybe this weekend. I don't know. Probably."

Mrs. Noma laughed, "If you don't want all the answers at once, Setsuko-chan, don't ask all the questions at once!" She nudged the house plan book across the counter towards her husband as the phone rang. "I do like that Open Country plan Setsuko found. See what you think while I get the phone."

Setsuko perched beside her father and waited for him to look over the house plan.

Mrs. Noma squeezed the phone between her shoulder and ear as she stirred something on the stove. "Oh, hi, Paula....Hmmm....Yes, I see....Certainly. I'd be glad to and it's no problem at all....I'm sure.... Right....7:30 tomorrow morning will be fine. Don't worry, Paula. I'm glad you called me. After all, what are friends for?...Okay, bye."

Mrs. Noma put the lid back on the pot and set the phone on the counter. "I do like this floor plan." Mr. Noma thumped the page in front of him. "It's really nice the way the kitchen is so open to the family room. The whole design appears to be well thought out, don't you think, Sweetheart?"

"Mmm-hmm, I do." Mrs. Noma joined her husband and daughter at the bar, but seemed preoccupied. "That was Paula Johansen on the phone. You know how hard she's been trying to turn her life around—working two jobs now, going to meetings to get help in controlling her drinking and to be a better mother. Well, apparently her old car quit, and the mechanics say it's no use to try fixing it anymore. She called to ask for a ride, to get the girls to school and her to work tomorrow."

Later, as the three Nomas sat around the supper table, Mr. Noma put down his fork. "You know, I keep thinking we ought to do something about Paula's car."

"You too?" Mrs. Noma smiled at her husband. "That thought keeps crossing my mind as well. It just seems like the right thing to do, doesn't it?"

"What do you think, Suzy-Q?" Both parents turned to Setsuko. "We wouldn't be able to go ahead with building a house for a while longer if we get a car for Mrs. Johansen. How would you feel about that?"

The half-chewed bite in Setsuko's mouth suddenly seemed like sawdust. "Uh, um. Well, we've, uh, been waiting so long already to get a real house..." Setsuko paused. She'd been going to say that it wasn't fair to have to wait any longer, but deep inside she knew what Jesus would do and wasn't she supposed to follow His example? She swallowed hard. "...so I guess since we've waited this long it won't hurt to wait a while longer." She even managed a small smile.

Mrs. Noma reached over and squeezed her hand. Mr. Noma grinned. "So it's settled. I'll talk to Judy tomorrow. She's one of my assistants at the hospital, and her husband repairs wrecked cars that are practically new otherwise, then sells them for a reasonable price." He picked up his fork, but paused before taking another bite. "Keep that Open Country plan handy, though. Sooner or later, we'll be ready to build."

After she'd crawled into bed that night Setsuko looked around her tiny room. She was disappointed about not getting a big new house right away, but she felt good about helping Sarah's mom. She noticed the special doll boxes stacked in the corner and grinned sleepily. She didn't need to worry about being doomed because of some dolls. All she had to do was love God and try to do what He would do. She could trust Him to take care of everything— including when the Noma family got their new house.

Discussion Time

2

Check understanding of the story and development of personal values.

- Why was Setsuko having trouble putting the special dolls away?
- Where had she gotten the dolls?
- The dolls were a part of the celebration of what special Japanese holiday?
- Why had Mrs. Noma bought the Home Plan Idea magazine?
- What kind of room did Setsuko want?
- Who called and asked for a ride?
- What did the Noma family decide to do to help Paula Johansen?
- Do you think they made a good choice? Why or why not?

A Preview

Write each word as your teacher says it.

Name _____

1. anchor
2. clerk
3. solar
4. energy
5. clever
6. West Virginia
7. New Jersey
8. version
9. deliver
10. charter
11. journey
12. major
13. burden
14. error
15. desert
16. deserve
17. molar
18. chapter
19. courage
20. adverb

Words with /ər/ or /ûr/

Lesson **26**

Scripture

Psalm 37:3

163

3 Preview

Test for knowledge of the correct spellings of these words.

Customize Your List

On a separate sheet of paper, additional words of your choice may be tested.

(Say) I will say each word once, use the word in a sentence, then say the word again. Write the words on the lines in your Worktext.

Correct Immediately!

(Say) Let's correct our Preview. I will spell each word out loud. If you spelled a word incorrectly, rewrite it correctly.

Progress Chart

Students may record scores. (Reproducible master provided in Appendix B.)

1.	anchor	She thoughtfully traced the **anchor** embroidered on her sleeve.
2.	clerk	The **clerk** pointed Mrs. Noma to the house plan books.
3.	solar	Many of the house plans were designed to use **solar** power.
4.	energy	The natural **energy** of the sun could heat and cool an entire house.
5.	clever	"What a **clever** design for a kitchen," her mom told Mr. Noma.
6.	West Virginia	Mrs. Noma was eager to receive a plan designed in **West Virginia**.
7.	New Jersey	Mrs. Noma's book was published by a **New Jersey** company.
8.	version	Dad really liked their **version** of a combination toolshed/workshop.
9.	deliver	"I hope the mail will **deliver** a second book today," Mrs. Noma said.
10.	charter	"It's from a **charter** company in energy-efficient house plans," he said.
11.	journey	"This **journey** to build a house is taking too long," complained Setsuko.
12.	major	"A car is a **major** expense, especially for the Johansens," reminded her mom.
13.	burden	"Why do their car problems have to be our **burden**?" she muttered.
14.	error	"Don't you think there is an **error** in your thinking?" her mom questioned.
15.	desert	"They're in the middle of a **desert**, so to speak, and we have the water they need."
16.	deserve	"We have been blessed with a lot we don't **deserve**," said her dad.
17.	molar	Setsuko ran her tongue over her new **molar** and tender gum.
18.	chapter	She read a **chapter** in her Bible and asked God for help with her attitude.
19.	courage	"Give me the **courage** to do right even when I don't feel like it," she prayed.
20.	adverb	She marked the last **adverb**, then put her grammar book in her backpack.

255

4 Word Shapes

Help students form a correct image of whole words.

Say Look at each word and think about its shape. Now, write the word in the correct Word Shape Boxes. You may check off each word as you use it.

(The sound of /ər/ or /ûr/ can be spelled with **ar**, **er**, **ir**, **or**, **ur**, or **ure**. Because spellers cannot rely on a phonetic way of remembering the various spellings, this sound is often difficult.)

Say In the Word Shape Boxes, fill in the boxes containing the letters that spell the sound of /ər/ or /ûr/ in each word.

Take a minute to memorize...

Psalm 37:3

B Word Shapes   Name _____

Using the word bank below, write each word in the correct Word Shape Boxes. Next, in the Word Shape Boxes, fill in the boxes containing the letter or letters that spell the sound of /ər/ or /ûr/ in each word.

Words with /ər/ or /ûr/

Lesson 26

1. solar
2. courage
3. major
4. clerk
5. anchor
6. charter
7. molar
8. desert
9. chapter
10. deliver
11. journey
12. burden
13. energy
14. version
15. West Virginia
16. clever
17. New Jersey
18. deserve
19. adverb
20. error

Word Bank

adverb	charter	deliver	error	New Jersey
anchor	clerk	desert	journey	solar
burden	clever	deserve	major	version
chapter	courage	energy	molar	West Virginia

164

Answers may vary for duplicate word shapes.

Be Prepared For Fun

Check these supply lists for **Fun Ways to Spell** - presented **Day 2**.
Purchase and/or gather these items ahead of time!

General
- Pencil
- Notebook Paper
- Spelling List

Auditory
- Pencil
- Notebook Paper
- Dictionary
- Spelling List

Visual
- Pencil
- Notebook Paper
- Spelling List

Tactile
- Clay
- Spelling List

C **Hide and Seek**

Name_____

Play Hide and Seek with your words. Fill in a box on the bar graph (left to right) for each word you spell correctly.

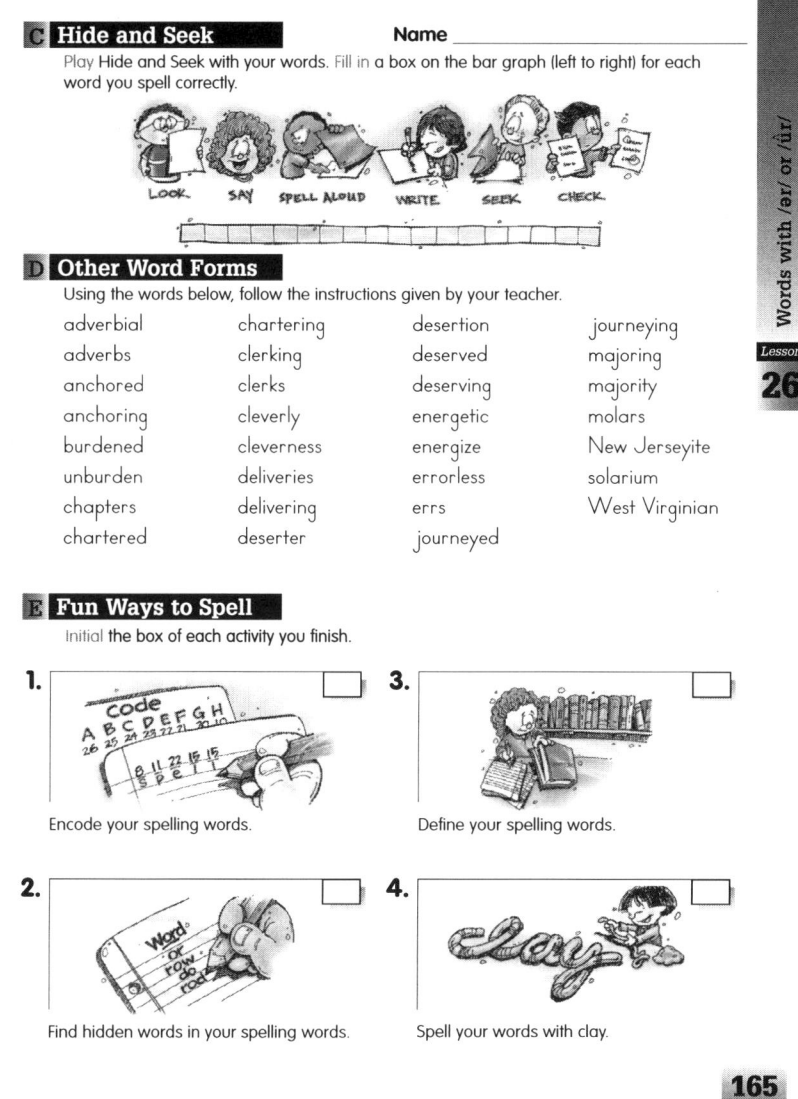

LOOK   SAY   SPELL ALOUD   WRITE   SEEK   CHECK

D **Other Word Forms**

Using the words below, follow the instructions given by your teacher.

adverbial	chartering	desertion	journeying
adverbs	clerking	deserved	majoring
anchored	clerks	deserving	majority
anchoring	cleverly	energetic	molars
burdened	cleverness	energize	New Jerseyite
unburden	deliveries	errorless	solarium
chapters	delivering	errs	West Virginian
chartered	deserter	journeyed	

E **Fun Ways to Spell**

Initial the box of each activity you finish.

1. ☐

Encode your spelling words.

2. ☐

Find hidden words in your spelling words.

3. ☐

Define your spelling words.

4. ☐

Spell your words with clay.

165

---

1 **Hide and Seek**

Reinforce spelling by using multiple styles of learning.

On a white board, Teacher writes each word — one at a time. **Have students:**

- **Look** at the word.
- **Say** the word out loud.
- **Spell** the word out loud.
- **Hide** (teacher erases word.)
- **Write** the word on paper.
- **Seek** (teacher rewrites word.)
- **Check** spelling. If incorrect, rewrite word correctly.

2 **Other Word Forms**

This activity is optional. Have students write original sentences using these Other Word Forms:

anchored
molars
deserving
cleverly

3 **Fun Ways to Spell**

Four activities are provided. Use one, two, three, or all of the activities. Have students initial the box for each activity they complete.

Options:

- assign activities to students according to their learning styles
- set up the activities in learning centers for the students to do throughout the day
- divide students into four groups and assign one activity per group
- do one activity per day

General
To encode your spelling words...
- Write the alphabet on your paper.
- Write your own code for each letter underneath it.
- Write your spelling words in your code.
- Trade papers with a classmate and decode the words.
- Check to make sure your classmate spelled the words correctly.

Auditory
To define your spelling words...
- Ask a classmate to look up a word from your spelling list in the dictionary and read the definition to you, but not the spelling word.
- Decide which word on your list matches this definition and write the word.
- Ask your classmate to check your spelling.
- Switch and continue taking turns.

Visual
To find hidden words in your spelling words...
- Choose a word from your spelling list.
- Write it on your paper.
- Find and write as many smaller words as you can that are contained within your spelling word.
- Do this with each word.

Tactile
To spell your words with clay...
- Roll pieces of clay into ropes.
- Use the ropes to make the letters of each word.
- Put them in the right order to spell each word.
- Check your spelling.

Familiarize students with
word meaning and usage.

Secret Words

The boxed letters in the
acrostic are a phrase
from the Scripture verse
for this week.

Say

Use the clues to write the
words in the puzzle. You
may use a dictionary to help
you. Then write the boxed
letters on the lines below to
find the secret words from
this week's Scripture.

Take a minute
to memorize...

Psalm 37:3

258

F Working with Words   Name _____

Secret Words

Use the clues to write the words in the puzzle. Then write the boxed letters on the lines below
to find the secret words from this week's Scripture.

Words with /ər/ or /ûr/

Lesson **26**

Puzzle answers:

1. b u r d e n
2. d e s e r v e
3. c l e r k
4. W e s t V i r g i n i a
5. e n e r g y
6. a d v e r b
7. s o l a r
8. a n c h o r
9. d e s e r t
10. c o u r a g e
11. e r r o r
12. j o u r n e y
13. d e l i v e r
14. c h a p t e r
15. m o l a r
16. m a j o r
17. t
18. c h a r t e r
19. c l e v e r
20. N e w J e r s e y
21. v e r s i o n

1. hardship, affliction
2. be worthy of
3. salesperson
4. Charleston is the capitol
5. power, force
6. modifies a verb
7. relating to the sun
8. weight for mooring a ship
9. wasteland, sand
10. bravery
11. mistake, blunder
12. expedition, trip
13. rescue from danger
14. division of a book
15. tooth for grinding food
16. dominant, primary
17. letter before **u**
18. founding, original
19. quick-witted, intelligent
20. Trenton is the capitol
21. account, report

Write the secret phrase:
B e   k i n d   a n d   g o o d   t o   o t h e r s .

Word Bank

adverb	charter	deliver	error	New Jersey
anchor	clerk	desert	journey	solar
burden	clever	deserve	major	version
chapter	courage	energy	molar	West Virginia

166

G Dictation

Name _____

Write **each sentence as your teacher dictates. Use correct punctuation.**

1. Mrs. Noma told her daughter a short version of the Girls' Day festival.

2. In the next chapter we will learn about adverbs.

3. The clerk will make plans to deliver the package.

H Proofreading

If a word is misspelled, fill in the oval by that word. If all the words are spelled correctly, fill in the oval by **no mistake**.

1. ● burdin
   ○ missile
   ○ crumple
   ○ no mistake

2. ○ angle
   ● ancher
   ○ particle
   ○ no mistake

3. ○ miracle
   ○ riddle
   ● clirk
   ○ no mistake

4. ○ courage
   ○ decimal
   ● sollar
   ○ no mistake

5. ○ chapter
   ● mollar
   ○ mumble
   ○ no mistake

6. ● new jersey
   ○ deserve
   ○ fragile
   ○ no mistake

7. ○ multiple
   ○ version
   ● journie
   ○ no mistake

8. ○ dribble
   ● majer
   ○ humble
   ○ no mistake

9. ○ energy
   ○ mingle
   ● eror
   ○ no mistake

10. ● desertt
    ○ charter
    ○ example
    ○ no mistake

11. ○ bundle
    ● West Virginya
    ○ double
    ○ no mistake

12. ○ adverb
    ○ clever
    ● delivr
    ○ no mistake

167

Dictation

Reinforce correct spelling by using current and previous words in context.

(Say) Listen as I read each sentence and then write it in your Worktext. Remember to use correct capitalization and punctuation. (Slowly read each sentence twice. Sentences are found in the Student Worktext to the left.)

Proofreading

Familiarize students with standardized test format and reinforce recognition of misspelled words.

(Say) Look at each set of words. If a word is misspelled, fill in the oval by that word. If all the words are spelled correctly, fill in the oval by **no mistake**.

3 Hide and Seek

Reinforce correct spelling of current spelling words. Repeat this activity from Day 2.

4 Vocabulary Extension

Have your students complete this activity to strengthen spelling ability and expand vocabulary. The reproducible master is provided in Appendix A as shown on the inset page to the right.

1 Posttest

Visit the **A Reason For** website to download free, printable Posttest pages.

I will say the word once, use it in a sentence, then say it again. Write your words on a separate sheet of paper.

Progress Chart
Students may record scores. (Appendix B)

Personal Dictionary
Students may add any words they have misspelled to their personal dictionaries. (Appendix B)

Hide and Seek

Play Hide and Seek with your words. Fill in a bar graph (left to right) for each word you spell correctly.

Vocabulary Extension

Trade-off

Choose a word from the word bank to replace the word(s) in parentheses. Write the word in the blank.

1. Several ways to _____preserve_____ (keep) food include drying, salting, freezing, and canning.

2. Each graduate left a short _____interval_____ (pause) before starting down the aisle.

3. The boys have been _____forbidden_____ (prohibited) to climb on the steep, jagged cliffs.

4. The _____primary_____ (main) reason for this meeting is to nominate a mayor for our town.

5. The intense basketball game caused the players to _____perspire_____ (sweat) profusely.

6. Our trip to the mountains turned into an exciting _____adventure_____ (experience).

7. Fog lay low over the valleys due to so much _____moisture_____ (dampness) in the air.

8. After you fill out the form, please place your _____signature_____ (written name) at the bottom.

9. Autumn gives me a lot of _____pleasure_____ (enjoyment) with its crisp air, colorful leaves, and hayrides at Grandpa's farm.

10. I thought the dog leash was _____secure_____ (fastened), but when I came home, Rover was gone.

11. There are several countries in _____Europe_____ (a continent) I would like to visit, such as Germany, Spain, France, and Italy.

12. _____Failure_____ (neglecting) to do your homework will result in bad grades.

Word Bank

adventure	forbidden	perspire	primary
Europe	interval	pleasure	secure
failure	moisture	preserve	signature

1.	clerk	The store **clerk** showed Mrs. Noma the house plan books.
2.	solar	Mrs. Noma liked the innovative use of **solar** power in many of the plans.
3.	energy	She wanted their new home to be **energy**-efficient.
4.	West Virginia	Her favorite plan was designed in **West Virginia**.
5.	clever	"This is a **clever** kitchen design, don't you think?" she asked her husband.
6.	New Jersey	"Did you request the plan book from that **New Jersey** company?" he asked.
7.	charter	"They were a **charter** company in the move to energy-efficient house plans."
8.	deliver	"I expect the carrier to **deliver** it today," his wife replied.
9.	version	"I really liked that one **version** of a detached workshop," said Mr. Noma.
10.	anchor	Setsuko fiddled with the **anchor** embroidered on her sleeve.
11.	molar	A new **molar** breaking through made her gum sore.
12.	journey	"Planning to build a house seems like an endless **journey**," she moaned.
13.	major	"The Johansens' need for a car is **major**," Mrs. Noma said with concern.
14.	burden	"Do we have to bear that **burden** for them?" Setsuko asked sullenly.
15.	courage	"We must have the **courage** and selflessness to give to others," replied her dad.
16.	error	She knew in her heart that her feelings were in **error**.
17.	desert	"They're in a **desert**, sort of, and need water; we've got just that!" said her dad.
18.	chapter	After reading a **chapter** in her Bible, she prayed for help with her attitude.
19.	deserve	"God, thank you for all I have that I don't even **deserve**," she prayed.
20.	adverb	Before closing her grammar book, she marked one more **adverb** she saw.

I Game

Name _____

Complete the secret phrase by spelling the words from this week's word list.

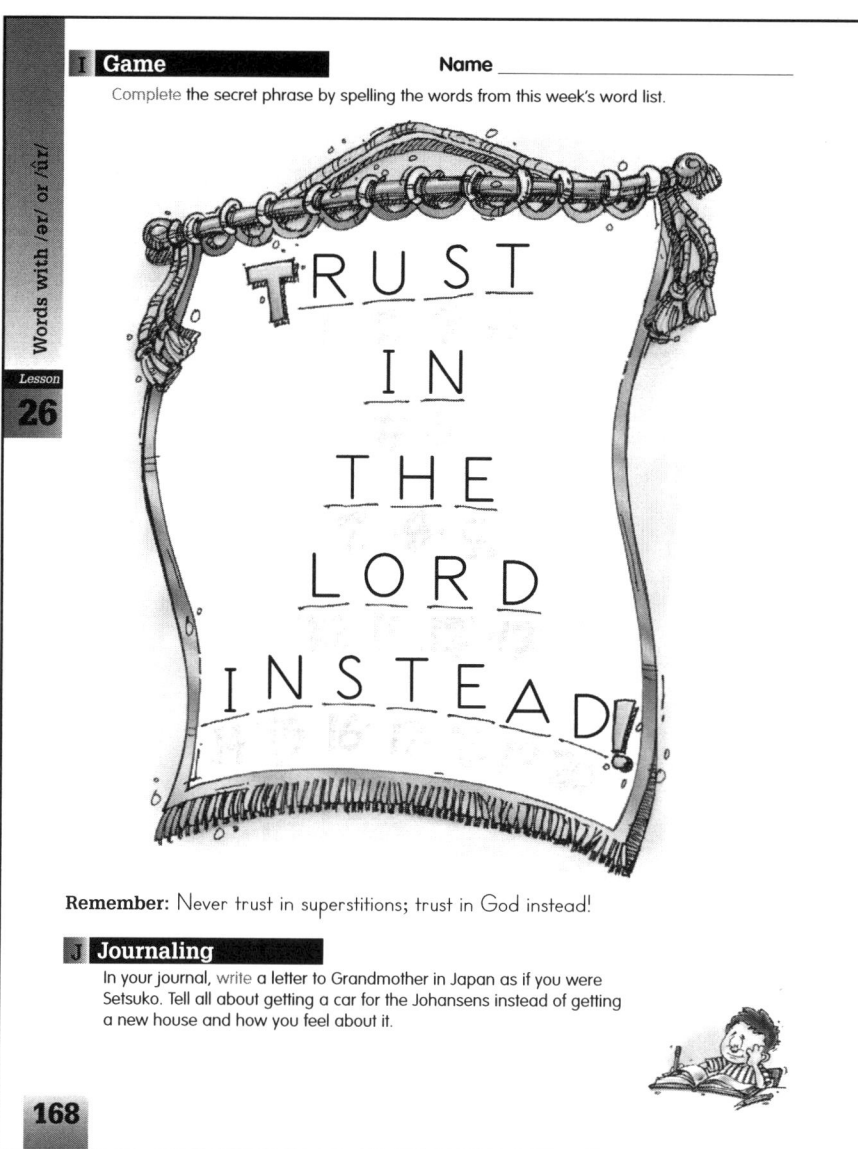

T R U S T

I N

T H E

L O R D

I N S T E A D!

Remember: Never trust in superstitions; trust in God instead!

J Journaling

In your journal, write a letter to Grandmother in Japan as if you were Setsuko. Tell all about getting a car for the Johansens instead of getting a new house and how you feel about it.

168

How to Play:

- Divide the class into two teams, and decide which team will go first.
- Have a student from team A choose a number from 1 to 20.
- Say the word that matches that number from the team's word list.
- Have the student write the word on the board.
- If correct, have each member of team A write the given letter in the matching space on his/her game page.
- Alternate between teams A and B having the students choose a number of a blank space.
- The team to complete the secret phrase first is the winner.

2 Game

Reinforce spelling skills and provide motivation and interest.

Materials

- game page (from student text)
- pencils (1 per child)
- game word list

Game Word List

Team A	Team B
1. burden (R)	1. clever (A)
2. anchor (U)	2. deliver (D)
3. clerk (S)	3. major (R)
4. courage (T)	4. energy (U)
5. solar (I)	5. error (S)
6. molar (N)	6. desert (T)
7. West Virginia	7. deserve (I)
8. (T)	8. charter (N)
9. New Jersey	9. chapter (T)
10. (H)	10. adverb (H)
11. version (E)	11. clever (E)
12. journey (L)	12. deliver (L)
13. major (O)	13. burden (O)
14. energy (R)	14. anchor (R)
15. error (D)	15. clerk (D)
16. desert (I)	16. courage (I)
17. deserve (N)	17. solar (N)
18. charter (S)	18. molar (S)
19. chapter (T)	19. West Virginia
20. adverb (E)	20. (T)

3 Journaling

Provide a meaningful reason for correct spelling through personal writing.

Review the story using discussion leads provided on the following page. Encourage students to apply the Scriptural value in their journaling.

- Why couldn't Setsuko find a place to put the dolls in her bedroom? (Her bedroom was small and what space there was had already been filled with other things.)

- What are her special dolls? (Elaborate Japanese dolls, including an emperor and an empress, that are displayed in the best room of the house for a few weeks before Girls' Day, when they are taken down.)

- Why did traditional superstition dictate that they had to be put away on Girls' Day? (The superstition was that the girls of the house would be doomed if the dolls were not put away on March 3.)

- Do you think the Nomas believed the superstition? Why or why not? (No. They believed in God.)

- Why were Setsuko and her parents waiting to look for a place to build a new house? (They were saving the money they would need.)

- What kind of car did the Nomas plan to get for Paula Johansen? (A car that had been wrecked when it was fairly new and then repaired so it would be a little less expensive but still dependable.)

- How did getting the car for the Johansens affect their plans for a house of their own? (They would have to wait and save some more money.)

My Journal

Homophones have one pronunciation and more than one spelling.

6-way homophone
air   are   heir   ere   err   e'er
(This pronunciation of "are" is for 100 square meters, i.e. 1/100 hectare. E'er is a contraction of ever. And of course there is also Jane Eyre.)

4-way homophone
right   Wright   rite   write

3-way homophones
aisle   isle   I'll
do   dew   due
for   four   fore

Table-Top Refuge

A flooded Mason Creek puts Heather and her family in danger.

"Come on, Heather! I can't hear with you practicing so loud." Collin grabbed sofa pillows and made himself comfortable in front of the TV. He added a few blocks to the tower the Jensen children had been building earlier. A boom of thunder competed with the keyboard, but Heather continued playing without missing a note.

Collin threw a pillow at his sister, just missing the back of her head. The ten-year-old girl was concentrating on the music and didn't even notice. Collin sighed and placed a few more blocks on the tower.

When she finished the song, Heather Starks gazed out the window at the glow of the streetlight. Curtains of rain rippled in windy gusts. She checked her watch. "It's raining again," she announced. "And I'm ready to watch the movie Mom said we could watch. Where's the remote?"

Collin laughed, "Welcome back to planet earth!"

"Here, let me see the remote," Heather directed.

Collin held the remote high. "I don't think so! I remember almost missing that home run because you were switching to nature shows during commercials."

"But you didn't, did you?" Heather smiled.

"Mom!" Heather yelled as she grabbed for the remote held just out of her reach. "I'm ready to start the movie—and he won't share the remote."

Mrs. Starks walked in with a huge bowl of popcorn. "I may take it away from both of you if it's such a bone of contention." Mom held out her hand for the remote. She punched in the right channel before she set the remote on the floor and dipped out bowls of popcorn.

The movie theme music drew their attention to the screen, and no more thought was given to the remote—or the rain.

Halfway through the movie, a flood watch started scrolling across the bottom of the screen.

"When does dad get back?" Collin asked as a commercial began.

"Tomorrow." Mom picked out the last kernels of popcorn from her bowl.

Collin looked out the window. "What if it keeps raining? Will Mason Creek flood?"

"I'm sure it could with all this rain," Mrs. Starks answered.

"How high do you think it'll get?"

"It depends. The longer it rains, the more saturated the ground becomes. Then the water starts running off and filling up all the storm drains, creeks, and rivers. When they get full, things start backing up. I hope this weather system will move through quickly." Mom refilled her popcorn bowl.

"Shhhhh!" Heather interrupted.

Collin was still looking at his mom. "It's not forecasted to."

Mom wiped her buttery fingers on a napkin. "It would take a lot of water to put this town in any kind of danger! I don't think we have anything to worry about, but Dad has to drive through...."

"Shhhh!" Heather interrupted again. "I can't hear the movie."

"Heather, aren't you worried about Dad?"

Moments later the movie disappeared from the screen. "We interrupt this program to bring you the latest report from the National Weather Service. Sebastian and Cole counties are under a flood watch throughout the night. Heavy rains are forecasted to continue. The Illinois River is expected to be out of its banks by late tomorrow morning. Please do not drive or walk into flowing water. If your car is stranded in water, do not stay in it! If you become trapped in your home, remain there until help arrives. Keep a flashlight and cell phone ready for emergency use. I repeat—get out of stranded cars, but remain in your homes. Stay tuned to this station for the latest updates."

Later Mom came into Heather's room to tuck her in for the night. She sat on the edge of the bed and smoothed back her daughter's hair. Rain still slashed against the window and lightning occasionally lit up the room.

"Are you worried about the creek flooding?" Heather asked.

"Not really. This house has been around for many years, and it's never been flooded before. God can keep us safe even if the river floods. Remember that Scripture verse you were practicing on the way home from school today?" Heather nodded.

Mom tucked the covers under her daughter's chin and kissed her nose. "I don't think we have anything to worry about. Here's your flashlight if you need it in the night."

Heather sat up in bed, not knowing how long she'd been asleep or what had awakened her. She rubbed her eyes and tried to shake the fog from her mind. It was still dark. She glanced at the clock beside the bed, but the hands weren't moving. She reached for her flashlight.

Heather was jolted to alertness when her toes felt icy dampness instead of warm carpet. The rain had stopped slashing against the window—but there was an ominous new sound.

Heather headed for the living room when she saw her mom standing at the front window. She aimed her flashlight across the living room floor. Water was seeping under the door, and a little rivulet was running across the wooden floor toward the block tower. She picked up the remote just before the water reached it. Mom

263

waved her toward the window. Their streetlight illuminated a rushing river of brown water. She gazed wide-eyed as objects bobbed through the pool of light and on downstream. They watched in stunned silence until the streetlight went out.

Heather ran to the side window, relieved to see their car still parked on the gravel driveway.

Mrs. Starks took a final look at the rising water before grabbing the phone and dialing her sister's number. "Maria! Maria!" she blurted as soon as her sister answered. "Yes. Our carpet is already wet. Has creek water reached your house yet?… Maria?…Maria!" she cried as the connection was broken. She hurriedly redialed the number—but got no answer.

Mrs. Starks joined her daughter at the back door. Collin followed, rubbing sleep from his eyes. The three stepped out onto the patio in time to see the eastern sky turning pink. "Will the water get any higher?" Heather asked.

"Probably. Even though the rain has stopped here, the smaller streams will keep draining into the river. And it might still be raining upstream. We need to get out of here, but I'm not sure how or where to go. The electricity is off…the radio in the car doesn't work… and my phone isn't working." She paused. "Let's move stuff out of the water before we leave."

"The TV weatherman said we're supposed to stay in our house and out of our cars!" Heather reminded them.

"This wasn't supposed to happen," Collin mumbled.

"Where will we go? How will Dad find us?" Heather prayed as tears rolled down her cheeks, "Lord help us."

The water was now ankle deep— and rising. Mom finally came up with a plan. "I want you both to get dressed. Put on your wool sweaters—they'll be warm even if they get wet. Then let's pick everything up off this wet floor."

Heather was the first to return to the living room. She

felt better with something purposeful to do. She picked up the blocks and put them on the dining room table. Mom looped the end of the drapes over the curtain rods. Collin brought in some cement blocks from the garage and the three of them lifted the couch out of the rising water. Just as they finished, a surge of muddy water pushed the back door open and lapped at the couch fabric. Heather watched the remote float off the coffee table and disappear into the murky water. Something in the water hit her leg, and she screamed. She sloshed to the dining room and climbed up beside the building blocks.

Mom and Collin soon realized the hopelessness of the situation and joined her. They watched numbly as the swirling brown water continued to rise. Heather spoke first. "I wonder why nobody warned us? Are all our neighbors gone?"

Mrs. Starks shrugged. "They're probably as surprised and unprepared as we are. I think the Rozells are out of town. Who knows where the Gunters are?"

"Do you think we should get up on the roof so someone will see us?" Collin finally said.

Mom wasn't sure what to do. "I'm thinking and praying," she finally explained. Heather added a silent prayer to her mom's. She watched as Collin began to build a tower with the blocks. As it got higher, her anxiety began to drain away. She started to hum the tune of a new praise song Mr. Canfield had been teaching them. Heather added a few blocks to Collin's tower. She thought she heard a car engine but realized it was impossible with the street covered with water. Everyone jumped when the front door crashed open and a familiar voice boomed, "What's for breakfast?"

"Dad!" Heather yelled. "You're home early. Where's your rig?"

"I'm a boat driver now, Heather, and I think we'd better eat out this morning!" Dad smiled as he surveyed his children sitting on the dining room table. He sloshed over and turned around so Heather could hop on his back.

"I'm glad you came, Dad." Heather

tightened her arms around him. "Our table seems to be shrinking, and this tower won't keep us out of the muddy water. And I couldn't figure out how God was going to get us out of here. I think sending you in a boat was a good idea."

Dad smiled and patted the arms that clung to his neck. "He's a powerful God, Heather. A powerful God."

Check understanding of the story and development of personal values.

- Talk about a flood you have seen or been in.
- Where is a safe place to be in a flood?
- How did Heather feel when something hit her leg in the swirling brown water?
- Where did Heather and Collin go as the water started to rise?
- Whom did Heather silently ask to help her?
- How did she begin to feel after praying?
- How can you tell her feelings were changing?
- Who came to rescue the Stark family?

A Preview

Write each word as your teacher says it.

Name _____

1. nucleus
2. obvious
3. radius
4. interest
5. fungus
6. cirrus
7. cumulus
8. octopus
9. mollusk
10. restless
11. stillness
12. witness
13. citrus
14. virus

15. congress
16. walrus
17. services
18. aimless
19. closeness
20. reckless

Words with /əs/ or /is/

Lesson **27**

Scripture

Psalm 59:16

169

3 Preview

Test for knowledge of the correct spellings of these words.

Customize Your List
On a separate sheet of paper, additional words of your choice may be tested.

(Say) I will say each word once, use the word in a sentence, then say the word again. Write the words on the lines in your Worktext.

(Say) **Correct Immediately!**
Let's correct our Preview. I will spell each word out loud. If you spelled a word incorrectly, rewrite it correctly.

Progress Chart
Students may record scores. (Reproducible master provided in Appendix B.)

Day 1

---

1. nucleus — The **nucleus** of the storm shimmered in green on the weather map.
2. obvious — It was **obvious** that this storm was potentially dangerous.
3. radius — The map showed the **radius** of the storm was increasing.
4. interest — Their **interest** in the weather bulletins grew as the clouds darkened.
5. fungus — "Wet carpet smells like some kind of **fungus**!" grimaced Heather.
6. cirrus — "Those aren't **cirrus** clouds," said Collin importantly.
7. cumulus — "They aren't **cumulus** clouds either," he said knowingly.
8. octopus — "It felt like an **octopus** just touched my leg," squealed Heather.
9. mollusk — "Maybe it was just a **mollusk**," Collin joked.
10. restless — As the storm grew worse, Heather and Collin grew **restless**.
11. stillness — In the **stillness**, the lapping of the water against the house seemed loud.
12. witness — "I've never had any desire to **witness** a flood firsthand," he said.
13. citrus — "Our little **citrus** tree is all under water now," noticed Heather.
14. virus — "This would be perfect weather to come down with a **virus**," Heather mused.
15. congress — "We should have a **congress** on the dining room table," directed Mom.
16. walrus — "I'm sure I look like a **walrus** on a rock," she said.
17. services — "We could use the **services** of a rescue party anytime now!" they agreed.
18. aimless — "Our prayers are not **aimless**!" encouraged Mom.
19. closeness — She thanked God for His **closeness** and asked for His help.
20. reckless — Now was not the time for **reckless** abandon.

Word Shapes

4

Help students form a correct image of whole words.

(Say) Look at each word and think about its shape. Now, write the word in the correct Word Shape Boxes. You may check off each word as you use it.

(The sound of **/əs/** can be spelled with **as**, **us**, or **ous**. The sound of **/is/** can be spelled with **es**, **ess**, or **ice**. Because spellers cannot rely on a phonetic way of remembering the various spellings, this sound is often difficult.)

(Say) In the Word Shape Boxes, fill in the boxes containing the letters that spell the sound of **/əs/** or **/is/** in each word.

Take a minute to memorize...

Psalm 59:16

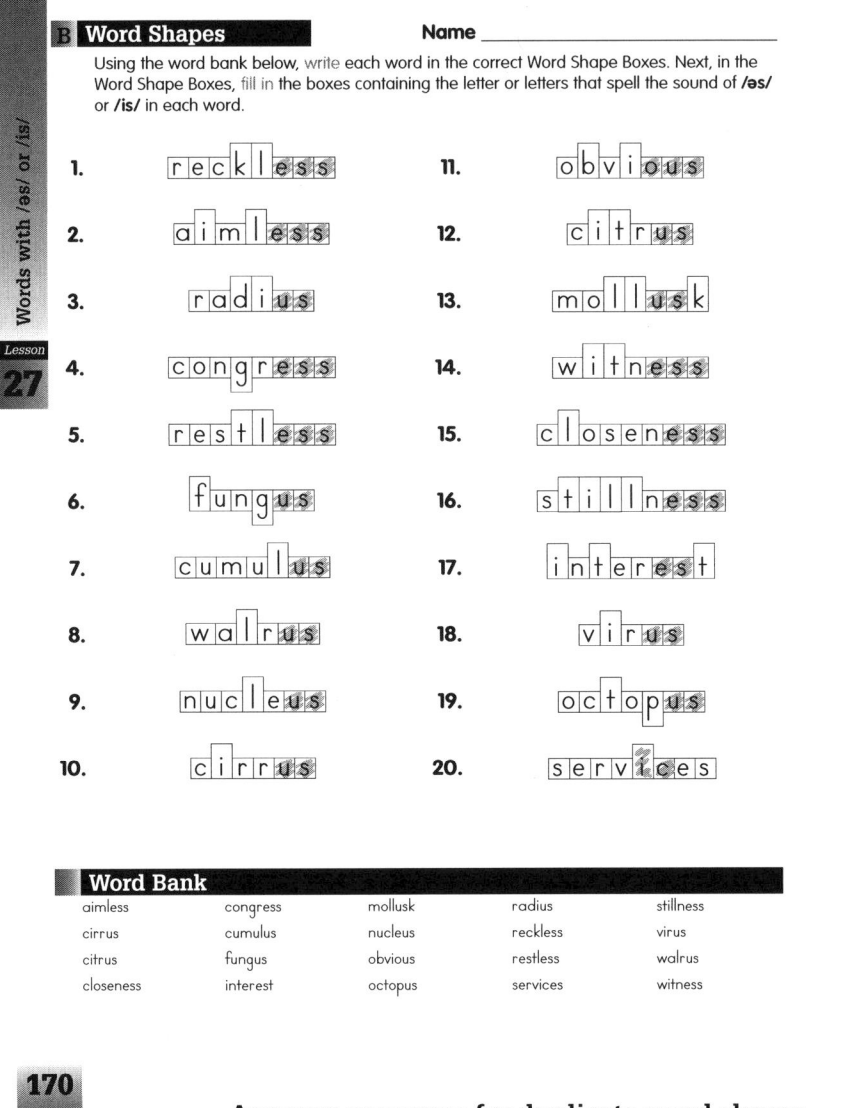

B **Word Shapes**

Name _____

Using the word bank below, write each word in the correct Word Shape Boxes. Next, in the Word Shape Boxes, fill in the boxes containing the letter or letters that spell the sound of **/əs/** or **/is/** in each word.

Words with /əs/ or /is/

Lesson **27**

1. r e c k l e s s
2. a i m l e s s
3. r a d i u s
4. c o n g r e s s
5. r e s t l e s s
6. f u n g u s
7. c u m u l u s
8. w a l r u s
9. n u c l e u s
10. c i r r u s

11. o b v i o u s
12. c i t r u s
13. m o l l u s k
14. w i t n e s s
15. c l o s e n e s s
16. s t i l l n e s s
17. i n t e r e s t
18. v i r u s
19. o c t o p u s
20. s e r v i c e s

Word Bank

aimless	congress	mollusk	radius	stillness
cirrus	cumulus	nucleus	reckless	virus
citrus	fungus	obvious	restless	walrus
closeness	interest	octopus	services	witness

170

Answers may vary for duplicate word shapes.

Be Prepared For Fun

Check these supply lists for **Fun Ways to Spell** - presented **Day 2**.
Purchase and/or gather these items ahead of time!

General
- Pencil
- 3 X 5 Cards cut in half (20 per child)
- Spelling List

Auditory
- Spelling List

Visual
- Pencil
- Notebook Paper
- Spelling List

Tactile
- Blackboard and Chalk
  -OR-
- White Board and Marker
- Spelling List

266

C Hide and Seek Name _____

Play Hide and Seek with your words. Fill in a box on the bar graph (left to right) for each word you spell correctly.

LOOK SAY SPELL ALOUD WRITE SEEK CHECK

D Other Word Forms

Using the words below, follow the instructions given by your teacher.

(aimlessly)	cumuli	obviousness	serviced
aimlessness	fungi	octopuses	servicing
cirri	(interested)	radii	stillest
closer	uninteresting	(recklessly)	viruses
closest	mollusks	recklessness	walruses
congressional	nuclei	restlessly	witnessed
congressman	(obviously)	restlessness	witnessing

E Fun Ways to Spell

Initial the box of each activity you finish.

1. match match Spell your words, then play "Concentration."

2. s_e_l_n w_r_s Decode your spelling words.

3. Johnny has a p-u-p-p-y!   Spell your words in a sentence.

4. .sp Play the game "Spelling Backwards."

171

Words with /es/ or /is/

Lesson 27

Day 2 | Lesson 27

1 Hide and Seek

Reinforce spelling by using multiple styles of learning.

On a white board, Teacher writes each word — one at a time. **Have students:**

- **Look** at the word.
- **Say** the word out loud.
- **Spell** the word out loud.
- **Hide** (teacher erases word.)
- **Write** the word on paper.
- **Seek** (teacher rewrites word.)
- **Check** spelling. If incorrect, rewrite word correctly.

2 Other Word Forms

This activity is optional. Have students find and circle the Other Word Forms that are antonyms of the following:

purposefully
carefully
not apparently
inattentive

3 Fun Ways to Spell

Four activities are provided. Use one, two, three, or all of the activities. Have students initial the box for each activity they complete.

Options:

- assign activities to students according to their learning styles
- set up the activities in learning centers for the students to do throughout the day
- divide students into four groups and assign one activity per group
- do one activity per day

General

Spell your words; then play "Concentration"...
- Write each spelling word on a card. Mix your cards and a classmate's cards together. Arrange them face down in five rows of eight. Pick up two cards. If the cards match, play again. If the cards do not match, turn them back over. It is your classmate's turn. Continue taking turns until all the cards are matched. The player with the most cards wins!

Visual

To decode your spelling words...
- Look at the first word on your list.
- Write every other letter of the word on your paper, putting a blank where each missing letter belongs.
- Trade papers with a classmate and fill in the missing letters.
- Check your spelling.

Auditory

To spell your words in a sentence...
- Ask a classmate to read a spelling word to you from the list.
- Spell the word aloud and use it in a sentence.
- Ask your classmate to check your spelling.
- Each correctly spelled word that is used properly in a sentence counts as one point.
- Switch and continue taking turns.

Tactile

To play the game "Spelling Backwards"...
- Ask a classmate to stand behind you and draw the letters to spell a word from your list on your back.
- Write the spelling word on the board as your classmate traces the letters on your back.
- Ask your classmate to check your spelling.
- Trade places and take turns until you have each spelled all the words.

267

Working with Words

Familiarize students with word meaning and usage.

Drawing Conclusions

Explain that to figure something out using logic is to draw a conclusion. On the board write:

You are learning the art of Japanese paper folding. You are learning _____.

Have a volunteer supply the word **origami**.

Complete each conclusion by writing a word from the word bank. You may use a dictionary to help you.

Take a minute to memorize...

Psalm 59:16

F **Working with Words**   Name _____

Lesson 27 · Words with /əs/ or /is/

Drawing Conclusions

Complete each conclusion by writing a word from the word bank.

1. You are studying snails and clams. You are learning about _____mollusk_____s.
2. The night is calm and quiet. Sitting on the porch, you enjoy the _____stillness_____.
3. You see a high-altitude cloud of thin, white patches. It is a _____cirrus_____ cloud.
4. You feel affection towards your parents. You feel a _____closeness_____ to them.
5. You feel like you are getting the flu. You may have caught a _____virus_____.
6. You see dense, fluffy clouds that are rounded on top. These are _____cumulus_____ clouds.
7. You are learning about yeasts, molds, and mushrooms. You are studying _____fungus_____.
8. Draw a line from the center of a circle to the edge. You have drawn the _____radius_____.
9. A doctor, lawyer, dentist, and repairman have something in common. They all provide _____services_____ for people.
10. Your savings account is earning money in the bank. It earns _____interest_____.
11. You are learning about DNA. You study about a cell's _____nucleus_____.
12. You easily understand a joke. The answer is _____obvious_____.
13. You go to the mall without money. Your trip is probably _____aimless_____.
14. You are buying oranges and lemons. You are buying _____citrus_____ fruit.
15. This mollusk has a soft body with eight tentacles. It may be an _____octopus_____.
16. You ride your bike very carelessly. You are being _____reckless_____.
17. You cannot relax or sit still. You are feeling _____restless_____.
18. You see a large marine mammal with long tusks. It is a _____walrus_____.
19. The national legislative body is meeting. It is a meeting of _____congress_____.
20. You saw an accident happen. You are a _____witness_____.

Word Bank				
aimless	congress	mollusk	radius	stillness
cirrus	cumulus	nucleus	reckless	virus
citrus	fungus	obvious	restless	walrus
closeness	interest	octopus	services	witness

172

Lesson 27 | Day 3

G Dictation

Name _____

Write **each sentence as your teacher dictates**. Use **correct punctuation**.

1. It soon became obvious that they could not leave the house.

2. Heather saw the nucleus of the huge storm on the screen.

3. In science class we learned the meanings of cumulus and cirrus.

H Proofreading

If a word is misspelled, fill in the oval by that word. If all the words are spelled correctly, fill in the oval by **no mistake**.

1. ○ chapter
   ● nuckleus
   ○ obvious
   ○ no mistake

2. ○ congress
   ○ New Jersey
   ○ fungus
   ● no mistake

3. ○ deserve
   ○ energy
   ● aimliss
   ○ no mistake

4. ○ cumulus
   ○ adverb
   ● molusk
   ○ no mistake

5. ● reckliss
   ○ restless
   ○ anchor
   ○ no mistake

6. ● cloesness
   ○ clerk
   ○ stillness
   ○ no mistake

7. ○ desert
   ○ witness
   ● octoppus
   ○ no mistake

8. ○ solar
   ○ cirrus
   ○ error
   ● no mistake

9. ○ interest
   ○ journey
   ○ major
   ● no mistake

10. ○ West Virginia
    ● vyrus
    ○ version
    ○ no mistake

11. ● wallrus
    ○ courage
    ○ services
    ○ no mistake

12. ○ citrus
    ● raddius
    ○ burden
    ○ no mistake

173

Dictation

Reinforce correct spelling by using current and previous words in context.

Say

Listen as I read each sentence and then write it in your Worktext. Remember to use correct capitalization and punctuation. (Slowly read each sentence twice. Sentences are found in the Student Worktext to the left.)

Proofreading

Familiarize students with standardized test format and reinforce recognition of misspelled words.

Say

Look at each set of words. If a word is misspelled, fill in the oval by that word. If all the words are spelled correctly, fill in the oval by **no mistake**.

Hide and Seek

Reinforce correct spelling of current spelling words. Repeat this activity from Day 2.

Vocabulary Extension

Have your students complete this activity to strengthen spelling ability and expand vocabulary. The reproducible master is provided in Appendix A as shown on the inset page to the right.

Posttest

Visit the **A Reason For** website to download free, printable Posttest pages.

I will say the word once, use it in a sentence, then say it again. Write your words on a separate sheet of paper.

Progress Chart
Students may record scores. (Appendix B)

Personal Dictionary
Students may add any words they have misspelled to their personal dictionaries. (Appendix B)

Hide and Seek

Play Hide and Seek with your words. Fill in a bar graph (left to right) for each word you spell correctly.

LOOK   SAY   HIDE   WRITE   SEEK   CHECK

Vocabulary Extension

Multiple Choice

Fill in the oval by the word(s) with the same or nearly the same meaning as the word in bold type.

1. conscious
- ● mentally awake or alert
- ○ thoughtful, attentive
- ○ showing self-importance
- ○ taking into account

2. delicious
- ○ easily damaged
- ○ ready-to-eat food products
- ● pleasing to the taste
- ○ harmful, poisonous

3. dangerous
- ○ hang loosely with a swinging motion
- ● likely to inflict injury
- ○ small missile used in a game
- ○ sharp pointed knife for stabbing

4. generous
- ○ unusually intelligent person
- ○ the origin or beginning of something
- ○ bend the knee in worship
- ● free in giving or sharing

5. precious
- ● of great value
- ○ undue hastiness
- ○ highly accurate
- ○ water that falls to earth

6. Celsius
- ○ thin transparent wrapping material
- ● scale for measuring temperature
- ○ relating to the sky
- ○ condemning sternly

7. emptiness
- ○ eternal, everlasting
- ○ threatened with extinction
- ○ wife of an emperor
- ● vacancy, void, hollow

8. loneliness
- ○ length of life
- ● isolation, lacking company
- ○ to hang around idly
- ○ not rigidly fastened

9. readiness
- ○ to understand written language
- ○ already made up for sale
- ○ information printed by a computer
- ● preparedness

10. ugliness
- ○ last in a progression
- ● disagreeableness, repulsiveness
- ○ an open sore that festers
- ○ resentment, taking offense

347

---

1. virus — "Collin, sometimes you're like an annoying **virus**," teased Heather.
2. restless — Heather felt **restless** as they watched the weather bulletin.
3. radius — The weather map showed the **radius** of the storm.
4. nucleus — The **nucleus** of the storm was highlighted in green.
5. interest — Their **interest** in the news grew as the storm worsened.
6. fungus — The smell of the wet carpet reminded Heather of **fungus**.
7. cumulus — "There aren't any **cumulus** clouds up there," Collin said knowingly.
8. aimless — They were not **aimless** in their efforts to keep the couch dry.
9. reckless — Now was not the time to be **reckless**!
10. closeness — No one enjoyed the **closeness** of the cold, muddy water.
11. witness — "I'd really rather not **witness** a flood firsthand," said Collin.
12. octopus — "An **octopus** would like it in here, but I don't!" he exclaimed.
13. mollusk — "Hey, I think I see a **mollusk** down there," he said, trying to be funny.
14. cirrus — There were no **cirrus** clouds to be seen in this severe thunderstorm.
15. citrus — The little **citrus** tree in their backyard was soon covered with water.
16. congress — "Let's have a little **congress** on the dining table," smiled Mom.
17. obvious — It was **obvious** that things were serious now.
18. walrus — "I feel like a **walrus** perched on a rock," joked Heather nervously.
19. stillness — In the **stillness**, Heather's mom asked the Lord to send help.
20. services — "Lord, we could use the **services** of a rescue team!" prayed Heather.

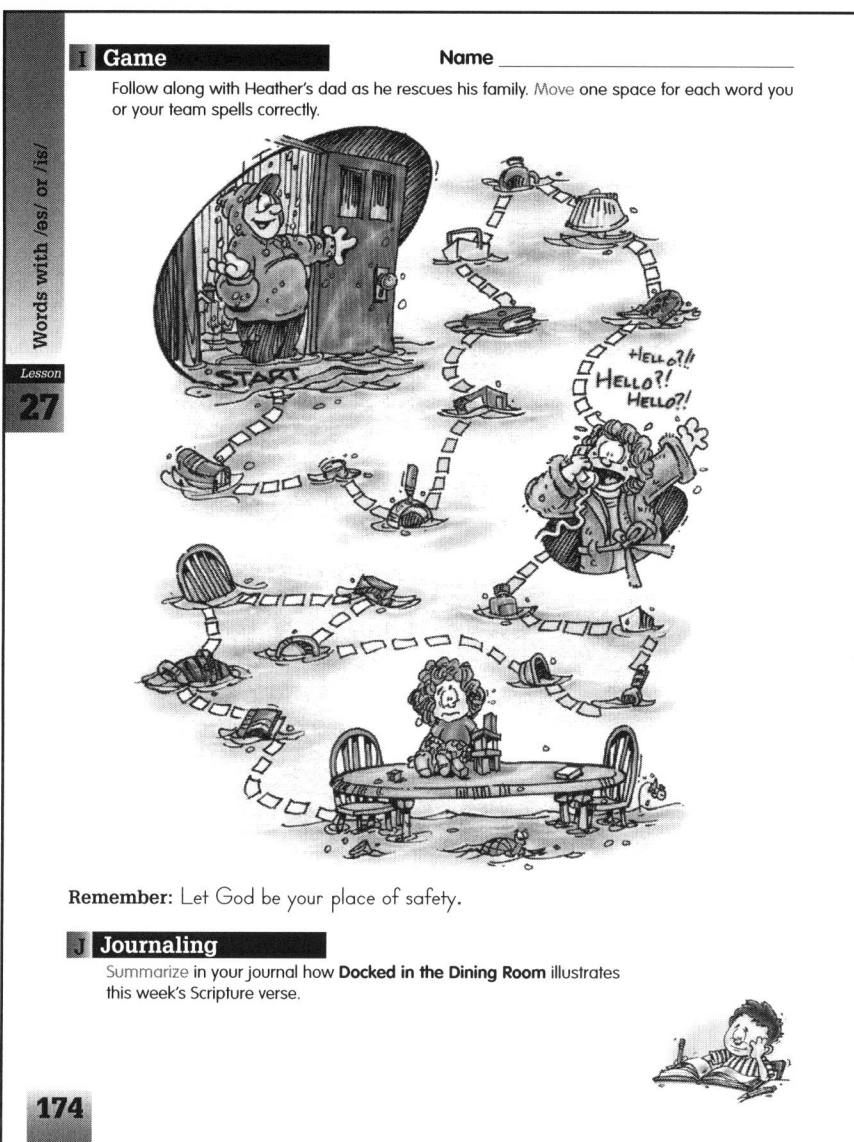

Words with /es/ or /is/

Lesson **27**

Follow along with Heather's dad as he rescues his family. Move one space for each word you or your team spells correctly.

Remember: Let God be your place of safety.

J **Journaling**

Summarize in your journal how **Docked in the Dining Room** illustrates this week's Scripture verse.

174

How to Play:

- Divide the class into two teams.
- Have each student place his/her game piece on Start.
- Have a student from team A go to the board.
- Say the spelling word.
- Have the student write the word on the board.
- If correct, instruct each member of team A to move his/her game piece forward one space.
- Alternate between teams A and B.
- The team to reach Heather and family first is the winner.
- **Small Group Option**: Students may play this game without teacher direction in small groups of two or more.

2 **Game**

Reinforce spelling skills and provide motivation and interest.

Materials

- game page (from student text)
- game pieces (1 per child)
- game word list

Game Word List

1. **New Jersey (E)**
2. **version (A)**
3. **journey (D)**
4. **nucleus**
5. **obvious**
6. **radius**
7. **congress**
8. **fungus**
9. **aimless**
10. **cumulus**
11. **mollusk**
12. **reckless**
13. **restless**
14. **closeness**
15. **stillness**
16. **witness**
17. **octopus**
18. **cirrus**
19. **citrus**
20. **interest**

Day 5

Lesson **27**

3 **Journaling**

Provide a meaningful reason for correct spelling through personal writing.

Review the story using discussion leads provided on the following page. Encourage students to apply the Scriptural value in their journaling.

271

Journaling (continued)

Say

- What is our Scripture this week? (Psalm 59:16)

- Why would King David (who wrote this Psalm) say a high tower was a safe place to be when he's distressed? (He was a soldier. Higher ground is preferred by soldiers because they can see the enemy better and it usually gives them an advantage.)

- Where did Heather go when muddy water pushed open the back door and swirled into the living room? (Up on top of the dining room table.)

- Where did Collin think they should go as the water continued to rise? (To the roof)

- What did Heather and Mom do while they waited for help to come? (Mom thought and prayed. Heather prayed and hummed a praise song while she helped Collin build a block tower.)

- How did Dad get to the house in the rising water? (In a boat)

- What did David sing about each morning? (God's power and mercy.)

- What did Dad say about God? ("He's a powerful God, Heather. A powerful God.")

My Journal

Dusting a cake with sugar means putting dust on it. Dusting the furniture means taking dust off it.

Word-Wow!

A Life Preserver

When a stranger's car is washed off the road by floodwaters, the Wright family has to act fast.

"Dozens of rivers and creeks in northwestern areas of the state overflowed their banks Friday and Saturday, forcing hundreds of people in four counties to flee their homes, with more flooding possible Sunday."

"Shhh, everybody!" Mr. Wright quieted the rest of his family. "Here's an update on the flooding." He reached over to turn up the volume on the car's radio.

"Officials estimate that 900 people have been forced from their homes. National Guard troops were called out Saturday and are still on the job helping people evacuate from low-lying areas."

"Governor Williams toured the flooded areas on Saturday. He declared a state of emergency for Fulbright, Cole, and Sedgewick counties. The Illinois River cut off access to the town of Winrock and was still rising Sunday as workers filled sandbags."

"According to Joy Moser, State Emergency Management spokeswoman, Aurora was hardest hit as water flowed over a 35-foot levee protecting the town from the Whitewater and Walnut rivers. Seven feet of water covered downtown streets Friday, but the level had fallen to three feet by Saturday afternoon as the river receded."

"About 300 homes and 30 businesses were inundated in Aurora. It will probably be Wednesday or Thursday before the waters recede enough for residents to return home. Officially, 8 inches of rain fell in Aurora by Friday night, but many locations across the area reported as much as 11 inches of rain."

"The flooding was spawned by a slow-moving storm system that hit late Thursday. Flooding elsewhere in the region has forced hundreds from their homes and caused millions of dollars in damage."

"One person has died; the body of 19-year-old Kate Tucker was found hours after water washed the car she and her mother were in off a road. Her mother was rescued and is hospitalized in stable condition. More after this."

Mr. Wright punched the "off" button and silenced the commercial blaring something about rushing over to Jerry's Fine Furniture for the deal of a lifetime.

Cory broke the lengthening silence in the car, "Dad, what if our house is full of water?"

"Yeah, maybe we should have stayed at Granny and Gramp's house." Christopher wriggled around to get a better view at the water-logged scenery.

Dad focused on his youngest son's question. "You know I have to get back to work, Cory. But I don't think our house will be flooded because Appleby Road is on pretty high ground."

Mom reached over and ruffled Cory's hair, "Don't worry about it, pumpkin. We'll deal with whatever we find when we get there."

"It won't be long now." Kristin pointed to a green highway sign, "Just 12 miles to go. Dad, could we stop by Rosa's house to see how she's doing? It's really not out of the way if we get off the highway sooner and take back roads."

Dad flipped on the right-turn blinker. "This exit, isn't it? We'll try, Kristin, but if the roads are covered with water, we'll have to turn around. It's not smart to try to drive through flooded areas."

"Wow, look at that grass stuck so high up in the trees!" Cory pointed out the front window as the car traveled more slowly down the rural road. "Is that how high the water was?"

"Yeah. Just think, Cory, we'd be totally under water if it was still flooded!" Cathy leaned over Christopher to get a better look.

"It is still flooded." Kristin gazed out the window on her side of the car. "The ditches on both sides of the road are totally full of rushing water. It's like we're right between two creeks."

"Uh, oh." Dad stopped the car. "Looks like your two creeks come together into a river up ahead. I just hope we can find a good place to turn around or we'll have to back up quite a way."

"Charles!" Mrs. Wright exclaimed, "that car in front of us is driving into the water!" The six Wrights stared as the small white car they'd been following crawled forward into the water rushing across the roadway. The water inched up the sides of the car as it drove ever deeper.

"Whew!" Christopher let out a relieved breath a minute or two later. "Look, she's giving up and is backing out."

But suddenly the white car lurched to the side. The family watched in horror as the current shoved the car off the roadway. They were close enough to see the terror on the woman's face as her car was swept away from the road into the rough waters beyond.

"Call 911!" Mr. Wright was out of the car before Mrs. Wright could grab her cell phone. He rushed along the edge of the swollen waters, splashing through the mud, heedless of his good clothes and leather dress shoes.

The children were silent while their mother gave the necessary information to the 911 operator. "That's right. As far as we could tell, the driver appeared to be the only passenger....Oh, I see.... Well, thank you." Mother pushed the button to end the call.

"How long till they get here, Mom?" Kristin twisted a lock of hair around her finger.

"All rescue units are out

right now so it may be a little while. Maybe too long." She rushed away to let Dad know. "You children stay in the car. Do you understand?"

"Is that woman going to drown?" Cory unbuckled his seat belt and turned around on his knees to face his brother and sisters in the back seat.

Christopher shrugged, "I don't know. Sometimes people do die in situations like this. Remember that news report we heard earlier?"

Kristin frowned across at her twin. "But she might be fine, Cory. Dad and Mom will do everything they can to help."

"We can, too." Cathy tickled her younger brother's tummy. "Let's pray." The children bowed their heads and Cathy began. Cory was just finishing his prayer when Mom and Dad came back to the car. "So dear God, please take care of that woman. Amen."

Mom opened Kristin's door. "Christopher, Kristin, come here, please, and help us undo the rope that's holding everything on top of the station wagon. Cory, you and Cathy may get out, too, but don't go near the water."

"We're going to try to rescue them," Dad explained as he frantically tugged at the knots securing the family's luggage under the plastic tarp.

"THEM?" Kristin dropped the end of the rope she was working on.

"Yes, there's a small child as well as the driver." Mother struggled with yet another wet and stubborn knot. "For now the car is stuck on its side against a couple of small trees."

"But if we don't get them out of there soon, it may be too late." Dad pulled another section of the rope loose. "The current is strong and may knock the car away. There, that's it." He began to wind the long rope in loops. "We'll tie this securely around a large tree on the bank and around my waist. Then I can safely wade out to the car. You kids can help Mom pull the rope if I need help getting back to

the shore. Okay? Let's go!"

Kristin's skin crawled when they got to the bank. The car was tilted on one side and most of it was hidden by the rushing brown water. The woman seemed to be standing with her feet against the driver's side window. Her face looked chalky through the window; she was clutching the child in her arms.

Mr. Wright secured the rope to a sturdy oak and handed his wallet and watch to Cory for safekeeping. After tying the rope around his own waist, he stepped into the torrent of water. Mom held the rope taut, ready to pull Dad back to safety in an instant. Minute by agonizing minute crawled by as Dad worked his way through the flood waters, careful to maintain his footing and balance. Finally, he reached the car.

Mom sucked in her breath when the car rocked slightly as Dad helped the woman out of the window. Kristin looked away. If the car should come loose, the strong current was sure to hurl it away, along with its passengers—and probably Dad. The rope could never hope to stop that. "Oh, dear God, protect them. Take care of Dad."

She didn't even realize she'd spoken aloud until she heard Mom say, "Amen."

When Kristin got the courage to look up again, Mr. Wright was torturously picking his way back toward the bank. The woman was riding piggy-back; he held the child against his chest. The muscles stood out along his neck. His face looked exhausted and strained as he concentrated on keeping his balance and finding firm footing. Kristin whispered her prayer over and over again.

Dad was out of the deepest water when he slipped! Cathy screamed. Even there, the current immediately swept the three downstream. "PULL!" Mom shouted, tugging at the rope. The children added their combined energy born of fear for Dad.

Finally, the raging waters lost and the three struggled onto the bank. Mom threw her arms around Dad, laughing and crying at the same time. Kristin was surprised to find tears running down her own face.

"Thank you. Thank you. Thank you." The bedraggled woman sat in the mud, holding her small daughter tightly. A sudden sharp crack caught the attention of everyone on the bank. One of the small trees holding the car had given way. In slow motion the white car turned in the water, then jerked loose and moved downstream.

"Oh, thank you." The mother repeated, "How will I ever thank you?"

The Wrights gathered in a family hug. Kristin squeezed her dad and smiled over at the little girl and her mother on the bank. "Thank you, God."

Discussion Time

Check understanding of the story and development of personal values.

- Where had the Wright family been when the flooding began?
- Why didn't Dad think they would find their house flooded when they got home?
- What happened to the white car the Wrights were following?
- Why couldn't an emergency rescue unit respond to the call right away?
- How many people were in the car?
- How did Mr. Wright help them?
- What did Kristin do while Mr. Wright was in the flood waters?
- What happened to the car after the people were safe on the bank?

A Preview

Write each word as your teacher says it.

Name _____

1. border
2. normal
3. Florida
4. dormitory
5. Georgia
6. North Carolina
7. formula
8. New York
9. North Dakota
10. Oregon
11. foreign
12. horror
13. orbit
14. forehead
15. corridor
16. format
17. ordeal
18. cornerstone
19. cornea
20. dinosaur

Scripture
Psalm 121:5-7

Words with /ôr/

Lesson 28

175

3 Preview

Test for knowledge of the correct spellings of these words.

Customize Your List
On a separate sheet of paper, additional words of your choice may be tested.

Say

I will say each word once, use the word in a sentence, then say the word again. Write the words on the lines in your Worktext.

Say

Correct Immediately!
Let's correct our Preview. I will spell each word out loud. If you spelled a word incorrectly, rewrite it correctly.

Graph

Progress Chart
Students may record scores. (Reproducible master provided in Appendix B.)

1.	border	"The state that shares our southern **border** was also hit hard," Dad said.
2.	normal	Rainfall was far above **normal** for this time of year.
3.	Florida	The **Florida** Red Cross was very helpful throughout this disaster.
4.	dormitory	They set up a cafeteria and first aid center in a **dormitory**.
5.	Georgia	The volunteers that came in from **Georgia** were a great help.
6.	North Carolina	**North Carolina** was unable to spare even one crew.
7.	formula	They did send a huge supply of baby **formula** to distribute to mothers.
8.	New York	The flood victims greatly appreciated the donations from **New York**.
9.	North Dakota	**North Dakota** sent two choppers and a huge supply of blankets.
10.	Oregon	An extra disaster relief crew from **Oregon** came in on Monday.
11.	foreign	The little white car was a **foreign** model.
12.	horror	They looked on in **horror** as the car floated through the water.
13.	orbit	Kristin's mind went into momentary **orbit** with fear.
14.	forehead	She could see the veins in Dad's **forehead** as he struggled through the water.
15.	corridor	Kristin wished the water would open into a **corridor** for Dad.
16.	format	Kristin did not worry about the **format** of her prayers!
17.	ordeal	She just begged God to help them through this **ordeal** safely.
18.	cornerstone	She knew God was the **cornerstone** on which she could trust.
19.	cornea	Mom felt sure the little girl had a scratched **cornea**.
20.	dinosaur	Cory handed the little girl his stuffed **dinosaur**.

Word Shapes

4

Say

Help students form a correct image of whole words.

Look at each word and think about its shape. Now, write the word in the correct Word Shape Boxes. You may check off each word as you use it.

(In many words, the sound of /ôr/ is spelled with **or** or **ore**. In a few words the sound of /ôr/ is spelled **our** or **aur** when it is at the end of a word or comes before a final consonant sound.)

Say

In the Word Shape Boxes, color the letters that spell the sound of /ôr/ in each word.

Take a minute to memorize...

Psalm 121:5-7

B **Word Shapes**   Name _____

Using the word bank below, write each word in the correct Word Shape Boxes. Next, in the Word Shape Boxes, fill in the boxes containing the letter or letters that spell the sound of /ôr/ in each word.

Words with /ôr/

Lesson **28**

1. forehead
2. North Carolina
3. Georgia
4. border
5. horror
6. foreign
7. normal
8. formula
9. cornerstone
10. Florida

11. ordeal
12. orbit
13. corridor
14. dinosaur
15. Oregon
16. format
17. New York
18. cornea
19. North Dakota
20. dormitory

Word Bank

border	dinosaur	foreign	horror	North Dakota
cornea	dormitory	format	New York	orbit
cornerstone	Florida	formula	normal	ordeal
corridor	forehead	Georgia	North Carolina	Oregon

176

Answers may vary for duplicate word shapes.

Be Prepared For Fun

Check these supply lists for **Fun Ways to Spell** - presented **Day 2**.
Purchase and/or gather these items ahead of time!

General
- Pencil
- Notebook Paper
- Spelling List

Auditory
- Pencil
- 3 X 5 Cards Cut in half lengthwise (20 per child)
- Spelling List

Visual
- Colored Pencils
- Graph Paper (2 sheets per child)
- Spelling List

Tactile
- Clay
- Spelling List

C Hide and Seek

Name _____

Play Hide and Seek with your words. Fill in a box on the bar graph (left to right) for each word you spell correctly.

LOOK   SAY   SPELL ALOUD   WRITE   SEEK   CHECK

D Other Word Forms

Using the words below, follow the instructions given by your teacher.

bordered   dinosaurs   Georgian   North Dakotan
bordering   dormitories   horrors   orbited
corneal   Floridan   New Yorker   orbiting
cornerstones   formatted   normalcy   Oregonian
corridors   formatting   normality
dinosaurian   formulated   North Carolinian

E Fun Ways to Spell

Initial the box of each activity you finish.

1. ☐

Classify your words according to syllables.

2. ☐

Spell your words on graph paper.

3. ☐

got a "fish"? NOPE!

Spell your words and play "Match-It."

4. ☐

Spell your words with clay.

---

1 Hide and Seek

Reinforce spelling by using multiple styles of learning.

On a white board, Teacher writes each word — one at a time. **Have students:**

- **Look** at the word.
- **Say** the word out loud.
- **Spell** the word out loud.
- **Hide** (teacher erases word.)
- **Write** the word on paper.
- **Seek** (teacher rewrites word.)
- **Check** spelling. If incorrect, rewrite word correctly.

2 Other Word Forms

This activity is optional. Have students find and circle the Other Word Forms that are most nearly synonyms of the following:

**expressed concisely
commonplaceness
circled
hallways**

3 Fun Ways to Spell

Four activities are provided. Use one, two, three, or all of the activities. Have students initial the box for each activity they complete.

Options:

- assign activities to students according to their learning styles
- set up the activities in learning centers for the students to do throughout the day
- divide students into four groups and assign one activity per group
- do one activity per day

General

To classify your words according to syllables...
- Write three headings on your paper:
  One-syllable, Two-syllable, and Three-syllable.
- Write the first word on your list under the proper heading.
- Draw a line through the word to divide it into syllables.
- Do this with each word.

Visual

To spell your words on graph paper...
- Look at the first word on your list.
- Shade in squares to form the letters of each word.
- Check your spelling.
- Do this with each word.

Auditory

To spell your words and play "Match-It"...
- Write each word on a card. Mix your word-cards and a classmate's together. Deal six cards to each player; the rest face down between you. Ask your classmate for a word-card. If the word-card matches, take it and play again. If not, draw from the stack, and it is your classmate's turn. Take turns until all cards are matched.

Tactile

To spell your words with clay...
- Roll pieces of clay into ropes.
- Use the ropes to make the letters of each word.
- Put them in the right order to spell each word.
- Check your spelling.

Working with Words

Familiarize students with word meaning and usage.

Rhyming Clues

Write the words **climber**, **climb**, **I'm**, and **china** on the board. Have a volunteer underline the two words that rhyme (**climb**, **I'm**). Tell students that, for this exercise, words need to rhyme on at least the last syllable to be considered rhyming words. Explain that students will be matching some of their spelling words to a rhyming word.

(Say) Write the spelling word that rhymes with each word below.

The OR's Have It

(Say) Each spelling word in this lesson has the /ôr/ sound. Answer each question with a word from the word bank. You may use a dictionary to help you. Write the word in the blank.

F **Working with Words**   Name _____

Similar Sounds

Write the spelling word that rhymes with the last syllable of each word below.

1. recorder — border
2. horrid — forehead
3. formal — normal
4. pulpit — orbit
5. unreal — ordeal
6. stegosaur — dinosaur or corridor
7. stork — New York
8. explorer — horror
9. saxophone — cornerstone
10. anymore — corridor or dinosaur
11. category — dormitory
12. doormat — format
13. stepson — Oregon
14. South Carolina — North Carolina
15. Minnesota — North Dakota

The OR's Have It

Answer each question with an /ôr/ word from the word bank. Write the word in the blank.

1. What /ôr/ word means the arrangement and layout of a publication? — format
2. What /ôr/ word is a state which has Raleigh as its capitol? — North Carolina
3. What /ôr/ word indicates an intense dislike and abhorrence? — horror
4. What /ôr/ word means the part that forms the outer edge of something? — border
5. What /ôr/ word is the part of the head between the eyebrows and the hairline? — forehead
6. What /ôr/ word is a narrow hallway, often with rooms opening onto it? — corridor
7. What /ôr/ word means from another country? — foreign
8. What /ôr/ word is the path of a celestial body as it revolves around another body? — orbit
9. What /ôr/ word is a state which has Atlanta as its capitol? — Georgia

Word Bank

border	dinosaur	foreign	horror	North Dakota
cornea	dormitory	format	New York	orbit
cornerstone	Florida	formula	normal	ordeal
corridor	forehead	Georgia	North Carolina	Oregon

178

Take a minute to memorize...

Psalm 121:5-7

G Dictation

Name _____

Write each sentence as your teacher dictates. Use correct punctuation.

1. Many people had the horror of cleaning up after the storm.

2. It would take a long time for things to get back to normal.

3. He walked down the corridor of the dormitory where his family had found refuge.

H Proofreading

If a word is misspelled, fill in the oval by that word. If all the words are spelled correctly, fill in the oval by **no mistake**.

1. ○ border
   ● ordeel
   ○ obvious
   ○ no mistake

2. ● corneea
   ○ aimless
   ○ cirrus
   ○ no mistake

3. ○ congress
   ● cornerstoan
   ○ corridor
   ○ no mistake

4. ○ dormitory
   ○ cumulus
   ● orbitt
   ○ no mistake

5. ● forhead
   ○ witness
   ○ foreign
   ○ no mistake

6. ● formatt
   ○ formula
   ○ closeness
   ○ no mistake

7. ● Floorida
   ○ interest
   ○ virus
   ○ no mistake

8. ○ radius
   ● Gorgia
   ○ fungus
   ○ no mistake

9. ● horor
   ○ restless
   ○ mollusk
   ○ no mistake

10. ○ normal
    ○ octopus
    ● North Carrolina
    ○ no mistake

11. ● North Dakoata
    ○ Oregon
    ○ stillness
    ○ no mistake

12. ● dinosor
    ○ New York
    ○ nucleus
    ○ no mistake

179

Dictation

Reinforce correct spelling by using current and previous words in context.

(Say)

Listen as I read each sentence and then write it in your Worktext. Remember to use correct capitalization and punctuation. (Slowly read each sentence twice. Sentences are found in the Student Worktext to the left.)

Day 4

Proofreading

Familiarize students with standardized test format and reinforce recognition of misspelled words.

(Say)

Look at each set of words. If a word is misspelled, fill in the oval by that word. If all the words are spelled correctly, fill in the oval by **no mistake**.

Lesson 28

3 Hide and Seek

Reinforce correct spelling of current spelling words. Repeat this activity from Day 2.

4 Vocabulary Extension

Have your students complete this activity to strengthen spelling ability and expand vocabulary. The reproducible master is provided in Appendix A as shown on the inset page to the right.

1 Posttest

Visit the **A Reason For** website to download free, printable Posttest pages.

 I will say the word once, use it in a sentence, then say it again. Write your words on a separate sheet of paper.

Progress Chart
Students may record scores. (Appendix B)

Personal Dictionary
Students may add any words they have misspelled to their personal dictionaries. (Appendix B)

Hide and Seek

Play Hide and Seek with your words. Fill in a bar graph (left to right) for each word you spell correctly.

Vocabulary Extension

Cause and Effect

Write a word from the word bank to complete each sentence.

1. If you are always talking, your parents say that you are _____forever_____ talking.
2. If you give up winning a race to help someone who has been hurt, you may _____forfeit_____ the trophy.
3. If you see something that is extremely large, you might call it _____enormous_____.
4. If you help a friend dress up for a skit, and she looks completely different, you have helped to _____transform_____ her.
5. If you visit the zoo and see a giant turtle that lives on land, you are watching a _____tortoise_____.
6. If you are learning the art of Japanese paper folding, you are learning _____origami_____.
7. If you are lying down instead of standing up, you are _____horizontal_____ instead of vertical.
8. If a submarine sends out an underwater missile that explodes when it hits a target, it is sending out a _____torpedo_____.
9. If nothing unusual happens today, I would consider it an _____ordinary_____ day.
10. If a violent, whirling column of air appears as a dark, funnel–shaped cloud, it is called a _____tornado_____.
11. If we are making small decorations to hang on a Christmas tree, we are making _____ornament_____s.
12. If you have won a prize for your science display, you have won an _____award_____.

Word Bank

award	forfeit	origami	torpedo
enormous	horizontal	ornament	tortoise
forever	ordinary	tornado	transform

---

1. normal — This much rain was not **normal** for this time of year.
2. border — "Even the states that **border** ours have been affected," Dad told them.
3. North Dakota — "Can it be snowing in **North Dakota** and raining here?" wondered Cory.
4. dormitory — The Red Cross set up a relief station in a nearby college **dormitory**.
5. Florida — The **Florida** Red Cross volunteered some of its people to aid in the crisis.
6. Georgia — The state of **Georgia** also sent in volunteers.
7. North Carolina — All the **North Carolina** volunteers were already in the field.
8. Oregon — **Oregon** was able to send one of its disaster relief crews and a chopper.
9. New York — The city of **New York** sent several semi trucks with food items.
10. foreign — The white vehicle in front of them was a small **foreign** car.
11. corridor — It seemed like they had walked through a **corridor** in time.
12. horror — They watched in **horror** as the car lurched and slipped off the road.
13. forehead — Kristin could see the veins bulging on her dad's **forehead**.
14. orbit — Kristin felt her mind go into momentary **orbit** with fear.
15. formula — There seemed to be no sure **formula** for success in this situation.
16. format — Kristin didn't worry about the perfect **format**; she just prayed.
17. cornerstone — Jesus is a solid **cornerstone** on which we can place our trust.
18. cornea — The little girl seemed to have a scratched **cornea**.
19. ordeal — She had had quite an **ordeal** and was very frightened!
20. dinosaur — Cory let her hold his stuffed **dinosaur**.

I Game

Name _____

Record points for each word you or your team spells correctly. Earn bonus points for each row in which all five words are spelled correctly.

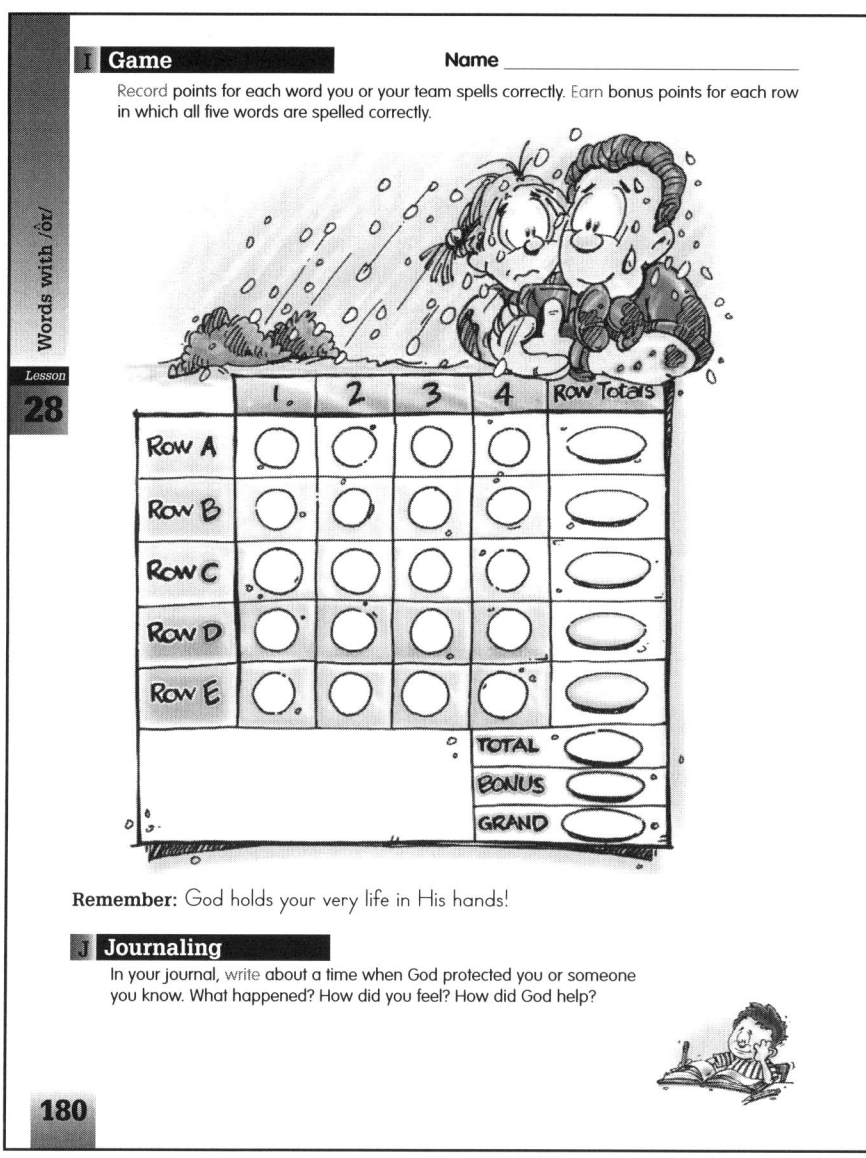

Remember: God holds your very life in His hands!

J Journaling

In your journal, write about a time when God protected you or someone you know. What happened? How did you feel? How did God help?

180

How to Play:

- Divide the class into two teams.
- Have a student from team A choose a square on the grid by indicating the row letter and number.
- Say the word that matches that row letter and number from the team's word list.
- Have the student write the word on the board.
- If correct, have each member of that team record the awarded points (in parentheses by the word) in the circle in that box. If the word is misspelled, have him/her put an **X** in that circle. That square may not be chosen again.
- Repeat this process with the second team.
- When all the words have been spelled by both teams, have each team tally its score. Award a bonus of 5 points for each row in which all four words were spelled correctly.
- Have the teams record their grand totals. The team with the highest score is the winner.

2 Game

Reinforce spelling skills and provide motivation and interest.

Materials

- game page (from student text)
- pencils (1 per child)
- game word list

Game Word List

Team A		Team B
E4	virus	A1
E3	walrus	A2
E2	services	A3
E1	border (3)	A4
D4	cornea (1)	B1
D3	cornerstone (2)	B2
D2	corridor (4)	B3
D1	dormitory (3)	B4
C4	forehead (4)	C1
C3	foreign (2)	C2
C2	format (1)	C3
C1	formula (2)	C4
B4	Florida (3)	D1
B3	Georgia (1)	D2
B2	horror (4)	D3
B1	normal (2)	D4
A4	North Carolina (1)	E1
A3	North Dakota (4)	E2
A2	Oregon (3)	E3
A1	orbit (3)	E4

3 Journaling

Provide a meaningful reason for correct spelling through personal writing.

Review the story using discussion leads provided on the following page. Encourage students to apply the Scriptural value in their journaling.

Journaling (continued)

Say

- Has it ever flooded in the community where you live? (Allow time to share experiences.)

- Why did the Wright family turn off the highway on their way home? (They decided to go home the back way in order to go by Rosa's house and see how she was doing.)

- Why did they have to turn around? (The flood waters were across the road.)

- Should you ever drive through flood water crossing a road? (No. It is NEVER safe, as it is hard to tell how deep and swift the water is.)

- Where did the Wrights get the rope to tie around Dad's waist? (They used the rope that was holding the plastic cover over the luggage on the top of their car.)

- Why didn't the Wrights wait for a rescue unit to come? (They were afraid the small trees the car was resting against wouldn't hold and the car would be swept away with the people still inside it.)

- Do you think God helped Mr. Wright save the woman and her child? Why or why not? (Yes. Because Kristin and the others were asking God for help and He has promised to help us whenever we ask.)

A good palindrome for a time of drought: Niagara, O roar again!

Word-Wow!

In a Bug's Eye

When his class studies insects, Tommy understands a bit better how awesome God really is.

"You're making a what?" Tommy Rawson stared suspiciously at the lumpy mass of soggy newspaper on the Simmonses' kitchen table.

"A model of the compound eye," Hubert Thornton Remington III repeated patiently. "Admittedly, it is a somewhat complex project, but well worth the effort. To begin with, I cut up 10 egg cartons into individual 'eyes.' Next, I inverted this large mixing bowl for a mold and covered it with two layers of newspaper. Then, using a glue gun, I attached the individual eyes to each other and to the newspaper covering the bowl. Naturally, the closer together the eyes fit, the better."

"Naturally," Tommy echoed, looking confused.

"Now I'm ripping newspaper into thin strips to be dipped in paper mâché paste. Application of these strips fills in and smoothes out the spaces between the individual eyes." Thorny carefully wove the dripping strip between the egg carton bumps and patted it into place.

"Since drying time may take several days, it's vital to complete this stage of the project today. Otherwise it would not be possible to finish the entire project in a timely fashion before our science project due date." Thorny applied another strip with precision.

"Uh, this stage, huh?" Tommy scooted down in the chair and rested his head on its back.

Thorny dipped another strip in the paste bowl. "After it's completely dry, I'll remove the compound eye from the bowl and apply a layer of paper mâché to the inside, again smoothing out and filling in spaces between the individual eyes. Once it's completely dry, I'll cover both surfaces with metallic blue paint. The finishing touch will be hot-gluing 120 mirrors on the concave side of the compound eye, one to the bottom of each individual eye. By looking into the compound eye, one can get a small indication of what an insect might see, although dragonflies have as many as 30,000 such lenses in each eye."

"Sounds good." Tommy picked up a stack of one-inch-round mirrors. "I wish our projects didn't have to be about insects, though. I know Heather disagrees, but insects are just so boring. If we were studying animals, or magnetism, or the ocean, or the human body, or anything else, it would be more fun!"

"What's black and red, hairy, with six legs and a long stinger?" Thorny paused to look across the table at his friend.

Tommy shrugged, "I don't know—what is it?"

Thorny shrugged too. "I don't know either, but there's one crawling on your shoulder."

"What? Where?" Tommy jumped up and craned his neck, trying to see his own shoulders.

"Gotcha!" Thorny chuckled and applied another strip of newspaper. "Then there's the one about the centipede complaining to his physician: 'Doc, when my feet hurt, I hurt all over.'"

"Awww." Tommy dropped back into the chair he'd vacated so swiftly. "No fair. Besides, you can't convince me that insects are interesting with a joke about a centipede. Even I know that real insects have six legs."

"Touché!" Thorny scratched his face with his thumb, leaving a blob of paper mâché paste on his chin. "How about 'Time flies like an arrow, but fruit flies like a banana.'"

Tommy groaned and clutched at his belly as if he were sick.

"Well, do you know what has four wheels and flies?" Thorny persevered.

"No, no! I don't know, and I don't think I want to know, either."

"As you wish." Thorny shrugged and proceeded in silence for a few seconds till Tommy couldn't stand it anymore.

"All right, I've gotta know. Tell me." Tommy braced himself against the table with his hands as if he were about to receive a blow.

"A garbage truck, naturally." Thorny laughed as Tommy flung his head back as if he'd been punched.

"AWWW! I should have seen that one coming."

"Seriously, there are things about the insect world that are fascinating." Thorny took a step back to look for uneven places on his project.

"Fascinating to you and Heather, or to someone like me?" Tommy propped one elbow on the table and rested his chin in that hand.

"Well, I admit that Heather piqued my interest, and when I began my own research, it became abundantly clear why she has such an enduring fascination with all manner of insects. Do you find it fascinating that mosquitoes of genus Malaya steal honeydew from the jaws of worker ants? Or that comparative studies show that humans have 792 distinct muscles, whereas grasshoppers have 900, and caterpillars may have as many as 4,000? Did you know an average man can pull about 0.86 times his own weight, but a leaf beetle can pull 42.7 times its own weight?"

Thorny kept peppering Tommy with facts. "There are more than a million species of insects—90,000 in North America. Insects outnumber all other animals four to one. Or what about the fact that 17 states have chosen the honeybee for the official state insect?"

Thorny paused for breath and Tommy just

283

stared at him. "Or have you ever wondered how far insects can fly? Painted ladies migrating from Africa to England travel more than 3,000 miles. Perhaps it might interest you that the longest insect is 24.5 inches long, a stick insect from southern China; the largest butterfly is the Queen Alexandra's birdwing from New Guinea (an endangered species), with a wingspan of 10 inches. Truly remarkable is the tropical owlet moth, with a wingspan of 12 inches; the smallest butterfly is our own country's Western Pygmy Blue, which has only a one-half inch wingspan. Would you care to hear more?"

Tommy grinned sheepishly, "Uh, sure. I guess these guys are pretty interesting. So what's the tiniest insect?"

"Well, the smallest insects are fairy flies, which are insects that parasitize or lay their eggs inside other insects' eggs. Fairy flies are only one-fifth of a millimeter long." Thorny began cleaning up the mess on the table.

"So, tell me more," Tommy prompted after a moment of silence.

Thorny held his hands out, in a gesture of innocence. "Just remember, you asked for it! Honeybees fly at about seven miles per hour, and have to beat their wings 190 times per second to do it. But that's nothing. The 'no-see-ums,' or very tiny midges, beat their hairy wings 1,046 times per second. Cockroaches are the fastest runners—almost a foot per second, or a little more than one mile per hour. Fleas jump 200 times their body length. In human terms, that would be like a human clearing a 70-story building. And finally, one of my personal favorites, the queen of a termite colony may lay 6,000 to 7,000 eggs per day, and may live 15 to 50 years. Does that baffle the mind or what?"

"Awesome." Tommy leaned back in his chair, one hand to his head. "So maybe this field trip to the Bug Bowl will be pretty interesting after all."

A few days later, Tommy discovered that "interesting" was only one of many words that would apply to the Bug Bowl. "Revolting" came to mind when he saw the Cajun-style fried mealworms, and "gag" seemed appropriate when he spotted the Grasshopper Fritters. Tommy took one look, and promptly decided that if he wanted to eat something crunchy, he'd stick to carrot sticks!

By making learning fun, kids discovered facts about insects and their value to people and the environment. The students got to hold three-inch-long Madagascar hissing cockroaches and three-horned rhinoceros beetles the size of hamsters. Displays showed the commercial uses for bugs, including an array of products based on honey and beeswax. The class saw red worms worth worth over $30 a pound to be used for composting—which with worms can be done indoors in small containers—and fish bait. Building their own butterfly hats was also fun.

But the cockroach races were the greatest. Huge two-tone Madagascar hissing roaches took an average of 35 seconds to complete one lap around a coffee-table-sized plastic track. However, the American cockroaches proved to be winners, and as crowds of children cheered for their favorites, the speedsters routinely raced around the track in 15 seconds.

By the end of the afternoon, the whole class was excited about insects and eager to complete their projects.

The day they turned their projects in to Mr. Canfield, the students went around the room admiring each one. Everybody wanted to get the bug's eye view with Thorny's compound eye. And they were amazed at the results of Tommy's project.

"Wow, Tommy I had no idea the Scriptures mentioned bugs so much!" Tony leaned over the counter where Tommy's project was displayed. "Hey, Laney!" he called, "Can you believe grasshoppers are mentioned in the Scriptures 10 times and locusts 28 times?"

Thorny admired the listing of insects mentioned in the Scriptures that Tommy had designed. "So, Tommy, you did come up with a project about insects. An impressive one at that."

"Thanks." Tommy grinned. "But you gave me the idea."

"Excuse me?" Thorny's eyebrows shot up under his sandy-colored bangs.

"When I thought about all those incredible insect facts you were spouting the other day, I thought about what an awesome God designed them all. I decided to see what the Scriptures said about them." Tommy hadn't noticed Mr. Canfield standing behind him till the teacher spoke.

"Well, boys, of all these excellent projects, both of yours are designed to help us see things from a little different perspective." He turned to walk away and spoke back over his shoulder. "See what I mean? Think about it!"

Discussion Time

2 Check understanding of the story and development of personal values.

- What was Thorny making for his science project?
- Can you remember any of the interesting facts Thorny told Tommy about insects?
- Where did the class go on their field trip?
- What kinds of races were held at the Bug Bowl?
- What other types of things did the students do at the Bug Bowl?
- What project did Tommy end up doing?

A Preview

Write **each word as your teacher says it.**

Name _____

1. compound
2. account
3. crouch
4. snout
5. scowl
6. browse
7. whereabouts
8. announcer
9. boundary
10. counterfeit
11. coward
12. willpower
13. clout
14. drought
15. foul
16. mountains
17. pronounce
18. South Carolina
19. South Dakota
20. scoundrel

Words with /ou/

Lesson **29**

Welcome to the BUG BOWL!

Scripture

Psalm 47:1, 2

181

3 **Preview**

Test for knowledge of the correct spellings of these words.

Customize Your List

On a separate sheet of paper, additional words of your choice may be tested.

Say

I will say each word once, use the word in a sentence, then say the word again. Write the words on the lines in your Worktext.

Correct Immediately!

Say

Let's correct our Preview. I will spell each word out loud. If you spelled a word incorrectly, rewrite it correctly.

Progress Chart

Students may record scores. (Reproducible master provided in Appendix B.)

1.	compound	"Your project of the **compound** eye of an insect is awesome!" said Tommy.
2.	account	Thorny was careful to take into **account** every detail in his design.
3.	crouch	Thorny started to **crouch** down and add another strip of paper mâché.
4.	snout	"Hey, you've got more paste on your **snout** than the bug's eye," teased Tommy.
5.	scowl	Thorny stood back up with a pretend **scowl** and wiped his face.
6.	browse	Mr. Canfield encouraged his students to **browse** through the Bug Bowl.
7.	whereabouts	"Do you know the **whereabouts** of the butterfly exhibits?" asked Heather.
8.	announcer	The event **announcer** pointed to the south side of the convention hall.
9.	boundary	The clear plastic walls provided a **boundary** or barrier for the racing roaches.
10.	counterfeit	It would be impossible to **counterfeit** God's creation.
11.	coward	"Don't be a **coward**, have a fried grasshopper," encouraged Daniel.
12.	willpower	"I'll have to summon all my **willpower**, but I believe I'll pass," smiled Setsuko.
13.	clout	One of the three-horned rhinoceros beetles delivered a swift **clout** to another.
14.	drought	"Wow! This bug can survive a long **drought**," marveled the boys.
15.	foul	"What is that **foul** stench?" questioned Thorny.
16.	mountains	"A toasted worm from the **mountains** of Colorado," noted Tommy.
17.	pronounce	"I can't even begin to **pronounce** its name, though," he said.
18.	South Carolina	"Tommy, did you see this cool insect from the **South Carolina** forest?"
19.	South Dakota	"Here's a neat one from **South Dakota**, too," continued Christopher.
20.	scoundrel	"This big guy is an ugly **scoundrel**," commented Laney.

4 Word Shapes

Help students form a correct image of whole words.

Say) Look at each word and think about its shape. Now, write the word in the correct Word Shape Boxes. You may check off each word as you use it.

(The diphthong **/ou/** is spelled **ow** or **ou**.)

Say) In the Word Shape Boxes, color the letters that spell the sound of **/ou/** in each word.

Take a minute to memorize...

Psalm 47:1,2

B **Word Shapes**   Name _____

Using the word bank below, write each word in the correct Word Shape Boxes. Next, in the Word Shape Boxes, fill in the boxes containing the letter or letters that spell the sound of /ou/ in each word.

1. crouch
2. snout
3. account
4. browse
5. foul
6. pronounce
7. boundary
8. drought
9. South Carolina
10. clout

11. compound
12. scowl
13. mountains
14. announcer
15. whereabouts
16. coward
17. willpower
18. South Dakota
19. counterfeit
20. scoundrel

Word Bank

account	clout	crouch	pronounce	South Carolina
announcer	compound	drought	scoundrel	South Dakota
boundary	counterfeit	foul	scowl	whereabouts
browse	coward	mountains	snout	willpower

182

Answers may vary for duplicate word shapes.

Be Prepared For Fun

Check these supply lists for **Fun Ways to Spell** - presented **Day 2**.
Purchase and/or gather these items ahead of time!

General
- Pencil
- Graph Paper (1 sheet per child)
- Spelling List

Auditory
- Pencil
- Notebook Paper
- Spelling List

Visual
- Colored Pencils
- Alphabet Stencils
- Paper

Tactile
- Uncooked Rice
- Art Paper (1 sheet per child)
- Glue
- Spelling List

C Hide and Seek   Name _____

Play Hide and Seek with your words. Fill in a box on the bar graph (left to right) for each word you spell correctly.

LOOK   SAY   SPELL ALOUD   WRITE   SEEK   CHECK

D Other Word Forms

Using the words below, follow the instructions given by your teacher.

accounted	clouting	crouching	scoundrels
accounting	compounded	droughts	scowled
announced	compounds	fouled	scowling
announcing	counterfeited	foulest	snouts
boundaries	counterfeiting	mountaineer	South Carolinian
browsed	cowardice	mountainous	South Dakotan
browsing	cowardly	pronounced	
clouted	crouched	pronouncing	

E Fun Ways to Spell

Initial the box of each activity you finish.

1.
acknnjes
bewordus
Infindinr
btmhxdrg
rmnosdrb

Spell your words in a "Word Find."

2.
Spell your words with stencils.

3.
M·i·s·s·i· s·s·i·p·p·i

Play "Spelling Tic-Tac-Toe."

4.
Arkansas
Spell your words with rice.

Words with /ou/

Lesson **29**

183

---

1 Hide and Seek

Reinforce spelling by using multiple styles of learning.

On a white board, Teacher writes each word — one at a time. **Have students:**

- **Look** at the word.
- **Say** the word out loud.
- **Spell** the word out loud.
- **Hide** (teacher erases word.)
- **Write** the word on paper.
- **Seek** (teacher rewrites word.)
- **Check** spelling. If incorrect, rewrite word correctly.

2 Other Word Forms

This activity is optional. Have students write original sentences using these Other Word Forms:

**accounted
cowardly
clouting
scowled**

3 Fun Ways to Spell

Four activities are provided. Use one, two, three, or all of the activities. Have students initial the box for each activity they complete.

Lesson **29** | Day **2**

Options:

- assign activities to students according to their learning styles
- set up the activities in learning centers for the students to do throughout the day
- divide students into four groups and assign one activity per group
- do one activity per day

General

To spell your words in a "Word Find"...
- Arrange your words on a piece of graph paper.
- Put one letter of each word in a square.
- Words may be written backwards, forwards, or diagonally.
- Outline your puzzle.
- Hide your words by filling in all the spaces inside the puzzle with random letters.
- Trade grids with a classmate and find the hidden words.

Auditory

To play "Spelling Tic-Tac-Toe"...
- Draw a Tic-Tac-Toe grid.
- Ask a classmate to read a word from the list.
- Spell the word aloud.
- If the word is spelled correctly, place your mark on the grid.
- Take turns with your classmate.

Visual

To spell your words with stencils...
- Look at the first letter of a word on your list.
- Place the stencil for the proper letter over your paper.
- Shade inside the stencil.
- Choose the proper stencil for the next letter of the word and shade it in next to the first letter.
- Finish the word in this way.
- Do this with each word.

Tactile

To spell your words with rice...
- Choose a word from your spelling list.
- Shape the letters of your word with rice.
- Glue the rice to art paper.
- Do this for each word on your list.

287

Working with Words

Familiarize students with word meaning and usage.

Scrambled Words

Write the letters **adeefhor** on the board. Have a student unscramble the letters to make the word **forehead**.

 (Say)

Unscramble each spelling word. Write the word correctly on the line. Remember to use capital letters where they are needed.

Word Clues

 (Say)

Use your word bank to help you match the spelling words to the clues. Some of the clues are synonyms, words that have the same meaning as the spelling word. You may use a dictionary or thesaurus to help you.

Take a minute to memorize...

Psalm 47:1,2

F | **Working with Words**   Name _____

Words with /ou/

Lesson **29**

Scrambled Words

Unscramble each word. Write the unscrambled word on the line. Use capital letters and spaces where they are needed.

1. abdnoruy	boundary		**11.** tosuh alaricon	South Carolina
2. acdorw	coward		**12.** husot atodka	South Dakota
3. acennnoru	announcer		**13.** abeehorstuw	whereabouts
4. beorsw	browse		**14.** aimnnostu	mountains
5. cacnout	account		**15.** cdelnorsu	scoundrel
6. cchoru	crouch		**16.** cennoopru	pronounce
7. cdmnoopu	compound		**17.** closw	scowl
8. ceefinorttu	counterfeit		**18.** eilloprww	willpower
9. dghortu	drought		**19.** flou	foul
10. tolcu	clout		**20.** nostu	snout

Word Clues

Match the spelling words to the clues. You may use a dictionary or thesaurus to help you.

1. strength of will	willpower		**10.** a fearful person	coward
2. location, site	whereabouts		**11.** false, fraudulent	counterfeit
3. nose, proboscis	snout		**12.** mixture, blend	compound
4. frown, grimace	scowl		**13.** influence, pull	clout
5. rascal, rogue	scoundrel		**14.** leaf or skim through	browse
6. enunciate, say	pronounce		**15.** border, confines	boundary
7. disgusting, offensive	foul		**16.** commentator, reporter	announcer
8. stoop, bend	crouch		**17.** lack of moisture	drought
9. high country	mountains			

Word Bank

account	clout	crouch	pronounce	South Carolina
announcer	compound	drought	scoundrel	South Dakota
boundary	counterfeit	foul	scowl	whereabouts
browse	coward	mountains	snout	willpower

184

G Dictation

Name _____

Write **each sentence as your teacher dictates.** Use **correct punctuation.**

1. Tommy <u>scowled as he thought about his</u>
<u>science homework.</u>

2. Thorny <u>gave an account of creepy crawly</u>
<u>details as he worked on the compound eye.</u>

3. <u>The announcer told about the drought in</u>
<u>the mountains.</u>

H Proofreading

If a word is misspelled, fill in the oval by that word. If all the words are spelled correctly, fill in the oval by **no mistake**.

1. ● wherabouts
   ○ formula
   ○ Florida
   ○ no mistake

2. ○ forehead
   ○ foreign
   ● browze
   ○ no mistake

3. ○ cornea
   ● boundery
   ○ cornerstone
   ○ no mistake

4. ● acount
   ○ corridor
   ○ dormitory
   ○ no mistake

5. ● counterfit
   ○ orbit
   ○ New York
   ○ no mistake

6. ○ South Dakota
   ○ border
   ● cowerd
   ○ no mistake

7. ○ drought
   ● fouwl
   ○ North Carolina
   ○ no mistake

8. ○ South Carolina
   ● mountins
   ○ horror
   ○ no mistake

9. ● anouncer
   ○ pronounce
   ○ Georgia
   ○ no mistake

10. ○ compound
    ● wilpower
    ○ normal
    ○ no mistake

11. ● scoundril
    ○ crouch
    ○ format
    ○ no mistake

12. ○ scowl
    ○ snout
    ● cloutt
    ○ no mistake

185

Dictation

Reinforce correct spelling by using current and previous words in context.

Say

Listen as I read each sentence and then write it in your Worktext. Remember to use correct capitalization and punctuation. (Slowly read each sentence twice. Sentences are found in the Student Worktext to the left.)

Proofreading

Familiarize students with standardized test format and reinforce recognition of misspelled words.

Say

Look at each set of words. If a word is misspelled, fill in the oval by that word. If all the words are spelled correctly, fill in the oval by **no mistake**.

Day 4

Lesson 29

3 Hide and Seek

Reinforce correct spelling of current spelling words. Repeat this activity from Day 2.

4 Vocabulary Extension

Have your students complete this activity to strengthen spelling ability and expand vocabulary. The reproducible master is provided in Appendix A as shown on the inset page to the right.

1 Posttest

Visit the **A Reason For** website to download free, printable Posttest pages.

Say

I will say the word once, use it in a sentence, then say it again. Write your words on a separate sheet of paper.

Progress Chart

Students may record scores. (Appendix B)

Personal Dictionary

Students may add any words they have misspelled to their personal dictionaries. (Appendix B)

Hide and Seek

Play Hide and Seek with your words. Fill in a bar graph (left to right) for each word you spell correctly.

LOOK SAY HIDE WRITE SEEK CHECK

Vocabulary Extension

Fill in the Blanks

Choose a word from the word bank that best fits each sentence clue.

1. There are more girls in class than boys; girls ____outnumber____ boys two to one.
2. My parents give me some money each week. This is my ____allowance____.
3. After the farmer cut his hay, ____countless____ birds flocked from all around to get hay seeds.
4. We bought our winter clothes on sale. Mom was glad to get a ____discount____ on them.
5. I love the huge hills around us. I always wanted to live in a ____mountainous____ area.
6. When Julie learned to play the clarinet, she was taught how to hold her mouth on the ____mouthpiece____ to get a clear tone.
7. I know you are upset, but you do not need to make such an ____outburst____ in the middle of class.
8. Before we write our three-point paragraph, we have to make an ____outline____ of the points we will cover.
9. When Heather writes a story, she uses so many ____pronoun____s that nobody can tell who is doing what.
10. We drove home by a different ____route____ because men were working on a culvert under one of the roads.
11. Jesus traveled to many ____outlying____ villages and towns, preaching and healing the people.
12. His mom says embarrassing things in public. She is much too ____outspoken____.

Word Bank

allowance	mountainous	outline	outspoken
countless	mouthpiece	outlying	pronoun
discount	outburst	outnumber	route

349

---

1. compound — "I am making a **compound** eye," explained Thorny.
2. snout — "Hey, you've got paste on your **snout**," he laughed.
3. scowl — Thorny gave Tommy a pretend **scowl**.
4. account — Thorny's attention to detail would **account** for his terrific project!
5. whereabouts — Heather was interested to find the **whereabouts** of the hissing roaches.
6. boundary — "It seems the creativity of the Creator knew no **boundary**!" Thorny commented.
7. browse — It was exciting and interesting to **browse** through the Bug Bowl.
8. counterfeit — No one can **counterfeit** God's magnificent handiwork.
9. crouch — A flea is so small you can't see it **crouch** down before it hops.
10. clout — "Can this insect deliver a fierce **clout** with its hind legs?" wondered Tommy.
11. South Carolina — "This insect inhabits the forests of **South Carolina**," said Heather.
12. drought — "This amazing insect can survive a long **drought**," Thorny noted.
13. foul — "What is that **foul** smell?" asked Tommy.
14. mountains — "A delectable stir-fried worm! This one is found in the **mountains**."
15. South Dakota — "Yeah, it says here that they live mainly in **South Dakota**!" said Tommy.
16. pronounce — Daniel got tickled as he tried to **pronounce** one of the names.
17. coward — "Don't be a **coward**; munch on a meal worm," teased Tommy.
18. willpower — "I'll exercise **willpower** and skip the meal worms," joked Tony.
19. scoundrel — "This three-horned rhinoceros beetle looks like a **scoundrel**," said Beth.
20. announcer — An **announcer** called for everyone to gather around the platform.

I Game

Name _____

Walk along with Tommy and observe some amazing insects. Move one space for each word you or your team spells correctly.

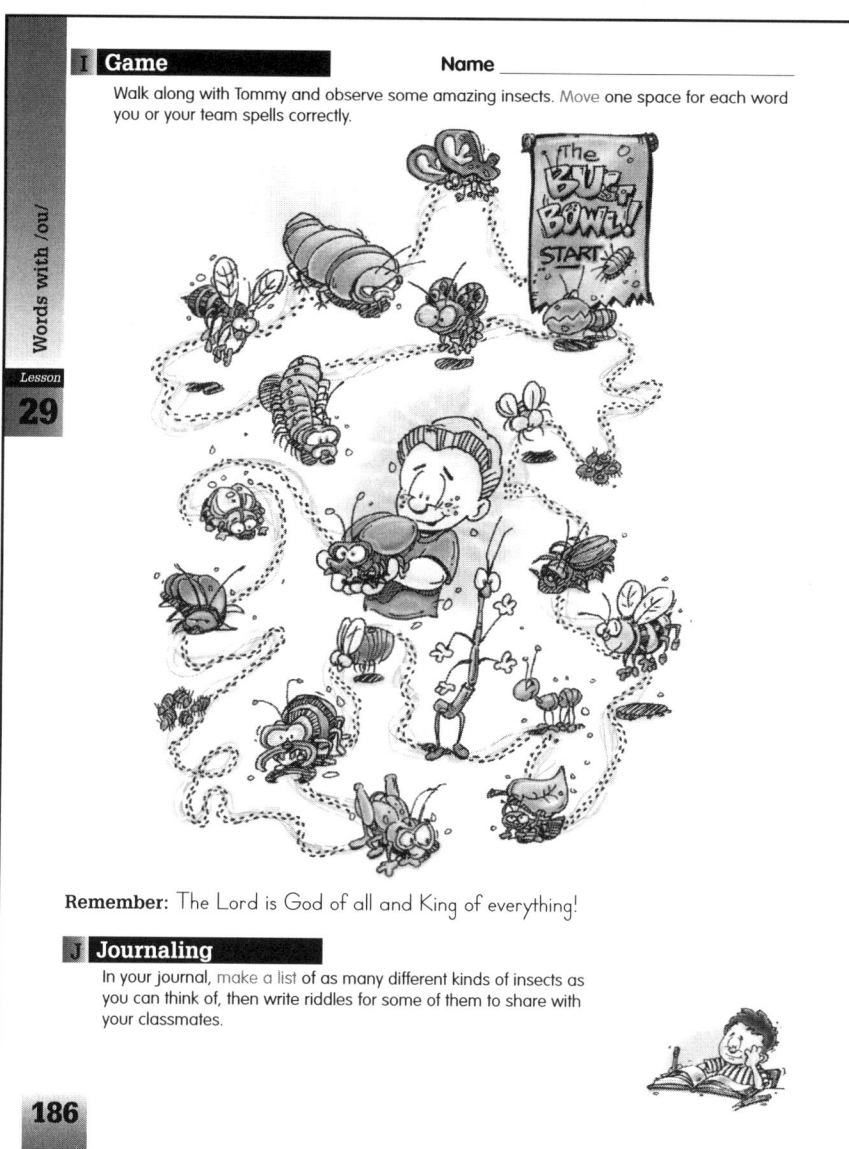

Remember: The Lord is God of all and King of everything!

J Journaling

In your journal, make a list of as many different kinds of insects as you can think of, then write riddles for some of them to share with your classmates.

How to Play:

- Divide the class into two teams.
- Have each student place his/her game piece on Start.
- Have a student from team A go to the board.
- Say the spelling word.
- Have the student write the word on the board.
- If correct, instruct each member of team A to move his/her game piece forward one space.
- Alternate between teams A and B.
- The team to reach the exit of the Bug Bowl first is the winner.
- **Small Group Option**: Students may play this game without teacher direction in small groups of two or more.

2 Game

Reinforce spelling skills and provide motivation and interest.

Materials

- game page (from student text)
- game pieces (1 per child)
- game word list

Game Word List

1. **ordeal** (4)
2. **dinosaur** (2)
3. **New York** (1)
4. **whereabouts**
5. **browse**
6. **boundary**
7. **account**
8. **counterfeit**
9. **coward**
10. **crouch**
11. **clout**
12. **drought**
13. **foul**
14. **mountains**
15. **announcer**
16. **pronounce**
17. **compound**
18. **willpower**
19. **South Carolina**
20. **South Dakota**

3 Journaling

Provide a meaningful reason for correct spelling through personal writing.

Review the story using discussion leads provided on the following page. Encourage students to apply the Scriptural value in their journaling.

Lesson **29** | Day 5

(Say)

- What was Thorny using to make his model of the compound eye? (Ten egg cartons cut apart, newspaper, paper mâché, and mirrors.)

- Why was Tommy having a hard time thinking of a science project to do? (The projects had to be about insects and Tommy thought insects were boring.)

- How did Tommy get the idea for the project he did? (From listening to Thorny talk about so many interesting facts about insects.)

- Have you been to an insect fair of some kind similar to the Bug Bowl which Tommy's class attended?

- Of the insect facts that Thorny told Tommy, which did you find most interesting? (Allow time for discussion.)

- How many insect species are there? (Over a million.)

- Imagine trying to create a million different kinds of insects—besides all the animals, plants, fish, birds, and other things God made! Isn't He an awesome God?

- Can you solve this riddle? While a colony is my home, Sometimes far away from it I roam, With other insects of my kind, I search for any food that I can find, My strong jaws lift loads others can't, Have you guessed by now that I'm an _____?

- You will write some riddles of your own in your journal today.

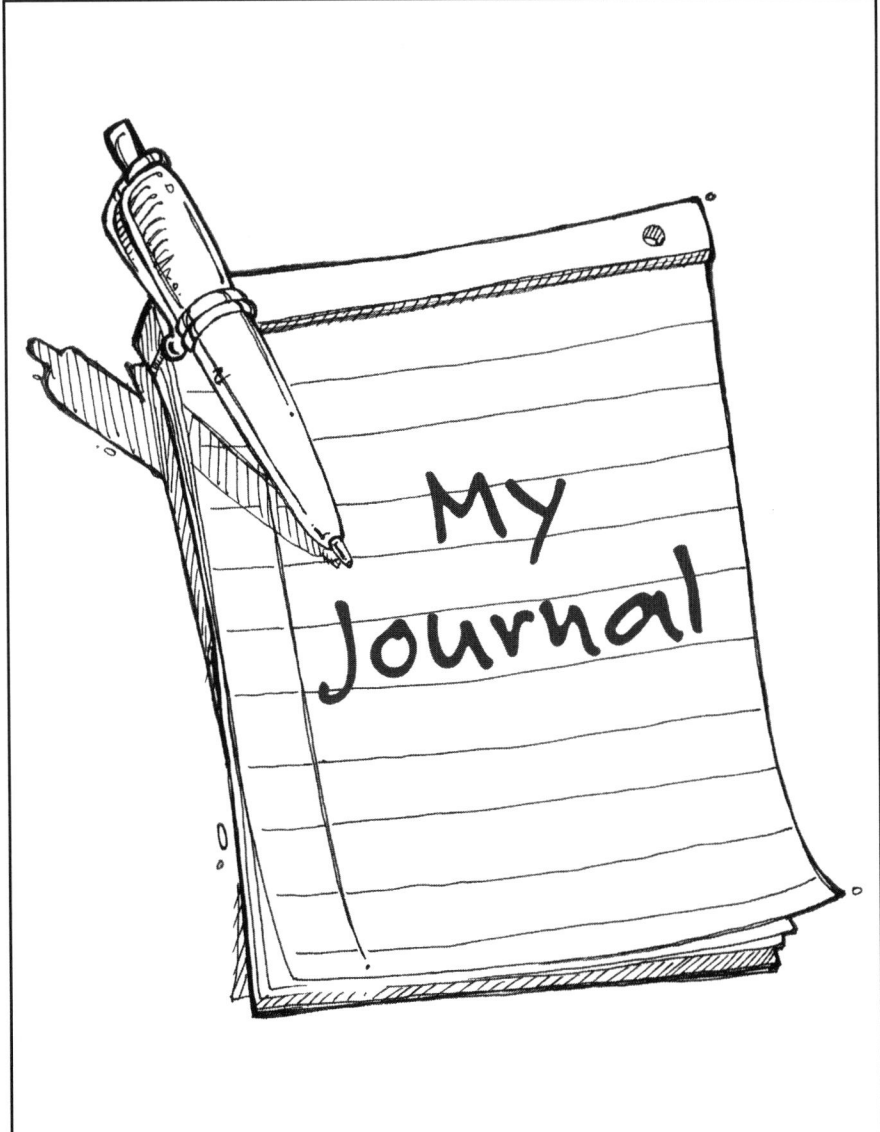

My Journal

Add-on!

en
sent
resent
present
presentation
representation
representational
nonrepresentational
nonrepresentationalism

Word-Wow!

No Luck for Liars

Katelynn lies about having her homework completed.

Katelynn turned the dead bolt in the red door and slid the safety chain into place before she headed toward the kitchen counter to check the list.

He adds more to this list every day! The dark-haired girl marched over to the window by the front door and yanked the blinds closed. The sunlit room darkened to match her mood.

She read the words at the top of the list her father had written. "Monday— Vacuum bedrooms. Empty dishwasher. Read for at least 20 minutes. Do homework. Write thank-you letter to grandparents."

Katelynn carried the list back to her bedroom and set it on the dresser. Her lucky money packet leaning against the mirror caught her attention. She picked it up and sat down on the edge of her bed. Her mother had given it to her at Chinese New Year. Katelynn fingered the gold characters on the red envelope that wished her good luck in the New Year.

She remembered her mom's excitement and anticipation about the holiday. February seemed like such a long time ago. Mom had been feeling good then. She'd prepared for weeks beforehand. First she cleaned the apartment from top to bottom. Then she'd decorated by stringing red firecrackers around the front window and hanging red good-luck banners on the front door. She bought special holiday foods, such as tangerines. She even purchased new clothes for everyone in the family.

"It's much more important than the New Year here," Mom had explained on one of their shopping trips. "In China, it's the biggest celebration of the year and lasts 15 days. It's the beginning of

spring—time for a fresh start. The color red is used everywhere to symbolize joy and happiness. There's a spectacular procession in the heart of the city. It was my favorite holiday when I was a little girl growing up in Hong Kong. Hong Kong was a British Colony then, you know," Mom had smiled, remembering. She didn't do that much any more.

A smile now spread across Katelynn's face as she thought of how delighted Mom had been when she found a kumquat tree. The fruit looked like a miniature orange but tasted a little sour. Mom had explained that its Chinese name is a play on the word lucky.

Mom had fixed a sumptuous feast for New Year's Day. The meal began with tea. It included a vegetable pancake and a sticky rice cake, which was Katelynn's favorite. The family had practiced using chopsticks and everyone laughed a lot. Mom was the only one who could get much rice to her mouth.

Even though Hatasaki was a name from the Orient, Katelynn's father wasn't sure from where or when his ancestors had immigrated. He'd grown up in California and had never left the continental United States. He was the worst with chopsticks. Big hunks of sticky rice kept landing in his lap. He'd finally asked for a fork. The meal had ended with tea. Mom was the only one that really liked tea, but they all drank it. Mom had been so happy.

The celebration had ended with the Festival of Lights. Mom's parents had come from their home in Maryland to be with them. *It all seems so long ago,* thought Katelynn.

She returned the red envelope to her dresser and picked up the list. *I'd*

better get started. Mom will be home soon.* She emptied the dishwasher and got the vacuuming done before she started to work on the thank-you letter. She'd just sat down at the kitchen table with her stationary when she heard her mom come to the door. She got up to unfasten the chain.

"Hello, dear. How are you?" Mom shut the door and walked over to the kitchen counter.

Katelynn looked over at her mother without answering. *She looks really tired,* she thought.

Katelynn finally spoke. "How am I? Fine, I guess." She went back to her letter writing.

"Have you done your reading and finished your homework?" Mom asked as she walked back toward the bedroom. She didn't even look at her daughter.

Katelynn didn't answer. She wanted to scream what she was thinking, *I've emptied the dishwasher. I've vacuumed the bedrooms. I'm writing a thank-you letter—but did you notice any of that? No! You'll probably go back to your room and sleep until Dad gets home and starts supper. You might come help then, Mom, but I doubt it,* Katelynn fumed to herself.

"Did you finish everything on the list?" Dad asked when he came in later.

Katelynn felt the anger rising in her again as she thought about what he'd said. *No "Thank-you for emptying the dishwasher," or, "The apartment looks nice—thanks for vacuuming," or maybe, "I'm glad you got that letter written. I'll mail it tomorrow. Supper smells good."*

Katelynn busied herself taking the muffins out of the oven and just nodded her head. She wasn't done with her homework. She still had her reading to do, too; but somehow she didn't care. She didn't care about the lie she had just told her father. She didn't care that her dad was tired. She was angry that her mom couldn't get herself together to fix supper and act like a normal mother. Katelynn shut the door to her bedroom. She felt guilty about the lies she'd just told, but her feelings of anger were stronger. She

293

didn't come out of her room until her sister called her to supper.

Father continued to leave a list of things for Katelynn to do every day, and Katelynn got in the habit of doing only the things he could easily check up on. He asked now and then if she had homework, or what she'd done at school. It got easier to shake her head no when he asked about the homework—even if it was a lie. She didn't tell him much about the unit on electricity they were working on at school, either. Whether she was reading or not didn't come up again, until one night when she was in her room working a jigsaw puzzle on the floor.

"So what book have you been reading, Katelynn?" Dad knelt down beside her and picked up a puzzle piece. "Is it something about electricity? You seem to be enjoying that unit at school."

Katelynn shook her head no, hoping he'd drop the subject or leave her room.

Dad looked at the lid of the puzzle box, then studied the piece he held in his hand. "So what's it about?"

"What's what about?" To avoid her father's eyes, Katelynn looked at the picture of Thomas Edison on the box.

"The book, Katelynn. The one you read every day when you get home. What's the name of it?" Dad tapped a puzzle piece into place.

Katelynn tried to put her puzzle piece in a couple of different places, but she was distracted and tried to put the silver piece in her hand on the brown hair of Thomas Edison.

Dad gently took the puzzle piece from her fingers and put it in the correct spot for her. "Katelynn, what's wrong? Why don't you want to talk about the book you've been reading? You usually love to read."

Katelynn looked down at the puzzle, hoping the water forming in her eyes wouldn't roll down her cheeks.

When the pieces blurred, she knew it was hopeless. "Dad,

I'm not reading any book. I didn't do my homework, either. I'm sorry I've been lying to you. It's just that I'm at school all day and then you leave me all this stuff to do when I get home. Mom doesn't fix lunches for us anymore or wash clothes. Jennifer's even been doing the ironing."

Dad found a place for a couple more puzzle pieces before he said anything. "Katelynn, I'm glad you've decided to tell me the truth, but being truthful is a constant action, not a one-time event. I have a feeling you've been lying about this for a while. Haven't you?"

Katelynn just nodded. Dad continued, "Trust is the reward for being truthful. I can't trust you now. Whenever you tell me something, I'll wonder if it's really true or if you're lying again."

Dad put his arm around his daughter. "I'm sorry about your mom. I'm worried about her, too. She's been talking to some people at work, and she's made an appointment to see a counselor. Maybe he'll be able to help her. I feel bad you've had so much to do lately. You can skip the reading for a while, but you do need to keep up with your homework. What are you doing in math now?"

Katelynn got her math book from her backpack. She looked her dad in the eye as she handed him the book. "It's the last chapter." He took the book, sat back down on the floor, and leaned against the bed.

When he got up to leave, he paused at the door and set the math book on her dresser. He picked up the lucky money envelope and turned it over slowly in his hands. He rubbed the gold Chinese characters with his thumb. "I like the Chinese New Year, but there's a lot more to a new start than luck, Katelynn. It has more to do with the choices you make. You don't have to wait until the new year for a fresh start. Shall we ask the Lord to give you a new, truthful start—beginning right now?"

Check understanding of the story and development of personal values.

- What was Katelynn supposed to do when she got home from school every day?
- What jobs are you responsible for at home?
- How did Katelynn feel about all the jobs she had to do?
- What did Katelynn's mom do when she got home?
- What did Katelynn's dad ask her when he arrived?
- What did Katelynn want her parents to notice?
- Why did Katelynn lie to her dad?
- What did Katelynn's dad tell her when she finally confessed to lying?

A · Test-Words

Name _____

Write each spelling word on the line as your teacher says it.

1. aimless
2. interest
3. normal
4. virus
5. burden
6. clerk
7. clever
8. forehead
9. energy
10. deliver
11. scowl
12. decimal
13. crumple
14. entitle
15. browse
16. compound

Review

Lesson
30

B · Test-Sentences

Write the sentences on the lines below, correcting each misspelled word, as well as all capitalization and punctuation errors. Two words are misspelled in each sentence.

wherebouts in orregon do you live she asked

1. "Whereabouts in Oregon do you live?" she asked.

down the museum coriddor he saw a huge dinosuar

2. Down the museum corridor, he saw a huge dinosaur.

in the state of florrida cittrus groves are numerous

3. In the state of Florida, citrus groves are numerous.

they had a bundel of crisp green counterfit bills

4. They had a bundle of crisp, green counterfeit bills.

187

4 · Test-Sentences

Reinforce recognizing misspelled words.

(Say) Read each sentence carefully. Write the sentences on the lines in your Worktext. There are two misspelled words in each sentence. Correct each misspelled word, as well as all capitalization and punctuation errors.

Take a minute to memorize...

Psalm 24:3,4

Review **30** | **Day 1**

3 · Test-Words

Test for knowledge of the correct spellings of these words.

(Say) I will say each word once, use the word in a sentence, then say the word again. Write the words on the lines in your Worktext.

1. aimless — Katelynn's mom was not cheerful and energetic, but **aimless** and tired.
2. interest — She seemed to have lost **interest** in life in general.
3. normal — "What's wrong with mom? She isn't acting **normal**," Katelynn thought.
4. virus — "Does she have a **virus** or something?" wondered Katelynn.
5. burden — Everything seemed like a huge **burden** to her mother these days.
6. clerk — At the grocery, Mrs. Hatasaki didn't even speak to or smile at the **clerk**.
7. clever — She usually had a **clever** wit and great sense of humor.
8. forehead — Mrs. Hatasaki just rubbed her **forehead** and headed for her bedroom.
9. energy — "I just don't have any **energy**," she mumbled as she lay down.
10. deliver — "I hope the carrier will **deliver** the package today," she replied.
11. scowl — Katelynn looked down at her math homework with a dark **scowl**.
12. decimal — She didn't care where the **decimal** needed to go!
13. crumple — She wanted to **crumple** up the page and throw it in the trash.
14. entitle — "Being tired does not **entitle** Mom to ignore all of us!" she said angrily.
15. browse — Mrs. Hatasaki used to really like to **browse** at the craft fairs.
16. compound — Instead of helping her, more sleep seemed to **compound** the problem.

295

1 Test-Dictation

Reinforce correct spelling by using current and previous words in context.

Say

Listen as I read each sentence, then write it in your worktext. Remember to use correct capitalization and punctuation. (Slowly read each sentence twice. Sentences are found in the student text to the right. The words **courage**, **snout**, **cornea**, and **octopus** are found in this unit.)

2 Test-Proofreading

Familiarize students with standardized test format and reinforce recognizing misspelled words.

Say

Look at each set of words. If a word is misspelled, fill in the oval by that word. If all the words are spelled correctly, fill in the oval by **no mistake**.

Review

Lesson

30

C Test-Dictation

Name _____

Write each sentence as your teacher dictates. Use correct punctuation.

1. The beautiful horse showed spirit and courage.

2. The dog pushed his snout deep into the grass.

3. The cornea of your eye should not be scratched.

4. An octopus, when afraid, can move very quickly.

D Test-Proofreading

If a word is misspelled, fill in the oval by that word. If all the words are spelled correctly, fill in the oval by **no mistake**.

1. ● fungis
   ○ aimless
   ○ interest
   ○ no mistake

2. ○ normal
   ○ virus
   ● boundery
   ○ no mistake

3. ○ burden
   ○ clerk
   ● misille
   ○ no mistake

4. ● nuclues
   ○ clever
   ○ forehead
   ○ no mistake

5. ○ energy
   ○ deliver
   ● forren
   ○ no mistake

6. ○ scowl
   ○ decimal
   ○ radius
   ● no mistake

7. ● wittness
   ○ crumple
   ○ formula
   ○ no mistake

8. ○ West Virginia
   ○ entitle
   ○ browse
   ● no mistake

9. ○ congress
   ○ fragile
   ○ crystal
   ● no mistake

10. ● cloute
    ○ double
    ○ ordeal
    ○ no mistake

11. ○ molar
    ○ compound
    ○ closeness
    ● no mistake

12. ○ mumble
    ● horrer
    ○ chapter
    ○ no mistake

188

296

E Test-Table

Name _____

If a word is misspelled, fill in the space on the grid.

crouch	multiple	restliss	sollar
New Jersey	adverb	services	cirus
centrall	Newyork	South Dekota	North Dekota
forrmat	North Carolina	coward	charter

F Writing Assessment

Make a list of things your parents do for you every day. Make another list of things they do on a weekly basis. Start a third list for things they do once or twice a year for you. You may add things to the list as you think of them. Make three more lists of things you do for your parents—daily, weekly, and yearly.

_____

_____

_____

_____

_____

_____

_____

_____

Scripture
Psalm 24:3, 4

189

A rubric for scoring is provided in Appendix B.

An ambigram is a word or words that can be read in more than one way or from more than a single vantage point. The classic ambigram is a 180-degree symmetric rotation, which means it reads the same upside down and right side up: MOM=WOW, NO=ON

1 Test-Table

Test mastery of words in this unit.

 Say

If a word is misspelled, fill in the space on the grid.

2 Writing Assessment

Assess student's spelling, grammar, and composition skills through personal writing.

 Say

- How do you feel when it's hard to tell the truth, but you choose to do it?
- Why did Katelynn lie to her dad? (She was angry about all the work he was asking her to do around the house and hurt that he didn't thank her.)
- What could Katelynn's parents have done to help her feel better even though she was working hard? (Acknowledged and thanked her for all the work she was doing so well.)
- Tell about the jobs you do at home.
- Do you think Katelynn did more jobs than you are required to do?
- Do you think it was okay for Katelynn to lie since her parents were insensitive to her needs because of their own problems? (Talk about Exodus 20:16. Does the ninth commandment make any exceptions?)

Test-Sentences

Reinforce recognizing misspelled words.

Say

Read each sentence carefully. Write the sentences on the lines in your Worktext, correcting each misspelled word, as well as all capitalization and punctuation errors.

G **Test-Sentences**

Name _____

Write the sentences on the lines below, correcting each misspelled word, as well as all capitalization and punctuation errors. Two words are misspelled in each sentence.

Review Lesson 30

while at a zoo in south carolina I saw a wallrus

1. While at a zoo in South Carolina, I saw a walrus.

Jesus taught us by exampel, how to be humbel.

2. Jesus taught us, by example, how to be humble.

the decaying molusk on the beach had a fuol smell

3. The decaying mollusk on the beach had a foul smell.

a journy through the deserrt can cost you your life!

4. A journey through the desert can cost you your life!

H **Test-Words**

Write each spelling word on the line as your teacher says it.

1. formula
2. fragile
3. crystal
4. double
5. ordeal
6. closeness
7. mumble
8. chapter
9. border
10. obvious
11. error
12. major
13. version
14. miracle
15. mountains
16. willpower

190

Test-Words

Test for knowledge of the correct spellings of these words.

Say

I will say the word once, use the word in a sentence, then say the word again. Write the word on the lines in your Worktext.

1. formula — "I wish there was magic **formula** to get Mom back to normal!" said Katelynn.
2. fragile — She picked up a **fragile** bowl out of the dish drain.
3. crystal — She was so mad she didn't care if she broke her mom's nice **crystal** bowl.
4. double — "We'll just have to **double** up on chores till she's better," Jennifer said.
5. ordeal — "I hate this whole **ordeal**!" Katelynn complained to herself.
6. closeness — She missed the **closeness** she usually had with her mom.
7. mumble — When her dad asked about her homework, Katelynn would **mumble** a reply.
8. chapter — "Which **chapter** are you reading in your book about castles?" he asked.
9. border — Katelynn looked guilty as she fiddled with the **border** of the puzzle.
10. obvious — By the look on her face, it was **obvious** to her dad that she had been lying.
11. error — Katelynn knew lying was not just an **error** in judgment; it was a sin!
12. major — "I consider your lying a **major** breach of trust," said Mr. Hatasaki.
13. version — "I don't want your **version** of the truth; I want the truth!"
14. miracle — "We need the Lord to work a **miracle** for Mom," Dad said.
15. mountains — "He can move **mountains** and help you and Mom, too!" he encouraged.
16. willpower — Don't trust in your own **willpower**; trust in God for help!

Test-Editing

Name _____

If a word is spelled correctly, fill in the oval under **Correct**. If the word is misspelled, fill in the oval under **Incorrect**, and spell the word correctly on the blank.

	Correct	Incorrect	
1. Goergia	○	●	Georgia
2. dormitory	●	○	
3. particle	●	○	
4. scoundrel	●	○	
5. acount	○	●	account
6. reckliss	○	●	reckless
7. dribble	●	○	
8. burial	●	○	
9. angle	●	○	
10. mingel	○	●	mingle
11. stillness	●	○	
12. drought	●	○	
13. riddle	●	○	
14. pronownce	○	●	pronounce
15. anchor	●	○	
16. deserve	●	○	
17. cornerstone	●	○	
18. anouncer	○	●	announcer
19. cummulus	○	●	cumulus
20. orbitt	○	●	orbit

Review
Lesson
30

191

3 Test-Editing

Reinforce recognizing and correcting misspelled words.

4 Action Game

Reinforce spelling skills and provide motivation and interest.

Materials

- two balls
- word list on certificate at end of unit

SPELLING ZIGZAG

Divide the class into two teams. Each team forms two lines which stand about eight feet apart facing each other. Choose a student to monitor each team. The first player on each team holds a ball. Call out the first spelling word to be reviewed. The first player on each team says the first letter of the word and tosses the ball to the player across from him. That player says the second letter of the word and tosses the ball to the player next in line on the other side. The pattern continues until the word has been spelled, the monitor for each team checking the team's spelling. The team to spell the word correctly first gets a point. The team with the most points wins!

Game

1

Reinforce spelling skills and provide motivation and interest.

Materials
- game page (from student text)
- colored pencils (1 per child)
- game word list

Game Word List
Check off each word lightly in pencil as it is used.

The Dragons

1. scoundrel
2. scowl
3. snout
4. fungus
5. boundary
6. missile
7. nucleus
8. foreign
9. radius

The Firecrackers

1. witness
2. West Virginia
3. congress
4. clout
5. molar
6. horror
7. crouch
8. New Jersey
9. central

The Lanterns

1. format
2. multiple
3. adverb
4. New York
5. North Carolina
6. restless
7. services
8. South Dakota
9. coward

J Game   Name _____

Score points for each review word or Other Word Form you or your team spells correctly.

Review
Lesson
30

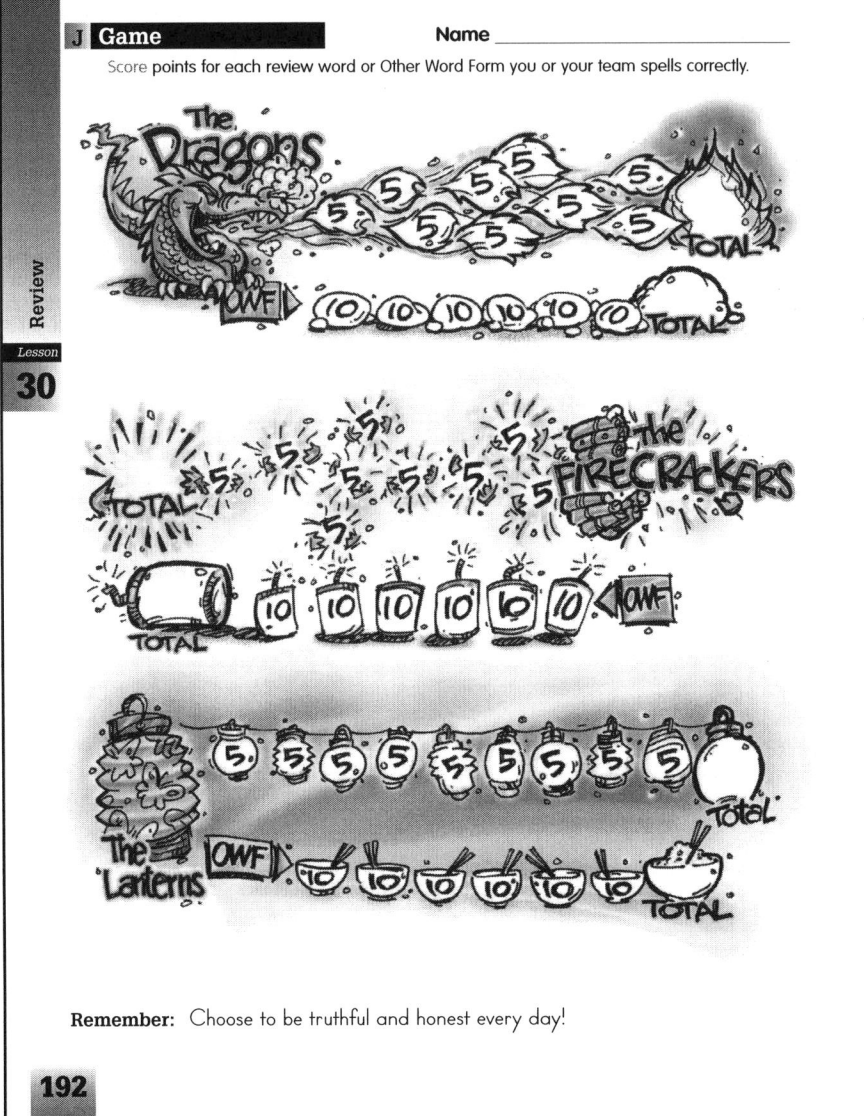

Remember: Choose to be truthful and honest every day!

192

How to Play:
- Divide the class into three teams. Name one team **The Dragons**, one **The Firecrackers**, and one **The Lanterns**. (Option: You may wish to seat students in groups of three, each student from a different team. They should share one game page.)
- Have a student from the first team go to the board.
- Say the spelling word.
- Have the student write the word on the board.
- If the word is spelled correctly, have each team member color a point symbol by his/her team name. If the word is misspelled, have him/her put an **X** through one point symbol. That word may not be given again.
- Repeat this process with the second team and then the third.
- When the words from all three lists have been used, the team with the most points is the winner.
- Play another round using Other Word Forms.

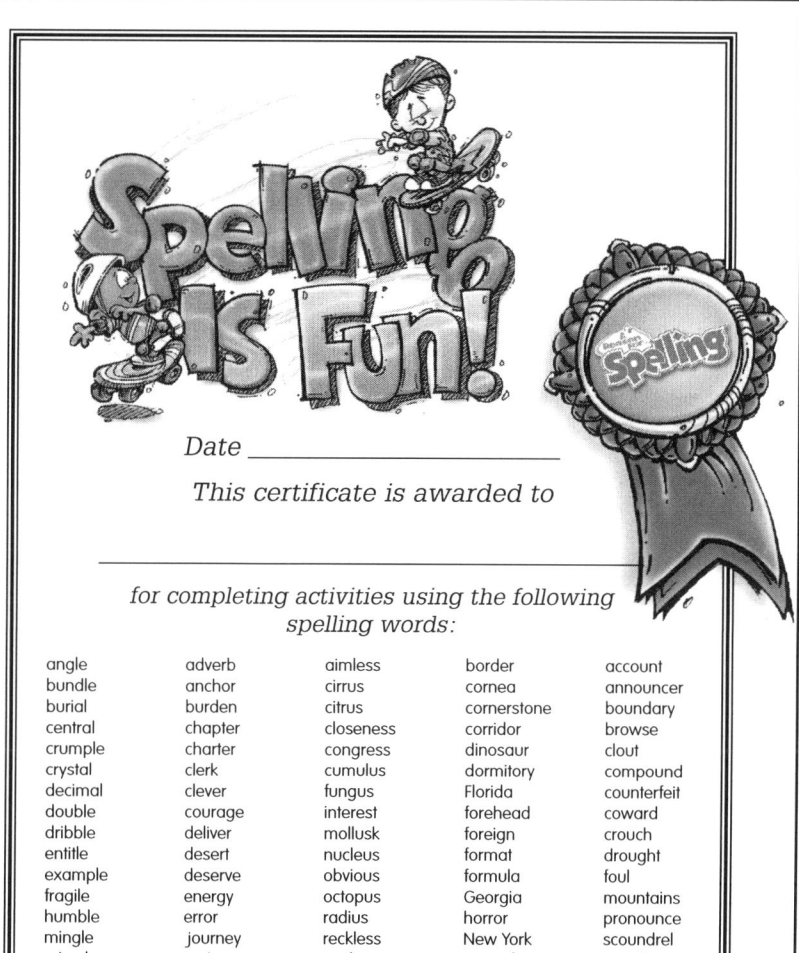

Date _____

This certificate is awarded to

_____

for completing activities using the following spelling words:

angle	adverb	aimless	border	account
bundle	anchor	cirrus	cornea	announcer
burial	burden	citrus	cornerstone	boundary
central	chapter	closeness	corridor	browse
crumple	charter	congress	dinosaur	clout
crystal	clerk	cumulus	dormitory	compound
decimal	clever	fungus	Florida	counterfeit
double	courage	interest	forehead	coward
dribble	deliver	mollusk	foreign	crouch
entitle	desert	nucleus	format	drought
example	deserve	obvious	formula	foul
fragile	energy	octopus	Georgia	mountains
humble	error	radius	horror	pronounce
mingle	journey	reckless	New York	scoundrel
miracle	major	restless	normal	scowl
missile	molar	services	North Carolina	snout
multiple	New Jersey	stillness	North Dakota	South Carolina
mumble	solar	virus	orbit	South Dakota
particle	version	walrus	ordeal	whereabouts
riddle	West Virginia	witness	Oregon	willpower

2 Certificate

Provide an opportunity for parents or guardians to encourage and assess their child's progress.

 Fill in today's date and your name on your certificate.

 Take a minute to memorize...

Psalm 24:3,4

3 Letter

Provide the parent or guardian with the spelling word lists for the next unit.

Give your parents or guardian this letter that lists your spelling words for the next unit. Put it where you will remember to practice the words together.

Dear Parent,

We are about to begin the last spelling unit of the year containing only one lesson. A set of twenty words will be studied next week. All the words will be reviewed the following week. Values based on the Scripture listed below will be taught.

Lesson 31

Connecticut	knock
doorknob	knuckle
flight	nighttime
highland	plight
Illinois	Rhode Island
khaki	rhyme
knack	sigh
kneel	slight
knitting	wharves
knives	wreck

Psalm 33:4, 5

Trivia and Trust

Laney questions why God would want Rachel to move.

Rachel tore open her yellow bag of candy and looked down at the magazine in her lap. "True or false? 'Names for Crayola® crayon colors come from official government books.'" Rachel turned to Laney and dumped some of the brightly colored candy in her friend's open hand.

"False," Beth guessed. "I don't think 'Razzmatazz' comes from a book the government wrote."

Rachel swallowed the chocolate morsels in her mouth before she pronounced judgment. "That's right!" She beamed as she surveyed her classmates' faces. "Okay, 'How many crayons are made in the Crayola® factories every day?'"

A thick cloud suddenly hid the sun. Laney picked the last chocolate from her hand and popped it into her mouth. There weren't ever enough pieces to satisfy her! She stood up to leave the group still sitting around the lone pine tree on the playground. She shivered as she put her jacket back on. It was cold now that the sun's warming rays had disappeared.

"One-hundred thousand," guessed Rosa.

"A million," Heather glanced up from her butterfly book.

"Guess again. No one's close." Rachel rubbed her hands together in anticipation.

"On a normal production day, I'd say somewhere in the proximity of 12 million, or roughly 3 billion a year." Thorny looked very serious as he joined the game. "Hypothetically speaking, in 16 months enough are made that when laid end to end they'd reach the moon. Of course the possibilities of proving that hypothesis

other than mathematically are remote. There is the problem of gravity in our atmosphere and the lack of it in space to consider.…" Thorny's voice trailed off as he started pondering his own thoughts.

Laney raised her eyebrows and frowned as she looked at her best friend, Rachel.

"He's right—about the 12 million part at least," Rachel announced with a happy face. "How did you know that?" Thorny didn't respond, so Rachel continued. "You must've read this. Okay. Here's the next one."

"'According to surveys, what is the all-time favorite crayon color?'"

"I say Tickle-Me-Pink or Mango Tango." Kristin guessed.

"Very good, Kristin. Those are Crayola® color names, but not the ones we are looking for! Do I have another guess?" Rachel finished the juice in her box with a noisy slurp.

Thorny was still considering the possibilities of a trail of crayons to the moon and didn't attempt to answer.

"Blue!" Beth yelled out her favorite color.

Rosa tried hers, "Red!"

"Blue it is! Beth is right! With two correct answers, you are a winner!" Rachel picked up the magazine again. "One final question. 'How many shades of wrappers are Crayola® crayons wrapped in?'"

Laney ran her fingers through her short hair and rolled her eyes. "Who cares?" She picked up her lunch bag and headed toward the trash can by the back door of the school.

"Twelve!" Thorny announced as Laney passed him. "And did you know that in five weeks there are enough

Crayola® crayons made to circle the earth at the equator?"

"Are you sure?" Laney taunted.

Rachel stood and pointed toward Thorny. "Who agrees with this gentleman in the blue T-shirt?" Everyone raised their hands. Hubert Thorton Remington III was always right.

"If your hand is raised you are…" Rachel paused for effect, "…right! And that concludes round one of Knowlton Knows Trivia Game! Beth and Thorny are tied with two correct answers each!"

Laney turned and looked over her shoulder at her friend's animated face. She watched her show the cover of the magazine to Thorny. She was too far away now to hear what Rachel was saying, but she could see Thorny laugh and open the magazine. Everyone else gathered around to look at the pictures.

I'm going to miss Rachel, Laney thought as she hurried on toward the trash can. *Montana is so far away the Jacobsons might as well be moving to the other side of the earth—or the moon, for that matter. I can't believe she's leaving in just three weeks. But it's true!*

Laney walked slowly to the other side of the playground and leaned against the warm bricks of the school. She wiped her eyes with the back of her hand. Sometimes she wanted to spend every waking moment with Rachel—making sure they did as many things together as they could before she moved. Other times she just wished the Jacobson family would hurry up and get out of town, so the hurt in her heart could begin to heal. *How could they know God wanted them at Shadow Creek Ranch in Montana?* she thought.

"What's wrong?" Rachel joined Laney against the sun-warmed wall a few minutes later. "Why'd you leave?"

"You're the one who's leaving," Laney snapped. "And you don't seem too unhappy about it."

"I will really miss all the people here, Laney—especially you. But I think God wants our family in Montana. I'm not exactly sure what it will be like living out there, but God loves us, and I guess I trust Him to plan only good things."

"What about me? You said we'd be best friends forever. If I can't trust you, how I can trust God?"

"God sent someone to buy Father's business and our house, and I've told you how much they need us at Shadow Creek Ranch. With more guests coming, they need me to help with the horses. It's a lot of work keeping a barn clean and 10 horses groomed."

"But I need you right here."

"Do you believe 12 million Crayola® crayons are made every day?"

"Yeah, that's what Thorny said. But what do 12 million crayons have to do with you leaving?"

"Don't you think the Bible is more reliable than a magazine?" Rachel handed Laney three pieces of candy.

"What do you mean?"

"I mean that if you trust Thorny when he tells us a magazine says 12 million crayons are made every day, you should trust God when He says He loves you and will take care of you."

The bell rang. The two girls lined up at the door with the rest of Mr. Canfield's class. Laney ate the last piece of chocolate in silence. The sun peeked out from behind the gigantic cloud and the bright rays began warming the playground again. She took the magazine from Rachel's hand and thumbed her way through it, looking for the crayon article.

"'When was the first box of colored wax crayons in the United States made, and how much did they cost?'" Laney smiled.

Rachel rapidly replied, "1903. A nickel for a box of eight."

"You're right! And you are a winner with two correct answers in the ongoing Knowlton Knows Trivia Game." Rachel laughed and felt the tension leaving her body.

"You're right about God, too, Rach," Laney said quietly. "And I'm glad you're my best friend even if you're moving. Now, 'What retired colors are placed in the Crayola® Hall of Fame?'"

Discussion Time

Check understanding of the story and development of personal values.

- Talk about a best friend you have had who no longer lives near you.
- How did it feel when you could no longer see him or her on a regular basis?
- How does Laney feel about her best friend Rachel moving to Montana?
- What game is Rachel leading during lunch hour?
- Who are some of the kids participating in the game?
- Why doesn't Laney play?
- What does Rachel tell Laney about trusting and relying on God?

A Preview

Write each word as your teacher says it.

Name _____

1. Connecticut
2. flight
3. nighttime
4. sigh
5. plight
6. Illinois
7. wharves
8. slight
9. Rhode Island
10. khaki
11. doorknob
12. kneel
13. knock
14. knives
15. knuckle
16. rhyme
17. knack
18. knitting
19. wreck
20. highland

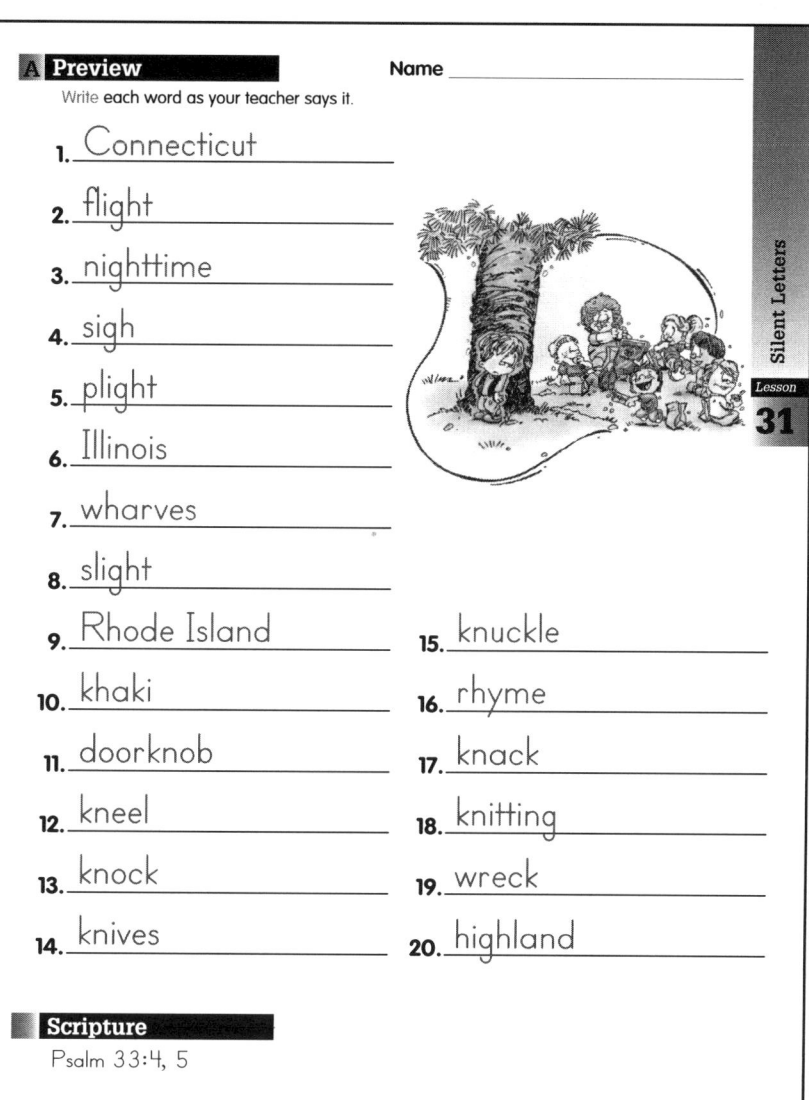

Silent Letters

Lesson **31**

Scripture
Psalm 33:4, 5

195

3 Preview
Test for knowledge of the correct spellings of these words.

Customize Your List
On a separate sheet of paper, additional words of your choice may be tested.

Say I will say each word once, use the word in a sentence, then say the word again. Write the words on the lines in your Worktext.

Correct Immediately!
Say Let's correct our Preview. I will spell each word out loud. If you spelled a word incorrectly, rewrite it correctly.

Progress Chart
Students may record scores. (Reproducible master provided in Appendix B.)

1.	Connecticut	Connecticut borders Laney's home state of New York.
2.	flight	She remembered the **flight** she made with her mom to visit Knowlton Elementary.
3.	nighttime	"It was **nighttime** when we arrived," she reflected.
4.	sigh	She let out a **sigh** as she remembered how nervous she was.
5.	plight	Laney felt God did not understand her **plight** of losing her best friend.
6.	Illinois	"Isn't there a ranch in **Illinois**? That's a lot closer!" she pleaded.
7.	wharves	Laney enjoyed looking at a painting of New England **wharves**.
8.	slight	She liked the look of a **slight** storm brewing in the sky.
9.	Rhode Island	Her mom had purchased the painting at a gallery in **Rhode Island**.
10.	khaki	She put on her **khaki** walking shorts and went out to play with Wicker.
11.	doorknob	Wicker bounded toward her when he heard her hand on the **doorknob**.
12.	kneel	She didn't want to **kneel** in the grass, so she sat on the lawn chair.
13.	knock	Mr. Canfield gave a quick **knock** on the podium to get the class's attention.
14.	knives	"Who can bring spreading **knives** to our class party?" he asked.
15.	knuckle	Rachel hit her **knuckle** on her desk as she tried to raise her hand.
16.	rhyme	"I want each of you to write a short, humorous **rhyme** to share at the party."
17.	knack	"You have real **knack** for cheering me up," Laney told Rachel.
18.	knitting	"I guess I can to take up **knitting** if you move," she told her.
19.	wreck	"I'm sure you won't be the **wreck** you think you will," said Rachel.
20.	highland	"The **highland** areas on and around the ranch are gorgeous," said Rachel.

305

Word Shapes

4

Help students form a correct image of whole words.

Say Look at each word and think about its shape. Now, write the word in the correct Word Shape Boxes. You may check off each word as you use it.

(A silent letter occurs when two letters spell the sound of only one letter or when one or two letters stand for a completely silent sound.)

Say In the Word Shape Boxes, fill in the boxes containing the silent consonant or consonants in each word.

Take a minute to memorize...

Psalm 33:4,5

B Word Shapes

Name _____

Using the word bank below, write each word in the correct Word Shape Boxes. Next, in the Word Shape Boxes, fill in the boxes containing the silent consonant or consonants in each word.

Silent Letters

Lesson **31**

1. k h a k i
2. k n e e l
3. k n o c k
4. p l i g h t
5. r h y m e
6. I l l i n o i s
7. s l i g h t
8. w h a r v e s
9. f l i g h t
10. w r e c k

11. k n a c k
12. k n i t t i n g
13. k n i v e s
14. h i g h l a n d
15. R h o d e I s l a n d
16. k n u c k l e
17. d o o r k n o b
18. s i g h
19. C o n n e c t i c u t
20. n i g h t t i m e

Word Bank

Connecticut	Illinois	knitting	nighttime	sigh
doorknob	khaki	knives	plight	slight
flight	knack	knock	Rhode Island	wharves
highland	kneel	knuckle	rhyme	wreck

196

Answers may vary for duplicate word shapes.

Be Prepared For Fun

Check these supply lists for **Fun Ways to Spell** - presented **Day 2**.
Purchase and/or gather these items ahead of time!

General
- Pencil
- Graph Paper (1 sheet per child)
- Spelling List

Auditory
- Voice Recorder
- Spelling List

Visual
- American Sign Language reproducible master (provided in Appendix B)
- Spelling List

Tactile
- Soccer Ball, Basketball, Tennis Ball, or 4-Square Ball
- Spelling List

C Hide and Seek Name _____

Play Hide and Seek with your words. Fill in a box on the bar graph (left to right) for each word you spell correctly.

LOOK SAY SPELL ALOUD WRITE SEEK CHECK

D Other Word Forms

Using the words below, follow the instructions given by your teacher.

doorknobs	knelt	plighted	slighted
flightier	knife	plighting	slighting
flightiest	knitted	Rhode Islander	wharf
highlander	knocked	rhymed	wreckage
Illinoian	knocking	rhyming	wrecked
khakis	knuckled	sighing	wrecking
kneeling	knuckling	sighs	

E Fun Ways to Spell

Initial the box of each activity you finish.

1. Create a crossword puzzle with clues.

2. Spell your words with sign language.

3. WORD
Spell your words on a voice recorder.

4. B·A·T·C·H
Bounce a ball as you spell your words.

197

Silent Letters

Lesson 31

Day 2 *Lesson 31*

---

1 Hide and Seek

Reinforce spelling by using multiple styles of learning.

On a white board, Teacher writes each word — one at a time. **Have students:**

- **Look** at the word.
- **Say** the word out loud.
- **Spell** the word out loud.
- **Hide** (teacher erases word.)
- **Write** the word on paper.
- **Seek** (teacher rewrites word.)
- **Check** spelling. If incorrect, rewrite word correctly.

2 Other Word Forms

This activity is optional. Have students find and circle the Other Word Forms that are most nearly synonyms of the following:

pier
rapped
intertwined
sighing

3 Fun Ways to Spell

Four activities are provided. Use one, two, three, or all of the activities. Have students initial the box for each activity they complete.

Options:

- assign activities to students according to their learning styles
- set up the activities in learning centers for the students to do throughout the day
- divide students into four groups and assign one activity per group
- do one activity per day

General
To create a crossword puzzle...
- Use a pencil to arrange your words on graph paper.
- Overlap words where letters are shared.
- Don't create any new words.
- Outline each word with a marker and number it.
- Write a clue for each word.
- Erase your words.
- Trade with a classmate and work each other's puzzles.

Auditory
To spell your words using a voice recorder...
- Record yourself as you say and spell each word on your spelling list.
- Listen to your recording and check your spelling.

Visual
To spell your words with sign language...
- Have a classmate read a spelling word to you from the list.
- Spell the word using the American Sign Language alphabet.
- Do this with each word on your list.

Tactile
To bounce a ball as you spell your words...
- Look at the first word on your list.
- Bounce the ball as you say each letter of the word aloud.
- Do this with each word on your list.

Working with Words

Familiarize students with word meaning and usage.

Hidden Words

Explain that the spelling words for this week are hidden in the puzzle. After finding each word, the student should write the word under the correct heading.

Say

Use the word bank to help you find each of the words in the puzzle. Words may go across, down, or diagonally. Circle, then write the words.

Take a minute to memorize...

Psalm 33:4,5

F **Working with Words**

Name _____

Hidden Words

Silent Letters

Lesson **31**

Use the word bank to help you find each of the words in the puzzle. Words may go across, down, or diagonally. Circle and write the words.

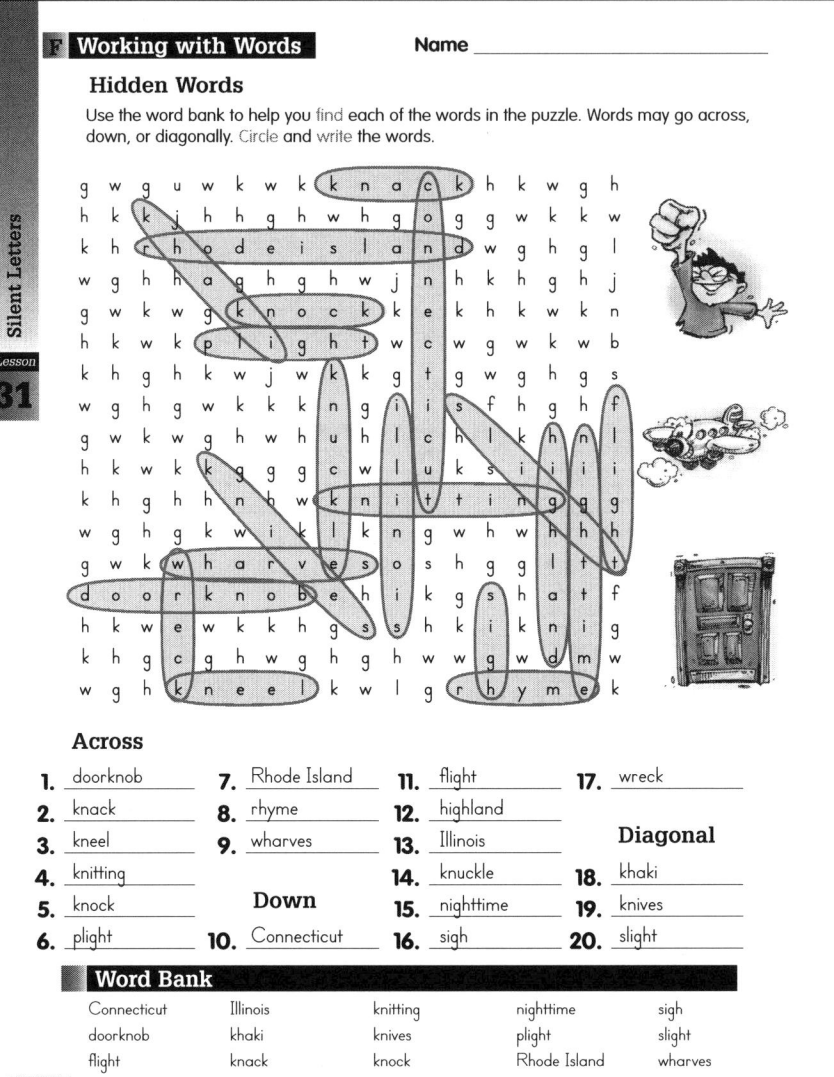

Across

1. doorknob
2. knack
3. kneel
4. knitting
5. knock
6. plight
7. Rhode Island
8. rhyme
9. wharves
11. flight
12. highland
13. Illinois
14. knuckle
15. nighttime
16. sigh
17. wreck

Down

10. Connecticut

Diagonal

18. khaki
19. knives
20. slight

Word Bank

Connecticut	Illinois	knitting	nighttime	sigh
doorknob	khaki	knives	plight	slight
flight	knack	knock	Rhode Island	wharves
highland	kneel	knuckle	rhyme	wreck

198

C Dictation

Name _____

Write **each sentence** as your teacher dictates. Use **correct punctuation.**

1. Laney <u>felt lonely as she let out a huge sigh.</u>

   _____

2. Thorny <u>cut his knuckle with one of the knives</u> <u>while he was playing with it.</u>

3. <u>She caught her khaki pants on the chair when</u> <u>she tried to kneel.</u>

H Proofreading

If a word is misspelled, fill in the oval by that word. If all the words are spelled correctly, fill in the oval by **no mistake**.

1. ○ wreck
    ● Conneticut
    ○ foul
    ○ no mistake

5. ○ slight
    ● kaki
    ○ clout
    ○ no mistake

9. ● kniting
    ○ knives
    ○ willpower
    ○ no mistake

2. ○ scowl
    ○ flight
    ○ crouch
    ● no mistake

6. ● rhime
    ○ Rhode Island
    ○ browse
    ○ no mistake

10. ○ knock
    ○ knuckle
    ○ compound
    ● no mistake

3. ○ highland
    ○ boundary
    ● nightime
    ○ no mistake

7. ○ doorknob
    ○ knack
    ○ snout
    ● no mistake

11. ○ announcer
    ● Ilinois
    ○ drought
    ○ no mistake

4. ○ plight
    ○ sigh
    ○ mountains
    ● no mistake

8. ○ South Dakota
    ○ kneel
    ○ coward
    ● no mistake

12. ● warves
    ○ whereabouts
    ○ pronounce
    ○ no mistake

199

1 Dictation

Reinforce correct spelling by using current and previous words in context.

(Say) Listen as I read each sentence and then write it in your Worktext. Remember to use correct capitalization and punctuation. (Slowly read each sentence twice. Sentences are found in the Student Worktext to the left.)

Day 4

2 Proofreading

Lesson **31**

Familiarize students with standardized test format and reinforce recognition of misspelled words.

(Say) Look at each set of words. If a word is misspelled, fill in the oval by that word. If all the words are spelled correctly, fill in the oval by **no mistake**.

3 Hide and Seek

Reinforce correct spelling of current spelling words. Repeat this activity from Day 2.

4 Vocabulary Extension

Have your students complete this activity to strengthen spelling ability and expand vocabulary. The reproducible master is provided in Appendix A as shown on the inset page to the right.

1 Posttest

Visit the **A Reason For** website to download free, printable Posttest pages.

I will say the word once, use it in a sentence, then say it again. Write your words on a separate sheet of paper.

Progress Chart

Students may record scores. (Appendix B)

Personal Dictionary

Students may add any words they have misspelled to their personal dictionaries. (Appendix B)

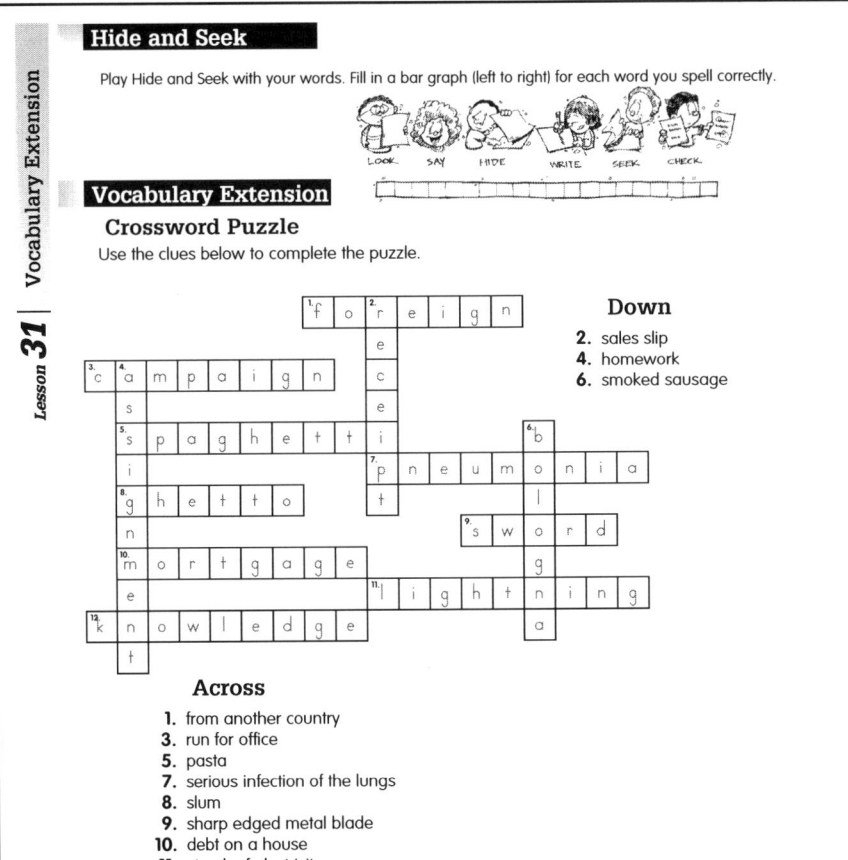

Lesson **31** | Vocabulary Extension

Hide and Seek

Play Hide and Seek with your words. Fill in a bar graph (left to right) for each word you spell correctly.

Vocabulary Extension

Crossword Puzzle
Use the clues below to complete the puzzle.

Down
2. sales slip
4. homework
6. smoked sausage

Across
1. from another country
3. run for office
5. pasta
7. serious infection of the lungs
8. slum
9. sharp edged metal blade
10. debt on a house
11. streak of electricity
12. understanding

Word Bank

assignment	foreign	lightning	receipt
bologna	ghetto	mortgage	spaghetti
campaign	knowledge	pneumonia	sword

350

1.	Connecticut	Laney's home state of New York borders **Connecticut**.
2.	highland	"Dad showed us some of the beautiful **highland** areas on the ranch," she said.
3.	flight	She recalled the **flight** that brought her and her mom here.
4.	nighttime	"It was **nighttime**, and I couldn't tell a thing about the town," she remembered.
5.	sigh	"Now I have a good friend here and she's going to move!" she said with a **sigh**.
6.	knitting	"Maybe I can take up **knitting** in my spare time," she thought mournfully.
7.	plight	"God, do you even care about my **plight**?" she asked.
8.	slight	"I feel a **slight** bit annoyed and grumpy about all of this!"
9.	Illinois	"Why Montana, Lord? Why not **Illinois** or someplace close like that?"
10.	khaki	After putting on **khaki** walking shorts, she went to see Wicker.
11.	doorknob	Hearing the **doorknob** turn, Wicker bounded toward the patio.
12.	kneel	Not wanting to **kneel** on the wet grass, she sat in a lawn chair.
13.	knuckle	"Want me to throw you a **knuckle** ball, Wicker?" she asked.
14.	knack	"You have a **knack** for making me feel better," she told the dog.
15.	Rhode Island	Laney showed Rachel a painting her mom had purchased in **Rhode Island**.
16.	wharves	"I love the colors of the sky and all the goods being unloaded on the **wharves**."
17.	knock	A **knock** on the podium by Mr. Canfield got the class's attention quickly.
18.	knives	"Who will volunteer to bring spreading **knives** to the class party?" he asked.
19.	rhyme	"Write a funny **rhyme** or two to share with the class at our party," he said.
20.	wreck	"Lord, help me not to be a total **wreck** when Rachel moves!" Laney exclaimed.

▌ Game

Name _____

Go along with Rachel to cheer up Laney. Move one space for each word you or your team spells correctly.

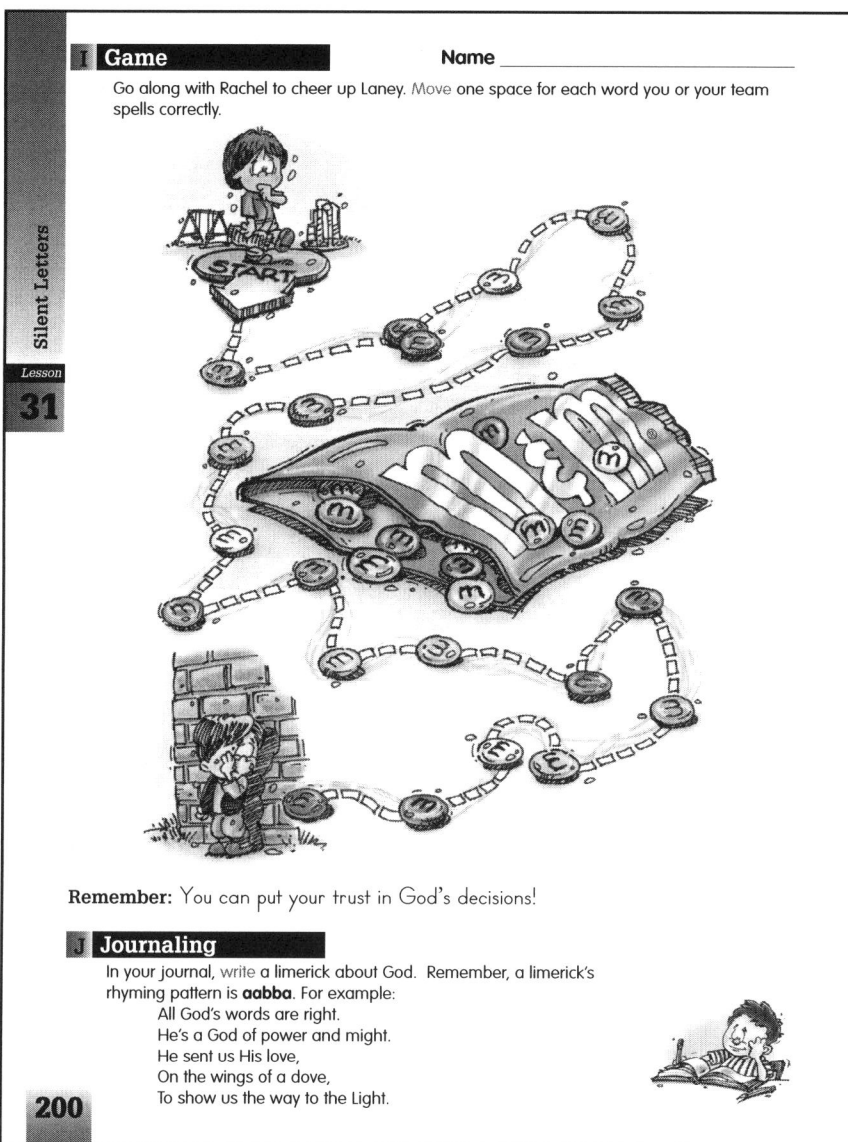

Remember: You can put your trust in God's decisions!

▌ Journaling

In your journal, write a limerick about God. Remember, a limerick's rhyming pattern is **aabba**. For example:

All God's words are right.
He's a God of power and might.
He sent us His love,
On the wings of a dove,
To show us the way to the Light.

200

2 Game

Reinforce spelling skills and provide motivation and interest.

Materials
- game page (from student text)
- game pieces (1 per child)
- game word list

Game Word List

1. **solar**
2. **cirrus**
3. **charter**
4. **Connecticut**
5. **flight**
6. **highland**
7. **nighttime**
8. **plight**
9. **sigh**
10. **slight**
11. **khaki**
12. **Rhode Island**
13. **rhyme**
14. **doorknob**
15. **knack**
16. **kneel**
17. **knitting**
18. **knives**
19. **knock**
20. **knuckle**

How to Play:

- Divide the class into two teams.
- Have each student place his/her game piece on Start.
- Have a student from team A go to the board.
- Say the spelling word.
- Have the student write the word on the board.
- If correct, instruct each member of team A to move his/her game piece forward one space.
- Alternate between teams A and B.
- The team to reach Laney first is the winner.
- **Small Group Option**: Students may play this game without teacher direction in small groups of two or more.

3 Journaling

Provide a meaningful reason for correct spelling through personal writing.

Review the story using discussion leads provided on the following page. Encourage students to apply the Scriptural value in their journaling.

(Say)

- How many crayons did Thorny say the Crayola® company made every day? (12 million….or roughly 3 billion a year.)

- How many shades of wrappers are Crayola® crayons wrapped in? (12)

- Who said there were 12 shades of wrappers when Rachel asked her classmates that question? (Thorny)

- Where did Thorny get his information? (From a magazine.)

- Why did Rachel ask Laney, "Don't you think the Bible is more reliable than a magazine?" (She wanted Laney to understand that if you trust Thorny when he tells us facts from a magazine, you should trust God when he says he loves you and will take care of you.)

- No one knows exactly where limericks came from; but Edward Lear wrote some that everyone liked in the early 1800's. Two examples of his limericks are:

  A flea and a fly in a flue
  Didn't know quite what to do
  Said the flea, "Let us fly."
  Said the fly, "Let us flee."
  So they flew through a flaw in the flue.

  There was an Old Man with a beard,
  Who said, "It is just as I feared!
  Two Owls and a Hen,
  Four Larks and Wren.
  Have all built their nest in my beard."

- The rhyming pattern of a limerick is always aabba. Lines 3 and 4 are often shorter too.

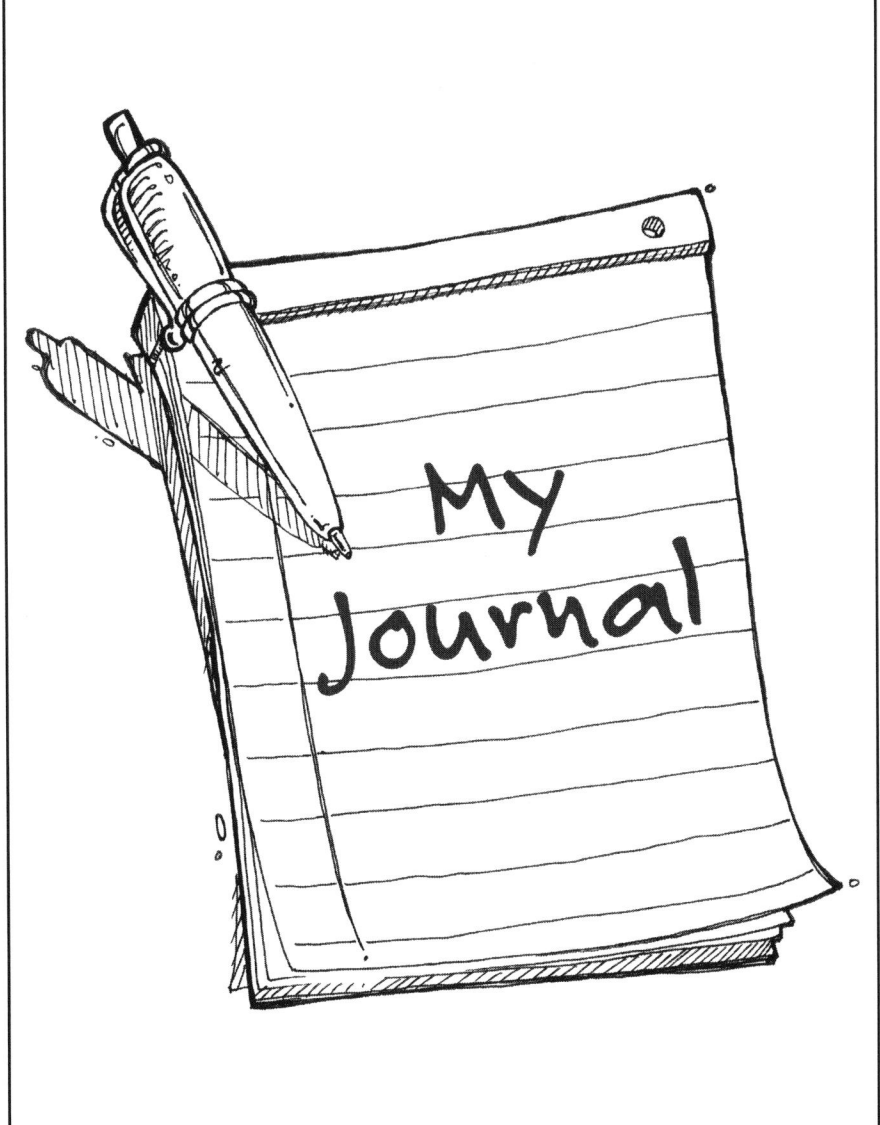

The plastic things on the ends of shoelaces are called aglets.

Good Times, Bad Times

Tommy gets a chance at a major role in a school play. When his grandmother dies, he loses the part — or was there another reason?

"Guess what, Mom?" Tommy bounded into the house when Mrs. Simmons dropped him off after school.

"Let's see, it probably has something to do with the baseball season coming up." Mrs. Rawson neatly folded an undershirt and reached into the dryer for another. "I know! You found out which team you'll be playing for in the city Little League!"

"No, not yet." Tommy put his math book down on the washing machine. "Our school is having an end-of-the-year program, and our class is doing a play. Guess who got a really big part?"

Somehow Mrs. Rawson kept a straight face as she guessed, "Daniel?"

"Aw, Mom." Tommy gently knocked his forehead against the door-jamb he was leaning against.

"So what part did you get?" Mom picked up a stack of neatly folded laundry and headed upstairs.

Tommy grabbed his math book and followed. "Well, see, it's about several inventor guys and how they never gave up and stuff—and I'm Thomas Edison."

"How fitting, Tommy Edison," Mom teased. "I'm impressed." She put a pile of clean clothes in the proper drawer in her bedroom. "That sounds like quite a responsibility. Do you have a lot of lines to memorize?"

"I've got it right here." Tommy pulled out several sheets of folded paper out of the math book. "I guess it's about five pages, but I'm not the one talking all the time."

Mom took the sheets and looked them over. "That's true, Tommy, but you have to know when to say your lines, and that's almost as hard as remembering what to say. There's really quite a bit here. When is this play?"

"Next week right at the end of school." Tommy refolded the papers and stuck them back in his book. "Mr. Canfield is having two people learn each part in case someone gets sick or something, but I'm Thomas Edison. Tony is my understudy like in a real production."

"I hope Grandma's doing better by then." A worried frown crossed Mrs. Rawson's face. "Lately she's gotten extremely agitated—sometimes even violent—if I'm not right here, even though she doesn't know who I am." She rubbed the back of her neck and smiled. "We'll work something out, though, because I can't miss Tommy Edison, actor."

Tommy gave his mom a hug. "Where is Grandma, anyway?"

"She's asleep downstairs in her room." Mom rested her chin on the top of Tommy's head. "She's been sleeping a lot and seems to have a harder time walking and talking." Tommy felt her sigh ruffle his hair softly. "I just don't know how much longer we can take care of her, even though I know it's better for her to be here with her family."

Tommy gave his mom a tight squeeze. He knew she worked awfully hard taking care of Grandma, and now that Grandma had to wear adult diapers, it was even harder. "Want me to finish the laundry?" He offered.

"Why, thank you, kind sir." Mom dropped a kiss on the top of his head. "You betcha I do. I'll go ahead and get started on supper." Arms looped around each other, they marched back downstairs in step.

After supper, Tommy fetched his math book. By the time his homework was done, he decided he was just too tired of using his brain to practice his Edison lines that night.

The next afternoon was one of those near-perfect days when it seems almost a crime to stay indoors. Tommy got out his pitch-return backstop and began sharpening up his baseball skills.

"Tommy the Terror!" Lisa called out the back door, "Mom said to remind you to practice your lines tonight. You've only got four more days to learn it all!"

"Okay!" Tommy called back over his shoulder. "I'll practice 'em in a little while." But it was a soft, beautiful spring evening and the ball felt good when it thunked into his glove. Tommy stayed outside till supper time, then he had to finish his homework and do his chores.

As soon as Tommy walked in the door the next afternoon, Mrs. Rawson insisted that he sit down and work on memorizing his lines. And he did, for a little while. Then the phone rang and it was Daniel telling him all about a multi-sport camp his parents were sending him to that summer. Somehow Tommy didn't get back to rehearsing his part. When he went to bed that night, it hit him. Three days! Three days to know it all by heart. He HAD to get busy and spend time memorizing those lines!

But school was almost over for another year and the days were busy. Tommy was embarrassed when they practiced the play at school the next day and he only knew the first page by memory. *At least no one else knows every bit of their parts perfectly yet, either,* Tommy consoled himself, even though he realized everyone else knew much more than he did.

He practiced well that evening—until a baseball game came on TV and he got sidetracked again. Lying in bed that night staring at the dark ceiling, Tommy promised himself that he'd drop everything

313

Story Continued

the next day and LEARN THAT PART.

Sometime in the night Tommy stirred. *Voices,* he thought sleepily, *Mom and Dad's voices.* It wasn't uncommon now for Grandma to get up and attempt major house cleaning in the middle of the night. Mom and Dad would handle it. Tommy rolled over and drifted into a deep sleep again.

The next morning, Tommy read through his lines as he felt his way foot-by-foot down the steps to the kitchen. "...so there must be an answer and I will find it!" he read in his best Thomas Edison voice. He stopped abruptly in the kitchen door when he looked up and saw the serious looks on Mom's and Dad's faces. "Was I that bad?"

Dad smiled a little. "Not quite, son. Come join us." Tommy took his chair at the round table between Lisa and his mom. Dad reached over and took Mom's hand. "Grandma fell last night and broke her hip. We took her to the hospital, but I'm afraid the trauma was just too much for her in her condition." He swallowed. "She died this morning about 5:00."

It was quiet for several seconds until Lisa choked back a cry and, jumping up from the table, ran upstairs to her room. Tommy wished tears would come. Instead he felt this awful, hot, choking thing in his throat and his eyes burned dry and bright. Mom started to get up, but Dad put a hand on her shoulder. "I'll go to her." He stood slowly. "Tommy, are you all right?" He leaned over his son. Tommy nodded stiffly. He couldn't get a sound past that horrid thing in his throat.

The play rehearsal at school later that morning was a disaster for Tommy. He couldn't even remember the few lines he did know. Mr. Canfield took him to one side and kindly let him know that Tony would be taking his place as Thomas Edison. No one made fun of Tommy.

Everyone thought it was just because of his grandmother, but deep inside Tommy knew there was more to it than that.

That evening, the Rawson family gathered in the living room. "So, we'll have a small memorial service day after tomorrow, then." Dad held a small pad of paper on his knee and jotted down notes. "Say 7:00 at the church?"

Mrs. Rawson nodded from her favorite chair. "That will work out well since the school program is tomorrow evening. I'm sorry this happened right before your program, son. I was really looking forward to seeing my son, the actor."

Tommy squirmed. "I didn't lose the part just 'cause Grandma died." He ran his fingernail along the jeans seam at the side of his leg as he admitted the truth. "I didn't take time to practice enough. I just wasn't ready. It seemed like time passed so quickly."

"Time does, son." Dad made little squiggles down the side of the pad. "It seems like just yesterday that I was your age and Grandma was making me eat my green beans!"

"Ugh!" Tommy grinned. "Remember when Grandma lived in that house with all the roses? She always had this huge garden every summer. I loved to stuff myself with corn-on-the-cob and tomatoes and stuff, but she always grew row after row of green beans, too!"

"Mmmmm." Lisa rolled over on her back on the carpet and rubbed her tummy. "I remember Grandma's strawberry pie. I've never tasted anything better."

"Grandma certainly had a green thumb, all right." Mom tucked her feet up under her. "She grew the best strawberries for miles around, not to mention everything else. And did she ever know her way around the kitchen!" Mom smiled across the room at Dad, "With all your mother's good cooking, it's a wonder you didn't weigh 300 pounds when I met you."

"I would've if she hadn't worked me so hard," Dad chuckled. "Grandma always was a stickler for keeping things neat and clean." His smile slowly faded.

"I guess that's why she kept trying to clean house at odd hours after the Alzheimer's changed her so."

"I miss her so much." Lisa sniffed.

"Me, too." Tommy moved across the couch and leaned against his dad. "Why couldn't everything just stay the way it used to be before Grandma got sick?"

"Time doesn't slow down for anyone, kids." Dad laid the pad and pen down on the table beside the couch. "None of us has much time on this old earth. Your Grandma had a full and fulfilling life. We'll miss her, but we can remember all the good times we had with her and remember to live wisely and well in the time we have."

Discussion Time

Check understanding of the story and development of personal values.

- What part did Tommy get in the school play his class was presenting?
- Why was Mrs. Rawson worried about Grandma?
- How come Tommy didn't learn his part well?
- What happened to Grandma during the night?
- Why did Tommy lose the part of Thomas Edison?
- What did Tommy's grandmother like to do before she got sick with Alzheimer's?
- Why is it important to use your time wisely?

A Test-Editing   Name _____

If a word is spelled correctly, fill in the oval under **Correct**. If the word is misspelled, fill in the oval under **Incorrect**, and spell the word correctly on the blank.

Correct Incorrect

1. highlind ⚪ ⚫ highland
2. flight ⚫ ⚪ _____
3. plite ⚪ ⚫ plight
4. kakki ⚪ ⚫ khaki
5. slight ⚫ ⚪ _____
6. Rhode Island ⚫ ⚪ _____
7. Conetticut ⚪ ⚫ Connecticut
8. rhyme ⚫ ⚪ _____
9. doorknob ⚫ ⚪ _____
10. nock ⚪ ⚫ knock
11. warves ⚪ ⚫ wharves
12. nightime ⚪ ⚫ nighttime
13. knack ⚫ ⚪ _____
14. kneel ⚫ ⚪ _____
15. sigh ⚫ ⚪ _____
16. kniting ⚪ ⚫ knitting
17. knives ⚫ ⚪ _____
18. knuckle ⚫ ⚪ _____
19. Ilinios ⚪ ⚫ Illinois
20. reck ⚪ ⚫ wreck

201

Take a minute to memorize...

Psalm 90:12

Review Lesson **32**

3 Test-Editing
Reinforce recognizing and correcting misspelled words.

Game

Reinforce spelling skills and provide motivation and interest.

Materials
- game page (from student text)
- game pieces (1 per child)
- game word list

Game Word List

1. **Illinois**
2. **wharves**
3. **wreck**
4. **Connecticut**
5. **flight**
6. **highland**
7. **nighttime**
8. **plight**
9. **sigh**
10. **slight**
11. **khaki**
12. **Rhode Island**
13. **rhyme**
14. **doorknob**
15. **knack**
16. **kneel**
17. **knitting**
18. **knives**
19. **knock**
20. **knuckle**

B Game

Practice your part in the play with Tommy and his classmates. Move one space for each word you or your team spells correctly.

Review Lesson **32**

202

How to Play:

- Divide the class into two teams.
- Have each student place his/her game piece on Start.
- Have a student from team A go to the board.
- Say the spelling word.
- Have the student write the word on the board.
- If correct, instruct each member of team A to move his/her game piece forward one space.
- Alternate between teams A and B.
- The team to reach the stage first is the winner.
- **Small Group Option**: Students may play this game without teacher direction in small groups of two or more.

Remember: Ask God to help you spend your time wisely!

203

Writing Assessment

Assess student's spelling, grammar, and composition skills through personal writing.

Say

- Have you ever had a special part in a play or program? (Allow time to share experiences.)

- What did Mrs. Rawson say was almost as hard as remembering what to say? (Remembering when to say your lines in a play.)

- What are some of the things Tommy did when he should have been focused on learning his lines? (Practiced his pitching, talked to Daniel on the phone, and watched a baseball game on TV.)

- How did Tommy feel when Dad told him Grandma had died early that morning? (Very sad. He wished he could cry, but just felt an awful, hot, choking thing in his throat and burning, dry eyes.)

- Why did Tommy's classmates think he wasn't doing the part of Thomas Edison anymore? (Because his grandma had died.)

- Was that the only reason Tony got the part instead of Tommy? Why? (No. He lost the part because he hadn't learned the lines.)

- What lesson do you think Tommy learned? (That time passes very quickly and we need to use every bit of it wisely.)

C **Writing Assessment**   Name _____

Write a short story about someone using their time wisely or unwisely. Don't forget to identify your characters, the setting, the plot or conflict, and the resolution.

Review

Lesson
32

_____

_____

_____

_____

_____

_____

_____

_____

_____

_____

Scripture
Psalm 90:12

204

The right side of a boat was called the starboard side due to the fact that the astro navigators used to stand out on the plank (which was on the right side) to get an unobstructed view of the stars. The left side was called the port side because that was the side you put in on at the port. This was so that they didn't knock off the starboard!

D ⬛ Proofing

Name _____

To better prepare for his role in the play, Tommy wrote a brief character sketch of Thomas Edison. Use the proofreading marks to show the errors in his report. Write the misspelled words correctly on the lines.

◯	word is misspelled	⋀	word or words missing
≡	capitalize letter	⊙	comma is missing
⊙	period is missing	ℓ	take out word
/	letter should be lower case	⋁	apostrophe is missing

Thomas edison, a famous inventor was born well over a ⟨sentury⟩ ago in Milan Ohio. Even as a little boy, Thomas very intelligent and extremely curious. A laboratory in his parents cellar allowed him to conduct ⟨dificult⟩ experiments and ⟨desine⟩ and ⟨cunstruct⟩ various ⟨divices⟩

When Edison became an ⟨udult⟩ he continued with his experimenting and inventing. Two character traits that Were apparent in his work were patience and diligence When an experiment failed, he did not ⟨panik⟩ become ⟨embarrased⟩ or give up. he would work all day long even when he was ⟨exausted⟩ Sometimes he worked late into the Night seeking the correct ⟨formyela⟩

Not everyone did supported Edison in his pursuits. a good many people did not ⟨rispect⟩ or ⟨udmire⟩ his ⟨metheds⟩, but thought he was the crazy and ⟨foolesh⟩ Only a few Men stood by Edison and ⟨asisted⟩ him in perfecting his ingenious inventions. They ⟨partnired⟩ with him, ⟨pledgeing⟩ to devote their ⟨inergy⟩ to ⟨gethering⟩ information and ⟨combineing⟩ their knowledge Together they ⟨uspired⟩ to invent ⟨quolity⟩ products and Then presented them to a skeptical public.

1. century
2. difficult
3. design
4. construct
5. devices
6. adult
7. panic
8. embarrassed
9. exhausted
10. formula
11. respect
12. admire
13. methods
14. foolish
15. assisted
16. partnered
17. pledging
18. energy
19. gathering
20. combining
21. aspired
22. quality

205

Proofing

Reinforce recognizing capitalization, punctuation, and spelling errors.

Write this sentence on the board: **tommy did not lern up his lines for the plae.** Have volunteers come to the board to insert the proofer's marks needed for a misspelled word, letter to capitalize, and unnecessary word.

(Say) You will be using these and other proofer's marks to show the errors in Tommy's report about Edison. Read his report, then use the proofer's marks to show the errors. Write the misspelled words correctly on the lines.

---

2 Action Game

Reinforce spelling skills and provide motivation and interest.

Materials

- masking tape
- four square ball
- word list on certificate at end of unit

BOUNCE BACK

Use tape to mark a two-square game grid on the classroom floor. Divide the class into two teams. Line up the two teams on opposite sides of the two-square court. The first player from each team steps into the court, one player holding a ball. Call out the first spelling word to be reviewed. The player with the ball says the first letter of the word as he or she hits the ball into the opposite square. The player in that square says the second letter of the word as he or she hits the ball back. This continues until the word has been spelled. If a player misspells a word by saying an incorrect letter, play stops and the other team gets a point. If the word is spelled correctly, both teams get a point. Give a new word to the next two players and continue in this pattern. The team with the most points wins!

Word Find

Familiarize students with word meaning and usage.

Write the letters **lleps** on the board. Ask the students to read the letters backwards to spell the word **spell**. Write the letters **sdrawkcab** on the board. Allow time for the students to decide that the letters spell the word **backwards**. The students will be challenged with some words that are hidden backwards in this puzzle.

Say

Read each of the sentences below. Find the bold words in the puzzle and circle them. Words may go down, across, forwards, or backwards.

E Word Find

Name _____

Find each of the bold words in the sentences below and circle them in the puzzle. Words may go down, across, diagonal, forwards, or backwards.

1. Tommy read a **chapter** on the **clever** Edison.
2. He wrote a **paragraph** or two about the inventor.
3. Dad told Lisa and Tommy about the **crisis** in the night.
4. Grandma's life was a **journey** that covered nearly a **century**.
5. She had grown very **restless** near the end.
6. Her care was not a **burden** to those who loved her.
7. Some of Grandma's old **photos** smelled of **peppermint**.
8. The memorial service was at seven **o'clock**.
9. There was an **awkward silence** when Tommy **mumbled** a line incorrectly.
10. Tommy felt **truly** foolish and felt sick in the **bottom** of his stomach.
11. He had to **humble** himself and **admit** he was not **prepared**.
12. **Perhaps** in the **future** he will make a real **effort**.
13. Tony was Tommy's **backup**, or understudy.
14. Some students are part of the stage **crew**.
15. Mr. Canfield did not **comment** on the **quality** of Tommy's acting.
16. The **audience** will enjoy seeing events from **history**.

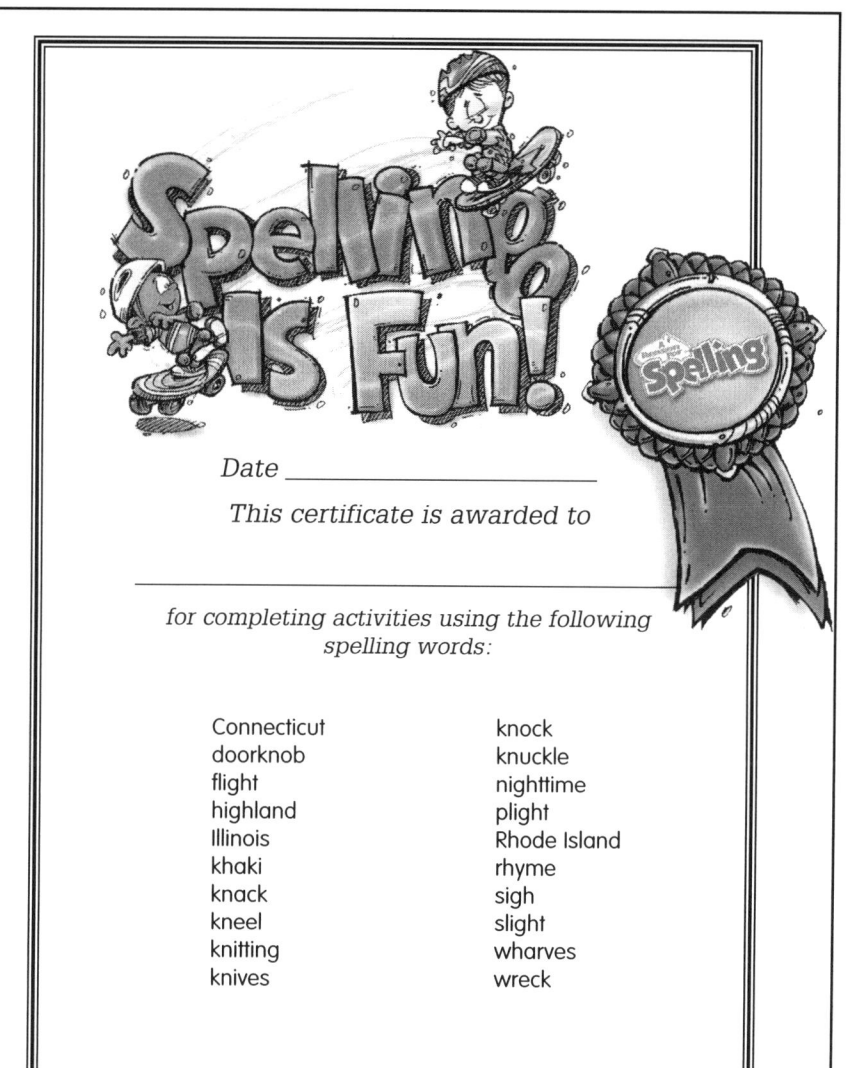

Date _____

This certificate is awarded to

_____

for completing activities using the following spelling words:

Connecticut	knock
doorknob	knuckle
flight	nighttime
highland	plight
Illinois	Rhode Island
khaki	rhyme
knack	sigh
kneel	slight
knitting	wharves
knives	wreck

2 Certificate

Provide an opportunity for parents or guardians to encourage and assess their child's progress.

 Fill in today's date and your name on your certificate.

Take a minute to memorize...

Psalm 90:12

PLEASE PHOTOCOPY!*

The following pages contain Black Line Masters for use with the *A Reason For Spelling*® Student Worktext.

*Photocopy privileges extend only to the material in this section, and permission is granted only for those class-rooms or homeschools using *A Reason For Spelling*® Student Worktexts. Any other use of this material is expressly forbidden and all copyright laws apply.

Hide and Seek

Play Hide and Seek with your words. Fill in a bar graph (left to right) for each word you spell correctly.

LOOK   SAY   HIDE   WRITE   SEEK   CHECK

Vocabulary Extension

Crossword Puzzle

Use the clues below to complete the puzzle.

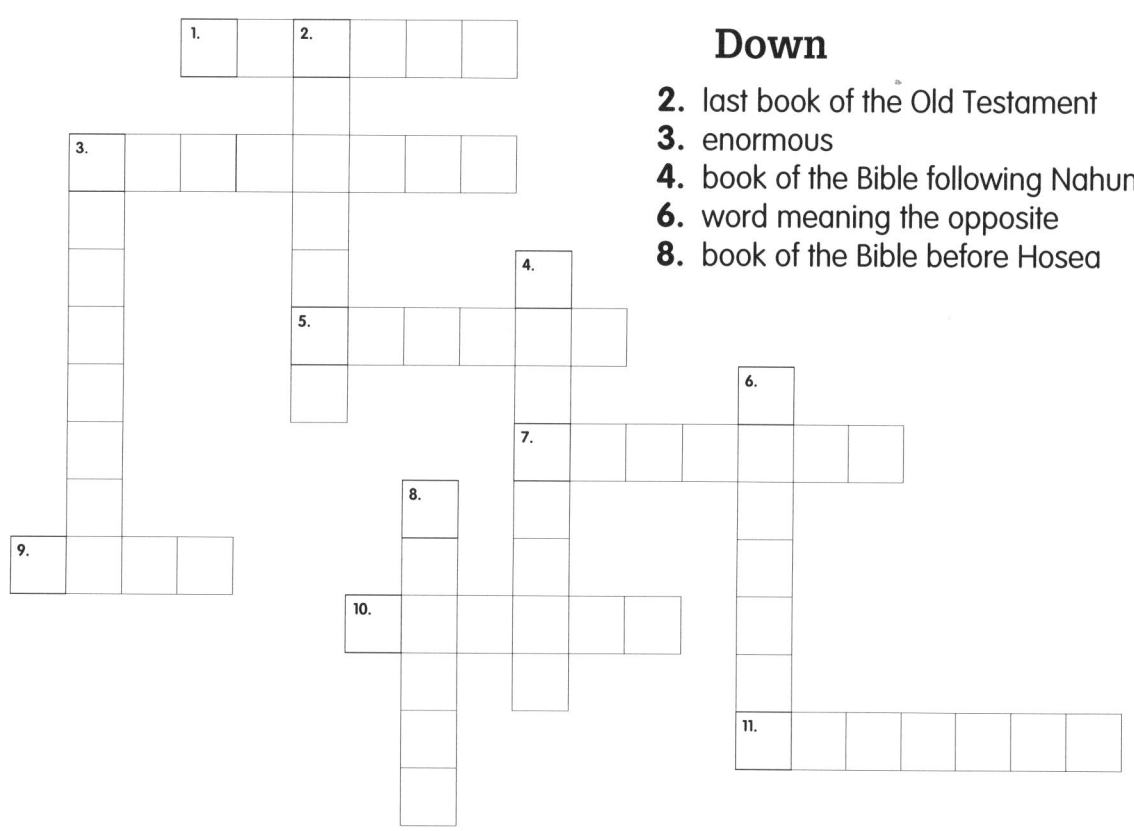

Down

2. last book of the Old Testament
3. enormous
4. book of the Bible following Nahum
6. word meaning the opposite
8. book of the Bible before Hosea

Across

1. book of the Bible that follows Ruth
3. motor fuel
5. book of the Bible between Zephaniah and Zechariah
7. move forward
9. fifth book of the New Testament
10. occurring every year
11. one of the four gospels

Word Bank

Acts	antonym	gigantic	Malachi
advance	Daniel	Habakkuk	Matthew
annual	gasoline	Haggai	Samuel

325

Hide and Seek

Play Hide and Seek with your words. Fill in a bar graph (left to right) for each word you spell correctly.

LOOK   SAY   HIDE   WRITE   SEEK   CHECK

Vocabulary Extension

Trade-off

Choose a word from the word bank to replace the word(s) in parentheses. Write the word in the blank.

1. _____ (book of the Bible meaning beginning) tells sacred history from the first day of creation to the death of Joseph.

2. I don't _____ (suggest) that you wait very long to begin your science project.

3. I have only a vague _____ (recollection) of when I was very little.

4. It is _____ (important) for you to understand how to work these math problems.

5. King Artaxerxes sent _____ (a priest) to set up civil and religious laws in Jerusalem.

6. Moses led the Israelites from Egypt in a grand _____ (departure) after they had been held in slavery for a long time.

7. The king sent a _____ (courier) to tell the other armies the news of the battle.

8. There is an _____ (index) at the end of the book that tells the definitions of your words.

9. This beautiful woman, _____, (Mordecai's cousin) became the Queen of Persia.

10. This table looks so old, I am sure it must be a _____ (authentic) antique.

11. We like to visit the _____ (graveyard) to read the names and dates on the tombstones.

12. You can easily peel the _____ (yellow fruit) at lunch time.

Word Bank

appendix	essential	Ezra	memory
banana	Esther	Genesis	messenger
cemetery	Exodus	genuine	recommend

Hide and Seek

Play Hide and Seek with your words. Fill in a bar graph (left to right) for each word you spell correctly.

Vocabulary Extension

Multiple Choice

Fill in the oval by the word(s) with the same or nearly the same meaning as the word in bold type.

1. consider
- ◯ ponder
- ◯ babble
- ◯ thoughtless
- ◯ balance

2. Timothy
- ◯ Old Testament book
- ◯ companion of Paul
- ◯ first king of Israel
- ◯ town in western Judah

3. convince
- ◯ chosen one
- ◯ lenses for your eyes
- ◯ prisoner
- ◯ persuade

4. Corinthians
- ◯ friends of Isaiah
- ◯ Old Testament book
- ◯ people who lived in Corinth
- ◯ Abraham's nephew

5. initials
- ◯ beginning letters of a name
- ◯ first book of the Bible
- ◯ important document
- ◯ good judgment

6. political
- ◯ ethical
- ◯ governmental
- ◯ noticeable
- ◯ license

7. friction
- ◯ smoothness
- ◯ disagreement
- ◯ roll carefully
- ◯ flattering

8. grimace
- ◯ expression
- ◯ enemy
- ◯ lonely
- ◯ frightening

9. minimum
- ◯ receive
- ◯ administer
- ◯ smallest
- ◯ record

10. Kings
- ◯ to take an oath
- ◯ to persuade
- ◯ prophet of Israel
- ◯ Old Testament books

Hide and Seek

Play Hide and Seek with your words. Fill in a bar graph (left to right) for each word you spell correctly.

LOOK SAY HIDE WRITE SEEK CHECK

Vocabulary Extension

Cause and Effect

Write a word from the word bank to complete each sentence.

1. If you are reading the fifth book of the Bible, you are reading _____.

2. If a machine runs by mechanical or computerized means,
   it is an _____ device.

3. If you are reading a collection of sacred hymns from the Bible,
   you are reading the _____.

4. If someone brings something to completion, they were able to _____ it.

5. If someone pretends to be very good but is not, he is guilty of _____.

6. If something is too small to see without using a special magnifying lens,
   it is _____.

7. If you are reading a poetical book of essays and practical statements,
   you are reading _____.

8. If you live where there is government rule by the people,
   you live in a _____.

9. If you want to learn about the reign of King David,
   you may read the books of _____.

10. If you wanted to read about Jesus' cousin,
    you would read about _____ the Baptist.

11. If you wanted to read a letter written by Paul,
    you could read the book of _____.

12. If you wanted to learn more about the man who led the Israelites after Moses,
    you would learn about _____.

Word Bank

accomplish	democracy	hypocrisy	microscopic
Chronicles	Deuteronomy	John	Proverbs
Colossians	electronic	Joshua	Psalms

Hide and Seek

Play Hide and Seek with your words. Fill in a bar graph (left to right) for each word you spell correctly.

LOOK   SAY   HIDE   WRITE   SEEK   CHECK

Vocabulary Extension

Fill in the Blanks

Choose a word from the word bank that best fits each sentence clue.

1. If you want the cookies to turn out well, you must follow the _____.

2. The seventh book of the Bible, _____, is named for the way Israel was ruled during this time.

3. I had to _____ to get the saddle on the huge horse, but I finally was successful.

4. _____, the fourth book of the Bible, begins with a census taken at Sinai.

5. The art class I want to sign up for allows a _____ of twenty students.

6. When our sink developed a leak underneath, we called a _____.

7. It felt absolutely _____ to go swimming in the middle of the hot day.

8. Someday she would like to travel to several other _____ for a visit.

9. The stray cat soon became a _____ visitor to our dog's bowl on the back porch.

10. The hotel where we stayed provided _____ service to the nearby attractions.

11. Several _____ sent me their catalogs of outdoor gear when I subscribed to a ski magazine.

12. Mom is looking forward to the _____ of a long soak in the whirlpool.

Word Bank

companies	Judges	Numbers	shuttle
countries	luxury	plumber	struggle
instructions	maximum	regular	wonderful

Hide and Seek

Play Hide and Seek with your words. Fill in a bar graph (left to right) for each word you spell correctly.

Vocabulary Extension

Crossword Puzzle

Use the clues below to complete the puzzle.

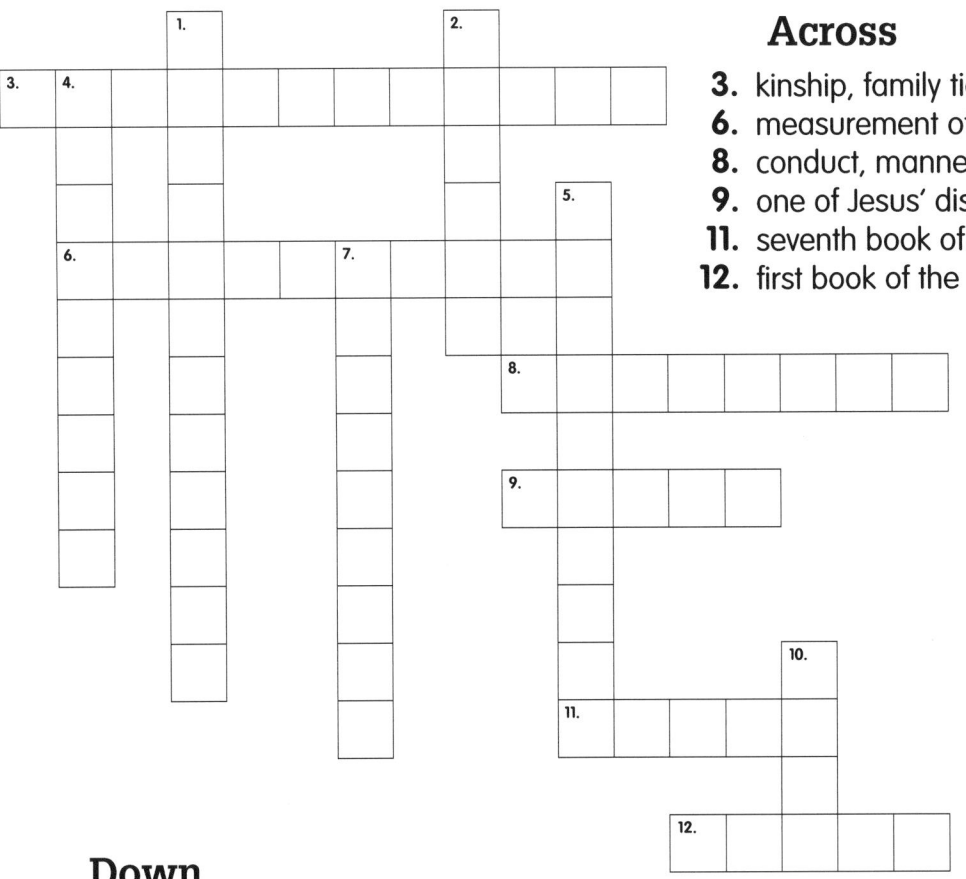

Across

3. kinship, family tie
6. measurement of temperature
8. conduct, manners
9. one of Jesus' disciples
11. seventh book of the Minor Prophets
12. first book of the Minor Prophets

Down

1. Old Testament book following Jeremiah
2. Old Testament book before Jeremiah
4. instruction, schooling
5. last book of the Bible
7. letter written by Paul
10. third book of the Minor Prophets

Word Bank

Amos	education	Isaiah	Nahum
behavior	Galatians	James	relationship
centigrade	Hosea	Lamentations	Revelation

Hide and Seek

Play Hide and Seek with your words. Fill in a bar graph (left to right) for each word you spell correctly.

LOOK   SAY   HIDE   WRITE   SEEK   CHECK

Vocabulary Extension

Trade-off

Choose a word from the word bank to replace the word(s) in parentheses. Write the word in the blank.

1. Descendants of Jacob became known as _____ (Israelites).

2. Levers, screws, pulleys, and gears are all simple _____ (devices).

3. Anne has always done very well. She will _____ (triumph) now.

4. Dad _____ (surrendered) to the other car so we would not have an accident.

5. When we go out in the _____ (excessive) cold, we dress in many layers of clothes.

6. Paul wrote a letter to _____ (Onesimus' master) asking him to treat the slave as a brother in Christ.

7. Brushing your teeth every morning and night is an example of good _____ (health habits).

8. _____ (Simon) was an eager, earnest, and courageous disciple of Jesus Christ.

9. We quickly called the police and hoped they would catch the _____ (burglars) who had robbed us.

10. I am teaching my dog how to _____ (fetch) a stick when I throw it for him.

11. _____ (Old Testament book) was written by King Solomon and tells his view of life.

12. She has the gift of _____ (administration), so she is the yearbook editor.

Word Bank

Ecclesiastes	hygiene	Peter	succeed
extreme	leadership	Philemon	thieves
Hebrews	machines	retrieve	yielded

331

Hide and Seek

Play Hide and Seek with your words. Fill in a bar graph (left to right) for each word you spell correctly.

LOOK   SAY   HIDE   WRITE   SEEK   CHECK

Vocabulary Extension

Multiple Choice

Fill in the oval by the word(s) with the same or nearly the same meaning as the word in bold type.

1. Obadiah
- New Testament prophet
- son of Ruth and Boaz
- the shortest book in the Old Testament
- the longest book in the Old Testament

2. sacrifice
- to commandeer an airplane
- an offering
- to communicate
- resemblance

3. satellite
- to soak thoroughly
- uncivilized
- an object that orbits a heavenly body
- sixth planet from the sun

4. Nehemiah
- Old Testament book before Esther
- Old Testament book after Esther
- New Testament book after Ezra
- follower of Jesus who called Peter

5. Jeremiah
- important city in the Jordan Valley
- city where the temple stood
- first king of Israel
- the "weeping prophet"

6. Micah
- an archangel
- a town near Bethel
- book of the minor prophets
- last Old Testament book

7. Zephaniah
- prophet in the days of King Josiah
- ninth book of the Bible
- last book of the Old Testament
- son of Zilpah

8. Zechariah
- next to the last book of the Bible
- Old Testament book following Haggai
- a man who climbed a tree to see Jesus
- a town in Shephelah in Judah

9. variety
- undue pride in oneself
- an animal considered a pest
- assortment of different things
- fine particles floating in the air

10. Titus
- the 10th part of one's increase
- letter written by Peter
- a covenant
- New Testament book before Philemon

332

Hide and Seek

Play Hide and Seek with your words. Fill in a bar graph (left to right) for each word you spell correctly.

LOOK   SAY   HIDE   WRITE   SEEK   CHECK

Vocabulary Extension

Cause and Effect

Write a word from the word bank to complete each sentence.

1. If you wanted to _____ someone, you would go up and talk to them.

2. If a family had lived in the city of Thessalonica,
they would be known as _____.

3. If you want to look at something that is very small,
you would use a _____.

4. If you want to read the book of the Bible between Hosea and Amos,
you would read the book of _____.

5. If you wanted to describe the brilliance that radiates from a heavenly angel,
you might use the word _____.

6. If a carpenter wanted to hold up the roof of a porch,
he might use pillars to _____ it.

7. If you wanted to describe someone who had suffered a lot,
you might compare them to a man in the Bible named _____.

8. If you want to go into a cave to discover what it is like, you will _____ it.

9. If you were telling a story about a man who had been swallowed by a large fish,
you would be telling the story of _____.

10. If you had written a letter to a friend and needed to mail it,
you would write the address on an _____.

11. If you challenged a friend to a game of tennis,
you would play at a tennis _____.

12. If your family were citizens of Rome, they would be known as _____.

Word Bank

approach	explore	Joel	Romans
court	glory	Jonah	support
envelope	Job	microscope	Thessalonians

333

Hide and Seek

Play Hide and Seek with your words. Fill in a bar graph (left to right) for each word you spell correctly.

LOOK   SAY   HIDE   WRITE   SEEK   CHECK

Vocabulary Extension

Fill in the Blanks

Choose a word from the word bank that best fits each sentence clue.

1. When I saw my brother playing with my yo-yo, I had to _____ that he had taken it.

2. We did not mean to _____ you; we accidentally left you out of the game.

3. Grandma always smells like a rose garden. I like the _____ she wears.

4. When my sister broke her leg, lots of people sent flowers to her. Their kindness was abundant and _____.

5. I am memorizing a verse in the 26th book of the New Testament. I am learning a verse in the book of _____.

6. My grandfather thinks I look very young. He comments on how _____ I seem.

7. I have good opinions and feelings about school. I have a positive _____.

8. My mother-in-law's name was Naomi. I was kind to her. I later married Boaz. My name was _____.

9. The round black part of your eye that lets light travel through it is called the _____.

10. I was a doctor and wrote the third gospel. I also traveled with Paul. My name was _____.

11. The earth, the planets, the stars and everything in space make up the _____.

12. My brother likes to make funny little drawings. He likes to draw _____s.

Word Bank

attitude	exclude	perfume	Ruth
cartoon	Jude	profuse	universe
conclude	Luke	pupil	youthful

Hide and Seek

Play Hide and Seek with your words. Fill in a bar graph (left to right) for each word you spell correctly.

LOOK   SAY   HIDE   WRITE   SEEK   CHECK

Vocabulary Extension

Crossword Puzzle

Use the clues below to complete the puzzle.

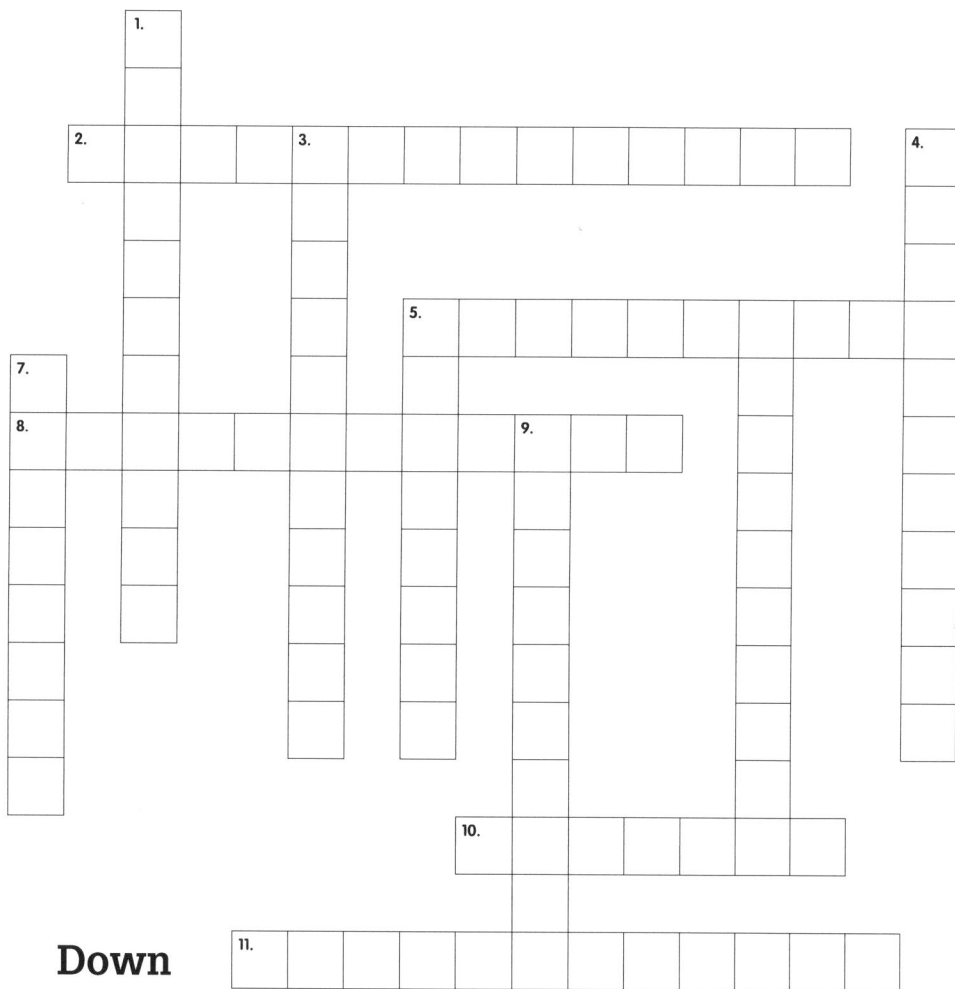

Down
1. questionnaire, test
3. add blood through a vein
4. done with extraordinary skill
5. catastrophe, misfortune
6. tenderness, mercy
7. six-pointed star
9. insufficient, imperfect

Across
2. writing or printing in uppercase letters
5. a person between childhood and adulthood
8. contentment, happiness
10. display, show
11. scarf, tissue

Word Bank

accident	capitalization	handkerchief	pageant
adolescent	compassion	inadequate	satisfaction
asterisk	examination	masterpiece	transfusion

335

Hide and Seek

Play Hide and Seek with your words. Fill in a bar graph (left to right) for each word you spell correctly.

LOOK   SAY   HIDE   WRITE   SEEK   CHECK

Vocabulary Extension

Trade-off

Choose a word from the word bank to replace the word(s) in parentheses. Write the word in the blank.

1. My teacher said that the _____ (essay) I wrote was really good.

2. There was a lot of _____ (conflict) to the plans for the new gymnasium.

3. The lawyer for the _____ (accuser) had plenty of evidence to convict the thief.

4. She was so upset that her arguments became very _____ (unreasonable).

5. The boys finally gave up on the go-cart they were trying to build. They decided it was _____ (hopeless).

6. The laws in our country that state the rights of the people and the powers of the government are known as the _____ (written laws).

7. The fraction 13/7 is an _____ (incorrect) fraction because the numerator is greater than its denominator.

8. I love to look at the _____ (pattern of stars) Orion in the sky on a dark night.

9. Jeans are the most _____ (most common) kind of clothes in my closet.

10. We need to be _____ (accepting) of others by showing respect for their customs, beliefs, or opinions.

11. I want to protect valuable things such as forests, wildlife, and natural resources. I believe in _____ (preservation).

12. If you have a _____ (discourse) with someone, you talk to them for a while.

Word Bank

composition	constitution	illogical	opposition
conservation	conversation	impossible	prosecution
constellation	dominant	improper	tolerant

Hide and Seek

Play Hide and Seek with your words. Fill in a bar graph (left to right) for each word you spell correctly.

Vocabulary Extension

Multiple Choice

Fill in the oval by the word(s) with the same or nearly the same meaning as the word in bold type.

1. pharmacist
- ◯ large, brightly colored bird
- ◯ person who prepares and sells medicines
- ◯ one who grows crops
- ◯ machine that reproduces sounds

2. carpenter
- ◯ thick floor covering made of fabric
- ◯ vehicle pulled by horses
- ◯ part of the engine in a car
- ◯ someone who works with wood

3. bargain
- ◯ discuss the price of something
- ◯ to trade food for other goods
- ◯ land where crops will not grow
- ◯ common cereal plant

4. margin
- ◯ something made of stone or cement
- ◯ dark reddish brown color
- ◯ place where people buy and sell food
- ◯ blank space down the edge of a page

5. article
- ◯ disease that makes people's joints swell
- ◯ false, not real or natural
- ◯ piece of writing published in a newspaper
- ◯ conceited and proud

6. charming
- ◯ enchanting and appealing
- ◯ document that states the rights of people
- ◯ raising money to help people in need
- ◯ deep crack in the surface of the earth

7. regard
- ◯ in spite of everything
- ◯ opinion; esteem
- ◯ to give money back to someone
- ◯ person who is forced to leave their home

8. darkened
- ◯ room with photography equipment
- ◯ someone who is dearly loved
- ◯ unpleasantly wet and damp
- ◯ caused something to be without light

9. enlarged
- ◯ made bigger or increased
- ◯ gave something all your attention
- ◯ mystery or puzzle
- ◯ made something better or greater

10. guardian
- ◯ person who is dirty or sloppy
- ◯ musical instrument with strings
- ◯ person legally responsible for a child
- ◯ direction or supervision

Hide and Seek

Play Hide and Seek with your words. Fill in a bar graph (left to right) for each word you spell correctly.

LOOK   SAY   HIDE   WRITE   SEEK   CHECK

Vocabulary Extension

Cause and Effect

Write a word from the word bank to complete each sentence.

1. If you promise that something will work, you _____ it.

2. If you study about the tubes that carry blood throughout your body,

you are learning about arteries, veins, and _____.

3. If you want to write a letter to someone,

you may write on some pretty _____.

4. If you do not know what a word means, you can look it up in a _____.

5. If you are riding an exercise bike,

it does not take you anywhere because it is _____.

6. If you are sent to teach people about Jesus, you are being a _____.

7. If you recite the details of something that has happened,

you are being a _____.

8. If you have a glass tank in which you keep fish, you have an _____.

9. If your mom says you must clean your room, it is _____ for you to do it.

10. If a country has a group of soldiers in the navy, air force, or army,

they are known as a country's _____.

11. If you are hired to handle records, mail, and routine work for another person,

you are their _____.

12. If you own a store that sells tools, bolts, nails, knobs, and other such things,

you own a _____ store.

Word Bank

aquarium	guarantee	missionary	secretary
capillaries	hardware	narrator	stationary
dictionary	military	necessary	stationery

Hide and Seek

Play Hide and Seek with your words. Fill in a bar graph (left to right) for each word you spell correctly.

Vocabulary Extension

Fill in the Blanks

Choose a word from the word bank that best fits each sentence clue.

1. I spoke to my mom in a rude manner. I'm afraid I was being _____.

2. I have learned to ride my mountain bike well. I am a good _____.

3. My dad had to get new glasses that have two sections in the lenses. He can see up close and far away with his new _____.

4. We had to change the plans for our tree house; however, we only needed to _____ them a little.

5. We visited a _____, a factory where raw materials are purified and made into finished products.

6. Your body needs foods that give you energy. Eat plenty of _____, such as bread, pasta, and potatoes.

7. We needed lightweight foods to take on our backpack trip, so Mom helped us _____ some in the food dryer.

8. Uncle Paul sure can eat a lot. He has a huge _____ because he works so hard.

9. My nephews play in the community orchestra. They are both good _____s.

10. I like to study about nature and the physical world. I really enjoy _____ experiments.

11. Some drivers travel too fast. This is a _____ of the speed limit laws.

12. We watched a play in which the story was told through gestures, body movements, and facial expressions instead of words. It was called a _____.

Word Bank

appetite	carbohydrates	modify	scientific
bicyclist	dehydrate	pantomime	violation
bifocals	impolite	refinery	violinist

Hide and Seek

Play Hide and Seek with your words. Fill in a bar graph (left to right) for each word you spell correctly.

LOOK   SAY   HIDE   WRITE   SEEK   CHECK

Vocabulary Extension

Crossword Puzzle

Use the clues below to complete the puzzle.

Across

1. changes sound into electric current
4. cold-blooded animal that lives in water when young and on land as an adult
6. study of the earth
7. working well
8. punctuation for possessive nouns
10. making pictures with a camera
11. doctor

Down

2. director, leader
3. musical instrument
5. booklet, brochure
6. wall writing, scribbling
9. prediction

Word Bank

amphibian	geography	official	physician
apostrophe	graffiti	pamphlet	prophecy
effective	microphone	photography	saxophone

Hide and Seek

Play Hide and Seek with your words. Fill in a bar graph (left to right) for each word you spell correctly.

LOOK   SAY   HIDE   WRITE   SEEK   CHECK

Vocabulary Extension

Trade-off

Choose a word from the word bank to replace the word(s) in parentheses. Write the word in the blank.

1. Dad bought Mom a _____ (small bouquet) to wear to the formal event.

2. The hungry deer had to _____ (search) for food during the harsh winter.

3. Medics are trained to act quickly and carefully in an _____ (crisis).

4. Michael forgot to put the milk back in the _____ (cooling appliance), so it soured.

5. Measles, chicken pox, and the flu are all _____ (infectious) diseases that can spread to other people.

6. A _____ (span of time) is said to be around 30 years between the births of parents and that of their children.

7. A _____ (member of the armed forces) was waiting at the train station.

8. Mom and Dad had made an _____ (agreement) for me to stay at a neighbor's house until they got home.

9. Getting used to his new school took some _____ (adaptation), but he soon made new friends.

10. We say a pledge to our country's flag to show _____ (loyalty) to the country we live in.

11. People train dogs with high _____ (aptitude) to serve as police dogs and seeing–eye dogs.

12. The traffic accident occurred because of the _____ (carelessness) of the driver who ran the stop sign.

Word Bank

adjustment	contagious	forage	negligence
allegiance	corsage	generation	refrigerator
arrangement	emergency	intelligence	sergeant

Hide and Seek

Play Hide and Seek with your words. Fill in a bar graph (left to right) for each word you spell correctly.

LOOK   SAY   HIDE   WRITE   SEEK   CHECK

Vocabulary Extension

Multiple Choice

Fill in the oval by the word(s) with the same or nearly the same meaning as the word in bold type.

1. comedian
- ○ process of catching fire and burning
- ○ punctuation used to split a sentence
- ○ booklet with cartoon stories
- ○ entertainer who tells funny stories

2. custodian
- ○ person who cleans a large building
- ○ dessert made of milk, eggs, and sugar
- ○ something you do regularly
- ○ arrested by the police

3. reflection
- ○ automatic action such as blinking
- ○ an image on a shiny surface
- ○ shelter from danger or trouble
- ○ to happen again

4. confidence
- ○ organize something and carry it out
- ○ to ask someone's advice
- ○ strong belief in your own abilities
- ○ say that something is definitely true

5. circumference
- ○ distance around something
- ○ cautious or careful
- ○ conditions of an event
- ○ move in a circle or pattern

6. conference
- ○ a famous Chinese philosopher
- ○ mistake one thing for another
- ○ doing what the law requires
- ○ meeting for discussing ideas

7. creature
- ○ living thing
- ○ something that has been made
- ○ using your imagination
- ○ model of the baby Jesus

8. culture
- ○ guilty of doing wrong
- ○ to develop by studying
- ○ way of life, ideas, customs, traditions
- ○ used to make sofas more comfortable

9. sculpture
- ○ confused and disorderly fight
- ○ figure made of wood, metal, or stone
- ○ to examine something closely
- ○ strong feelings about right and wrong

10. accuracy
- ○ performs gymnastic acts
- ○ skin condition from clogged pores
- ○ to admit something
- ○ precision, exactness

Hide and Seek

Play Hide and Seek with your words. Fill in a bar graph (left to right) for each word you spell correctly.

LOOK   SAY   HIDE   WRITE   SEEK   CHECK

Vocabulary Extension
Cause and Effect

Write a word from the word bank to complete each sentence.

1. If you are using a piece of clear, triangular glass that breaks light up into colors, you are looking through a _____.

2. If you want to measure something very precisely, you want it to be _____.

3. If you are reading the book of the Bible that comes before Daniel, you are reading the book of _____.

4. If you _____, you try to make something seem bigger, better, or more important than it really is.

5. If you are reading a booklet that has news, articles, photographs, and advertisements, you are reading a _____.

6. If you are a detective , you will _____ the evidence carefully.

7. If a company makes, sells or provides a service, it is known as a _____.

8. If you have painted some pictures that you want to show to the public, you would set up an _____.

9. If were reading Paul's letter to the people who lived in Ephesus, you would be reading the Bible book of _____.

10. If you were living in a war zone and heard the sounds of guns and bombings, you would be hearing _____s.

11. If you are about to dive into a lake that you know is cold, you may pause or _____ before jumping in.

12. If you live in a neighborhood, you are considered a _____.

Word Bank

business	exaggerate	explosion	magazine
Ephesians	examine	Ezekiel	prism
exact	exhibit	hesitate	resident

343

Hide and Seek

Play Hide and Seek with your words. Fill in a bar graph (left to right) for each word you spell correctly.

LOOK   SAY   HIDE   WRITE   SEEK   CHECK

Vocabulary Extension

Fill in the Blanks

Choose a word from the word bank that best fits each sentence clue.

1. Someone who is attractive in appearance is said to be _____.

2. This book of the Bible, _____, comes just before the book of Isaiah.

3. This pancake recipe calls for three teaspoons of baking powder.

   This is the same as one _____.

4. A beautiful flower is blooming in the garden. Dad took a _____ shot

   of it to get all the details.

5. The sauce didn't taste quite right, so Mom added a _____ of salt.

6. When the factory workers went on strike, many people formed a _____

   to keep anyone from entering the building.

7. My older brothers both married, so I have two _____.

8. The team captain organized his _____ for the ice hockey game.

9. We have a computer lab at school. We are learning to type faster

   on the _____.

10. The new boy in our class likes to draw pictures of airplanes and _____.

11. One of my favorite classes is physical education.

   We are learning how to play _____.

12. We are going camping when school gets out on Friday.

   It will be a great _____.

Word Bank

close–up	picket line	spacecraft	teaspoon
handsome	sisters–in–law	tablespoon	volleyball
keyboard	Song of Solomon	teammates	weekend

Hide and Seek

Play Hide and Seek with your words. Fill in a bar graph (left to right) for each word you spell correctly.

LOOK   SAY   HIDE   WRITE   SEEK   CHECK

Vocabulary Extension

Crossword Puzzle

Use the clues below to complete the puzzle.

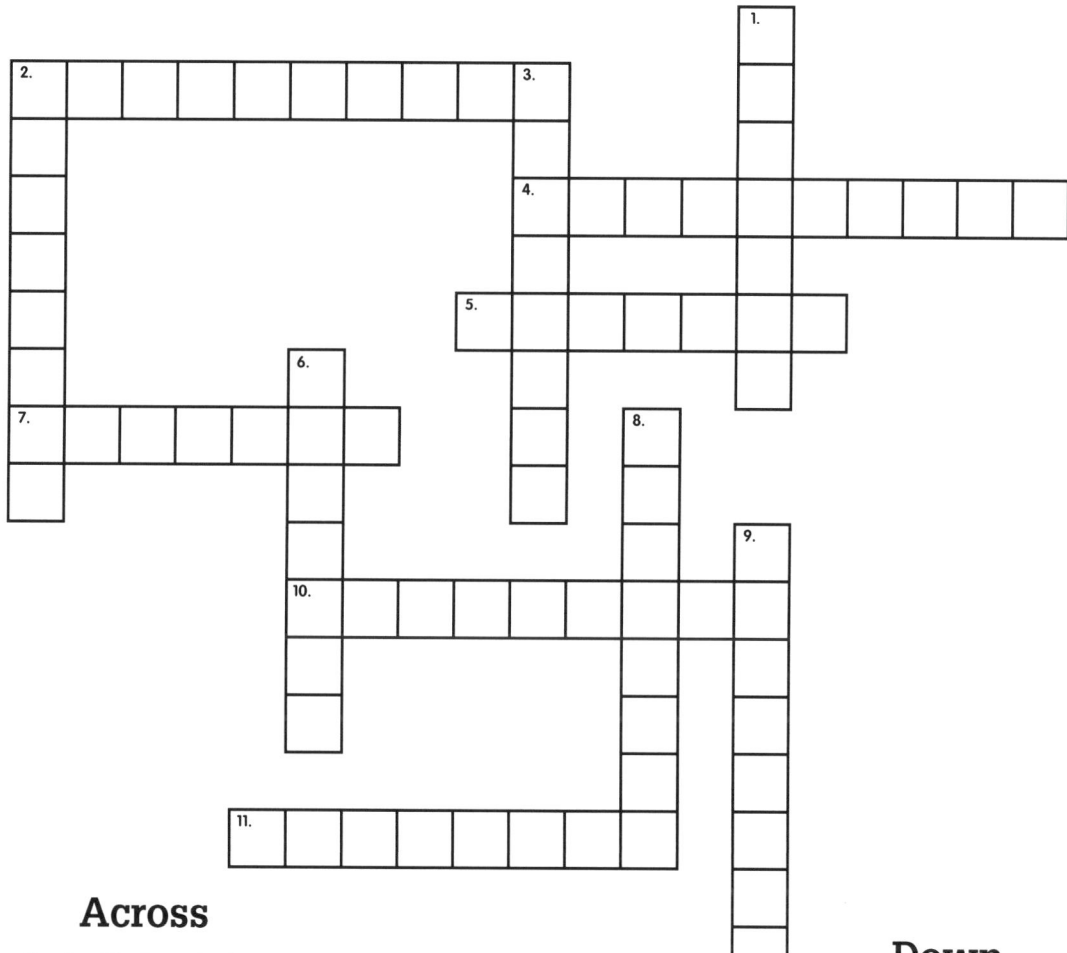

Across

2. half of a circle
4. a tent sanctuary used by the Israelites
5. step-by-step, creeping
7. reasonable
10. quadrilateral with four right angles
11. voluntary

Down

1. diary
2. struggle
3. on the outside
6. normal
8. unique, fresh
9. upright

Word Bank

external	logical	original	semicircle
gradual	natural	rectangle	tabernacle
journal	optional	scramble	vertical

345

Hide and Seek

Play Hide and Seek with your words. Fill in a bar graph (left to right) for each word you spell correctly.

LOOK   SAY   HIDE   WRITE   SEEK   CHECK

Vocabulary Extension

Trade-off

Choose a word from the word bank to replace the word(s) in parentheses. Write the word in the blank.

1. Several ways to _____(keep) food include drying, salting, freezing, and canning.

2. Each graduate left a short _____(pause) before starting down the aisle.

3. The boys have been _____(prohibited) to climb on the steep, jagged cliffs.

4. The _____ (main) reason for this meeting is to nominate a mayor for our town.

5. The intense basketball game caused the players to _____ (sweat) profusely.

6. Our trip to the mountains turned into an exciting _____ (experience).

7. Fog lay low over the valleys due to so much _____ (dampness) in the air.

8. After you fill out the form, please place your _____ (written name) at the bottom.

9. Autumn gives me a lot of _____ (enjoyment) with its crisp air, colorful leaves, and hayrides at Grandpa's farm.

10. I thought the dog leash was _____ (fastened), but when I came home, Rover was gone.

11. There are several countries in _____ (a continent) I would like to visit, such as Germany, Spain, France, and Italy.

12. _____ (neglecting) to do your homework will result in bad grades.

Word Bank

adventure	forbidden	perspire	primary
Europe	interval	pleasure	secure
failure	moisture	preserve	signature

Hide and Seek

Play Hide and Seek with your words. Fill in a bar graph (left to right) for each word you spell correctly.

Vocabulary Extension

Multiple Choice

Fill in the oval by the word(s) with the same or nearly the same meaning as the word in bold type.

1. conscious
- ○ mentally awake or alert
- ○ thoughtful, attentive
- ○ showing self-importance
- ○ taking into account

2. delicious
- ○ easily damaged
- ○ ready-to-eat food products
- ○ pleasing to the taste
- ○ harmful, poisonous

3. dangerous
- ○ hang loosely with a swinging motion
- ○ likely to inflict injury
- ○ small missile used in a game
- ○ sharp pointed knife for stabbing

4. generous
- ○ unusually intelligent person
- ○ the origin or beginning of something
- ○ bend the knee in worship
- ○ free in giving or sharing

5. precious
- ○ of great value
- ○ undue hastiness
- ○ highly accurate
- ○ water that falls to earth

6. Celsius
- ○ thin transparent wrapping material
- ○ scale for measuring temperature
- ○ relating to the sky
- ○ condemning sternly

7. emptiness
- ○ eternal, everlasting
- ○ threatened with extinction
- ○ wife of an emperor
- ○ vacancy, void, hollow

8. loneliness
- ○ length of life
- ○ isolation, lacking company
- ○ to hang around idly
- ○ not rigidly fastened

9. readiness
- ○ to understand written language
- ○ already made up for sale
- ○ information printed by a computer
- ○ preparedness

10. ugliness
- ○ last in a progression
- ○ disagreeableness, repulsiveness
- ○ an open sore that festers
- ○ resentment, taking offense

347

Hide and Seek

Play Hide and Seek with your words. Fill in a bar graph (left to right) for each word you spell correctly.

LOOK   SAY   HIDE   WRITE   SEEK   CHECK

Vocabulary Extension

Cause and Effect

Write a word from the word bank to complete each sentence.

1. If you are always talking, your parents say that you are _____ talking.

2. If you give up winning a race to help someone who has been hurt,

you may _____ the trophy.

3. If you see something that is extremely large, you might call it _____.

4. If you help a friend dress up for a skit, and she looks completely different,

you have helped to _____ her.

5. If you visit the zoo and see a giant turtle that lives on land,

you are watching a _____.

6. If you are learning the art of Japanese paper folding,

you are learning _____.

7. If you are lying down instead of standing up,

you are _____ instead of vertical.

8. If a submarine sends out an underwater missile that explodes when it hits a target,

it is sending out a _____.

9. If nothing unusual happens today, I would consider it an _____ day.

10. If a violent, whirling column of air appears as a dark, funnel-shaped cloud,

it is called a _____.

11. If we are making small decorations to hang on a Christmas tree,

we are making _____s.

12. If you have won a prize for your science display,

you have won an _____.

Word Bank

award	forfeit	origami	torpedo
enormous	horizontal	ornament	tortoise
forever	ordinary	tornado	transform

Hide and Seek

Play Hide and Seek with your words. Fill in a bar graph (left to right) for each word you spell correctly.

LOOK   SAY   HIDE   WRITE   SEEK   CHECK

Vocabulary Extension

Fill in the Blanks

Choose a word from the word bank that best fits each sentence clue.

1. There are more girls in class than boys; girls _____ boys two to one.

2. My parents give me some money each week. This is my _____.

3. After the farmer cut his hay, _____ birds flocked from all around to get hay seeds.

4. We bought our winter clothes on sale. Mom was glad to get a _____ on them.

5. I love the huge hills around us. I always wanted to live in a _____ area.

6. When Julie learned to play the clarinet, she was taught how to hold her mouth on the _____ to get a clear tone.

7. I know you are upset, but you do not need to make such an _____ in the middle of class.

8. Before we write our three-point paragraph, we have to make an _____ of the points we will cover.

9. When Heather writes a story, she uses so many _____s that nobody can tell who is doing what.

10. We drove home by a different _____ because men were working on a culvert under one of the roads.

11. Jesus traveled to many _____ villages and towns, preaching and healing the people.

12. His mom says embarrassing things in public. She is much too _____.

Word Bank

allowance	mountainous	outline	outspoken
countless	mouthpiece	outlying	pronoun
discount	outburst	outnumber	route

Hide and Seek

Play Hide and Seek with your words. Fill in a bar graph (left to right) for each word you spell correctly.

Vocabulary Extension

Crossword Puzzle

Use the clues below to complete the puzzle.

Down

2. sales slip
4. homework
6. smoked sausage

Across

1. from another country
3. run for office
5. pasta
7. serious infection of the lungs
8. slum
9. sharp edged metal blade
10. debt on a house
11. streak of electricity
12. understanding

Word Bank

assignment	foreign	lightning	receipt
bologna	ghetto	mortgage	spaghetti
campaign	knowledge	pneumonia	sword

350

PLEASE PHOTOCOPY!*

The following pages contain Black Line Masters for use with the *A Reason For Spelling*® Student Worktext.

*Photocopy privileges extend only to the material in this section, and permission is granted only for those classrooms or homeschools using *A Reason For Spelling*® Student Worktexts. Any other use of this material is expressly forbidden and all copyright laws apply.

Spelling Progress Chart

Fill in the five lesson numbers for the unit in the first row of blocks. Use the first half of the column under each block to record the score for the Preview, and the second half of the column for the Posttest. To record the score, begin at the bottom of the column and color the blanks to show the number of words spelled correctly. Use one color for Preview and another for Postest.

Lesson Numbers

	Preview	Posttest	Preview	Posttest	Preview	Posttest	Preview	Posttest	Preview	Posttest
20.										
19.										
18.										
17.										
16.										
15.										
14.										
13.										
12.										
11.										
10.										
9.										
8.										
7.										
6.										
5.										
4.										
3.										
2.										
1.										

Words Spelled Correctly

You may wish to use this rubric at the end of each unit to track student progress.

	Standard	Usually	Sometimes	Not Yet
1.	Writes all letters correctly and legibly (upper and lower case)			
2.	Uses correct spelling on words from current and previous lessons			
3.	Writes a paragraph in response to a prompt			
4.	Uses appropriate punctuation			
5.	Uses capital letters correctly			
6.	Writes complete, coherent, and organized sentences			
7.	Includes descriptive language			
8.	Forms plurals correctly			
9.	Subjects and verbs agree			
10.	Uses a logical sequence of events			

Level **E** | Appendix B

American Sign Language

The American Sign Language alphabet is widely used in communicating with the hearing impaired.

American Sign Language

The American Sign Language alphabet is widely used in communicating with the hearing impaired.